THE SEVENTH
AND
THREE ENEMIES

The late Lieutenant-Colonel F. W. BYASS, D.S.O., M.C.

THE SEVENTH
AND
THREE ENEMIES

The Story of World War II and
the 7th Queen's Own Hussars

by

Brigadier G. M. O. DAVY, C.B., C.B.E., D.S.O.

The Naval & Military Press Ltd

Published by

The Naval & Military Press Ltd
Unit 10 Ridgewood Industrial Park,
Uckfield, East Sussex,
TN22 5QE England

Tel: +44 (0) 1825 749494
Fax: +44 (0) 1825 765701

www.naval-military-press.com
www.military-genealogy.com
www.militarymaproom.com

In reprinting in facsimile from the original, any imperfections are inevitably reproduced and the quality may fall short of modern type and cartographic standards.

Dedicated
by Gracious Permission
to Her Majesty
Queen Elizabeth the Queen Mother

Foreword

By Field-Marshal The Earl Alexander of Tunis, k.g., g.c.b., g.c.m.g., c.s.i., d.s.o., m.c.

The reputation which the 7th Hussars had earned in the desert was already known to me when I first met them in Burma. Their excellent work, their consistently high morale and their exemplary discipline during the long and arduous march to India were what I expected of them. Their willing co-operation and stout fighting in very trying conditions earned them the respect of their British, Gurkha, Indian and Chinese comrades alike. In Italy again they had hard and prolonged fighting from the time of their arrival until the final victory and added further distinction to their name. I remember the satisfaction I felt when, just at the time of the final surrender, I was told that the leading squadron of the 7th Hussars had entered Venice. This was a fitting end to their six years of war on three continents.

I first knew George Davy in the Middle East. He himself took part in all the major desert battles of which he writes. After eighteen months in the desert he became Director of Military Operations at General Headquarters and served in this capacity for nearly two years, with my predecessor, myself and my successor. With the last, General Wilson, he then moved on to Allied Force Headquarters at Algiers, where he remained for six months before being given command of the newly formed independent raiding formation, Land Forces Adriatic. Throughout these years he was closely concerned in all the complexities of the Mediterranean scene and he is therefore fully qualified to comment on the events which he describes.

One of the aims of the book, as declared in the preface, is to explain to the soldiers "the reasons why they were there." It is therefore something more than an ordinary regimental history. While it lacks nothing in the human touch where the actions of troops and individuals are concerned, it provides in addition some candid comments on the higher aspects of war and politics and shows how the fortunes of the trooper may be influenced by distant events and by decisions taken many miles away. This should commend it not only to all soldiers, but to a broad section of the reading public as well.

Alexander of Tunis
F.M.

Ministry of Defence,
Christmas, 1952.

Author's Preface

"In peace there's nothing so becomes a man
As modest stillness and humility.
But when the blast of war blows in our ears,
Then imitate the action of the tiger."

Henry V.

The 7th Hussars, had they been known to Shakespeare, might have inspired these lines. Distinguished as they were in war, too few of their exploits have survived the test of their humility in peace. Such personal stories as have found their way into these pages may be taken as typical of hundreds, modestly withheld or lost for ever in the silence of a knocked-out tank. This book, if it conveys to those who took part and to their relatives the reasons why they were there, the atmosphere in which they lived and the sense of achievement to which every one of them was entitled, will have fulfilled its purpose.

The writing of it has given real pleasure to the author, who is grateful to Colonel T. A. Thornton, C.V.O., and the officers for inviting him to do it, to the past and present members of the regiment who have helped in research, to Brigadier H. B. Latham and the staff of the Historical Section of the Ministry of Defence for their unfailing co-operation, to the Imperial War Museum for their help with photographs, to the Officers in Charge of Records at Enfield and Droitwich for their patience, to Prince Eugene Lubomirski for obtaining valuable information from Polish records, to Major Edward Ainger for his expert guidance with the background of Japan, to Miss Sheila Kinnear for her solid and efficient work with the draft, to A. P. Hay, Esq., C.V.O., and Lieutenant-Colonel W. M. Cunningham, M.V.O., O.B.E., M.C., for reading and criticizing the typescript, and finally to Miss McGlinchy of Camberley for her admirable typing.

Houghton,
Huntingdon.

Christmas, 1952.

Contents

		Page
Foreword by Field-Marshal the Earl Alexander of Tunis.		vii
Author's Preface.		ix

Part I: The Desert

Chapter		
I.	The End of Peace	3
II.	Operations on the Frontier	26
III.	The Battle of Sidi Barrani	49
IV.	From Bardia to Beda Fomm	69
V.	The Summer of 1941	94
VI.	"Crusader" Begins	134
VII.	"Crusader" Goes On	165

Part II: Burma

VIII.	The Third Enemy	191
IX.	Southern Burma	207
X.	Central Burma	246
XI.	From Burma to India	274

Part III: Italy

XII.	Iraq to Italy	307
XIII.	The Struggle up the "Calf"	339
XIV.	Round the Apennines	377
XV.	A Watery Winter	407
XVI.	The Battle of the Po Plains	426
	Roll of Honour	453
	Honours and Awards	456

List of Illustrations

	Facing page
The late Lt.-Col. F. W. Byass, D.S.O., M.C.	Frontispiece
An armoured car at the wire	34
"Several vehicles brewed up"	34
Mr. Eden's visit to 7th Hussars	58
Italian C.V.3 tank	58
Personal maintenance in the desert	74
Fort Capuzzo	74
The wreck of an army—Beda Fomm	90
Knocked-out vehicles—Beda Fomm	90
Tank maintenance	106
Tanks in a duststorm	106
A.10 Cruiser tanks	138
"Crusader" tank and transporter	138
German Mark III tank	178
Rommel	178
Sergeants' Mess Group	210
Pegu—burning haystacks	226
Indian refugees	226
Tharrawaddy—A Squadron's leaguer	258
Sgt. Brown's crew	258
The Padigon road	266
Gen. Cowan and Col. Fosdick	266
Revd. Metcalfe	282
The Ava Bridge	282
Carrying Gurkhas	290

List of Illustrations (continued)

Crossing the Chidwin	290
Some Officers of R.H.Q.	298
A Squadron tanks at Shwegyin	298
The Krak des Chevaliers	314
5th Troop, C Squadron	314
Capt. Low and Maj. Thornton	330
Christening at Lanciano	330
The King and Lt.-Col. Jayne	362
Captains Barton, M. M. Stanley Evans and White	362
Poles Crossing the Metauro	378
7th Hussars tank at Pesaro	378
River Marecchia	402
"The weather intervened"	402
Troop post on the Lamone	418
Lord Alexander with C.O. and R.S.M.	418
Fantail crossing the Po	442
Sherman crossing the Adige	442
Indian infantry in the pursuit	450
B Squadron in Venice	450

Maps

		Page
I.	Western Desert and Cyrenaica	39
II.	The Frontier	47
III.	Sidi Barrani	67
IV.	Eastern Cyrenaica	77
V.	Mechili	83
VI.	Beda Fomm	91
VII.	Operation "Crusader"	161
VIII.	Burma	213
IX.	Rangoon	243
X.	Prome	271
XI.	Yenangyaung	283
XII.	Mandalay	295
XIII.	Central Italy	335
XIV.	Adriatic Sector	351
XV.	Battles for Ancona	361
XVI.	River Misa	371
XVII.	Rivers Cesano and Metauro	375
XVIII.	Rimini	383
XIX.	Battle of Croce	403
XX.	Mouths of the Lamone and Senio	425
XXI.	Argenta to Venice	447

PART I—THE DESERT

CHAPTER I

The End of Peace

Last years at home—move to Egypt—mechanization—Italian imperialism—Middle East defence—war with Germany—training in the desert—back in the Delta—final preparations—move to the desert—the war in Europe—Italy declares war.

Map I

World War I had ended at an interesting period in the evolution of the army. For two centuries organization had changed little; the lengthening of the range of fire-arms and inventions such as shrapnel and the machine gun had caused only slight and occasional alterations to unit establishments. But the invention of the internal combustion engine and the exigencies of the struggle for existence between 1914 and 1918 brought about rapid and wholesale changes. For transport and intercommunication the horse was supplemented and partly replaced by the lorry and motor cycle, and in 1916 armour, which had hitherto been used only on a few wheeled motor-cars and on railway trains, was built on to specially constructed tracked vehicles, capable of moving across country, and christened, for the sake of secrecy on their first rail journey from the factory, "tanks."

If the war had lasted another year, there might have appeared upon the battlefields of Europe whole formations of armoured units, some of them manned by cavalry. But when the war ended, a blanket of economy fell upon the application of advanced military thought, and the value of horsed cavalry in war remained the subject of critical, but purely theoretical, study. So the consequences of a clash between large armoured forces and an army composed mainly of cavalry, infantry and artillery were consigned to the imagination; and, as the thought was disagreeable and the remedy expensive, most people preferred to leave it at that. It was not until 1939 that the devastating power of armour on the battlefield was to be demonstrated to the world, an all-British idea executed with all-German thoroughness.

In the absence of a realistic proof of this kind it was not easy, between the wars, for the progressives to convince the more conservative elements of the army that the horse in battle was dead—or quickly would be. Those who raised their voices too loudly were silenced and the more timid were unheard. Such glimpses of the controversy as reached the cavalry regiments themselves aroused mixed feelings. Many had been brought up from the cradle with the horse as their "best friend" and none cherished the idea of the horse being mangled on a modern battlefield. On the other hand, in peace time the horse played an immense part in the pleasures as well as in the character-development of potential war-time leaders. It was difficult to reconcile the opposing lines of thought and both were used with weight in the arguments which preceded the mechanization of cavalry.

In the first few years after the war, the 7th Hussars were only on the fringe of the problem. It was mentioned in lectures and on training; there was a demonstration at manoeuvres in 1925, in the vicinity of Savernake Forest, in which an attempt was made to show how tanks and cavalry could co-operate in the attack, but this was not very convincing. For several years mechanization only penetrated the cavalry as far as its transport. In March, 1927, however, it went a little further, in theory; a new organization was announced and a cavalry regiment was to consist of two sabre squadrons and a machine gun squadron. The transport was to be mechanized at once and the machine gun squadron was to be mechanized in due course.

Some of the transport arrived during manoeuvres the same year and no time was lost in trying it out with the machine gun squadron. The lorries met with approval when used for administrative purposes but had a cool reception in the machine gun squadron. Some of course saw in them the brighter side; the prospect of learning something in the army which would help afterwards in civilian life; no more stables on Saturday afternoons and Sundays; no more sitting in sodden clothes in a rain-soaked saddle. From the tactical point of view however the new vehicles met mainly with criticism. They were large, conspicuous and vulnerable; they had usually to stop some way from the selected gun position, which meant a long carry for the guns and ammunition both into and out of action; they were slow on hills and "were easily left behind by the horses." Nevertheless a beginning had been made in mechanization; the first shock was over and the way was paved for open discussion of the problems involved and for the gradual evolution of the armoured regiment.

* * * *

In September 1935, after twelve happy and successful years at home —Edinburgh, Tidworth, Colchester, Aldershot and Hounslow—the 7th Queen's Own Hussars moved to Southampton, to embark for another tour of foreign service. A farewell inspection was carried out by Major-General A. P. Wavell, General Officer Commanding the

2nd Division. While the regiment had been training with the 2nd Division it had made its first acquaintance with a commander with whom it was to be closely associated in several periods of the war. No special parade was held, but he saw the recruits at riding school and the machine gun troop at training, and visited the stables. He seemed satisfied but he said little. He never wasted words.

*   *   *   *

The move to Egypt was part of the ordinary routine of peace time. Every year a cavalry regiment went from the United Kingdom to Egypt, replacing another which went from Egypt to India, while a third left India for home. It is true that Mussolini was flouting the League of Nations in Africa and that Hitler's Germany was threatening the peace of Europe. But so far the activities of these dictators had not altered the normal change of station among regiments of the British army. There was only the merest shadow of war and, among the troops, nobody gave it more than a passing thought.

The military occupation of Egypt dated from 1882, when British troops had intervened to suppress a rebellion against the Khedive's authority. The Khedive Ismail, who, by his profligate extravagance, had incurred vast debts abroad, had been forced to accept an International Debt Commission, and the prospect of unwelcome economics had brought about Arabi Pasha's short-lived rising. After Tel-el-Kebir the British troops remained. Meanwhile the opening of the Suez Canal in 1869 had greatly enhanced the significance of Egypt as a centre of communications, and Great Britain had acquired a large block of canal shares from the Khedive. The stability of Egypt was therefore of paramount importance to those countries whose finances were involved and in particular to the British Empire.

Aided by a succession of able British administrators, Egypt evolved from a condition of chaos into an orderly state, in the government of which the Egyptians themselves played an ever-increasing part. World War I brought the end of Turkish suzerainty and Egypt emerged as a sovereign country under King Fuad. Still however there were reserved subjects which required final settlement and agreement. These included the security of empire communications, defence against external attack, protection of foreign interests and minorities, and the Sudan. But these outstanding problems were not to be resolved for some time, and still the British troops remained. A resort to violence and the murder of the Sirdar in 1924 only served to prolong the occupation and it was not until 1936 that a treaty was signed; the British troops were in future to be confined to the canal zone. But before the Egyptians could build the new barracks World War II had broken out and Egypt was to become the hub of the vast military machine of the Middle East.

With the Egyptians the British occupation was unpopular—at least in theory. Among a few of the more ambitious the xenophobia was genuine, but among the poverty-stricken masses it was practically non-existent. Except when stirred up by their newspapers and a few piastres in cash, they were generally disinterested. A few indeed saw in the British a kind of indefinable guarantee against more intensive robbery by the less scrupulous of their own exploiters. On the whole the population accepted the British kindly and many of all classes reaped considerable financial benefits from their presence and the incidental advantages which they attracted in the way of winter visitors.

The voyage to Egypt was uneventful. Most of the men were at sea for the first time and found the conditions strange. From the day he joined every man had to make up his bed in the morning, not, as at home, with the idea of sleeping in it the following night, but in a fashion peculiar to army life and quite unrelated to either sleep or comfort. At sea the day began with the same event, but in aggravated form, as the hammocks had to be taken down and stowed away. This left bare boards in the mess decks and a small space on the decks above as alternatives for the crowded troops in their leisure hours.

Mornings were taken up with roll call, cleaning up, boat drill, inspections, individual training and education. Several of the men had crown and anchor sets; these and an occasional concert occupied the evenings. The sea was calm and the weather pleasantly warm, so the voyage was reasonably comfortable.

The Nevassa called at Gibraltar and there were several opportunities for bathing. When she sailed on, in company with S.S. *Somersetshire*, they were escorted—an ominous sign of the times—by the cruiser H.M.S. *Exeter*.

Few members of the regiment had been to Egypt. One or two of the old hands had memories of a dusty transit camp near Suez, where the returning cadre had spent two days on its way from Mesopotamia to the United Kingdom in 1919, and of a grimy railway journey from there to Port Said. Some had seen the expanse of sand on both sides of the Suez Canal, as the Troopship *Zeppelin* took them to India in 1920. Some had spent a few hours and too much money among the tawdry displays and shameless souvenir vendors of Port Said, on their way home again in 1923. These were now old soldiers. To the great majority Egypt had been an image in the distance. Doubtless the daily round of stables, riding school and the rifle range would go on as usual, but this time against a background of Moses in the bullrushes and the railway stations' incentives to "Visit Egypt for Health, Sunshine and Romance."

The "health" aspect was belied by the inoculations which seemed to be necessary before embarkation, and the common house fly was soon to prove itself a more constant companion of man than either his horse or his dog. The Egyptian fly has one thing, besides its appearance, in common with its British cousin; it is adept at dodging the human hand. The British fly, more nervous, stops worrying after one attack, but the Egyptian persists, dodging successive swipes and repeatedly settling on the same exasperated spot. Its habits when in contact with human food need not be related here, although they were explained with relish by the medical officers in their talks on hygiene. Briefly, the fly was the cause of much of the disease in Egypt, including "Gyppy Tummy," which almost all were to experience at least once, and the more serious but less common affliction, dysentery.

Nobody could deny that there was sunshine; often there was far too much and the sight of a good grey cloud was very refreshing.

Romance was according to taste. Some found it in their visits to to the tombs and temples of the ancient Egyptians, although not many undertook the long journey to Luxor. Some sought it, in a different form and with indifferent success, in the more sordid quarters of the large cities. Others left their romance at home, at the end of the tenuous threads of the mail service, which came and went twice a week.

Social life for the troops was very limited. The officers were fortunate. They usually had leave to the United Kingdom every summer—at their own expense of course—and in the winter a number of tourists came out to Egypt, some indeed for their health, but not all. For the men, however, there were few opportunities for making friends outside the immediate circle of their comrades. They led a fairly full life in their military duties and in organized games and sport. Efforts were also made, in so far as finances and opportunity permitted, to provide other recreations for them in reasonable surroundings. Dances were organized, visits to the Pyramids, mosques and other places of interest were arranged and a regimental concert party was formed.

All the families and most of the men went to a seaside camp near Alexandria for a few weeks' rest and change of air in the hot weather, and were able to enjoy the sea bathing. The band also went, but that was something of a busman's holiday, as it had to perform. But although much was done to keep the soldiers occupied in their leisure hours, there was a good deal of boredom and it is hardly surprising that there were a number of them who looked forward to nothing so much as the passage home at the end of their service.

*　　　*　　　*　　　*

In March 1936 the regiment was photographed, mounted, in line of squadron columns. On the 23rd, Brigadier Friend carried out the annual inspection and the regiment marched past. Although it was not realized at the time, this was the 7th Hussars' last ceremonial parade with horses.

Soon after the regiment landed in Egypt Brigadier Friend, commanding the Cairo Cavalry Brigade, had opened the subject of mechanization with Lieutenant-Colonel Weatherall. The Commanding Officer did not discuss it with the officers until it became a definite policy. It was clear to everyone that if war came the first moves would be in the desert. Although cavalry regiments had operated against the Senussi as far west as Sidi Barrani in World War I, the horses had suffered very severely and nobody thought seriously of using them in prolonged operations against the mechanized Italian Army. So a decision was eventually taken and in May 1936 it was announced that the regiment would have tanks.

Among the officers there was at first a certain amount of dismay, but they quickly adjusted themselves and entered wholeheartedly into the business of oil and spanners. One young officer was heard to say something about Indian cavalry and was at once told, by an equally young officer, that they must all go into mechanization together and make a job of it—as indeed they did. A census was taken of the men, to find out which of them wished to stay with horses. Sixteen elected to do so, and most of these were eventually transferred, out of a total of 531 other ranks.

At the beginning of May mechanization began. With the help and co-operation of the 6th Royal Tanks, courses were held throughout the summer.

By April 1937 the only horses left in the regiment were officers' chargers. Young officers were still given riding instruction however, every day before breakfast, on horses borrowed from the Remount Depot.

Training with tanks was limited by the strict controls on engine and track mileage. Nevertheless, by January 1938 the regiment was feeling fairly sure of itself and was able to take part in brigade training. The last two of the brigade schemes were carried out in the Western Desert and provided a first taste of the strange variety of its surface—

dust, gravel, slabs of rock, patches of hummocky scrub and, in some places, sand.

In February, Lord Athlone and Princess Alice passed through Cairo on their way to Saudi Arabia. They dined with the officers and their wives in the mess. When they returned from Arabia, Lord Athlone spent three days with the regiment, inspecting it on parade, going round the cookhouse and dining halls, and attending the Sergeants' Mess dance. On his last morning he inspected the regiment mounted (in tanks) a few miles out in the desert. He was obviously satisfied with all he saw and after his visit sent a message to the regiment:

"Will you please convey to all ranks how happy I was as Colonel to see the regiment on parade and I congratulate all ranks on what has been achieved in under two years in the change over to tanks. From all I saw the regiment has the same spirit as it always has had in the past, which is second to none."

*   *   *   *

In December 1934 there had been a clash between Italian and Abyssinian soldiers at some wells on the borders of Abyssinia and Italian Somaliland. Trivial though it was, this was the opening incident which led to the eventual rape of Abyssinia. It gave Mussolini an excuse to increase, as he thought, his own and Italy's prestige in the world, and to round off the eastern portion of Italy's African Empire.

Italian military preparations began at once and in March 1935 the Emperor of Abyssinia appealed to the League of Nations. This body, which had already—by default—condoned the Japanese aggression in Manchuria, was getting weaker and weaker. Having no force with which to back its decisions it could only censure an erring state and one after another the aggressors found themselves strong enough to ignore it in pursuing their private ambitions. So when, in 1935, the League of Nations was confronted with another problem of aggression, it was quite incapable of taking effective action.

Mussolini had in the first instance done much to raise the spirits of the Italian people, depressed, although on the winning side, by the ravages of World War I. But he had gone a little too far, and in creating an ambitious and offensive spirit in his compatriots he had made Italy an armed nation with ideas of territorial aggrandisement which must inevitably bring her into conflict with the League. The latter, however, was already faced with another crisis. Hitler, whose power had grown even more rapidly than Mussolini's, had just announced the re-constitution of the German Air Force and the creation of an army based on compulsory service. The German threat to peace was regarded as greater than the Italian and Mussolini himself shared the apprehensions of the other members of the League regarding Hitler's intentions. Anxious to placate Mussolini and to retain his support against the greater menace, the other powers took one more bound down the slope to ruin and virtually condoned his attack on Abyssinia.

The effect was just the opposite of what the League had hoped. None of this escaped the watchful Führer. Although he was not to count Mussolini as his ally for several years to come, he yet saw, in the Duce's dealings with the League, a sure sign of its increasing weakness, and appreciated that he too could go a long way towards his goal without serious interference.

So in spite of Haile Selassie's appeal to the League, Mussolini's preparations went on undisturbed. Troopships and freight ships carrying guns and all manner of war material passed daily through the Suez Canal, as they were entitled to do by the terms of its charter. Mussolini was nevertheless taking a chance. The two terminal ends of the canal and the whole of the narrow Red Sea could very quickly be closed to him by the British navy, and his army would then be cut off and at the mercy of the Abyssinians. He must have had a brief moment of suspense when the League of Nations, under the lead of Great Britain, resolved to impose sanctions, but his fears were soon allayed.

There followed an exchange of views which defined how far sanctions could go without causing war, and the solution was broadly that nothing must be done which would interfere with the Italian campaign in Abyssinia. So only minor economic sanctions were imposed, which hit the people of Italy and caused bitterness against the League in general and Great Britain in particular, but contributed nothing whatever to the cause of peace. With the help of the modern devices of warfare, including gas, the campaign began in October 1935 and was carried through to its conclusion. One member of the League swallowed another member while all the rest looked on.

*   *   *   *

The British forces in the Middle East were widely scattered in the British colonies, protectorates, mandated territories and in the friendly kingdom of Egypt. Their strength and dispositions had, until 1935, been governed by the needs of internal security and it had always been assumed that the troops in Egypt might be able, in certain conditions, to provide a small reserve for use elsewhere. As Mussolini's plan of imperial expansion unfolded however, those responsible for the defence of British interests in the Middle East had to take into consideration the possibility of a clash with the Italians. Such a possibility was all the more dangerous because, while the Italians were building up their forces in East Africa and Libya and the threat to British and allied territories became more pronounced, the condition of the British defences remained static.

In the United Kingdom at this period there was an influential minority which clamoured for peace at any price and lent its support to the cry of the amateur pacifists, who declared that to arm meant war and weakness meant peace—cold comfort to a goat in the presence of a tiger. Consequently little help was to come in the form either of reinforcements or equipment and the British authorities had to make the most economical use of the small forces available, and make them as efficient as time and equipment would allow. Little could be done to improve dispositions; it was impossible to be strong anywhere. But there was one point which, to some extent, offset this military weakness—the inhabitants of all the Middle East territories disliked the Italians far more than they disliked the British.

The backbone of the defence of the Middle East would be the armoured force in Egypt. This was very small and its equipment was antique, but every effort was made to develop it on sound lines. When the Munich crisis came in 1938 preparations were pushed a stage further and the organization of the armoured division began. First the Matruh Mobile Force was formed under Brigadier H. E. Russell, commander of the Cairo Cavalry Brigade. It was based on Mersa Matruh fortress—a little enclosure with only four miles of depth and overlooked from the escarpment to the south and west. Its task was to support the garrison (mixed British and Egyptian) by operating in the neighbourhood of "Charing Cross." This was the name given to the road junction where the Siwa track joins the road to Sidi Barrani, on the plateau, about six miles outside the Mersa Matruh defences.

The force and equipment are worth noting. The 3rd Regiment, Royal Horse Artillery, was equipped with 3·7-inch mountain howitzers towed by "dragons." The 7th Hussars had two squadrons of light tanks, mixed Marks III, VIA and VIB, but had no ·5 ammunition for the heavy machine guns. The 8th Hussars had 15-cwt. Ford trucks with Vickers-Berthier light machine guns on improvised mountings. The 11th Hussars had old Rolls Royce and Morris armoured cars; many of the former had seen service in this area in World War I. The 1st Battalion Royal Tank Regiment was complete to establishment in light tanks, which it had brought out from the United

Kingdom in March 1938, when they were already old, but all there were. This was an era when a tank's fitness for operations was measured by the mileage left in its tracks, which, in the case of the 1st Royal Tanks, was very little; tracks were scarce and such spares as existed would not fit. The mobile force was completed by No. 5 Company, R.A.S.C. and the 2nd/3rd Field Ambulance. The remaining unit, the 6th Battalion, Royal Tank Regiment, equipped with old medium and light tanks, had been left in Cairo for internal security. Such was the nucleus of the Mobile Division (Egypt), and shortly after the move to Matruh, Major-General P. C. S. Hobart arrived to take command.

In October 1938 the tension relaxed and the embryo division returned to Cairo. Here it was joined by the 1st Battalion The King's Royal Rifle Corps, commanded by Lieutenant-Colonel W. H. E. Gott, M.C., and recently arrived from Burma. Training continued throughout the winter and in March 1939 the division went out again to Gerawla, a few miles east of Matruh, for a month's collective training. During 1939 the division was organized into:—

Light Armoured Brigade (Brigadier H. E. Russell; 7th, 8th and 11th Hussars).

Heavy Armoured Group (Lieutenant-Colonel H. R. B. Watkins; 1st and 6th Royal Tanks).

Pivot Group (Lieutenant-Colonel W. H. B. Mirrlees, R.H.A., later Lieutenant-Colonel W. H. E. Gott; 3rd R.H.A., F Battery, 4th R.H.A., 1st Battalion K.R.R.C.).

The 3rd R.H.A. had discarded their 3·7-inch howitzers and were now part anti-tank and part 25-pounders. F Battery had 25-pounders. There were still no cruiser tanks, and the first of these, A.9's, were not issued until October 1939.

While the forces were being organized and modestly built up, plans were being made for their use in defence of the vital delta area. The "Egypt War Plan" was in two phases, each with a code name in the interests of secrecy and simplicity. In the precautionary stage ("Umbrella") units were to be placed at notice to move. In the emergency stage ("Scram") the now re-named "Armoured Division Egypt" was to move to the Western Desert.

As the end of August approached the state of tension in Europe grew worse. The "peaceful penetration" of Danzig was followed by the announcement of a Russo-German non-aggression pact, even while staff talks between the British, French and Russians were still in progress. The secret clauses of this pact, providing for the fourth partition of Poland, were not of course known till later, but the non-aggression part of it, and the evident duplicity of the Russians, boded ill for the peace of Europe, and war seemed inevitable.

As regards the Middle East, it was the attitude of Italy which mattered most in the immediate future and this was far from certain. The strength of her army and air forces in North and East Africa were such that all possible precautions had to be taken to ward off a sudden attack on the important centre of communications round the Suez Canal and the Nile Delta. On 23rd August, therefore, Headquarters, British Troops in Egypt, ordered "Umbrella" and the next day "Scram." This placed the Armoured Division in the area round Mersa Matruh; the 11th Hussars, a company of the 1st Royal Tanks and P Battery, 3rd Royal Horse Artillery were still located forward, near the frontier.

Every precaution was taken in case the Italians should be given an excuse by some accident or incident on the frontier and the injunctions of the British Minister at Alexandria were carefully observed—"It is of the highest importance at this juncture that there should be no incidents in which Italian forces either land, sea or air are involved." So the division took up its dispositions on the 24th and the 25th, and next day the Divisional Commander (Brigadier J. A. L. Caunter, deputizing for Major-General P. C. S. Hobart, who had not returned from leave in the United Kingdom) assumed command of all troops in the desert west of Maaten Bagush.

On 23rd August and for the third time in twelve months, the 7th Hussars received the order to mobilize. Two days later the regiment left for its preliminary war station at Mersa Matruh. Most of the officers and all the tanks with their crews went in two trains, leaving Abbassia in the early morning of the 25th. They reached Mersa Matruh soon after midnight and moved up to Charing Cross. As a camp site Charing Cross might have been worse. The low scrub grew fairly thickly in the light dry soil and not far away was an unusual feature—a tree. This was a smallish bushy tree, a solitary descendant from the primeval forests long since devastated by the aborigines and their goats. Known erroneously as the fig tree, it was useful as a landmark and may have had some value to those who contemplated it for just what it was—a tree, though not much of one.

The next afternoon the road party arrived, 52 lorries and 145 all ranks under Captain Davies-Gilbert. The tented camp was completed and the next few days were spent in applying the finishing touches, in particular the slit trenches—disrespectfully referred to in the war diary as "funk-holes"—and anti-aircraft pits for the Bren guns. The ground was very stony and the weather hot, so the proximity of Mersa Matruh and its bathing facilities was fortunate, and everyone was able to bathe several times a week.

* * * *

On the morning of 1st September news came of the invasion of Poland. On the night of the 2nd a practice blackout was held and next day Great Britain declared war on Germany.

* * * *

September was devoted to squadron training and a number of exercises were held. Among the regimental exercises was one in "mosquito tactics"—the harassing of large enemy forces by small and enterprising detachments—and one in "leaguering." Leaguering was the process of settling in for the night in desert conditions where the nearest neighbouring unit might be many miles away and the enemy might approach from any direction. There were several methods, but all armoured regiments worked more or less on the same principle. Armoured vehicles were stationed on the perimeter and soft vehicles in the middle. The distance between vehicles was anything from ten to forty yards depending on the state of the moon and the prospect of air attack. Some favoured a triangular formation with one squadron on each face, some a rectangular one. There was generally a coloured light at each corner, to be shown when required for the benefit of incoming vehicles, and units made their own arrangements for identifications by simple flash codes. It was remarkable how many people hit upon three flashes as the signal, and how often this caused confusion and disappointment until identification was more carefully organized. The system of leaguering adopted by the regiment was triangular and continued practice in this, once more active operations had started, proved it to be simple, quick and effective.

Among the formation exercises were a divisional recovery exercise, a B Echelon evacuation exercise, and an exercise for A and B Echelons in refilling and replenishing. The Royal Air Force gave a demonstration to show the various types of aircraft then in use; this was to be most useful later in enabling all concerned to distinguish our own from enemy aircraft. The only other event of importance was an inspection of the whole British Force, the Armoured Division and the 7th Division, by King Farouk, on the flat open space south of the wire at Matruh. His impressions are not recorded, but the sight of two divisions on a single parade ground was very encouraging to the troops themselves, who had seen nothing like it before, except in newspaper photographs from totalitarian sources.

At the end of October the band rejoined in its war paint. It had spent two months at the depot being trained, and came up with four Bofors 2-pounder anti-tank guns, mounted on 3-ton chassis, and three 15-cwt. trucks.

Trucks took some of the men down to Mersa Matruh every afternoon. The inhabitants were very friendly. There was beer and food, such as eggs and bread, which could be bought for cash. An even more popular, though quite irregular method, was barter, and undoubtedly some of the ample rations of tea and bully beef found their way into Matruh in exchange for eggs.

On the night of 10th November there was a severe storm. It rained in torrents and the camp was flooded. The pegs lost their hold in the sodden mud and the gale blew the tents flat on their inmates. The cinema, too, was blown down. Major Fielden, then second-in-command, came round and ordered a rum issue, which was some consolation. The next two days were spent by the brigade in pulling itself—and its tents—together. Movement was virtually impossible and some of the tanks had to be used to drag out those of the 8th Hussars, who were on still worse ground.

Early in December the 7th Hussars left the desert and moved back to Maadi, about ten miles south of Cairo. As the "phoney war" progressed the fear of immediate Italian participation receded somewhat, and the troops were gradually placed at longer notice to move, from four hours, when camp was first established at Charing Cross, to forty-eight at Maadi. This gave a certain amount of latitude for short leave and recreation, and the troops had opportunities for resuming old contacts in Cairo in their leisure hours.

The three months in the desert had been very valuable. They had enabled the men to become accustomed to desert conditions, including a good deal of dust and heat and a brief but long remembered bout of storms. They had been practised in the handling of their full war equipment on the kind of ground where they would have to use it.

Among other sequels to the outbreak of war were certain changes in personnel. A number of officers and warrant officers returned prematurely from leave or temporary duty in the United Kingdom. Lieutenant-Colonel L. P. Payne-Gallwey, O.B.E., M.C., Captain W. T. Kevill-Davies and Lieutenant N. M. H. Wall were the first to arrive. Others at home were struck off the strength. Lieutenant R. C. Watson was attached, as camp commandant, to the headquarters of the Light Armoured Brigade. In October Captain A. I. C. Cameron rejoined the regiment and was posted to A Squadron, Second-Lieutenants T. R. S. Thornton and R. D. G. Oates joined from the Royal Military

College and were posted respectively to B and C Squadrons. In November five second-lieutenants joined from the Supplementary Reserve of the Royal Tank Regiment and were posted, C. G. Dean and L. H. Gray to A Squadron, A. E. White to B, and W. Huckin and G. G. Hill to C. In December all the newly joined officers attended a young officers' course at the depot.

Until the outbreak of war, armoured regiments in Egypt had depended upon the Royal Tank Regiment's school at Bovington for the technical training of regimental instructors. Several officers and warrant officers had had spells of duty there, which were welcome in more ways than one. But the outbreak of war had made it necessary to start schools and courses in the Middle East and the staffs had to be found from whatever resources were locally available. The first young officers' course was taken by Brigadier Russell, Commander of the Light Armoured Brigade, assisted by Captain R. Younger. The school staff however was built up on a more permanent footing. The school opened on 20th November with Colonel H. R. B. Watkins, Royal Tank Regiment, as Commandant and Captain P. Pitman-Butler as adjutant. Among the instructors of the gunnery wing were Captain C. G. Davies-Gilbert and Lieutenant J. Congreve. The regiment also provided for the staff fifteen warrant officers and N.C.O.'s.

In November Major-General P. C. S. Hobart had been succeeded by Major-General M. O'M. Creagh, who had served for some years in the 7th Hussars before transferring to the 15th Hussars, shortly after World War I. Major-General Hobart had formerly been one of the stoutest advocates of the all-armoured theory; this envisaged the use of formations from which all unarmoured vehicles would be excluded. While in Egypt he had welded the miscellaneous armoured units, with their miscellaneous old equipment, into something like a fighting force. He had spared no pains to bring the cavalry and the Royal Tank Corps into harmony with one another. He had laid the foundations of sound desert-craft for armoured formations and all officers of the division had become familiar with the western desert and some of its idiosyncracies.

The desert had already been admirably mapped by the Egyptian Survey Department under British officers, and the 1/100,000 gridded map, although sometimes criticized by those who had lost their way, was never proved wrong. General Hobart added to its usefulness by establishing distinctive beacons at a number of points in the area of possible operations and painting on them their map references, as aids to weak "navigators." These "Hobo beacons," being of metal and no good as firewood, will long remain in the desert, with the hundreds of derelict tanks, to mark the visits to Africa of twentieth-century Europeans. They will make an interesting contrast—not altogether in their own favour—with the cisterns, irrigation systems and other relics of civilization which mark the Greek and Roman visits two thousand years before.

One of the most essential accomplishments in the desert was that of finding one's way about. The Arab's uncanny knack of arriving at the next well, perhaps scores of miles away in what seems to be a featureless desert, is a matter of fact as well as of fiction, but the European who thought he could do it too was soon disillusioned. A so-called bump of locality was a dangerous thing. With a few artificial aids, however, such as map, compass and speedometer, and enough determination to stick to the facts which they showed, in spite of other people's "instincts," it was unnecessary to go wrong.

Although every officer had had to own a compass from the time he was commissioned and had had to know how to use it, it had never played an important part in his military life. In the desert, however, the features were few and, with the exception of the major escarpments and the sand sea, there were practically no obstacles to movement east of the Gebel el Akhdar ("Green Mountain"). Sometimes identifiable features were so far apart as to be invisible from one another, so that a map was of little value without a compass and speedometer. The commonest landmarks were the "Birs" (pronounced "beer") or rock cisterns; these, unless they were concealed by a chance fold in the ground, were usually visible for some distance, as the original spoil hewn out of the rock lay in a heap at one side of the cistern. On arrival one often found they were dry, or perhaps full of quite attractive looking water which was too salt to drink. In the later stages of the war they might be found contaminated with oil, to deny their use to the enemy. But as landmarks they were useful.

Then there was the "Gabr" or tomb, usually a heap of stones covering the bones of a dead Arab, and the "Alam" or mark—generally a poorish sort of cairn. A "ghot" was also frequently marked on the map, being a faint depression, a foot or two below the level of the surrounding desert, in which water collected after rain. This increased the stature of the scrub and also enabled the Arab to scratch up and sow a patch of soil; he would come back and collect a scant crop of barley two or three months later.

Spot levels, in metres, were marked in many places by the Egyptian Survey Department and were usually somewhat ill-defined on the ground as small cairns. A few tracks were marked, but these were apt to be misleading; any column of vehicles, or even a single vehicle, would churn up the dust and make track marks. These would be made more or less permanent by a subsequent shower of rain and the baking effect of the following sunshine. Tracks could therefore seldom be relied upon, and a movement across the desert could only be carried out with real accuracy by the use of the compass and speedometer, usually on a straight line, or if an obstacle or a piece of bad going was known to intervene, on two or more "legs." Over featureless desert for much of the way a march might be on a "dead reckoning," that is, for a measured distance on a bearing. But the wise man took every reasonable opportunity of checking his position whenever he saw a good landmark or thought he ought to be passing within sight of one. In this way any error in steering could be corrected at once and he could start off from a new and accurately identified spot. There was thus a similarity between the methods of the army in the desert and the navy at sea, and the process came to be known as "navigation."

There was one great disadvantage to the ordinary magnetic compass. It was badly affected by the proximity of iron or steel, and, although standing on the turret of a tank sometimes gave reliable readings, it was safer to dismount and move some ten yards away. To overcome the disadvantages and delays of the frequent halts, a sun compass was devised. This was of great value in daylight but could be somewhat inaccurate if mis-used, as the movement of the sun (some would say the movement of the earth) altered the direction of the cast shadow and the compass had to be adjusted every few minutes. Other navigators made use of any odd shadow cast by part of a vehicle on its bonnet or wings, in order to keep direction, and these less accurate methods were often good enough on short journeys by day. On long journeys however, and at night, the most punctilious accuracy was necessary. The stars were of value at night and some of them, in the east and west, only changed their bearing very slowly. But there were many instances of men going hungry and vehicles being short of petrol through navigators of transport columns taking chances with Venus or the Moon.

*   *   *   *

At Maadi the 7th Hussars continued individual training well into January. Training then took on a new aspect, as C Squadron was to be completely equipped with A.9 cruisers. Two-pounder instruction therefore became very important, not only for C Squadron, but also for A and B, as it was probable that cruisers would be issued more generously once the flow of new production started to come in. The divisional school had taken a number of the regiment's best instructors and many others were absent as students on courses—100 men were away in December. So the instructors who remained had their hands full.

As fresh units and equipment arrived, the armoured division was gradually built up in the form in which it was eventually to fight. To provide the Light Armoured Brigade with defence against tanks, D and J Batteries, 3rd Royal Horse Artillery, were attached to it, armed with 2-pounder anti-tank guns mounted on 3-ton chassis, facing aft. In the Heavy Armoured Group (now Brigade) the heavy cruisers and close support tanks were gradually replaced by light cruisers (A.9) as these became available. In January 1940 the 2nd Battalion of The Rifle Brigade arrived from Palestine and the Support Group was formed of the 4th Regiment, Royal Horse Artillery (C and F Batteries) and the two Greenjacket battalions, under Brigadier W. H. E. Gott.

With this organization a full scale divisional exercise was carried out west of the Pyramids of Giza early in February. The conclusion reached at the end of the exercise was that the division with its own resources could operate for seventy-two hours, provided that extra petrol was carried for the heavy armoured brigade.

The organization of the brigades themselves was now changed, as a division consisting of a light brigade, a heavy brigade and a support group had proved somewhat complicated to handle. On 1st April, Headquarters British Troops in Egypt authorized re-organization of the armoured formations into two homogeneous brigades, although the names of the headquarters were not yet changed. The 7th Hussars went to the heavy brigade, their place in the light brigade being taken by the 1st Royal Tanks. At the same time a re-organization of the cavalry regiments took place and both were to have two squadrons of light tanks and one of A.9 cruisers. More cruisers were gradually coming out from England and A.10's were expected to arrive at the rate of ten per month from July onwards. Meanwhile A.9's were being issued.

Unfortunately some of these arrived without their 2-pounder guns and by the beginning of May, when the twilight war was changing to lightning war in Western Europe, and the attitude of Italy was more menacing, the tank situation in Egypt was by no means satisfactory. It was the cruisers that would count in operations against the Italians, who were known to have a number of armoured units, and the cruiser situation in the division was bad. In the 4th Armoured Brigade (the new name for the heavy brigade) the headquarters had four, the 7th Hussars seven (out of sixteen) and the 6th Royal Tanks twenty-three (out of thirty-six). In the 7th Armoured Brigade (formerly the Light Armoured Brigade) the headquarters and the 8th Hussars had none, while of the twenty-three in the 1st Royal Tanks, eight were without their 2-pounders. This was a lamentable condition in which to go to war.

*   *   *   *

By the early spring of 1940 the first episode of the war in eastern Europe seemed to have ended. Having divided the spoils in Poland, the Germans began their westward concentration for the next phase. Mussolini, however, still confined himself to the war of nerves, which was bolstered up with increased movements of troops. On 28th August, 1939, it was reported that air force reinforcements had reached Benghazi. On 1st September Italian metropolitan troops were reported to have moved eastwards to Tobruk and Bardia. On the 2nd the Italian Government informed the British Government that on 9th September they were going to reinforce Libya with four infantry regiments (i.e. brigades) and two artillery regiments. Why this information was given is not clear, but it may have been at Germany's suggestion, in order to draw British troops away from northern Europe.

In fact a movement on this scale had already begun on 3rd September, when 5,000 infantry were reported to have landed at Benghazi and 8,000 at Tripoli, and the British intelligence staffs knew of this move long before the 9th. The Italian strength in Libya on the 3rd was estimated at 85,000 Metropolitan and 17,000 Libyan native troops.

Although Cyrenaica remained quiet, reinforcements from Italy continued to arrive. The garrisons of Bardia and Tobruk were reinforced and by the beginning of October it was estimated that there were 129,000 Metropolitan troops in the country, including three corps headquarters and a composite mobile force.

This uneasy neutrality continued throughout the winter. In Rome, the British Ambassador, Sir Percy Loraine, was welcomed in the Royal Box at race meetings by the King, with whom he shared an affection for the turf, but ignored by Mussolini. In Cairo and the desert little news came through of warlike operations in Europe—only an odd patrol clash on the French frontier. There was no devastating air attack on London. Only from the sea came occasional news of engagements, and these mostly with submarines. The war seemed to lack reality—it was like an unpleasant dream. Cairo was its old self. Life in the hotels, cafés and streets was as gay, noisy, lurid and squalid as ever. Only the intensive training and occasional episodes such as an inspection of British troops by the French General Weygand in April, kept the men from forgetting there was a war on.

With the invasion of Norway Italy's attitude became more offensive and the tone of her press more anti-British. On 12th April, General Wilson informed Major-General Creagh that the Western Desert Plan might have to be put into operation at short notice. At this time the troops were at ninety-six hours' notice and it was still important not to precipitate Italian action by any sudden change in our dispositions. So the notice to move was reduced throughout the command to twenty-four hours by carrying out successive practice mobilizations of units and keeping them mobilized.

Final touches were put to the Western Desert Plan and small adjustments were made to a few details of desert technique. As units were generally below strength, personnel to be left out of battle (L.O.B.) were to be calculated on a basis of existing strengths and not of establishments. L.O.B. personnel left at the base had to include all ranks and trades, so that no unit could be seriously crippled by casualties in any particular category. Those left behind were used to train recruits and changed over periodically with personnel from their respective regiments. The minimum number of officers to go to battle with each squadron was laid down as three, and a troop might be commanded by a sergeant. L.O.B. personnel had to include three officers fitted to be squadron leaders, one competent as adjutant, three subalterns and the second-in-command. Spare crews to replace those who might become casualties were to be carried in unit B Echelon. Gas clothing, which took up a great deal of room on a tank, was to be discarded.

On 1st May the final mobilization parade was held and the brigade commander, Brigadier J. A. L. Caunter, inspected the regiment. On returning to camp it was learned that there was another Italian scare, so all tanks and lorries were kept loaded and a black-out was ordered. A black-out in Egypt was easy to order but not to enforce. The troops of course carried it out effectively, but the gaol at Maadi and the civil population seemed to ignore it altogether; there was never any effective black-out except in parts of Alexandria and the Suez Canal area.

There were still no pronounced changes of the situation in Cyrenaica. No Italian reinforcements had been noticed since March and the training of the new formations appeared to have reached its natural culmination in large scale manoeuvres between Derna and Tobruk. But the political situation left no further room for doubt that Mussolini was only biding his time and that the time was not far off. A covering force consisting of the Support Group and the 11th Hussars was therefore ordered to move to the Western Desert at once to cover the concentration of the rest of the division, if it should be moved out, and to establish a dump of three days' supplies and fuel for the division at Sidi Barrani.

On 2nd May ten light tanks were handed over to the 8th Hussars and three of the allotted seven cruisers arrived. Next day three more came. All three were in a deplorable condition, with no machine guns and no interior communication. It was learnt afterwards that other people's cruisers had no 2-pounders, which was even worse. All had long lists of deficiencies which were "to follow."

* * * *

On 12th May the move to the desert began. The tanks and crews entrained at Maadi and left for Matruh. Travelling by train in Egypt was a dirty and dusty experience even in the best of civilian trains. In May it was liable to be very hot as well, and on 12th May there was a "khamsin." This is a hot southerly wind which usually blows violently for fifty hours or so (khamseen means fifty) and carries with it the fine desert dust. This penetrates everywhere—eyes, throat and lungs. It is consumed in quantities with food and drink and does nobody any permanent harm, although it causes considerable discomfort and may spoil the temper, even of the most placid. It drives far out to sea on the wind, and the snow on the mountains of Crete, 200 miles away, often gets a faint yellow tint from the thin coating of African dust. In a railway carriage the wind seems to swirl round under the seats and to drag out any particles of old dust and rubbish which the railway sweeper's brush has not found; it goads the now dust-coloured flies to greater efforts, and they become more adhesive and persistent than ever; and when a carriage is crowded to capacity, and changing one's cramped position usually means kicking somebody else, there is no particular pleasure in the journey.

The 13th was a little cooler, which was fortunate, for the engine broke down, and instead of arriving early in the morning, the train only reached Matruh in the late afternoon. The regiment first concentrated at Gerawla, reaching the leaguer area as it got dark. The transport, which had left Maadi on the 13th under Captain Cameron, arrived complete on the 14th. Major Fielden was now in command, and was shortly to be promoted to lieutenant-colonel. Major Byass, as second-in-command, was sent back to the base (L.O.B.). A and B Squadrons were taken over respectively by Majors R. B. Sheppard and N. L. L. Palmer, on their arrival from the United Kingdom.

Among the hardest worked of the officers was the technical adjutant, Lieutenant J. F. Astley-Rushton; his efforts in hunting for cruiser spares were rewarded with very fair success.

As a precaution against a sudden air attack all the troops dug slit trenches alongside their vehicles. This was strenuous work as the ground was rocky and the weather very hot—there were three khamsins between 10th May and 10th June. Sidi Barrani landing ground was blocked against enemy air landings by vehicles from 9 a.m. to 6 p.m. every day and one troop of the 7th Hussars was stationed at the landing ground at Qasaba to help the detachment from the 22nd Infantry Brigade to protect it against sabotage or landings. So as to increase the mobility of the division, transport being none too plentiful, a dump was established on the high desert at Bir Digneish, in addition to that at Sidi Barrani.

On 20th May the 7th Armoured Division, which was still short of the 7th Armoured Brigade, took over all troops in the Western Desert, pending the arrival of headquarters of the 6th Division from Palestine. This was to form the Headquarters Western Desert Force under Lieutenant-General Sir Richard O'Connor, and opened as such on 7th June.

On 4th June the 11th Hussars sent a troop to Salum, but it was not allowed to go west of the barracks; every precaution was being taken to avoid creating an incident. Nevertheless there was no thought of passive defence once hostilities should begin; the intention was to seize the initiative and keep it, and a plan had already been made for the capture of Fort Capuzzo.

* * * *

Bad news from Denmark and Norway in April had been followed by worse news in May. Every broadcast of the B.B.C. had some fresh misfortune to tell and the cold dispassionate tone of the narrative did not conceal the gravity of the situation. The long expected offensive in the west opened on the night of 9th/10th May. Holland and Luxemburg were quickly overrun. Belgium was attacked at the same time and the British and French forces advanced to her aid. But she had refused staff conversations until it was too late and, under the vigilant eye of the German Military Attaché, had done little about her defences.

The Belgians had resisted as well as could be expected in view of their unreadiness—better in fact than most of their allies had dared to hope. It was from the French that the greatest disappointment was to come.

Between the wars France had built the Maginot Line, a line beyond which "Ils ne passeront pas"; there was to be no more devastation of France by prolonged battles on French soil. So everything was concentrated on a line—something which had length without breadth.

The Maginot Line stretched along the Franco-German frontier from Switzerland to Belgium and was nowhere more than four miles in depth. There was an anti-tank ditch in front and another at the back and the system was divided into compartments by anti-tank obstacles every few miles joining the two. There were small works, containing one or two anti-tank guns, 37 mm. or 47 mm. There were large works with miles of underground tunnelling and just a few guns and machine guns poked out of cupolas on top, badly camouflaged or not camouflaged at all. The system was extended after the war began until it reached the sea, but the extension lacked the major works. Otherwise it was much the same except along the Meuse at Sedan and Mézières, where the river itself was the anti-tank obstacle. Except on the short British front, where the defences were about twenty miles long and fifteen miles deep, there was no depth in the position at all. Furthermore, there was scarcely a trench or a gun emplacement between the Maginot Line and Paris. Those divisions not in the line were sitting close behind it in general reserve, but not organized as a mass of manoeuvre. They were intended rather for carrying out reliefs than for a counter-offensive and the bulk of them were in the Metz salient.

The French official point of view was that the Maginot Line was impregnable and there was therefore no need for defence in rear of it. The most weakly held sector was on the Meuse at Sedan and Mézières, where the river was certainly a formidable obstacle. But here the Forest of the Ardennes gave confidence to the French, despite the fact that in 1914 over ten German divisions had passed that way. They thought the roads through the forest too few to carry German armoured forces.

Then, on 16th May, the Germans seized these crossings. At one stroke the Maginot Line was turned and the bottom fell out of the French defensive plan. This was the moment, in this hectic month, of the military defeat of France. By 24th May the Germans had reached Boulogne. Their tanks, closely accompanied by artillery, infantry and engineers, had penetrated deeply, though not in very great strength, and with little regard to their main unarmoured armies in the rear. The Germans were using methods which had been foreseen by the original British armoured staffs during World War I, methods shelved when the war had ended, in the interests of economy.

The French armies rapidly lost cohesion and no effort by the single British armoured division had the remotest chance of restoring the situation, except locally and temporarily. The extrication of the B.E.F. was no small achievement. Its left was protected by the Belgians until their front was broken on 27th May, but elsewhere it had to cover its own movements almost from start to finish. By the night of 2nd/3rd June the evacuation was complete. On 4th June the B.B.C. announced that 335,000 of the B.E.F. had been brought back across the Channel. The men were available for the defence of Great Britain; their weapons however had been left behind.

Even before the days of aircraft it was an axiom of British strategy that a hostile power could not be tolerated on the coasts of Flanders or northern France. This British anxiety had been the basic cause of more than one war with a too powerful neighbour across the Channel. Now France was our ally, but in the early days of June it was obvious that she was on the verge of final collapse. We should then be left without an ally in the world and with the German air force and army just across the Channel. It was at this moment, on 5th June, that Mr. Churchill made his call to the nation, which brought forth the derision of the Axis, but gave to the oppressed people of Europe a gleam of unexpected hope :—

> "We shall fight on the beaches;
> We shall fight on the landing grounds;
> We shall fight in the fields and in the streets;
> We shall fight in the hills;
> We shall never surrender."

This invigorating message came to the soldiers in the desert only a few days before Mussolini joined in.

On 10th June the 7th Armoured Division held aquatic sports on the seashore. These were just ending when the news came that the "Duce" had made a speech to the Italians on the iniquities of England and we were now at war with Italy.

CHAPTER II

Operations on the Frontier

First clashes—capture of Capuzzo—operations at Sidi Azeiz and Madelena—operation S.W. of Capuzzo on 16th June—lull—second operation against Capuzzo—skirmishes without artillery support—skirmishes with artillery support—rest.

Maps I, II

At 11.20 p.m. on 10th June, 1940, a warning order came that the division was to concentrate forward in the area Bugbug, Sidi Barrani, Bir el Talata, Dar el Hamra. The 4th Armoured Brigade, less the 6th Royal Tanks, was to move to Bir Habata via Bir el Istabl, arriving on 12th June. The move was completed successfully by the evening of 11th June.

Orders were issued to the brigade for the general conduct of operations. It was not anticipated that there would be any enemy activity except in the air. The 7th Armoured Division was to control the frontier by vigorous aggressive action without committing itself to an organized offensive. The task given to the 4th Armoured Brigade was to establish complete patrol superiority in the frontier area between Capuzzo and Sidi Omar. The 11th Hussars were to destroy the wire wherever possible, to penetrate into Italian territory and if possible to harass enemy communications on the roads Capuzzo-Bardia, and Bardia-Tobruk.

The troops under the 4th Armoured Brigade for the offensive patrolling and guerilla warfare on the frontier were, besides the 7th Hussars and 11th Hussars, J Battery Royal Horse Artillery (2-pounders), one troop of C Battery Royal Horse Artillery (25-pounders) and B Company of the 1st Battalion, The King's Royal Rifle Corps. All these were concentrated at Dar el Hamra by the evening of the 12th except four cruisers and two light tanks of the 7th Hussars which fell by the wayside; spares were still very short. A plan was at once made for an operation, with Royal Air Force co-operation, to capture Capuzzo.

The 11th Hussars were the first troops in action. On 12th June they captured two Italian officers and fifty-nine native troops a few miles north east of Sidi Omar. The officers were surprised, offended and furious at being captured by British troops based on Egyptian territory. On the same day the Italian Consul at Salum protested to the Mamour (equivalent to a mayor) against the bombing of Tobruk and Derna by British aircraft based on neutral Egyptian territory.

The situation of Egypt was certainly somewhat unusual. Ever since 1882 Great Britain had guaranteed her security against aggression and she was now to play a passive, but on the whole very helpful, part and remain neutral while British, Rhodesian, New Zealand, Australian, South African, Indian, Transjordanian, French, Belgian, Greek, Polish, Jugoslav and Sudanese troops struggled on her soil against Italians and Germans.

The Italian forces on the frontier were estimated as follows:—

Amseat (Capuzzo), two motor machine gun companies and one garrison machine gun company.

Sidi Azeiz, three companies Libyan infantry and 15 guns.

Bir el Gubi, two companies Libyan infantry.

Fort Madelena, one company Libyan infantry, one garrison machine gun company.

Melfa, one company Libyan infantry.

Giarabub, two motor machine gun companies, one garrison machine gun company, a few tanks and anti-aircraft artillery.

As expected, there was no enemy activity except in the air. On 13th June bombing and machine gun attacks inflicted casualties on the Egyptian frontier troops, who withdrew. But the Italian land forces on the frontier stayed in their defences and only came out at night to repair gaps made in the wire by the 11th Hussars, or to lay mines in them. This must have been depressing work, as the number of gaps increased daily. The wire was fifteen years old and although densely coiled and in some places drifted up with sand, gave way fairly easily under the persuasion of a grappling hook and tow-rope.

* * * *

The operation against Capuzzo was to take place on 14th June. Fort Capuzzo stood on the flat plateau four miles west of the wire. It was connected by tarmac roads with the frontier post at Musaid and with Bardia. From the Bardia road a track branched north-westwards about two miles from Capuzzo and led to Sidi Azeiz—an insignificant tomb which was probably not noticed by most of those who were fated to spend days and nights in the area—and thence westwards to El Adem and beyond. This track was known as the Trigh Capuzzo;

it was wide and clearly defined and seemed to have been levelled by bulldozers and metalled in places, but without tarmac; the surface soon broke up as successive armies advanced and retreated along it. Other tracks ran off in southerly and westerly directions from the fort, some with a purpose, as in the case of that leading to Sidi Omar, others merely the result of some convoy or column going off for an exercise or expedition in the desert.

The fort itself, if first seen in the flickering mirage of a sunny day, looked like a Byzantine city with white domes and minarets. This illusion was quickly dispelled as one approached it, and the whole edifice turned out to be only a barracks block scarcely more than a hundred yards square, and a few low walls and buildings round it. Where the plaster was chipped off by splinters and bullets the rough construction of the main walls showed beneath. Outside the fort and glowering towards Egypt, was a plaster eagle on a hollow plaster plinth, a reflection of the ambitions of its creator and designed perhaps to inspire ardour in the garrison.

In the desert round the fort defences had been prepared. These consisted of infantry posts and gun pits, the stones thrown up in excavating the trenches being used to build sangars. In the early stages there was little wire and there was no anti-tank ditch, but a few mines had been laid.

No. 253 Wing, Royal Air Force (Group Captain Brown) was to bomb Capuzzo and Madelena in the morning. The 4th Armoured Brigade was then :—

(1) To exploit the success of the Royal Air Force and seize and destroy Fort Capuzzo.

(2) To do likewise if possible to Fort Madelena.

(3) To attack the enemy at Sidi Azeiz.

The orders for the operations were very hasty. On the afternoon of the 13th Brigadier J. A. L. Caunter, M.C., the Commander of the 4th Armoured Brigade, went to divisional headquarters and on the way passed the bearer of the orders without their recognizing each other— they may even have been out of sight. So orders were late and had to be issued to the troops during the night. Mechanical troubles kept forty per cent. of the cruisers and twenty per cent. of the light tanks off the road, track pins being the chief trouble of the light tanks; but the rest of the regiment was ready for the move in good time and all were keen and rather excited at the prospect of the first serious engagement.

Task (1) was carried out by a force consisting of the 7th Hussars less C Squadron, one company of the 1st Battalion, The King's Royal Rifle Corps, and one field troop of the 2nd Field Squadron, Royal Engineers. The attached troops reported to Lieutenant-Colonel Fielden at 6.15 a.m. at Sidi Suleiman. The force crossed the frontier three miles south of Capuzzo at 8.15 a.m. just as the Royal Air Force Blenheims bombed the fort. They bombed it again at 8.50. The air attack undoubtedly scared the enemy, although the nearest bomb was 100 yards away.

B Squadron 7th Hussars (Captain P. Pitman-Butler) was sent round west and north of the fort to prevent the retreat of the garrison and interference from Bardia. The squadron came under shell fire but suffered no damage. At about 9.10 a.m. A Squadron, which had six cruiser tanks (Major D. C. Seymour-Evans) and A Company of the 1st Battalion, King's Royal Rifle Corps, closed on the fort from the south-west. They came under machine gun fire and engaged the fort with 2-pounders and machine guns from tanks and carriers, circling round it. This was enough to keep most of the Italians' heads down.

The riflemen dismounted about 1,400 yards away and advanced rapidly on foot. The enemy did not await their arrival, but put up a white flag and surrendered—16 officers, 10 Italian N.C.O.'s and 200 Libyan infantry. The 60th entered the fort and mounted the walls and the prisoners were marched off to Salum—except the officers, who were taken off in a truck. The 7th Hussars meanwhile moved two miles north towards Bardia to cover the preparation of demolitions. There was no interference except from the Italian air force. This soon arrived on the scene and attacked anything visible in the area of the fort, including the 7th Hussars and the Italian prisoners. The attacks continued spasmodically until the withdrawal. No damage was done to the regiment.

The casualties in this operation were two men of the 7th Hussars wounded, when their 8-cwt. truck hit a mine after the operation was over. One man of the 60th was killed, one of their carriers was destroyed and another was damaged by mines.

At 12 noon orders were received for the withdrawal and at 12.30 demolitions were carried out. These were as thorough and effective as time and resources would allow, but Fort Capuzzo still had four sturdy walls. These stood up, a tawdry landmark, through many changes of fortune until they were flattened by the South Africans as practice—and perhaps also as fun—for their engineers in 1942.

The withdrawal was linked up with that of Combe Force, at Sidi Azeiz. This force having penetrated farther into enemy territory, was ordered to withdraw first. But as Lieutenant-Colonel Combe had asked permission to stay out longer, Colonel Fielden's force was withdrawn as soon as the demolitions had been carried out.

*   *   *   *

Lieutenant-Colonel Combe with his own regiment (11th Hussars) less one squadron, C Squadron 7th Hussars (Major R. F. G. Jayne), one troop of C Battery Royal Horse Artillery (25-pounders) and J Battery Royal Horse Artillery less one troop (2-pounders) had been ordered to cross the wire at 7.45 a.m. and attack Sidi Azeiz immediately after the bombing of Capuzzo was over, at about 9 o'clock. He was then to send patrols to find out whether Bardia was held and other patrols to get astride the Bardia-Tobruk road to harass enemy transport.

Combe's force crossed the wire earlier than ordered, about 7.10 a.m. At 8.5 the advance guard squadron of the 11th Hussars came under fire from nine to twelve guns near Sidi Azeiz, still three or four miles to the northward. One squadron was sent round to the west of the enemy, and the other, followed by regimental headquarters and the rest of the force, worked round to the east. Both the armoured car squadrons drew fire and enemy infantry were observed on the ridge two miles east of Sidi Azeiz. C Squadron 7th Hussars attacked the enemy infantry, who fled when they saw the tanks. But these ran on to a minefield and three, the leading tanks of three different troops, struck mines. The tanks were damaged beyond repair. Trooper Leslie Webb was killed, but the rest of the crews were evacuated undamaged.

At the same time the squadron of the 11th Hussars which had gone round to the west of the defended area had found enemy with heavy automatics on gently rising ground just south-west of Azeiz. But the ground was flat and mirage made observation difficult, so the 25-pounders could do little to help. A patrol sent to reconnoitre Bardia reported infantry in position in the defences.

When, at 12 noon, orders were issued for withdrawal, Lieutenant-Colonel Combe asked and was given permission to withdraw later. He had a squadron watching the Bardia road and another watching the Bardia-Tobruk road. The enemy did not move at all until the withdrawal began. Then the easterly squadron of the 11th Hussars was chased by light tanks (2-man Fiat Ansaldo, C.V.3) but shook them off at the frontier. The westerly squadron saw twenty-four, of which six attacked it. One of these was destroyed and its crew of two captured. This squadron was also subjected to a ruse which the Italians were to try several times later. A white flag was put up, and when the squadron went to investigate it came under artillery fire. There was however no damage.

The third operation of this day was at Fort Madelena. This was bombed by the Royal Air Force soon after 9 a.m. when they had finished with Capuzzo. The squadron of the 11th Hussars advanced on the small fort, which surrendered with one officer and seventeen other ranks.

*   *   *   *

The first excursion in force into Italian territory had resulted in the capture of the two principal frontier forts and about 250 prisoners, for the loss of two men killed, one officer and three men wounded, three light tanks, a carrier and a truck. One interesting point emerged from these operations. The enemy prisoners only had one respirator among them, a significant pointer to their intentions on gas warfare.

There was not long to wait for the next operation. Early on 16th June a patrol of the 11th Hussars on the frontier saw enemy movement and crossed into Italian territory to investigate. It found a column of enemy motor transport, with C.V.3 tanks in front and behind, some ten miles west-south-west of Capuzzo. It made a wireless report and engaged the enemy. The squadron moved towards the area and the regimental commander moved more patrols in that direction.

The prompt action of the 11th Hussars made the enemy halt and de-bus and he occupied a position on a slight ridge. The report said 1 gun, 12 tanks and 300 M.T. (this may have been 30). Brigade headquarters ordered up A Squadron (cruisers) of the 7th Hussars and one troop of J Battery Royal Horse Artillery (2-pounders). These were to come under command of the 11th Hussars and Lieutenant-Colonel Combe was told that the opportunity seemed good for offensive action—advice which he never really needed. The brigade second-in-command, Colonel C. H. Gairdner, was sent forward with a skeleton report centre, and the rest of the brigade was put at fifteen minutes' notice.

At 8.42 a.m. the 7th Hussars received the order. At 9.5 A Squadron was on the move, with the troop of J Battery. By 11.50 they had covered twenty-nine miles and were engaged with the enemy. The Italian column had six guns, which were well served, but their infantry mostly got away before the main battle began. The appearance of the cruisers was a shock for the crews of the C.V.3's, some of whom abandoned their little tanks before they were shot to bits. The 11th Hussars with their Boys rifles knocked out five and the cruisers of the 7th Hussars twelve enemy tanks. Many of the C.V.3 tanks' crews, manned by a former cavalry regiment, fought very gallantly. At one moment Major Seymour-Evans heard a sort of rattling noise down behind his tank. Turning round he saw a little C.V.3 blazing away at him with a machine gun. He put on speed until his gun could depress on to it, and one 2-pounder shot wrecked it.

Twenty enemy dead were counted and 200 prisoners were taken, including the colonel commanding the column. The prisoners had not heard of the capture of Capuzzo two days before. One tank, two guns and five lorries were brought in, but the rest of the enemy equipment was destroyed. There was no interference from the air and there were no casualties. On the same day a patrol of the 11th Hussars on the Bardia-Tobruk road captured a general and his staff, fifty in all, including four women.

The moral effect of these opening operations on the frontier was far greater than the physical. Of the British force, only a mere handful were veterans of World War I. For the rest, battle was a new experience, and the successful outcome gave them supreme confidence from the start.

The effect upon the Italians was equally noticeable. They went mentally upon the defensive. When they moved out of their defended areas it was in compact columns apparently without reconnoitring detachments and the whole expanse of desert between the defended areas was at the disposal of the British patrols. Thus the initiative was gained at the outset and, with one brief interval of four days in September, when the reluctant Marshal Graziani trundled his vast army forward to Sidi Barrani, was held until the Germans arrived ten months later.

But the effect was more than local. The news of these British successes, small as they were in comparison with the disasters in Europe, seemed to show the outside world that there was, after all, something in what Mr. Churchill had said. They were a blow at the morale of the Italians and gave a flicker of encouragement to the people at home when perhaps it was most needed. For on 17th June news came to the desert that the French had formally asked for an armistice. Somebody murmured that Waterloo was a day earlier this year, but there was no surprise and little comment.

Operations had been active and enterprising but somewhat heavy in wear and tear of equipment. In order to conserve track and engine mileage—the latter affecting transport as well as tanks—the enemy was now to be drawn forward before being attacked. Offensive patrolling and guerilla warfare were to continue, but no operations on as large a scale as hitherto, and the enemy was not to be attacked except when outside his defences. There was thus a comparatively quiet period. On the right the Support Group took over from the 2nd Battalion The Highland Light Infantry and watched the frontier from the sea to Salum. The 11th Hussars patrolled from the south and west across the wire and made frequent contacts with the enemy. The Italians patrolled the road east and west of Gabr Saleh with strong columns of tanks and lorried infantry and sometimes had considerable forces there including, it was believed, a divisional headquarters. But no enemy crossed the frontier and all contacts were on Italian soil.

The principal enemy activity was in the air. Operating from Menastir, close to Bardia, his aircraft were within a few minutes flying of attractive targets such as the 11th Hussars patrols and Salum barracks. They were seldom interfered with by Royal Air Force fighters, which were then based at Qasaba, 150 miles away.

The weather was at its hottest and the troops sat sweltering in the shade of their tanks or lorries. It was a great relief when, on 26th June, a regular leave scheme was started, eight days' leave to Cairo for two officers and five per cent. of other ranks per unit. On this first occasion priority was given to married men, so that they might see their families before these left for Palestine. Men on leave were replaced while absent by L.O.B. personnel. The leave system became a permanent institution. It was later calculated so as to give each man five clear days in Cairo instead of eight away from his unit, because some units were farther afield than others and there were many hazards and possibilities of delays on the journey. Before long someone called it the "five clear days and six cloudy nights."

* * * *

As the second half of June was producing very little fighting, on the morning of the 27th the Brigade Commander decided to form a force for the capture of Giarabub. At 6 a.m. on the 29th the following were to come under Colonel C. H. Gairdner, the brigade's second-in-command, for the operation:—

    B Squadron, 7th Hussars (light tanks) under Captain P. Pitman-Butler.
    One squadron 11th Hussars.
    One troop 3rd Royal Horse Artillery (2-pounders).
    One troop 4th Royal Horse Artillery (25-pounders).
    One troop 2nd Field Squadron Royal Engineers.
    One company 1st Battalion, The King's Royal Rifle Corps.

The operation against Giarabub did not however take place, as it was reported early on the 28th that Capuzzo had been re-occupied by the

Italians. B Squadron of the 7th Hussars was therefore put under command of B Squadron of the 11th Hussars, to be used for a fighting reconnaissance to discover the enemy location and strength at Capuzzo and Sidi Azeiz. First reports from the air, which were quickly confirmed by the 11th Hussars, showed forty-eight M.T. at Sidi Azeiz and fifty M.T. and four tanks at Capuzzo. Meanwhile the rest of the regiment, still at Khreigat, fifteen miles south of Capuzzo, was put at thirty minutes' notice.

Next morning, 29th June, Lieutenant-Colonel Fielden was ordered by the brigade commander to attack first Capuzzo and then Sidi Azeiz. The 4th Armoured Brigade's Operation Instruction No. 3, dated the 29th, reached the 7th Hussars at Khreigat at 8.30 a.m. and at 9.10 a.m. the regiment was on the move. In the instruction it was stated that the enemy had 400 men and 48 M.T. at Sidi Azeiz, 50 M.T., 6 medium and some light tanks at Capuzzo. There was a line of defended posts two miles long to the east of Capuzzo. Of our own troops, the 2nd Battalion The Rifle Brigade was at Musaid. B Squadron, 11th Hussars, were in the Sidi Azeiz area and would co-operate with the 7th Hussars. B Squadron, 7th Hussars, reverted to regimental control at once. The rest of the 4th Armoured Brigade was put at thirty minutes' notice to move against the enemy forces reported in the Bir El Gobi area, if these should stir.

The role of O.C. 7th Hussars was given, "to clear the enemy from Fort Capuzzo and Sidi Azeiz." He was ordered to advance from Khreigat astride the track leading northwards, to Boundary Post 38, two miles south of which he was to meet the commander of B Squadron, 11th Hussars. Fort Capuzzo was to be dealt with first and Sidi Azeiz afterwards. The regimental bivouac area was to be moved seven miles farther north to the vicinity of Sidi Suleiman. Fighter cover had been arranged for the operation, but this could not be strong or continuous as the fighters were still stationed at Qasaba and they were kept busy in escorting the occasional tactical reconnaissances, which were carried out by the slow and vulnerable Lysanders.

At 10.45 a.m. the regiment crossed the wire at Boundary Posts 38 and 39. B Squadron, crossing at B.P. 39, advanced to a point about two miles west of B.P. 38 and came under shell fire from an enemy battery somewhere between Point 195 and Point 204. C Squadron moved north up the west side of the wire and came under fire from a battery north-east of the fort. Thus both the light squadrons were in contact and held off by enemy artillery which could not be engaged because there was no artillery support.

An armoured car of the 11th Hussars at the wire at Sidi Omar, July, 1940.

"Several vehicles brewed up and casualties were inflicted." An 11th Hussars armoured car investigating damage after an engagement.

Colonel Fielden's first task was to drive the enemy out of Fort Capuzzo. With this object in view he decided to attack first from the south-west. A Squadron were accordingly ordered to attack the guns which were engaging B Squadron. But cruisers are scarcely more suitable than light tanks for attacking guns in position and the guns have every advantage. If the tanks halt so as to engage the guns accurately, they in turn become stationary and easy targets for the guns. If they do not halt, they are still quite good targets and at the same time nothing but a fluke shot from the moving tank would hit an enemy gun.

A Squadron, with the light tanks in front, advanced a mile and came under artillery fire from at least twelve guns. The commanding officer very wisely ordered the squadron to withdraw a short distance to the wire at B.P. 38, while he reported the situation by radio-telephone to brigade headquarters. Meanwhile B Squadron, which had moved round farther to the west as A advanced, engaged some enemy motor cyclists on the front of the enemy guns and one was seen to fall. At about noon C Squadron advanced on the other side of the fort to the vicinity of the customs house and again came under artillery fire, in face of which it fell back slightly. It appeared that there were at least three enemy batteries in position round the fort, all well concealed.

At 1 p.m. a message was received that the 6th Royal Tanks were coming to the support of the 7th Hussars. They were not to be allowed to attack guns. At 2.15 p.m. a further message was received, that a troop of C Battery Royal Horse Artillery would bombard from 6 p.m. to 7.45 p.m., ending up with smoke, in support of the 7th Hussars and at targets to be selected by them. At 4.45 the troop commander of C Battery arrived in an armoured O.P. and carried out his reconnaissance and at 6.6 p.m. the troop opened fire.

Meanwhile the enemy artillery had engaged both B and C Squadrons intermittently all the afternoon and at 3.30 there had been an attack by five bombers and three fighters. No damage was done, and the most interesting feature of the attack was that one of the fighters seemed to be armed with "some kind of pompom." The enemy also carried out one move of artillery, a battery west of Capuzzo being moved into position north-west of the fort near the aerodrome.

While the troop of C Battery was engaging the enemy, B Squadron worked farther round to the west and C prepared to carry out another advance. At 6.50 p.m., when the four 25-pounders of C Battery had been engaging the enemy for forty minutes, and their fire stopped, C Squadron advanced to within 1,500 yards of the fort on the east side.

The enemy's fire became heavy and accurate and the squadron withdrew, with one tank damaged. Four guns could scarcely have been expected to subdue the far greater number of the enemy, and closing with the enemy guns in daylight would have been very expensive and quite profitless.

The Brigade Commander now decided that the 7th Hussars should attack in the half dark. They were to make a converging attack from three sides. C Squadron was to attack from the east, the light tanks of A Squadron and regimental headquarters from the south, B Squadron from the west. The tanks were to "advance at speed against the enemy batteries using Vickers machine guns continuously during such advance." After reaching the guns the tanks were to destroy them and withdraw. The attack was to be timed "at a moment when it is so dark that the enemy guns cannot lay over open sights against moving tanks over 200 yards (range) but yet light enough to allow of drivers being able to see where to drive." The space of time between the former condition beginning and the latter condition ending is very short; the driver of a closed down light tank never had a good view, even in broad daylight. However it was decided that such a moment might occur at precisely 8 p.m. and the attack was planned for that hour.

The troop of C Battery, which was always ready to help anyone at any time, exceeded its instructions by staying on with the 7th Hussars. It engaged the enemy until about 8.15, so that the attack was postponed until 8.20, by which time it was much darker than had been intended. The regiment then advanced, more slowly than had been expected, and it was fifteen minutes before the tanks were near the fort. C Squadron had meanwhile closed in too far to the left and was jostling the right of A. All squadrons now halted and opened up with machine guns on the fort, A and C being within 500 yards of it.

Two red Verey lights went up and the enemy opened fire with all he had got. The outline of the fort was clearly shown up by the flashes of the numerous weapons of all calibres from field guns to rifles. The coloured tracer of the Bredas was the most spectacular, red, blue, green and white. The nearest enemy fire seemed to come from guns and machine guns in the area just south of the fort and some of these were apparently firing on fixed lines. The commanding officer's tank and the adjutant's were both hit and Colonel Fielden was wounded. Major Byass took over command and Lieutenant Wall, intelligence officer, opened up as the reserve rear link wireless. Both C and A Squadrons were very near enemy batteries but quite unable to deal with them in the dark and confusion. The squadrons were therefore ordered to withdraw to their original positions.

B Squadron, attacking from the west, advanced much faster across the aerodrome and penetrated the enemy anti-tank and field gun positions on the west side. These were in pits, partly excavated out of the rocky ground and partly built up with loose stone walls. The tanks, firing their machine guns, drove in among the batteries and one tank went into a gun pit and crushed one of the gun crew while the others were shot as they ran by the troop leader with his revolver. Troop Sergeant-Major Clarke's tank was hit by a shell, but did not stop, and a few moments later it was rammed by three enemy M.11 medium tanks. One of these fired its gun into the driver's glass at short range, but the shell did not penetrate. The ·5 machine gun was jammed—no unusual occurrence with this gun—so the ·303 machine gun was fired at the enemy tanks, which obligingly backed slowly away. The ·303 would not have penetrated their armour even from behind, where it was thinnest. Clarke's tank would not move forward, so he backed it away about 100 yards. It was then hit again and caught fire. Corporal Pegler, who had sent his gunner off to get another machine gun lock, came to Sergeant-Major Clarke's help and took off the crew. For this action he was awarded the Military Medal.

Another party of enemy tanks moved on to the aerodrome and seemed to be attacking the squadron headquarters, but two of them rammed each other and they withdrew and disappeared. The squadron did considerable damage to enemy guns and motor transport found in the area, but was somewhat split up in the darkness. The squadron leader (Captain Pitman-Butler) gave the order to rally about the same time as his rear link was receiving the order from the regiment to withdraw, but the two headquarters tanks were out of touch with one another, so the order to withdraw did not reach the troops when it should have and the squadron returned to its position rather later than expected.

On withdrawal the tanks of the adjutant and navigator were missing, also one from A Squadron, five from B and three from C. All came in during the night except one from A and the one from B which had been hit and burnt out. The missing tank from A Squadron had been hit early in the operation and all its crew wounded; it moved slowly out of action but was hit again; this time Corporal William S. Fabry and Lance-Corporal William Lewis were killed. The enemy continued shelling long after the withdrawal, sometimes using star shells, but the only shells which fell near the regiment were at B.P. 38 and in C Squadron's area about Musaid; these did no harm.

Next morning B Squadron moved out at dawn to search the area south-west of the fort for A Squadron's missing tank. It was not in fact in that area. The enemy's motor transport was still in the neighbourhood of the fort. At 7 a.m. the squadron was attacked by aircraft. At this period of the war very ineffective bombs were used for low flying attacks, a mixture of small anti-personnel and incendiary bombs which fell close to the tanks without doing any harm. Low flying attacks were however unpleasant and the absence of air cover was not at all appreciated by the troops. It was causing some anxiety in higher quarters too; a successful enemy air attack on the divisional transport would have had a most serious effect on the mobility of the division as there was literally no reserve of vehicles in the country. But there were in fact good reasons for conserving our diminutive air strength, as will be seen later.

The report of the 4th Armoured Brigade states—"The operation, despite the mistakes which occurred, was a success." It was thought that the enemy was badly shaken by the night attack; that much material damage must have been done by the volume of fire; that the Italians would never again feel safe at night and could be harassed and deprived of sleep and ammunition by a single troop of tanks using searchlights. To this extent something may have been achieved. But the enemy still remained in possession of Fort Capuzzo.

Mistakes would be difficult to avoid in an operation whose origins were so fortuitous. For a force of all arms had been organized for an attack on Jiarabub, and this project was only abandoned in favour of the attack on Capuzzo and Sidi Azeiz on the morning of the 28th, when it was heard that the fort had been re-occupied. The 7th Hussars were then ordered to eject the enemy the next morning.

No infantry were allotted and no artillery support. The heaviest weapons were the 2-pounders in the six cruiser tanks. The light tanks had only ·5 and ·303 Vickers machine guns. Their armour was proof against nothing except shell splinters and small arms fire. In these circumstances the Commanding Officer was wise not to press his attack against the strong artillery and anti-tank defences.

When artillery was allotted in the afternoon, it was only a troop of four guns, placed in support for a limited bombardment from 6 to 7.45 p.m., at the conclusion of which it was to withdraw. It is not quite clear why, at 6.50 p.m., when the bombardment was still in progress, an attack was launched with one squadron only, but it is evident that it would have been unwise to press this home against opposition which four 25-pounders could not possibly have suppressed in the time. In the circumstances co-ordination between the tanks and

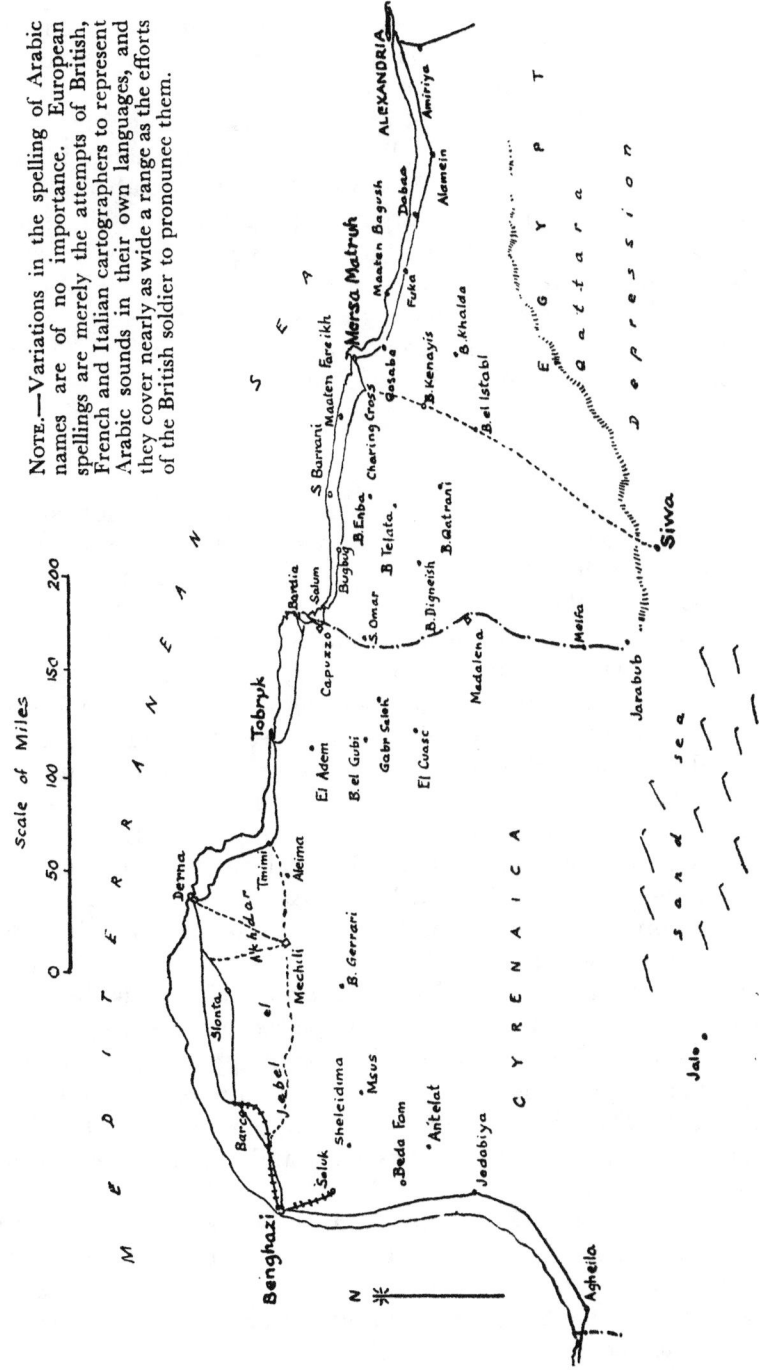

Map I — Western Desert and Cyrenaica

the artillery might have been easier if the four guns had been placed "under command" of the 7th Hussars instead of "in support," or alternatively if brigade control had been less remote.

The night attack may have had its value for harassing purposes and causing anxiety for the future. But a converging attack is always somewhat hazardous at night. As it was, A and C Squadrons bumped one another. If all three had driven right home into the enemy's artillery positions they might have suffered severely not only from the enemy's guns but from each other. It was certainly a day of unusual operations and it was probably due to the discretion of the Commanding Officer that the cost was not heavier, two killed and four wounded, among the latter the Commanding Officer himself.

*   *   *   *

On 1st July the regiment settled down to several days' much needed maintenance. On the frontier a slight adjustment was made in the boundaries, the Support Group being made responsible from the sea to Musaid, the latter and Capuzzo and all to the south being within the boundary of the 4th Armoured Brigade. The Brigade's new task was "while conserving personnel, to harass the enemy and delay any attempt he may make to re-establish himself on the frontier."

On the 2nd the German wireless announced that the Italians were going to take Salum. Whether this was designed to inspire their allies to offensive action or to deter the British does not matter, but no attack came off. The only movement seen next day was reported by the Rifle Brigade, a column of thirty mechanical transport moving north-eastwards along the wire about B.P. 29. At 11.15 a.m. Colonel C. H. Gairdner, second-in-command of the brigade, ordered the 7th Hussars, 6th Royal Tanks and J Battery Royal Horse Artillery to move forward. One squadron of the 6th Royal Tanks was ordered to attack the column. They endeavoured to do so, but actually passed between Fort Capuzzo and the enemy. The mirage was bad and apparently neither side saw the other. Consequently the combat was limited to exchanges of artillery fire. The 7th Hussars patrols which went to the Salum aerodrome made no contact with the enemy and that night the regiment leaguered two miles south-east of B.P. 38.

For the first four days of July the operational task of the regiment was to watch the wire from Musaid to B.P. 39. On the 4th the regiment crossed the wire just before 6 a.m., with what intent is not stated. It came at once under shell fire and withdrew, in accordance with instructions, to the vicinity of B.P. 38.

On the 5th, at 10 a.m., Colonel Gairdner visited the Commanding Officer with orders for a fresh task. The 7th Hussars were to move to the west and north of Capuzzo, keeping out of range of the guns. On arrival in the area north of the fort the regiment was to be prepared to attack and harass any small enemy columns which approached the fort from Bardia or Sidi Azeiz. The start was delayed, as it was necessary to move the regiment a little to the rear in order to replenish. Why replenishment was not carried out the evening before, in accordance with the usual practice, is not explained, but the regimental war diary records that "This error annoyed brigade headquarters somewhat."

At 1 o'clock the regiment moved in two columns. B Squadron was sent east of the wire, which it was to cross at B.P. 28. From that locality it was to patrol the Bardia-Capuzzo road. From B.P. 28 the squadron moved north to B.P. 25. It was immediately attacked by M.11 tanks covered by artillery fire. The squadron moved away, farther to the north, in the direction of Bardia; here it remained more or less "in check" for the rest of the afternoon, as it had no effective means of engaging the M.11's. At 6 p.m. it withdrew to B.P. 28 and re-crossed the wire.

The rest of the regiment went west-about round Capuzzo and lay in the area between the fork roads leading respectively to Bardia and Sidi Azeiz. C Squadron was to the eastward, watching the Bardia road. A Squadron was watching the Sidi Azeiz road and was also available to come to the support of C.

The regiment was in position by 3 p.m. but nothing happened. There could of course be no surprise, as there had already been a clash between B Squadron and the Italian tanks, and the troops in Capuzzo must unavoidably have seen movement going on to the west and north. It appears, however, that the enemy had every intention of getting a convoy through to Capuzzo. He waited to see whether the tanks moved back to the frontier and at 6 p.m., as they had shown no signs of doing so, he took steps to force the convoy through. First he attacked with aircraft. Regimental headquarters was the target, and was attacked repeatedly from 6 p.m. for twenty minutes. A large number of small anti-personnel and incendiary bombs were dropped and the tanks were hit many times. There was a little superficial damage, and splinters made holes in bedding, mugs, water-tins and rations, but there were no casualties.

The convoy, of about thirty transport vehicles, came in view of C Squadron about 7 p.m. C Squadron advanced to attack and halted when it came under shell fire from the covering artillery, which had evidently come into action before the convoy advanced; the order to avoid shell fire was still in force. Long range machine gun fire, even with the ·5, was not effective enough to stop the enemy. Most of their vehicles were thought to be hit, but they drove on fast and reached Capuzzo.

At 9 p.m., after placing two patrols, one on each road, the regiment withdrew to B.P. 41 to leaguer. There was an error in navigation and it was 1 a.m. before everything was in place and settled down for the night. The wireless operator on the rear link was still busy however. There was a lot of traffic on the rear link frequency all the evening. Between traffic congestion, atmospheric interference, which is often very tiresome in the desert after dark, and being rather spasmodically on the move, the report of the day's operations did not get through to brigade headquarters until 2 a.m. Says the diary "This was to cause a lot of unpleasantness." The 7th Hussars do not seem to have given much satisfaction on this day.

At 4.30 a.m. on the 6th the regiment, less B Squadron, began to move forward again to the area north of Capuzzo. B Squadron was sent back to the regiment's original leaguer area for a day's maintenance. Both the night patrols had had engagements. Lieutenant Llewellen Palmer's troop of C Squadron on the Bardia road had intercepted two cars, destroyed both and captured an officer and two other ranks. Lieutenant Oates' troop of C Squadron, on the Azeiz road, had headed off a convoy evidently bound for Capuzzo. On being fired upon the convoy withdrew towards Sidi Azeiz. As day broke the troop followed up this convoy and found it halted three miles east of Sidi Azeiz. By 10.15 it was clear that the enemy had taken up a defensive position on the ridge. Lieutenant-Colonel Byass decided to attack, using the same tactics as previously. The attack was to be carried out by A Squadron and one troop of C.

At 11 a.m. the attacking troops drove up the road and on coming within range of the enemy, wheeled right in line ahead and drove round his position, keeping up a continuous fire. Several lorries were hit and disabled and the rest fled. The guns, standing out clearly against the desert, were an obvious target and the volume of machine gun fire was too much for some of the gunners; many were hit as they ran from them; others continued in action and kept firing at the tanks. There was, however, no intention of closing with the enemy guns, which were supported by heavier artillery in the neighbourhood of Sidi Azeiz. So the order was given to withdraw.

A Squadron started to rally and to find its whereabouts, covering itself with smoke from its smoke bombs. In a mobile action of this kind it is not easy to navigate accurately and people get confused in a constantly revolving turret. While the squadron was sorting itself out it came under fire both from the guns at Sidi Azeiz and from the guns of the enemy column. Colonel Gairdner, with one cruiser tank and one light tank, saw the enemy gunners running back to their guns and engaged them effectively, thus helping to cover the withdrawal of A Squadron. At 7.30 p.m. the regiment withdrew from the battle area and made for the leaguer area east of the wire.

This time the enemy had been prevented from sending a column to Capuzzo and the day was quite successful. One cruiser was damaged and had to be towed home. One light tank was missing, with Corporal Ram and Troopers Cooney and Sims of C Squadron; it had in fact struck a mine, and Trooper Edward Cooney was killed and the other two were taken prisoner. The satisfaction of a good day's work was somewhat marred by a letter from brigade headquarters "condemning the action of the previous day."

The next few days were spent in the same area, the regiment remaining concentrated about Point 208 between Capuzzo and Sidi Azeiz, with patrols watching the two roads. On one of these patrols Troop Sergeant-Major Hatherall cut the pipe line which supplied water from Bardia to Capuzzo. On his last patrol he had shot up an enemy convoy and had been somewhat nettled by a note of unbelief in his report's reception at brigade headquarters. So this time he cut the pipe line with his ·5 machine gun and cut a section right out of it. He made this fast to his tow rope and dragged it all the way back to the leaguer area, observing, "Now the —— will believe me."

On the 7th there was a brief moment of anxiety when a report from brigade headquarters said the enemy had got between the regiment and the wire. The regiment was ordered to move away eight miles to the westward for safety, but the report was soon found to be incorrect. On the 8th no enemy movement was seen. On the 9th an enemy column was seen on the Bardia road and engaged by the troops of Lieutenant Oates and Troop Sergeant-Major King of C Squadron, supported by Major Seymour-Evans with two cruisers of A. Again the tanks were held off by artillery and anti-tank fire. The long range fire did some damage to the enemy, but probably not much. It was recorded on this day that the 2-pounders on the cruisers were a failure, their shooting being inaccurate.

* * * *

The 10th was another blank day but the 11th brought a welcome change in tactics. Hitherto the tank had operated unsupported against its most effective antidote, the gun. Small wonder that its operations had given little satisfaction. Now a troop of C Battery Royal Horse Artillery was attached to the regiment. A success was scored at once. A column of 100 transport vehicles was engaged by the 25-pounders and prevented from reaching Capuzzo; the enemy gunners however found no target at all. For two days after that the Italians never ventured out.

The 7th Hussars were now given a new task—to find good targets for C Battery Royal Horse Artillery. They did so and on the 14th and 15th C Battery "did great damage to the enemy." But the attachment of guns meant more than that. The regiment was now able once more to act offensively. Instead of having to stand off in order to avoid too heavy losses from shellfire, it could press home its attacks to within effective machine gun and 2-pounder range. To make an effective all-purpose fighting force, there were now lacking only infantry and an engineer demolition party.

On the 16th orders were received to attack and destroy some damaged lorries and stores at the road junction two miles north of Capuzzo. These were the result of C Battery's action two days before. The attack was to be covered by a troop of C Battery Royal Horse Artillery, which was to neutralize the enemy guns. B Squadron formed up in line about 3,000 yards to the west of the objective, A and C together 3,000 yards north-west of it.

At 7.30 a.m. visibility was bad, but slowly improving until, at 8.20, it was clear enough and the attack went in. When about 2,000 yards from the enemy B Squadron came under artillery and anti-tank fire from the fort and from the area of the road junction. A few moments later C Squadron also came under fire. The advance continued, aided by the effective supporting fire of C Battery, which undoubtedly kept down the enemy's artillery fire and also hit some of the lorries. B Squadron drove right in among an enemy anti-tank battery and shot down a number of the gunners. The Italian gunners, both Metropolitan and Libyan, frequently gave a very good account of themselves in action and were not easily driven from their guns.

C Squadron were now approaching the area of the objective, but the fire of their right troop was masked by B, who were mopping up the remaining enemy personnel, about a dozen prisoners. Captain Pitman-Butler and Second-Lieutenant Murray Smith of B Squadron dismounted from their tanks—no infantry being available—and with their revolvers made the prisoners march in front of the tanks. But the prisoners' morale had now quite given way and as the batteries at Capuzzo were keeping up a steady fire they fell flat as every shell arrived. Progress was so slow that they were then taken on board the tanks and driven away. B Squadron had destroyed three enemy anti-tank guns, but there were other enemy still active in the area and it was an armour-piercing bullet which, at this stage, penetrated the turret of Captain Pitman-Butler's tank, mortally wounding him and wounding Corporal Cowley, the wireless operator.

Meanwhile C Squadron's left troops had penetrated among the lorries and shot up sixteen of them. The enemy's artillery fire was now getting heavier. The stores in the lorries were damaged as much as possible—no engineers being available—by machine gun fire from the tanks, and perhaps also by the enemy's own fire, but not completely destroyed. The troop of C Battery Royal Horse Artillery did all that four guns could do. At 9.30 a.m. the squadrons withdrew. All the tanks were in running order and only three of them damaged. The casualties to personnel had been four in all; besides those already mentioned, Second-Lieutenant T. R. S. Thornton and Lance-Corporal H. Bancroft were wounded.

The 7th Armoured Brigade was now coming forward to take over from the 4th. Patrolling continued as usual by day and night. No major contact was made with the enemy but one successful night ambush was brought off by Second-Lieutenant C. T. Llewellen Palmer's troop. On the night of 19th/20th July he laid mines on the Bardia road and lay up 100 yards away. A lorry came along from Bardia and stopped on reaching them. A number of men got out and went to look at the mines. Some picked them up. At this moment the tanks opened fire. A few of the Italians rushed back to the lorry, which got away. Six or seven remained and surrendered.

On the 20th Captain G. Harbord's squadron of the 8th Hussars arrived and came under command of the 7th Hussars. Next day C Squadron the 7th Hussars and B Squadron the 1st Royal Tanks (attached to the 8th Hussars) went out together, again without incident. On the 22nd the regiment handed over its task on the frontier to the 8th Hussars and marched back a few miles to Sidi Suleiman, leaving only B Squadron forward, on an independent mission west of Sidi Azeiz. From an area near the aerodrome B Squadron was to report any enemy movements and to shoot up aircraft. For two days it remained about Sidi Azeiz and reported enemy movements, but was unable to attack enemy aircraft without prejudice to its primary task. The squadron was then withdrawn to rejoin the regiment.

The regiment less C Squadron was now ordered back to Sofafi, moving by night without lights. Before hostilities began there had not been much practice in moving across the desert by night without lights. Since then the transport had done a good deal of it, in replenishing, and the tanks had done a little in recent operations. The most satisfactory method was in line ahead, or in two columns of line ahead. The distance between vehicles was then regulated by the visibility. On a very dark night it might be only ten yards, on a moonlight night it could be fifty. If there was a gentle cross breeze to take the dust away a night march was not too bad, but if there was no breeze at all, or it was dead fore and aft, it was misery. The most important thing was to keep touch with the tank in front. Unless the commander of a tank which lost touch was very alert, he could easily go astray before anyone discovered he was wrong, and in this case everything behind him would follow. Something of this kind now happened to A Squadron, which got lost, and so caused a delay of about one-and-a-half hours in arriving at the destination. The next night C Squadron rejoined with the Light Aid Detachment of the Royal Army Ordnance Corps, which had been left behind for it at Sidi Suleiman.

There now followed twelve days of rest. This meant work as hard as ever for the fitters and the Light Aid Detachment. Their strenuous efforts, under the guidance of Lieutenants Dean and Astley-Rushton of the regiment and Warrant Officer Calder of the Royal Army Ordnance Corps, put every vehicle on the road again by the end of the tenth day. Meanwhile the tank crews started leave in succession to Cairo, and others who could be spared were sent off for forty-eight hours' picnic at the sea, some twenty miles away.

Health on the whole was good. The main trouble was septic sores —a condition more tiresome than painful, due to something lacking in the "hard" rations. It affected most people at some time or other. The slightest tap would remove the skin of a knuckle or other projection and it would not heal up, but stayed as a damp yellow mess which had to be kept in a bandage. The scientific meaning of it all has doubtless been set forth by others.

So ended the regiment's first period of combats with the Italians. Several decorations had been won, including the Military Medal for S.S.M. Swain and Corporal Cowley. Much experience had been gained. At first the regiment had been used for attacking targets discovered by the 11th Hussars. Then it had found its targets with its own patrols, while it lay concentrated in the area between Capuzzo and Sidi Azeiz, ready to strike. Then its patrols had found targets for the artillery to engage. Finally a successful operation was carried out with artillery support.

Whenever it had an opportunity, C Battery Royal Horse Artillery was always most co-operative and enterprising. That the battery was absent from many of the engagements was no fault of its gallant commander, Major Geoffrey Goschen, but the serious ammunition situation in the Middle East no doubt had a great deal to do with it.

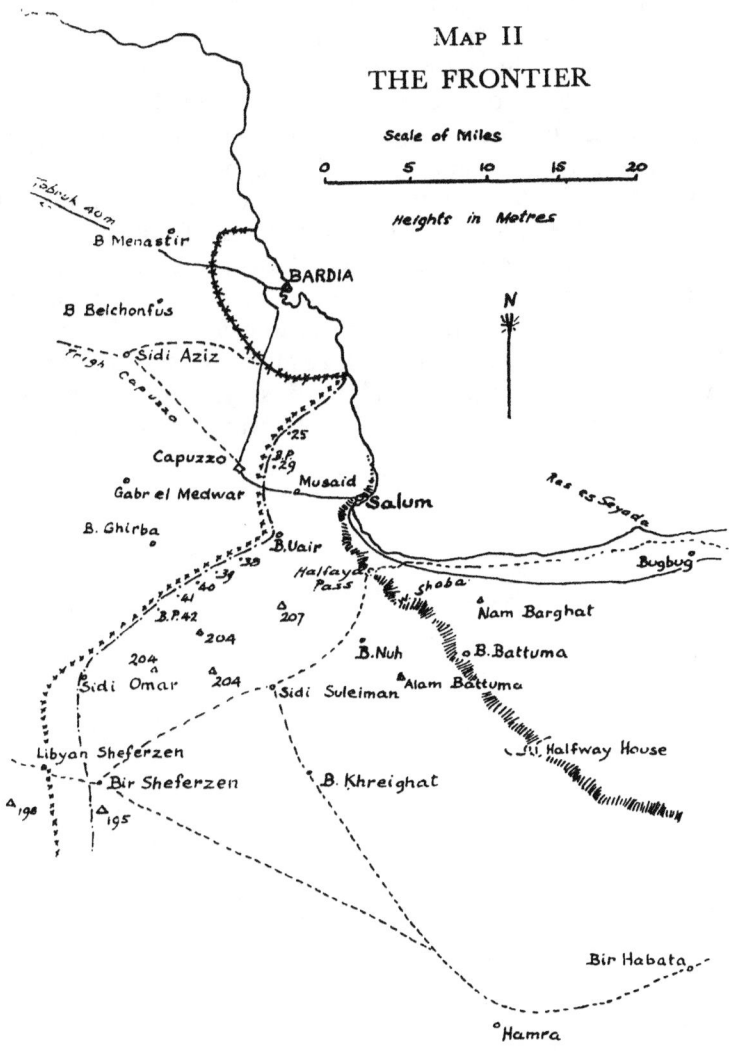

Some of the operations were of an unusual character—infantry attacking a fort supported by tanks but no artillery—tanks attacking a fort without infantry or artillery—tanks attacking guns. But the tank had a moral effect of its own, which only began to wear off beyond the wire when the enemy gunners realized that they were really in a very strong position if attacked by tanks in the open desert.

At first the enemy marched his guns with the convoys and they came into action when the convoy was attacked. Then he started a kind of caterpillar movement, sending guns into action ahead, then moving the convoy up to the guns, then bringing up his tail artillery which had stayed in action during the movement. Then he evolved a third method and picketed parts of the road with batteries before starting his convoy off. These tactics made it difficult for tanks to close, and as they were ordered not to incur losses they could not do so. The addition of C Battery's 25-pounders however made a considerable difference and largely restored the offensive power of the tanks.

During this opening period the enemy was hard put to it to maintain his garrison in Capuzzo and had very little control in the Bardia-Capuzzo-Sidi Azeiz triangle. In the first six weeks he lost 500 men in prisoners alone and the total loss of the 7th Armoured Division was only five killed, twenty-seven wounded and eight missing. Four of the dead and half the others were 7th Hussars. Still, it was a satisfactory start.

CHAPTER III

The Battle of Sidi Barrani

Desert routine—Italian invasion—defensive preparations south of Matruh—preparations for the offensive—concentration—operations on 9th December—operations on 10th December—pursuit to Bardia—attack on Sidi Omar.

Maps I, II, III

By this time the soldier's daily life in the desert had settled into an established routine. Naturally the routine varied in accordance with the circumstances, and during periods of fighting lapsed altogether. But under normal conditions, when in contact with the enemy, it was somewhat as follows. As it grew dark the regiment would come into close leaguer. There would be an hour or two to wait for the replenishment vehicles, which avoided travelling the last few miles in daylight because of the enemy's control of the air in the forward zone. Rations and, when necessary, petrol and ammunition would then be issued to the troops, and each tank commander would satisfy himself that his petrol tank was full, his ammunition complete, that he had his reserve of petrol and his three days' reserve of rations and water for each man, and that his wireless battery was replaced by a newly charged one if necessary. When all was in order the crew lay down alongside its tank in a row on the sheltered side and slept till it began to get light.

At the first streak of dawn the regiment dispersed, each squadron moving perhaps a mile and then opening out to 150 yards between vehicles. This made contact between commanders and their troops somewhat laborious, but the enemy airmen, if bent on the offensive, usually went for the most closely huddled target, so dispersion was worth while.

On arrival at the dispersal spot, breakfast was made at once. A neat little petrol cooker was carried on every tank, but it was rather more trouble to light and keep going than the simpler method of a slight hole dug in the sand. About half a pint of petrol was poured in the hole and a match set it alight. If the flame died down a slight stir with a track pin or sprig of scrub would bring up more of the petrol. It was dangerous however to throw more petrol on and several people were burnt that way. First water would be boiled for tea. The tea was dropped in, then some tinned milk and sugar—and plenty of it.

Next the tinned bacon or bully beef would be put on to fry and perhaps marmalade on biscuit would finish the breakfast. A fearful pale yellow substance called "Margarine with Butter Content for Tropical Climates" was always offered with the rations. Occasionally a tin was accepted and opened just to see if it was the same as the last; it always was.

After breakfast each man attended to his personal economy, stepping out a short way into the desert with the tank's shovel. The latter was an indispensable piece of domestic furniture which kept the North African fly out of its improper place. Whenever misfortune led British troops into an area which had recently been contaminated by enemy occupation (the Italians did not understand the use of shovels) an outbreak of dysentery or Gyppy Tummy invariably followed.

Then came a shave. Of the gallon of water—sometimes reduced as low as half a gallon—issued daily for all purposes, a little would be heated up for a shave and a few spoonfuls were used for brushing the teeth. Washing was a problem. Some washed a very little every day, some washed a little more every other day, some washed the top half one day and the bottom half three days later. If anywhere near the sea and not in the dead of winter, some never washed in fresh water at all; there were a few who bathed even in the winter months, when frequently one awoke with hard droplets of ice covering the bedding; these winter bathers were usually prominent in outbreaks of jaundice. It was not easy to organize the small water supply for washing oneself and one's clothes, as well as for drinking and cooking.

Lunch and supper were much the same as breakfast, a brew of tea, bully beef and biscuits. Sometimes there was an issue of rice, or tinned potatoes. N.A.A.F.I. stores included tinned fruit. The evening meal was either cooked and eaten in daylight before going into leaguer, or brought up cooked, in heatproof containers, with the replenishment vehicles and issued to each man from the vehicle. There was practically never an issue of bread or fresh meat except when back near the railhead.

The British soldier is never slow in adding a little to his comfort when opportunity permits and it is remarkable how quickly beds, tables and chairs appear from nowhere, even in a desert. When, early in August, the regiment was moved back to Maaten el Firikhat, twenty miles west of Matruh, a higher standard of living slowly crept in. The shovel was displaced by the squadron latrine and beds found their way into improvised tents, rigged out of groundsheets or tarpaulins against the sides of tanks. Even a real tent or two found its way into the regimental area. There was an infamous case where a tent was loaded into a lorry by one officer while another officer "passed the time of day" with the responsible ordnance authority who was losing it. Both being good officers, they observed the eleventh commandment, "Thou shalt not be found out."

Life was further brightened by the arrival of a mail from the United Kingdom. None had come by the Mediterranean route since early in June, so there had been a gap of nearly nine weeks while the June letters steamed round the Cape. This first arrival meant that the new flow had started and more could be expected with every convoy.

As the 7th Hussars arrived in the new area they took over tanks from the 6th Royal Tanks, who were returning to Cairo. No tanks were moved more than was absolutely necessary and all were put into good order, as far as their age and availability of spares would permit. Of the seven cruisers only three could be made serviceable. Five light tanks were deficient, five scout cars and two 3-tonners.

The operational duty of the regiment while at El Firikhat was to support the coast watching detachments of the Arab Legion, in case of an enemy landing, on a stretch of twenty-five miles of coast line westwards from Mersa Umm el Rakham. Liaison was maintained with these posts and one squadron was kept at one-and-a-half hours notice to move, with one troop at thirty minutes. Nothing ever happened, but in view of the possibility of a quick move, crew-messing continued.

The move to El Firikhat coincided with a change of plan for action in case of an enemy advance in force. All the tanks in the desert had been worked fairly hard and it was desirable that all should be made ready for the decisive battle in the Mersa Matruh area if the Italians should come on. Both the armoured brigades were therefore to be placed on the general line Maaten el Firikhat—Bir el Kenayis, while dummy tanks were erected in the forward area. The Support Group was to remain in the forward area and to harass and delay the enemy's advance, without becoming seriously committed.

In order to leave the Support Group a free hand and to avoid what the divisional diary calls "cluttering up the desert," the headquarters of 7th Armoured Division were established at Bir el Kenayis. Brigadier Gott, commanding the Support Group, had a liking for elbow room. But between Mersa Matruh and the frontier the probable area of operations was something like 5,000 square miles and there were not as many as 5,000 men in the Support Group, so "cluttering up" was perhaps hardly the word. It would however obviously be better if he did not have to feel a sense of responsibility for covering an extra headquarters, which in any case could contribute little to the Support Group's battle.

Reconnaissances were carried out in the area west of the Siwa track, with a view to finding hull-down positions where the enemy could be engaged at an advantage. "Hull-down" is another expression borrowed from the Royal Navy, who, on a clear day, often see the enemy and each other's funnels and superstructure, the hulls being hidden below the horizon. A tank with only its turret and gun showing is not only less conspicuous than in the open, but, against flat trajectory weapons like a tank-gun or an anti-tank gun at fairly close range, less vulnerable. There were a good many tiny but fairly steep escarpments in the desert which afforded convenient positions of this kind and if they happened to be on the enemy's line of advance they could be useful.

The four weeks from the middle of August to the middle of September were passed in comparative inactivity and not very much comfort. There was a certain amount of sickness, caused by the dirtiness of the camp site. But this was gradually cleaned up, and by the time the Italians advanced most of the Gyppy Tummy had disappeared.

Skirmishing continued in the Capuzzo area throughout August and into September. The enemy bombed Mersa Matruh regularly. He shelled Musaid, Salum and the surroundings every day between 8 and 11 a.m. and between 6 and 7 p.m. The soldiers used to speculate on the routine in the intervening periods, coffee, spaghetti, siesta and finally more spaghetti. On the 6th there was a change in the enemy's routine, and he did a little night firing. This was thought to be practice of defensive fire.

The first move in the impending advance into Egypt began in the early hours of the 10th September. The sound of engines was heard during the night and on the morning of the 10th, under the watchful eyes of the 11th Hussars, 450 vehicles were on the move slowly from the north camp at Gabr Saleh towards Sidi Azeiz. In the afternoon about the same number were counted in the area Capuzzo—Musaid; about a 100 crossed the wire at B.P. 26 and men began to dig gun positions. Enemy aircraft were active and twenty-six of their fighters were in the air at intervals during the day, some of them carrying out low flying attacks on the forward troops. These activities all seemed to herald a grand operation.

No alterations were made in the dispositions of the division and leave parties proceeded as usual.

The next day further preliminary operations took place. Three large columns, amounting in all to 1,000 vehicles, moved from Gabr Saleh towards the frontier, in the general direction of Sidi Omar and

Sheferzen, but halted several miles short of it. A similar number were seen in the Capuzzo area and motor cycle patrols were seen moving on the aerodrome. On the 12th the enemy was found to be digging in along the frontier from Musaid to Sidi Omar, some twenty posts, each with about fifty men. The enemy camps at Gabr Saleh, Sidi Azeiz and Bir el Gobi were reported empty and the whole Italian army seemed to have concentrated on the frontier.

Thinning out of the Support Group now began according to plan and all was made ready for harassing the enemy's advance. In the evening our patrols were driven away from Musaid by five enemy medium tanks and the enemy then bombarded the Musaid area and occupied it.

There had been three days of very obvious concentration in the forward area before the advance began. The moves had been accurately reported by our tactical reconnaissance aeroplane, which was attached to the division with six protecting fighters and was allowed to reconnoitre up to ten miles across the frontier. All reports were confirmed by the 11th Hussars.

At 7 a.m. on the 13th the enemy crossed the wire near Capuzzo. The 3rd Battalion of the Coldstream Guards withdrew according to plan and the Italians occupied Salum barracks. Another Italian formation moved forward to the Helfaya Pass area, covered by motor cyclists. This column, in the high desert south of the escarpment, was harassed by the 1st Royal Tanks. It made its way to the top of the pass and pushed out a covering force to Bir Nuh. By the evening the enemy was feeling his way down the escarpment at Salum and Helfaya.

Throughout the day the British forward troops had been attacked continuously by aircraft and no fighter protection was available. It is recorded that on this day the enemy dropped "bombs very like thermos flasks." These were later to have a certain nuisance value. As they hit the ground something was actuated in the mechanism which made them detonate the next time they were moved, however slightly. The first three victims were men of the 11th Hussars, but news of the thermos bomb was quickly circulated and there were very few casualties from it afterwards.

On the 14th the enemy advanced down Helfaya Pass, losing considerably from the accurate fire of C Battery Royal Horse Artillery, for which his densely packed column was a perfect target. The same day he repaired the craters in Salum hill and by the evening had advanced to a point ten miles east of Salum, with the bulk of his force on the summer track, nearest the coast, and a smaller column on the main road. His halting places for the night were accurately located and he was harassed by the artillery, now increased to two batteries by the move forward of F Battery Royal Horse Artillery (Major H. C. Withers).

On the 15th the advance continued, harassed by our artillery and that of the Free French on the coast road. That evening the enemy halted about the north and south line through Bugbug, from which the Support Group had withdrawn. On the 16th, still being harassed all the way, he reached the general line Sidi Barrani and south. He then began preparing defences, and the next day the Italian wireless announced that all the services in Sidi Barrani were restored and the trams running as usual. Sidi Barrani consisted of three or four huts for the peace-time accommodation of a patrol of Egyptian Frontiers Administration camel police—a score of Sudanese—and a few wells and cisterns.

The salient features of the operation had been the enemy's dense concentrations and his very limited reconnaissance. He seemed to have no armoured cars and his motor cyclists seldom reconnoitred more than a mile from his main columns. His losses in vehicles alone were 200. If aircraft had been available to attack him his packed columns would have suffered severely. British casualties in the withdrawal were under thirty, killed, wounded and missing. The Free French made an excellent impression on their British allies and were to be become firm friends of the regiment.

*   *   *   *

On the 15th, just as the enemy reached Bugbug, orders were given for the armoured brigades to concentrate in their battle areas, which extended from Bir Khalda, thirty-five miles due south of Matruh, westwards for fifty miles to El Qatrani. The 4th Armoured Brigade was to be about the middle of the area, at Bir el Kenayis on the Siwa track, and the 7th Armoured Brigade at el Qatrani.

The move was carried out in a great hurry, as there was no saying how far Graziani might advance. This was where the high standard of living was an embarrassment, especially for the light tanks. It was very distressing to abandon beds and chairs which had become cherished possessions and seemed to be part of the tank's furniture. But no light tank had the space outside to carry them. The cruisers were more fortunate and the squadron leader's tank of A Squadron was perhaps the most interesting of all, if carefully investigated. It had a goat, a cage of partridges, three chairs and a bedstead (not his own). Dress was also somewhat mixed. Some were caught out with their washing wet and others were in any case getting a little variegated in their plumage. The Hon. D. R. C. Chichester was perhaps above average in this respect; his trousers had shrunk so far that they only reached to his calves; he was without socks and had a white sandshoe on one foot and a brown one on the other. Hitler might have been even more misled if he could have seen the move of the 7th Hussars to Bir el Kenayis.

After one night in the new area the brigade was ordered back to the neighbourhood of Charing Cross, where it occupied a site which had been in use before; it was infested with flies. It was also on the main route of the unfortunate Bedawin.

In accordance with a pre-arranged plan the Bedawin had been ordered back towards Amiriya, near Alexandria, as soon as the Italian advance began. At the same time all the wells within thirty miles of the coast were either blown in or salted, so as to make life as difficult as possible for the Italians. Pathetic little family processions came constantly through the regimental area. Each party was generally in the order of its economic importance, men and camels first, then goats, then women. They offered eggs and emaciated hens in exchange for water, bully beef and tea. The women would stay well away while the men came up to the tanks with their simple greeting for Europeans "Sayeda!" repeated several times by both sides with grins and handshakes, and some embarrassment because that was usually the limit of conversation. Occasionally they would frown and say "Mussolini," and draw the finger significantly across the throat. They were mostly of the Senussi sect and had an unfeigned hatred for the Italians, who had, in the past twenty years, treated their brethren across the frontier with particular brutality, especially in their desert campaigns in 1930. Now, with their camels and goats, they were to go back to the edge of the delta until the Italians were driven out.

The Arab wanted nothing so much as to be left alone. With his age-long social system, his camels and goats and the patch of depression in the desert where it was customary for each family to throw in its annual barley, he was content, because Allah and the Prophet said he was to be. While he hated the Italians, it would not be right to say he loved the British. But in spite of the many advances and retreats of the next few years, the Arabs in enemy occupied territory as well as those in Egypt were of the greatest help. Many soldiers, sailors and airmen owe their escapes, when shot down or cut off, to a friendly reception by the Arabs and their frugal but brave and generous hospitality. Whenever possible the Arabs were subsequently rewarded.

September and October were uneventful. The Italians made occasional pompous pronouncements. About 24th September they said that by the 30th the British would be in full flight. They also spoke of the pincer movement which would drive the British out of the Middle East, the other half of the pincers being in the Balkans.

By 22nd September it was clear that the enemy was settling in. He built and blasted entrenched camps in a semi-circle from Sidi Barrani, southwards and westwards, through Nibeiwa and Rabia to Sofafi, some within supporting distance of each other, others not. All of them were protected at least on three sides by loose stone walls, such as are to be found all over Italy, as anti-tank obstacles.

The enemy's Balkan drive took the form of an invasion of Greece on 28th October. The Greeks put up a splendid resistance and the Italians made even less headway in the mountains than they had made in the African desert.

At the end of September a fast convoy of armoured units arrived in Egypt, having come round the Cape. This included the 3rd Hussars (light tanks), the 2nd Royal Tanks (cruisers, A.10 and A.13, of which more later) and the 7th Royal Tanks (infantry tanks—Matildas). The 3rd Hussars went to the 7th Armoured Brigade, the 2nd Royal Tanks to the 4th. In order to give each of these regiments something which it had not got, each transferred its B Squadron temporarily to the other. They knew each other very well after a five weeks' voyage, and this was better than trying to train a squadron of the 3rd Hussars in cruisers in the short time available before they would have to go into action.

The enemy in the meanwhile continued his defensive preparations and showed no signs of continuing his advance. At night patrols from motor battalions reconnoitred his positions from all sides so that very full details were known of his defences. By day the 11th Hussars kept him under constant observation and not only reported the movements of vehicles outside the camp, but, until the shimmering of the mirage spoilt the view, saw a great deal of what was going on inside. The numbers of vehicles in the camps were accurately reported and the location of one particular vehicle was always followed with interest. It was recognized by its size and had a cargo of ladies.

The enemy seldom ventured forward from his camps except in force. His precise reasons for such excursions are not clear. They may have been reconnaissances, or they may have been designed in deference to the theory of keeping up the offensive spirit.

Of the two newly arrived armoured regiments, the 2nd Royal Tanks had already seen fighting in France, but the 3rd Hussars had not. The latter were accordingly sent forward to the Support Group for experience and in November had two actions with Italian offensive columns. In the second of these they destroyed five medium tanks and captured a number of prisoners for the loss of one officer and one man killed by air attack.

In this period of rest and boredom the 7th Hussars had little to do but seek amusement where it could be found. The tanks could not be moved and the less they were tinkered with the better. There was a good deal of shooting with the machine guns and 2-pounders. One exercise was held on 25th and 26th November in conjunction with the 4th Indian Division, which gave the tanks a much needed spin. A few reconnaissances were carried out and the officers improved their knowledge, and occasionally the menu of their mess, by going out to shoot gazelle and bustard. Bathing parties were organized near Matruh as far as transport facilities would permit.

As the weather grew cooler the need was felt for warmer clothing and the battle dress of the newly arrived regiments, who had brought it with them from the United Kingdom wisely but against orders, was the envy of the older hands. The "comforts" sent up from the delta through the efforts of Colonel and Mrs. Fielden and the goodness of the knitting ladies of Cairo, were a most welcome addition to the wardrobes of all and added a colourful and even fragrant touch to the usually rather drab and odorless character of the desert. Blue, red and yellow mufflers or silk scarves, magenta and green cap-comforters or balaklava helmets, all were worn freely and without question and the word uniform ceased to have much meaning.

During this period several new officers joined. Among them were the Rev. N. S. Metcalfe, the new chaplain, and Captain W. Low, the new medical officer. These two were to remain with the regiment for the rest of the war, and gained the admiration and affection of all ranks. The new subalterns were Second Lieutenants M. M. and P. B. Stanley Evans and J. L. C. Williams. The first two had arrived in Egypt at the end of August and been on a long course at the Royal Armoured Corps Depot at Abbassia. It is a comment on the danger of the Italian threat to Egypt in September that no courses were shortened and the leave parties continued as usual.

The senior military commanders were never very defensively minded, and during the whole of this static and somewhat defensive period plans were being made for an offensive—by 30,000 troops against six times their number.

*   *   *   *

The plan for the operation was simple and embodied the spirit of every one of the rather long-winded words and phrases called the Principles of War. It was to be a limited offensive, of which the object was to destroy the enemy in the group of camps round Sidi Barrani. Success would be exploited according to circumstances, but it was not expected that operations would last more than four or five days.

The enemy had two Libyan divisions in the area, the 1st at Sidi Barrani and Maktila and the 2nd in the Tummar camps. Each was 6–7,000 strong. In addition, at Nibeiwa, there was the Maletti Group, some 3,000 Libyans under the vigorous and enterprising Colonel Maletti. The nearest neighbouring troops were the 63rd (Metropolitan) Division at Rabia and Sofafi camps, on top of the escarpment. These camps were nearly twenty miles away from the main operation, so interference from the 63rd Division was not expected.

The 4th Indian Division was to carry out the attacks, in close co-operation with the 7th Battalion the Royal Tank Regiment, and D Day was fixed for 9th December. Nibeiwa was to be attacked first, at 7 a.m., then the Tummars at about noon. The attacks were to be carried out from the north-west and west, where the defences were weakest and attack would be least expected. On the north flank the Matruh garrison was to contain the enemy in Maktila and the Royal Navy was to bombard Maktila and Sidi Barrani.

The 7th Armoured Division was to prevent interference from the west and south. The Support Group was accordingly given the task of neutralizing the enemy in Rabia and Sofafi by occupying a general line extending some six miles westwards from the vicinity of Bir Enba and harassing Rabia at dawn on the 9th. The 7th Armoured Brigade was kept in reserve. The 4th Armoured Brigade, with which we are most closely concerned, was to prevent interference from the west.

Preparations and preliminary moves were conducted with the greatest possible secrecy. The cosmopolitan atmosphere of the big cities of Egypt was ideal for the work of spies and informers and their task might have been made easier by the large number of non-British personnel working in the base installations and lines of communication. It is only fair to say, however, that the vast number of men and women who might technically be termed camp followers, were almost without exception exceedingly loyal—a tribute both to the security service and to the appeal of the British way of life.

Passive deception was effected by concealing troop movements as much as possible and in particular the forward move of tanks. The Matildas of the 7th Royal Tanks, which were to play the leading part

The Secretary of State for War (Mr. Anthony Eden), General Sir Henry Maitland Wilson, Lt.-Col. F. W. Byass and Brigadier J. A. L. Caunter talking to a 7th Hussars Sergeant, October 1940.

Italian light tank C.V.3 knocked out beyond the frontier.

in the opening attack, were carefully housed in large tents until the last moment. Leave continued unbroken. Geese and turkeys and all that goes with them were placed on order by the end of November so as to ensure their delivery in time for the Christmas dinner, which in the event turned out to be bully and biscuits. The gradual move forward was cloaked with mystery and the 7th Hussars operation order of 29th November began with the deceitful statement: "Although no definite movement of the enemy has been reported, from various sources it seems possible that the enemy may be preparing to advance."

* * * *

On the 30th Lieutenant-General O'Connor visited the regiment and spoke to a number of the men. Next day the regiment carried out the first stage of its forward movement, to a featureless area twenty-five miles west of Charing Cross. It advanced at 8 a.m., widely dispersed, with B Squadron right, C left and A, with its seven cruisers, following regimental headquarters. B Echelon travelled behind A Squadron. The troops of D Battery Royal Horse Artillery (2-pounders) remained with the squadrons to which they were now more or less permanently attached, B and C. The regiment was ordered to send one troop of tanks to be attached to the 3rd Battalion The Coldstream Guards at Matruh; to avoid breaking up the squadron organization, this troop was improvized, one light tank being taken from each of B and C Squadrons and regimental headquarters, the crew for the latter being provided by A Squadron.

On the 6th orders were issued for the final moves, in stages, to a point about three miles north of Hagfet el Inhaba (otherwise Bir Enba), some eight miles south-south-west of the Italian camp at Nibeiwa. The 7th Hussars were to reach this point by 10 p.m. on the 8th and might expect to advance again on the morning of the 9th. The last part of the move was to be carried out in the dark. In order to economise transport every article which could be dispensed with was to be left behind at an improvized camp where it could be collected after the operation.

On the 7th visibility was very good all day, and as the dust stirred up by tanks is visible to aircraft many miles farther than the tanks themselves, the march only started at 4.30 p.m. Twelve miles were covered and soon after dark the regiment leaguered. At 8 a.m. on the 8th the march continued. By 11.30 the regiment had done twenty miles, and it now halted for three hours, brewed up and rested. At about 3 it moved on another ten miles and halted again. A hot meal was provided at 5 o'clock and at nightfall the 7th Hussars' B Echelon left to join the brigade B Echelon farther in rear. There remained only the topping-up vehicles and a cooks' lorry to provide hot tea and breakfast next morning—an abnormal procedure, necessary because the crews would have no opportunity to cook in daylight and no lights or fires could be allowed in the dark.

At 6 p.m. it was still dark except for the moon and the march was resumed, the destination, three miles north of Enba, being reached at about 8. All vehicles were topped-up and everyone lay down for a good night's sleep. No enemy aircraft had been seen all day. Fighters had been patrolling over the moving troops and it had been well worth while conserving them for this occasion instead of frittering them away in aid of the earlier skirmishing operations. As it was, their numbers were small, and the somewhat fitful periods of movement on this day had been carefully regulated so as to coincide with the available air cover.

By 10 p.m. the 4th Armoured Brigade was concentrated north of Bir Enba, ready to advance at dawn next day. Its main task was to prevent the enemy interfering from the west or north-west with the attacks of the 4th Indian Division. Subject to this it was to destroy any enemy tank forces which might be found within reach, and any forces of any nature which were in the Azzizia area—on the main road half way between Sidi Barrani and Bugbug.

From the high ground near Enba a clearly defined ridge descends fairly evenly, first just west of north and then north-westwards towards Bugbug, into the rather indeterminate undulations of the hummocky and scrub-covered coastal plain. To the eastward lies another ridge, on which stood the Italian camp at Nibeiwa, and which quickly loses itself in the untidy and insignificant features of the gradual slope to the coast. Between the two ridges is a broad shallow valley, where the going is good for some twelve miles north of Enba. From that point however the valley, in its lower stretches called the Wadi el Kharruba, is more sharply defined, and its dry water course, cut out by the winter spates, becomes an effective obstacle to mechanical vehicles.

*   *   *   *

The Nibeiwa attack was to go in from the north-west at 7 a.m. The 4th Armoured Brigade therefore was to start its move at 6 a.m., and to advance nearly due north, down and across the valley, with the 6th Royal Tanks on the right, missing Nibeiwa by about three miles, and the 7th Hussars on the left. The 2nd Royal Tanks and a company of the 1st Battalion The King's Royal Rifle Corps were to follow in reserve. The 6th Royal Tanks were to move on Sanyet el Khadra.

The 7th Hussars were given successive tasks; to destroy any enemy troops guarding dumps in the Wadi el Kabsh; likewise in the Wadi Kharruba; then to occupy a battle position facing north-west, astride the Wadi el Kharruba and about five miles from the main road at Azzazziya.

Colonel Byass ordered B Squadron to advance on the right and C on the left. B was to move with its right on the brigade centre line, through Alem el Agrad, and to occupy the right half of the battle position. C was to carry out the two tasks of destroying the enemy guarding dumps and to occupy the left half of the position, astride the Wadi el Kharruba. Wireless silence was not to be broken before 6 a.m. The map reference code was to be used for all purposes except when referring to the enemy's positions.

At 5 a.m. every man had a breakfast of hot tea, tinned bacon and biscuits. No lights were visible anywhere and there was complete silence all around. At 6 a.m. engines were started and the regiment formed up; at 6.15 the advance began.

At 7.15 a patrol of the 11th Hussars reported the Wadi el Kabsh clear of the enemy and at 7.35 Major Jayne, commanding C Squadron, confirmed the report as he passed through. The 11th Hussars then reported the steep part of the Wadi el Kharruba to be held, and the 7th Hussars were ordered to push on and to destroy the enemy. C Battery Royal Horse Artillery (Major Goschen) was put in support of the regiment and C Squadron was to do the job.

At 7.55 the leading troops reached the wadi. There were no enemy in its upper reaches, but the right troop of the squadron came under fairly heavy shell fire from guns in position at Alam el Rimth, the high ground two miles to the north. Lieutenant-Colonel Byass and Major Seymour-Evans (A Squadron) joined Major Jayne and carried out a reconnaissance. The enemy was holding a position running roughly east and west on the north-eastern bank and about two miles south of Alam el Rimth. He had a few anti-tank guns forward and field guns farther in rear. At 8.15 Major Goschen arrived at regimental headquarters. His battery, however, went too far to the left, to the west of the Wadi el Kharruba, and came under heavy fire from the guns at Alam el Rimth. One troop came into action at once over open sights to cover the withdrawal of the other and eventually both came round to the east of the wadi, having had one gun knocked out and twelve men wounded. At 8.50, covered by the fire of C Battery, the regiment swung its right forward to within three miles of the main road and occupied a line facing west, a mile or so from Alam el Rimth. The right troop of B Squadron made contact with the left of the 6th Royal Tanks, who had also moved forward.

The enemy in the vicinity of Alam el Rimth and Azzaziya seemed to take only limited interest in the proceedings. At 9.30 a patrol of B Squadron reported twenty-five lorries on the road, stationary and apparently empty. There were also about a hundred men on the high ground near the road, but they showed no signs of taking up a position. Half an hour later they got into the lorries, which moved off westwards, and B Squadron advanced at speed to intercept them. The enemy went too fast, but the troop of D Battery Royal Horse Artillery came into action and scored a hit on one lorry before they disappeared. As the squadron approached the road, a small enemy camp was encountered, occupied by seventy men with a few machine guns. The squadron headquarters made straight for the enemy, who at once surrendered. The telephone wires were cut before the squadron moved off the position.

At 11.15 there were still a good many vehicles and men in the neighbourhood of Alam el Barragi, but there were no signs of a heavily held position. Colonel Byass accordingly decided to attack. C Squadron, leaving Lieutenant Llewellen Palmer's troop to watch the enemy in the Wadi el Kharruba, was to go in from the north-east. A Squadron was to move farther round the enemy, behind the high ground to the north of him, and to go in from the north-west. Regimental headquarters moved to a point south of Alam el Barragi.

At 11.40 the attack went in. There was no resistance until the tanks were quite close and then the enemy opened fire with machine guns. But they had no anti-tank weapons and so never had a chance. A number were killed and the rest made haste to surrender. One fanatic, having surrendered, picked up a rifle and fired at Major Jayne; he was promptly shot dead by a tank gunner.

While the prisoners were being rounded up the guns at Alam el Rimth opened fire again, at comparatively short range and with considerable accuracy. So the twenty lorries that had been captured were not brought away. At 11.55 the squadrons were withdrawn to their positions south of the road. Some of the 140 prisoners were made to walk in front of the tanks, some were given a lift. Their presence did not stop the enemy guns firing from el Rimth and the blue-grey mass, accompanied by apparently blue-grey tanks of unusual shape, even drew the attention of C Battery's guns until it was explained over the wireless, through brigade headquarters, that they were the 7th Hussars with their prisoners. The only casualty in the 7th Hussars in this operation was Corporal Waite slightly wounded. By 12.10

the whole regiment was back in its position three miles south of the road, where it remained for the rest of the day. At night the squadrons concentrated into leaguer in the same area as before, C on the right and A, with regimental headquarters, on the left, B a little farther to the south, or rear.

From early dawn on the 9th a cloud of black smoke and dust had been visible, drifting south-eastwards from Nibeiwa. But news of the main battle only came through slowly. The attack had succeeded. It had been a complete surprise and the Matilda had swept all before it. Every form of Italian projectile bounced off its thick armour and it just rumbled slowly along to the end of its course. Among the killed was the commander of the garrison, Colonel Maletti. This officer was well known by name among the British troops, as he had shown more enterprise than other enemy commanders in organizing offensive operations outside the perimeters of the camps. The soldiers did not rejoice at the news of the death of their most dangerous Italian enemy. They had respected his courage and, having no spite, would rather he had been one of the 2,500 prisoners.

After the capture of Nibeiwa the British artillery was moved at once to positions from which it could engage the Tummar Camps. The attack on Tummar West was to have been staged at 11.15, but preparations could not be made in time. It was launched at 2.30, again from the west, but with fewer tanks, as some were suffering from superficial damage; it met with equal success. The group of works known as Tummar East was captured by the same methods before nightfall and everything had gone according to plan. The prisoner of war cage had only provided for 2,000 prisoners and already four times this figure were on their way to it.

It was significant that throughout the day no attempt had been made by the garrison of any Italian camp to go to the help of its neighbour. Each one remained passive until it was, in its turn, overwhelmed.

*   *   *   *

As day dawned on the 10th the squadrons of the 7th Hussars broke leaguer, to the accompaniment of violent firing from Alam el Rimth by field and anti-tank guns and small arms of all kinds. Everything fell so far short that the general opinion was that it was aimed at something else—or at nothing at all. The regiment was now ordered to send one squadron to the road at Alam el Barragi. C Squadron accordingly advanced and the leading patrol reported no signs of enemy there. At 10.50 a patrol went farther west to investigate reports of enemy movement in the area north-west of Sawani el Khur.

The squadron followed in support, as a dust storm had begun to blow up and by 11.30 visibility was very bad. No enemy were found in the area, but there were still plenty of Italians in their positions around Alam el Rimth. During the morning, so long as he could see, Major Goschen engaged these with C Battery.

At 1 o'clock the brigade commander suggested that, in view of the density of the dust storm, it might be possible to round up the enemy at el Rimth, attacking him from two sides. Heavy casualties were not to be incurred and the decision whether to attack or not was left to the Commanding Officer. Lieutenant-Colonel Byass at once carried out a personal reconnaissance. He found the enemy holding a number of quite strong localities to the west of Alam el Rimth, and from there towards Sawani el Khur there were several positions less well defended. He thought casualties would be inevitable and consequently recommended that the operation should not be carried out. At 2.45 C Squadron was withdrawn, taking back a few prisoners and leaving two patrols on the road, one at Barragi and one three miles farther west.

At 6.15 p.m. night dispositions were taken up, B Squadron on the track three miles east of el Rimth, C Squadron on the road south of Barragi, A and headquarters between the two. At 7 p.m. the patrol of C Squadron on Alam el Barragi was shelled—without damage. Apart from this the night was quiet. Orders for the 11th were to move westwards at dawn and work north of the Bugbug road. But at 3 a.m. these were cancelled and the regiment was ordered back to Bir Enba, whence it had started on the morning of the 9th.

The operations of the 4th Indian Division on the 10th had again been extremely successful. In the Sidi Barrani area fighting had been fierce, but by 5 p.m. all positions had been captured, with thousands more prisoners including the General commanding the group of divisions. The 2nd Royal Tanks of the 4th Armoured Brigade had taken an active part in the attack on Sidi Barrani, north of the main road, and had captured 1,700 prisoners. The operations had been successful beyond everyone's hopes and nobody, from General Wavell downwards, was going to leave it at that.

During the night of the 10th/11th the garrisons of Rabia and Sofafi left their camps and moved to Bugbug, en route for the frontier. On the 11th the 7th Armoured Brigade, hitherto held back in reserve near Nibeiwa, was launched in pursuit along the coastal plain and went off at great speed. A troop of the 11th Hussars went off in advance, and the 3rd Hussars led the pursuit of the 7th Armoured Brigade. They passed through an abandoned gun position astride the Sofafi track just south of Bugbug; there was every sign of a hasty withdrawal of the detachments, who had taken out the breech blocks and fled, for no apparent reason; the fires where they had recently brewed up were still smouldering. The troop of the 11th Hussars turned west along the main road for Salum, and headed off a huge column, capturing some thousands of prisoners. The 3rd Hussars moved northwards to the summer track and, a few miles west of Bugbug, encountered a fresh force of metropolitan troops who had not hitherto been engaged. Their dispositions were appropriate to the Napoleonic wars, guns and infantry being interspersed along the crest of an L-shaped ridge, astride the summer track and overlooking the main road in the distance. In ten bloody minutes and at a cost of twenty-five casualties the 3rd Hussars killed fifty-two Italians and captured 4,000, with fifty-eight field and medium guns and a hoard of lesser weapons.

While the 7th Armoured Brigade and the 11th Hussars were thus vigorously exploiting the victory, the 4th Brigade was preparing to advance across the desert south of the escarpment—back to the old familiar region of the frontier.

The 7th Hussars moved off from the Barragi area at 7.45 a.m. on the 11th, and reached the vicinity of Bir Enba three hours later. There was a severe sandstorm and the day was spent in maintenance. That evening the remainder of the brigade moved off at 8.30 p.m. in a south-westerly direction, heading for Bir Habata, a few miles west of Sofafi. The 7th Hussars stayed where they were, having been brought into divisional reserve.

The rest was very brief. At 11 o'clock next morning, the 12th, a liaison officer arrived from divisional headquarters with orders. He said that the enemy seemed to be leaving Bardia and that the 7th Hussars were to move so as to reach Hamra (twenty-five miles north-east of Madelena and forty miles from Enba) by 2 a.m. on the 13th. Here it was to come under the 4th Armoured Brigade again. The move began at 4 p.m. and was completed at midnight.

On the 13th no further orders were received until 12.20 p.m. The regiment was then ordered to move at once to a spot six miles east of the wire, opposite Sidi Omar. It moved off at 12.45 and reached its destination at 4.45 p.m. It was then ordered to replenish and be ready to move at 5 p.m.

The brigade was now organized in two columns. Combe Force, consisting of the 11th Hussars (less two squadrons), the 2nd Royal Tanks and the 4th R.H.A. (less one troop) was to take up positions watching the Bardia-Tobruk road. Birks Force was to protect Combe Force from the east, south and west, and consisted of two squadrons of the 11th Hussars and the remainder of the 4th Armoured Brigade. The route was given in great detail, including the precise bearing and distance for each leg of the advance. But the move did not begin at 5 p.m. The replenishing party did not arrive until after midnight, and the regiment marched off at 3.30 a.m.

Good progress was made to Point 204, the assembly area. This was a short leg of only six miles. Here the columns completed their organization. The march was then resumed and the wire was reached at B.P. 42, half way between Capuzzo and Sidi Omar, both of which were expected to be held by the Italians. There was some congestion at the gap, but by daybreak the brigade was clear of the wire and on its way north-westwards.

The 7th Hussars were responsible for the navigation of Birks Force and Lieutenant Napier was navigator. The destination was Bir el Hariga, ten miles west of Sidi Azeiz. There was no incident until 8.45 a.m., when an 11th Hussar's patrol reported thirty enemy vehicles to the right front. The 7th Hussars were ordered to increase speed and knock them out; but they proved to be the 4th R.H.A., with Combe Force, which was just ahead.

At 9.15 enemy air attacks began and were incessant throughout the day; thirty-six attacks were counted. There was one satisfactory minute when three of our fighters were seen to shoot down three of the enemy. At noon the 7th Hussars regimental headquarters were attacked. Lieutenant Astley-Rushton and the fitters had just arrived, and one of their 15-cwt. trucks was knocked out, Trooper Jackson being killed and Sergeant Gowan wounded.

By about 11.15 the destination was reached and patrols were established facing east on an eight-mile front astride the Trigh Capuzzo about eight miles west of Sidi Azeiz. At about 3 p.m. Lieutenant Llewellen Palmer's troop was sent to report on Sidi Azeiz and found it clear of the enemy. The patrol was ordered to stay there the night and hand over to the 7th Armoured Brigade in the morning. No enemy movement was seen all day and the night was quiet.

The 15th was uneventful, except for more bombing, which did no damage, and the capture of four prisoners by C Squadron. "They were unarmed, so they were allowed to go." To C Squadron, we must suppose, so paltry a catch was not worth keeping. At about 1 o'clock Second-Lieutenant Murray Smith, who had relinquished command of B Squadron on Major Younger's return from L.O.B., was sent off with two troops to get in touch with a patrol of the 11th Hussars about ten miles south-east of Gambut. Enemy aircraft, personnel and stores had been reported on a landing ground a little farther on and he was to destroy them. On investigation however it was found that the report was incorrect and the landing ground had not been used for some time, so he rejoined the regiment.

*   *   *   *

On the 16th the regiment was ordered to move to Sidi Azeiz and take up a position a little to the east, the rest of the brigade being to the south-west. Squadrons moved off down the Trigh Capuzzo and by

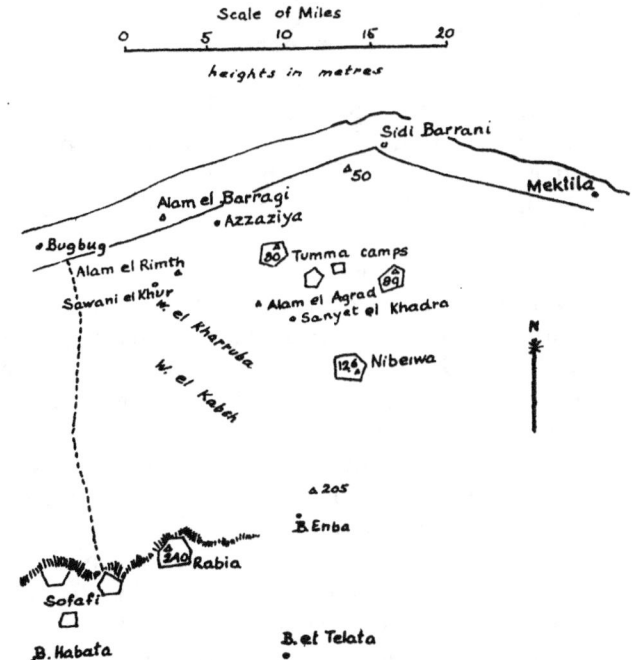

Map III

SIDI BARRANI

8.25 a.m. were in position. At 11 o'clock regimental headquarters were bombed—without damage; this was becoming the usual hour for air attacks. Shortly afterwards the order came to move to an area south and west of Sidi Omar, to be in position there by 3 p.m. and ready to take part in an attack.

Hardly had the move begun when a column of enemy motor transport was reported ten miles south-west of Sidi Omar, moving west, and the regiment was ordered to move as quickly as possible to cut them off. But the enemy had the advantage of speed and the going was good. By 2.55 it was apparent to the Commanding Officer that he could not catch the enemy and if he tried any longer to do so, the speed would have a serious effect on the tanks. Brigade headquarters therefore agreed to the chase being given up and ordered him to be at Sidi Omar by 3.30.

The turn to the west in pursuit of the enemy column had made it impossible now to cover the distance in the time available; as the order gradually came through over the wireless, it became clear that there would be no time for reconnaissance and it was even doubtful if the regiment could reach Sidi Omar in time to take part in the operation at all. Sidi Omar was to be shelled from 4.15 to 4.30 p.m., and during the bombardment the 7th Hussars were to close in from the south and west and the 2nd Royal Tanks from the north. At 4.30 both regiments were to attack the defended area. Lieutenant Napier's navigation was as usual excellent, and at 4.5 p.m. the regiment was in its allotted place, with ten minutes only in which the commanding officer might reconnoitre and give his orders. Then happily the attack was postponed for fifteen minutes, so there was time for the plan to be explained to squadron leaders.

At 4.30 the bombardment opened and seemed to be very effective. C on the right advanced from the south, B on the left from the southwest; A Squadron and regimental headquarters moved between C and B, slightly behind them. There was only light artillery fire from the enemy during the approach, and when the bombardment stopped the few posts which opened machine gun fire were quickly suppressed. Many of the enemy abandoned their positions and weapons when they saw the tanks coming. B Squadron went through their positions to the north of the fort, A, C and regimental headquarters to the south and the whole regiment rallied east of it. Deploying again, the squadrons moved back through the positions but by this time the enemy had ceased resistance altogether and were surrendering freely. Rallying again west of the fort the regiment then collected the prisoners, some 900, and a quantity of weapons and material. No casualties were incurred either to personnel or equipment.

Meanwhile B Echelon had been bombed by ten Italian aircraft. About fifty bombs were dropped. One 15-cwt. truck was damaged beyond repair and four other vehicles were hit by splinters. The only casualty was one trooper who had shock. There would undoubtedly have been more had it not been for the slit trenches alongside each vehicle. Trooper Brown with his Bren gun showed great coolness and disregard of danger. He remained at his gun throughout the attack.

Twice he and it were knocked down by the blast of bombs falling close and each time he set it up on its tripod again and continued to engage the enemy. For this action he was subsequently awarded the Military Medal.

The enemy still had a fair measure of control of the air in the forward zone and daily attacked some target or other. On 22nd December twenty-five enemy aircraft machine-gunned the replenishing party. But dispersion was good and Italian marksmanship very poor, for not a single casualty occurred and there was no damage to the vehicles.

When the mopping up of Sidi Omar was finished the regiment was ordered to deal with the enemy in Sheferzen. His strength was believed to be several hundreds, and an intercepted message had indicated that he was likely to leave during the night. Accordingly the regiment moved south soon after dark and formed a cordon on the north, west and south sides, with a troop in position about every two miles. If the enemy had moved out he would have been heard. Actually he had not waited so long. A patrol early in the morning found the place empty and very little kit had been left behind. So the small enemy detachment must have left in an orderly fashion some time the previous day. About 11.30 a.m. the regiment moved to a leaguer area east of Sidi Omar where much needed maintenance was carried out for the rest of the day.

CHAPTER IV

From Bardia to Beda Fomm

Capture of Bardia—capture of Tobruk—advance to Mechili—Italian tank attack—Italian withdrawal—advance to Beda Fomm—battle of Beda Fomm.

Maps I, IV, V, VI

On 18th December the 7th Hussars moved forward about twelve miles to Bir Beder, three miles South of Sidi Azeiz. An order to protect the left of the Australian Division was cancelled, and the regiment continued maintenance in the same locality until the 21st. That evening an order for a patrol arrived, but too late to be acted on the same night, and the following morning fresh orders were received from brigade headquarters. The headquarters of an Australian Brigade were some three miles south-east of the regiment's leaguer area, and required protection. In order to give early information of enemy movements, and in particular of the movements of his tanks, one squadron was to patrol the north and south grid line from a point on the escarpment, overlooking the Tobruk road and half a mile from the Bardia perimeter, to a point four miles farther south and about a mile from the perimeter. This line, as the map clearly indicated, lay along a forward slope descending gently from the ridge of Bir Belchonfus, three miles to the west, to the forward line of the Bardia defences half a mile to the east. If enemy tanks came out of Bardia they were to be prevented from reaching the Australian gun positions in the area north-west of Capuzzo.

On the 22nd B Squadron moved out on this task. There was nothing to report except a few men and motor transport to be seen moving within the perimeter and occasionally just outside it. The patrols, which were in a very exposed area, were shelled whenever they moved, the northern one especially.

There seemed to be only one way from the Tobruk road up the escarpment, at a point just over a mile from the perimeter. From 25th December this was watched by a standing patrol which was relieved every evening. Little movement was seen except inside the perimeter. Twice a dozen enemy medium tanks appeared, once inside and once outside, near the Tobruk road. But they did not venture far.

Christmas Day (bully and biscuits) passed almost unnoticed and everyone was living in an atmosphere of expectation, waiting for the attack on Bardia to begin. The nights were bitterly cold, especially for those tank crews who were out on patrol and whose duty as escort to the artillery meant extra alertness and perhaps sitting up in cramped positions in the turrets all night. It was rather a surprise when one morning during this period a golden voice announced that all the thoughts of those at home went out to our troops "sweltering in the desert heat." That morning there were little droplets of ice on the tanks, and every day men stood or sat huddled in the shelter of their vehicles while the cold wind howled past. But the B.B.C. seldom made mistakes of that kind and it was from them that much of the news came about our own operations. On 20th December it was announced that since the 9th of the month 30,000 prisoners had been taken and we had lost 72 killed and 760 wounded.

On the 29th the regiment moved to a point about three miles north of Sidi Azeiz. This was more convenient for patrolling, as the reliefs had shorter distances to travel. There was still little activity except in the air. Every night there were spectacular coloured lights from the Bardia defences, the "flaming onions" being the most favoured. These were coloured tracer ammunition fired from the Breda anti-aircraft machine gun. By day an array of enemy aircraft known as "the circus" used to come over fairly regularly at 11 a.m. At first they had over a dozen bombers escorted by twenty-one fighters. They bombed any group of vehicles which was in close formation. One day the Hurricanes got into them and within six minutes six of the bombers were smoking wrecks on the ground. Two or three enemy fighters also appeared nearly every day and attacked targets on the ground in the forward area.

On the 31st of December the 4th Armoured Brigade's Operation Order was received, giving the plan for the attack on Bardia. The operation was to be carried out on 2nd January by the 6th Australian Division, attacking from the west, parallel with the Tobruk road. The remaining thirty serviceable Matildas of the 7th Royal Tanks had trundled forward from Sidi Barrani to take part in the assault.

The 7th Armoured Division was to hold the ring and a little more besides. First it was to attack the garrison by day or by night if it tried to escape before the assault. Secondly it was to help the assault by a demonstration, supported by artillery fire, to contain that part of the garrison which was in the sector north of the Tobruk road. These two tasks were primarily the concern of the Support Group.

The third task of the division was to prevent the movement of enemy forces eastwards from Tobruk in the direction of Bardia. Fourthly, the division was to be prepared to advance to the area of El Adem with a view to cutting off Tobruk from the west as soon as Bardia was captured. These last tasks were given to the 7th Armoured Brigade. The 4th Armoured Brigade was to move to the area north-west of Sidi Azeiz and be ready to help either the Support Group or the 7th Armoured Brigade in their tasks. On the 31st the 7th Hussars moved a few miles southwards to the new area.

Next evening it was heard that the attack had been postponed until the 3rd. At the same time the regiment was ordered to provide a squadron to protect the left of the Australian Division against a possible tank attack up the escarpment south from the Tobruk road. C Squadron (Captain Congreve) was detailed for the job and was to take up positions in the wadis overlooking the road, moving out at dusk. In the interests of secrecy however it was decided to postpone the move until the following morning. The absence of wind at night made sound travel long distances and the noise of tanks was unmistakable. The enemy had now got used to the sight of light tanks in this sector, but the sound of them at night might arouse his suspicions and draw attention to the point where the assault was to be delivered. Accordingly at 6.15 a.m. the squadron moved out and troops got to their positions without apparently being seen. The following day and night were quiet and nothing indicated the imminence of an attack.

Just as dawn broke on the 3rd the bombardment began and a few minutes later the assault went in. The enemy replied with defensive fire from his artillery. A few shells fell near Second-Lieutenant W. Huckin's troop, which was the most easterly, but no damage was done. The bombardment was heavy for those days, but as ammunition was scarce it could not be compared with corresponding bombardments later in the war. The 25-pounders were limited to fifty rounds each per day during the operation, a mere tenth of what they were to use in later battles.

Nothing could be seen of the progress of the attack owing to the smoke and dust, but at 8.30 it was reported to be going well and 8,000 prisoners had been taken. In the afternoon the Support Group made their demonstration and this could be clearly seen by C Squadron from the top of the escarpment. In the evening B Squadron relieved C. The battle inside the defences continued for three days but little news of it penetrated to the regiment. Nobody had any doubts about the outcome, but they were impatient to be told and wanted to get on with the next job, as this one was obviously finished as far as the 7th Hussars were concerned.

Patrols continued and several troops were used for protecting the gunners, who really had no further need of them. There were no incidents and even trivialities seemed important. A 15-inch naval shell came rollicking across the desert from seaward, thought to be from H.M.S. *Warspite*, and narrowly missed Lieutenant Huckin's troop on one of its bounces. And Corporal Hipsey's tortoise died and was buried.

* * * *

On the evening of the 4th arrangements were made for the 4th Armoured Brigade to make contact with the eastern and southern defences of Tobruk while the 7th Armoured Brigade moved round to the west of it. Early on the 5th one troop of 7th Hussars was sent ahead to Gambut to make contact with the 8th Hussars of the 7th Armoured Brigade, who were moving on westwards. The troop leader, Lieutenant M. M. Stanley Evans, was ordered to take over the blocking of the Bardia road just outside the Tobruk perimeter and to reconnoitre an enemy aerodrome which was to be attacked next day. He arrived about noon, took over from the 8th Hussars and found two aerodromes deserted.

The regiment marched in the afternoon and came up with the patrol at 2 a.m. on the 6th. C Squadron, with the company of Durham Light Infantry and their dummy tanks, stayed a little way in the rear and put up the dummies before dawn. Patrolling and tapping-in on the eastern sector of the perimeter continued for several days without incident, beyond occasional shelling and a firework display from the Tobruk defences when our bombers attacked each night. News then came of the fall of Bardia and the capture of more than 40,000 prisoners. For the second time General O'Connor's little army had destroyed a force larger than itself and arrangements were already in progress to do it again.

On 8th January the 7th Hussars handed over on the east sector of Tobruk to the 19th Australian Brigade and moved farther westwards. When the Australians came up to take over from B Squadron they seemed to doubt whether the enemy was still in his positions. Second-Lieutenant M. M. Stanley Evans, who had been reporting enemy movements at intervals all day, was therefore ordered to take his troop towards the perimeter. The tanks edged forward slowly, the troop leader in front. The enemy held his fire until they were about a thousand yards from the defences and then let go with all he had. The withdrawal was more hurried than the advance. One enemy gun position was spotted by Corporal Pratt, who gave it a belt from his machine gun. Fortunately the enemy failed to score a hit with anything but machine gun fire and this did only superficial damage. The object was achieved—the Australians were convinced.

The outline plan for the capture of Tobruk was very like that for Bardia. The attack was to be carried out by the 6th Australian Division with the remaining Matildas of the 7th Royal Tanks. The 7th Armoured Division was to isolate the garrison. The 11th Hussars were to give early warning of an enemy approach from Mechili; the 7th Armoured Brigade was to prevent reinforcements coming from Derna or Mechili. The Support Group was to prevent the garrison escaping westwards on the sector between Acroma and the sea. The 4th Armoured Brigade was to protect the left of the Australians and the right of the Support Group.

At 9.15 a.m. on the 9th the regiment moved off, taking with it the Durham Light Infantry and their dummy tanks, and reached the new area, five miles south-west of Medawar, at 5.15 p.m. In the moonlight the Durham Light Infantry once more erected their dummies and arrangements were made for C and B Squadrons in turn to keep standing patrols watching the sector south-east of Medawar. C's patrols went out at first light on the 10th to the ridge south of Medawar and were shelled at once as they topped it. These patrols continued in twenty-four hour rotation until the attack was delivered on 21st January.

Whenever the tanks came in sight the enemy shelled them and reconnaissance was generally carried out by troop leaders advancing a few hundred yards on foot over the ridge, leaving their tanks under cover. The patrol on the right flank was usually shelled most, as at this point the ridge is closest to the perimeter. Patrols were kept out all night and occasionally raids were carried out inside the wire. Twice a patrol of the Durham Light Infantry was sent in to investigate the defences. On the night of the 11th they found that some of the enemy guns were dummies. Next night a similar patrol was seen and shot at by the enemy and failed to get through the wire.

On the night of the 17th a patrol of B Squadron was ordered to carry out a mock attack in the Medawar sector. It was quite simple, first a few flares, then a burst of fire from all the machine guns of the troop. The noise was improved by dragging a few empty petrol tins on the tow ropes. The result was satisfactory. The enemy put down his defensive fire, sent up lights and for half an hour the air was full of flashes and metal. No harm was done, and when a few more belts were fired the enemy refused to be stirred up again.

B Squadron at "personal maintenance." Sergeant M. H. Brown's tank near Capuzzo, with himself on the turret, Tpr. Delaney having half a bath in half a petrol tin, Tpr. Chaplin shaving.

Carriers of the 1st Battalion The King's Royal Rifle Corps at Fort Capuzzo.

The last activity in the Medawar sector before the attack was a diversion on the final night. This was carried out by a party of Royal Engineers and Durham Light Infantry who blew bangalore torpedoes under the wire and penetrated into the defences. The party was heavily shelled. Three of the four engineers were wounded, but the detachment of Durham Light Infantry, including Major Johnson in command of the company, disappeared. Captain Congreve and Captain Low, Royal Army Medical Corps, went out to look for them but could find no trace.

On the 21st the attack was delivered early in the morning, in the south-eastern sector. In the Medawar sector the enemy opened heavy shell fire on our patrols, without effect. When this ceased, in the afternoon, the patrols moved forward to reconnoitre and the enemy at once engaged them with anti-tank and artillery fire.

The same night a limited operation was carried out to ascertain the situation in the sector. The 2nd Royal Tanks on the right and the 7th Hussars on the left were to send patrols across the wire and they were to attack and destroy any enemy who seemed to offer a suitable target. The order was worded in a way which reflects the concern often felt by commanders at this period—to have the job properly done, but at the smallest possible cost. A good deal of ingenuity was needed in framing such orders, and an intimate knowledge of the subordinate and the way he would be likely to respond. On this occasion the order included the two phrases "No unnecessary risks" and "bold and offensive patrols." But there was no particular difficulty this time. When the two troops advanced about 2 a.m. they both came under heavy fire of all natures before they reached the perimeter and it was clear that the positions were still held in strength and the enemy was on the alert.

On the 22nd C Squadron was providing the patrols. The 2nd Royal Tanks had penetrated the wire farther eastwards and were reported to be held up in the sector opposite the most easterly 7th Hussars patrol. This patrol (Lieutenant Llewellen Palmer) accompanied by the squadron leader (Captain Congreve), went forward a short distance and engaged the enemy with machine gun fire; about 300 Italians came across the wire and surrendered.

Farther to the left Second-Lieutenant P. B. Stanley Evans was less fortunate. His troop came under intense fire of all kinds when it had only advanced a few hundred yards. Sergeant Cleere, the troop sergeant, spotted three enemy anti-tank breda guns inside the perimeter, which consisted of a deep anti-tank ditch and a thick barbed wire entanglement. Stanley Evans reported the situation to his squadron leader and was ordered to press on. In face of the heavy fire he himself took the lead, the other two tanks being slightly refused to his right and left. Firing their machine guns as they advanced, the tanks went straight for the enemy.

As they approached the wire the troop leader's tank disappeared in a cloud of black smoke, having run on to a mine. Trooper Davenport was killed and the troop leader looked under the tank and found the sprocket was blown off. Sergeant Cleere engaged the enemy vigorously while Corporal Magill drove up to the troop leader to take his tank in tow. Stanley Evans and Magill hitched on the tow rope and the latter was shot in the knee while getting back into his tank. While he was being helped inside the troop leader got his guns going at the enemy, and as the tanks slowly withdrew all guns were firing hard.

After a mile and a half, and still fully exposed to the enemy's fire, the damaged tank, which had no track on one side, dug itself into the ground and could not be straightened up. None of the wireless was now in action, so Magill was sent back to squadron headquarters to report. Cleere's tank was now hit again and Trooper Yoxall was wounded. As the damaged tank could not be taken in tow the troop leader now mounted Cleere's tank and moved away, all the time being shelled, for another half mile. Here he halted and continued to observe the enemy. This tank also was in a somewhat battered state. The rations, kit and all exterior parts were riddled and all bars and frames were bent, but the tank stayed with the regiment and was present later at the battle of Beda Fomm. For this action Sergeant Cleere was later awarded the Distinguished Conduct Medal.

* * * *

At 11.55 a.m. the patrols were withdrawn and the regiment was concentrated. The attack on Tobruk had gone well and all was now ready for the next stage—the advance to Mechili. Preparations had been going on for some time. The 8th Hussars and 6th Royal Tanks had handed over their remaining tanks—with crews complete until these could be replaced—to other units of the division. Eight tanks had come from the 8th to the 7th Hussars. Meanwhile a force was being formed on the nucleus of the 4th Armoured Brigade, for an advance on Mechili.

This little fort lies at the foot of the south-eastern slopes of the Gebel el Akhdar. The gebel is only passable for transport along the recognized tracks; elsewhere, although there are stretches of good going, steep sided wadis are liable to be met with and all movement stopped. South of Mechili lie rough and undulating hills consisting of loose slabs of rock, very punishing to the tracks of tanks and the springs of wheeled vehicles. Through the gap between the gebel and the rocky hills lay the best route towards the coastal plain south of Benghazi and the road to Tripoli. If therefore Mechili could be seized quickly the enemy in the gebel would be threatened from another angle. The garrison was thought to be small and it was hoped that it could be

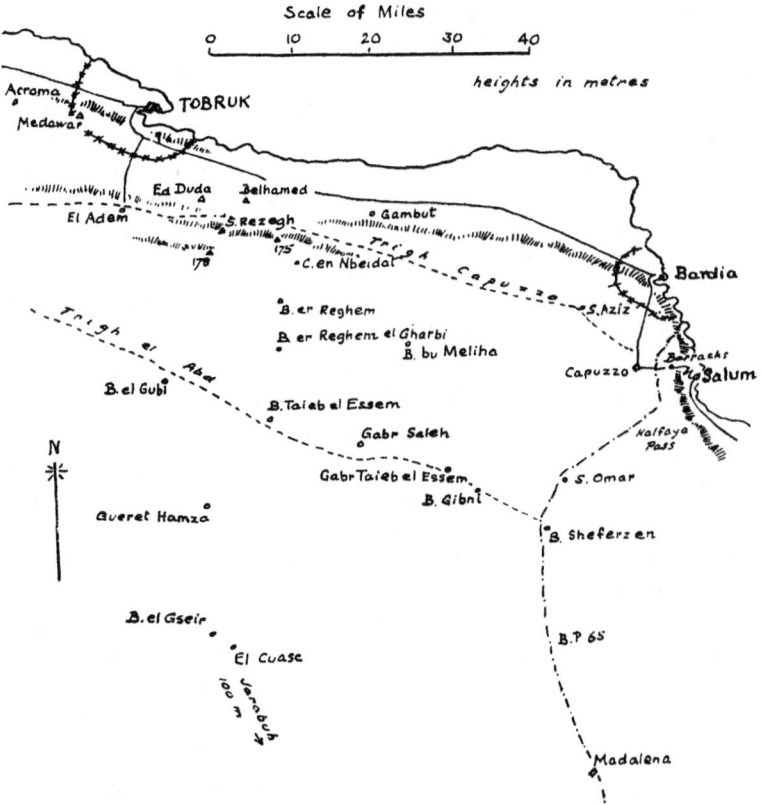

MAP IV
EASTERN CYRENAICA

swept up in one rush before reinforcements could reach it from Derna. The march, once begun, was to be continuous, Mechili was to be surrounded on three sides and detailed reconnaissance for an attack was to be made on arrival.

The 11th Hussars were to reconnoitre up to and beyond Mechili, reporting particularly on the going. The 3rd Hussars were to move independently to block the western approaches to Mechili. The rest of the 4th Armoured Brigade Group was to move to an area ten miles east of Mechili and be prepared to attack in accordance with orders to be issued on arrival. The 7th Hussars were to lead, with two troops of the 155th Light Anti-Aircraft Battery under command and followed by brigade headquarters, a company of 2nd Battalion The Rifle Brigade, the 2nd Royal Tanks and the 4th Royal Horse Artillery. The 3rd Hussars were already out west of Gazala. The main force was to assemble seven miles south of Acroma, march southwards to the Trigh Enver Bey (the westward continuation of the Trigh Capuzzo), and thence along the Trigh for thirty-five miles, thence north-west for fifteen miles to Bir Aleima and due west for another thirty miles. Zero was to be signalled as "Venus....hours." All tanks were to be topped up daily at 2 p.m. and petrol lorries were to remain with the fighting troops so that they could be topped up early on the morning of Day 2 of the move. A field supply dump was established at Bir Aleima, forty miles east of Mechili. On D 1 there was to be a long halt from 6 p.m. to 2 a.m., during which the evening meal was to be "consumed." Breakfast was to be consumed between 7 and 8.30 a.m. on D 2. The order ended with the customary and encouraging paragraph, "All burials will be *in situ*."

Colonel Horace Birks, commanding the force in the absence of Brigadier Caunter on leave, received the order to move at 12.30 p.m. on 21st January. This was rather an awkward time, as the replenishment vehicles were due to reach units at 2 p.m. and were now on the move up. So he ordered the move to start at 2.30 p.m. and the vehicles were then to accompany their units on the first stage of the march. Everything went according to plan and by 6 p.m. the brigade had covered twenty miles.

The night was then dark and cloudy, so further movement was postponed to 6 a.m. But at 1.30 a.m. the clouds thinned out somewhat and it was decided that the march should be resumed at 2 a.m. in accordance with the original plan. But the night darkened again and progress was very slow. Part of the brigade headquarters, with the petrol lorries, became separated from the rest of the column and by 6.30 a.m., when a halt was called for breakfast, only sixteen miles had been covered. What was worse, the 1/500,000 map, of Italian origin, was positively misleading and units' locations were not always accurately judged. There were many blank squares on the map where large wadis and escarpments ought to have been marked. In other squares hachures on the map indicated obstacles which did not exist. It was not until 10.30 a.m. that the whole force was collected on the brigade centre line and the march continued.

Meanwhile the 7th Hussars had moved on ahead. C Squadron had been sent forward to reconnoitre the going towards Bir Aleima and Mechili. The rest of the regiment followed. At 4 p.m. on the 23rd the brigade halted about twenty miles east of Mechili and the Commanding Officers of the 7th Hussars, 2nd Royal Tanks and 4th Royal Horse Artillery were summoned to a conference. Colonel Byass did not arrive, because of difficulties with the map. So orders to the 7th Hussars as well as to the 3rd Hussars, who were already in their correct position west of Mechili, were issued by wireless. The 7th Hussars were to move to the Got Breiber, four miles north-east of Mechili and to block the roads running north and north-west from Mechili against enemy movement in either direction. The 2nd Royal Tanks were to occupy the area Baltet Seif, a mud flat ten miles east of Mechili and south of the 7th Hussars. The 4th Royal Horse Artillery were to put one battery into action in the Got Breiber, with a view to engaging the Mechili defences and the roads north and north-west of the fort. The other battery was to remain in reserve. The company of the Rifle Brigade was to go to the 7th Hussars area and to move on to the wadi north of Mechili at dawn on the 24th. Brigade headquarters was to move to a position just east of the 2nd Royal Tanks.

Most of these moves were carried out the same evening and on the following morning most units thought they were in their allotted places. Some of them were, but not the 7th Hussars. The order to go to the Got Breiber had been received at 4.45 p.m. The regiment was to move as quickly as possible and to place one squadron six miles north of the Got across the Derna track and patrols on the two more westerly tracks. The march had hardly begun when it was cancelled and the regiment was ordered to a point just south of the Baltet Seif, where it was to rendezvous with the Commanding Officer.

On arrival at what was thought to be, but was not, the rendezvous, there was no sign of the Commanding Officer and it was now dark. But everyone on the wireless was very helpful and brigade headquarters said a guide should be left there and the regiment should go at once to Got Breiber. Major Sheppard was reluctant to do this move in the dark, as the going was bad in patches, and he obtained permission to put it off till daylight. The Commanding Officer was still missing and the replenishment vehicles did not turn up.

At 5 a.m. on the 24th the regiment moved off and an hour later reached the Got Breiber—or so it thought. At 7.15 a.m. some of the replenishing party arrived. They had driven almost on to the defences of Mechili during the night, and many had become separated when the enemy opened heavy artillery fire. Colonel Byass had been with them and at 7.30 he drove up to B Squadron. Almost at the same moment a dozen enemy bombers came over and dropped a few bombs, but these did no damage.

There followed a discussion on the actual position of the regiment. Far from being in the Got Breiber it was actually eight miles south of it, so the allotted task was not being fulfilled and the roads from Derna and Giovanni Berta to Mechili were open to the enemy. The situation was the more serious because the few lorries which had joined up were only enough to re-fuel part of A Squadron and regimental headquarters.

* * * *

At 9.20 the regiment moved northwards. C Squadron (Major Jayne), who were already a few miles to the north and had been ordered to block the more westerly roads, was in the lead, and the Commanding Officer with them. At about 10.15 C Squadron reported a large column of transport escorted by twenty-four medium tanks moving towards Mechili down the road from Derna. At the same time some more of the regimental transport joined up and A Squadron, who had three cruisers, were topped up again and as many tanks as possible took on rations. The regiment was now about four miles south of the Got Breiber, and C Squadron about two miles farther north.

A few minutes later C Squadron reported that twelve to fifteen enemy tanks had broken away from the rest and were attacking. In face of this attack, in which the Italians were using their 47-millimetre guns on the move with fair accuracy, C Squadron patrols were ordered to withdraw. Brigade headquarters were informed and a squadron of the 2nd Royal Tanks was ordered to stand by. But the enemy came on fast, and as C Squadron withdrew towards regimental headquarters, their leading tanks came within close range. Second-Lieutenant P. B. Stanley Evans' tank was hit and caught fire. The crew were picked up by Major Jayne. Second-Lieutenant Huckin's tank was hit and he himself was wounded in both arms. Lieutenant Llewellen Palmer's tank was hit and Trooper Barlow was wounded. As the enemy followed C Squadron over the ridge his 47-millimetre and machine gun fire spattered among the replenishing vehicles and these were steered to a safer place by Major Rash, of the 5th Royal Tanks, who was doing a preliminary visit to the desert in advance of his recently arrived regiment.

The situation was now serious and at about 10.50 a.m. A Squadron was ordered to move up and attack the enemy's right. Their three cruiser tanks quickly got into action but one of them was knocked out at once. Sergeant Thomas Thompson was killed and Corporal Woodcock severely wounded. In another the 2-pounder jammed. Captain Seymour-Evans in the third one held out for ten minutes on his own and, for an ammunition expenditure of 55 rounds, knocked out two of the enemy and enabled both his other tanks to be withdrawn. Although at close range the enemy seemed unable to hit him and he came away only when they were within 300 yards.

Meanwhile the rest of the regiment had moved slowly south-eastwards. The Commanding Officer had asked brigade headquarters for the help of the 2nd Royal Tanks, but the message was barely through when the second rear link tank was hit and Lance Corporal Blenkisop of the Royal Signals wounded. So Colonel Byass did not know whether the message had been understood, and if it had, whether the 2nd Royal Tanks were coming or not. He therefore sent over Lieutenant Llewellen Palmer of C Squadron, whose tank was very low in petrol (C had not topped up) to the 2nd Royal Tanks to explain the situation. Their Commanding Officer was somewhat taken aback; the story of Italian tanks advancing was almost unheard-of. The Commanding Officer consulted brigade headquarters on the wireless and in a few minutes the 2nd Royal Tanks had both their cruiser squadrons on the move towards the enemy. One moved north under cover of a small ridge and attacked the enemy from the north-east. The other moved through the 7th Hussars and attacked him from the east.

The enemy had meanwhile halted with his tanks on a ridge, where they presented an excellent target. Of the eight which had penetrated so far from home seven were knocked out by the 2nd Royal Tanks and only one got away. In ten minutes it was all over and by 11.30 the 7th Hussars were reorganizing just south of the Baltet Seif. Those whose tanks had been knocked out, including Major Sheppard and Captain Kevill-Davies, rejoined and the fitters got busy with the damaged tanks. For their part in this action Major Jayne was later given the immediate award of the Distinguished Service Order and Trooper Barlow the Distinguished Conduct Medal.

* * * *

The next two days were quiet, but not very enjoyable, as the water ration was down to half a gallon per man. Patrols were out north of Mechili by day and night and were occasionally shelled. But the enemy seemed to be fairly strong. On the 26th a big concentration of enemy transport on the hills north of the fort was successfully shelled by the 4th Royal Horse Artillery. Then, on the morning of the 27th, it was found that the enemy had left during the night by the roads leading north-westwards. The 7th Hussars were ordered to follow up and moved off with C Squadron in the lead.

About eight miles north-west of the fort the regiment was halted. The going was very bad as the track led across a number of deep wadis up into the highest part of the gebel. B Squadron (Major Younger) was sent on a little farther and Second-Lieutenant M. M. Stanley Evans' troop reported the enemy's tail some six miles ahead. He was sent forward another five miles, but the enemy was moving away rapidly and disappearing in the gathering darkness, covered by medium tanks. No engagement took place. Patrols were left out and suffered considerably from the cold, wet and windy night. The enemy also halted about the same time and next morning his rearguard was again spotted by B Squadron patrols twenty miles north-west of Mechili.

A force consisting of B Squadron and a troop of D Battery Royal Horse Artillery (2-pounders) was now ordered to move westwards on to a track south-west of the enemy's position in order to prevent him withdrawing in that direction. But the steep country made it quite impossible to get round him on that side, and such a manoeuvre could only have been carried out by moving back round the south of Mechili into the plain. Then C Squadron was ordered to try and also failed to find a way through. The enemy continued his withdrawal and touch in this sector was lost.

Meanwhile the Australians had completed the capture of Tobruk, with over 30,000 prisoners, on the 22nd. They at once began moving up to Derna and establishing themselves on a line in the hills to the south of it. The enemy's intentions were still not clear and it was thought possible that he might try to counter-attack against our troops in the Mechili area. The regiment spent four days patrolling in the area north and north-west of Mechili, and on 1st February an operation instruction was received from headquarters 7th Armoured Brigade, under whose orders it was to come on the 2nd. The task of the brigade was to co-operate with the 4th Armoured Brigade in preventing the Italians from recovering Mechili by advancing from Derna or Giovanni Berta.

The movements executed the next day proved in fact to be fruitless, cost a lot in wear and tear of vehicles and need not be described in detail. While the 3rd Hussars moved all the way round from south of Mechili, the 7th were drawn back nearly to the fort before being sent north again ten miles, almost to the point they had left; and patrols were sent on a further six miles to the north. Positions were reached with difficulty over the steep and rocky country and patrols stayed out all night.

The enemy's only offensive action was from the air and his circus, now only two or three bombers and half a dozen fighters, confined itself mainly to dropping thermos bombs in promising areas well away from the troops. His intentions on land, however, were becoming more and more clear. On the 1st and 2nd, even while our defensive

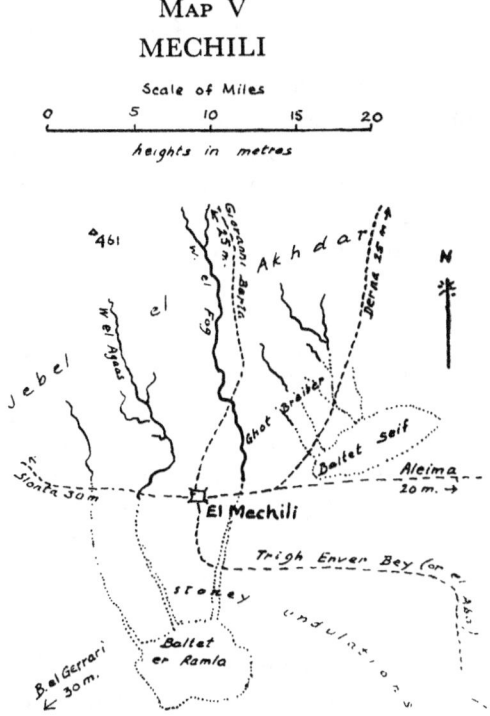

Map V
MECHILI

precautions were being taken round Mechili, there were indications that he was withdrawing on Benghazi. There was much speculation as to whether he would try to hold on there, relying on the use of the port if the Tripoli road were cut, or whether he would continue his retreat to Tripolitania.

Preparations to meet the latter eventuality were put in hand on the 2nd. A column from the Support Group was sent off from Mechili towards Slonta, but it could not get through the hills. The 4th Armoured Brigade was told to prepare itself for a move to Msus, eighty-five miles to the west, any time after mid-day on the 3rd. A field supply dump was being established half way between Mechili and Bir el Gerrari and preparations were made to establish another at Antelat, forty miles south-west of Msus.

From now until the end of the campaign the regiment was commanded by Major Sheppard, with Major Jayne as second-in-command. C Squadron was commanded by Captain Congreve and Lieutenant-Colonel Byass was L.O.B. in Cairo. At 1.30 a.m. on the 3rd February the 7th Hussars received the order to be ready to move at noon on Msus. A good many of the tanks were now very shaky and the rough going north of Mechili had proved too much for four of them, which had to be left behind. The morning was spent in maintenance and minor repairs—all that were possible—and by noon twenty-six light tanks and the solitary cruiser were ready. At 2.15 p.m. the regiment moved for the rendezvous, six miles west of Mechili, where it arrived at 6 p.m. and reverted to the command of the 4th Armoured Brigade. It was a rough and dusty march, but all tanks arrived safely and all was ready for the culminating act of the campaign.

*   *   *   *

On 3rd February air reconnaissance reports indicated that the enemy meant to quit Cyrenaica. His forces in the gebel were now believed to consist of the special armoured brigade, the 60th Division and artillery elements of the 17th and 27th Divisions, whose infantry were thought to be still in Tripolitania and moving eastwards. The 7th Armoured Division issued orders for the move to Msus, which was to take place on the 4th. The 11th Hussars were to be sent in advance and the main body was to march in the order 4th Armoured Brigade, divisional headquarters, 7th Armoured Brigade (1st Royal Tanks only), Support Group.

During the night the headquarters XIIIth Corps (the new name of General O'Connor's command) came to the definite conclusion that a full scale retreat from Cyrenaica was in progress and the 7th Armoured Division was ordered to move at speed to the area Soluch-Agedabia to cut the enemy off. Thus the scope of the operation was at once enlarged and General Creagh was given a wide choice—sixty miles in fact—of frontage on which he might operate. From now onwards speed and mobility were all-important and the time of starting was advanced by an hour.

At 6.50 a.m. on the 4th the 7th Hussars began the march to the appointed assembly area west of the Baltet el Ramla. Regimental headquarters moved in front, C Squadron on the right, B on the left and A in rear. Presently there was a bang and a cloud of black smoke enveloped the rear link tank, which had run on to a thermos bomb.

The suspension was damaged but the crew were unhurt. It was found that a large number of thermos bombs lay about in the area and caution was necessary in dodging them. So the regiment was ten minutes late reaching its appointed location.

At 8.50 a.m. the march began, the 7th Hussars being on the left of the brigade axis, the 3rd Hussars on the right. The route lay past No. 14 Field Supply Dump—just established—Bir el Gerrari and Msus. The regiment marched on a five-mile frontage, C Squadron on the right, B on the left. The going was extremely bad, over loose slab rock. For the first fifteen miles, as far as the Field Supply Dump, progress was slow, although damage to tracks was remarkably slight.

At 10.40 the brigade halted and replenished. The halt here was longer than expected because an order reached the brigade from the 7th Armoured Division that a flying column was to be formed under Lieutenant-Colonel J. F. B. Combe of the 11th Hussars. The latter were already at Msus; here they had narrowly missed the garrison, which fled in two lorries at the approach of the armoured cars. Now the 2nd Battalion of the Rifle Brigade and C Battery 4th Royal Horse Artillery, were ordered to push on as fast as possible and to come under Colonel Combe, who was to block the enemy retreat about Sidi Saleh.

The 2nd Battalion the Rifle Brigade were in rear of the column and it took two hours to replenish the units and provide extra transport from the armoured regiments so as to give the special force an endurance of 300 miles. By 12.40 p.m. it was on its way and at 1 p.m. the 4th Armoured Brigade Group resumed its march. The going was still bad. It was in fact easier for tracks than for wheels and very soon the leading regiments found themselves catching up and delayed by the tail of the Rifle Brigade. But after an hour it became more gravelly and the motor battalion gradually drew away out of sight.

As the going improved, so did the pace. If a whip had been needed, it would now have been pulled out. General Creagh said that speed was more important than anything, so halts were cut down to the minimum. The brigade was to reach Msus that night. The pace was exhilarating and even those who, in moments of boredom during the preceding four weeks, had secretly looked forward to a rumoured re-fit in the delta, forgot their cares in the excitement of the rush.

At 5.30 p.m. there was another halt for topping up. The march should have continued at 6.30, but the replenishment party could not find the regiment in time, so the rest of the brigade moved on and the regiment followed at 7 p.m. It soon caught up and was up in its place. Another thermos area was now encountered, so the brigade halted for the night seven miles east of Msus.

During the 5.30 halt Lieutenant Astley, the regimental liaison officer at 4th Armoured Brigade Headquarters, had brought orders for the 7th Hussars to move to Soluch, the terminus of a railway running south for thirty miles from Benghazi, on the following day. It was to report on several intermediate bounds and then to surround and isolate the railhead. At 6.50 a.m. on the 5th all was ready for the move, which was then postponed to 7.30. At 7.30 however the orders for the move to Soluch were cancelled and the regiment was ordered to move south-west in advance of the brigade and to make good successive bounds to a line just west of Antelat.

This march of fifty miles was finished by 3 p.m. without incident. The regiment was then ordered to send patrols to the Beda Fomm area to report whether it was held. If not, it was intended that the brigade should move there before dark and leaguer for the night. Otherwise it would leaguer where it was, at Antelat. There was not a moment to lose and the patrols went off at once.

At 5 p.m. on the 5th, just as the patrols were approaching Beda Fomm, news came that a large column of enemy transport was on the move southwards down the main road. The regiment was ordered to attack them provided that the reconnaissance found the Beda Fomm area unoccupied. At 5.15 B Squadron reported the area clear and the regiment moved west-south-west towards the road. Tanks were very low in petrol. A little was taken from the vehicles of the troop of D Battery Royal Horse Artillery, and this was a help. But in the circumstances all risks were justified, and in fact several tanks ran out of petrol on the way to the battle.

The regiment moved with C Squadron on the right and B on the left. At 6.15 the leading troops found the enemy, who had halted and were cooking their evening meal. They were completely surprised. Both squadrons rushed on the enemy and crossed the road. B turned south and shot up the long string of vehicles along the road. C continued westwards, chased and captured or destroyed a number of vehicles which tried to escape into the sandhills near the sea. Unfortunately darkness supervened and the engagement could not be driven to a conclusion.

Helped by the light of an enemy petrol lorry set on fire by Lieutenant Murray Smith, 800 prisoners were rounded up and twelve lorries were driven away. Thirty more were destroyed and sixty to seventy had to be left, as there were no drivers for them and the darkness made mopping-up operations difficult. The troop of D Battery was very useful and did much of the work which more properly belonged to infantrymen. Captured petrol was put into two tanks which had run dry on the battlefield and into the single cruiser of A Squadron, which had run dry two miles short of the road.

The enemy prisoners were quite co-operative in their rounding-up. Lieutenant Fox's troop picked up 300 of them. In the darkness the tanks became separated and tank commanders dismounted, revolver in hand, to sort out the catch. One Italian officer came forward to help, speaking fair English and explaining that he had spent eleven years in America. Another was equally helpful when he saw that Sergeant Cleere was walking around with a Verey light pistol, which he had picked up in a hurry instead of the more lethal kind, and gave him his own automatic.

At 9 p.m. the regiment moved into leaguer two miles south-west of Beda Fomm, having left the prisoners under an escort of Lieutenant Pilkington and six light tanks, a few miles farther west. Wishing to take no chance the brigade headquarters ordered them to be marched into the leaguer and they came in during the night.

*   *   *   *

Just before dawn a strong south wind began to blow and by daylight there was a howling gale and heavy rain. Empty petrol cans left by the tanks after replenishment during the night danced noisily across the leaguer area and everyone was cold and wet. It was a boisterous opening to an eventful day.

The stage was now set for the final destruction of Marshal Graziani's Army of Egypt. Combe Force was firmly astride the road west of Sidi Saleh. The Support Group, consisting now only of the 1st Battalion the King's Royal Rifle Corps, and the 7th Armoured Brigade, 1st Royal Tanks only, were in the vicinity of Scheleidima, which was held by the enemy. The 4th Armoured Brigade Group was about Beda Fomm, whence it could strike at the retreating enemy at any point it chose on the road. For the first time the Royal Air Force were absent from a major engagement as there was no time to establish facilities for them within reach of the road. Oddly enough it was on the same stretch of road that two years later the Royal Air Force attacked the retreating Rommel, having established their own forward landing grounds at Msus, nearly a hundred miles ahead of the army.

At 9 a.m. on 6th February the 7th Hussars, less B Squadron, moved north-westwards with orders to locate and harass the tail of the enemy column on the road. B was left as escort to F Battery Royal Horse Artillery, four miles south of Beda Fomm. At 9.30 F Battery (Major Withers) was ordered to move to help the 2nd Royal Tanks, who were about to engage the enemy, and B Squadron rejoined the regiment.

F Battery was to have a very successful day with ideal targets of enemy tanks and transport. Sitting in his 8-cwt. truck alongside the Commanding Officer of the 2nd Royal Tanks, with the southern half of his fine moustache drooping at full depression in the weather and the northern half at its usual angle, Major Withers pounded the enemy transport and tanks as hard as the ammunition situation and the close fighting of the 2nd Royal Tanks would allow.

By 10.30 a.m., in poor visibility, B Squadron had joined C on the main road near the road-house (sometimes referred to incorrectly as a block-house) almost due west of Beda Fomm. As visibility improved B Squadron shot up the enemy in the area of the road-house and C Squadron engaged the transport on the road farther south. It seemed that the enemy's tail had been found. But at 11.15 a.m. a more formidable body of the enemy was seen by the most northerly patrol of C Squadron, advancing down the road from Benghazi. It was preceded by three motor cyclists and an armoured car (ex-11th Hussars) and escorted by twelve medium tanks. Lieutenant Llewellen Palmer advanced on the enemy with his troop. Two of the motor cyclists were shot and he rammed the armoured car and killed its crew—two Italians and a Libyan. But in face of the medium tanks the regiment was forced to withdraw.

At 12 o'clock the 7th Hussars were asked to find a place suitable for the 3rd Hussars to attack the enemy column. The 3rd Hussars still had four fit cruisers in their attached squadron of 2nd Royal Tanks. The points recommended were on either side of the road-house and at 12.15 the 3rd Hussars were ordered to attack and the 7th to help them. A few moments later however a further twenty-five enemy mediums appeared moving down just east of the road. These could not be ignored. They halted, which was perhaps fortunate, as the single cruiser of A Squadron (Lieutenant Guthrie) cast a track within 2,000 yards of the enemy. The troop of D Battery stood by the cruiser during a precarious twenty-five minutes, not opening fire in case the enemy should retaliate. When the repairs were completed the party fell back successfully on the regiment.

The 7th Hussars were now ordered to move north round the enemy and to tap in on the road, again on his tail. With B and C in the lead the road was crossed once more, five miles north of the road-house, and the regiment turned south. They found the enemy rearguard, shot two motor cyclists and prepared to attack a concentration of enemy vehicles south and south-west of the road-house. The time was now about 2.45

p.m., and just as the attack was about to begin twenty-eight medium tanks were seen moving back to the road from the direction of Beda Fomm. They were in fact just returning from an engagement they had had with the 3rd Hussars, whom they were trying to keep at a distance from the column, and they were too formidable a force for the 7th Hussars to attack.

The head of the enemy column was now in difficulties fifteen miles to the south, and although the Italians fought their tanks with determination, they were unable to stave off disaster. When they made their next attempt to drive off the British on their flanks, the Italian tanks were met by the cruisers of the 2nd Royal Tanks and almost wiped out. The 2nd Royal Tanks had a splendid day. Of the eighty-three enemy tanks found abandoned or destroyed, the 2nd Royal Tanks knocked out forty-eight. They fired from stationary hull-down positions, and they withdrew several times behind a ridge to fill up with ammunition and returned to the battle in a matter of minutes.

As the light began to fail the enemy's rear was gradually drawing up towards his front, leaving behind a stricken trail of burning and abandoned vehicles, dead and wounded, and shaken stragglers. At 5.45 p.m. the 7th Hussars were ordered to leaguer four miles south-west of Beda Fomm. The regiment was well on the way when brigade headquarters suggested that if it moved by the road a few prisoners might be picked up. But it was already late and would be quite dark before the road could be reached, so permission was given for the movement to continue on the same bearing.

At dawn the following morning the enemy made his last attempt, with his remaining medium tanks, to break out to the south. Some of his tanks were destroyed practically on the muzzles of C Battery Royal Horse Artillery and the few anti-tank guns with Combe Force, and the attempt failed. At 6.45 the 7th Hussars sent Lieutenant Fox's troop on patrol to the road south of the road-house, but he found nothing but a mass of battered and abandoned vehicles and tanks. Moving north to the road-house he met with no resistance; the only human beings were Italian medical personnel and wounded, and Arab looters.

Throughout the battles of the previous day a tribe of Arabs had remained in and around their square black tents, some venturing out among the troops to sell eggs, their camels quietly grazing and, like their owners, taking no notice of all the metal screaming over their heads from both directions. It would have taken more than that to drive the Arabs away from the very evident prospect of good and early looting. The regiment too moved north-westwards again, through the scene of the 2nd Royal Tanks' action, where thirty-one M.13's were counted, their dead crews lying all round.

At 9.10 the 7th Hussars were ordered to cross the road and cut the coastal track through the sand dunes. The coastal track was reached at a point where old strands of barbed wire told the story of the last resistance of a handful of Turks when the Italians seized Libya in 1912. Before a way could be found through the sand dunes news came that the battle was over.

Berganzoli was among the prisoners. For the fourth time in eight weeks General O'Connor's little army had captured a force bigger than itself, this time with only the much depleted 7th Armoured Division. A hundred-and-sixty miles had been covered in thirty hours and had caused much wear and tear to the vehicles, but in the ensuing battle the losses of the whole force were only three tanks as battle casualties, one man killed, and two officers and four men wounded.

The 4th Armoured Brigade war diary records that "The work of the 7th Hussars was also most praiseworthy." Brigadier Caunter had already written a letter of thanks to Lieutenant-Colonel Byass on 2nd February, when the regiment was transferred—only temporarily as it happened—to the 7th Armoured Brigade. This letter was greatly appreciated:—

> "I am very sorry to lose the 7th Hussars, as the regiment has shown itself in battle and maintenance, etc., to be first class. You have the right to be well satisfied with its past performances and its present state of efficiency. I have watched its progress very carefully from the early days around Capuzzo until now with great satisfaction. It has been tested severely on numerous occasions and has come through such tests with great success. I wish you and the 7th Hussars every success in the future. . . .
> J. A. L. CAUNTER."

While armoured cars were sent off to the Tripolitanian frontier at Agheila, the work of clearing the battlefield began at once. The 7th Hussars were given the area from the road-house to the Pimple Mound. The latter was inclusive to the 3rd Hussars and included the bulk of the knocked out tanks. Priority was to be given to burying the dead, work which the prisoners were to do, and clearing vehicles off the road. Those which were serviceable were parked at selected places and taken into use. Others were pulled off the road by tanks and left. For fifteen miles the road and its verges were a mass of wrecked and abandoned guns, tanks and vehicles, their contents strewn widely about by the looters and the wind.

The wreck of an army. Part of the fifteen miles of wrecked and abandoned guns, tanks and vehicles at Beda Fomm.

Knocked-out vehicles at Beda Fomm, with an M.13 Italian tank, and Arabs looting.

From the 7th to the 16th the clearing of the battlefield went on, the only incidents being the occasional visits of German aircraft, which dropped a few bombs and machine gunned the parks of captured vehicles and the road. There was rain at intervals throughout this period and the leaguer area, north of Beda Fomm, was chiefly

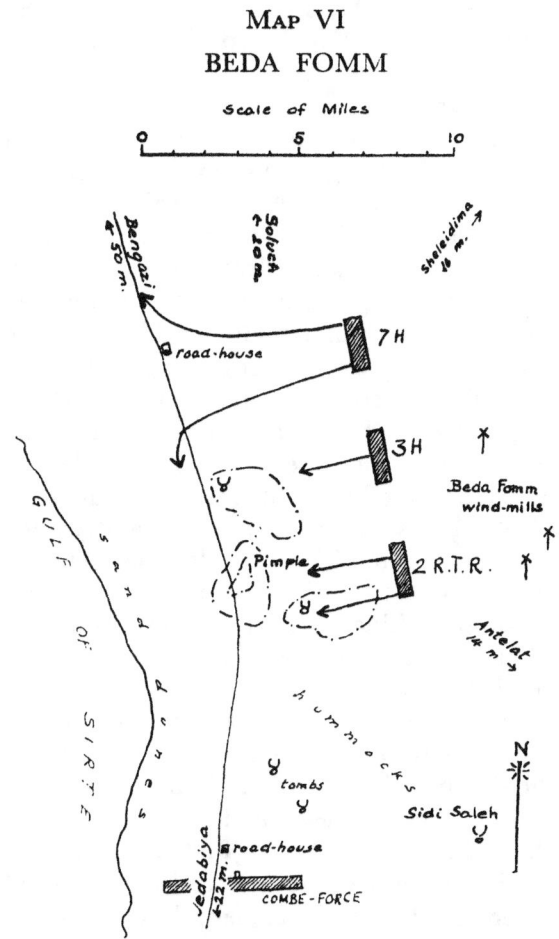

MAP VI
BEDA FOMM

notable for mud and scorpions. Nevertheless, the standard of living improved a little. Once more shelters of tarpaulins or ground-sheets went up alongside the tanks. Most were fortunate enough to find a few eggs in exchange for tea and biscuits. The most important luxury of all was an issue of fresh meat for the first time since the campaign began, made possible by the opening of the port of Benghazi.

At the same time as the battlefield was being cleared up the force was being reorganized. The headquarters of the 3rd Armoured Brigade came up and this was to take over the 3rd Hussars and the 6th Royal Tanks, the latter having returned from a short spell in the delta. The former were to be equipped with the best of the surviving light tanks, the latter with the captured Italian M.13's. Then one squadron of the 3rd was given M.13's—a decision of questionable wisdom as their clearing area had included the grisly mess on the Pimple.

On 17th February the 7th Hussars handed over their twelve best light tanks to the 3rd and prepared to march back to Mena. The march began on the 22nd. The regiment kept its wheeled transport and scout cars and was lent six extra R.A.S.C. lorries for carrying the crews. Each squadron took with it a captured Italian vehicle as a reserve. The route was past Msus and Mechili to Tmimi and thence by the coast road. Tobruk was passed on the 25th and on this day the journey was marred by a very unfortunate accident. Trooper H. Fields, of C Squadron, was struck by a passing trailer. He was rushed into hospital but died before he could be operated on.

On the 28th Amiriya was reached and an officer was sent off with eight R.A.S.C. lorries to collect the superfluous baggage left behind in the desert just before the battle of Sidi Barrani. The last night of the eight-day journey of 600 miles was cold and wet and eight vehicles had to be left, stuck in the mud, to be dragged out later. At about noon on the 1st of March the bulk of the regiment arrived rather bedraggled in the Jubbulpore Lines at Mena, where Major Sheppard and Lieutenant and Quartermaster Blake had done everything possible to make the camp comfortable.

There followed three weeks of rest, resuscitation and leave to Cairo, punctuated with individual training and courses. But there was no equipment and when, on 17th March, four light tanks were issued, these were the only ones in the brigade. But there were other and more dreary jobs to be done. On the 21st orders were received to take over guard duties at Tura Caves and Helwan, south of Cairo.

The Tura Caves were made by the ancient Egyptians when they hewed out the rock for the pyramids. They were of great value to the Survey and Ordnance departments, and easy to guard. So they presented no problem. But the 130,000 Italian prisoners were a shock to the administrative system of the Middle East with which it had not been fully able to cope. They were lodged in improvised camps at Helwan. Two hundred and thirty men were required to guard them and a considerable staff was required for their administration. The 4th

Armoured Brigade set up a board of officers to check the equipment of the camps. C Squadron was then made responsible for their administration and B Squadron, with all the spare men from A and regimental headquarters, for the guards. On 26th March the new draft from the depot, 130 men, was sent direct to Helwan to make up the numbers for guards. So there were left at Mena only a few officers and men required for training and courses and these were accommodated in Calcutta Lines with the 7th Armoured Division Signals. Besides the new draft, eight young officers joined the regiment, Lieutenant R. Nickels, and Second-Lieutenants B. P. Barton, A. P. Mills, J. E. Parry, M. J. E. Patteson, P. J. Stevens, D. M. Allen and V. L. John.

Immediate awards received for the campaign included the Distinguished Service Order for Lieutenant-Colonel F. W. Byass, M.C., Major R. B. Sheppard and Major R. F. G. Jayne, the Military Cross for Lieutenants G. W. Murray Smith and J. Napier, the Distinguished Conduct Medal for Sergeant Patrick Cleere and Trooper Barlow; the Military Medal for Sergeant Widdowson, Sergeant Glendinning Troop Sergeant-Major Hatherall, Sergeant Austin, Trooper Brown, Trooper Bell, and Corporal Spreadbury of the Royal Corps of Signals.

CHAPTER V

The Summer of 1941

B Squadron goes to the desert—the German advance—operations on the frontier—columns—the coastal plain—Amiriya—Middle East problems—Greece—Crete—Iraq—Syria—Tobruk—attempts to relieve Tobruk—change in Middle East command—7th Hussars at Charing Cross—21st Panzer Division advances to Rabia—forward concentration begins—B Squadron's raid at Sheferzen—gunnery practice.

Maps I, II, IV

Late on the evening of Saturday, 5th April, the 7th Hussars were ordered to provide a squadron for the occupation of Giarabub. B Squadron (Major R. Younger) was chosen and every effort was made to get it ready by the evening of Monday the 9th. Additional driver-mechanics were selected to accompany the squadron and also a detachment of Royal Corps of Signals under Corporal Spreadbury, M.M.

During the preceding month, since Beda Fomm, all serviceable equipment and vehicles had either been handed back to Ordnance or passed on to other units. So the squadron had to be completely re-equipped in a very short time. Ten light tanks were drawn from the 8th Hussars and three from Royal Army Ordnance Corps Workshops. The wheeled vehicles were collected straight from a ship at Suez. All equipment was new except four tanks and the Bren guns. It was a rush, but the squadron was ready in time.

At 6.30 p.m. on the 7th the train carrying the tanks left Abbassia siding for the desert. Next morning the road party left, six 3-tonners, six 15-cwt. trucks, a 220-gallon water tanker and one 8-cwt., accompanied by a recovery detachment. On the 9th the train party left, carrying most of the personnel. These detrained the same evening at Matruh and Major Younger went off to the 3rd Battalion Coldstream Guards to get information.

The squadron set out at once by road for Salum. Shortly before midnight it reached Sidi Barrani; the road party joined up and the squadron bivouacked for the night. No tanks had fallen out.

Next morning the march was resumed and at 12.30 a halt was made at the foot of Halfaya Pass. Wireless sets were not fitted; there had been no time to do this before the start and the sets had been carried, crated, in the turrets. A hundred and thirty-five miles had been covered in twenty-two hours and by 5 p.m. all tanks were up except one. So far little news had reached the men, but all knew that the Germans had arrived somewhere in the Tobruk area, having advanced very rapidly from Agheila in the preceding fortnight.

*   *   *   *

In spite of his recent victory, which had surpassed everyone's most optimistic forecasts, the few months following Beda Fomm were one of General Wavell's most difficult periods. The campaign in Greece was now added to the already heavy calls on the forces in the Middle East. So Cyrenaica, where a victory had just been won and the threat of retaliation, if apparent at all, was 700 miles from the vital spot, became a front where economy of force was practised to the point of danger. General Neame had taken over from General Wilson, and, if he were to be attacked, his instructions were to fight a delaying action and withdraw if necessary.

It was always expected that the enemy would some time resume the offensive, but there was no indication that he would be ready so soon, or that the main punch of his counter-stroke would be German armour. Messerschmidts had indeed been active in the forward area for some weeks; after the battle of Beda Fomm they carried out sporadic attacks on our troops clearing up the battlefield and assembling the captured equipment. In February, somewhere near Agheila, a German officer was present at the interrogation of a British corporal who escaped soon afterwards. But apart from this there was no news of German land forces arriving in North Africa, nor even of their passage through Italy.

The policy of placating the Italians had in fact led to neglect of the elementary precautions for getting information in time of war—the establishment of a widespread information service before war breaks out. So the arrival and strength of the German forces and the vigour of Rommel, their commander, came as a complete surprise.

The days when the enemy could be counted upon to stay snugly in his entrenched camps or to move carefully and ponderously on well charted routes, were coming to an end. Rommel understood desert warfare as well as our own commanders and the Germans were well ahead of us in the development of armour and in experience of handling armoured forces in conjunction with other arms. From now onwards the Germans were the dominant partners on the enemy's side and the character of his strategy and tactics changed accordingly.

On 25th March the German air force attacked the landing ground at Jedabiya with JU 87's (Stuka dive-bombers) and JU 88's, escorted by Messerschmidts. His armoured forces, closely supported by infantry and artillery, advanced at the same time against the light forces about Agheila and these slowly withdrew, the artillery taking every opportunity of harassing the German columns. The enemy as usual concentrated the whole of his air force in close tactical support of his leading troops and considerable damage was done to the British and Australian forces as they withdrew.

The Australians moved by the coast road to Benghazi and Derna and the more mobile troops across the desert by Msus and Mechili. On 3rd April, our troops evacuated Benghazi and the area round Msus.

The main difficulties were in the desert. Transport was short owing to the calls of other theatres. Unit and Royal Army Service Corps transport worked hard, and all might have been well if the fuel dump at Msus had not been prematurely destroyed by the unit guarding it, owing to a misunderstanding of the situation. Besides petrol, there had been diesel oil for the Italian tanks—the backbone of the little armoured force. From now onwards every drop of petrol counted and as a vehicle broke down its petrol tank was drained before it was abandoned. One after another the Italian tanks ran out of fuel and were destroyed.

When the two main components of the force reached the general line Derna—Mechili, where it was hoped that the withdrawal might stop, there was such an acute shortage of armour that the left flank in the desert was completely exposed. The Germans could, and did, exploit the advantages of their armoured mobility. On 7th April they surrounded the Indian Motor Brigade, whose three splendid regiments, only partially trained in the ways of the desert and partially equipped, extricated themselves with much difficulty and heavy losses. The Germans tapped in with small armoured detachments at many points on the road between Benghazi and Derna and forced the Australians back on Tobruk. They captured much of the headquarters of the 2nd Armoured Division, including its commander, Major-General Gambier-Parry. They captured Lieutenant-Generals Neame and O'Connor and Lieutenant-Colonel Combe. General O'Connor, having commanded the forces throughout the previous campaign, had an unrivalled knowledge of the desert and its ways. He had been sent up to visit the new Commander, "just to hold his hand" in the emergency.

On 7th and 8th April General Wavell flew to Tobruk and decided that it should be held. The forces in Tobruk amounted to some 40,000 men, the majority Australians. In view of the speed of the enemy's advance and the shortage of transport it would not have been easy to move them back to the frontier area, or to Matruh, and in any case the enemy's preponderance of armour would have enabled him, once he could use the harbour, to out-manoeuvre our forces again and again. Other important factors influencing the decision were the many base installations such as workshops and a large quantity of stores which it would be impossible to evacuate. It was anticipated that the armour situation would shortly improve and that reinforcements now on the way from the United Kingdom would enable operations for relief of the garrison to be undertaken in the not distant future.

By 11th April the enemy had completely invested Tobruk. The garrison had set to work at once on the defences. They were thus ready for the enemy's first impromptu attack, which penetrated the perimeter at one point but was then successfully stopped.

The remainder of the British troops, including the Support Group of the 7th Armoured Division, had withdrawn past Tobruk to the frontier at Salum and Sidi Omar. Here the position was in process of stabilization. The 22nd Guards Brigade was about Salum and Capuzzo, the Support Group a little farther inland. The withdrawing troops were quickly sorted out and reorganized, and control, temporarily lost when the senior commanders had been captured a few days earlier, was restored. Armour was entirely lacking, and it was to supply this need that B Squadron of the 7th Hussars had been so hurriedly equipped and sent forward to the foot of Halfaya Pass.

*   *   *   *

On arrival the squadron came under the orders of Lieutenant-Colonel J. Moubray, 3rd Battalion The Coldstream Guards. It was ordered to co-operate with his battalion in defending the dumps at Salum against raiding parties. After dark on the evening of 10th April the squadron moved by the main road up the escarpment at Salum, past the barracks on the plateau 600 feet above and bivouacked near Musaid. A surprise and welcome guest that night was Major A. I. C. Cameron, who had escaped from Mechili.

Early on the morning of 11th April three patrols were sent out to observe the western approaches to the Capuzzo area, respectively to Sidi Azeiz, Bir Charruba and Bir Ghirba. Squadron headquarters moved up to the familiar triangle north of Capuzzo. In the afternoon the squadron came under command of Brigadier Ian Erskine, commanding the 22nd Guards Brigade. No enemy were seen that day.

The 11th of April was a day of rumours. This is hardly surprising, as it was the day the enemy finally completed the investment of Tobruk and the units and elements of units arriving on the frontier were somewhat lacking in cohesion. There were many alarmist and defeatist reports of a kind which are always associated with retrograde movements in war. The increasing membership of the "last survivors' club," as hapless lorry drivers became detached from their unit and sought security on the frontier wire, led to the operation being christened irreverently "the Matruh Stakes."

A few may have moved a little farther eastward than was really necessary, but on the whole the drivers who became detached, British, Australian and Indian, took the only sensible course. In the almost featureless desert the vagrant detachment or individual with no wireless, no compass and no map, and with only a limited reserve of water, rations and petrol, had little hope of finding a parent unit whose location was not known and which was probably also on the move. The only unmistakable features were the sea coast, the coast road, and the frontier wire, and all were put right when they reached one or the other.

Apart from the material inconvenience, however, a considerable moral effect is produced by the combined circumstances of a withdrawal and being lost. Quite rational human beings become engrossed in the importance of their own anxieties and wish to spread the load of their feelings to others. This is done by the exaggeration of their experience and the magnification of the enemy's strength. In the armies of temperamental races such conditions have often produced panic. But here there was no panic and individual stories were given their true value by the troops in rear.

After dark one troop of B Squadron was sent to Bardia to support the 2nd Battalion, Durham Light Infantry. During the night the water supply installation was destroyed and Bardia was evacuated without enemy interference.

Next morning the squadron was placed under the 4th Royal Horse Artillery, commanded by Lieutenant-Colonel J. C. Campbell, D.S.O., M.C., at Musaid. His force included one company of the 1st Battalion King's Royal Rifle Corps, F Battery Royal Horse Artillery and a troop of anti-tank guns of the 3rd Royal Horse Artillery.

It was a foul day. The air was full of driving sand and the atmosphere, again, of rumours. Two patrols were sent out, one to observe the southern exit from Bardia and the other to Sidi Azeiz. The latter saw nothing. The former (Lieutenant J. Napier), approaching Bardia defences in the sandstorm, ran on to a German anti-tank gun.

Shots were exchanged, but in the low visibility—scarcely 10 yards—the troop extricated itself without damage. Both troops remained in position after nightfall.

About 1 a.m. the anti-tank guns at the road junction north of Capuzzo opened fire on what appeared to be enemy vehicles approaching from the north-west. The "enemy" drew off, and it was not known until later that they were in fact a troop of 11th Hussars. Happily no damage was done.

As the Germans were arriving in the area, orders were now given for the isolated troop of anti-tank guns to withdraw, its flanks being protected by the two 7th Hussars patrols. This movement was successfully carried out and by 3 a.m. the troop and the patrols were in position just east of Fort Capuzzo. During this withdrawal a small party of German infantry, either a reconnaissance patrol or a raiding party sent out to attack the guns, was encountered by Lieutenant Llewellen Palmer's troop, which captured seven, including two officers.

In the morning fresh patrols were sent out. One observed a small enemy column emerging from the Bardia perimeter. This was engaged by our artillery and retraced its steps. Then a larger column of about 100 vehicles approached from the direction of Sidi Azeiz. This also was engaged by artillery. Covered, however, by its own guns, the enemy column continued its advance and occupied the Fort Capuzzo area about 1 p.m. The artillery continued to engage the enemy, the guns and observation posts being protected by troops of the 7th Hussars. The enemy made no attempt to advance beyond the frontier and set to work to establish himself in the neighbourhood of the fort.

At 6 p.m. the squadron leader was sent for and the squadron was told to be ready to move at 10 p.m. Major Younger went with Colonel Campbell to Brigadier Gott's headquarters. Orders had been received that the offensive was to be resumed at once. The enemy was thought to be at the end of his tether. He was doubtless using Benghazi as a port by this time and perhaps getting a little help from the small facilities at Derna. But Tobruk was denied to him and his leading elements had only entered Bardia a few days before. His activities in the frontier area must surely be restricted by his administrative situation.

British forces for "resuming the offensive" were hard enough to find, but it needed difficulties less trivial to stop the indomitable commander of the 7th Support Group. A plan was made to recapture Fort Capuzzo with the 1st Battalion the King's Royal Rifle Corps, supported by the 4th Royal Horse Artillery and led by B Squadron the 7th Hussars—light tanks playing in the role of Matilda.

The squadron marched off at 10 p.m. and soon after midnight reached the rendezvous at Sidi Omar. The motor battalion, however, had a long way to come and was unable to arrive in time to carry out the operation as planned. It was nevertheless considered necessary to take some sort of offensive action. The squadron was therefore ordered to sweep round Capuzzo. A course was chosen, passing west and north about, round the defended area, and returning down the frontier wire to the gap at B.P. 41. The sweep was carried out and nothing happened; not even a sniping shot came from the enemy positions. The squadron went back to Sidi Omar and then at 4 p.m. moved back to Haqfet el Nas, just south of Halfaya Pass, for the night.

The 15th was spent in maintenance and by noon all seventeen tanks were in good order. Some of the transport, which had been sent back to Bugbug on the 12th for safety, as the situation in the frontier area had then been a little fluid, was brought up again. Next morning, 15th April, the task of the squadron was first to act as escort to the artillery observation posts and secondly to prevent the enemy moving south and south-west along the wire.

At 6.45 a.m. two patrols and squadron headquarters moved out to positions about three miles short of the wire, south-east of Capuzzo. The rest of the squadron was put at fifteen minutes' notice. Nothing happened all day, so in the evening the whole squadron demonstrated towards Musaid. It was hoped that this, and the shelling by the 4th Royal Horse Artillery which was to take place at the same time, would provoke enemy retaliation and so provide good targets for the gunners.

At 6 p.m., supported by guns of D Battery Royal Horse Artillery (anti-tank), the squadron, less two troops, advanced in line to within about 1,500 yards of Musaid. A short and heavy burst of firing brought no response except one German deserter and the squadron went back to its bivouac area. The enemy were evidently not to be drawn on by troops standing off at long range. Accordingly at a conference at 10 p.m. orders were issued for a more forceful operation. B Squadron 7th Hussars, accompanied by four guns of D Battery Royal Horse Artillery, was to cross the wire at B.P. 41 and at first light on the 17th to do as much damage as possible to enemy transport in the Capuzzo-triangle area. F Battery would support the operation from about B.P. 39.

Three tanks had to be left behind for essential maintenance and a patrol of two was required for another task. So at midnight the squadron and the anti-tank troop set off, twelve tanks and four 2-pounders. The march was slow and uneventful—it was never safe to move more than six to seven miles an hour at night. On this night conditions were good. The wire was crossed just before dawn and it was light by 6 o'clock when the squadron reached its assembly position four miles north-west of Capuzzo. One tank had dropped out on the way.

Major Younger carried out a quick reconnaissance. He decided to advance on the fort and triangle area from the north-west, in line. He would then order "tanks right" and sweep past the north-west, and west sides of the fort in line-ahead. Eight tanks were to carry out the attack, two were to stay in reserve with orders to go to the help of any which got into difficulties and the eleventh was used as an armoured observation post for the battery.

At 7.30 a.m. the attack went in. Two enemy vehicles were set on fire in the triangle area and several enemy were seen to fall to machine gun fire. When the squadron was about 800 yards short of the line of sangars in front of the fort, the squadron leader gave the order "tanks right." The troop of D Battery continued to engage the enemy transport in the triangle while the squadron, under heavy anti-tank and artillery fire, engaged any target which presented itself. One enemy armoured car was destroyed and one ammunition dump blew up. F Battery Royal Horse Artillery gave effective covering fire on the enemy guns at the western corner of the fort just when it was most needed. Squadron Sergeant-Major Lawrence Swain was killed when his tank was hit, and his crew, Corporal Cossins and Trooper Clayton, were wounded and captured. Their tank was out of sight of the reserve tanks at the time, so details of these casualties were not known until later.

Swain had been a keen horseman before the war and for some years had been in the regimental jumping team. He had also been a popular member of the sergeants' mess and a brilliant darts player. On mechanization he quickly adapted himself to the new conditions and at the time of his death was squadron navigator. In navigation he became a real expert, very quick and supremely confident—a quality which was of great value to his squadron, who never had any doubts about their position.

The squadron leader's tank was hit twice and another of the tanks four times, Corporal R. Hipsey and Trooper Canby being wounded. Others brought to notice for gallant conduct on this day were Sergeant Harding and Corporal Pegler. At the end of the action the squadron returned to its leaguer area to refit.

The next two days were spent in maintenance and were generally uneventful except for a sandstorm. On the 18th Brigadier W. H. E. Gott visited the squadron and congratulated it on its achievements of the day before. By the end of the 19th fourteen tanks were serviceable. Of the others, one had been lost in action, one damaged and another was mechanically out of order, both these beyond the capacity of regimental fitters and their equipment. The four troops were now commanded by Lieutenant C. T. Llewellen Palmer, Lieutenant J. Napier, Second-Lieutenant R. Nickels and Sergeant Harding. Second-Lieutenant P. B. Stanley Evans was B Echelon commander. Two patrols were sent out daily to support the observation posts and protect the gun positions.

On the 22nd it was decided that the advanaced forces should now try to "dominate the triangle" as in the previous June and July. Accordingly the squadron started at 5.30 p.m. on a short march of fourteen miles to a position of assembly, five miles south of B.P. 40, and went into bivouac.

At first light a patrol under Lieutenant Napier was sent to B.P. 39 as escort to an observation post. The rest of the squadron moved at 2.15 at very short notice via B.P. 45 to the area of Gabr el Meduar. From here two patrols were sent out, one to protect an observation post and the other as escort to guns, while a troop of C Battery Royal Horse Artillery engaged a party of enemy motor transport on the Trigh Capuzzo, just west of its junction with the Bardia road. Lieutenant Llewellen Palmer's patrol was attacked by three enemy armoured cars and withdrew slightly. The cars were driven off by the Bofors troop of D Battery and by a Breda of the 11th Hussars and the patrol resumed its position.

In the evening a demonstration was carried out by the squadron together with a squadron of the 11th Hussars. This party moved north to Bir Beder and then a short way eastwards, but provoked nothing except a little ineffective artillery fire. At 7 p.m. the squadron moved back to Gabr el Meduar and leaguered for the night. Enemy aircraft attempted to attack the leaguer with incendiary bombs, but missed by a considerable distance.

On the 24th two patrols were again sent as escort to the observation post and guns of C Battery, and the artillery shoot against enemy transport was again reported to be effective. The enemy retaliated by a low flying attack by Messerschmidts 110. These did no damage to the 7th Hussars, but three cars of the 11th were hit and the Royal Horse Artillery had several casualties. In the evening the squadron returned to its leaguer area, south of the wire.

Next day the morning was spent in maintenance. At 2.15 however an order was received to move at once to a spot near the gun positions, as the enemy was showing more activity than usual. Accordingly the squadron moved four miles to the north. The enemy's aircraft had in fact been active again and the 11th Hussars had lost a further three cars. So Lieutenant Napier's troop was sent to back them up. Nothing else unusual occurred. An evening shoot was to have taken place, and the squadron provided the usual escorting patrols. But there was a breakdown in the artillery communications and the guns did not arrive.

The 26th of April opened with a khamseen wind. Two patrols were sent out to supplement the screen of the 11th Hussars, as they were getting short of armoured cars. Their orders were to watch for, and if possible stop, any enemy movement south of the 380 grid, which runs east and west about three miles north of Capuzzo. Nothing was seen until 3 p.m. when the dust cleared a little and Lieutenant Llewellen Palmer, whose patrol was about three miles north-west of the fort, observed in his rear a strong enemy column approaching the gap at B.P. 39 from the north-east. With him were an observation post and a section of Bofors guns. To avoid being cut off, he withdrew all these and his troop to B.P. 41.

In order to ensure the safety of the guns in action about B.P. 40, the rest of the squadron moved a few miles north-eastwards. The enemy crossed the wire about B.P. 38 and moved southwards towards Sidi Suleiman. Lieutenant Nickels' troop, with a section of Bofors guns, was sent to observe his movements. Sergeant Harding's troop was still out some eight miles north of the wire. Another troop was left as rearguard to the guns, and the squadron headquarters and remaining troop retired with the guns about four miles southwards. The enemy halted at the old Italian camp at Point 207. In the evening the squadron rejoined the transport, which had already been sent back to Bir el Khreigat when the enemy advance began. By nightfall all troops were in.

Some anxiety had been felt for Sergeant Harding, who only rejoined after dark. His march had been difficult as one of the tanks had broken down and he had had to tow it for five miles.

Lieutenant Napier's troop, with two Bofors guns, was sent out to block the track junction south of Sidi Suleiman for the night. This sounds an odd sort of task when the surrounding desert is all just as passable as the track itself—and not half so dusty. But it was quite usual for the enemy to follow tracks when he moved at night, so a troop on a track might at least be able to give warning of his approach.

At 9.30 p.m. orders were received that the whole force was to move back to Bir Enba. The enemy had advanced about eight miles. Our own light forces, some of which had been operating on his flank, had withdrawn a corresponding distance. Now however they were ordered to go back a further sixty miles. The enemy, by occupying the old positions about Point 207, now denied us the use of Halfaya Pass. From this point to Sofafi, some thirty-five miles, the escarpment is impassable to vehicles except at Halfway House, where there was a rough track which had not yet been made really safe. From Sofafi eastwards the escarpment gradually fades away into the desert and Bir Enba lies in a wide tract of reasonably good going. So an enemy force at Capuzzo, able to dominate Halfaya Pass and to make use of Salum hill, could operate at will either in the coastal plain or on the tableland. Our own forces in these two areas could not however support one another without a move back to the Sofafi area. This no doubt influenced the decision to withdraw so far—a decision which was ultimately reversed when the pass at Halfway House had been improved.

At midnight the eastward march began. It was a very dark night and three changes of bearing were necessary. SQMS Widdowson had now become acting SSM and his navigation was very good. By 10 a.m. all the tanks had arrived in the new area. A number of the transport drivers however were short of experience in night driving and some of them got lost, but they all rejoined by 1 p.m. on the 27th. The squadron then did maintenance, which was much needed. One troop was kept out on patrol watching the Bir el Telata track, and was relieved daily.

On the morning of the 28th Major Younger and Lieutenant Murray Smith went on a reconnaissance with the force commander, Lieutenant-Colonel J. C. Campbell, D.S.O., M.C. If the enemy were to attempt any further advance, the desert south of the escarpment offered more scope than the coastal plain. The latter was very bad going off the road. The fine dust lay deeper over the slab rock, the scrub grew more strongly and the wind drifted the dust round its stems into more pronounced hummocks than on the higher desert. In order to ensure rapid reinforcement of the column south of the escarpment by the only tank squadron, it was therefore decided to move it three miles farther westwards.

At the same time another reconnaissance was carried out by Lieutenant Napier and an officer of the 1st Battalion The King's Royal Rifle Corps in order to find the quickest way to get to the main lateral line of communication, the track between Sofafi and Bugbug. This track had been levelled by the Italians. Bulldozers had driven a line through the coastal plain and cut off the hummocks, leaving a flattish surface which was fairly good going although very deep in dust.

The force was now organized into "columns." There were Big Brother and Big Sister, and Little Brother and Little Sister. Generally, these were founded on a motor battalion and a battery or troop of horse artillery. The idea was active and mobile defence.

When the Italians were in the desert alone, and stayed staunchly in their entrenched camps, columns could work at will in the intervening gaps, get a great deal of information and generally dominate the open desert. But when Rommel came conditions changed. Here there was a great driving personality. He generally knew where he wanted to go and why he wanted to go there. He also had a very good idea of how to do it. When he advanced, he did so in comparatively compact formation, all arms operating in intimate co-operation. He was not to be diverted by "Jock Columns," as they came to be called (after the commander of the 4th Royal Horse Artillery) which could at the best only harass and withdraw in face of his concentrated mass.

The column system was in fact drawing to the end of its usefulness, even if it had not already passed that point. The difficulty was to find an alternative. In the desert there were almost limitless opportunities for wide turning movements. Only in a few areas, such as el Alamein, were both flanks protected, one by the sea and the other by the escarpment of the Qattara Depression, and the frontage here was sixty miles. When there were more troops, as in 1942, it was reasonable to regard this as a potential defensive position beyond which the enemy should not be allowed to pass. But in 1941 there was no point in establishing a fortified line with a spare end hanging in the empty desert. Nor was there any point in preparing a series of defended localities across a belt of desert unless they were able to support each other, as each could be attacked in turn, just as the Italian camps had been attacked at Sidi Barrani. Defensive positions were not the answer. The fact was that the side which had the more powerful armour had control of the desert over as wide an area as its administrative facilities would allow it to operate.

At this time Rommel had tanks whose front plates were proof against all British weapons smaller than the 25-pounder and even their side plates kept out the 2-pounder at ranges over 600 yards. The German tank guns on the other hand penetrated our light tanks and cruisers at 1,500 yards, and their 88-millimetre anti-aircraft gun at any range, as though they had no armour at all. Moreover the enemy used all arms in close co-operation with one another. In such circumstances the best that could be hoped for from our diminished forces in the frontier area was harassing the enemy whenever an opportunity arose or could be made, and, in the event of his advancing, causing him a certain amount of delay.

The gallantry and enterprise of the artillery and motor units, who penetrated often deeply behind the enemy in order to harass his forward troops and their communications were beyond praise. Often columns of smoke were seen, indicating that vehicles were hit and on fire. There is no doubt that the enemy found the raids by our columns and tanks a nuisance and that they made him take defensive precautions which against a more passive opponent would have been unnecessary. On the Italians there was also doubtless a good moral effect. But the Germans always had the measure of our columns. On them the moral effect was small, as they had a superiority in tanks and reasonable confidence that our lightly armed and generally unarmoured columns would be unlikely to close with them. Beyond "brewing-up" a few enemy vehicles with direct hits—by no means easy to obtain on the widely dispersed targets usually offered—the material damage inflicted on the enemy was usually slight, and, as there was seldom an opportunity of counting up the corpses, there was scope for a good deal of wishful thinking.

The part of B Squadron 7th Hussars in these column operations was usually protection of the artillery observation post and guns, one troop to each. The rest of the squadron would usually be held at short notice in rear, ready to go to any area of interest if the column should seem to be getting into trouble. On occasions the squadron was used on a "sweep," an operation usually intended to inflict damage on the enemy and provoke retaliation, which might show targets to our guns. Sweeps too had a certain nuisance value, but usually resulted in some damage to tanks, sometimes a few casualties and always considerable wear and tear of equipment.

*   *   *   *

On the evening of 29th April orders came for the squadron to go to Bugbug and come under command of the 22nd Guards Brigade. Only ten tanks were fit. Three of the others were left at Sofafi, to come on when the fitters had repaired them. B Echelon moved by Bir Enba to Sidi Barrani.

Two patrols were sent out to the area of the Ghot Ogrein some ten miles south-west of Bugbug, thus taking over part of the front watched by the 11th Hussars, who had had further casualties. One patrol

Robinson, a fast bowler, doing maintenance on his Mark VIB light tank in the desert.

7th Hussars tanks outside Tobruk; a dust storm is just beginning.

was near an observation post of F Battery, for its protection. The squadron headquarters was at Bugbug, close to the 2nd Battalion the Scots Guards and B Squadron the 11th Hussars. Lieutenant Murray Smith (Squadron second-in-command) was at headquarters 22nd Guards Brigade, a couple of miles away, for purposes of inter-communication. No movement was seen south of the coast road and a few enemy armoured cars which moved eastwards along the road and the summer track withdrew when fired on by artillery.

On 1st May a readjustment was made between the 7th and the 11th Hussars. The country south of the coast road was unsuitable for light tanks, so the 7th Hussars squadron took over the front from the coast road to the sea. The coast road is metalled, although the surface had been destroyed over much of its length, leaving bare hardcore foundation and pot-holes. It was however passable all the year round.

Nearer the sea was the so-called summer track. This was merely a trail, skirting and crossing the treacherous salt marshes which lie between the white sand-dunes on the sea shore and a low stoney ridge bordering the sparse patches of cultivated ground on the coastal plain. The salt marshes are very deceptive. In appearance they resemble the "ghots," or cultivable patches of the open desert which, being a foot or so below the level of their surroundings, hold the water a little longer and grow rather bigger scrub. There is one important difference however. In the salt marshes near the sea there is a very high water-table, only six to eighteen inches below the surface, according to the rainfall or the height above sea level. The going may appear to be good, but a heavy vehicle is liable at any moment to sink through the crust.

Two patrols were sent out, one along the road and the other along the summer track to a point about four miles west of Ras el Seiyada. The patrol on the summer track passed the wrecked hulks of the 3rd Hussars tanks, partly submerged in a salt marsh, and a permanent relic of their miniature and rather costly victory of the previous December. A little farther on, one of Second-Lieutenant Llewellen Palmer's tanks went through the crust in the same way. It was only after two days of hard work and by using three Scammell lorries together, that it was pulled out.

The patrols were ordered to work westwards to where the coastal plain narrows to about two miles, shortly before reaching the Halfaya Pass. Each was supported by a section of 25-pounders and anti-tank guns. Enemy armoured cars had been seen on the road and track on the two previous days.

The patrols moved out at first light and reached the line ordered. But the enemy cars did not come out. A plot was then made in conjunction with the Scots Guards for laying an ambush, but this could not be done as the anti-tank guns were mounted in lorries and suitable concealed positions could not be found.

The Guards Brigade was now relieved by the 7th Support Group, and the squadron came under command of the 2nd Battalion The Rifle Brigade (Lieutenant-Colonel A. S. G. Douglas). The squadron leaguer was moved about two miles to a fresh site, the old one being dusty and dirty.

As the war went on, many camping sites became dirty and foul. The popularity of a camping site was usually governed by its name and its conspicuousness on the map, or in the minds of those who had been there before. Bugbug had little to commend it except that it was marked in quite thick type, and the name itself somehow caught the imagination. There was no building of any kind, but only a few rather brackish wells, perhaps slightly more productive than other groups of wells, and the rather ill-defined area had been heavily camped upon. B Squadron's fresh site however was clean and remained so. It had the further advantage of thicker scrub, which gave better concealment from the air.

Reliefs of patrols were now arranged to take place in the early afternoon, both to give the returning troops an opportunity to bathe and because the mirage at that time of day helped to conceal the movement from the enemy.

On the 4th our guns engaged an enemy observation post on the escarpment and what was believed to be an armoured car. The enemy had very few armoured cars, and never seemed to hazard them far afield. He was known to have an eight wheeled car and much importance was attached to capturing one of these. A plan was accordingly made. As the enemy cars had not ventured into the coastal plain since British armoured patrols had been operating forward, the latter were ordered not to go so far. A spot was chosen on the road, mines were laid and a platoon of the Rifle Brigade and two Australian anti-tank guns were placed under command of B Squadron for the operation.

On 6th May a sandstorm spoiled visibility and nothing was seen. On the 7th, however, Lieutenant Nickels reported two enemy armoured cars advancing down the road towards him. The troop withdrew slowly towards the guns, keeping about 1,000 yards between themselves and the enemy, who was coming on nicely. The artillery unfortunately opened fire while the cars were still some way off and although the first shot was not very accurate, it turned the enemy back at high speed. During the afternoon the enemy did a little shelling from his battery positions somewhere about Halfaya Pass.

On 8th May the commander of the Support Group ordered a demonstration to be made towards Halfaya and Salum, in conjunction with operations being carried out by three columns south of the escarpment. A carrier platoon of the Rifle Brigade and a section of Australian anti-tank guns were put under command of B Squadron. The patrols on the road and track, each supported by a troop of the 8th Field Regiment, Royal Artillery, moved forward to points from which they could observe all movements in the Salum and Halfaya area, about three miles east of the pass. The rest of the squadron and attached troops moved to Alam Barghat.

Information about the operations to the south was entirely lacking. The enemy had guns above and below the escarpment at Halfaya Pass and it would have been unwise to penetrate deeply into the defile unless these could be located. The carrier platoon of the Rifle Brigade was sent to reconnoitre the Wadi Shaba and found it empty. Their move was covered by Second-Lieutenant P. B. Stanley Evans' troop. They were just preparing to stalk on foot an enemy battery beyond it when they were ordered to withdraw on account of a shoot which was to be carried out by the artillery.

The enemy's activities in the coastal plain were nothing more than a brief shelling of the summer track in the vicinity of the 7th Hussars patrol. He showed no signs of withdrawing in face of the operations of the three columns above the escarpment. At nightfall the detachment withdrew slightly, behind the cover of road blocks formed by the anti-tank guns. As the enemy was expected to withdraw during the night from Halfaya and perhaps also from Salum the Rifle Brigade patrolled constantly. But he did not do so and it was clear that the operations south of the escarpment had been a disappointment. The enemy was not to be turned out of positions whose value was obvious by the sporadic artillery fire or flanking threats of British columns.

At 4 o'clock in the morning of the 9th a south wind got up and at 7 the desert dust was travelling with it. Temperatures reached 118 degrees and this was the most unpleasantly hot day anyone was to experience in the desert. As the operations south of the escarpment were over, orders came at 11 o'clock for normal dispositions to be resumed.

The 3rd and 4th Troops were left out on patrol and the rest of the squadron started to move. Although there were only a few miles to go, ten at the most, conditions were such that the squadron only reached its old area at 4.30. Engines over-heated and tank crews suffered severely from physical exhaustion. Water in water bottles and cans was hot and slabs of chocolate assumed the consistency of oil paint, liberally treated with sand. It was the kind of day which was too much even for the rare enthusiast who said he liked the desert.

Quite suddenly at 5.30 p.m. the wind turned about and blew from the north, cool and refreshing. Very soon after it was heard that D Squadron of the 3rd Hussars had arrived in the area and would be taking over. In the circumstances nobody was very sorry at the prospects of leaving the desert.

On the 10th, when the squadron was on its last patrols before handing over its tanks to the 3rd Hussars, two enemy cars advanced down the road. Lieutenant Napier, who had just taken over with his troop, was temporarily out of touch with the artillery observation post. He was ordered to withdraw slowly to cover the guns, and meanwhile Major Reed, attached from the United States Army, and accompanying his patrol as a spectator, went back to the 8th Field Regiment and told them what was happening. The enemy was engaged by the artillery when still at long range and promptly withdrew.

In the evening, the cars came forward again to Alam el Barghat, but withdrew before being shelled. At about 9 p.m. a report came through that there were more motor transport than usual in the Capuzzo area and an attack was expected. Arrangements were made accordingly, the particular problem being the carrying of personnel of the 3rd Hussars who had been lorried up and were now dismounted. However, no attack materialized and at the next day's relief the tanks of the new patrols were manned by 3rd Hussars.

*   *   *   *

When the relief was complete the move to the delta began. The signal detachment under Corporal Spreadbury, M.M., Royal Corps of Signals, was left behind with the 3rd Hussars. All equipment and transport were handed over except oil compasses and the squadron depended entirely on borrowed transport for its return to railhead at Matruh.

The first stage, on 12th May, was in lorries of the Rifle Brigade and the 11th Hussars. One party changed at Sidi Barrani into a Royal Air Force lorry, which took them straight to the transit camp at Mersa Matruh. The rest were put down at Kilo 87, about halfway. From here they were taken by the Australian Divisional Ammunition Company to Kilo 50. They were given a meal by the hospitable

Australians, including the nearly forgotten luxuries of fresh meat and real butter.

The last fifty kilometres were done by "lorry hopping" on any vehicle which was heading in the right direction, and all troops were in the Leave and Transit Camp at Matruh by 5 p.m. At 6.30 a.m. they entrained for Amiriya. A railway truck on fire caused some delay and after a hot and dusty journey the squadron arrived in the hot and dusty Leave and Transit Camp at Amiriya at 5 p.m. At almost the same time the rest of the regiment, on its way up to the desert, arrived in another equally unpleasant camp at Amiriya and next day B Squadron moved across and joined it. Officers and men of B Squadron were then sent off on leave.

*   *   *   *

We left the regiment in April, with its headquarters at Mena and most of the men looking after the prisoners of war at Helwan. On 15th April this rather monotonous task was taken over by the New Zealanders and the regiment—less B Squadron—concentrated at Mena. Training then began in a more realistic fashion, although shortage of equipment was a serious handicap. It was nevertheless encouraging to learn that the next equipment would be cruisers and the rumour said A.13's. These were the fastest tanks in the country and the last word in cruisers. The 2nd Royal Tanks had had one squadron of them in the recent campaign and had found them satisfactory.

The change from light tanks to cruisers involved a good deal of re-training in driving, maintenance and gunnery. Gunnery in particular was a subject which could only be superficially dealt with in the few months likely to be available before the next engagement and tank gunnery was still in a somewhat experimental stage even in 1941.

The 2-pounder in the cruiser tank, although too small to deal effectively with German tanks, was in fact an excellent gun of its type and extremely accurate in the hands of a commander and gunner who understood it. But in the period between the wars the evolution of the tank itself and the ability of its crew to get it to the vital spot in time on manoeuvres had perhaps had more attention than the science of gunnery. Tank gunnery was not a science which could be learned in a few weeks.

The elementary handling of the gun, loading, aiming and firing, were taught in a succession of short courses. On 27th April forty-four gunners and fifty drivers were sent to the Base Depot for training in their respective spheres, the former for fourteen days only, the latter for twenty-one. These were followed by another batch. Two men were sent on a fitters' course, two on an electricians' and three on a technical storeman's course. These specialist courses lasted twelve weeks.

The move from Mena to Amiriya in the middle of May was an untidy one, as there was a shortage of transport and the stores had to be moved in several lots. The rail party marched to Mena and went by tram to Giza, where they entrained. It was an unpleasant day—khamseen wind and sandstorm. The road party went by the tarmac road across the desert. Several vehicles were driven off the road and had to be towed out of sand drifts. The rail party reached Amiriya at 1.30 p.m. and the road party half an hour later.

The camp was a bad one. It had evidently been occupied by troops who had not understood the importance of hygiene and the flies were described in the diary as "appalling." Many wished for the pleasant emptiness of a nice fresh leaguer area in virgin desert. However, there were compensations. It was good to see B Squadron again, with stories to tell of their latest experiences in the frontier area.

On 15th May it was expected that the final establishment would be thirty-two A.9's and twenty A.10's. The latter had a little more armour and were generally more solid, and it was something of a disappointment that there were to be so many A.9's and that there should be no mention of the A.13. However, it was a beginning, and the arrival of the first seven tanks gave a lot of encouragement. They were very deficient in equipment and frequent visits to store depots at Abbassia, Tel el Kebir and Tura only partially made up the shortages.

The joys of being real tank owners were short-lived. On 31st May an order was received from Headquarters, Western Desert, to send all tanks up to Mersa Matruh as replacements for the 2nd Royal Tanks. The mysterious "They" were blamed as usual for inconsistency—order, counter-order, disorder. Nobody ever quite knew who "they" were. They were as remote as a bearded deity sitting on a cloud. Some people had a mental picture of drooping white moustaches crowned with red hat bands, sitting round tables in palatial offices and working out just how the regimental soldier could be frustrated once more. But the much maligned staff and services in Cairo were doing their best to make every reasonably fit tank available for a serious effort to relieve Tobruk. At 9 a.m. next day the tanks were entrained. It was disheartening to lose them, and it was unsatisfactory that they should be handed over with such serious deficiencies to another unit. SSM Wilson in particular had worked unceasingly to make these up, but had only partially succeeded and it seemed that the missing parts were not in the country.

The fortnight had not been wasted. All officers and troop leaders had been through a driving and maintenance course under Warrant Officer Calder, Royal Army Ordnance Corps, and a gunnery course under SSM Wilson. The seven tanks had earned their living while they were there. Another draft of forty-four men arrived, but still this left the regiment a hundred men short. Another seventy were posted in June, thirty of these from the 1st Army Tank Brigade. When the tanks were gone, attention was given to gas training and other subjects not dependent upon missing equipment.

In June the tank situation was little better. By Waterloo day only two had arrived, A.10's. As the monotonous month wore on it became apparent that no more than one squadron would be equipped and it was decided that C Squadron should come first—Major J. Congreve. By the end of the month twelve tanks had come and all the wheeled vehicles except scout cars and a Ford "utility." The tanks were already veterans, but destined nevertheless to prove themselves good reliable old files.

*   *   *   *

The spring and summer of 1941 were among the most critical periods of the war in the Middle East. The campaign in the desert was only one of six conducted by General Wavell between April and July. Nevertheless by using every resource of ingenuity, mobility and improvization the situation in the theatre was not only preserved, but improved as the summer wore on.

In Greece and Crete there was never a chance of tactical success, although each had its value, strategically, in the long run. Operations in Iraq and Syria were quickly over and resulted in the consolidation of our position to the north and east. The mopping up of the Duke of Aosta's forces in East Africa was completed and the final result was that by the autumn all available resources could be concentrated in the desert, which was the only remaining scene of active operations.

In October 1940 Greece had been attacked by Italian forces based in Albania and had repulsed them. In January 1941 military help was offered to Greece by the British government. The Germans had consolidated their hold on Bulgaria and Rumania and were building up forces in those countries for their spring campaign.

The Greeks refused this offer in case it should provoke aggression. Nevertheless preparations were made to send a force to Greece, consisting of the 6th Australian Division from Cyrenaica, the 2nd New Zealand Division, and the 1st Armoured Brigade (4th Hussars and 3rd Royal Tanks) of the 2nd British Armoured Division, just out from home. Lieutenant-General Sir H. M. Wilson was given command, a headquarters was scraped together and the Signals were hastily improvized.

In March the Germans were bringing pressure upon Jugoslavia and the threat to Greece was increased. So it was decided to send the force. The information from Italy and Libya was so scanty that the balance of opinion in intelligence circles was that German troops had not arrived in Libya and were not even on the way through Italy. General Wavell thought it would be May before he need worry about his position at Agheila. The force was landed in Greece during March and by the time the Germans attacked on 6th April was mainly up in Northern Greece, except the 6th Australian Division, which was still disembarking.

There followed a campaign lasting three weeks. About the tenth day it was apparent that without air support there was no prospect of resisting the German advance and it was decided to evacuate the force. From the first day of operations the German airmen had dominated the battlefield and the communications in rear. They could not fly by night, as the mountains overhanging the landing grounds made these difficult enough for modern aircraft even in daylight. But among the troops the demoralizing paralysis of the day-time did not always wear off at nightfall and movement along the mountain roads was slow and difficult. The small and inadequate British air contingent was rapidly overwhelmed, the last remaining fighters, carefully nursed to cover the evacuating ships, being destroyed in a huddle on their airfield just as the evacuation began. So our troops, amply equipped with transport, fell back rapidly from northern Greece to the beaches as the German forces, covered by their aircraft, relentlessly advanced.

The Greeks had fought well against the Italians, but the German invasion was a moral and physical blow which, with the very limited scale of British help, they were unable to withstand. Some fought on as guerillas, with British help, for years, but as the British forces embarked, the gallant Greek army melted miserably away.

The good results of this campaign were not to be realized for some time, but its bad results were at once apparent. The Anzac Corps, re-formed for the first time since the epic summer of 1915 at Gallipoli, was involved in an evacuation in face of an overwhelming enemy.

The evacuation had been more successful than those concerned in it had dared to hope, and the losses to the dominion troops had been small. But in order to ensure that the greatest possible number of men should be got away, all equipment had to be left behind. The political effect in the dominions was serious and the loss of so much equipment, including 8,000 lorries, when we had so little, and when the Mediterranean was closed to our shipping, was a severe blow.

Nevertheless the campaign had several effects which, in the long run, were to prove that it had been worth while. It had shown the world that Great Britain and the Commonwealth, though still alone in the struggle, were determined to honour their obligations and in no mood to give in. Secondly it had cemented the friendship between the British and Greek people of which the foundations had been laid over a century earlier, in the time of Byron. As the troops left Athens on the way to the beaches, the Athenians, who had greeted their arrival with flowers, again threw flowers into the loaded lorries. The only apparent achievement of the force had been to delay the enemy's advance by a few weeks and this must be one of very few occasions in history when an unsuccessful army, in the act of abandoning a friendly people to their fate, has been paid the tributes usually reserved for liberators.

Politically, therefore, the campaign had a certain measure of success. But strategically, its effects on the course of the war may well have been greater than has yet been acknowledged. The Germans had planned their offensive against Russia and were now in process of securing their Balkan flank. The delay imposed by this small British expedition caused them to postpone by two or three fatal weeks the start of their great Russian adventure. These few weeks were enough to enable winter to stop operations when they were on the threshold of a success which the Russians, without the weather, could scarcely have prevented.

When the troops were evacuated from Greece many of them, to shorten the turn-round of the cruisers, destroyers and merchant vessels engaged in the operation, had been landed in Crete. It was then decided to hold Crete. The troops were reorganized and equipped and dispositions were taken up for the defence of the island—the last remaining free soil of Greece.

Late in May German parachutists landed at Herakleion and secured the airfield for the landing of glider-borne troops. They did the same at other aerodromes and followed up with seaborne troops. They made up for shortage of craft for landing guns by using their air force in the role of artillery. The British had no air support and the island had to be evacuated.

Again much equipment was lost and again dominion troops were involved in an unsuccessful operation. There was, however, one satisfactory outcome of the operation. The enemy's single airborne division, the apple of his eye, was practically destroyed and never again carried out a large scale airborne operation.

*   *   *   *

Simultaneously with the evacuation of Greece and the operations in Crete other troubles were developing in Syria and Iraq.

Iraq was pledged by treaty with Great Britain to afford rights and facilities for the transit of troops. The Royal Air Force maintained two aerodromes in the country, one at Habbaniyeh, forty miles west of Baghdad, and the other at Shaiba, near Basra; there were however no operational aircraft, as these had been withdrawn at the outbreak of war.

The Iraqi government had broken off relations with Germany but had omitted to do the same with Italy. Baghdad, with the Italians unmolested, was a hotbed of espionage and anti-British propaganda.

Iraq was of great importance in the conduct of the war. Not only was the oil necessary, but a rail and road route from Basra via Baghdad and the desert had been developed as an additional chain of communication with India. If the enemy should establish any measure of control in Iraq, these advantages would be lost and there would be yet another threat towards the Suez Canal area. So when Rashid Ali, said to be in Nazi pay, seized power in Iraq, something had to be done.

On 31st March the Regent heard of a plot to arrest him, took refuge on a British warship and had himself transferred to Transjordania. In the middle of April an Indian brigade was landed at Basra in accordance with treaty rights for the passage of troops. When Rashid Ali was told that another brigade was coming, he sought to refuse permission until the previous brigade should have moved on. But already his mind was made up and, encouraged by German successes, he now started to take action against the British force at Habbaniyeh.

The British women and children in Baghdad had already been moved to Habbaniyeh for safety, at the end of April, when the situation began to seem threatening. The British force was only 350 infantrymen, 1,000 R.A.F. details with 18 armoured cars, and 6 companies of the British-paid Iraq Levies. There was no artillery.

Rashid Ali's forces, a brigade group consisting of some 9,000 men with 50 guns, took up positions on slightly higher ground between the aerodrome and the lake of Habbaniyeh. On 1st May the A.O.C. considered the position so threatening that he took action with the few old aircraft left on the station and bombed the Iraqis. The latter replied with artillery fire and the Iraqi Air Force carried out an attack on the aerodrome. Another British battalion was flown up from Basra and air reinforcements were sent which destroyed the Iraqi Air Force. On 7th May the garrison made a successful sortie and captured 400 prisoners and the enemy withdrew to Fallujah.

Meanwhile a force had been scraped together in Palestine for use in emergency against any enemy threat in that area. It was a motorized cavalry brigade, somewhat incomplete and without much artillery. General Wavell was instructed to send this across to relieve the garrison of Habbaniyeh. It captured Rutbah wells and reached Habbaniyeh on the 18th. Fallujah was captured on the 19th. On the 22nd the Iraqis counter-attacked and retook Fallujah, but another British attack drove them back and they withdrew towards Baghdad. The British force then advanced on Baghdad, some 1,200 men with 8 guns. Although there was a whole Iraqi division intact, the Rashid Ali régime broke up. He himself left and by 1st June legitimate government was restored and the Regent was back in Baghdad.

There was no further trouble. Iraq now became a training area for several Indian Divisions and British troops. At the same time as they trained they had an operational role, though perhaps a rather shadowy one; as the Germans advanced across Russia, a distant threat to the Middle East developed through the Caucasus.

Even before the operations against Rashid Ali began, the Syrian problem was also coming to the front. The Germans were known to be infiltrating into the country and, if they established air bases there, the threat to the Suez Canal would be dangerous, Cyprus would be untenable and communication with Turkey would be severed. Early in May therefore General Wavell was ordered to prepare a force to bolster up the French in Syria, if they should resist the Germans. The only troops available were the incomplete British cavalry brigade and the weak Free French Division which General de Gaulle insisted should be used. Then suddenly, in the middle of May, the cavalry brigade had been sent to Iraq. In order to make it mobile, other units had been denuded of transport and left immobilized in Palestine and much of the civil transport had gone too. The Commander-in-Chief, still being pressed to enter Syria, had therefore to use troops which would otherwise have been available in the desert.

The troops allotted to General Wilson for the operation were the 7th Australian Division (less one of its brigades in Tobruk), a small remnant of the Cavalry Division including the Royal Scots Greys, the 5th Indian Infantry Brigade, freshly returned from Eritrea, and the Free French. Transport and signals were the main difficulty. The signals were as usual scratched together. Transport vehicles were taken over by the troops as they were unloaded at Port Said. The only aircraft available were used for the protection of the naval Squadron operating along the coast, so the land forces had no air support. The plan was to advance on a wide front, the 5th Brigade directed on Deraa, the Free French on Damascus and the Australians on Beirut. The advance began on the 8th June.

To oppose this attack the French had very superior forces, including ninety tanks, and they were under the control of the pro-Vichy General, Dentz. As the Vichy French realized the weakness of the attacking troops their resistance stiffened. Where they met the Free French their resistance was bitter. It was also thought that the regular elements of the army were driven further than they need have been by professional pride. Anyway, the French fought stubbornly. They delivered several heavy counter-attacks with tanks and the advance was checked. A brigade of the British 6th Division was consequently sent up to Palestine to help.

On the 21st the 5th Indian Brigade and the Free French captured Damascus after heavy fighting and with considerable casualties. Elsewhere resistance continued and a plan was made for a number of converging advances. Towards the end of June two more Indian brigades which were now in Iraq were directed up the Euphrates on Aleppo. General Clark, commanding "Habbaniyeh Force" had finished with Rashid Ali and was directed on Palmyra and Homs. The 6th Division (now two brigades) was directed from Damascus towards Rayak. The 7th Australian Division was to assault the last Vichy position covering Beirut.

General Clark captured Palmyra after a stiff fight. The Australians had a hard battle at Damour and the 6th Division met strong resistance on the road to Rayak. But the determination of the Vichy men was weakening and on 11th July they asked for an armistice. This was signed on the 14th.

*   *   *   *

The situation in the desert after the investment of Tobruk was not unlike the situation after the investment of Kut el Amara shortly before the 7th Hussars arrived in Mesopotamia in World War I. Owing to inaccurate estimates of the available supplies at Kut, two attempts at relief were made while the relieving forces were still too weak and both failed; Kut fell. In the case of Tobruk it was not shortage of supplies that counted, but rather the strain on the Royal Navy in maintaining the supplies through waters where no air cover was possible, and the strain on Commonwealth politics because most of the troops were Australian. Two attempts were made at relief, both with inadequate forces, and both failed. But here the similarity ended, for Tobruk was to be relieved, as an incident in a campaign of broader intentions, a few months later.

Tobruk was out of range of effective fighter protection and right from the beginning of the siege the Germans enjoyed unchallenged and leisurely control of the air over the fortress and the neighbouring waters. Any interesting episode in the harbour at once drew a spectacular though not always effective attack by dive bombers. The approach by sea was in easy reach of aircraft based on El Adem and the Gambut group of airfields, and slow vessels which were forced to pass the dangerous waters in daylight were frequently attacked. So communication with the outer world was confined as far as possible to destroyers and small vessels, bringing in a limited quantity of ammunition and stores on their decks during the hours of darkness. These were quickly unloaded, sometimes during air attacks; a return cargo, usually consisting mostly of wounded, was taken on board and within two hours and sometimes less the vessel was on its way again.

In this fashion the most dangerous waters were passed in the dark. There was no question of ships spending the day in the harbour unless special arrangements for concealment could be made. The occasional tankers which took two or three days to unload were laid up and concealed under nets alongside one of the many sunken hulks lying half submerbed on the harbour bottom. Before the end of the siege the losses in vessels of the Royal Navy alone were over seventy and many acts of heroism at sea passed unseen and unrecorded in maintaining this precarious traffic.

The garrison consisted mainly of Australian troops, the 9th Division and one brigade of the 7th. The Commander was Major-General Leslie Morshead. There were several regiments of British artillery, an Indian motorized cavalry regiment, a scratch collection of armour comprising the remnants of the 3rd Armoured Brigade, a squadron of Matildas of the 7th Battalion the Royal Tank Regiment and most of the King's Dragoon Guards (armoured cars). They were fine troops.

The Australians had had little experience of fighting, and the rapid withdrawal from Agheila and the Jebel was not a good introduction for new troops. But they lacked nothing in spirit and determination and responded admirably to the vigorous leadership of their commander. They soon had a chance to show their mettle and they successfully repelled two German assaults, delivered shortly after the investment of the fortress and when neither the assault nor the defence had been fully prepared.

From then onwards the improvement of the defensive plan and counter-attack developed quickly, the armour was reorganized and exercises were carried out to practice successive infantry battalions in co-operation with the squadron of infantry tanks. A plan was made to break out to Sidi Rezegh and Ed Duda in conjunction with forces advancing from the frontier. On the perimeter and in the reserve line the defences were strengthened and improved. Unserviceable tanks were dug in for use as anti-tank guns. Numerous captured Italian guns were put into action, some of them organized as batteries. Every infantry platoon supplemented its normal equipment with at least one Italian field gun or anti-tank gun, manned by infantry crews who had received elementary instruction from the gunners. The real gunners, restricted by the need to save up 25-pounder ammunition, listened with envy to the harassing fire carried out so light-heartedly by the "bush artillery."

*   *   *   *

During the spring attempts had been made to re-form the 7th Armoured Division and to equip it with tanks from both the United Kingdom and the base workshops. General Wavell's idea was to drive the enemy back from the frontier at least as far as Tobruk. On 1st May he ordered Lieutenant-General Sir Noel Beresford-Peirse, now commanding in the desert, to prepare to carry out an offensive operation as soon as his armoured strength would allow, probably early in June. Then, in the middle of May, there seemed to be a fleeting opportunity, lasting only a few days, during which it might be possible to take the offensive before the arrival of enemy reinforcements, while the German armour on the frontier was still weak and their supply position precarious. The only British tanks available were thirty cruisers and twenty-five infantry tanks.

The operation was fixed for 15th May. Salum and Capuzzo were to be captured with a view to securing a jumping-off place for a large offensive at a later date. It was thought possible that Tobruk might be relieved at the same time, but most of those who thought of this kept it to themselves.

Salum and Capuzzo were captured at little cost, but the enemy brought up armour in unexpected strength and our forces were compelled to withdraw.

Meanwhile tanks were slowly arriving and being off-loaded. They all had to be overhauled, sand filters and sand channels had to be fitted and they had to be painted. The troops had their tanks by the first week in June, but they had been without equipment since February and badly needed a few weeks training with their new equipment. But this was not to be. Operation "Battleaxe" was to begin on 10th June. General Creagh managed to secure a further five days for training and it was finally fixed for the 15th. At the same time a mixed force, consisting mainly of the 3rd Armoured Brigade with an Australian battalion attached, was made ready in Tobruk, and would carry out a sortie as soon as the 7th Armoured Brigade was within supporting distance.

The Germans were thought to have about 300 tanks in Cyrenaica, of which about 100 were on the frontier and 200 near Tobruk. The strength of the forces on the frontier was about 14,000 and round Tobruk 27,000, rather less than half in each case being Germans.

Our own forces consisted of the 7th Armoured Division and the force on the coastal sector, founded on the headquarters of the 4th Indian Division (Major-General F. W. Messervy) and comprising the 22nd Guards Brigade and 11th Indian Infantry Brigade. The 7th Armoured Division was unbalanced. The 11th Hussars were there as usual. The 7th Armoured Brigade consisted of two cruiser regiments; its radius of action was 80 to 100 miles at 15 miles per hour. The 4th Armoured Brigade had two infantry tank regiments; its radius of action was forty miles at five miles per hour. If the opposing armoured forces should both concentrate on the battlefield the enemy would outnumber our own tanks by 300 to 200.

The plan was to advance in three columns. On the coastal plain the Central India Horse and the 11th Indian Infantry Brigade were to capture Salum, co-operating if necessary with the attack on the Halfaya area. The centre column consisted of the 22nd Guards Brigade and the 4th Armoured Brigade and was to move south of the escarpment, cross the frontier well south of Salum, and to attack Halfaya, Capuzzo, Bir Waer and Musaid from the south. The 7th Armoured Brigade was to protect the left of the centre column and to attack enemy tank forces wherever met. An armoured battle was expected and if the result were successful the 7th Armoured Brigade was to advance to the Tobruk—El Adem area. "La Belle Alliance," where Brigadier Russell's 7th Armoured Brigade and Colonel Davy's mixed British and Australian force from Tobruk were to join hands, was to be Sidi Rezegh.

The attack was launched on the 15th and that day met with fair success. The centre column captured Capuzzo and Bir Waer, with a hundred prisoners. The attack on Halfaya was repulsed however and several infantry tanks were lost through mines and direct hits from the enemy 88-millimetre anti-aircraft gun. This weapon was henceforth to be a serious nuisance to our armoured forces. Although an indifferent anti-aircraft gun, it was accurate and powerful as an anti-tank gun and well and boldly handled.

Farther to the left the 7th Armoured Brigade, operating on the left of the Centre Column, had heavy casualties when several of its squadrons advanced across the Hafid Ridge, west of Capuzzo on to an antitank position. One squadron of the 2nd Royal Tanks lost all its tanks.

On the 16th the enemy brought up more troops and a force with tanks began an outflanking movement towards Sidi Omar. It was engaged by the 7th Armoured Brigade. Next day, the 17th, the situation deteriorated. The enemy had brought up considerable forces, including much armour. During the night 16/17th General Creagh had asked General Messervy to release the 4th Armoured Brigade for an attack from the north against the enemy at Sidi Omar, while the 7th Armoured Brigade, now only twenty cruisers, attacked from the south. But as soon as the 4th Brigade moved a strong enemy armoured force threatened the flank of the Guards Brigade at Capuzzo and the 4th Brigade had to be stopped. A further attempt at the same manoeuvre led to a similar enemy reaction. Meanwhile the 7th Armoured Brigade was pressed back from Sidi Omar to Sidi Suleiman and an enemy armoured force advanced eastwards from Sidi Omar towards Halfaya, which the Germans still held.

In view of the enemy's greatly increased armour, now estimated at 200 tanks in the forward area, and our own losses, the situation was becoming dangerous. The Centre Column was ordered to withdraw from the Capuzzo area and the offensive was abandoned. We had destroyed a few enemy tanks and captured 220 Germans and 350 Italians. Our own casualties were 150 killed, 600 wounded, 250 missing. We lost twenty-five cruisers and seventy infantry tanks. A large proportion of the latter were abandoned in the withdrawal from the Capuzzo area merely on account of mechanical breakdowns; there were no transporters.

The failure of the operation has been attributed to the varied assortment of armour and to the lack of training of the troops with their new equipment, including training in maintenance. General Wavell also comments on the enemy's rapid concentration of armour in the forward areas. But it is difficult to avoid the suspicion that political pressure caused the operation to be launched before an adequate force was ready. When the operation was over, the British armour was reduced again to dangerous weakness. But Rommel made no attempt to exploit his success. His plan was first to get possession of Tobruk, whose garrison now resigned itself to continued months of siege.

*   *   *   *

On 15th July 1941 Sir Archibald Wavell handed over the Middle East to Sir Claude Auchinleck and took his place as Commander-in-Chief in India. All fronts were for the moment stable and reasonably secure. There was a rather vague threat from the Caucasus, but the only front which required immediate attention was the desert. The urgency of relieving Tobruk was prominent among the arguments in favour of resuming the offensive and when the change of command took place a fresh offensive had already been decided upon in principle.

Throughout his tenure of command in the Middle East, General Wavell had been skating on thin ice. Although for the last year Great Britain had stood alone against Germany and Italy, and her major strategy was inevitably defensive, the forces in the Middle East had carried out a succession of aggressive campaigns. General Wavell's remarkable achievements with his very limited forces were only made possible by the ingenuity of the staff and services. These had made every possible use of the slender resources of the theatre and the supplies and material brought from overseas, and laid the foundations of the great base which was eventually to serve the whole Mediterranean theatre and to contribute substantially to the maintenance of the campaigns in Asia. In this General Wavell had been ably assisted by his Deputy Quartermaster-General, Major-General B. O. Hutchison. General Hutchison was an old 7th Hussar, who had spent eight of his early years of service in the regiment before transferring to the 10th. Soon after the departure of General Wavell he went as Governor-General of the Sudan, and later became Quartermaster-General in India.

The new Commander-in-Chief, Sir Claude Auchinleck, was already known by reputation among the regular officers. As a brigadier he had commanded an expedition on the North West frontier of India in which every principle of mountain warfare had been correctly followed. For the first time in our long frontier history a campaign had been brought to a successful conclusion without anyone being able to find fault with it. At the Staff Colleges it was regarded as a classic and Auchinleck's name stood high.

He arrived in the Middle East at a time when some of the experienced troops were being taken away. The Japanese menace had caused anxiety in the Pacific and the 6th and 7th Australian Divisions were allotted to that theatre. This however was compensated by the ending of Italian resistance in Abyssinia and Eritrea, which would release South African and Indian troops. Before long other Indian troops would be sent to Iraq in considerable numbers to train and in emergency to meet the threat through the Caucasus. New British troops and tanks were on the way from the United Kingdom and the steady stream of equipment was expected to continue. So a number of troops and new equipment were at any rate in sight. But it would take some time to assemble them and to build up a sufficient administrative machine to maintain them during prolonged operations. Consequently there must first be a period of several months on the defensive while preparations were being made.

* * * *

On 6th July orders were received for the 7th Hussars, less B Squadron, to move to the Western Desert on the 8th, the destination being Charing Cross. On arrival one squadron of the 2nd Royal Tanks was to come under command. B Squadron stayed behind at Amiriya and were equipped with the first of their A.13 cruisers.

Nobody was sorry to see the last of the camp at Amiriya. The flies were never under control, the dust was more than ordinarily disagreeable, and the sense of disappointment at being partly equipped, and then deprived of tanks was not relieved by any amenities or entertainments. Alexandria, with its bathing and social life, was too far away.

The move took place on the 8th as ordered. There were as usual three parties. The road party, under Major F. R. C. Fosdick, consisted of the wheeled vehicles and stores. The tanks with a small escort of crews went by train. The bulk of the officers and men travelled in another train which was, as usual, very crowded and uncomfortable. As they detrained at about midnight they were greeted by a stick of bombs, but no damage was done.

All but two of the tanks arrived at the new bivouac area near Charing Cross, and on the 9th fourteen more A.10's were taken over from the 2nd Royal Tanks. By the evening of the 9th A Squadron had A.10's and C Squadron had A.9's brought up from Amiriya. C Squadron 2nd Royal Tanks (Major John Marsh, M.C.) had A.13's. This squadron came under command and the remainder of the 2nd Royal Tanks left for the delta, where they were to be re-equipped with A.13's.

The rest of the month was spent in training. There were two administrative exercises and a scheme was gradually evolved whereby in battle some of the petrol and ammunition reserves were kept further forward than previously. Part of the petrol and ammunition lorries were split from B Echelon during active operations and moved with Brigade headquarters as an immediate reserve. This system worked satisfactorily and ensured replenishment with a minimum of delay for any regiment or squadron which had been heavily engaged. Tank training was less easy, however, owing to engine mileage restrictions.

On 24th July B Squadron rejoined with its seven A.13's and the regiment was together again. There was general satisfaction at being partially re-equipped, although most of the tanks were a bit old. The Siwa track was a monotonous sort of place, but less obnoxious than Amiriya and bathing facilities at Mersa Matruh were excellent. Some bathed in the harbour area and some at other beaches in the vicinity. The water ration was the usual gallon a day and the luxury of a bathe several times a week kept everyone in good spirits.

Further awards were announced at this period, including the Military Cross for Major R. Younger, Captain C. T. Llewellen Palmer and Major W. T. Kevill-Davies, and Member of the British Empire for Major C. G. Davies-Gilbert and Lieutenant and Quartermaster S. A. Blake. Corporal Pegler, M.M., was awarded the Distinguished Conduct Medal, and was the first man in the Middle East—if not in World War II—to win both decorations. Corporal Pegler was shortly afterwards given a commission. He joined the 8th Hussars and died of wounds received in France in 1944. He was a very brave man of fine character and a magnificent leader. Sergeant Harding got the Military Medal. Captain M. C. S. Phipps was given a Testimonial for Gallantry by the Free French General Catroux, and the following were mentioned in despatches: Captain F. H. St. J. Fairhurst, Lieutenant The Hon. S. N. Astley, Lieutenant C. G. Dean, SSM E. Winney, Sergeants J. Connelly, Jones, L. Martin, P. O'Brien, Corporals Gowan and Whitehouse and Troopers A. Pye and J. Steele.

There were several changes among officers in regimental headquarters. Major W. T. Kevill-Davies, M.C., relinquished the duties of adjutant, which he had performed admirably for two-and-a-half years, and went to command B Echelon transport. Lieutenant J. Napier, M.C., became adjutant, his place as regimental navigator being taken by Second-Lieutenant P. B. Stanley Evans.

The regiment was now under the command of the 7th Armoured Brigade, with the 2nd and 6th Royal Tanks, both somewhat battered after their battles in June. The operational role of the 7th Armoured Brigade was defensive. With the exception of an armoured car regiment there was no other armour in the desert, and if the support group and the 4th Indian Division in the forward area were to be forced back it was the intention that the enemy should be stopped by the mobile defence of the 7th Armoured Division on the general line of the Siwa track. Matruh was to be held, as a pivot on the right, by the 1st South African Division.

During the summer training continued and officers and men became proficient in the handling of cruiser tanks and their 2-pounder armament. In the delta staffs and ordnance worked hard to provide the tanks. These came up slowly. By the end of August A Squadron (Major Seymour-Evans) was completely equipped with well worn A.10's. B Squadron (Major R. Younger) was getting A.13's, but only seven had been issued. C Squadron (Major J. Congreve) also had only half their tanks, mixed A.9 and A.10. The regiment was not in fact in a very battleworthy condition.

At the beginning of August Brigadier H. E. Russell became head of the Armoured Fighting Vehicle directorate at General Headquarters in Cairo. He was succeeded in command of the 7th Armoured Brigade by another ex-gunner, Brigadier G. M. O. Davy, 3rd Hussars, who had just been commanding the armour in Tobruk. The new brigadier visited the regiment several times and saw each troop and then the B Echelon.

Inspections in the army mean a lot of work and seldom seem funny at the time, but they have their humorous aspects—if you look for them. It was recorded in a private document (since fallen into the hands of the author): "The new brigadier came to inspect the Camp this morning and was very impressed; I must say it was really very good and Bill (Kevill-Davies) is delighted. We went round in three staff cars. . . . I took no part in the proceedings except in allowing the monkey at the cookhouse to undo my bootlace as a sort of sideshow. It really was rather funny to see everyone in sort of tableaux bent over their respective jobs as we approached, the cooks squatting with knives poised over potatoes in the act of peeling them, the fitters bent over a radiator, a spanner in one hand and an oily rag in the other, wearing overalls they had never put on before in their lives. The only natural creature was the puppy in C Squadron office, which slept blissfully through the entire inspection"—and the next day—"I am almost alone in the camp. Nearly everyone has gone down to spend a day on the beach as a reward for the success of the inspection yesterday." In fact the inspection was not all "eye-wash." B Echelon was efficiently organized and administered and the few extra frills were in no way misleading.

Training was confined mainly to tactical exercises and gunnery. The first shoot with 2-pounders took place on the 15th August. The results were regarded as fairly satisfactory for a first effort. A tactical exercise without troops was carried out to study the role of the brigade in the battle of the Siwa track, if this should take place, and the Colonel held a subsequent exercise to study the role of the regiment on the same lines, within the brigade plan.

Most of the tanks were veterans with a very considerable mileage to their credit. So engine mileage had to be strictly conserved and extensive training with tanks was entirely ruled out. Some movement was essential in order to reach field firing areas for 2-pounder and Besa practice, but exercises were held as close as possible to leaguer areas. Every effort was made to ensure that no tank travelled a mile without someone getting training in the process.

Up to the middle of September only one tactical exercise with tanks took place. This was a two-sided exercise between the 7th Hussars and the 6th Royal Tanks on 12th September, a few miles south of the leaguer area. On the way back next day squadron training was carried out and in the afternoon a number of men went down to the sea to bathe. This, although they did not know it, was to be their last swim in the Mediterranean for nearly two years.

*　　　*　　　*　　　*

In the stillness of a desert night, when nothing is moving and the listener is well sheltered from the gentle breeze, an engine, even of a single vehicle, can be heard for many miles. When an armoured division starts up and moves off there is a deep and unmistakable rumble. This, it is said, was heard at the headquarters of the 4th Indian Division in the early hours of the 14th September when the nearest enemy armour was forty miles away. On this day the 21st Panzer Division carried out what appeared to be a reconnaissance in force in the direction of Rabia and Sofafi, the two old Italian camps on the edge of the escarpment.

It was thought at the time that the object of the reconnaissance was to find out the strength and location of the British armoured forces in the forward area. If so, the information obtained was of a negative character, because in fact the 7th Armoured Brigade was still on the Siwa Track south of Mersa Matruh, and on the frontier there was only the 4th South African Armoured Car Regiment. This had been a few weeks in the forward area, and its withdrawal in contact with the 21st

Panzer Division was a high test of resourcefulness and ingenuity for a newly arrived regiment. It was also good practice for the November battle, in which this regiment was to be closely associated with the 7th Hussars and to play a gallant and most valuable part.

As the enemy armoured column advanced, the armoured cars and mixed columns of infantry and artillery withdrew in front of him, harassing him with gunfire. When he reached a point a few miles south of Rabia the enemy halted to refuel. Whether he intended to continue his advance, or whether he regarded his task as performed and meant to withdraw to the frontier, is not known. But that afternoon and evening he was subjected to several most effective air attacks and some artillery fire. Next morning he withdrew whence he had come, followed up by armoured cars and mixed columns, who resumed their former positions on the general line Alam Battuma-Bir el Khireigat-Sheferzen.

The air attacks gave much encouragement to the troops. This was the first time that our bombers in strength had engaged a truly tactical target on the battlefield. The Germans had practised this form of co-operation from the beginning and only abandoned it in the later stages of the war when allied fighters had established complete mastery of the air over the battle area.

Hitherto our own air force had not had the resources for extensive tactical co-operation. But as its strength was built up the technique of tactical support was studied with enthusiasm by the South African bomber squadron in the desert. One of the difficulties was how to guide the bombers to the target and how to indicate the location of the forward troops nearest the target. Several exercises and trials had been held on the Siwa track in the past few weeks, the 7th Armoured Brigade and the 7th Hussars taking part in the trials. When the test came, conditions were ideal and the attacks were an unqualified success.

The enemy armoured force, although well in rear of the forward troops, was easy to identify. The first attack caught it with petrol lorries in many cases close alongside the tanks and the force in a huddle. Our own troops were well clear of the target. The bombing was very satisfactory and the enemy lost five tanks and twelve vehicles destroyed and abandoned—a spectacle of wreckage which was enjoyed by all who saw it as they passed a few days later.

* * * *

On 14th September, as the result of the enemy's advance, the brigade was put at three hours notice to move. Next day the move to the selected battle area took place, fifteen miles to the southward into the area east of Bir el Kenayis. Dispositions were taken up in accordance with the pre-arranged and rehearsed plan. The enemy's withdrawal on the same day made these dispositions superfluous, but his reconnaissance—if such it was—afforded an excuse for building up our forces in the forward area. Even if the movements were to be seen from the air, they might well be interpreted as defensive precautions rather than preparations for an offensive. Nevertheless every effort was made to ensure secrecy. Every tank now wore a "sun shield," canvas stretched over tubular steel rods bent roughly to the shape of the top of a lorry. The four wheels per side of the A.13 and five of the A.15 still gave them away, so the second wheels of A.13 and second and third of the A.15 were painted black and they looked from the air very like six-wheeled lorries.

The first formation to move up was the 7th Armoured Brigade. The area selected was south of Sofafi, where the brigade would be in a favourable situation to attack the enemy if he should advance again south of the escarpment and would also be able to cover the establishment of the forward dump in the Bir el Talata area, an essential preliminary to the offensive. A and C Squadron moved on their tracks. B Squadron (A.13's) moved on transporters.

The move was successfully carried out and most of the tanks arrived without trouble. The distance was about a hundred miles and the march was of immense value for training officers and men in the driving and maintenance of cruisers, with which they had had all too little experience. The only incident was an attack by a single aircraft on Major Fosdick and his reconnaissance party on the 18th September. The car was hit but there were no casualties. Reconnaissances were made in the possible area of operations and a plan was made for a raid to be carried out by B Squadron in the Sheferzen area, in conjunction with units of the Support Group.

During September the tank situation was still far from satisfactory. B Squadron had thirteen A.13's; C had eight A.9's and A.10's. A Squadron had so many tanks due for a major overhaul that the best four were handed over to C and the Squadron was sent back to Gerawla to refit in the railhead area. From this point things began to look better. First there came a rumour and then the order that A Squadron was to have A.15 cruisers (Crusaders). During October the Squadron sent most of its officers and crews back to the base for a course. By the end of the month, very pleased with itself, it was completely equipped with Crusaders and on its way back to the regiment.

The Crusader was rather an aristocrat among tanks. It was expensively built, had a good line as far as appearances were concerned and moved at high speed and very smoothly even over hummocky going. It was the latest thing in cruisers and the envy of all who were not equipped with it. Meanwhile C Squadron handed in its A.9's and was completed to establishment in A.10's. By the end of the month the regiment was up to strength in tanks, although each squadron had a different variety.

On 3rd October there was a small move forward of about six miles. This was in order to make room for the concentration of more troops behind the regiment and west of the dumping area. The word "concentration" is a little misleading, because although a great strategical concentration was in fact beginning, a regiment would cover an area at least two miles square and each vehicle would be some 150 yards from its nearest neighbour. In this way it was made as difficult as possible for the enemy airmen to estimate the strength of the force and no profitable target was offered for air attack.

Among the fresh troops now appearing in the desert was the 22nd Armoured Brigade, just arrived from the United Kingdom and fully equipped with Crusaders. This brigade had little time in which to get accustomed to the new conditions, but it made the best use of the remaining six weeks. Many officers and a number of warrant officers and non-commissioned officers, were attached to their opposite numbers in the 7th Armoured Brigade. The thought of a whole brigade of Crusaders was impressive. Their brigadier, however, expressed his concern that two of his 160 tanks had done 600 miles. The old "desert rats" on the other hand, had scarcely any which had done less.

To the 7th Hussars came Lieutenant-Colonel W. G. Carr (a regular 12th Lancer commanding one of the regiments of County of London Yeomanry) and three of his officers. They were enthusiastic to learn about the desert. It must have been a surprise to them to see so motley a collection of tanks—to say nothing of the variegated sartorial fashions. But with great good taste they appeared not to notice these things.

There was now in the desert a company of tank transporters. These were a useful adjunct to an armoured unit, especially to one whose tanks were getting elderly. A little training in their use was required, and for this purpose a section was attached to the regiment in the middle of October. They were used in the preparatory period for conveying tanks to the field firing range, and eventually they carried the slow moving old tanks of C Squadron nearly up to Sidi Rezegh.

*   *   *   *

The raid which had been planned on Sheferzen took place in the early morning on 12th October. The raiding force, all under Major R. Younger, consisted of B Squadron the 7th Hussars (thirteen A.13 cruisers), one troop of the 2nd/7th Royal Australian Artillery Regiment, a section of carriers of the 2nd Battalion The Rifle Brigade, one troop of the 4th South African Armoured Car Regiment who were already operating on the frontier and a small detachment of Royal Engineers for mine reconnaissance in the gaps.

In the preceding weeks Major Younger and the South African Armoured Car Regiment had carefully studied the enemy's habits and knew pretty well what he was likely to do. The object was to destroy or capture as much as possible of the enemy patrol which visited Libyan Sheferzen daily in the early morning. There are actually two Sheferzens, one known as Bir Sheferzen, on the real frontier, the other as Libyan Sheferzen, just on the enemy side of the wire which at this point is three miles west of the frontier.

The plan was to place the artillery in position about four miles east of Libyan Sheferzen, with the carriers and the 3rd Troop of B Squadron as escorts. This troop was also to attack the enemy if opportunity arose. The rest of the squadron was to cross the wire about eight miles south of Sheferzen, when the engineers had cleared the mines, to move up west of the wire to a point about two miles south-west of Libyan Sheferzen, and there to lie up behind the undulation at Point 198. The armoured car troop was to act as a decoy in case the enemy did not advance far enough.

The artillery with its escort moved up to within four miles of its position soon after dark and leaguered. It was in action before first light. The squadron moved out at midnight and at 1.30 a.m. reached a point near the gap in the wire after a 16-mile march. Here it topped up, while the engineers reconnoitred the gap, which they reported clear. At 4 a.m. the advance was continued and accurate navigation by Lieutenant White brought the squadron to its precise position behind 198 before first light. The squadron leader and second-in-command went on foot to the cairn, from which there was a good view to the north and east. One troop was ready to advance northwards to the right of the cairn and two north-westwards to the left of it.

At 6.10 a.m. four enemy vehicles, including a captured Marmon-Herrington armoured car, appeared from the west and halted at a point three miles north of 198. After ten minutes they moved south-eastwards, apparently meaning to reconnoitre the low ground east of 198. This was what Major Younger expected and he ordered the right troop to engage the enemy frontally while the other two moved rapidly north-westwards and then north-eastwards, behind a fold in the ground, to cut off the enemy if he should try to get away to Sidi Omar. The right troop claimed hits, but none of the enemy were stopped. One enemy artillery vehicle was destroyed by the other party north of Sheferzen and its crew of four, all wounded, were taken prisoner. An ammunition lorry was set on fire. Eight other vehicles appeared from the west, but they withdrew again, and although pursued for some way could not be caught.

Some delay was then caused in withdrawing because the squadron leader's tank cast a track. This was eventually repaired, with the help of Trooper G. Chaplin, who, although scalded on the eyes and face when his tank had boiled over during the night march, had insisted on staying in action. Another delay was caused when the medical officer, summoned up from the battery to attend to the German wounded, took his armoured car through an unexamined gap at Libyan Sheferzen. It was blown up on a mine, both his ankles were broken and the car, an old Rolls-Royce of World War I, had to be abandoned.

As the withdrawal began, the 4th South African Armoured Car Regiment began getting reports from one of its cars of tanks in the area of Sheferzen. For a time B Squadron tended to chase its own tail until it was realized that it was its own tanks that were being reported.

The only fatal casualty was to an Australian fighter pilot, shot down.

The operation had been in some ways a little disappointing but it provided useful identifications which were badly needed. Lance-Corporal S. Lee was congratulated by the Corps Commander for saving a valuable document from a prisoner before he could destroy it. Unfortunately a few weeks later he was badly wounded at Sidi Rezegh and died in hospital.

During October training consisted mainly of range practices with the 2-pounder. It had been noticed that on measured ranges, when the telescope sights had been tested as laid down in the Tank Gunnery text book, an accurately laid shot fired at a target 1,000 yards away fell 300 yards short, or 11 feet vertically below the point aimed at. If, therefore, the range to a precision target such as an enemy tank had been judged accurately the shot would miss. The importance of hitting with the first shot was now vigorously emphasized. It was reasonable to expect occasionally to achieve surprise, but surprise would finish with the first bang and, if this were inaccurate, the chances of a hit with the second shot would be much reduced. Tank gunnery teaching had glossed over this point. It had been taught that a hit should not be expected with the first shot, but that the strike of the first should be used as a guide for the second and so on. When the enemy had a superior weapon the "cock-her-up-a-bit-Bill" system was not good enough. The error was found, the correct method was propagated and the last few weeks before operations began were occupied largely in perfecting the shooting.

The 2-pounder was a very accurate weapon when fired from a stationary tank. Firing on the move was now forbidden as it was so inaccurate as to be quite useless against ordinary targets and merely a waste of ammunition. But something more than accuracy was required for the task with which the 2-pounder was soon to be faced. That was hitting power, and the 2-pounder had not got it. The many dents in those enemy tanks which were left on the battlefield testify alike to its inadequacy in weight and to the excellence of the shooting.

CHAPTER VI

"Crusader" Begins

Characteristics of the offensive—enemy forces and intentions—British forces—the plan—final enemy dispositions—final preparations—advance to Sidi Rezegh—the first three days—decision to launch the sortie from Tobruk—orders for the 21st November—first engagement on 21st November—other engagements on 21st November at Sidi Rezegh—the sortie from Tobruk.

Maps IV, VII

Operation "Crusader" was to be the last in which the 7th Hussars took part in this theatre of war. It was a soldiers' battle, in which much was to depend on the individual weapon and the man in the tank. Hard fighting resulted in a victory, though it was an expensive one.

In the past, when the range of weapons was short, armies formed up in tidy rows as on a parade ground; even in the 1914-18 war they might still maintain some sort of order after the battle had begun. But in the battle of Sidi Rezegh, although wireless communication between formations and units was usually maintained, and control and command were generally effective, all outward semblance of tidiness was lost in the first few days. The desert between the frontier and El Adem was crossed and re-crossed in every direction by columns of both sides, some of fighting troops, some administrative, some mixed. In the early stages it was easy to recognize friend from foe, but as in the various encounters each side captured transport from the other, the type of transport ceased to be a reliable guide to identity and the most certain test was the shape of a tank. Another indication was that the Germans tended to move concentrated and the British to move dispersed. This however was rather deceptive, as it was found that the South Africans also moved in much closer order than the British.

There were a few instances of friendly troops firing on one another and in the circumstances it is not to be wondered at. Nobody can be blamed. It was due in some measure to the lack of exchange of information and the limit of vision on so vast a battlefield. But if every unit had had enough wireless sets to hear the situation of all others in its vicinity the army would have consisted mostly of wireless operators.

Much, therefore, depended upon local reconnaissance and however good this might be there were plenty of unexpected encounters. There were also instances of hostile columns passing close to one another, by day as well as by night, without engaging. Perhaps they failed to recognize each other as enemies, or perhaps each was bent on a task it was ordered to fulfil. Doubtless there were occasions when a hasty glance revealed that discretion was the better part of valour. The armoured cars of the 11th Hussars, King's Dragoon Guards, and 4th South African Armoured Car Regiment covered most of the thousand square miles of this battlefield. They seldom made a mistake in their reports, though sometimes these sounded so improbable that the recipients seemed to doubt their word.

The sites occupied by both the advanced and rear headquarters of the 30th Corps were overrun, but this headquarters was so flexible and mobile that little damage was suffered and business continued as usual. One divisional headquarters was overrun, but another showed such agility that it escaped a similar fate. Most of a Panzer Division passed through the area of a Field Maintenance Centre on the lines of communication, but did little damage and failed to discover a thousand prisoners in their cage. Many individuals and small groups of administrative vehicles became detached from their parent units and showed discretion in reforming in safer areas east of the wire. One brigadier's staff car went to Jarabub to refuel and returned the next day. For those who asked the way, the bad old advice "Follow the track—you can't miss it" meant nothing at all, because there were tracks everywhere and they led anywhere.

The exceptionally volatile nature of this battle was something which had never been experienced before, even in the 1940 campaign in France. It is not easy to explain how this occurred, but perhaps some element of cause may be found in the conception of the original plan. There were some who likened it to an exploitation carried out before the battle instead of after it. This was not by any means the intention, as will be evident from a study of the evolution of the plan in the ten weeks preceding the opening of the offensive. It will be seen, however, that the initial British dispersion and the contrasting enemy concentration created a series of interesting situations. Not the least interesting was an engagement lasting eight hours between two British armoured regiments—one of them the 7th Hussars—and a battery of Royal Horse Artillery, on one side, and two German Panzer Divisions on the other.

* * * *

General Rommel was the supreme commander of the enemy forces in North Africa and his headquarters was called Panzer Gruppe Afrika. The German Africa Corps (Crüwell) included the 15th Panzer Division (Neumann-Silkow), the 21st Panzer Division (von Ravenstein), and the 90th Light Division (Sümmermann). The Italians had a motorized corps of three divisions, the 21st Corps of three infantry divisions and the frontier group of one division.

The failure of the "Battle Axe" Operation in June had left Rommel in a very satisfactory position. The two groups of British forces in the desert were separated from one another by over seventy miles. Their armour had been severely handled and their air force now never flew over Tobruk. Rommel had little confidence in his Italian Allies, but if stiffened by a few German detachments, they were of value in a defensive role for containing the British in their positions on the frontier and inside the fortress.

This left the bulk of the German Africa Corps free to re-fit in the area between Bardia and Tobruk. Here it was favourably placed either for a blow against one of the groups of British forces or for a counter-attack, if the British should make another attempt to relieve Tobruk. Rommel was not particularly afraid of such an attempt and he himself planned to take the offensive as soon as his forces were ready and his administrative position was satisfactory. He was still awaiting the arrival of the Italian Mobile Corps and the lorried infantry regiment of the 21st Panzer Division.

Rommel's intention was first to seize Tobruk. If he succeeded he would thereby eliminate 40,000 good British troops and obtain possession of a port and advanced base which would give him administrative facilities for operating deeply into Egypt. For three months after the June operation the situation was in his favour. Tobruk would certainly have been a very tough proposition and it is doubtful if he could have taken it. But during that period he had the only effective armoured force in the desert and, although he could not have realized it, it was to be nearly a year before he would have such a chance again. He preferred, however, to complete his build-up and preparations, and to defer his attack until the end of November. He was just too late, for by September the British forces were increasing more quickly than his own. By October his superiority had disappeared and Tobruk had been reinforced by a number of infantry tanks; these were put in at the same time as the Australians were replaced by British and Polish troops. In November the British attacked, a bare few days before his assault on Tobruk was due to take place.

*   *   *   *

On 10th September, 1941, Headquarters Western Army was formed in Cairo, under Lieutenant-General Sir Alan Cunningham. The Army Commander had just arrived from East Africa, fresh from the victory he had shared with Sir William Platt at the expense of the Duke of Aosta. He at once began to make a plan for carrying out Sir Claude Auchinleck's intention, "to drive the enemy out of North Africa." Operations were to start about the 1st November.

Reinforcements were arriving and old formations were being re-equipped and trained after their various experiences of this eventful summer. The 1st and 2nd South African Divisions had arrived and were training in the desert. The 1st Armoured Division was on its way from the United Kingdom. The 70th British Division replaced the 9th Australian Division in Tobruk.

On 25th September General Cunningham's headquarters moved out to Maaten Bagush. Next day it became Headquarters Eighth Army and took control of all troops in the desert. A month later Tobruk passed under Eighth Army command and the Western Desert Force became the 13th Corps.

The troops allotted to the Eighth Army are shown in the following table:—

13 Corps (Lieutenant-General A. R. Godwin-Austen)—1st Army Tank Brigade, New Zealand Division, 4th Indian Division.

30th Corps (Lieutenant-General C. W. M. Norrie)—7th Armoured Division, 4th Armoured Brigade Group, 22nd Guards Brigade, 1st South African Division (less one brigade).

Oasis Group—29th Indian Infantry Brigade, 6th South African Armoured Car Regiment.

2nd South African Division (El Alamein and Line of Communications).

2nd South African Brigade (Matruh fortress; detached from the 1st South African Division).

Long Range Desert Group.

Tobruk garrison, consisting of 70th British Division, Polish Carpathian Brigade Group and 32nd Army Tank Brigade (founded on the remains of the old 3rd Armoured Brigade and boosted with 100 infantry tanks).

Most of these troops had fought the Italians either in the desert or in East Africa—the 4th Indian Division actually in both. The New Zealand Division, parts of the 7th Armoured Division and the Carpathian Brigade had had some experience against the Germans. The South African troops were strangers to the conditions of the North

African desert and found it was by no means easy to handle their somewhat generous allowance of transport with its Basuto drivers. Their 1st Division had had experience against the Italians in East Africa, but the 2nd was less advanced in training and it was not proposed to use it in the early stages of the offensive. If all the British forces, including the Tobruk garrison, were taken into account, therefore, the comparison of strengths in terms of divisions was about ten to nine in favour of the enemy; but only three of his divisions were German.

There were other factors which had an important bearing on the issue of the campaign. First, our air force in the Middle East had been built up in fighters and bombers, and after much hard work a technique had been evolved for close co-operation between land forces and aircraft for attacking enemy targets on the ground. Thus not only did we enjoy first class protection against enemy air attack and even against his air reconnaissance, but our bombers intervened successfully more than once in the land battle.

Secondly, no comparison of strengths is complete without looking with some care into the tank situation. A numerical comparison is misleading and it was most annoying to the British armoured soldiers, as they struggled against superior equipment in the battles which followed, to hear and read in the news that the material odds were weighted in their favour.

The enemy had some 460 tanks, including 50 Mark I, 244 Mark II, III and IV, 5 captured British Matildas, 27 armoured gun carriers and 138 Italian M.13's. The British had 455 cruisers in the 30th Corps and 210 infantry tanks in the 1st and 32nd Army Tank Brigades. British cruiser strength was in fact about equal to the enemy's total strength, and if the infantry tanks, slow and with heavy armour, but armed with the same 2-pounder gun, were counted, we had a numerical superiority of about three to two.

But in quality the comparison was very different. The Italian M.13 was certainly less effective than the cruiser, which had already proved its superiority at Mechili and Beda Fomm. The German Marks I and II were about equal in armour and fire power to the cruiser, though slower; it had been with these tanks, now obsolescent, that the Germans fought their successful campaigns in Poland in 1939 and in France the following spring. But since then the Mark III and Mark IV had been produced in numbers. The Mark IV was armed with a short barrelled 75-mm. gun of low velocity and firing an HE shell which was effective against unprotected troops and soft vehicles, but it only did superficial damage to armoured vehicles except in the

A.10 Cruiser tanks.

A "Crusader" tank (A.15) and transporter.

case of very lucky hits. It was the Mark III which turned the balance in quality of armour in favour of the enemy. There were only about 150 of these in the two divisions, but they were protected in front by an extra thickness of armour and they were armed with a 50-mm. high velocity gun, firing a 4½ lb. shell or shot.

These guns could penetrate our cruisers at 2,000 yards range, whereas the 2-pounder with which all our British tanks were armed, had no effect whatever on the enemy's front plates and only penetrated his sides at ranges under 600 yards. The 37-mm. guns in the American General Stuart tanks, were no better than the 2-pounder in penetrating power and less good in accuracy. The 50-mm. gun in the Mark III tank, especially when backed by the 88-mm. anti-aircraft gun used in an anti-tank role, made the numerical comparison academic and the enemy could stand off and shoot our tanks to bits before they could get close enough to do him any harm. It was therefore unfortunate that the "all armoured idea" was not quite dead in the British army, that the conception of fighting armour deliberately with armour still prevailed and that infantry and anti-tank artillery were allotted to armoured formations in lamentably small numbers with quite inadequate hitting power. In the operations about to take place it was probably the 25-pounder, not designed as an anti-tank gun at all, which proved itself the most effective destroyer of the German tanks.

* * * *

The Commander-in-Chief had expressed his intention in geographical terms—to drive the enemy out of North Africa. This showed a new trend in military technique. In the past it had been more usual, when engaged with the modern army of a first class power, to regard the destruction of that army as the prime and main object. If that could be done, other desirable conditions, such as the occupation of territory or incarceration of the enemy ruler, followed as natural sequels. But the power of armour was now tending to draw the army into a system of strategical thinking which had been practised with success in the navy but not, until now, in the army. This became clear as the Commander-in-Chief amplified his intention. "The object of driving the enemy out of North Africa was to be accomplished in two phases. The re-capture of Cyrenaica was to be followed by the conquest of Tripolitania. The primary objective was to be the destruction of the enemy's armoured force, since by that means alone could these two aims be achieved." (Quoted from Eighth Army Report.)

It was the selection of a part of the enemy's force for destruction which was new for the army. In naval strategy it had been common practice for some years to choose for destruction one particularly dangerous vessel, or class of vessels, such as the *Graf Spee* or the *Bismarck*, and to disregard the smaller fry except in so far as they might interfere with the main task. That a similar selective strategy should now be adopted by the army was a perfectly logical sequel to modern developments in land warfare. For it had become clear that in the desert the army with the best armoured force—quality and quantity both taken into consideration—had a very great, if not a decisive, advantage over its opponents. In November, 1941, as neither side had an overwhelming preponderance in armour, the early establishment of superiority by the destruction, or at least heavy reduction of the enemy's armour was an essential preliminary to success and the extent of the victory would then be limited only by the possibilities of administration.

Two alternative suggestions were made as to how the first stage of the intention—clearing the enemy out of Cyrenaica—might be tackled and General Cunningham was instructed to prepare plans for both. The first alternative, for which a detailed plan had already been prepared at G.H.Q. and shown to him for his information, was soon discarded. This entailed leaving a holding force on the frontier, to advance westwards as opportunity offered, while the main blow was delivered at the enemy's communications in the Gialo-Benghazi area by forces based on Jarabub. An operation bearing some resemblance to this had been carried out as an exploitation against a demoralized and half beaten enemy when General O'Connor exterminated the Italians at Beda Fomm. But to divide the available forces to such an extent in the presence of an unbeaten and approximately equal enemy would have been too hazardous. The operation in the south was therefore not further considered except as a feint, and even in this capacity it was not taken seriously by Rommel.

The second alternative suggested was an attack in the coastal sector south of the escarpment, while a feint was made in the Jarabub area. This plan was adopted.

The Army Commander hoped that he would be able to avoid issuing written orders and intended to convey his instructions to the troops in a succession of conferences. The conferences took place, and minor adjustments were made as the situation changed or corps commanders brought up fresh problems. Eventually a simple directive was issued to corps commanders and operation orders were issued in the lower strata.

The first of the Eighth Army conferences took place on 6th October, and the Army Commander unfolded his plan to his corps commanders. He stated his object, to drive the enemy out of North Africa. He said his immediate object was to destroy the enemy's armoured forces, which would be accomplished by threatening the forces investing Tobruk in order to make the enemy deploy his armour. This task was allotted to the 30th Corps, which consisted of the 7th Armoured Division (7th and 22nd Armoured Brigades and 7th Support Group), the 1st South African Division, less one brigade, and the 22nd Guards Brigade.

The 30th Corps was therefore directed on Tobruk, the relief of which was to be effected as a secondary object, in conjunction with a sortie by the garrison. The 13th Corps was given the task of cutting off and isolating the enemy's positions on the frontier and preventing any possibility of an enemy break-through to the east and south. Subsequently the 13th Corps was to drive westwards to join up with the 30th Corps and clear the enemy out of the intervening area. No direct attack was to be carried out in the first instance against the enemy defences in the Salum and Sidi Omar areas. These were merely to be isolated and dealt with later as opportunity offered.

Then came the problem of the protection of the left of the 13th Corps. It was decided that a centre force should be formed consisting of the 4th Armoured Brigade Group and an armoured car regiment, to operate under the 30th Corps. It was given the tasks of protecting the left flank of the 13th Corps, of drawing off superior forces of enemy armour towards the 7th Armoured Division and of attacking enemy armoured forces if they advanced with inferior strength.

Two diversions were to be carried out. A force of armoured cars and lorried infantry was to advance from Jarabub on D minus 1, to capture Jalo. Secondly, enemy aircraft were to be attracted away from the area of the advancing 30th Corps on D day by a naval demonstration on the coast.

Minor adjustments to this plan were made at subsequent conferences. The next one, on 15th October, was attended by Major-General Scobie, the Commander of Tobruk Fortress. It was decided that the sortie should take place on a code word to be issued by Commander 30th Corps at the time judged most suitable by him, and that the Tobruk forces should come simultaneously under his command. The moment was to be chosen when the 1st South African Division should have arrived on the escarpment at Sidi Rezegh and should be in a position to join hands with the troops making the sortie. This again would depend upon the outcome of the armoured battle, as the South

Africans were only to be brought up when the enemy armour had been destroyed or hemmed in.

At the next conference, on the 21st, General Norrie proposed that he should concentrate all the armour in some central position, whence it could strike, concentrated, in any direction. But he could not procure the release of the 4th Armoured Brigade Group from its task of protecting the left of the 13th Corps; it was however to remain under the 30th Corps in carrying out its role.

Before the final conference on 29th October, a few changes took place in the enemy's dispositions. Two of the divisions of the Italian Mobile Corps were known to be moving eastwards through the Jebel el Akhdar, Trieste towards Mechili and Ariete towards Gazala, but of course their final destinations were not yet known. The 21st Panzer Division had been completed by the arrival of its lorried infantry regiment.

These changes did not result in any major alterations to the British plan. It was suggested, however, that the 7th Armoured Division could take on the whole German armour single handed and should therefore be sent straight to Tobruk. This was turned down and it was decided that it should be sent to some central battle position round Gabr Saleh on the first day, starting from an area as far behind the wire as possible, in the interests of surprise. Armoured cars were to push on in front to the Trigh Capuzzo to observe the few crossings of the escarpment. The 13th Corps was to do the absolute minimum until indications were received of the direction taken by the enemy's armour. The Corps Commander expressed himself ready to take on the enemy's armour if he were attacked, but still the 4th Armoured Brigade was tied to the protection of his flank.

The decision on the direction of the next move of the 7th Armoured Division, after reaching Gabr Saleh, was reserved by the Army Commander to himself, and would depend on the reactions of the enemy armoured forces to the opening gambit.

There was from the beginning considerable difference of opinion regarding the wisdom of spreading the armour on so wide a frontage and of postponing the action of the 13th Corps for so long. To force an armoured battle upon the enemy by occupying ground vital to him was regarded as a masterly strategical conception. But it has been suggested that the advantages of this stroke may to some extent have been neutralized by the failure to concentrate our efforts either in time or space at the vital point. The result was a series of engagements, most of them within five miles of Sidi Rezegh, in which the enemy was eventually worn down and defeated, but in many of which he had the advantage of fighting with his armour concentrated against comparatively isolated British forces of inferior strength.

* * * *

The enemy's dispositions at the opening of the offensive were known with considerable accuracy, although his subsequent manoeuvres could not of course have been foretold. During October and November the Italian motorized corps was moving up and when the operations began it was in a protective role covering the investment of Tobruk against interference from the South. Trieste Division was in the Bir Hacheim area and Ariete at Bir el Gubi. The third division of the Mobile Corps, Trento, was with the 21st Corps, investing Tobruk.

The frontier group, consisting mainly of Savona Division, was facing the Indians in the Salum and Sidi Omar area. Both the 21st Corps and the Frontier Group were stiffened with elements of German units, but in the main the Africa Corps was held in reserve, part of it destined for the attack on Tobruk, and the whole of it for counter-attack if the British should take the offensive first.

* * * *

By the beginning of November, as more and more troops arrived in the forward area, it became clear to everyone that something would happen shortly. The 1st Army Tank Brigade came up on the right of the 7th Armoured Brigade, the 22nd Armoured Brigade on the left. A Squadron of the 7th Hussars arrived on the 3rd November with their A.15's and spent all their time shooting their 2-pounders. Training now entered the final phase and exercises merged into rehearsals.

Major Kevill-Davies organized a series of competitions for B Echelon, which was now in a high state of proficiency. The 7th Armoured Division held a petrol-dumping exercise, which was in reality a rehearsal for the filling up of tanks on the first day's march in the offensive. On 10th November the brigade moved a further seven miles westwards, and three days later the regiment was ordered to move one mile south-eastwards. The latter move seemed somewhat unnecessary at the time, but apparently more room had to be left for some other unit. The final touches were put to preparations in a wireless exercise held at divisional headquarters on 10th November. On the 16th the Colonel and Adjutant attended a conference at brigade headquarters, where the brigadier gave out his orders for the operation.

The brigade plan was simple. It was to advance on D1 (as D Day was then called) to the vicinity of Sidi el Reghem el Gharbi, with one regiment leading and one on each flank. The move for D2 was not definitely fixed but it was almost certain to be an advance to Sidi Rezegh, which was regarded as ground vital to the enemy. A strong British force placed in this area would threaten the rear of the forces investing Tobruk and would deny to the enemy the use of the Trigh Capuzzo, hitherto the most convenient route for supplying the Frontier Group and the Africa Corps. The corridor between Sidi Rezegh and the Tobruk defences was only ten miles wide and unescorted convoys would be exposed to considerable risks from both directions. The enemy could not possibly ignore such a threat. It was therefore probable that sooner or later he would attack any British troops in the area and that there would be a battle between tanks. What strength of forces on either side would be engaged in such a battle was not predictable, but it was apparent from the start that at least one of the British armoured brigades would be held back for another task and that neither of the army tank brigades would be there.

On the night of the 16th orders were issued verbally by Lieutenant-Colonel Byass to the squadron leaders. The advance was to begin at first light on 18th November.

The 17th was spent in packing up and preparing the tanks and B Echelon. C Squadron (Major Congreve) loaded all its tanks on transporters, which were to carry them on the first stage of the march. Colonel Byass addressed each squadron in turn, read out a message to the men from the Brigadier and wished them luck.

At dusk squadrons moved into leaguer close beside regimental headquarters and in the formation in which the advance was to begin the following morning. It was a wild night with much thunder and lightning, but no rain fell in the immediate neighbourhood. Men lay down with a feeling of pent-up excitement. All knew that they were going to meet German armour for the first time. They had confidence in their newly acquired armour and skill in the use of their weapons. Morale was therefore high.

Whether their confidence was justified and whether their skill made up for the inadequate power of their weapons will become apparent as the story unfolds. The intention was to fight armour with armour and it was clear from the Colonel's address that no easy victory was expected. The end of the Brigadier's message read "This will be a tank commanders' battle. No tank commander will go far wrong if he places his gun within killing range of an enemy."

Major Fosdick went off on the evening of 17th November in charge of the petrol dumping operation for the brigade. This operation was covered by A Company, 2nd Battalion the Rifle Brigade

(Major C. Sinclair, M.C.) which prepared twelve gaps a few miles north of Madelena for the passage of the petrol party and the brigade. This task was successfully accomplished and the petrol point was laid out according to plan. All was ready by the time the brigade arrived.

At 5.40 a.m. the regiment advanced. It was just getting light and the desert was almost flat. To the left front the 2nd Royal Tanks could be seen, to the left brigade headquarters, conspicuous by its armoured control vehicle, and beyond it the 6th Royal Tanks in the distance. British aircraft were in evidence but there was no sign of an enemy in the air.

The wire was crossed at about 8 and the gaps had been so well made that there was scarcely a pause as the squadrons converged on them and passed through. At 9 o'clock each squadron was alongside its petrol dumps re-fuelling and only one tank had fallen out. By 9.45 the regiment was ready to move on. It had never been intended that there should be a long halt here, but somewhere or other in the division there was a hitch in the refuelling arrangements and the order to resume the advance did not come until 11.30. Unforeseen delays are not the same as planned halts, as everyone is momentarily expecting the order to move on and nothing can be done about maintenance, whether of vehicle or man. They cause, in fact, a sort of exasperation and are not in any way a rest. So it was with a feeling of relief that the march continued.

B Squadron (Major Younger) was leading, followed by regimental headquarters. A Squadron (Major Seymour-Evans) was on the right, the open flank of the force, and C on its transporters was following regimental headquarters and keeping well up in its place. The course of the march was now north-westwards and the pace a good twelve miles in the hour. In the early afternoon the brigade reached its destination in the area of Bir el Reghem el Gharbi. From Gabr Saleh onwards the going was boggy, owing to heavy rain which had fallen during the night.

There was no sign of the enemy until about dusk. Then a considerable number of M.T. were observed by B Squadron to its left front. These were at first thought to be the 2nd Royal Tanks, but when Lieutenant G. S. B. Palmer was sent with his troop to investigate, he found that they were enemy. He opened fire and knocked out two armoured cars and six lorries. The rest of the enemy escaped. He brought back a total of fifteen prisoners, including the crews of both cars, a number of maps and documents and an eight-wheeled armoured car. B Squadron lost one tank, which caught fire for some reason or other and burnt out its engine.

It was too dark to pursue the enemy and the regiment went into leaguer, not without difficulty, on account of the boggy ground. C Squadron had dismounted from its transporters, but it was impossible for the replenishing lorries to make their way through the sodden desert in the dark, so replenishment was postponed until the morning.

If Rommel himself had been captured the news would scarcely have spread more rapidly—at least in the armoured division—than the news of the eight-wheeled armoured car. It had been seen in the distance and had aroused great curiosity in armoured circles. People who were interested in armoured vehicles now drove miles to see it, some bringing their cameras. One used to hear of primitive peoples being impressed by visiting warships, not because of their speed, armour or firepower, but for the number of their funnels. The German eight-wheeler had somehow acquired an importance, in the imagination of its opponents, which nothing but its eight wheels could have justified. It was a poor thing, with thin armour and few weapons, and in the light of day the once formidable myth collapsed.

At 6 p.m. on the 18th the 7th Armoured Division issued orders for the following day. The brigades were to proceed to battle positions, that of the 7th Armoured Brigade being Sidi Rezegh. The three armoured car regiments, having hitherto been under divisional control, were allotted to brigades in accordance with the pre-arranged plan, the 4th South African Armoured Car Regiment (Lieutenant-Colonel Newton-King) coming under the 7th Armoured Brigade. The move to Sidi Rezegh was to take place at a time which would be notified the following day.

At first light on the 20th all squadrons opened out as usual and the transporters left for the rear areas. Two patrols were sent out eastwards from A Squadron, one under Lieutenant the Hon. D. R. C. Chichester and the other under Lieutenant J. L. C. Williams. They found a number of abandoned vehicles and took a few prisoners, the aftermath of B Squadron's engagement the evening before. They also located an enemy camp or leaguer about five miles away.

A reconnaissance was at once carried out by the Colonel and the Brigadier. Meanwhile the 7th Hussars and DD (Jerboa) Battery RHA were warned to prepare for an attack. But the reconnaissance revealed the presence of enemy tanks and very boggy conditions in the approaches to the enemy leaguer. While the reconnaissance was in progress the expected orders came for the brigade to move on Sidi Rezegh and the idea of an attack on this enemy detachment was abandoned. The patrols withdrew cautiously on the treacherous ground and at 2.15 p.m. the advance began.

By now the sun had had its effect and the going was firmer, though not very good. The pace ordered was eight miles in the hour. It was scarcely a twenty mile march, and there was no incident until the last moment before arrival. The 6th Royal Tanks were leading, followed by Brigade Headquarters, 7th Hussars on the right, 2nd Royal Tanks on the left.

As the brigade topped the gentle undulation of the desert about three miles south of Sidi Rezegh the aerodrome came into view, with a couple of aircraft just taxi-ing along, preparing to take off. The rear link intercepted the word "gallop" from brigade headquarters, but the 6th Royal Tanks needed no encouragement. Crusaders could touch forty miles an hour on good going and the going was good. The 7th Hussars had a fine view of the finish as the 6th Royal Tanks overran the aerodrome. Three aircraft managed to take off and two of them made several fruitless dives on the attackers. Nineteen serviceable aircraft were captured on the ground and all the pilots and ground staffs, some eighty in all.

It was now getting dark and the brigade leaguered, the 6th Royal Tanks, A Company, 2nd Battalion The Rifle Brigade and Brigade Headquarters at the aerodrome, 7th Hussars and DD Battery two miles to the south-east, 2nd Royal Tanks and F Battery R.H.A. on the escarpment a mile to the south-west. No opposition was encountered during the advance but just as the regiment was leaguering a few shells burst among the tanks, without doing any damage.

The night was quiet, but as dawn broke on the 20th there was a burst of firing in the area of the 2nd Royal Tanks, who had three tanks hit and withdrew slightly from the southern escarpment. There were in fact several enemy posts on the edge of the escarpment a mile south-west of the aerodrome in carefully concealed and entrenched positions. They included anti-tank guns, and in one case a captured British 2-pounder. The previous evening there had been no sign of the enemy. During the night however the 2nd Royal Tanks had heard voices, but there were no infantry for a job which clearly called for a dismounted patrol. The enemy had waited until there was enough daylight and then quietly run up the 2-pounder and sniped three tanks as they were silhouetted against the eastern sky. They did no damage to "soft" vehicles, as these had been cautiously withdrawn at 5 a.m.

Meanwhile in the vicinity of the aerodrome the enemy was beginning to react. His first concern was to recover the use of the Trigh Capuzzo. This runs at the foot of an escarpment which drops steeply down on the north side of the aerodrome plateau. German infantry and anti-tank guns wormed their way up the re-entrants in this escarpment and started sniping the 6th Royal Tanks. Major Sinclair's company was too small to hold them off and several tanks were hit.

Next, having established an anti-tank screen to protect his movements the enemy advanced with a battalion from the west. The 7th Hussars were ordered to the aerodrome in case an opportunity should arise to counter-attack. The enemy, however, was stopped by artillery fire, which caused him a number of casualties, and as he was covered by anti-tank guns in both escarpments and these would have been on the flanks of the attacking tanks, the opportunity was not favourable.

Shortly before mid-day the Support Group began to arrive and during the afternoon endeavoured to establish itself north of the aerodrome with observation over the Trigh Capuzzo. But the enemy already held the lip of the escarpment with self-propelled and other anti-tank guns and infantry and this gave him good observation and a field of fire along the flat tableland. The Support Group was thus unable to secure the observation over the Trigh Capuzzo which was so necessary if it were to be effectively cut, and which could have been secured with no trouble if it had arrived a few hours earlier.

In the late afternoon the 7th Hussars and brigade headquarters were attacked by Stuka bombers. No damage was done to the regiment, but an unexploded bomb lay in the middle of B Squadron's area. At dusk the regiment moved about two miles eastward to the vicinity of its previous night's leaguer, and settled down for the night.

* * * *

For the first three days the offensive had gone according to plan. By the end of 18th November the 7th Armoured Division had reached the Gabr Saleh area and the 1st South African Division had advanced to El Cuasc. No contact other than reconnaissance had been made with the enemy except by the 7th Hussars, as already mentioned. The Army Commander had then taken the decision which he had reserved to himself, and which depended upon the success of the first day's move and the enemy's reactions. The latter were still undetermined, but General Cunningham had nevertheless decided that the 7th Armoured Division should move north-west to Sidi Rezegh.

It will be recalled that the 4th Armoured Brigade had the task of protecting the left of 13th Corps. It had been arranged by General Norrie (30th Corps) with General Gott, that all three armoured brigades should start off under command of the 7th Armoured Division but that if the 7th and 22nd were both operating west of the 440 grid (about five miles east of Sidi Rezegh) the 4th Armoured Brigade should pass to direct command of the 30th Corps. The north-westerly move of the division took it a long way west of the 13th Corps and the 4th Brigade had of necessity to be left well back. It was nevertheless still under the 7th Armoured Division when it became engaged with the main enemy armour on the morning of the 19th.

The first reaction of the enemy's striking force (his armour) was a southerly move, presumably directed at what he thought was the main force threatening him from the desert. The first serious engagement took place between advanced elements of the 4th Armoured Brigade and some sixty German tanks in the area north of Bir Gibni. The 22nd Armoured Brigade also had an engagement with the Italians at Bir el Gubi and knocked out forty-five of their tanks—mostly M.13's—at the cost of twenty-five of their own damaged. At about noon on the 19th the Commander 30th Corps ordered one brigade of the 1st South African Division to Gueret Hamza and another to Ber el Gseir, respectively thirty and forty-five miles south of Sidi Rezegh, and they reached these positions during the day.

By nightfall on the 19th the 7th Armoured Division was disposed with the 7th Armoured Brigade at Sidi Rezegh, the Support Group some fifteen miles south of it, the 4th Armoured Brigade east of Gabr Saleh, thirty miles away to the south-east, and the 22nd south-west of Bir Gubi, twenty-five miles to the south-south-west.

On the 20th the enemy's reactions began in earnest. At 7 a.m. the 4th Armoured Brigade, in view of the presence of German armour in its vicinity and the distance which separated that brigade from the others, was taken under direct command of the 30th Corps as arranged. The difficulties which had always been foreseen in the gap between the 13th and 30th Corps now became real. The 4th Armoured Brigade, which was protecting the left of the 13th Corps, found itself in fact protecting the right of the 30th Corps as well.

At about 8 a.m. air reconnaissance reported 200 enemy tanks moving south-east some 10 miles north of the 4th Armoured Brigade and at 8.20 a.m. 600-800 transport moving eastwards astride the Trigh Capuzzo a little farther north. Next, at 9 a.m., the 4th Armoured Brigade reported that the enemy were forming up to attack them. This was confirmed at 11 a.m., when army headquarters reported that the two enemy armoured divisions had joined up and were preparing to attack the 4th Armoured Brigade, probably at 12 noon. At the same time, on instructions from the 30th Corps, the 22nd Armoured Brigade was ordered to move eastwards from Gubi to the Gabr Saleh area and to reconnoitre thence north-east and eastwards with a view to co-operating with the 4th Armoured Brigade.

At about 3 p.m. the enemy attack developed towards Gabr Taieb el Essem, with about 100 tanks. The 4th Armoured Brigade was heavily pressed. The 22nd Armoured Brigade was now ordered to come in on the enemy's western flank in the Gabr Saleh area, and shortly afterwards the 30th Corps handed back control of the 4th Armoured Brigade to the 7th Armoured Division. The 22nd Brigade was unable to make contact until 6.30 p.m. when one regiment engaged the enemy. Fighting continued after dark and both sides spent the night in uneasy proximity to one another.

* * * *

Meanwhile the fateful decision had been taken by the 30th Corps Commander, with the Army Commander's approval, that the sortie from Tobruk should begin the following morning. First air reports on the 20th indicated a general westerly movement of the enemy, heavy columns of transport being observed moving west on the Trigh Capuzzo, the Bardia—Tobruk road, and from El Adem towards Mechili, This was interpreted as an indication that the enemy was slipping away. Early reports from the 4th Armoured Brigade that the enemy armoured units in their area seemed unwilling to engage, tended to confirm this impression and the later activities of the German armour seem to have been taken for "savage-rabbit tactics" designed to cover a withdrawal.

Everyone was looking forward to the moment when Tobruk should be relieved. In the early days of the siege the 7th Armoured Division had tried twice with inadequate resources and failed. Now it was making its third attempt, this time with far greater resources and was full of confidence and eager for the event. At 10 a.m. the G.O.C. 7th Armoured Division was consulted and said he thought that the Support Group, which was then on its way to Sidi Rezegh, should be able to join hands with the 70th Division if it began the sortie the next morning.

General Gott and Brigadier Campbell of the Support Group had spent the previous night, 19th/20th, with the 7th Armoured Brigade near Sidi Rezegh aerodrome, possibly in an atmosphere of too easy optimism, for the ground vital to the enemy had been reached almost without opposition and there were practically no enemy to be seen. In such circumstances it was difficult to advise postponement of the event for which all were so anxious.

Yet scarcely any of the conditions for the sortie, as laid down at the army conference of 15th October, had been fulfilled. The Support Group was only just joining the 7th Armoured Brigade at Sidi Rezegh. The South Africans had not yet reached—or even been ordered forward to—the escarpment at Sidi Rezegh; even their most advanced brigade was still thirty miles away, and it had never been intended that they should be ordered up until the enemy's main armour had been either destroyed or hemmed in.

The 15th and 21st Panzer Divisions had indeed been located with precision and there was no reason to suppose that touch would be lost. They had been engaged with the British armour, had had casualties (which were in fact over-estimated) and had shown no particular vigour in pressing home the advantage of their superiority in protective armour and fire power. But they could not be considered as destroyed and they were not hemmed in.

These factors however were offset by fears that the enemy might get away. General Norrie accordingly ordered the South Africans to move their 5th Infantry Brigade to Sidi Rezegh, where it was to arrive at 7 a.m. on 21st November. It was put under command of G.O.C. 7th Armoured Division and would be available either for its original role, to join hands with the 70th Division or, as seemed to be General Gott's intention, to replace the Support Group in a defensive task while the latter moved forward to meet the sortie.

Early in the afternoon of the 20th General Norrie sent the code word "Pop" to Tobruk. The 5th South African Brigade began its forward move, but by nightfall had only reached the Trigh el Abd, some twenty miles south of its destination, having been three times attacked by enemy aircraft.

*   *   *   *

On the evening of 20th November the G.O.C. 7th Armoured Division had command of five brigades, disposed in three main groups. The 7th Armoured Brigade and the Support Group were at Sidi Rezegh, in possession of ground vital to the enemy. The 4th and 22nd Armoured Brigades were in the Gabr Saleh area, both having been engaged with German armour and one with the Italians at Bir el Gubi on the previous day. The 5th South African Infantry Brigade was east of Bir el Gubi on its way to Sidi Rezegh, but was halted when still twenty miles short of its destination. The rest of the 1st South African Division had not yet moved north from el Cuasc. Next day, the 13th Corps was due to carry out an attack in the frontier area and the 70th Division to carry out its sortie from Tobruk.

On the enemy's side, Rommel had reacted more or less as expected. He had concentrated his two armoured divisions and after his engagement with the 4th and part of the 22nd Armoured Brigade on the 20th, remained for the night in the vicinity of Bir Bu Meliha.

The 7th Armoured Division's orders for 21st November were as follows. At first light the 22nd Armoured Brigade was to occupy a battle position facing north and east in an area about four miles square to the east of Gabr Saleh. Then, in the words of the divisional narrative :—

"4th Armoured Brigade and 22nd Armoured Brigade will reconnoitre with a view to attacking enemy as soon after first light as possible, time of attack to be arranged between commanders. Should enemy show signs of withdrawing he will be relentlessly pursued.

"7th Armoured Brigade and Support Group will remain in the area south of Sidi Rezegh and will put in a limited attack on the following day (21st November) with the object of assisting Tobruk garrison who are making a sortie to secure El Duda.

". . . 5th South African Infantry Brigade . . . to continue its advance and assist in the Sidi Rezegh attack."

At about midnight General Gott arrived at the headquarters of the 7th Armoured Brigade to co-ordinate the operation for a junction with the 70th Division, whose sortie had been ordered to begin at 6.30 a.m. Placing the Commander of the 7th Armoured Brigade in command of all troops in the Sidi Rezegh area, he ordered him to recapture the lip of the escarpment the next morning, so as to restore observation over the Trigh Capuzzo and to send forward a force across the Trigh Capuzzo to join hands with the 70th Division on El Duda. He then returned to his headquarters.

At 2 a.m. Lieutenant-Colonel Byass attended a conference at which orders were given for the attack. This was to be carried out by the 1st Battalion of the 60th on the right and A Company of 2nd Battalion The Rifle Brigade on the left. The 6th Royal Tanks were to lead the latter in close co-operation and to establish themselves on an objective beyond the Trigh Capuzzo. A special detachment of the 6th Royal Tanks was to be prepared to advance to El Duda to join hands with the 70th Division. The 2nd Royal Tanks were to continue to watch the approaches from the south and west. The 7th Hussars were to be in reserve, but placed rather to the eastward of the attacking troops so that they would afford protection to the right flank of the 60th. The whole of the guns of the Support Group (forty-two 25-pounders) with Brigadier Campbell of the Support Group acting as Commander Royal Artillery, were to support the attack and it was hoped that they would be able to give adequate cover against the anti-tank guns on the escarpments. Zero was fixed for 8.30 a.m.

This plan was fairly reasonable in so far as the reoccupation of the lip of the northern escarpment was concerned. But it seems to have been a tactical error to have ordered the 6th Royal Tanks to go beyond the Trigh Capuzzo to an objective which was not immediately to be occupied by our own riflemen and before there was reasonable certainty of being joined on it by the leading troops of the 70th Division.

* * * *

On the morning of 21st November, at first light, the 11th Hussars reported a large enemy column of some 150 tanks and transport moving south-westwards direct for the 22nd Armoured Brigade and only a few miles off. The 4th Armoured Brigade was within supporting distance and it looked as if the enemy were about to become engaged simultaneously with both these British armoured brigades. But, on making contact with the 22nd Armoured Brigade on the old Italian track joining El Adem with Sheferzen on the frontier, he turned north-westwards.

The 4th Armoured Brigade, whose strength was now ninety-seven tanks, made contact and engaged the tails of several enemy columns moving north-west and north. It succeeded in destroying a number of transport vehicles and a few tanks. The 22nd Brigade conformed to the movement of the enemy and followed up north-north-west with the object of engaging his left flank from the south. It was prevented in this, however, by difficulties with petrol. The 11th Hussars observed the enemy all the time and the 4th South African Armoured Car Regiment were in contact continuously from about 8 a.m. at which hour the German armour was just approaching the isolated British force at Sidi Rezegh.

At Sidi Rezegh all was being made ready for the attack which was to secure observation over the Trigh Capuzzo and to join up with the 70th Division on Ed Duda. As the outlines of the tanks in the 7th Hussars' leaguer began to show against the dawn, the squadrons opened out as usual and cooked breakfast. When it was light enough to see there was a little artillery fire as the gunners registered their targets, but otherwise all was quiet. The regiment was due to move to its battle positions, some two miles northwards, at 8.20, ten minutes before zero hour.

All was ready and squadrons were only awaiting the final signal, when suddenly at 8.10 the order came to stand fast; this was followed immediately by an order to face south-east and engage 200 enemy tanks reported approaching from that direction.

From the point of view of the 7th Armoured Brigade the problem was clear-cut. The sortie from Tobruk, according to the instructions received the previous night, had already begun and the leading troops of the 70th Division should now be approaching Ed Duda. The attack must take place as planned. But the arrival of German armour from the south-east was a threat to the main project and had to be dealt with at once. Other troops, known to be operating farther to the south, would soon be able to intervene and it was important that the smallest possible number of troops should be diverted from the attack towards Ed Duda.

Accordingly the Brigade Commander placed Brigadier Campbell in command of all the troops allotted for the northern operation and ordered him to carry out the attack as planned. The 2nd Royal Tanks were in reserve and available to meet the new threat, but alone they would not be enough. So the 7th Hussars and F Battery R.H.A. were withdrawn from the attacking force and Brigadier Campbell was told to make his own arrangements for the protection of his right flank, which was now left somewhat exposed to the eastward by the removal of the 7th Hussars.

The 7th Hussars were ordered to locate and delay the advance of the enemy tanks and the 2nd Royal Tanks were to move to a position near F Battery about two miles south-east of their present location. Brigade headquarters moved to the 7th Hussars.

The regiment advanced south-eastwards at once, B Squadron on the right, A on the left and C in reserve. A moved off a few minutes before the others as the threat seemed to be developing most dangerously from the east. At 8.20 the enemy were sighted on the horizon moving westwards, and some of the Support Group's transport passed through the regiment, having removed itself from the enemy's path in something of a hurry. A Squadron was directed south-eastwards and B southwards, C Squadron moving behind and close to regimental headquarters. F Battery engaged the enemy while the squadrons advanced and the forces rapidly drew closer together.

At about 8.30 the range was about 2,000 yards and the enemy opened fire with artillery and anti-tank guns on the leading squadrons. Part of his force, consisting of about fifty tanks, had moved north to meet the regiment and both leading squadrons came under very heavy fire. The enemy tanks were accompanied and in some cases preceded by anti-tank guns which were not at first recognized as hostile as they were mingled with British trucks and lorries. Some of these guns were very boldly handled and scored hits before their presence had been noticed among the other vehicles. B Squadron formed line, swung a little to the right and engaged both front and centre of the enemy main column and his flank detachment. C Squadron were moved up to the right flank to help B. After a severe engagement the enemy detachment rejoined the main German column which was by this time heading almost due north and showing no signs of stopping.

The enemy also appeared to detach another body of tanks from the rear of his main column. This, advancing among a number of withdrawing British transport vehicles, interposed between A Squadron and regimental headquarters. A Squadron engaged the enemy vigorously but the odds were too great and it was quickly overwhelmed. Major Seymour-Evans' tank was hit and he ordered Captain R. C. Watson to take command. There was no reply, as Captain Watson's tank had also been hit and he himself wounded. Control in A Squadron ceased.

Colonel Byass now ordered C Squadron to move across to the left to help A and to protect the left flank of the regiment. Regimental headquarters were themselves heavily engaged at close range and both the rear link tanks were knocked out, thus severing wireless contact with brigade headquarters. The brigade tactical headquarters, consisting of four tanks, were in fact now among the tanks of the 7th Hussars and trying in vain to be heard.

Captain Napier's tank had its steering wrecked and could only move in circles. Having circled towards the advancing enemy, he and his crew dismounted. All except Lieutenant P. B. Stanley Evans took cover behind the tank and were killed. Stanley Evans however decided to run for it and eventually reached another tank, unscathed.

Major Congreve, on receiving the order to move C Squadron to the left flank, was giving this order over his wireless when half the microphone was shot out of his hand and his wireless mast carried away. Consequently only a part of C Squadron got the order and the rest of the squadron, out of his control, withdrew a little to the north-east.

From the moment of the first shock B Squadron was heavily engaged with the enemy's main column and had considerable casualties. Major Younger's tank was hit early in the engagement and he was burned and slightly wounded. His driver, Trooper Crone, formerly a remount rider and one of the first men in the regiment to become a tank driver, was killed. His wireless operator and gunner, Corporal Doyle and

Lance-Corporal Walsh, were badly burned. Mounting his second-in-command's tank Major Younger withdrew the remainder of his squadron gradually towards regimental headquarters. He reported in person to the colonel and transferred to his tank.

All tanks were now closely engaged with the enemy, whose advance had at last been stopped. At this juncture the colonel's tank was hit by a 50-millimetre shot and he was killed instantly. Major Younger signalled to the second-in-command, Major Fosdick, who took over command and ordered the remainder of the regiment to rally to him and withdraw slightly northwards. Most of the tanks complied, but a few rallied to the brigadier's tank instead.

Wireless contact had not been re-established with brigade headquarters, so while Major Fosdick and a dozen tanks withdrew to the north-eastwards, two or three others withdrew with the brigade headquarters tanks to the vicinity of F Battery's position and, with F Battery, and a troop of DD Battery, which was ordered to point its guns in the new direction, prepared to take on the enemy if he should resume his advance.

These diverging withdrawals put the enemy between the regiment and the rest of the brigade. Major Fosdick hoped to rejoin round the north, but was prevented from doing so both by the main enemy armoured force which followed him up a short distance and by enemy in position on the high ground about Point 175, east of Sidi Rezegh aerodrome. His total strength was now twelve tanks and most of these had been hit and damaged. Several had their guns out of action, others had only a few rounds of ammunition left, and all were carrying survivors of other tanks on the outside, a number of them wounded. The regiment was thus in no condition to fight its way back to Sidi Rezegh and Major Fosdick now tried to rejoin the brigade by moving southwards.

First he reorganized his party under cover in a wadi at Carmuset en Nbeidat. He kept a close watch on the Germans, who presently occupied a position overlooking the wadi from the south-west and west with infantry. These dug themselves in while their artillery opened fire on the tanks. One A.10 of C Squadron was hit and destroyed and the rest of the tanks were moved farther eastwards. The enemy was now blocking the direct route to the south, so Major Fosdick decided to move still farther eastwards before taking a southerly course.

At 11 a.m. Corporal Phillips, who had been the Commanding Officer's wireless operator and was now in a tank with Major Younger, re-established rear link communication. Orders were received that if it were impossible to rejoin its own brigade immediately, the regiment should join the 4th Armoured Brigade which was known to be operating somewhere in that area.

The enemy seemed to be everywhere and there were only two scout cars with which to reconnoitre. Eventually Major Fosdick managed to lead the regiment through between two enemy columns, one of which engaged it with artillery. This fire was apparently observed from a vehicle moving on a parallel course about 3,000 yards away and was unpleasantly accurate.

At about 5 p.m., after moving twelve miles due south, the regiment encountered an officer of the 22nd Armoured Brigade with a number of replenishing vehicles. All tanks were now running very low in petrol as well as being short of ammunition and it was hoped that they could be refilled. But unfortunately the drivers of the vehicles thought the regiment was the enemy, made off to the southward and touch was lost.

Major Fosdick now turned westwards and the next contact was made, two miles farther on, with a troop of the 8th Hussars (4th Armoured Brigade). This troop tried to obtain medical help for the wounded and passed a message from the 7th Armoured Brigade to the 4th Armoured Brigade that help at Sidi Rezegh would be appreciated. The 4th Armoured Brigade was on the move, in a northerly direction, and as it was equipped with American M.3's (Honeys) and the 7th Hussars were restricted to the pace of the slowest horse (A.10) contact was soon lost in the gathering darkness.

At about 6 p.m., Major Fosdick decided to leaguer. His position was now once more at Bir Sidi Reghem el Gharbi, almost the spot where the eight-wheeler had been captured three days before. There were now only ten tanks, mostly A.10's, these old veterans having stood up to the three days' operations better than their more luxurious successors. There was petrol for some fifteen to twenty miles only and the regiment was separated from its brigade by twelve miles of desert and two German armoured divisions.

It had been an expensive day. Lieutenant-Colonel Byass, Lieutenant J. L. C. Williams and fourteen men had been killed. Twice as many more had been wounded and as many again were missing. But the object had been achieved. We still held Sidi Rezegh, the attack on the escarpment had succeeded and had been carried out without interference from Rommel's armour.

* * * *

Freddie Byass was educated at Wellington. He joined the 19th Hussars in France in the second half of World War I and was awarded the Military Cross. When the cavalry was reorganized after the war he transferred to the 7th Hussars. He at once found his feet in his new regiment and was soon prominent in all things connected with the horse. He won a number of point-to-points and some steeplechases and was for several years in the regimental polo team, including the last year at home when it won the inter-regimental. He will always remain a vivid memory to those who knew him. Quiet and even shy, he had a keen sense of humour and an equable temperament which made him a delightful companion. Young at heart, and with a natural gaiety, he had a particular appeal to young people, who in peace as well as in war regarded him as a friend. Yet nobody took liberties with him, for his light-hearted energies ran side by side with a strong sense of duty and a willing readiness to put himself out for others. In war he set a code of conduct, both before and during his tenure of command, which remained as an example and an inspiration long after his death. As a commanding officer he was ideal and seemed to get his way with no effort or fuss. Under him the regiment was happy and successful. His loss was deeply felt, not only by every officer and man in the regiment, but by his many friends outside.

*   *   *   *

At Sidi Rezegh the battle had continued from dawn until 4.30 p.m. When the enemy had first appeared from the south the 2nd Royal Tanks had also been ordered in that direction to meet him. The plan was to concentrate them to the west of F Battery and bring them in against the enemy's left flank as he advanced on the 7th Hussars. In the event the 2nd Royal Tanks became engaged, at the same time as the 7th Hussars, with some fifty German tanks, of which they destroyed 15. This part of the enemy force, the most westerly, halted and then sheered off north-eastwards, covered by a screen of anti-tank guns. It was probably the detachment referred to above, which B Squadron noticed as it merged again with the enemy main body.

The 2nd Royal Tanks were now drawn in rather closer to F Battery and made ready to deliver a counter-attack when the enemy should again decide to advance. The latter was meanwhile topping up, covered by a strong screen of infantry and anti-tank guns. When soft vehicles were observed in any numbers among his tanks they were harassed by F Battery; but the range was about 4,000 yards and no damage could be inflicted on the tanks themselves.

At about 3.15 p.m. the final attack came, tanks and infantry, supported by considerable artillery fire. F Battery and DD Battery Royal Horse Artillery engaged the enemy vigorously. The 2nd

Royal Tanks, in spite of strong anti-tank fire, advanced on the enemy's flank and claimed six enemy knocked out. They lost eleven of their remaining tanks, however, most of them before they were within 2-pounder range of the enemy and almost all of them burnt out. The detached troop of the 7th Hussars also advanced on the enemy and lost two of its three tanks.

There was now no further reserve left, and the enemy was still advancing. At this moment, however, Brigadier Campbell, whose operations in the north had ended successfully, arrived with Captain Longworth. The latter, the senior surviving officer of the 6th Royal Tanks, had organized the remaining tanks of his regiment, most of which had been destroyed in the northern attack, into a composite squadron. He now led this gallantly against the German armour and at the same time the remaining Brigade headquarters tanks advanced in the gap between the 2nd and 6th Royal Tanks. The enemy attack was halted. He withdrew his armour several hundred yards and remained in his positions until nightfall, covered by his usual screen of infantry and anti-tank guns.

That he halted was perhaps fortunate. The brigade had lost very heavily and there was no reserve of any kind left for an emergency. If he had come on, he might have suffered losses from the 25-pounders, which still had plenty of solid shot, but if he had managed to evade these or to neutralize them with his artillery and machine guns, he would have had little opposition except from the small number of 2-pounders with the Support Group. Apart from the 7th Hussars (nine tanks) now on the opposite side of the enemy, the only "runners" in the 7th Armoured Brigade were one of the 7th Hussars, six of the 2nd Royal Tanks, one of the 6th Royal Tanks and three of Brigade Headquarters, and most of these had been hit more than once. The vigorous defence had undoubtedly checked and misled the enemy, although it had probably not done him much material damage.

Of the attack in the north, in which the regiment had originally been allotted a minor part, little need be said. It was successful in reaching all its objectives and observation was restored over the Trigh Capuzzo. The 60th and A Company, the Rifle Brigade, lost heavily and the 6th Royal Tanks, who descended the escarpment and crossed the Trigh Capuzzo in accordance with their orders, lost every tank which went over the edge, including all their headquarters. The attack was most gallantly carried out and it was unfortunate that it coincided with the beginning of the sortie from Tobruk instead of with the arrival of troops from the garrison on the commanding features about El Duda and Bel Hamed. Six hundred prisoners were taken, but the position overlooking the Trigh could not be maintained by the depleted Support Group against the increasing enemy opposition. It is doubtful whether the gain of prisoners was balanced by the loss of the greater part of an armoured regiment and about 200 riflemen.

By 4.30 p.m., heavy fighting had ceased in the Sidi Rezegh area and both sides were repairing the damage.

Throughout the day efforts had been made to get the help of other formations. The 22nd Armoured Brigade was known to be not very far away to the southward and it seemed as if there was a good opportunity to inflict severe damage on the main enemy armour. This was fully occupied fighting the 7th Brigade in the north and an attack in flank or rear by another formation might prove decisive. The brigade major (Major N. M. H. Wall, 7th Hussars), who manned the brigade rear-link wireless set, made frequent reports and representations to the staff of the 7th Armoured Division, but without result. General Gott spent most of the hours of daylight visiting his formations, some of which were twenty miles from his headquarters. The staff, tied to their armoured control vehicles and offices, were able to record accurately the locations of troops and the estimated damage inflicted on the enemy. This however was often over-estimated and at so great a distance from the chief centres of activity it was quite impossible for the staff to keep touch with reality.

At 10 a.m., realizing that the situation at Sidi Rezegh, where the 15th and 21st Panzer Divisions had concentrated, was becoming critical, General Gott himself had ordered the 4th and 22nd Armoured Brigades to press on with all speed to the area of Point 175 and the aerodrome respectively. But both brigades were in need of replenishment. At 12.40 the 4th Brigade reach Gabr Slima and replenished. At 4.30 it made contact with the enemy near Bir er Reghem, where it was held up by an anti-tank screen which it engaged until last light.

The 22nd Brigade replenished at about 1 p.m. and soon after 3 p.m. hopes were raised at Sidi Rezegh when this brigade was seen on the horizon. It was sighted first by the 2nd Royal Tanks and then by the rest of the force, about four miles south of the battlefield, moving north-westwards. It looked as if it were arriving at an opportune moment, as the afternoon battle had just begun. All were watching for the northward turn which would bring it into the battle, now reaching the most critical stage. But as the brigade held to its course hope gave way to doubt and doubt to disappointment as it was realized that it was getting farther away; it finally disappeared over the horizon.

The 2nd Royal Tanks sent first one liaison officer and then another, but these came back with the news that the brigade had been given some other task. It had, in fact, been ordered "to clear 4239 of enemy tanks" (30th Corps Report). This square was some seven to ten miles west of the battlefield, towards El Adem. No enemy had been reported in that area during the day, so it is not clear why or by whom General Gott's original order for the brigade to go to the Sidi Rezegh aerodrome should have been altered.

MAP VII

OPERATION "CRUSADER"

Opening British moves on 18th and 19th November and Rommel's reactions on 20th and 21st.

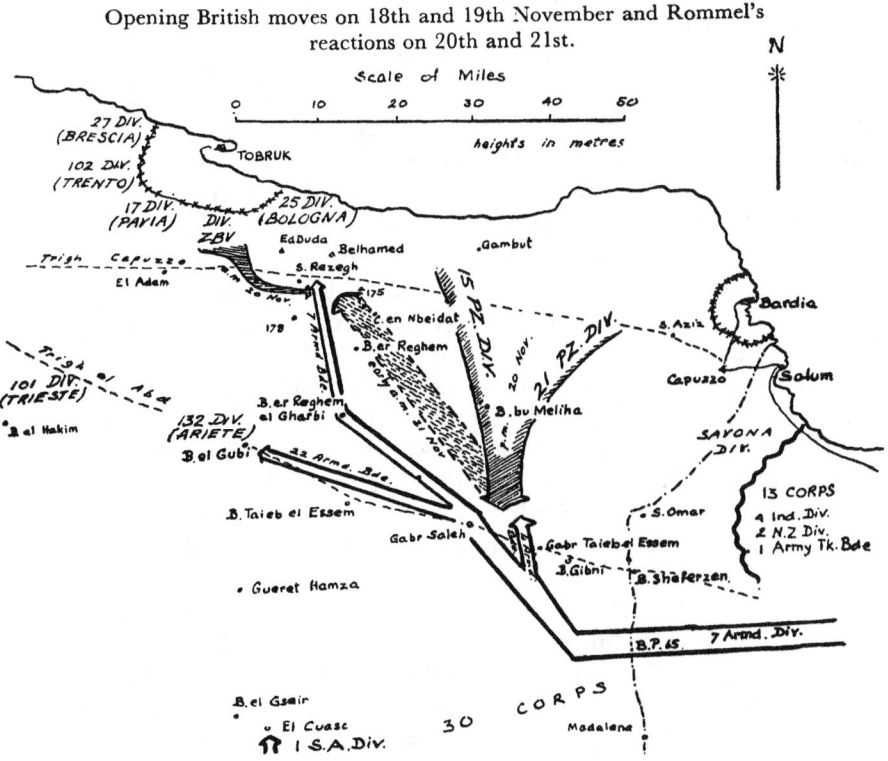

At mid-day and in the early afternoon General Gott was visiting a South African headquarters near Taieb el Essem and, owing to a wireless hitch, was out of contact both with his own headquarters and with his brigades. It was entirely by chance that, at about 1.30 p.m. he met one of the commanding officers of the 22nd Brigade and was able to send for the brigadier over the brigade wireless net. Brigadier Scott-Cockburn duly arrived at the rendez-vous, with part of his headquarters, but when they moved on again they bogged down in soft sand and were stuck for some time. So the three Yeomanry regiments reached the end of their abortive journey without their brigade commander and chafing at having obviously by-passed a bloody battle without being able to intervene.

The battle was at its height and nearly all the remaining tanks of the 2nd Royal Tanks were on fire, when the 22nd Brigade faded into the distance. Major Wall once more asked the headquarters of the 7th Armoured Division for the co-operation of the 22nd Brigade. But it was now too late for it to intervene usefully on this day. Having found nothing in the area it had been sent to, the brigade turned back eastwards and at about 5 p.m. halted about two miles west of the smoking battlefield.

Thus, instead of being able to help in destroying a tired and moderately battered enemy, the 22nd Brigade was destined, on the following day, to have an experience very like that of the 7th. It had to engage the resuscitated and still concentrated German armour for some hours with very little support and it suffered severely in the process.

After dark the 7th Armoured Brigade closed towards the Support Group and leaguered. F Battery's guns were in action facing the German armour, and the prisoners were guarded by the Support Group. The situation was in hand, but only just. At the end of a day of savage fighting the ground vital to the enemy was still held, although the gains of the morning had been partially lost. The enemy, although checked, was still there, surrounding the depleted British force on three sides. On the north and east was the 90th Light Division. On the south-east and south were the 15th and 21st Panzer Divisions.

A report had to be made to the 7th Armoured Division, still near Gabr Saleh, and the wording of it over the radio, in clear language, was a delicate problem. It would have been a mistake to let the enemy know the real situation as regards our strength. It would, on the other hand, have been a pity to paint too rosy a picture for divisional headquarters. Accordingly, a somewhat over-optimistic report was made first, and this was followed by a cryptic one to say it was over-optimistic. The head of the Armoured fighting vehicle directorate at GHQ was known to his friends as "Rosey Lloyd." That made it easy. The message was "The situation is not so Lloyd as previously reported. Brink's Boys (i.e. the 5th South African Brigade) will be welcome." The message was acknowledged and understood.

The fitters worked solidly throughout the night and achieved a total of twenty-eight runners in the brigade by the morning. No praise is too high for the regimental fitters and the Ordnance—later R.E.M.E.—personnel. They may have been exposed to less frequent danger and they were generally left out of the glamour which shone on the tank crews, but their vigorous efforts throughout the chilly nights, and their endurance often for several days on end with practically no sleep, earned for them the greatest respect of all who depended upon them.

*   *   *   *

The operations of the 7th Hussars on the 21st November had been closely linked with the sortie from Tobruk. Yet there had been no sign of the 70th Division arriving at El Duda. Even on the 22nd the news from Tobruk was scanty, but it was realized that something had gone wrong.

The sortie opened with two feints, designed to draw off the enemy's reserves; the Polish Carpathian Brigade Group and the 23rd (British) Infantry Brigade carried out limited attacks in the western and southern sectors. Then at 6.30 a.m. the main attack was launched in the south-eastern sector and a few minutes later the first objectives were occupied. But the capture of subsequent objectives was delayed by the obstinate defence, especially of one post on the axis of advance. Owing to the several belts of minefields put down by the enemy in the preceding six months, it was necessary to confine the frontage of the attack to a narrow corridor where the mines could be swept. Space for manoeuvre was thus somewhat limited. Further, in the past ten days the enemy had been gradually moving up German troops of the Africa Corps into the area opposite the south-eastern sector of Tobruk, as this was the point selected for the German attack on the fortress.

So the progress of the 70th Division's attack was less rapid than had been anticipated. Nearly 1,000 prisoners were taken, but the enemy counter-attacked from both flanks and drew the 32nd Army Tank Brigade into the fight before it was intended. This brigade was to have been kept in hand and it had been General Scobie's intention to use it for the attack on El Duda, destined to take place at 2.30 p.m. This unavoidable engagement of his most powerful formation deprived General Scobie of the main punch for his afternoon operation.

He received a further blow in the middle of the morning, when the 30th Corps informed him that no support could be given from Sidi Rezegh that day, as a heavy armoured battle was in progress. So the attack on El Duda was reluctantly postponed. This left the 70th Division in a somewhat precarious position, as the leading troops were about four miles outside the perimeter at the end of a long corridor of which both flanks were vulnerable to counter attacks.

In the evening the Army Commander offered a New Zealand Brigade and a squadron of Valentine tanks—the cheaper but quite effective infantry tank—to the 30th Corps. General Norrie refused the New Zealanders as he felt that, with the South African Division's two brigades, he had plenty of infantry. But he accepted the "Valentines." These were slow and like all other British tanks, had only a 2-pounder gun. But they had good armour and could withstand knocks which would have destroyed cruisers. They were to prove of great value in the Sidi Rezegh area during the next few days.

The fourth day of the offensive had been, on the whole, disappointing. The losses inflicted to date on the enemy were believed to be considerable, but were probably less heavy than was thought. Contact had not been established between the 30th Corps and the garrison of Tobruk. Instead, the 7th Armoured Brigade and the Support Group had only just been able to hold on to the enemy's vital area at Sidi Rezegh and were now so much reduced in strength that Rommel was beginning to recover a great measure of the initiative.

CHAPTER VII

"Crusader" Goes On

Enemy recovers Sidi Rezegh area on the 22nd November—fighting south of Sidi Rezegh, 23rd November—operations on the frontier—Rommel goes to Sheferzen, 24th November—a night engagement—7th Hussars leave the desert—comments on the battles—progress of the offensive—re-organization in the delta.

Map IV

Up to this point the battle had been comparatively tidy and everyone knew more or less who his neighbour was. But from now onwards the movements of individuals and even of formed bodies of troops became exceedingly confused. Both sides were switching troops from here to there and back again. Numerous vehicles became detached from their parent columns and, as they endeavoured to rejoin their units, ran into the enemy. So many vehicles had changed hands that an apparently friendly column might turn out to be German and only the tanks provided a certain clue to identity. Yet the armoured car regiments, with patrols operating all over the area amidst the apparent confusion, seldom made a mistake and the enemy's main movements were reported with remarkable accuracy.

In the area where the regiment had leaguered on the 21st November the night had been cold and wet. It was however satisfactory to have evacuated the wounded and dismounted men, who had been taken back by the replenishment vehicles of the 22nd Armoured Brigade. Early on the morning of the 22nd November wireless contact was obtained with the 7th Armoured Brigade and the position was reported. Orders were received to rejoin at Sidi Rezegh as soon as the B Echelon had arrived. B Echelon had had an exciting time moving through an Italian camp somewhere in the vicinity of Bir el Gubi, but they escaped unscathed and arrived about 8 a.m.

Shortly after noon the regiment reached the brigade near Point 178 on the southern escarpment. Lieutenants Llewellen Palmer and White and three tanks rejoined. They too had had a busy time and had been constantly in action; their losses included Sergeant Walford and Corporal Weaver killed. The regiment now consisted of twelve tanks, and these took up positions facing west and north-west, about a mile from brigade headquarters.

The brigade was nominally in reserve, but all the serviceable tanks were on the aerodrome engaged in support of the Support Group. As the result of strenuous efforts during the night, the indefatigable Captain Longworth of the 6th Royal Tanks had managed to get five or six of his tanks fit by the morning of the 22nd. He towed his crocks to the 2nd Royal Tanks area. The latter regiment had got thirteen of theirs fit. All these tanks were on the aerodrome in time for the enemy's next effort.

At 7.30 a.m. the enemy, with some fifty tanks, again attacked the Support Group and the remnants of the 7th Armoured Brigade. He was driven off, and desultory fighting continued on all sides of the aerodrome until noon, when the German tanks were seen to be forming up again for an attack both on the north and on the south of the aerodrome.

The 4th Armoured Brigade, which had been engaged with parties of the enemy to the south-east of his main concentration, was ordered to close to a point three miles south-east of Point 175, and to be prepared to assist in the Sidi Rezegh area. The 22nd Armoured Brigade was ordered to take up a battle position south of Sidi Rezegh and to assist the Support Group if required.

At 2.30 p.m. the enemy made a very heavy attack on the aerodrome from the west and north-west with not less than 100 tanks, accompanied, according to his custom, by lorried infantry and numbers of anti-tank guns and supported by artillery fire. Within fifteen minutes the 22nd Armoured Brigade was engaging him closely with all three regiments and had heavy casualties. By 4 p.m. two regiments of the 4th Armoured Brigade were also engaged. Fighting continued until after dark and the enemy succeeded in recapturing the aerodrome area. The 1st Battalion The King's Royal Rifle Corps, who had already lost severely the previous day, were overrun on the northern escarpment.

By the end of the day the situation was no more satisfactory than it had been twenty-four hours earlier. The fighting had been severe and losses were heavy on both sides, although difficult to assess in the smoke, dust and confusion. The enemy had retaken the ground vital to his communications. The sortie from Tobruk had been checked in the north and the advanced British troops at Sidi Rezegh had been pressed back several miles in the south, thus widening the gap which the British had hoped to close finally the previous day. German lorried infantry, covered by anti-tank guns, had taken up positions on all sides of the aerodrome.

By the evening the 7th Armoured Division was disposed roughly along the southern escarpment, south of the aerodrome. The 4th

Armoured Brigade (about 100 tanks) on the right, then the remnants of the Support Group, then the 5th South African Brigade set slightly behind the rest, and the 22nd Armoured Brigade (45 tanks) on the left. The remains of the 7th Armoured Brigade (10 tanks) were two miles farther south, in reserve, and looking after the 700 prisoners captured on the 21st.

Earlier in the day the brigade had been ordered to move farther south, taking the prisoners. These however were in very poor condition, suffering severely from exhaustion, hunger and thirst, and could not be moved except by transport. As none could be obtained—actually the lorries arrived late in the evening—the brigade stayed where it was. At dusk it concentrated in a single leaguer three miles to the south. Replenishment vehicles came up, and Lieutenant Nickels and SSM Lowe rejoined the 7th Hussars from the base. There was no tank for Lieutenant Nickels so he stayed with brigade headquarters.

*   *   *   *

As the result of the battle on the 22nd, General Gott appreciated that no further offensive operations were possible with the forces at his disposal. With the exception of the 4th Armoured Brigade and the 5th South African Brigade, casualties had been high. He therefore decided to secure the southern escarpment with the Support Group (reinforced by most of the 2nd Battalion Scots Guards) and the 5th South African Brigade, the 4th and 22nd Armoured Brigades protecting the right and left flanks respectively. The 7th Armoured Brigade was ordered to move to Sidi Er Reghem el Gharbi, fifteen miles to the south, taking the prisoners, and to remain in reserve. Captain Longworth with a mixed squadron, was with the Support Group, and the brigade consisted only of ten tanks of the 7th Hussars, a few crocks of the 2nd Royal Tanks and three of brigade headquarters.

The brigade ordered the 7th Hussars A1 Echelon, the crocks and the prisoners, these escorted by crocks of the 2nd Royal Tanks, to go off at 7.30 a.m. on the 23rd. The rest of the regiment was to follow brigade headquarters and be ready to move at 8. On reaching the destination the regiment was to reorganize and do maintenance.

At 8 p.m. the 7th Armoured Brigade, having put 700 prisoners into the 10 3-ton lorries and sent them off just ahead, began its march southwards. Almost at once the 4th South African Armoured Car Regiment reported a strong enemy column including a large number of tanks moving south-west a mile away on a course which looked as f it would lead them into a direct collision with the brigade. Captain de Beer, adjutant of the Armoured Car Regiment, said afterwards that he had been very anxious as he knew the report would sound improbable and he was afraid it would not be believed and that the enemy would run straight into the brigade and the prisoners. Fortunately the prisoners, whose overloaded lorries could barely crawl along, were clear by about two miles. They were all Germans and it would have been a pity to lose them. The brigade headquarters accelerated and passed across the head of the enemy column, the tanks engaging the enemy on the move. One of the cruisers was knocked out, but no other serious damage was done. The 7th Hussars halted and engaged the enemy's northern flank, scoring a number of hits.

This column was one of several which seemed to be concentrating in the area south-west of Sidi Rezegh. One of these, at 7 a.m., had already bumped into the leaguer of the 5th South African Infantry Brigade. It halted on being engaged by artillery. The column which the regiment was now engaging covered its flanks in the usual style with anti-tank guns and, as it joined up with the other enemy force, also came to a halt. This was the opening move of the principal fighting on the 23rd, which centred round the South African Brigade's leaguer, while the regiment spent a rather unsatisfactory day on the southern outskirts of the main battle.

Having concentrated and found an apparently static and satisfactory objective, the enemy began to make his plans for attacking it. He worked his way south-west and west round the leaguer. This was very conspicuous and clearly definable. The South Africans were equipped with a generous scale of transport and all their troop-carrying lorries and their B Echelon vehicles had remained in the leaguer throughout the night and were still there.

As the enemy moved round, the South Africans prepared to defend their position from the south, west and north. The 22nd Armoured Brigade (now only 48 tanks) was ordered to reconnoitre to the south-west of the leaguer with a view to engaging any enemy who might threaten it from that direction. The 4th Armoured Brigade, although strong in tanks (119), was not fully under control owing to a night attack on the brigade headquarters leaguer. The brigade headquarters had lost several officers and men and various wireless links, both internal and external. It was not therefore possible to concentrate the division for the ensuing battle.

During the morning there were sporadic exchanges of artillery fire in the Sidi Rezegh area. At 1.30 p.m. the enemy began bombarding the northern face of the South African leaguer and shortly afterwards enemy infantry advanced to attack. They were stopped by the machine gun and artillery fire of the defence and were never nearer than 1,000 yards.

Meanwhile there were clear indications that enemy armoured forces were forming up a few miles south-west of the leaguer with a view to attacking it from that direction. But as the attack did not take place once, it is possible that the operation in the north was an effort on the part of the 90th Light Division to draw the attention of the defence, and more particularly of its artillery and anti-tank guns, away from the main effort. At any rate the attack was not pressed. It was at 3.30 that the main blow was delivered, from the south-west.

The defence was at considerable disadvantage. A large proportion of the artillery was in the central area of the leaguer, especially the 25-pounders. From their positions the latter could concentrate their fire on any sector which was threatened, but only while the enemy were still some way outside the leaguer. As the range shortened the guns were badly masked by the mass of transport.

The enemy tanks advanced under cover of heavy artillery fire and closely accompanied by lorried infantry and anti-tank guns. As they advanced the 22nd Armoured Brigade fell upon their left flank, but in face of the anti-tank screen the now rather weakened brigade could not prevent the enemy advancing. It took toll of his tanks, however, and destroyed or damaged a number of them, but at considerable cost to itself.

The enemy pressed on and entered the leaguer area. As they penetrated resistance stiffened and the South African Gunners fought most gallantly. Often their first view of the enemy tanks would be at only a few yards range as they emerged from the smoke and dust among the bewildered transport. It was believed that some fifty enemy tanks were destroyed by the South Africans and the 22nd Armoured Brigade, but no pick-up was possible as the enemy, who over-ran the leaguer completely, remained in possession of the battlefield. He therefore managed to recover a high proportion of his casualties. The South African losses amounted to 2,000 men, the majority of them captured. The rest of the brigade made its way south-eastwards and the enemy was held off by the vigorous work of the 22nd Armoured Brigade.

We now return to the 7th Hussars, who at 8.30 a.m. were engaging the northern flank of a large German column. The move of this column through the line of march of the 7th Armoured Brigade in the morning had separated the regiment from its own brigade once more. Numerous smaller columns and individual vehicles, some of them British vehicles in German possession, some the reverse, were on the move all over this part of the desert. The situation was in fact somewhat obscure, as it was bound to be, since the initiative had, for the time being, passed to the Germans.

A few miles to the east of the South African Brigade was the Support Group of the 7th Armoured Division. They were seriously depleted by the three days fighting, but the 2nd Battalion, The Scots Guards, had been ordered to join them and was on its way forward.

When Brigadier Campbell saw from a distance the 7th Hussars engaged with the enemy column he ordered them to close on him and come under his orders. The officer he sent across said they were urgently wanted to help to get the Support Group and some South Africans out, as enemy tanks had got among their soft vehicles. Major Fosdick, knowing the predatory instincts of Jock Campbell, insisted on first getting permission from his own brigadier, now several miles off on the opposite side of the enemy, but still in wireless contact. This was given and Major Fosdick, with the 7th Hussars' tanks and a few others he managed to collect, covered the withdrawal of the Support Group in a southerly direction. The tanks, as they fell back, fired steadily at the enemy tanks and stopped them advancing.

All the time elements of other units were gravitating towards the Support Group including several of the 11th Hussars' armoured cars. One or two of their cars and a few of the guns got stuck in some boggy ground and some of the tanks of the regiment helped them out. While this was being done a dozen Italian light tanks appeared from the blue and drove straight at the regiment. It was a very gallant but fruitless attack, as every one of them was knocked out. They were followed up at a distance by some M.13's, but these withdrew on being engaged by 25-pounders and before coming within range of the tanks.

The headquarters of the 22nd Armoured Brigade now joined up with the Support Group and it was decided to move northwards. The tanks were replenished from the 22nd Brigade's B Echelon and the whole force moved northwards to about the area where the regiment had leaguered the previous night. Here it was expected that Colonel Carr's 4th County of London Yeomanry would be found.

The enemy's attack on the South African leaguer was now in full swing and for a time it was intended that the regiment should go into the battle. It would, however, have been difficult to intervene, as there was no possibility of informing the South Africans, with whom there was no direct wireless contact, and the arrival of a strange body of armoured troops might have added to the confusion. So the Support Group remained halted and the 7th Hussars were placed out in front as a defensive screen.

About this time they were joined by the headquarters of the 7th Armoured Brigade, which, having borrowed a battery of 25-pounders from the 1st South African Brigade at Taieb el Essem, had moved up with these and a few resuscitated tanks of the 2nd Royal Tanks to help in the battle. The battery came into action but did not open fire as it was by no means clear whether the vast quantity of vehicles moving eastwards were friendly or hostile—or both. A few shells fell among the tanks of the regiment, coming from the general direction of the moving vehicles, and just before sunset, when the light was getting difficult, about half a dozen A.15 crusaders arrived at great speed from the same direction.

This was one of the unfortunate mistakes which are so easy to make and cannot be helped. It was doubtless due to a combination of failing light and the general uncertainty created by the confused nature of the fighting. The crusaders fired as they came, but as they did not halt their shooting was not very accurate and only two hits were noticed, one of which did considerable damage to Major Congreve's cupola but caused no casualties. Having a better light, the 7th Armoured Brigade and the 7th Hussars realized the mistake from the beginning and did not open fire. In the words of the regimental diary, "This was a bad end to a bloody day."

The regiment leaguered at nightfall a short distance away, while the rest of the 7th Armoured Brigade (three tanks of brigade headquarters and three of the 2nd Royal Tanks) escorted the borrowed battery to its parent South African Brigade and leaguered a few miles north of it.

* * * *

It is now necessary to review briefly the principal events in the frontier area since the beginning of the offensive, as during the next few days the centre of interest was momentarily to shift in that direction.

It will be remembered that the 13th Corps was not intended to play a major part in the opening phases. Its role was to prevent the enemy breaking through to the east or south and to take no further action until the threat of armoured attack against its left had been removed. On 18th November therefore limited operations were carried out by the 4th Indian Division against the eastern, southeastern and southern faces of the enemy's frontier defences. Next day the 7th Indian Infantry Brigade moved farther round and occupied an area to the west of Sidi Omar, thus threatening the rear of the Savona Division. These operations provoked artillery fire but no other reaction. In the afternoon of the 19th the New Zealand Division moved on to the Trigh el Abd ready to advance when the order should be given. Its task was then to isolate the enemy forces on the frontier and move westwards via the Trigh Capuzzo and the Bardia—Tobruk road.

On the morning of the 21st (D4 of the offensive and the day of the first armoured battle at Sidi Rezegh), the enemy armour was known to be well away to the west, and at 9.40 a.m. the 13th Corps was told to begin active operations that afternoon. Accordingly at 1 p.m. the New Zealand Division advanced, with one squadron from the 1st Army Tank Brigade under command of each infantry brigade. At dusk an enemy post at Sidi Azeiz was rushed and fifty prisoners were taken. Next morning at dawn Capuzzo was taken with 200 prisoners. The water supply to the Halfaya position was cut and the main signal communications of the frontier groups were broken. During the morning advanced elements of the New Zealand Division cut the Bardia—Tobruk road. Such tanks as were encountered did not fight, presumably because they were crocks or reinforcements in the base area of the Africa Corps.

At noon on the 22nd the 4th Indian Division, supported by the 1st Army Tank Brigade, attacked the enemy position at Sidi Omar. It met strong opposition and had severe losses, but took its objectives.

The New Zealand Division was now operating over an extensive tract of desert which was by no means clear of the enemy. In the evening it was given permission to clean up the situation around Bardia. At dawn on the 23rd Musaid and Salum were captured.

As the result of these operations there remained of the enemy Frontier Group only isolated areas of resistance round Sidi Omar and about Halfaya Pass, and a considerable number of administrative troops inside the Bardia perimeter and in the neighbourhood of Gambut.

On the evening of 23rd November the Eighth Army Commander decided that the situation in the area El Duda—Sidi Rezegh required the use of infantry. He accordingly made the 13th Corps responsible from a minute before midnight on the 23rd for the command of all infantry north of the 390 east-west grid (which passes about ten miles south of Sidi Rezegh) and placed the 70th Division under the 13th Corps. The task of the 13th Corps was to capture Sidi Rezegh and El Duda at all costs and to exploit westwards on the El Adem road. The 30th Corps was to reorganize and be prepared to go to the help of the New Zealand Division in case of a concentrated enemy tank attack, in particular to secure their rear around Bir el Gubi. It was considered that the tank strength reported by the 30th Corps on 22nd November "should make comfortable allowance for this without prejudice to the main role of the armoured forces which is to destroy enemy tanks." The 30th Corps was further instructed to give all possible protection to the 1st South African Division against tank attack.

As far as the 30th Corps was concerned, none of the original infantry of the Corps was north of the 390 grid, so the only major change of command was the passing of the 70th Division (the garrison of Tobruk) from the 30th to the 13th Corps. The 1st South African Division had only one effective brigade, the 1st, and this had not yet been engaged. It was now ordered to occupy an all-round defensive position in the neighbourhood of Taieb el Essem and to organize two mobile columns to reconnoitre the track between El Adem and the northern outskirts of the Italian position at Bir el Gubi. The 7th Armoured Division was to rally in a central area between the Trigh Capuzzo and the Trigh el Abd.

*   *   *   *

The 24th November was the seventh day of the offensive and no less eventful than the preceding six, for on this day Rommel led his two armoured divisions approximately along the line of the Trigh El Abd to Sheferzen. His object is still not clear. General Norrie thought at the time that it was the last desperate fling of a gambler. But this was perhaps to under-rate the nature of Rommel. He had already led the Africa Corps in one daring and spectacular advance—from Agheila to Salum. The risks he took were not however the products of a rash or frivolous nature, but carefully calculated. Once a plan was decided upon, he was ruthless in its execution and would himself be in the forefront to drive it to its conclusion. In defence he was dogged and obstinate. Like his master and subsequent murderer, Hitler, or perhaps under his persuasion, he was slow to recognize defeat and reluctant to give ground.

On 24th November there were several factors in the situation which may have induced Rommel to choose the course he did. First, he saw the prospects of his own projected offensive being frustrated. He had expended much energy and lost a number of tanks in maintaining his position. He had recovered Sidi Rezegh and re-opened his communications and the count of destroyed British tanks he found on a succession of battlefields was impressive.

On the other hand, detachments on the frontier and at Bardia were isolated and the administrative area around Gambut had been overrun. If he could restore the position on the frontier and free the area between there and Tobruk of the many British formations which appeared to be swarming over it, he might still be able to overwhelm the garrison of Tobruk and take possession of the valuable harbour and base. He may have hoped that, by following the Trigh el Abd, he would so disrupt and disorganize the administrative arrangements of the 30th Corps that it would be compelled to withdraw behind the frontier again. That he achieved very little was doubtless due in large measure to the imperturbable characters of Generals Norrie and Gott and to the agility of their headquarters and the various formations and units of the 30th Corps.

At dawn on the 24th the 7th Hussars opened out as usual. Orders were received at 6.30 a.m. to rejoin the 7th Armoured Brigade, which was north of Bir Taieb el Essem. Ten tanks were fit for action and these started off. The crocks followed with the fitters.

Just before the march was completed orders came to send all the fit A.13 and A.15 tanks to the 22nd Armoured Brigade, which was in the area east of Sidi Rezegh. There were only four of these, three A.15's and one A.13, and they were sent off under Lieutenant Glendinning, who had just returned to the regiment as an officer. Only two of the tanks finished the journey. With these Lieutenant Glendinning took part in the operations round Belhamed in the next phase of the battle of Sidi Rezegh, until the 26th, when he handed them over to the composite squadron of the 2nd Royal Tanks under Major Yule.

The remaining six fit tanks, A.10's, two of regimental headquarters and four of C Squadron, arrived at their destination about a mile from brigade headquarters. They were replenished and in the couple of hours which followed everyone had an unusually peaceful breakfast and a shave; beards were in some cases quite long. During this interlude orders came to send off the six remaining A.10 tanks to the headquarters of the 7th Armoured Division.

Meanwhile the brigade was ordered to go to protect the 62nd Field Maintenance Centre, some fifteen miles south of the divisional headquarters at Gabr Saleh, and it was decided that the six A.10's should be detached from the brigade as it passed Gabr Saleh and should in the meanwhile act as rearguard, as it was reported that several enemy columns were on the move.

The brigade was nearing Gabr Saleh when a lorry being driven at high speed eastwards, subsided with a broken axle in a slit trench, to the evident consternation of its Basuto driver. Shortly afterwards General Brink of the 1st South African Division called at the armoured control vehicle and said that enemy tanks were approaching and that there were a number of British tanks in the vicinity which seemed to be doing nothing about it. He was asked if he had any guns to lend and explained that he had not. There followed a mass of transport all moving fast in an easterly direction and in the distance could be seen the black smoke of bursting shells.

The brigade B Echelon transport was ordered to continue its south-easterly movement towards No. 62 Field Maintenance Centre while the regiment, which had hitherto been covering the transport, was ordered to close on brigade headquarters, which would be identifiable by its two remaining A.15's. Fortunately the six A.10's of the 7th Hussars had not yet been sent off to divisional headquarters and these were to be the mainstay of the subsequent operations.

The regiment at once accelerated in the direction where brigade headquarters was known to be, but in the welter of dust stirred up by the masses of hurrying South African transport it was at first difficult to find the A.15's. As the atmosphere cleared Lieutenant Thornton, in a dingo, found them. Two tanks were engaging the enemy and the other two were in tandem, one towing the other. Four Bofors guns of the 1st Anti-Aircraft Regiment were also engaging the enemy, whose tanks numbered about forty.

The 7th Hussars came up into line. The range was now long as the enemy were going rapidly eastwards. One enemy tank was knocked out and the crew dismounted. They were captured by an officer in a dingo who at the same time completed the destruction of the tank. Officers of the regiment who could no longer be mounted in tanks were useful for purposes of inter-communication. Major Congreve, and Lieutenants P. B. Stanley Evans and Thornton and a dingo driver, Trooper Horsecroft, did invaluable work in helping the brigade commander to establish and maintain control of the several units who now joined in the chase.

First to be found was the Protection Squadron of the 30th Corps Headquarters. These amounted to about a dozen American M.3's (Honeys). Major Congreve organized as many as he could lay hands on and helped to get them into action.

There was no wireless link for controlling the force except that between Brigadier Davy's tank and the adjutant's tank of the 7th Hussars. But this link was short lived because the brigadier, looking at the enemy instead of where he was going, collided with the other brigade headquarters tank and both were put out of action by the impact. Sergeant Murphy, 7th Hussars, the brigadier's driver, was killed by a machine-gun bullet while gallantly trying to fix the towing gear to his disabled tank. Lieutenant P. B. Stanley Evans then took the brigade commander to one of the Honeys. This, however, was unsatisfactory as it had no ammunition—there was an acute shortage of 37-millimetre ammunition and the Protection Squadron was not very generously supplied. So Stanley Evans' dingo became the brigadier's charger for much of the day.

The next unit to join in the chase was a mixed battery of about eight guns of the Northumberland Hussars, with Major J. Cookson, Major Benson and Captain Williamson. Their real task was the protection of the 4th Armoured Brigade's B Echelon, but having seen this get clear, after it had passed obliquely through the South African transport, Major Cookson attached himself and his guns to the 7th Armoured Brigade.

At first only two guns came into action. One of these had its regular crew. That of the other gun had been killed the previous day, and this was manned by Captain Williamson, a sergeant-major and a sanitary orderly. The two guns stayed in rear of their own soft vehicles and then, when they saw headquarters 7th Armoured Brigade in position, pulled out to join it. Together the party advanced to meet the Germans, but these, keeping up a fairly heavy shell fire, sheered off slightly south-eastwards and continued their movement. The enemy's strength in tanks still seemed to be about forty. Another enemy tank was knocked out at nearly 2,000 yards range and burst into flames.

Six more guns of the Northumberland Hussars then came into action on the left of the 7th Hussars and engaged the enemy. The 7th and the 30th Corps Protection Squadron moved past them and tried to head the enemy off. But the Germans were going so fast that all the regiment's A.10's could do was to come in on their flank. Then the Northumberland Hussars pulled out and the leapfrog process continued all the afternoon.

When the guns were getting short of ammunition the adjutant (the Duke of Northumberland) went off to try to find B Echelon of the 7th Armoured Brigade. He found a "most helpful sergeant of the 7th Hussars," pulled his truck out of the moving convoy and took it to the guns. Having handed out all his ammunition the sergeant returned with his truck, driving straight through a straggling column of enemy tanks without being touched. If it had not been for this ammunition the Northumberland Hussars could not have continued the action. Major Congreve also managed to find the regimental B Echelon of the 7th Hussars and he brought up more ammunition for the tanks, but by 4 p.m. only two tanks had serviceable guns, so little ammunition was needed.

For thirty miles some part of the force was always in action against the enemy. In the early stages, owing to his speed of movement, he could only be attacked in flank. But at last, at about 4 p.m. he seemed to be split up into several parties and to be well headed off. One party of about twelve German tanks halted to refuel, watched by a troop of Northumberland Hussars, which had been happily placed by Major Benson right across the enemy's line of advance. The rest of the force had leapfrogged a mile or two farther.

Everything which was mobile and had serviceable weapons was now moved two miles or so westwards again, towards the enemy, to support the Northumberland Hussars. This was in fact only two cruisers of the 7th Hussars, two armoured cars, eight Honeys, the two remaining anti-aircraft guns and two cars of the 4th South African Armoured Car Regiment. Before they reached the position however the enemy was again on the move, this time in a north-easterly direction and obliquely across the front of the position. The Northumberland Hussars held their fire and then quickly knocked out two tanks. The enemy halted and opened fire and the guns on the right flank were forced to withdraw. The enemy drew off westwards again, halted out of range, and disappeared from view in the failing light.

* * * *

The party now assembled again on the crocks and took stock of the situation. The American tanks were very low in fuel and the two remaining cruisers of the 7th Hussars only had about twenty miles of petrol. All were short of ammunition. Of the five cruisers only two had guns which could fire and one of these two could not reverse. The Duke of Northumberland went out to look for his regimental transport, which would have provided both petrol and ammunition, but could not find it. This was hardly surprising in the circumstances.

As the party was not very mobile it was decided that it should stay where it was; if an enemy column came within close range in the dark it should be fought. The leaguer was arranged so that soft vehicles—they were very few—were in the middle and the tanks and anti-tank guns on the outside, the five tanks of the regiment being on the western perimeter. The guns of the Northumberland Hussars were on the perimeter, interspersed between the tanks and armoured cars. Any enemy who passed by would be assessed on their merits (strength and distance being the principal factors) and the signal for battle would be given by the brigadier shouting "Fire" from the top of the adjutant's tank.

There was half a moon and visibility was about 200 yards, or three times as much through field glasses. Most people managed to have a bite of food, but there could be no brewing up or smoking and there was no chance for sleep as obviously the area was infested with enemy columns. Soon after dark three of these were observed on the move, as the separated detachments of the 21st Armoured Division converged on Sheferzen. At intervals the enemy put up white lights, much brighter than the British Verey light, and quite unmistakable, presumably for the purpose of being given a bearing by wireless from his destination. By taking the magnetic bearing of each successive light, it was thus quite easy to determine the direction of each enemy column.

One column was obviously passing well clear of the position to the eastward. Another was evidently passing it on the west side, but not missing it by much. The third, some minutes later, was going to bump straight into the leaguer as the bearing of its lights never varied.

The first of these three columns was ignored as it was too far off. At about 8.30 p.m. the second column passed by, missing the leaguer by about 200 yards to the westward. Major Fosdick, the brigade commander and the adjutant went out to look at the tracks and picked up a straggler, described as a "poor specimen," left behind from a lagging tank. This tank moved off, but a few hundred yards farther on it stopped again and metallic hammerings were heard. Lieutenant Murray Smith snatched the tommy gun from Major Fosdick and ran in the direction of the noises, but before he got there the tank moved on again. Then a truck drove up to within 100 yards of the leaguer and a German approached with a tommy gun. He was made prisoner by Captain Williamson of the Northumberland Hussars but the truck drove off into the darkness.

The third enemy column was now very near and fingers were itching on the triggers. Presently it could be seen, headed by half a dozen tanks, on a course which would pass the leaguer at a range of about fifty yards—some said less. The brigadier waited until it drew abreast so that the guns could penetrate the thinner armour of the enemy's flanks. The Germans were just about at the best possible position and apparently suspecting nothing, when they put up one of their periodical lights. As it went up the order to fire was given and immediately every trigger was pressed.

All manner of metal sped through the air and the enemy tanks turned their front plates towards the leaguer. Only one of them was knocked out and the rest stood fast to cover the withdrawal of their soft vehicles. For a few moments the flashes of the guns lit up the little circle of the battle and then the fires of burning vehicles provided a more constant light.

Armour and weight of shell again prevailed. Much damage was done to the enemy's transport as it moved away, but the front plates of his tanks were impenetrable. These stood their ground. They

A German Mark III tank, destroyed by South African airmen, September 1941.

The Enemy.
General Rommel interviewing a captured New Zealand officer, Brigadier George Clifton, D.S.O. Known to his friends as "the buccaneer" because of his outstanding enterprise, Clifton made many attempts to escape and although badly wounded eventually succeeded.

kept up a steady fire which knocked out one of the guns of the Northumberland Hussars, the remaining anti-aircraft gun, whose towing vehicle added to the glow as it burned, and one tank of the 7th Hussars. Trooper Robson was killed and Trooper Brennan, the driver, was wounded.

The 7th Hussars were almost out of ammunition; the Honeys, followed by those guns of the Northumberland Hussars which were on the eastern and southern side of the leaguer drew round to the southwest but did not manage to engage the enemy, whose tanks now began to move forward. As there was nothing to stop them the Brigade Commander ordered the 7th Hussars and Northumberland Hussars to withdraw slowly and rendezvous one mile towards the moon.

The enemy now sent up powerful flares which hung for some time in the air. It was not therefore easy to disengage and there were a number of exciting incidents. Two of the tanks were just drawing away, one towing the other, when Major Benson of the Northumberland Hussars, looking for his truck, ran between them, fell over the tow rope and narrowly escaped being crushed. Squadron Sergeant-Major Marshall, whose tank was knocked out, jumped on to the next tank he saw, where already someone else was standing. "This is a rum go isn't it?" he said, and on getting no reply he saw he was talking to a German. He knocked him out at once, jumped off the tank—a German one—and ran off into the desert. He was picked up next day, thirsty and footsore, but otherwise in good order.

Two more tank crews, those of Lieutenants Fox and Allen, were missing and the regiment was reduced to four tanks. One of these could not reverse, one could steer to the right but not to the left, one could go both forwards and backwards but its turret was jammed and this one was towing the fourth, which was a crock. Lieutenant P. B. Stanley Evans and Sergeant Weaver were also present with their scout cars. The others who reached the rendezvous were one unserviceable tank of brigade headquarters, one South African armoured car, and two guns of the Northumberland Hussars. The rest of the force had vanished.

Petrol was important and in order to obtain replenishment it was decided to make for the wire. One column going north-westwards was passed at a few yards distance and words were exchanged—English and German. To the Germans the tanks doubtless appeared more dangerous than they were and both sides passed on. The wire was reached at B.P. 65, eight miles north of Madelena. Here a detachment of the Royal Air Force was found. They provided petrol and evacuated the two wounded men, who had been travelling on the back of a tank. All then lay down and got an hour or two of shivering sleep, two to a blanket, until dawn.

* * * *

Somewhere among the German armour round Sheferzen was the "A1" Echelon of the 7th Hussars. At this period of the war in the desert, regimental transport was split into three échelons, A1, A2 and B. A1 always accompanied the regiment and included the medical officer's truck and the first re-fill of ammunition. After the 21st November it was to be almost a week before the regiment saw this échelon again, not because A1 was "lost"—it always knew where it was—but because for two days it could find no trace of the regiment and it was then caught up in the withdrawal of the South African transport. In trying to extricate itself A1 went and leaguered in what appeared to be a nice peaceful bit of desert, but was in fact about the middle of the area occupied by a German armoured division.

On the morning of the 21st, as the German tanks advanced on the regiment, Lieutenant M. M. Stanley Evans moved A1 a mile or so to the northward. Here it had a good view of the attack by the 6th Royal Tanks and the Support Group. In the afternoon it replenished the few tanks of the 7th Hussars which remained in the area and then moved southwards, to the west of the German armour, hoping to find the rest of the regiment. Wireless touch had been lost and, as no news could be obtained, A1 leaguered at dusk with some South African gunners near Taieb el Essem.

During the next two days A1 must have been close to the regiment more than once, but without wireless communication it was not easy to make contact among the many thousands of vehicles moving here and there over the immense battlefield. It was still searching hopefully when Rommel made his dash for the frontier on the 24th. Inevitably it was caught up in the rush for the wire and, with the seething mass of transport, passed through one of the gaps. The congestion and confusion were indescribable. Some of the transport was maintaining cohesion and under control in its groups, but many vehicles were just "going spare." In such conditions news was more difficult to get than ever; information was swamped by rumour; rumour took charge.

On passing through, Stanley Evans moved his échelon a few miles northwards up the wire and leaguered. After dark he went in quest of information, with his 15-cwt. truck and Trooper Strickland, and accompanied by Lieutenant John. They went south along the wire, to see what was happening at the gap. About halfway there they passed another truck on the opposite side of the wire and both stopped. After a short and anxious silence a soft voice from the other truck said "I do hope you're not German." The unknown voice had just come from the gap, where confusion still reigned, so the party returned to leaguer.

The next few days were spent in trying to dodge the Germans, who seemed to be everywhere. As each movement merely led to another encounter, the échelon remained halted as much as possible, but always ready to move quickly away from any approaching enemy columns. One night the leaguer just escaped being over-run, as an enemy column passed within 200 yards without apparently spotting it.

Each time the échelon halted in a new place Stanley Evans drove round the area to try to make contact with a British unit. On one occasion he and John saw what they thought was a derelict enemy eight-wheeled armoured car; why they thought it was derelict is not clear. This type of vehicle was still an object of interest and, from sheer curiosity, they said "Let's go and have a look at it." As they approached they were horrified to see the turret turning. The truck swerved round and beat the speed record, pursued and hit by bullets, but without serious damage. When out of range a gunner subaltern complained that he had lost his hat, which had fallen off at the first swerve. However, he declined the offer of the 15-cwt. to go back and retrieve it.

Being at one time not very far from Sidi Omar, Stanley Evans decided that he would try to make contact with the British or Indian troops which were probably still there; he might obtain information and also get some measure of protection. Leaving the transport tucked away in a wadi, he drove to Sidi Omar. He was received with sympathy, but could get no information about the 7th Armoured Brigade and was firmly refused asylum. The area was already over-crowded with transport columns which had had the same idea, and the local commander was concerned about the prospect of air attack.

One thing was obvious—A1 was in the middle of a German armoured formation and unless it moved out it must eventually fall into enemy hands. Stanley Evans determined to move out.

Scarcely had the échelon left the Sidi Omar area when a powerful German column headed by tanks was seen to the right front, and almost immediately another to the left. Before it could turn or manoeuvre A1 found itself in the embarrassing situation of driving westwards in flat open desert between two German armoured columns driving eastwards and neither more than a thousand yards away.

That they did not open fire may have been due to fear of hitting one another with the overs or, more probably, to their singleness of purpose; this was the opening of the attack on the Indians, in which the Germans lost a number of their tanks through the accurate shooting of British gunners.

Eventually news of the regiment was obtained; it was already east of the wire and under orders to return to the delta. The temporary loss of A1 had been only a slight inconvenience. In the absence of Captain Low, other units' medical officers had been available to attend to the wounded; B Echelon had been in contact with the regiment during most of the period and, in view of its depleted condition, had been more than adequate for its needs.

Early on the 25th the headquarters of the 7th Hussars left B.P. 65 and moved a few miles south of army headquarters in order to get in touch with the 7th Armoured Division and receive instructions. These were to go to 62nd Field Maintenance Centre, twenty miles to the north-west. Soon after the march began one of the three remaining tanks broke down. It was sent back on tow to army headquarters, with a dingo and any spare men who had been riding on tanks. Captain Murray Smith, the adjutant, was also sent back to try to find A Echelon. The regiment now consisted of two tanks and a dingo, but two miles farther on Major Fosdick's tank broke a fan chain and had to be left.

So with one tank and one dingo the regiment arrived at 62nd Field Maintenance Centre at about 11 a.m. Here it was joined by two more tanks. The remains of the brigade were then moved to a point about eight miles west of Madelena. All three 7th Hussars tanks were handed in next day, as all were unserviceable. On the 26th Captain Murray Smith, Lieutenant Fox and Lieutenant Calder, the Ordnance Mechanical Engineer, rejoined, bringing fifteen lorries full of supplies. The day was spent trying to account for the many officers and men who were missing.

On the 27th the brigade moved back to railhead, seven miles east of Bir el Telata. Here for two days crews were organized for delivering tanks to the other brigades and personnel who had become detached in the confusion of the last few days, or who had been manning the serviceable tanks sent to the 22nd Armoured Brigade, rejoined.

On the 28th the 7th Hussars were ordered to form a squadron to man Honeys. This was the regiment's first introduction to the American M.3 tank, which was very different in design, construction, armament and handling from anything it had met before. There was little time. The squadron was formed under Captain Pilkington, with

Lieutenants Nickels, Palmer, Barton and Patteson, Squadron Sergeant-Major Lowe and Sergeant Crew. In the afternoon it went to railhead and had four hours of concentrated instruction under American officers and next day it moved off to Army Headquarters and took over its tanks. The squadron was never used in active operations and the personnel rejoined the regiment in Cairo a month later, after doing a good deal of work in clearing the battlefield.

On 29th November orders were received to proceed to Cairo, where the regiment would be re-equipped. Major Fosdick and Captain Murray Smith went off in advance. The road party followed under Major Kevill-Davies and a rail party of 150 under Major Congreve. On the 30th the regiment arrived at Abbassia and went into barracks for the first time for two years. It was an agreeable change and, as always happens when men who have lived in the open suddenly go into barracks, nearly everyone got a cold.

*   *   *   *

Mention has been made of the strategy of the campaign in so far as it influenced the experiences of the 7th Hussars. Tactically there are numerous lessons, but here it is only necessary to relate the opinions of the new Commanding Officer as recorded by him on his return to the delta. His first reference is to "the importance of keeping sufficiently concentrated to maintain numerical superiority in the initial engagement against the enemy's main force." In contrast, he draws attention to the enemy's habit of moving in concentrated masses, more vulnerable perhaps to air attack than troops in very open formation, but infinitely more powerful when the hostile forces meet.

This leads to his second point: "Unless and until we have a tank gun which can equal that on the most modern German tanks opposed to us, 25-pounder support under direct control of regimental commanders is essential. At 2,000 yards over open sights, the 25-pounder is a good anti-tank weapon." The Army Commander when he visited the regiment and F Battery Royal Horse Artillery a few days before the battle, had told the gunners (his old regiment) that he expected them to fire to the muzzle and as long as they destroyed tanks he did not mind losing a few 25-pounders, as these were not difficult to replace. Where the 25-pounders got their chance they took their toll and it was a pity, as Major Fosdick observes, that F Battery could not have moved up in line with the 7th Hussars when they had their fiercest battle on 21st November. But 25-pounders are not very mobile and such a move, carried out when the enemy was advancing at high speed more or less direct for the gun position would have been very hazardous. As the enemy did not penetrate far enough he never came within range of their solid shot on the 21st. A few days later, however, when the 21st Panzer Division attacked the 4th Indian Division on the frontier, one field regiment knocked out seventeen enemy tanks for the loss of four guns.

The shortage of an effective anti-tank gun was indeed a major defect in our army. Probably as a result of the old "all-armoured" idea the conception still prevailed that the proper role of armour was to fight armour while anti-tank guns were principally of value for the protection of infantry in the more static phases of the battle. But in the absence of anti-tank guns British armour, including the 7th Hussars, was used more than once specifically as a screen to protect infantry against enemy armour. In this capacity it was conspicuous, vulnerable and only partially effective. In contrast, the enemy used his tanks, intimately supported by infantry, anti-tank guns and artillery, to penetrate our positions and as soon as he halted he covered his tanks with a screen of infantry and anti-tank guns. Yet such was the belief among our own infantry that tanks were the remedy for tanks and such was their consciousness of lack of anti-tank protection, that they were never happy unless they could actually see their own tanks.

General Gott, in a subsequent lecture on the operations, stressed the shortage of infantry. This was noticeable on many occasions, and conspicuously so during the first four days at Sidi Rezegh. But without adequate anti-tank guns infantry were liable to become only an added responsibility to the armoured forces, as General Norrie realized when he refused the offer of a New Zealand Brigade on 21st November. The real lack was the high velocity gun—both in a tank and on the ground—capable of penetrating the enemy's armour.

There was one further point which gave rise to much comment and some criticism of our equipment among the troops. It was noticeable that when British tanks were hit they more often than not caught fire, whereas German tanks seldom did. For some time it was believed that the Germans were using an incendiary filling in their shells. Apparently this was not the case, however. They used solid shot and a high explosive shell. Some weeks later, as the result of careful investigations, it was established that the fires were caused by splinters breaking up the cartridge cases of the ammunition. The Germans stowed their ammunition in carefully segregated compartments, protected by metal lids. We stowed ours in exposed compartments with no lids and often added a few dozen rounds as a sort of unauthorized but not unapproved reserve, in any part of the tank where space could be found. So a splinter might break through several cartridges and its heat would set light to the scattered cordite, thus completing the destruction of the tank and increasing the casualties.

From the beginning this campaign had its critics and the mistakes, both in pre-war policy in armoured development and on the battlefield, may perhaps be studied by the soldiers of future generations. But from all quarters came nothing but praise for the regimental soldier. It was a very general feeling which was expressed by the Commander of the 30th Corps, Lieutenant-General Norrie, in his report on the operations :—

The Human Element

"There has been no spectacular tank battle, with the whole of the armoured forces of both sides engaged at once. Nevertheless, the enemy's armour has been reduced to a mere skeleton of its former proportions. This has been achieved not by superior weapons or superior armour, for the enemy had better of both. It was the man in the tank and the man behind the weapon that won a succession of smaller combats. Bit by bit, with wonderful gallantry and dogged determination, he wore down and destroyed the enemy forces."

* * * *

When the regiment left the desert the battle of Sidi Rezegh was still in full swing. The New Zealanders had advanced westwards to Belhamed and had joined hands with the 70th Division, but not with the 30th Corps on the left. Then contact with the 70th Division was severed by the enemy, who attacked the New Zealand Division at Belhamed. The New Zealanders were withdrawn southwards and preparations were then made for an attack towards El Adem.

Meanwhile the German armour was still concentrated in the Gambut area and Rommel made one more attempt to reach his frontier detachments, it is believed with convoys of supplies. This failed and he withdrew those of his forces which were still east of Tobruk, through the gap between Sidi Rezegh and the 70th Division. They were harassed as they went, but there was no body of troops sufficiently powerful to stop their escape.

On 4th, 5th and 6th December the Indians attacked the Italians at Bir el Gubi. On the 7th the 7th Armoured Division joined hands with the 70th Division and the enemy was withdrawing by degrees to the Gazala position. All his troops were clear of the perimeter by the 10th. He held Gazala until the 16th and during this period carried out two determined counter attacks against the 4th Indian Division. Then Rommel resumed his withdrawal.

He moved both by the coast road through Benghazi and also across the desert by Mechili, covered by rearguard positions, and held no main position until he reached Agedabia (Jedabiya). He was harassed all the way by mobile troops, and by the remaining tanks, when these were not delayed by petrol difficulties or bad going. By Christmas the army had again occupied Benghazi and advanced elements of the 7th Armoured Division were in contact with the enemy at Agedabia. Once again the opposing forces faced one another near the Tripolitanian frontier.

Cyrenaica had been cleared of the enemy except on the Egyptian frontier, where Bardia and Halfaya held out until January. So the first phase of the plan had been carried out. The second phase—the conquest of Tripolitania—could not at once be undertaken as the losses had been too great and it would take time to build up the force and to make the necessary administrative arrangements. Before this could happen however Rommel had launched his counter-offensive.

*   *   *   *

Among the immediate awards resulting from the battle of Sidi Rezegh were the Distinguished Service Order for Major J. Congreve, Bar to Military Cross for Captain G. W. Murray Smith, M.C., Military Cross for Major N. M. H. Wall and Lieutenants M. Fox, T. R. S. Thornton and M. J. E. Patteson, Distinguished Conduct Medal for Squadron Sergeant-Major W. Marshall, Bar to Military Medal for Sergeant Cowley and Military Medal for Sergeant Austin and Lance-Corporal Glenn.

Of those casualties reported missing, nothing was heard for some time. Most of the officers and tank crews of A Squadron were taken prisoner, including Major Seymour-Evans, Captain R. C. Watson, who died of his wounds in a hospital in Italy a month later, Captain Chichester, Lieutenant MacGill and Squadron Sergeant-Major Wilson.

At Abbassia adjustments were made in the personnel in consequence of the severe casualties. Lieutenant-Colonel F. R. C. Fosdick was confirmed in command. Major R. Younger became Second-in-Command and Captain G. W. Murray Smith, Adjutant. Major N. M. H. Wall accompanied Brigadier Davy back to the desert to the staff of the 30th Corps and the Second-in-Command, Colonel J. H. Anstice, D.S.O., took over the brigade.

Smartening-up parades were held and attention was paid to dress—the last very necessary after so long in the desert. The usefulness of smartening-up parades in wartime has often been called into question, especially by those who have not themselves been closely concerned with men in war. But the value of drill has been recognized from the earliest times. Its effect is not so much physical as mental. It confirms and strengthens the spirit of the regiment and closes the gaps left by the battle casualties.

When, a fortnight after reaching Abbassia, a service of thanksgiving and memorial was held in Cairo Cathedral, the 7th Hussars, as they marched past, were clearly proud of themselves and their achievements, and ready for their next venture, whatever it might be.

PART II — BURMA

CHAPTER VIII

The Third Enemy

Ancient Japan—the new era—neutrality—Pearl Harbour—opening moves—defences of India and Burma—invasion of Burma.

Operation "Crusader" was still in full swing when news came of the Japanese attack on Pearl Harbour. Although the United States were now at war, there were no grounds for complacency about the situation in the Far East, and calls were at once made on the resources of other theatres for help in stemming the tide of Japanese invasion. The first contribution from the Middle East was to be the 7th Armoured Brigade, and Lieutenant-Colonel Fosdick was told of this, confidentially, a few days before Christmas. The precise destination had not been determined and would depend upon the developments of the situation. The brigade was in fact already at sea before the decision was finally taken to send it to Burma.

Of the new enemy little was known. To the British people, Japan had always seemed a long way off and, except in a limited section of the business world, contacts between the British and the Japanese had been rare. The older generation remembered the Russo-Japanese war of 1904/5, but this had passed into obscurity, overshadowed by the more dynamic events of World War I. The middle-aged had vague recollections of an earthquake, and kind English ladies collecting subscriptions to relieve distressed Japanese victims. More widely known were the cheap Japanese goods which had been on the market for some years. They were cheap because of the simple needs and low wages of Japanese workers and they were also damaging to many British industries—to the Lancashire cotton industry in particular.

It was not until the Manchurian incident and the beginning of the war with China in 1932 that the Japanese were forced upon the political consciousness of the world at large. People in Britain were shocked at what seemed to be unprovoked aggression and dismayed at the impotence of the League of Nations. Japan, in her dealings with the League, quickly found that she had in fact several points of common interest with Hitler and Mussolini and it became clear that, in the event of war, she might eventually join her fortunes with theirs. But there were many conflicting factors and opinions among her people and for two years after the outbreak of the war in Europe she maintained a nominal neutrality. The reasons why she took her disastrous decision and why her military operations were besmirched with acts of apparently wanton barbarity, which even the short-memoried British will be long in forgiving, can be traced from her early history, but would require a volume in themselves. Here it is only possible to give a bare outline of the forces by which she was impelled; ancient mysticism, touched but never uprooted by imported religions; a disciplined and often harsh feudal system which in theory had been superseded by a constitution adapted from the European pattern, but of which the warlike spirit remained; a stark realism born of economic necessity; and finally an underlying resentment against the white races which had never quite learnt to conceal their disdain for the yellow.

The primitive beliefs of the Japanese were in the divine origin of their race and the divine descent of the emperor from the sun-goddess; consequently the emperor could do no wrong. When Buddhism was introduced from China, the native cult came to be known as Shinto—the way of the gods—to distinguish it from the way of Buddha. Shinto was merged with, rather than replaced by, Buddhism and when, in the middle of the nineteenth century, Japan came out of her isolation, it recovered its place as a sort of national religion, governing the manners and behaviour of the people.

Side by side with Shinto ran a social system which glorified the carrying of the sword, and even its use. The samurai—the warrior class—were in a stratum of their own, far removed from the rest of the population. They were forbidden to work at anything except the perfection of martial skill and the cultivation of the associated virtues of courage, stoicism, frugality and loyalty to their superiors and to their family. Their self-discipline often reached the point where they were able to commit suicide by a revolting process of disembowelling, an act which was practised by the samurai both as the normal method of self-execution for a delinquent and as a polite form of protest for the shortcomings of others. The rest of the population were considered of little account. At the bottom of the scale were the merchants, and only a little higher were the agricultural community and the artisans.

Under a social system of this kind it is perhaps hardly surprising that the early history of Japan—since records began in the eighth century A.D.—is little more than a story of wars between feudal chiefs, each of whom had his own body of warriors. There was little contact with the outside world except desultory trade with China and Korea, which led to one or two military expeditions. Attempts to attack Japan were made only twice, by the Mongols, and both times they were driven back. With the West there was no contact at all until the sixteenth century, when the accidental "discovery" of Japan by the Portuguese led to nearly a century of commercial and religious contact with Europeans.

The Portuguese made their trading conditional upon the free movement and speech of the Jesuits they brought with them. British and Dutch traders arrived soon afterwards; these too were Christians, but obviously at loggerheads with the Portuguese.

The Christian religion was at first regarded by the Buddhists with dignified tolerance and even respect. A number of Japanese were converted by the Jesuits, including some of the chieftains—although in their case the encouragement of trade probably weighed more heavily than spiritual conviction. But before long news of the savage tortures inflicted by Christians upon one another in the name of religion, and squabbles between Christian sects in Japanese ports over apparently trivial differences of doctrine, alarmed the Japanese. After nearly a century of contact with the militant Christian races, they decided to drive them out and to cut themselves off entirely from the outer world.

It was decreed that Europeans, with the sole exception of a carefully controlled handful of Dutchmen, should leave the country, that all Japanese Christians should revert to Buddhism, that no Japanese should leave Japan, that none who had left should return, and that no ship should be built capable of leaving island waters. The penalty for infringement of these decrees was death. Very few Europeans were executed, but a considerable number of Japanese. In general, however, the order was obeyed, because punishment in Japan was carefully devised as a deterrent and executions were of fiendish barbarity; it must be admitted however that they were no more outrageous than those in fashion in contemporary Europe. Within twenty years Christianity was almost, though not quite, eliminated—and so was foreign trade.

Japan now lapsed into two centuries of self-imposed isolation, during which she had peace, but not prosperity. For many reasons, among them the redistribution of wealth, the introduction of coinage as currency instead of rice, and the enforced indolence of the samurai, the country fell into a state of economic stagnation. By the end of the eighteenth century starvation among the peasants was so acute that the population had to be kept down by infanticide—a practise which was not regarded as a crime. In contrast with this widespread poverty was the recently acquired wealth of a few of the merchants; this gave them a standing which the samurai could resent but could not resist.

In between these extremes were the useless samurai and the unused artisans. The country was not in fact lacking in arts or in potential industrial capacity, but it had reached a point where its circulation could be restored only by the resumption of foreign intercourse. Raw materials must be imported and there must be an outlet for manufactured goods. Although these facts were widely realized among the Japanese themselves, isolationism persisted to the middle of the nineteenth century, and it was only when pressure came from without, to meet the pent up forces within, that Japan was able to emerge into the modern world.

* * * *

In 1853 an American naval squadron arrived in Japanese waters, seeking to arrange for trading facilities. There was no religious condition attached and there were no Jesuits, but, as several similar approaches in the previous few years had been rejected, argument was reinforced by modern warships. Soon afterwards a British squadron arrived on a similar mission, and persuasion was backed up by bombardment. Japan opened her doors.

The next few years saw rapid changes. European and American ideas were hastily assimilated, western methods of administration were imitated, western culture was studied. Selected individuals were sent on courses of study and education, instructors were sent from Europe to Japan. The thirst for knowledge was intense and the world was eager to help. Among the models for imitation were the German legal system, the French and then the German army, the British navy. The speed with which modern methods were adopted was a surprise to everyone and the world powers smiled indulgently at the progress of the new pupil. In half a century transformation into a modern state seemed, on the surface, complete. But side by side with this material evolution an internal process was taking place, which was in some measure responsible for the sequence of events which led to the collapse of the whole structure. In 1868 Shinto was restored to its position as the state religion; but it was more than this, as it provided also the unseen backbone for the modern constitution; the emperor was once again placed at the pinnacle of the state, secluded, infallible.

The new Japan's first trials of strength came with China in 1895 and Russia in 1904. In both ventures she was highly successful and her armed forces, raised on a conscript system, proved that military prowess was characteristic of the race and not merely of the old warrior class. On both occasions her territorial ambitions were curbed by the intervention of the Western powers, who realized with growing anxiety that Japan's latest exploits had placed her on an equal footing with themselves. With Great Britain she signed a treaty in 1902. In 1914 she honoured her obligations by entering the war on the Allies' side, and played a small though effective part in eliminating the German garrisons in China and the Pacific.

At the end of World War I Japan held firmly to her treaty with Great Britain. It was perhaps unfortunate for her and for others when, in deference to American opinion and on the theoretical assumption that offensive and defensive treaties were redundant among members of the League of Nations, the treaty was abrogated. If the league had been a living reality, with power to keep the peace, this would not have mattered. The treaty however had forged a close and personal link between the Japanese and a truly democratic western people and it had exerted a restraining influence on the ambitions of the young state. Its sudden removal and the change from the personal sympathy of one friendly country to the impersonal and often chilly relationships of the league, came at an unfortunate time, when the spirit of expansion was already manifest in Japan and restraint was most needed.

In the new and prosperous Japan the birthrate had risen so quickly that the islands could scarcely support the population; covetous eyes were cast upon the vast and sparsely populated areas of Manchuria and Australia, and the rich but undeveloped islands of the East Indies, almost all under European domination. Oil and raw materials for the principal industries, such as cotton, had to be imported, which was a serious economic and strategical weakness. The ending of the Anglo-Japanese treaty seemed to accentuate the dangers and the government of the day lost much of its popularity. But this was not all. By the terms of the Washington Treaty of 1922, a restriction was imposed on Japanese naval strength. Both these events were regarded by the people as failures on the part of their government—therefore they must have been against the will of the emperor—and of course of the gods.

As the popularity of the government declined, that of the military authorities rose in proportion. It was they who inspired the occupation of Manchuria and the operations against the eastern Chinese provinces in 1932, and it is generally accepted that they began hostilities without the instructions of their government. The tide of militarism was rising in Japan and the world was alarmed. But the League of Nations was already effete and a few protests evoked nothing but contempt.

Japan now sought friendships among nations whose interests were more akin to her own, and to whom, incidentally, she had shown how easy was the way of the aggressor. In 1936 she signed the Anti-Comintern Pact with Germany and Italy. This gave her some measure of guarantee against Russia, whom she regarded as her most dangerous neighbour, and in this added security she set her course firmly for the elimination of European influence in the Far East. This time however the underlying objects were not retirement and seclusion, but imperial expansion and the domination of eastern Asia and the Pacific.

*   *   *   *

As the storm gathered over the world, there were tremors of anxiety among certain classes and individuals in Japan. The business community in particular viewed with concern the possibility of a breach with the United States and the western powers. Even after hostilities in Europe had begun, there were occasional setbacks to the headstrong. The first of these was the discovery of Hitler's pact with Stalin over the partition of Poland. Momentarily the reputation of those who had negotiated and applauded the Anti-Comintern Pact was tarnished, and for a time Japanese foreign policy seemed to mellow. On the collapse of France she did not, like Mussolini, join in to devour the carcase, but at first merely started negotiations with the Vichy government for the use of air bases in Indo-China.

The second cause for hesitation was Hitler's prolonged delay in launching his promised invasion of England. As time wore on it seemed to some that, if the British had managed to establish a solid defensive system in the air and on the land, they might be able to spare a fair proportion of their fleet for use in the Pacific; the combined British and American fleets would be a formidable obstacle to Japanese designs, in all of which sea power was of paramount importance.

But the voice of caution was muffled in discussion, largely because of a peculiarity—it has been called a flaw—in the constitution. The appointments of Minister of War and Minister of Marine could only be held by serving members of their respective services and no cabinet decision was valid without the approval of these two. As no general or admiral would approve a measure not acceptable to his service, and as nobody would be found willing to replace him if, on a matter of principle, he should resign, the services had virtual control of Japanese policy in all its aspects. The military faction gradually recovered its confidence; forces of occupation were sent to Indo-China, and Japan thereby entered the final phase of her conflict with democracy. This sealed the fate of an era in her history, begun less than a century before, and destined to end four years later under the first and fearful impact of atomic bombs.

In July 1941, following the occupation of Indo-China, the United States, Great Britain and the Netherlands government in London imposed economic sanctions. The most important commodity affected by the restrictions was oil, for which Japan depended entirely on imports, largely from the United States. She was faced with two alternatives, either to reach agreement with the United States or to go to war before her limited oil reserves ran out. Counsels were still divided, but on the whole the imposition of sanctions hardened opinion somewhat in favour of the Axis. In September 1941 the Tripartite Pact was signed with Germany and Italy, by which Japan undertook to join the Axis if the United States should come into the war on the British side.

The United States were in no mood for conciliation. They insisted that, before sanctions were removed, all Japanese forces should be withdrawn from China and Indo-China. The occupation of the latter was a direct threat to the Burma road, by which lease-lend equipment and supplies had been and still were reaching China, to aid Marshal Chiang Kai Shek in his resistance. Discussions were prolonged into the early winter of 1941, but in the last few weeks were devoid of reality, for Japan had already taken the decision. On 22nd November, four days before the final meeting at which Japanese counter-proposals were to be discussed, the carrier fleet was assembled in the Kurile Islands, and all was ready for the opening blow against the American fleet in Pearl Harbour. The date had already been fixed for 7th December, and although the attack could have been called off by wireless, there is no convincing evidence of any intention to do so, whatever turn the talks might have taken.

During these troubled months British opinion was solidly with the United States. There were nevertheless doubts and anxieties. Although Great Britain had announced that if Japan attacked the United States, she would at once declare war on Japan, no reciprocal utterance had come from across the Atlantic; not quite a high enough proportion of the people of the United States had yet come to realize the degree of the threat to their freedom. So there still lurked in the background the danger that Japan's entry into the war might be in a manner calculated not to provoke American action. In such circumstances nothing could be done to save Malaya, the Dutch East Indies and perhaps Burma; India would be in danger and even Australia and New Zealand would be threatened. The safety of all these depended upon United States intervention and upon her fleet remaining, in naval language, "in being."

*   *   *   *

On 6th December 1941 a large force of Japanese transports was seen moving from Indo-China across the Gulf of Siam in the direction of Malaya. There was no sign of any threat to American territory.

Late at night on the 7th Mr. Churchill received a telephone call from President Roosevelt; the United States battle-fleet lay shattered on the bed of its anchorage in Pearl Harbour.

*   *   *   *

At once all fears about America's attitude were dispelled. But although the United States were now with the Allies in every sense, and splendidly angry, one of their great assets had been wiped out in the first two hours. Another naval disaster followed; on 10th December Japanese aircraft sank the British battleship *Prince of Wales* and the battle cruiser *Repulse*. The enemy now had almost undisputed control of the Pacific and could bring overwhelming strength against any British or allied force which should venture out from its base.

It was at once apparent that the period which would elapse before the Allies could seek their revenge would be measured in years, rather than months. Hopes were at first concentrated on the degree of delay which could be imposed by the remote garrisons in the Far East, many of them already cut off from any possibility of supply or support. United States aid to Britain, Russia and China would have to be adjusted in relation to her own needs as a belligerent, and no major offensive could be undertaken until the necessary naval strength had been built up. Moreover priorities had to be determined between the two principal theatres of war, and for a number of reasons the European theatre was put first. So the course of the war in the Far East was to be a hard one for the British, the Americans, the Dutch and the Chinese, and the enemy scored one success after another with amazing rapidity.

Within a few hours of the attack on Pearl Harbour Japanese troops landed in Malaya and aircraft attacked Singapore and Hong Kong. On the 8th Great Britain and the Netherlands government in London declared war. On the same day Japanese aircraft bombed the United States naval base in the Philippines and two days later troops were landed; on the 21st the main forces were landed and began the systematic occupation of the islands, against stout but diminishing resistance.

The landings in Malaya were accompanied by destructive attacks on the British airfields. By the 12th the advancing enemy was being engaged in northern Malaya by the better part of an Indian division, but was still making progress. On the 17th Penang was captured and by Christmas there was already anxiety for Singapore, where reinforcements were still being thrown in. In the middle of December Borneo was invaded and on Christmas Day Hong Kong fell after a gallant and determined defence. Siam was invaded on 8th December and her token resistance died in twenty-four hours; by Christmas the enemy's hold on the country was established and his advanced elements were on the frontiers of Burma. The latter was now threatened by sea also, as there were only light naval forces—soon to be seriously depleted in the battle of the Java Sea—and a few well handled Dutch submarines, to oppose a seaborne expedition against the Burma coast.

Such was the measure of advantage enjoyed by the aggressor. Throughout the years of doubt and discussion the Japanese had pressed their military planning and preparations with unrelenting vigour. They were able to adapt their vast war machine, much of it already experienced in China, to the new task, to plan in detail every one of the numerous operations which together made up one of the largest and swiftest land-grabs in history, and to train selected units and formations for the particular country in which they would be used.

For jungle training Formosa had unsurpassed facilities, as well as providing perfect security against leakage of information. Successive divisions from China were trained there for use in Burma. They were given the most suitable equipment—and not too much of it—and they became experts at moving through hilly jungle both by day and night. Each man carried a bag of rice—nominally his rations for five days, but often eked out much longer. He was told to make his ammunition last, so he seldom fired except at a visible target. Replenishment in battle was therefore almost non-existent and maintenance was carried out every few days by porters and pack transport; this was supplemented in occupied territories by captured mechanical transport, in so far as roads would permit. There was no medical service to speak of and the Japanese took almost as little account of their own wounded as they did of the British—which was nil. They made full use of anything they captured and had no fear of being shot if taken in enemy uniform as, if captured, they would hope to be shot in any case.

Discipline was rigorous and primitive, non-commissioned officers having the right to inflict summary corporal punishment. Relationships between officers and men and even among officers themselves, were formal and lacking in humanity. Much of the disciplinary system had come down from the German teaching at the end of the

19th century, but some of it was inherently Japanese. Every man was first and foremost a fighting man, including those at the base; there were few non-combatants as other armies have known them. And the individual officer and man seemed able to endure unlimited discomfort and privations and to fight without respite for days on end. Under the harsh discipline of his superiors and the constant inculcation of samurai virtues, the Japanese soldier became a fanatic; to grumble was unpardonable, to be captured was unthinkable, and to die was the only alternative to success.

* * * *

In contrast with the prolonged and detailed planning of the Japanese, almost no counter-preparation had been made by the authorities in India and Burma. So long as the United States had had a fleet in the Pacific as a counter-weight, to discourage any offensive intentions Japan might have in south-eastern Asia, Burma and India had seemed fairly safe. A British naval force based on Singapore was a further deterrent to attack by sea. An overland approach seemed equally improbable, and even if Siam conceded the use of air bases and of her indifferent communications, the rugged frontier region was a formidable barrier to the movement of a modern army.

If Burma was free from danger, India was doubly so, for Burma itself was a natural bulwark against invasion from the east. All the principal physical features run north and south, each river and each range of hills forming an obstacle. In the north of Burma, largely for political reasons, no effort had been made to improve communications with India and the only contact was by jungle paths, on foot. In the circumstances it is hardly surprising that India should have turned her attention to the West rather than the East. From the outbreak of war her whole effort was concentrated on providing and maintaining large contingents of Indian troops in east Africa and the Middle East.

For Burma the problem was somewhat different. Unlike India, she had no martial races on which to draw for her military forces; on the contrary, she had to rely on India to provide men for her own internal security units. Even in peace time her defensive arrangements were scanty and when war broke out she had no means of improving them except from outside sources or by the expansion of the Burman units. The new Burma Army was formed in 1937, when the country was separated politically from India. In 1939 there were four battalions of infantry; a further four were raised after the outbreak of war. It takes years to train a Burman to become a soldier and it was never really expected that these troops would stand up to a first-class modern enemy. There were also six battalions of the Burma Frontier Force. These consisted of a number of detachments spread over hundreds of miles along the frontier, trained not as soldiers but as gendarmerie, for keeping order among the frontier tribes. The men were of the best Indian fighting races but there were only three British officers in each battalion and the training and environment of the detachments did not suit them for moulding into fighting units at a moment's notice. In December 1941 there were also two British infantry battalions and two Indian infantry brigades, the latter mainly consisting of young soldiers.

As a result of the new threat, on 10th January 1942 the headquarters of the 17th Indian Division and another infantry brigade arrived from India. Like other Indian troops, this headquarters and the brigade had been trained for desert warfare, and wide open spaces had been sought as training areas. Conditions in the jungle were entirely strange and transport was wheeled. This was a great disadvantage in a country where, until the large-scale development of air supply, pack or porter transport alone could enable troops to operate away from the sparse network of roads. Only a few old soldiers had seen active service, and that had been in the very different conditions of the North-West frontier; and two of the brigades eventually brought under this headquarters were strangers to the divisional commander and staff. Finally, none of the higher commanders or staffs in Burma had had experience in working together. The headquarters of the Burma Army had been improvised in the emergency and were required to come into action at once, themselves unpractised and with forces of little experience, unsuitably trained, short of much equipment which was needed and encumbered with some which was not.

When hostilities began, the situation of the air force was even worse than that of the army. The R.A.F. had one fighter squadron of old Brewster Buffaloes. The single bomber squadron had no aircraft, as its Blenheims were in Malaya. There was no adequate warning system against air attack, and no warning system at all once Rangoon was evacuated. Only the providential presence in Burma of part of the American Volunteer Air Force (raised for operations with Marshal Chiang-Kai-Shek and on its way to China) saved the British troops from complete Japanese domination of the air—and that was only for the first few weeks. After the enemy attack on Magwe aerodrome on 21st March, all aircraft and personnel were withdrawn to China and later to India; from that time onwards Japanese control of the air was undisputed. The moral and material results, above all on the civilian services and the main towns and communications, were devastating. The effect on the military operations was hardly less serious; the Japanese commanders had all the advantages of unhindered air reconnaissance, which was entirely denied to the Allies; troops in the forward area were under constant air attack during daylight hours, or, which is almost as demoralizing, under the threat of it; and perhaps most depressing of all was the fact that no British aircraft were ever seen; this, as the campaign wore on, added to the feeling of isolation already engendered by disappointment when an Australian division failed to arrive, and by the lack of mail from home.

The absence of air reconnaissance would have mattered less if there had been alternative methods of obtaining information. There was however no intelligence organization and there were no means either of feeling the political pulse of the population or of obtaining news of enemy movements. The lack of intelligence from across the frontier was due partly to the fear of irritating an outwardly friendly neighbour and partly to motives of economy. The lack of internal information was due to nothing but peace-time parsimony. The tactical effect on military operations will be apparent on every page of the story and requires no emphasis. The political effect may have been less obvious at the time, but the fog of uncertainty was demoralizing for the troops and a constant anxiety to the commanders.

The mixed population of Burma was not only a problem in itself, but a problem which was by no means fully understood, and the attitude of the inhabitants to the invaders was a matter largely for speculation. Of a total population of fourteen millions, about one million were Indians, who provided the most stable element in the business and administrative spheres. They were unpopular with the Burmans and were probably wise in deciding to flee the country, judging that otherwise they would be murdered. Of the rest, the true Burmans were perhaps the least reliable of all, and they deserted wholesale, with the single exception of those in the army signal units. Some of the races however were remarkable for their loyalty, notably the Chins, Karens and Kachins. There were many desertions, especially among those whose homes were farthest away from the Indian frontier, but there were few established cases of these races actively helping the enemy.

There was undoubtedly widespread disaffection, created by Japanese propaganda and only gradually dispelled by closer acquaintance with the Japanese forces of occupation. A number of Burmans were used as spies and guides and some were given weapons and organized as units, or incorporated into Japanese formations. Disaffection may also have been partly the cause of the rapid and wholesale disintegration of the civil administration, although apathy and fear, among people long accustomed to a life of idleness and peace, were probably responsible to an equal degree. Without an information service it was impossible to foresee the extent of the breakdown or to assess the size and scope of the subversive movement; consequently no preparatory steps had been taken to deal with these difficulties when they arose.

Finally a word must be said about the climate and geography of Burma, as these played an important part in the planning and conduct of military operations.

The climate has two main phases, the monsoon, which lasts from May to about the end of August, and the dry season, which is the rest of the year. By February it is beginning to get hot, although the nights are seldom oppressive. The river valleys and the ricefields are hard, dry and parched. But there is no shortage of water, and wells are to be found in every village.

A comparatively dry belt, with a rainfall similar to that of London, runs from east of the Chindwin to the plains around Meiktilla. But to the west of this, from the hills of Assam to Southern Burma, the rains which break in May, turn the country into a sea of mud and water. There is a constant and depressing drip from every leaf and twig of the jungle, and mildew settles on the boots and equipment in a night. Everything becomes damp and soggy, including the spirits.

Geographically Burma is a country of wide variety. Stretching four hundred miles down the coast of the Malayan Peninsula is Tenasserim, a strip thirty to sixty miles wide, a tangle of jungle-covered hills bordered on the east by Siam. Burma proper begins with the delta of the Irrawaddy, a flat, sparsely populated region, where movement is almost entirely by boat along the numerous creeks. The villages are of bamboo huts, raised on piles to keep them above the level of the floods in the monsoon season.

North of the delta the country is divided roughly into six strips, three belts of hill country alternating with three river valleys. On the west, rising out of the Bay of Bengal, are the Arakan Hills. These are densely wooded and the few tracks across them are fit only for pack transport. The rainfall is very heavy, especially in the north near the Indian frontier. The Arakan Hills fall gradually to the valley of the Irrawaddy, which is more open and, in places, park-like. The valley is about thirty to fifty miles wide and dotted with villages of a few hundred inhabitants, generally a cluster of bamboo huts, with a Buddhist temple and a well, in a clump of trees. There is scarcely anything deserving the name of a town, although bazaars have grown up in the neighbourhood of the European settlements and the larger centres of habitation have enormous pagodas. To the east of the Irrawaddy are the Pegu Hills, much like the Arakan Hills and equally impassable, but not quite so high. The Pegu Hills fall away to the Sittang Valley, east of which are the Karenni and Salween Hills and finally the rugged Salween Valley, almost on the borders of Siam.

Communications generally follow the river valleys. In 1942 there was no entry into Burma except through the port of Rangoon, or by the one road from China; elsewhere the frontiers could be crossed only on foot or with pack transport over the roughest of mountain paths. From Rangoon northwards the Irrawaddy and its navigable tributary, the Chindwin, have always been the principal means of communication of the country and for commercial traffic they still are. In the Irrawaddy Valley therefore the railway only runs 180 miles from Rangoon, and stops at Prome. The principal railway of the country runs through Pegu, up the Sittang Valley, through Pyinmana and Mandalay, across the Irrawaddy at the Ava bridge and up the valley to Myitkyina. Three branches run off on the east side, one down the Tennasserim strip, one to Taunggyi and the third to Lashio, and three on the west side, to Kyaukpadaung, to Myingyan and through Monywa to Ye-U.

The road north from Rangoon splits at Taukkyan, whence one route leads up the Irrawaddy Valley on the east bank of the river, the other through Pegu and up the west bank of the Sittang. From where they divide, which is only fifteen miles north of Rangoon, there is no connecting road fit for vehicles for 250 miles; the few tracks through the intervening Pegu Hills are generally overgrown with jungle.

South of Mandalay there is a fairly extensive network of roads in the triangle formed with Meiktilla and Yenangyaung. Parts of the Shan states also have reasonably good road systems, but these have very few links with the roads elsewhere. From Mandalay the road to China follows the railway to Lashio and thence winds its way northeastwards to the frontier. At Sagaing, ten miles below Mandalay, the Irrawaddy is crossed by the Ara bridge, and there is a road north through Shwebo, and another from Shwebo through Ye-U to Monywa on the Chindwin. From Ye-U to the Indian frontier, more than 100 miles as the crow flies, there were merely jungle tracks through the hills; this inhospitable region was soon to witness the depths of human misery as the thousands of refugees struggled against hunger, thirst, malaria, dysentery, cholera and exhaustion in their attempts—too often vain—to reach the sanctuary of India.

* * * *

The opening act of the invasion of Burma took place in early January, when a party of Japanese occupied Victoria Point in the extreme south of the Tennasserim strip. In the first skirmishes with detachments of the Frontier Force the invaders at once showed their skill in jungle fighting and the isolated frontier posts fell one after the other. The first large engagement, between the 16th Indian Infantry Brigade and an enemy force estimated at a thousand men, began at Kawkareik on the 20th. So that it should not be cut off, the brigade was ordered back to Moulmein, and began its withdrawal on the 22nd. There now occurred the first misfortune of this unlucky phase of the campaign; owing to the sinking of a ferry boat, the brigade had to abandon all its mechanical transport and much of its animal transport; in consequence it lost some of its weapons and most of its signal equipment.

On the 25th the 46th Indian Infantry Brigade was moved up to Bilin; this brigade had only arrived in the country on the 16th, its transport did not arrive until the 30th and it was not fully trained. On the 30th Moulmein was attacked. Next day the force at Moulmein was evacuated by sea and the whole of 17th Indian Division, except a few parties of stragglers, was then west of the Salween River.

On 3rd February the 48th Indian Infantry Brigade, which had arrived in Burma on 31st January, also partly trained and without transport, was moved forward to Bilin. It was hoped that the division would manage to hold the line of the Salween. But on 11th February the Japanese crossed the river in two places and cut off one Indian battalion. The front was very extended, the situation obscure and on the 15th the division began withdrawing to the Bilin River. At the same time a few units of the Burma Division were moved down from the north as far as Nyaunglebin, so as to ensure an effective watch, and it was hoped also defence, of the Sittang River; this was the last great natural obstacle protecting Rangoon. In addition, a small force was formed at Pegu, as an insurance against a Japanese landing on the west bank of the lower reaches of the river.

For a time the situation seemed to be stabilized. But the lull did not last long. On 18th February the Japanese attacked the Bilin position, forced a crossing of the river and outflanked the position on the right. They were thought to be bringing up larger forces to deliver a serious attack, and the British and Indian troops were now very tired. Accordingly a withdrawal was ordered to the strong position on the Sittang.

The only crossing of the lower Sittang was the railway bridge at Mokpalin, which had been decked in so as to take road traffic. For 100 miles above this there was nothing but an occasional ferry; and one extra ferry, capable of carrying lorries and guns, had just been improvised close to the railway bridge. A bridgehead position was established so as to prevent the crossings being rushed by Japanese from the jungle, and was held by one company of British infantry, one Indian and one Burman battalion.

On 20th February, after three days of close fighting on the Bilin, the withdrawal to the Sittang began.

Such, briefly, was the military situation in Burma as the convoy carrying the 7th Armoured Brigade crossed the Bay of Bengal on the last stage of its journey from Egypt. The campaign which followed was of unusual pattern; most of those who took part claimed to have withdrawn to India and a few to have advanced there. The base, Rangoon, fell to the enemy early in the proceedings and thereafter the force subsisted on stores which had been hurriedly transferred from Rangoon and dumped at convenient spots on the route to the north. For the greater part of the campaign the troops fought mainly facing their previous base and sometimes, when their movement was blocked by the enemy, facing India. At no time was there a feeling of security, because the enemy's habit of penetrating the jungle might bring him into anybody's camp without notice, and the attitude of the local inhabitants was at the best doubtful. Added to the uncertainty was the strange, often hot, dark and damp atmosphere of the jungle itself. The combination produced a neurotic condition known as "jungle-happiness," which was prevalent both among the European and the Asiatic troops before India was reached, especially among those with no previous experience of battle. That the army reached India with the British and Indian units still more or less intact, although short of nearly everything except their personal weapons, was a remarkable achievement by the leaders concerned, their improvised staffs and the troops themselves, inexperienced as most of them were. The part played by the 7th Armoured Brigade is summarized by Lord Wavell in his report:—

"Particular mention should be made of the 7 Armoured Brigade under Brigadier J. H. Anstice (7 Hussars, 2 Royal Tank Regiment, 414 Battery (Essex Yeomanry) R.H.A., A Battery 95 Anti-Tank Regiment), who, from their arrival in Burma in the third week of February till the end of the campaign, formed the mainstay of the Burma Army, and kept up a very high standard of morale and efficiency."

CHAPTER IX

Southern Burma

Embarkation—the voyage—arrival at Rangoon—the Sittang disaster—first operations round Pegu—threat to Rangoon—Pegu again—fighting on 6th March—Pegu road block—evacuation of Rangoon—rest at Tharrawaddy.

Maps VIII, IX

In Egypt the New Year found the 7th Hussars still without tanks, doing guard duties round Cairo and Heliopolis. But the brief period of comparative luxury in barracks was coming to an end; on 3rd January orders came to move to Tahag and the move took place on the 5th.

Tahag lies in the eastern desert, not far from Tel el Kebir, and in close proximity to the base depots and workshops set up specially to deal with American tanks. The camp was isolated and dusty, the weather cold, sandstorms frequent and conditions generally austere after the month at Abbassia. Tanks and trucks began to arrive at once, the tanks being the General Stuart or "Honey" with which the 4th Armoured Brigade had been equipped in the desert. With the exception of the scratch squadron under Captain Pilkington, which had suddenly been thrust into Honeys at the end of November, the regiment had no experience of these American light tanks. Training was therefore intensive and shooting on the ranges with the 37-millimetre gun was carried out every day. Time was short, as embarkation was due to start on the 22nd.

On the 20th General Gott visited the brigade. He presented ribbons to those whose awards had recently been announced and then gave a lecture on operation "Crusader." This was the last the regiment was to see of its former divisional commander, for a few months later he was killed, when he had just been designated commander of the Eighth Army, and the slow and elderly aircraft in which he was returning from the desert to Cairo was shot down. From the earliest days in the desert, when he had passed from the 1st Battalion of the 60th to command of the Support Group, the regiment had known and admired the large, genial figure who was to be seen driving everywhere in an open cut-down car. No crisis ever seemed to disturb his equanimity or to suppress the smile which revealed the happiness of his nature and endeared him to all those who served with him.

For the 7th Hussars the move from Egypt was something more than a move from one theatre of war to another. Egypt had been the regiment's peace station for four years before the outbreak of war and a number of the original officers and men still had ties in the country. Nevertheless it was for most a pleasant prospect to be going somewhere new, away from the desert, with its long periods of dusty monotony.

The regiment had a fine record of achievement in the Middle East. First it had been one of the most irritating thorns in the flesh of the Italian garrisons of Capuzzo and the frontier. Then it had played its part in the offensive which opened at Sidi Barrani and ended with the destruction of the remnants of Marshal Graziani's army at Beda Fomm. Finally it had met something like the equivalent of a German armoured division almost single handed and had done its job—despite heavy losses—in holding the Sidi Rezegh area. So now it left for a new theatre with gaps in its ranks but in good spirits and with a splendid reputation which its next campaign was destined further to enhance.

On the 22nd the transport vehicles left for Suez to be loaded in M.T. ships, followed two days later by the tanks. On the night of the 26th the regiment entrained for Suez and arrived there the following morning. After a brief stay in a disagreeable transit camp it embarked in the *Ascanius* of the Blue Funnel Line. Colonel and Mrs. Fielden, Brigadier Hewer, Mrs. Younger and Mrs. Murray Smith came down to see the regiment off. The arrival of the ladies caused momentary concern to the ship's staff, but it was quickly explained that they were not expecting to travel. Mrs. Fielden was as usual laden with gifts and "comforts" such as books and games. From the earliest times she had been tireless in organizing welfare and as a token of very genuine appreciation of the efforts of Colonel Fielden, who was later to be appointed Colonel of the regiment, and herself, the warrant officers, N.C.O.'s and men now presented them with a silver salver.

On 28th January the *Ascanius* sailed.

*　　*　　*　　*

On the first day out from Suez, as the rugged and forbidding mountains of Sinai faded from view, the officers and the ship's company were busy organizing the usual safety arrangements and anti-boredom activities. Not many had had the experience of travelling as a unit; it was far pleasanter to be one of a family party instead of a mere name and number in a reluctant draft. There were the same boat-station drills and the captain was just as particular as all captains about cleanliness in the mess decks and wash places. For the first few hours of the morning—which began early enough, as the crew sluiced down the decks—everyone's chief concern was scrubbing and rubbing things, and the standard was high. A little individual training was possible and every day there was a lecture of some kind on a more or less military subject. The padré organized the entertainments and himself acquired more than one black eye in the boxing ring. Visits to the engine and boiler rooms were permitted, one troop at a time, and nobody doubted that the hottest day in a tank in the desert was better than the boiler room of the *Ascanius* in the Red Sea.

There was plenty of time for letter writing and a large mail was ready for despatch at Aden but, much to everyone's surprise, the ship only stayed at anchor there for a few hours and then sailed on without making any contact with the shore. The weather grew hotter and hotter and at night, as a precaution against submarines, the deadlights had to be shut; so the atmosphere below was exceedingly stuffy. There were, of course, complaints about the food, but these were few and where more than two persons feed together the absence of criticism would be unnatural. On the whole the voyage was a peaceful relaxation and there were many who enjoyed it as such, in anticipation of a rather bleak and uncertain future.

The first indication of the destination—a wrong one—came the day after leaving Aden; maps of Singapore and Sumatra were issued to the officers. Some wondered afterwards whether it was hoped that maps left about in cabins or careless talk in Colombo might lead to the leakage of false information; but no such subterfuge had been devised. Originally General Wavell had intended that the brigade should be used in Malaya, and it was only on 6th February, when the situation there was beyond redemption and he had been to the front in Burma, that he decided that it should be diverted to Rangoon.

The approach to Ceylon was in daylight. The luscious green and blue of the hills and the dense growth of palm trees right down to the water's edge were a restful contrast with the barren beaches of Africa and Aden. The country looked fertile, prosperous and peaceful. But the realities of war soon re-asserted themselves when the *Ascanius* dropped anchor in Colombo harbour. Nearby were the liner *Empress of Japan*, in which wives and families had just been evacuated from Singapore, and two damaged cruisers, the British *Glasgow* and the United States *Houston*.

Everyone went ashore and a few of the officers spent several nights in hotels and met some of the British community. Among these they found little confidence. There was not indeed much cause for optimism; in Africa Rommel was now eighty miles east of Benghazi and still moving eastwards; in Asia the Japanese had landed on Singapore Island. The mounting volume of bad news had produced an atmosphere of gloom over Colombo which the billowing black smoke of a huge oil fire did nothing to dispel.

By 12th February the ships carrying the tanks, transport and stores had come in and the convoy was assembled; on the 14th it sailed, six merchant vessels, with an escort of the cruiser *Cornwall*, two destroyers and two sloops. One day out from Colombo it was announced that the destination was Rangoon and the next day it was learned that Singapore had surrendered.

The importance of this great naval base and the tremendous toil and treasure expended on its defences in the years before the war, were common knowledge. The fortress had a large garrison and had been considered almost impregnable. That it should have fallen so quickly was a shock, not only to those in high places, but to every officer and man, and they wondered what might be the secret of these startling Japanese successes; the Japanese soldier was in fact gaining a reputation to which he was only half entitled but which was to stand him in good stead in his engagements with the inexperienced troops in Burma.

By daybreak on the 21st the convoy was in the Rangoon estuary. Only then was it learned that a Japanese naval force was operating towards the Andaman Islands and had passed, not far from the convoy, during the night.

The country on either hand was disappointing—bare, flat paddy fields, with here and there a group of huts or a small clump of trees. The buildings of the oil refineries and tanks on the east bank made no contribution to the beauty of the scene and the passing of a shipload of Royal Air Force personnel on their way back to India was no encouragement to the spirits. Still more depressing were the views of the pilot, who spoke with feeling of the cholera epidemic, the state of the docks, the military situation and his personal conviction that the ships might as well turn round and go back.

* * * *

The *Ascanius* docked at 11.30 a.m. in an eerie silence, broken only by the clanking of the ship's donkey engines and once by the wail of an air-raid siren. The scene was one of gigantic desolation. Huge warehouses stood with their doors open and vast quantities of stores of all kinds, lease-lend weapons for China, lorries, food, ammunition, beer and champagne, lay intermingled, half in and half out, some of the cases broken open and their contents scattered over the ground. There were no guards, no labourers, nobody to organize the unloading.

Warrant Officers and Sergeants who sailed for Burma, January 1942.

4th row—Sgt. Roberts, Sgt. Hampton, Sgt. Cleere, D.C.M., Sgt. Chadwick, Sgt. Whitehouse, Sgt. Walton, Sgt. Hunt, Sgt. Hil, Sgt. Archer, Sgt. Sanderson, Sgt. Weaver.
3rd row—Sgt. Williams, Sgt. Kelty, Sgt. Silcock, Sgt. Yeomans, Sgt. Campbell, Sgt. Cowley, M.M., Sgt. Davies, Sgt. Kane, Sgt. Brown, Sgt. Patterson, Sgt. Newton.
2nd row—Sgt. Hipsey, Sgt. Connolly, Sgt. Crew, Sgt. Smith, Sgt. Sykes, SQMS. Stratton, SQMS. Collier, SQMS. Dunscombe, Sgt. Adams, R.A.O.C., Sgt. Martin, Sgt. Bridges.
Front row—MQMS. Webb, SSM. Lowe, SSM. Marshall, D.C.M., RSM. Brown, Capt. and Adj. G. Murray Smith, M.C., Lt.-Col. Fosdick, Capt. and QM. Blake, M.B.E., RQMS. Keen, TQMS Tate, ORQMS. Jones, SSM. Ainley, SSM Robinson.
Absent from photograph :—SQMS. Blackshaw, Sgt. H. Smith, Sgt. Austin.

For the first time in its history the great port of Rangoon was idle, derelict and deserted.

It had been like this for two months, since the air raids of 23rd and 25th December. These had apparently been directed against the docks and the power station, but most of the damage had been among the flimsy and crowded wooden houses of the neighbouring part of the town. More than 2,000 people had been killed and a large proportion of the population had fled into the country, including practically all the dockers, labourers, menials and servants, and most of the subordinate staffs of business houses and government installations. In consequence the hospitals, the local administration, the ordnance, works and transportation services, were totally dislocated just when they were most needed.

Among the few figures waiting on the quay was Brigadier Anstice, who came on board at once and explained the military situation. He himself had just returned from Java, where he had flown to see General Laverack, commander of the land forces in A.B.D.A. Command (short title for American-British-Dutch-Australian). The supreme commander, General Wavell, had once more become Commander-in-Chief, India, and Burma was back under India's control. In view of the rapid Japanese advance through Siam and the inexperience of the British troops—mainly Indians—the position in Burma was becoming serious and the 7th Armoured Brigade was required for active operations immediately.

Once the silence was broken by the wail of the air-raid sirens. Within a few minutes the tranquil river sprang to a new life and hundreds of little native boats crossed over from Rangoon to the west bank, laden almost to foundering point with hitherto unseen human beings. There was no further disturbance of the peace and during the afternoon they gradually found their way back again.

At 1 p.m. disembarkation began. The men from the *Ascanius* were driven away in Indian Army lorries to a rubber plantation near Mingaladon aerodrome, some fifteen miles north of the city. A rear party was left to bring the baggage, which arrived quite soon afterwards. For a few hours the men had little to do and they sat about under the trees, commenting on the beautiful shade and the obviously ample supply of water; later they were to have too much of both.

For nearly two days the vital point was the docks. The equipment had been loaded in the standard manner, on the assumption that it would be off-loaded at a base port with normal facilities. The guns were in mineral jelly—admirable for preventing damage by sea water but difficult to clean off—the ammunition was in boxes and not with the tanks. There was a lot to be done before the regiment could be ready for action. But worst of all was the total absence of dock labour, both skilled and unskilled, and it was no small achievement by the soldiers and the merchant seamen that in little more than forty-eight hours the ships were cleared.

The first freightship alongside was the *Birch Bank*, loaded with tanks, lorries, ammunition and stores. The gangway went down at about 11 o'clock. One of the troopers had been a crane operator in civil life and one of the electric cranes was still in working order. The ship's crew were first class and, besides working themselves, they taught the soldiers how to handle the donkey engines and winches. Under the tireless leadership of Captains Dean, Calder and White the men warmed to the task, and unloading was better and better as they got into the swing of it. As it grew dark the lights were switched on and it was decided to continue through the night, in spite of the chance of an unheralded air attack. About midnight a case of beer was provided for each hold, and the ship seemed to disgorge her cargo at an even greater speed. All the troops worked without a break until the last piece of equipment was off, just as the sun rose. Quite a lot of 7th Hussars felt they had earned dockers' rates of pay in those twenty hours.

Elsewhere the unloading went less smoothly, as there were not the same facilities and work had to continue through the heat of the second day. The liquor on the quay was a great temptation; some of it found its way into the ships, some of it was consumed on the spot and there was considerable diversion of effort among the less disciplined of the unloading parties. With a few exceptions the men of the 7th Hussars were extraordinarily good and gave a first taste of the steadiness and discipline for which the regiment was later to be commended. One exception was an old soldier who had been many years in the regiment; he found a bottle of "Pim's"—a deceptive sort of cocktail mixture in common use among Britons in oriental countries; it is about the colour of beer and he tackled it in much the same way, only to discover his mistake, when he returned painfully to consciousness, some hours later.

At 1.30 a.m. on the 22nd Captain Dean arrived in the rubber plantation to ask for guards for the warehouses, as the situation was getting out of hand. Accordingly Captain Llewellen Palmer and Lieutenant John with a party of men went off to take control of the docks area. An hour later the regiment was ordered to send another forty men to unload the ships, and these were taken by Lieutenant P. B. Stanley Evans. Work went on with renewed vigour and by 8 a.m. the first tanks began to arrive in the leaguer area. Regimental headquarters, B and C Squadrons, were soon complete. A Squadron's

SOUTHERN BURMA

Map VIII
BURMA

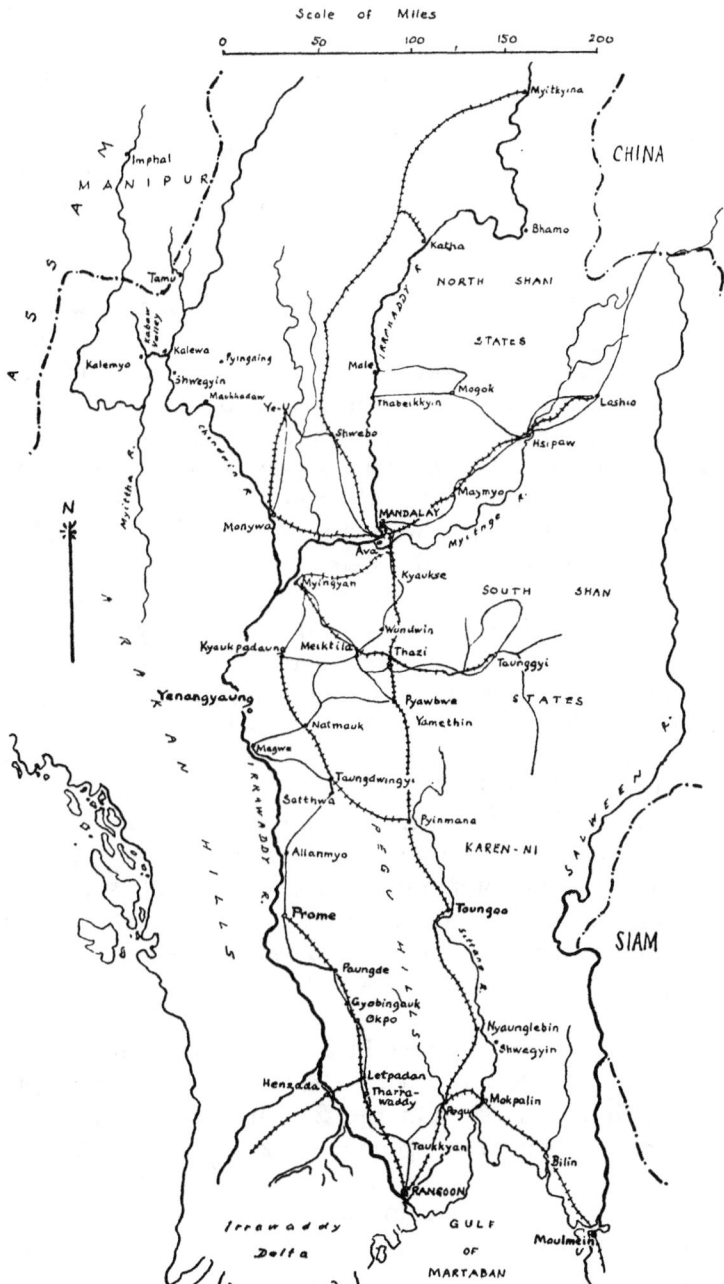

tanks however, except four, were not off the ship until the morning of the 23rd. But they were quickly ready for action because Lieutenant Glendinning, who had been with them in the ship, had had the guns cleaned while waiting.

Throughout the 22nd and the 23rd officers and men worked without ceasing, cleaning the guns, belting ammunition and packing the tanks. All the while a stream of refugees filed past along the road, some in vehicles, some on foot. Among them was a fire engine, complete with its crew, and extra passengers to capacity; this was seen again two months later, nearly 500 miles to the north, abandoned in a paddy field near Shwebo.

By nightfall on the 22nd B and C Squadrons could have moved, in an emergency, and by noon on the 23rd the whole regiment was ready. The final touches included a small issue all round of foodstuffs and minor luxuries, systematically acquired from abandoned stores dumps. In the absence of a canteen service these were a welcome reward for two good days' work. A few extra lorries were also attached to the regiment. These had been parked in the zoo by the Royal Air Force when they embarked for India and were discovered by Captain Calder, with the co-operation of the Revd. Metcalfe, when they were on a joint reconnaissance. The city was almost deserted, but their course took them, for some unexplained reason, to the lunatic asylum and the leper colony, which were both fully tenanted although without their junior staffs. The human element of the zoo had gone altogether, and it had been reported that the dangerous animals had been destroyed. The padré was considering a momentary rest on a convenient log of wood, when it blinked an evil alligator's eye, and they also found a boa constrictor suspended in a tree. Some of the less attractive carnivora were in fact alive, at large, and possibly hungry.

At 4 p.m. on the 23rd the commanding officer was hastily summoned to brigade headquarters. The situation on the Sittang was critical, Rangoon was in danger, the brigade was to move at once.

*   *   *   *

The 17th Indian Division was now in a very grave position. The withdrawal from the Bilin River, briefly referred to in the last chapter, had begun on 20th February. On the 21st it had continued and some of the transport had been brought back across the Mokpalin bridge to the west bank. On the morning of the 22nd however, movement over the bridge was stopped for three hours by a lorry which had run off the roadway in the dark; a long train of vehicles closed up in a dense column, waiting to cross. Then, at 8.30 a.m., the enemy attacked the Burmans holding the north-east sector of the bridgehead and penetrated almost to the bridge itself. A counter-attack restored the situation, but the attack was repeated, again succeeded temporarily, and the enemy was again driven back. The situation had several times appeared so serious that the ferry boats had been destroyed and the bridge remained as the only means of crossing the river; the Sittang at this point is 500 yards wide and very rapid.

Besides the troops in the bridgehead, there were still two complete brigades on the east bank, several miles away and closely engaged with the enemy. Their situation was not accurately known, but reports from the numerous stragglers indicated, in most cases quite wrongly, that units were disintegrating. Meanwhile fighting in the bridgehead continued and by the early hours of the 23rd the position seemed so critical that the order was given to blow the bridge. It went up at 5.30 a.m. with the best part of three infantry brigades and the artillery still on the east bank.

The British and Indian troops in the bridgehead had carried out frequent counter-attacks against the enemy, but pressure was constantly increasing. Although units of the two brigades from Bilin were now coming in, they were very tired and scarcely fit to fight; the only possible course was immediate withdrawal to the west bank.

A number got across the river by swimming, others with the aid of ropes across the gap in the bridge, others on improvised rafts. A large number were drowned and many were killed in the attempt, as the crossing, in the final stage, was under small arms fire. Some who could not swim made their way up the east bank and crossed the river on rafts and boats some miles to the northward. Almost none brought their weapons with them and many were without boots and clothing. All were exhausted and wild-eyed from want of sleep and their harassing experiences. It is not to be wondered at that the sorry spectacle of half naked Indians, some in lorries and some on foot, should at first shake the confidence of the newly arrived units in the fighting value of the Indian troops.

At the end of the Tennasserim episode the 17th Indian Division was deficient of half its proper establishment of officers, two-thirds of its men, four-fifths of its rifles, five-sixths of its automatics, most of its ammunition and all its guns. One brigade was so depleted that it had to be broken up. The other two were re-armed and re-clothed as far as possible, some of the weaker units being amalgamated. Those for whom there were no weapons were evacuated by lorry and train to the north, to be re-posted later, when rested and re-equipped. For raw Indian troops this was a gruelling finish to a depressing withdrawal.

It was no small credit to those who survived and to their leaders that they were so quickly in action again and able, in the subsequent operations, to play a part which quickly restored to them the esteem and respect of their British comrades.

*   *   *   *

When he returned from the brigade conference on the evening of the 23rd, Lieutenant-Colonel Fosdick briefly outlined the situation on the Sittang, as far as it was then known, and issued orders for the move. The 2nd Royal Tanks were to join their squadron which was already in the vicinity of Payagyi. The 7th Hussars, with D Troop 414 Battery Royal Horse Artillery under command, were to move to the Pegu area, where they would for the time being remain in reserve, close to brigade headquarters. B Echelon would be on the Pegu-Rangoon road, eighteen miles south of Pegu. Stress was laid upon the importance of holding Rangoon, so that the landing of reinforcements and stores might continue; not the least important of the expected reinforcements was an Australian division.

Lieutenant P. B. Stanley Evans was sent ahead to select leaguer areas, and the regiment moved at 2 a.m., B Squadron in the lead, then C, headquarters, A Echelon, D troop 414th Battery and A Squadron. The march was uneventful and the guides were waiting at the appointed spot, on the bridge at Pegu, when the regiment arrived about an hour before dawn. Squadrons split and went to their allotted areas. Headquarters went into a large white house in Pegu, which proved to be a girls' school—without the girls; there were twenty-four hours of comparative luxury, with hot baths and iced drinks, until the electricity was cut off. Each squadron went into cover in copses not above a mile away. In the darkness A Squadron crashed through a hedge into an enclosure which seemed to be a village of some sort; hens and Burmans scuttled about for a few minutes; then all was quiet and everyone tried to snatch a brief sleep. An order to switch on all wireless, however, woke up any who had dropped off; some wondered if this indicated the presence of the enemy, but nothing came of it and for another half hour there was peace.

At dawn it was realized that the squadron was in the grounds of a temple. The chief priest seemed quite friendly, but was taking no chances and all the women were despatched to a neighbouring village. One Burman who spoke English came up to Major Kevill-Davies and asked, "Are you on manoeuvres?" "No," indignantly, "we are fighting a war." "Oh! well, have a cigar." It seemed necessary somehow to justify the presence of tanks in a monastery garden and amends had to be made for the lack of ceremony with which they had entered. Amicable discussions went on for some time between the squadron leader and the priests and eventually everything was put right by the head priest, who formally blessed the tanks. Patrols went out and returned, and occasionally the whole squadron, but the priests, with their orange robes and shaven heads, were the peaceful and friendly hosts of the squadron for several days and nights. They seemed to take the tanks as a matter of course and the soldiers were given strict orders not to chase the chickens or in any way to desecrate the holy ground.

During the morning patrols were sent out from all squadrons to reconnoitre the country for "going" and to make contact with any of the enemy or our own troops who might be in the area, and Major Younger took out the seconds-in-command. All patrols were in scout cars. The information available was extremely scanty, as is inevitable when contact with the enemy has been lost. Of the three British battalions west of the Sittang, the 1st Gloucesters were in Rangoon, engaged largely in prevention of looting; the 1st West Yorkshires were about Thanatpin, giving slender cover against a possible enemy crossing of the Gulf of Martaban; the 1st Cameronians were round Pegu. The last named were now placed under command of the 7th Armoured Brigade, who allotted two companies to each armoured regiment; A and D companies came under the 7th Hussars.

Major Younger's party moved to Thanatpin, where they made contact with a company of the West Yorkshires, and then along the east bank of the canal to Waw. None of the bridges were fit for tanks. One of the squadron's patrols can best be described in the words of the patrol leader:

"I had hoped to get a bit of sleeping done to make up for last night, but at about eleven o'clock I was sent for by the Colonel and told to take out two dingoes (scout cars) and a motor bike on a ground-reconnaissance-cum-patrol. Just before I left the order came through that nobody was to go about by himself and everyone was to carry arms as a British lieutenant-colonel had just had his throat cut by a Burman fifth-columnist while he was in a state of exhaustion after swimming the Sittang. I set off on my patrol and went along the road for nearly twenty miles, which took me within a couple of miles of Waw. Here I turned south-east and tried to reach the Pegu-Sittang canal across the paddy fields. The divisions were too high for a dingo to negotiate and we had to follow any tracks we could find. I tried for several hours to reach the canal, but although I could see where it was, I never got to it. All the time I was meant to be on the look-out for the enemy, but I could never get near enough to any of the villages to investigate them and I shall never know who some horsemen, on the other side of the canal, were. It was unbelievably hot and we got choked with dust. Eventually the other dingo broke a spring and I had to tow it back to the road. It is hopeless country for dingoes. There are large stretches of paddy field, interspersed with copses and woods in many of which are villages. My dingo was running out of petrol, so I had to go down to Waw to get some from a 2nd Tank squadron who are in the village. They were blowing up the bridge over the canal there this afternoon. All day small groups of Indian stragglers were coming back along the road; they had no arms and looked helpless and hopeless to a man. The motor bike next got a puncture that Hancock couldn't mend. I left him on the road with Solomon and the other dingo and set off with my dingo to try and reach the canal again. We bellied down hopelessly on a paddy hump when we were still quite near the road and I had to go back on foot to fetch the dingo with the broken spring, which crawled over to tow us out; after a bit the effort was successful.

All day I had been keeping Burmans at a respectful distance, and at this juncture one carrying a sort of hoe raised it (obviously to put it on his shoulder) when he was rather near me. Mindful of the dead officer, and not wishing a notice to be given out that evening that "no one was to go more than ten yards from his tank, as a subaltern in the 7th Hussars was chopped to pieces to-day by a hostile Burman with a hoe," I clapped my right hand over to my holster, wild west style, and the poor little Burman ran until he was almost out of sight. I made one final attempt to reach the canal with the dingo, but I was afraid of getting it stuck again a long way from the road and, as Leathwood and I were both pretty beat, I eventually gave it up and started home, having neither reconnoitred nor patrolled the canal as ordered, but having found out a good deal about the country. There were still a lot of Indians straggling back. My party presented a sorry spectacle; I had the bike on the back of my dingo and was towing the other dingo so our progress was slow and we had to have frequent halts. At one of these I looked up into a tree (I often did this, as there were rumours that the Japs sat up trees armed with long spears for spearing the passing British) and saw thirteen vultures sitting in it—if that's an omen I doubt if it's a very good one. I got back and reported to the Colonel about an hour before dark. . . ."

On the 25th similar reconnaissances were carried out in tanks. The roads were now crowded with refugees, some moving northwards towards Toungoo, some moving southwards towards Rangoon, loaded with babies and any belongings they could carry, and with the aimless and hopeless expressions of any human being, of whatever race, fleeing from an unknown terror. There was no sign of the enemy, despite rumours that they had crossed the canal at Waw.

The principal information gained from these reconnaissances was that the paddy bunds were a very serious obstacle to the tanks. The rice growing country, now hard and well baked, had looked very promising and from the moment when it was known that the brigade was coming, every effort had been made to increase the scope of its movement by strengthening the bridges. The paddy bunds are small banks of earth, little more than a foot high, moulded up round the fields for controlling irrigation. Each field is only about an acre in extent, so the bunds occur every fifty to a hundred yards. They reduced the speed of the tanks to about four miles in the hour, greatly increasing petrol consumption and causing irritation and much distress to the crews.

On the evening of the 25th C Squadron was sent off to Thanatpin, to come under the 1st West Yorkshires; as this battalion was the only unit watching a coast line of sixty miles, the enemy, had he been so inclined, could have landed almost anywhere and cut the communications between the Sittang front and Rangoon. In the event, however, he stuck to the jungle and cut them from the opposite direction.

At 1 a.m. on the 26th reports were received of Japanese troops in the villages to the east and north of Payagale, and of others moving south towards Pegu. The enemy had already cut the road and established a block at Pyinbongyi, and there was a gap of thirty miles between the remnants of the 17th Division, now concentrating in the Waw-Pegu area, and the most southerly brigade of the 1st Burma Division at Nyaunglebin. Through this gap the enemy could penetrate at will into the dense jungle of the Pegu Hills, west of the road. He did not however seem to relish the idea of meeting tanks, and most of his movements were at night. In consequence very little was known about his activities, or in what strength he had crossed the road.

The 2nd Royal Tanks were in the Payagale area, and the 7th Hussars were now ordered to send a squadron to a point about two miles north of Pegu to guard the approaches by the road and the two railways from Waw and Payagyi. A Squadron was sent, and searched north-eastwards for some distance; no enemy were discovered, only a large number of refugees. Sergeant Hunt of A Squadron thought, for a moment, that he was being stalked, and opened up with his Browning into the ditch by the roadside. A lot of chattering broke out and he switched on his lights. The ditch was full of Gurkhas, who emerged bedraggled but unharmed, and were soon smiling again. Before noon both A and C Squadrons were recalled to Pegu.

On the 27th, at about 10, some aircraft were heard overhead, but as the tanks were entirely hidden under the trees, nobody took any notice. Suddenly a fearful screaming began and those who could dived for cover in the traditional manner, under their tanks. There followed a few faint pops in the distance, which were probably small anti-personnel bombs of which the worst feature was the scream. The only engagement on this day was between the 2nd Royal Tanks and a body of traitor Burmans armed with Japanese weapons, near Payagale. Fourteen of the enemy were killed and six captured. The Japanese themselves were little in evidence, although reports of their penetration into the Pegu Hills became more and more persistent. Anxiety was already being felt for Rangoon and for the communications northwards up the Irrawaddy Valley. Accordingly the 7th Hussars were ordered to send a squadron to Tharrawaddy, seventy miles north of Rangoon.

For some days a dumping operation had been in progress, as a safeguard in case of an eventual evacuation of the port. Stores had been transported by river, rail and road to selected points in the direction of India, so that the force could be withdrawn gradually northwards, first to positions covering the oilfields round Yenangyaung, thence to the Irrawaddy south-west of Mandalay and ultimately to India if this should be necessary. The first main area for dumps was at Tharrawaddy, which was quite unprotected, and it was for this reason that Major Congreve's C Squadron was now sent there, with one company of the 1st West Yorkshires. The Japanese however made no attempt to raid the dumps and the squadron had a peaceful week.

*   *   *   *

For the command in Burma the last few days of February were fraught with difficulty. Changes were impending, and it must have been extremely hard for General Hutton to determine a course of action which would leave to his successor, General Alexander, freedom to carry out whatever policy might have been determined for him by the higher authorities. General Wavell was flying from the Dutch East Indies to Colombo, India and thence to Burma. General Alexander would not arrive from England for several days. Rangoon was threatened, and news was received that the Australian division, upon which its safety so much depended, might not be coming after all.

The military situation was in fact very serious. It was certain that the Japanese had entered the Pegu Hills in some strength and all efforts to dislodge them from the road block at Pyinbongyi and the neighbouring villages had failed. If they should seize Rangoon before the Australians could land, or even establish themselves firmly across the route of withdrawal up the Irrawaddy Valley, the troops round Rangoon and Pegu would be in grave danger. These included the greater part of the Burma Army—the 17th Indian Division, which was in no state for hard or prolonged fighting, the 7th Armoured Brigade, the recently arrived 63rd Indian Infantry Brigade, three British battalions and the 1st Indian Field Artillery Regiment. The only other troops in the country were the 1st Burma Division, which included one Indian brigade, on the road between Mandalay and Nyaunglebin, and the greater part of this division was of doubtful reliability.

In the circumstances it was not surprising that some of the ships carrying stores and reinforcements to Rangoon were turned back and that preparations for putting into effect the denial scheme in Rangoon and at the oil refineries were speeded up. In its reports of the night 27th/28th February the 7th Armoured Brigade war diary speaks of orders and counter-orders, and some of the troop movements in the Pegu area must certainly have puzzled the troops themselves. It is clear however that the main ideas underlying the redistribution of the forces were the covering of the eventual demolition and evacuation of Rangoon and the safety of the route to the north.

The principal adjustments now ordered provided for a somewhat closer defence round the city. The weak 16th Indian Infantry Brigade was ordered back from the Sittang. The headquarters of 7th Armoured Brigade and the 2nd Royal Tanks remained in the Pegu area. The 7th Hussars, with the 1st West Yorkshires under command, were ordered to hold an eleven-mile front from the ferry at Dabein to the bridge at Hlegu. This was an awkward position, in dead flat country, with bad lateral communication, numerous canals which interfered with tank movement, and no artillery was available. Later on the 28th the brigade headquarters moved back to Hlegu and the brigade's B echelon transport to Taukkyan.

The move back to the Hlegu position was not very encouraging to the spirits. Even more depressing was the news—now definite—that the Australians were not coming at all. On this particular point comments among the troops were exceedingly bitter and a feeling was prevalent, for a time, that the war in Burma must now be regarded as a lost cause and that they would be left to their fate. There followed some lively speculations on what that fate might be, as this was a period when little trust was placed in any of the inhabitants. Rumour said that there were bad men in a neighbouring village near Dabein; one troop leader noted with satisfaction, next morning, that when his men were woken, no heads rolled away from their bodies. In this slightly disheartened atmosphere, it was all the more encouraging for the men when they were told that their old friend General Wavell was coming to see them.

General Wavell arrived in Burma and gave firm instructions that Rangoon was to be held, and that all ships with troops or stores, recently diverted from Rangoon, should continue to come in. So a somewhat more aggressive policy was adopted and the commander of the 7th Armoured Brigade was authorized to reinforce the 2nd Royal Tanks in the Pegu area, if he saw fit to do so. He thereupon decided to move the rest of the brigade up to Pegu again the following day. One modification was made; as General Wavell intended to visit the brigade the next morning, the 7th Hussars were at first only to move a short distance, to a locality north of Hlegu bridge.

At 9.30 General Wavell arrived. In the words of the war diary, "His visit was much appreciated by all ranks; it was indeed kind and considerate of him to go round all the regiment when he had so little time to spare." At one moment the formality of the proceedings was relieved by the precipitous arrival of a pig, which narrowly missed the General. It was closely followed by a sergeant of the 7th Hussars—nobody would have known it as he wore no shirt—armed with an improvized spear. General Wavell seemed not to notice the diversion. He was a human man in more ways than one and two officers heard later that he had sent messages through his daughter in Cairo to their wives, saying that he had seen them and they were well.

On his way back to Delhi Sir Archibald Wavell met Sir Harold Alexander, who was on his way out to take command of the Burma Army, and gave him a verbal directive, which was faithfully carried out and which explains much of what happened in the remainder of the campaign. He stated that "the retention of Rangoon was a matter of vital importance to our position in the Far East and every effort must be made to hold it. If, however, that was not possible, the force must not be allowed to be cut off and destroyed, but must be withdrawn from the Rangoon area for the defence of Upper Burma. This must be held as long as possible in order to safeguard the oilfields at Yenangyaung, keep contact with the Chinese and protect the construction of the road from Assam to Burma." (From General Alexander's report.)

*   *   *   *

On 2nd March, after General Wavell's inspection, the regiment waited for the order to move forward to Pegu. A Squadron were fortunate enough to find a deserted village and they were able to save several pigs and quite a number of hens and ducks from a lingering death by starvation. The move was carried out in the afternoon, and, for some obscure reason, at a very high speed. It was exceptionally hot and dusty. Headquarters and both squadrons leaguered together in an orchard a mile south of Pegu.

Next morning, the 3rd, the regiment was to relieve the 2nd Royal Tanks. The day was spent at half-an-hour's notice, everyone ready to move, but the 2nd Royal Tanks were so closely engaged with the enemy that the relief had to be postponed until the following day.

In the previous forty-eight hours the Japanese had in fact been pressing forward. On the night of 2nd/3rd March they advanced from Waw to Kyaikhla. During the 3rd the 2nd Royal Tanks did their best to dislodge them both from there and from the road block at Pyinbongyi and several tanks were lost in the attempt. Shortage of infantry and artillery were the chief troubles; without adequate help from other arms the tanks could not easily clear villages or road blocks, especially when these were defended with anti-tank guns.

On the evening of the 3rd the 2nd Royal Tanks concentrated south of Payagyi village and two companies of the 1st Cameronians were covering the approaches to Pegu by the line of the railway south-west of Kyaikhla. The hour for the relief was fixed at 6.45 a.m. and Captain Gray's company of the 1st Cameronians was to come under command, in the area south of Payagyi, at the same time.

At 5.45 a.m. the regiment moved off with B Squadron in the lead (Major Gilbert Davies-Gilbert), followed by headquarters, D Troop Essex Yeomanry and A Squadron. Captain Dean and the fitters came forward, but the rest of A Echelon stayed in the orchard. By 6.45 the relief was complete and in a very short time both squadrons were engaged with the enemy, who had, in the night, pressed forward to Payagyi and Shanywagyi.

One troop from A Squadron was ordered to patrol to Pyinbon, to reconnoitre the road block. Lieutenant M. M. Stanley Evans started off just before dawn, in a thick mist. As he approached Payagyi there suddenly emerged through the mist several lorry loads of infantry withdrawing from the village. As they were unable to pass the tanks, which were blocking the road, the Cameronians dismounted and from the ditches by the roadside opened fire in the direction of the enemy, two of the tanks joining in. When the mist cleared there was a little sniping, but no Japanese were visible.

B Squadron in the same area engaged some enemy infantry in the paddy fields east of the road and they were able to observe at a distance much of the road between Waw and Payagyi; close observation of this road was not possible, however, as there was an impassable "chaung" (the Burmese equivalent of a nullah or wadi) between the patrol and the road. It was something of a surprise when they reported twenty enemy tanks moving towards Payagyi. Major Younger questioned the report and the troop leader conceded that they might possibly be elephants. In view of what happened later it seems possible that he saw both tanks and elephants, but his friends made quite unkind remarks about the condition people must be in before they see elephants.

As the mist cleared it was realized that B Squadron was too close to the wooded area round Payagyi. There was a good deal of sniping; Lieutenant Patteson had a bullet through his cap and a graze on the head and Trooper Abrahams was slightly wounded. In order to get a better field of fire the squadron was withdrawn to a position about a mile south of the village. As visibility improved, there were opportunities for the guns; Captain Shorten, of the Essex Yeomanry, mounted in a 7th Hussars' tank which he handled with skill and boldness, was able to engage several targets; hits were obtained on at least one gun and one mortar. It was not, however, possible to stage an attack with the forces available, as in such close country more infantry were required.

While B Squadron were busy on the Payagyi road, A Squadron were engaged with the enemy along the Waw railway. He had now occupied Shanywagyi village, in rear of our infantry positions near Naungpattaya. Although Sergeant Patterson's troop was able to keep the Japanese pinned in the village and wood, nothing could be done about driving them out, again because there were no infantry available. He did however succeed in setting the village and part of the wood on fire, and more petrol was sent forward on the outside of tanks to keep the fire going.

The enemy's hold on Payagyi and Pyinbongyi not only kept the 17th Indian Division separated from the 1st Burma Division, but it assured him the use of a wide corridor for further penetration into the Pegu Hills. The anxiety which this caused for the safety of the Burma Army has already been emphasized. Accordingly the divisional commander, now Major-General Cowan, ordered the 7th Armoured Brigade to carry out an attack on Payagyi. Lieutenant-Colonel R. H. Thomas of the Cameronians was to command the operation, and the attacking troops were to be one squadron 7th Hussars and two companies of the 1st Cameronians. Fire support was "an intense artillery concentration" by 414th Battery Essex Yeomanry (eight guns) from 3.50 to 4 p.m. and a "heavy aerial bombardment" by twenty Blenheims between 4 and 4.10, at which hour the attack was to go in.

The artillery did all that eight guns could do, but only two bombers arrived and each dropped two bombs. The brigade commander considered this preparation was inadequate and cancelled the attack. This was a relief to many, as the approaches to Payagyi were over very open ground, the tanks would have been hampered as usual by the paddy bunds and the enemy was well concealed.

In the late afternoon everything seemed very quiet at Payagyi and Lieutenant Geoffrey Palmer's troop was sent forward to reconnoitre, followed by infantry patrols. He reached the far side of the village without interference and engaged an enemy mule column moving from east to west outside the village. The infantry patrols penetrated the near edge of the village and found a few of the enemy still there. Before withdrawing they inflicted some fifteen casualties, including five Japanese surprised and killed at their evening meal. The village was set on fire and the troops withdrew; there were no casualties. The 7th Hussars spent the night in leaguer about three miles north of Pegu, covered by A Company, 1st West Yorkshires.

The infantry kept up continuous patrolling during the night and at about 1 a.m. on the 5th one of their patrols was ambushed by an enemy detachment which shot up its truck and caused several casualties. The enemy had advanced about two miles south of Payagyi and occupied a wood. Lieutenant Young's troop was sent forward at once and he opened fire in the direction of the enemy, to cover the evacuation of the wounded; these were all brought away and were dressed by Captain Low. No further action was taken until dawn when Lieutenant Young began continuous patrolling of the road as far as Payagyi and the regiment moved forward to its positions of the previous day. A road block was seen at the village cross roads and the village itself was again strongly held. The wood where the ambush had taken place was still suspect, and in order to make sure of it, Lieutenant Glendinning's troop was sent forward with a strong fighting patrol of infantry; they found no enemy in the wood, but there was a satisfactory quantity of torn Japanese clothing and blood, so it seemed that Lieutenant Young's fire had had some effect.

About 9.30 a.m. an enemy tank and two lorries were seen by B

Squadron, moving along the road from Waw to Payagyi. Later the tank was foolish enough to come within range of a troop of B Squadron. It was knocked out, and proved to be a small two-man affair not unlike the Italian C.V.3.

Meanwhile A Squadron, and a company of infantry, were clearing the woods round Shanywagyi and any Burmans remaining within were to be treated as enemy. Only three emerged, an elderly couple who were left unscathed and an obviously simple Burman, who hurried away, frightened; every care was taken to miss him. The villages and houses were set on fire; one haystack went up with a minor explosion and was found to have a car hidden in it.

While these operations were taking place to the north-east of Pegu, there were ominous alarms to the west and south. First, a patrol of the 2nd Royal Tanks, sent up the west bank of the Pegu River towards Sitpinzeik, was fired on by an anti-tank gun, well concealed in the jungle; the leading tank was hit seven times before it could turn round. A detachment of Cameronians was sent to capture the gun, but all sign of it had gone and no enemy were found.

Secondly, throughout the morning soft vehicles moving up and down the main road south-west of Pegu were fired on from the jungle. Little damage was caused, but there was no longer any doubt that the Japanese were aiming at the communications of the Pegu force. Later on the 5th they established a road block and temporarily all traffic was stopped. But a troop of the 2nd Royal Tanks cleared it quickly and without much difficulty and contined to patrol the most threatened part of the road; normal movement was resumed.

At 3.30 p.m. on the 5th a liaison officer from divisional headquarters arrived at 7th Armoured Brigade with orders that the division was to withdraw to Hlegu that night, the 7th Armoured Brigade acting as rearguard. Instructions were issued at once to the regiment and squadron leaders were called to a conference. But the orders had barely reached squadrons when they were cancelled. The divisional commander had now come up to brigade headquarters, fresh from an interview with General Alexander; the latter's directive from General Wavell is already known. Verbal orders were issued at once for the 48th Indian Infantry Brigade, 7th Hussars, 414th Battery Essex Yeomanry, 1st West Yorkshires and 1st Cameronians to defend Pegu; the 63rd Indian Infantry Brigade, in the words of the brigade diary, "were due to join the throng in Pegu the following morning." Headquarters 7th Armoured Brigade and the 2nd Royal Tanks were to move back to Hlegu at 9 p.m.

News of its fresh task reached the regiment just before dusk, when it

Burning haystacks near Pegu, showing typical "paddy bund" in foreground.

Indian refugees from Rangoon on the way to Prome.

was concentrating north of Pegu and preparing to cover the withdrawal At 6 p.m. enemy aircraft attacked the bridge at Pegu. They narrowly missed the commanding officer and intelligence officer; the latter, Lieutenant P. B. Stanley Evans, was sitting on the bridge in his dingo at the time. The town was less lucky, and much of it went up in flames. To the troops, as they came back to the concentration area, Pegu seemed a good place to be leaving. A town on fire on the enemy's side of the line is as good as a bonfire on the 5th of November, but a town just behind one, especially when the jungle round may be full of the enemy, is quite a different thing. To many it seemed as if the present position was precarious. Some people were consequently a trifle surprised—even dismayed—when the change of plan was realized; regimental officers enjoyed their usual grouse about vacillation in high places, although it was generally recognized that a firmer policy was a change for the better.

The regiment settled down for the night with A Squadron and headquarters just north of Pegu and B Squadron with a company of the Cameronians just south of Payagyi. At dawn on the 6th A Squadron was to relieve B in the forward area.

*   *   *   *

For the 7th Hussars, the 6th of March was one of the most eventful days of the campaign. At dawn there was a dense mist. A Squadron moved out along the road to relieve B, closely followed by regimental headquarters. The latter resumed its position of the previous day, and, as the mist was still thick, vehicles remained in a huddle and everyone dismounted. It was probably unwise to go to the same spot three days running, but by day the sun was very hot and in this particular area there were not many copses to give shade and, which was equally important, cover from aircraft.

Crews brewed up and breakfast was just beginning when a shell arrived in the leaguer, followed quickly by others. In the mist nobody could see where they were coming from. The Japanese had either brought up some guns under cover of the mist, stalking the headquarters by the noise it made, or come up the night before to lie in wait in case the same spot should be occupied again. No time was lost in re-mounting and the headquarters moved back half a mile—with more speed than dignity. There were no losses except the breakfast and the only damage to vehicles was a superficial hit on Corporal Marlow's tank of B Squadron and a track blown off the commanding officer's tank.

As soon as the mist cleared D Troop, 414th Battery Essex Yeomanry, engaged the enemy with good effect and A Squadron, supported by a company of the West Yorkshires, was ordered to clear the copse of the enemy. Lieutenant M. M. Stanley Evans' troops was selected to lead, and the mentions of this officer on this day in the regimental war diary are almost monotonous; later he received a well-earned Military Cross. At the time he was out in the paddy fields watching the Waw-Payagyi road, where he had just relieved Sergeant Brown's troop of B Squadron. Fortunately he broke all the rules and kept a diary, and his own half-humorous account of the day, written that same evening, is quoted with his reluctant permission:

". . . I had only been in position for about an hour, and had seen nothing of note, when shooting started on the Pegu road behind me. I learnt later that some Japs who were concealed in the copse where A Squadron headquarters had been yesterday, had opened upon regimental headquarters and B Squadron with anti-tank guns and hit two tanks. A general withdrawal was ordered and we were told to pick up the infantry on the way back, but, much to their credit, they refused to move, as they said they were quite happy. The 25-pounders opened up on the Jap position and, when they had finished, I was sent in to capture the guns and mop up the position. On the way to the copse I came across two Japs lying face down in the paddy field; they weren't in a very 'dead' attitude and, taking no chances, I opened fire with the tommy gun; one was very much alive, but not long enough to do any harm. Sergeant Williams ran his tank into a hole, so I had to tell Sergeant Walton to tow him out, and arrived at the copse by myself. I saw four guns, with quite a few dead Japs lying round them, but suspected that some must still be alive in the copse, and went in on foot with the tommy gun—thinking it over now it was really rather courageous of me, but oddly enough I did not seem to mind much at the time. The first two I saw that looked alive to me were lying face down, looking the other way, by the bole of a tree. I fired a few shots at them, and, much to my chagrin, the left hand one squirmed round to the other side of the tree. I felt that that phase was over and went back to my tank, before going in from a different angle. It really had its funny side, as I would suddenly remember that I hadn't looked up into the tree just behind me, and would slowly turn round and peep into it, rather like Donald Duck when he suddenly realizes that there is an enormous and infuriated she-bear just behind him, ready to pounce. When I got out into the field again, I saw the infantry calmly taking the guns back to the road, and called the nearest three over, to help me first. One of them threw a grenade into the copse, and I said, 'Come on now, we'll rush it' (third term at my prep-school), but when I had got to the edge of the copse, not one of them had left the cover of the tank. I swore at them and, just as they joined me, a Jap fired at us from a range of a few yards with a rifle of some sort; I'm ashamed to say we all scampered back behind the tank. At that moment Francis (company commander) came up and Sergeant Walton's tank arrived too. A Jap broke out of the other side of the copse and ran for it, but everybody fired at him and he didn't get far. Francis and I then went through the copse side by side and saw no other living thing. My troop was then ordered to clear another copse to the north-east. We combed it, four of us with revolvers and three with tommy guns, but there were no Japs in it. We then set it on fire and returned to squadron headquarters on the road."

Stanley Evans was next used to support the infantry in clearing a large wood; the tanks fired into the wood until the infantry entered it and then went round to the other side to shoot anything that bolted. At eleven o'clock he was about to do the same at another wood, when he was ordered to return to the position where he had originally been on patrol; there were enemy tanks there, being engaged by Lieutenant Barton's troop.

Wireless messages showed that there was some doubt about the identity of the tanks, which might have been B Squadron's. When Stanley Evans saw three tanks near some haystacks, with two dismounted men standing by them, he thought they might be Barton's troop. This was quickly checked, and Barton reported that none of his men were dismounted. So Stanley Evans advanced in arrowhead formation and quickly came under fire from the tanks. At 800 yards he halted and engaged them, advanced another 100 yards, and opened fire again. Trooper Clare fired the 37-millimetre gun at the dismounted men by mistake and they ran off into a bushy gully.

Stanley Evans now co-ordinated an attack between himself and Barton, who engaged the enemy from a hull-down position. The enemy was still firing, either from the tanks or with an anti-tank gun, and Stanley Evans' tank was hit when about 300 yards from the objective. Bridges, the driver, was temporarily blinded; and he put his hands to his face and left the tank to run on by itself. He was then told to pull the left stick so as to get to a safer range while another driver took control. However, he quickly recovered, and all three tanks closed in on the enemy. The troop leader and tank commanders cautiously dismounted. Several Japanese lay dead. The enemy tanks were badly mauled and two were on fire. Sergeant Williams took the remaining tank in tow, and under a certain amount of small arms sniping the troop withdrew a short distance and remained in observation.

The Japanese tanks were very similar to the Honeys in appearance and also had a 37-millimetre gun. They were smaller, however, their armour was thinner and they never again in any Burma campaign faced British armour in the open.

During this engagement Lieutenant Glendinning's troop was sent forward to investigate some lorries reported on the road between Waw and Payagyi. On his way he passed close to the tank battle just described and he himself was fatally wounded by an unlucky shot from an enemy tank gun. Glendinning had been twelve years in the regiment. He had been outstanding as a tank commander in the desert and had obtained a commission soon after the Wavell campaign. After a few months as a subaltern in the 3rd Hussars he came back to the 7th shortly before they sailed from Egypt and proved himself a splendid troop leader.

* * * *

Things were now beginning to go wrong in and around Pegu, which was defended by the four weak Gurkha battalions of the 48th Indian Infantry Brigade (Brigadier Hugh-Jones). At first light the enemy began to attack Pegu from the north-west. Part of the 414th Battery (Essex Yeomanry) were surrounded in their leaguer area, but burst their way into Pegu in the mist.

Sometime during the morning of the 6th the enemy blocked the road about two miles south of Pegu. Among the first casualties at the road block was Lieutenant Alan Smith, 7th Hussars, who was liaison officer with the 7th Armoured Brigade Headquarters. He had just come up from brigade headquarters to explain the outline of the plan for the defence of Rangoon, involving the ultimate move of the 7th Hussars to Mingaladon. On his way back he was ambushed at the road block and killed when covering the escape of two ammunition lorries. Smith had joined the regiment just before leaving Egypt, having previously been a corporal in the Welch Guards. He was a great asset to the regiment and a most promising officer.

The first serious effect of this new block on the operations was the holding up of the 63rd Indian Infantry Brigade, which was due to reinforce the troops in the Pegu area that morning. The reconnaissance party, consisting of the brigade major and the commanding officers, had gone ahead into Pegu. When it was realized that there was a road block a squadron of the 2nd Royal Tanks at Hlegu was allotted to the brigade, so as to help it through. On reaching the vicinity of the road block, however, the brigade was halted and the infantry began to dig in.

By the early afternoon the decision had been taken to withdraw the whole force to the Hlegu area. One troop of the 2nd Royal Tanks was accordingly ordered to break through into Pegu and bring back the senior officers of the 63rd Brigade. It got through without difficulty, but on the way out the party was badly shot up by an anti-tank gun, small arms fire and, apparently, by individual Japanese perched up trees with grenades. Against such methods the carriers in which the infantry officers were travelling afforded little protection and all the commanding officers and the brigade major were killed or wounded.

Little information was exchanged between the troops on either side of the block, because wireless communication between the divisional headquarters and the 48th Brigade had broken down. An effort was made to keep contact through the 7th Armoured Brigade and the 7th Hussars, who had sent a tank to 48th Brigade Headquarters as a wireless link. But the 7th Hussars near Pegu and the armoured brigade, whose headquarters were near Hlegu, were twenty miles apart and the operators had had little experience of the new Number 19 set, so communication was somewhat spasmodic.

At 3.40 p.m. 7th Armoured Brigade Headquarters, on instructions from the 17th Indian Division, ordered the 7th Hussars to abandon their role of defending Pegu from the north-east and to concentrate in the northern part of town. After making contact with the 48th Brigade the regiment was to break out through the road block with the tanks and dingoes, one troop of 414th Battery and the senior officers of the 63rd Brigade—it was not then known that they were already casualties. The regimental transport was also to be brought out if the commanding officer thought it possible to do so without serious losses. At this point wireless touch between 7th Armoured Brigade and 7th Hussars again broke down and was not re-established until the following morning. It appears however that the regiment was ordered to come under command of the 48th Brigade on reaching Pegu and also that no instructions for the withdrawal of the 48th Brigade itself were included in the message, as far as it went.

While orders were being issued to squadrons, Major Younger went off to make contact with the headquarters of the 48th Brigade. Brigadier Hugh-Jones was found after some difficulty, as he was with one of his battalions. He knew nothing about orders to withdraw, but agreed that it was desirable to cross the bridge as soon as possible, because it had been bombed all day and there were no anti-aircraft guns to protect it. It seems, however, that, later in the evening, the decision was taken that the whole of the brigade should be withdrawn, as it is recorded that the brigade commander was anxious that the road block should be passed in the hours of darkness on account of the 190 vehicles of the brigade which had to go through.

It was nearly 5 o'clock in the evening when forward troops were called in. The area south of Payagyi was quite quiet. Squadrons concentrated just outside Pegu, on the north side, and re-fuelled. A machine-gun attack by a few fighters, while this was taking place, did no damage, and the regiment set off for the bridge. Lieutenant M. M. Stanley Evans was sent ahead with his troop to find the road block. At the river bridge he was diverted by the party of engineers preparing it for demolition. He crossed the river by a ford a few hundred yards to the south and tried to regain the main road. This however was impossible as the jungle on both sides of the road was burning fiercely and he could not cross the railway. He re-crossed to the east bank of the river and found another ford to the north, by which the rest of the regiment also crossed.

The reconnoitring troop had advanced nearly two miles down the road from the railway crossing when it was fired at by mortar, anti-tank gun and machine-gun fire. This was in the vicinity of the road block, but it was now quite dark and nothing could be seen. The regiment, as soon as it had crossed the main railway line west of the town, turned down a lane and halted, while Major Kevill-Davies and one of his officers did a reconnaissance, to see if the railway line itself would serve as a route for the withdrawal, instead of the main road. It was not, however, considered suitable for a large force and there would have been unavoidable delays and difficulties at the undecked bridges over the many streams and ditches. Nor was the lane a suitable place to spend the night. It was apparent that no action could be taken against the road block in the dark, so a plan was made to attack it in the morning and meanwhile the regiment moved across the road into a small clearing, surrounded by jungle, and settled down for an uneasy night.

Sniping began at once and several of the tanks, including the commanding officer's and the second-in-command's, opened fire into the jungle. In spite of the glare from the fires in Pegu and the neighbouring woods, it was impossible to see what was going on. Major Kevill-Davies set off to walk a short way up the main road, but had only gone a few yards when he was hit, and died very shortly afterwards. He had joined the regiment in Aldershot and had been adjutant and commander of B Echelon before obtaining his squadron after the battle of Sidi Rezegh. He was a most gallant and popular officer and his loss was keenly felt by everyone.

The next few hours were some of the most unpleasant of the war. To the north and east there was a raging inferno; to the south there was a road block; all round there was jungle and there were no infantry to provide outposts. Some of the crews became jumpy—the only occasion in the campaign—and there was a good deal of firing at the jungle. Most people had a few hours of fitful sleep, disturbed only by mortar fire; nothing fell very near and only the noise was tiresome.

At about 2 a.m. the colonel went off to 48th Brigade Headquarters, where a plan was being made to force the road block at dawn. The regiment was to support a frontal attack by the West Yorkshires and the Cameronians. On account of the jungle, only one troop could be used—along the road. Once the block was forced it was to be kept open until all troops from Pegu had been withdrawn through it.

*   *   *   *

Dawn came on the 7th with the usual dense fog. This had its advantages, as it kept the Japanese aircraft grounded. It nevertheless added somewhat to the confusion, because there seemed to be Gurkhas everywhere, and when little men suddenly loomed up at close quarters through the mist, more than one finger fondled a trigger; but there were fortunately no mishaps. Two other surprise callers were war correspondents, seeking a lift in a tank through the road block. One belonged to a popular British daily paper and the other was an Australian. They were given their lift and were surprised and grateful to the Regimental Sergeant-Major when, on arrival at Hlegu, he returned them their jeep, which he had driven through himself. They at once went on to Rangoon whence one of them, at least, despatched a highly imaginative account of his doings to his paper, and came back later with a welcome present of champagne.

At 7 a.m., while it was still very thick, the regiment formed up on the only track leading to the main road, and moved off with B Squadron in the lead. As the advance began, Major Pereira's 414th Battery opened a vigorous fire on the road block and almost at the same time a long column of transport of the 48th Brigade came down the road from Pegu; the leading vehicles intermingled with the tanks of B Squadron and there seemed to be every prospect of another kind of road block. There were no military police for traffic control purposes, and somehow the transport had got out of hand. However, the drivers met their match in the person of Captain Richard Thornton, second-in-command of the squadron, who halted them and sorted them out so that the road was kept clear.

Lieutenant Geoffrey Palmer's troop was chosen to lead the attack. He reached the road block, which consisted of burnt-out lorries dragged across the road. Corporal Barr, in the leading tank, tried to push them to one side, but a sticky-bomb knocked out his tank and set it on fire. The crew baled out with only slight damage; Japanese marksmanship was, as usual, poor. The troop leader and Sergeant Davies then made the attempt; after a few anxious minutes they were successful in clearing a passage for vehicles, and they led the way through. Meanwhile the infantry cleared the jungle on either side and drove the enemy away from the immediate vicinity of the block. But they had a number of casualties, including Major Stephen Francis of the West Yorkshires, who was severely wounded. He had earned great admiration among all ranks of the 7th Hussars and was given an immediate D.S.O. for his gallantry in the Pegu operations, but died of his wounds a few days later.

Apart from some sniping, the road was now open and the regiment drove through to Taukkyan, losing Trooper A. P. Clarke, who was killed, and two men wounded in B Echelon. The transport of the 48th Brigade followed, and most of the infantry withdrew on foot, supported by 414th Battery.

The story of the fighting round Pegu ends appropriately with the exploits of the Reverend Metcalfe, who was among the last to leave the burning town. Metcalfe never waited for things to come to him; wherever there was a job to be done, in his own line, he would find it. On the morning of the 6th March he had been carrying out the burials of several Cameronians who had been ambushed, and he was driving from Pegu towards the brigade B Echelon at Hlegu. Suddenly he was stopped by an officer of the Cameronians, who shouted that there was a Japanese road block a mile farther on. Without this warning he would probably have run into it and been killed, like the other unlucky people who had done so already. He parked the car and with Trooper Mansell, his driver, attached himself to the combined regimental aid post of the Cameronians and the West Yorkshires.

The two doctors and the padré of the West Yorkshires were at full pressure, bringing in and dressing the wounded. The medical officer of the West Yorkshires was soon killed by a sniper from a tree and a mortar knocked out the ambulance. So Metcalfe drove some of the wounded to Pegu hospital in his car. The hospital was crammed with wounded, and just after he arrived the situation was made worse by a bomb which destroyed one wing, and added to the casualties.

Metcalfe and Trooper Mansell set up an improvised canteen and provided hot tea and biscuits for some of the wounded.

In the evening several 7th Hussars tanks stopped outside the hospital and he learned that the regiment was pulling out of Pegu that night and going to force the road block; the wounded could then be evacuated. He sent Trooper Mansell and his car back to the regiment and stayed on to help in the hospital and to give as decent a burial as possible to the quickly mounting number of dead. During the night the Cameronians provided some lorries and at dawn, with the help of Mr. Mansfield, the Sergeant-Major of 414th Battery Royal Horse Artillery, the wounded were loaded up in these and one or two motor ambulances. Metcalfe sat beside the driver of the last ambulance and the convoy made for the Hlegu road.

At the last bridge over the railway, which the rear party of the Cameronians was just about to blow up, the ambulance broke down. Metcalfe ran up the road and persuaded the driver of the only vehicle in sight, a lorry, to back his vehicle on to the bridge and give the ambulance a tow. This started the engine, and he sent the ambulance on to catch up the convoy, while he himself stayed with the lorry driver. The lorry was then knocked out, and Metcalfe, now dismounted again, took the driver under his wing and they joined forces with the rearguard, under Major Gray. It is said that he had by now set aside ecclesiastical prejudice and taken up a rifle. Under heavy Japanese fire, the party was compelled to take cover under the last remaining lorries. These, however, were soon destroyed and the position, with the Japanese almost encircling them, was quite untenable. Accordingly they began to withdraw, taking what cover they could in the ditch beside the road, and eventually they reached the vicinity of the road block.

Here there was a scene of indescribable carnage, wrecked and burnt-out lorries and vehicles of all sorts, with their dead occupants in, half out of, and around the vehicles. His first thoughts being for their relatives, Metcalfe tried to establish the identity of the dead. But the Japanese, now back in the area, at once opened fire with a mortar and the first shot was so near that it blew him back into the ditch, scratched and deafened, on top of a party of Cameronians. In the lull that followed, the party slipped away into the jungle and made for Hlegu, twenty miles to the south-west. Thanks to the darkness of a moonless night, they arrived safely next day, without the loss of a man.

Metcalfe said that he would always remember that march for two things. One was the soreness of his feet. He had lost both his shoes in the hectic rushes from Pegu bridge to the road block, and found the jungle paths "extremely unsympathetic"; the other was his sense of gratitude to the crew of a knocked out tank which they passed, as its food chest provided a much needed meal. A large number of wounded of several races and creeds owe their lives to the devoted action of Metcalfe, and he was awarded a well deserved D.S.O.

* * * *

General Alexander had arrived at Rangoon on 5th March. His first impression was that the port might still be made secure. Preparations for immediate evacuation were therefore suspended and steps were taken, as already described, to strengthen the forces at Pegu. On the following day, however, a number of factors combined to convince him that, with the forces at his disposal, Rangoon could not be held much longer. First, a considerable stretch of the road between Nyaunglebin and Pegu was in enemy hands; the 1st Burma Division had made no progress towards Pegu, and an unknown number of Japanese had already passed westwards across the road; at least two thousand had been reported at Paunggyi, thirty miles north of Hlegu. The intentions of this force were not clear, but if they succeeded in establishing themselves across the Prome road, the situation would be, at the best, precarious. Secondly, a large part of the army, including the bulk of the best troops, was cut off by the enemy road block at Pegu. Thirdly, there were reports of Japanese and traitor Burmans under Japanese officers, landing in the lower parts of the Rangoon estuary. There was a small detachment of British infantry at the Syriam oil refineries but no other troops were available to protect Rangoon from the south. Accordingly General Alexander came reluctantly to the conclusion that his primary task could not be fulfilled. At midnight of 6th/7th March orders were issued for the Rangoon Denial Scheme to be put into operation.

Preliminary steps had already been taken for the evacuation. Petrol, ammunition and stores of all kinds had been sent northwards to Tharrawaddy, Prome (the terminus of the Irrawaddy branch) and by road and river farther to the north. Most of the key civilians had been evacuated some weeks earlier, but a number of these had trickled back when the holding of Rangoon again became an established policy; this added greatly to the congestion and confusion when the decision was once more reversed.

The denial scheme was effectively carried out and little of immediate value was left for the enemy. On 7th March Army Headquarters and all administrative units not required for demolition purposes started for the north, a great mass of vehicles, intermingled with a host of civilian transport and cars of all descriptions, loaded to capacity—and beyond—with men, women, children, animals, food, baggage and furniture, all hooting their way through a seething mass of overladen Indian refugees who had no transport but their own legs and had delayed too long the start of their pitiful flight. The column was led by a protective detachment consisting of a troop of C Squadron, 7th Hussars, a company of infantry and a troop of 25-pounders.

The troop of C Squadron, under Lieutenant D. M. Allen, had been sent down from Tharrawaddy the previous day, accompanied by Captain Nickells, the second-in-command, who provided an extra wireless link with the headquarters of the 7th Armoured Brigade. On its way south the troop had seen no signs of the enemy. On its way north again it likewise met with no opposition. The protective detachment then branched off the main road along the Paungde track, to carry out its allotted task of protecting the column against any threat developing from that direction. It was only after it had covered several miles that the troop heard of a road block having been established on the main road between the detachment and the main body. The enemy had in fact lain low and allowed the protective detachment to pass.

The main body of the column was now in motion, and at 11 a.m. the leading vehicle of Army Headquarters ran into the block, three miles north of Taukkyan. Everything behind piled up, nose to tail, double-banked. The densely packed column stretched far back, past Taukkyan, down the Rangoon road.

An hour later the leading troop of B Squadron also arrived at the cross roads at Taukkyan, and the rest of the column from Pegu was rapidly closing up, although its tail was scarcely clear of the Pegu road block. As the regimental headquarters passed Hlegu, Colonel Fosdick called at 7th Armoured Brigade Headquarters to ask for orders. Nothing had been heard of the trouble in front, and he was told to go to a rubber plantation north of Taukkyan, to leaguer there, replenish and rest.

For forty-eight hours the regiment had been constantly on the move, with little chance for sleep or for brewing-up, and the prospect of a square meal and a brief lull was pleasing. But these orders had scarcely been received when B Squadron reported by wireless what they had found at the road junction. Fortunately the area consists largely of rubber plantations, in which the trees are regularly spaced and undergrowth is cleared; this allowed vehicles to disperse off the roads and at the same time provided good cover from the air. There was nevertheless a scene of great confusion and there were no military police to sort it out. However, there were plenty of willing amateurs and the regiment was privileged to witness the unusual spectacle of two lieutenant-generals (Alexander and Hutton) acting as traffic-control police.

Orders had been issued at 11-12 a.m. to 7th Armoured Brigade, to send a squadron to Taukkyan, and a squadron of 2nd Royal Tanks was sent. But, as B Squadron 7th Hussars had just arrived there, they were used at once—their second road block experience in one morning. They were ordered forward to investigate the block.

Lieutenant Young's troop went off in the lead and as he came in view of the block, which was situated round a bend where the jungle was dense on both sides, his tank got a direct hit from an anti-tank gun. His guns were damaged but the shot did not penetrate and there were no casualties. Captain Shorten then engaged the road block, not with his own troop of 414th Battery—this, with A Squadron 7th Hussars, had been stopped by the 63rd Brigade north-east of Hlegu—but with some 25-pounders he managed to borrow.

Throughout a very hot afternoon there followed a succession of attempts to break through. Frontal attacks were carried out by the 1st Gloucesters, by a composite battalion of the Duke of Wellington's Regiment and the King's Own Yorkshire Light Infantry, and by the 2nd/13th Frontier Force Rifles, each attack supported by B Squadron. The dense jungle made it impossible for the armoured troops to advance except on a one-tank frontage down the road, and there was one gun very cleverly sited in a culvert, which defied all attempts to destroy it and scored direct hits on several tanks. Late in the afternoon a squadron of 2nd Royal Tanks took over from B Squadron; but at nightfall no impression whatever had been made on the enemy.

On the evening of the 7th Major Congreve was ordered to come south from Tharrawaddy next morning to see what he could do to help. It was a march of sixty miles and the road was in fact open before C Squadron could arrive.

The troop of C Squadron which was already operating under the Officer Commanding the Protective Detachment in the Taukkyan area had had a somewhat unsatisfactory day on the 7th. Soon after leaving the main road wireless touch was lost and the detachment spent most of the day on the outskirts of a village on the Paungde track. The inhabitants were unfriendly and would give no information. At dusk the party moved back to the main road with the 7th Hussars troop in the lead. As it approached the road the troop came under mortar fire. The commander of the detachment decided that no offensive action could be taken in such close country in the dark and tanks and infantry settled down to a watchful and uneasy night.

At about 1 a.m. a column of infantry was seen moving westwards along the main road. It turned off southwards into the jungle and a patrol sent to investigate found that it was Japanese. The infantry of the protective detachment were then withdrawn northwards and Lieutenant Allen's troop remained in observation near the road. The rest of the night was quiet and early on the morning of the 8th Lieutenant M. M. Stanley Evans' troop appeared from the south-east and the road was clear.

We now revert to the story of the main column which, on the night of 7th March, was still held up around the Taukkyan road junction. The regiment had spent the night of the 7th close to Army Headquarters at the road junction. The situation was grim. Not only were the enemy firmly established across the only line of withdrawal, but the whole area was thronged with civilians for whom there was no possible protection if the Japanese should emerge from the jungle in the night. Officers and men were all tired after several days of strenuous fighting, and, to people who have eaten little but bully and biscuits for some weeks, it was somewhat tantalising to be downwind of an officers' mess cook-house; a Burmese cook described with relish to two tired and hungry officers of the 7th Hussars the menu he was preparing for the Chief of Staff. As if this were not enough, one young officer of Army Headquarters seemed to enjoy drawing a contrast between his present predicament and the Dorchester Bar as he had left it only three nights before.

At 9 p.m. Colonel Fosdick was summoned to a Conference at Army Headquarters and General Alexander gave out orders for the following morning. The commanding officer returned at about 11 p.m. and issued orders to two very sleepy squadron leaders and a sleepy adjutant. The rest of the regiment were having a fairly restful night, which was much needed.

Next morning an attack was to be delivered on the enemy at the road block, supported by every available gun and by the 7th Hussars. Two battalions of the 63rd Indian Infantry Brigade, the 1st/10th Gurkhas and the 1st/11th Sikhs, were to carry out the operation, one from the right and one from the left flank and both had to undertake a march of some miles through the jungle, mainly in the dark. The 7th Hussars were to advance along the road so as to arrive at the block at the same time as the infantry and C Squadron from Tharrawaddy was to come south to co-operate. A Squadron was selected for the operation, B remaining in reserve except one troop, required to provide local protection for D Troop, 414th Battery. The Pegu flank was to be watched by the rest of the 63rd Brigade and the 2nd Royal Tanks, of which one squadron remained at Hlegu in case the 48th Infantry Brigade, marching on foot back from Pegu, should get into difficulties.

The night was quiet except for a little spasmodic small arms fire away to the north. At 7 a.m. on the 8th the troop of Essex Yeomanry, with its escort from B Squadron, moved off to the selected gun position in a clearing about four miles south of the target. The rest of the regiment, much refreshed after a good night's sleep, had an unusually leisurely breakfast and at 8.15, with A Squadron in the lead, set off up the road. B Squadron's tanks were spaced out, with groups of soft vehicles between them, so as to give extra protection while passing the road block area.

A report that Japanese in considerable numbers were coming southwards along both sides of the road proved entirely false. Colonel Fosdick himself went forward with the infantry commander who brought the report, but there was no sign of any enemy. On the contrary, Major Bonham-Carter, commanding the forward squadron of the 2nd Royal Tanks, which had relieved B Squadron 7th Hussars the previous evening, reported that he had been on foot to the road block and had been unable to find any enemy there. The enemy had in fact left during the night. Their departure had actually been witnessed by the protective detachment, as told in a previous paragraph. A Squadron therefore found no opposition and the immense column resumed its northward march.

It was perhaps fortunate that the Japanese relaxed their grip on the road, as the arrangements for the attack had gone seriously wrong. One of the battalions had been bombed and never reached its position of assembly at all; the other got there, but eight hours late. The night march was indeed a severe test for two battalions who had no battle experience and no adequate jungle training.

The Japanese had in fact only established the road block as part of a flank-guard operation, covering the movement of a strong force through Paunggyi, across the road and railway, to an area north-west of Rangoon; this force was actually entering the city from that direction while General Alexander's army was still passing through Taukkyan. If, instead of going first for Rangoon, the enemy had continued to block the road and had then taken advantage of the situation in the Taukkyan area, the story of the rest of this campaign might have been very different.

For a few miles the march went well, but at Hmawbi, about five miles on, A Squadron suddenly halted. Actually, there was an abandoned vehicle blocking the road and the delay in fact was only short. But the effect was unfortunate, as the rest of the regiment closed up nose to tail before it was realized that there was a hold-up, and the whole column behind was brought to a standstill. Wireless sets were soon busy asking and answering questions about the delay and Captain Murray Smith, on the regimental rear-link tank, dismounted and went to ask the colonel how he should answer the brigade's question.

Most of the column was more or less concealed by the jungle, but the regimental headquarters were closely congested in a treeless area and formed an ideal target for air attack. And to everyone's dismay, there suddenly appeared fifteen Japanese fighter-bombers, circling round and just about to attack. Those who could dived for cover, the adjutant under the colonel's tank, from which he emerged, he said, scared but unscathed, a few minutes later. A large number of bombs fell with much noise—and some effect—among and around the headquarters vehicles and there were six casualties. Trooper Littlewood, driving Lieutenant P. B. Stanley Evans' dingo, was severely wounded in the arm; the remainder were less serious. Captain Low, the medical officer, was knocked over and shaken by a near miss. One tank and one dingo were damaged, the Scammel recovery vehicle and two lorries were damaged beyond repair, and the commanding officer's staff car had several bullets through it. By the time the attack was over the obstruction in front was removed and the march continued without further interference. A few miles farther on contact was made with the leading troop of C Squadron.

The regiment was now ordered to select a leaguer area four miles south of Taikkyi, while the rest of the column passed through. The tail was still more than forty miles down the road. The 48th Infantry Brigade from Pegu were the last big body of infantry and they were feeling the strain of continuous fighting and marching.

The 2nd Royal Tanks acted as rearguard and only passed the road junction at 3.45 p.m. At about noon the 7th Hussars were ordered to patrol the whole road between Taukkyan and Tharrawaddy. This was a distance of sixty miles. B Squadron went back to the section between Taukkyan and Hmawbi, from the latter to Taikkyi was patrolled by A, and thence to Tharrawaddy by C. There was only one incident, when, at about 3.30 p.m., the enemy tried to establish machine guns near the Hmawbi road junction. A troop of A Squadron was a sufficient deterrent.

This patrolling was a considerable strain on the crews and on the tanks, as they were constantly passing or overtaking vehicles; one troop covered 120 miles on a 10-mile stretch of road. But the sight of an occasional tank was of great moral value to the column and it was well worth while for this alone. As the 2nd Royal Tanks moved northwards, each successive troop of the 7th Hussars was relieved and went back to its squadron, and both A and B Squadrons moved into the regimental leaguer at Taikkyi.

In the evening C Squadron returned to Tharrawaddy. After an exhausting and anxious day, the troops settled down to another peaceful night, while the column still rumbled past. Not the least satisfactory feature of the evening was the appearance of the regimental B Echelon, which came through without mishap.

Just after breakfast next morning General Alexander arrived and congratulated the regiment on its conduct on the previous day. He also revealed his plans for the future. His intention was to use both the 17th Indian and the 1st Burma Division in the Irrawaddy Valley, while a Chinese army would take over the Toungoo front in the Sittang Valley. For the moment the 17th Indian Division was to hold a line astride the road just south of Tharrawaddy. The adjutant has recorded that he felt somewhat sceptical about the plan, as so much seemed to depend on the Chinese; a Chinese "army" was no larger than a British corps, a division was the equivalent of a British brigade, they were miserably short of equipment, had no tanks, few guns and little mechanical transport; their administrative organization was understood to be worse than sketchy; he even doubted whether General Alexander himself felt as confident as he looked.

Few people—if any—have seen General Alexander looking anything but confident. Yet his anxieties at this stage of the Burma Campaign can scarcely have been much less than on the beaches at Dunkirk two years before. Tactically, the enemy's habit of penetration was a nuisance, and lack of intelligence was a serious handicap. But it was the administrative situation which now gave the greatest cause for concern.

The loss of Rangoon had been a very severe blow and the sudden reversal of the lines of supply called for adminstrative gymnastics with which no Staff College instructor would have dared to confront his students. The more rapid the withdrawal, the higher the speed at which the back-loading of stores had to continue. Further loss of stores and supplies, with no prospects of maintenance from India, might jeopardise the fighting capabilities of the force and even its existence. So a great strain was thrown on the transportation services, and the dumps already established at Prome and elsewhere had to be cleared to the north as fast as transport could be made available.

One of the chief difficulties was petrol and lubricants. The loss of the Syriam oil refineries deprived the army of the source of its petrol

Map IX
RANGOON

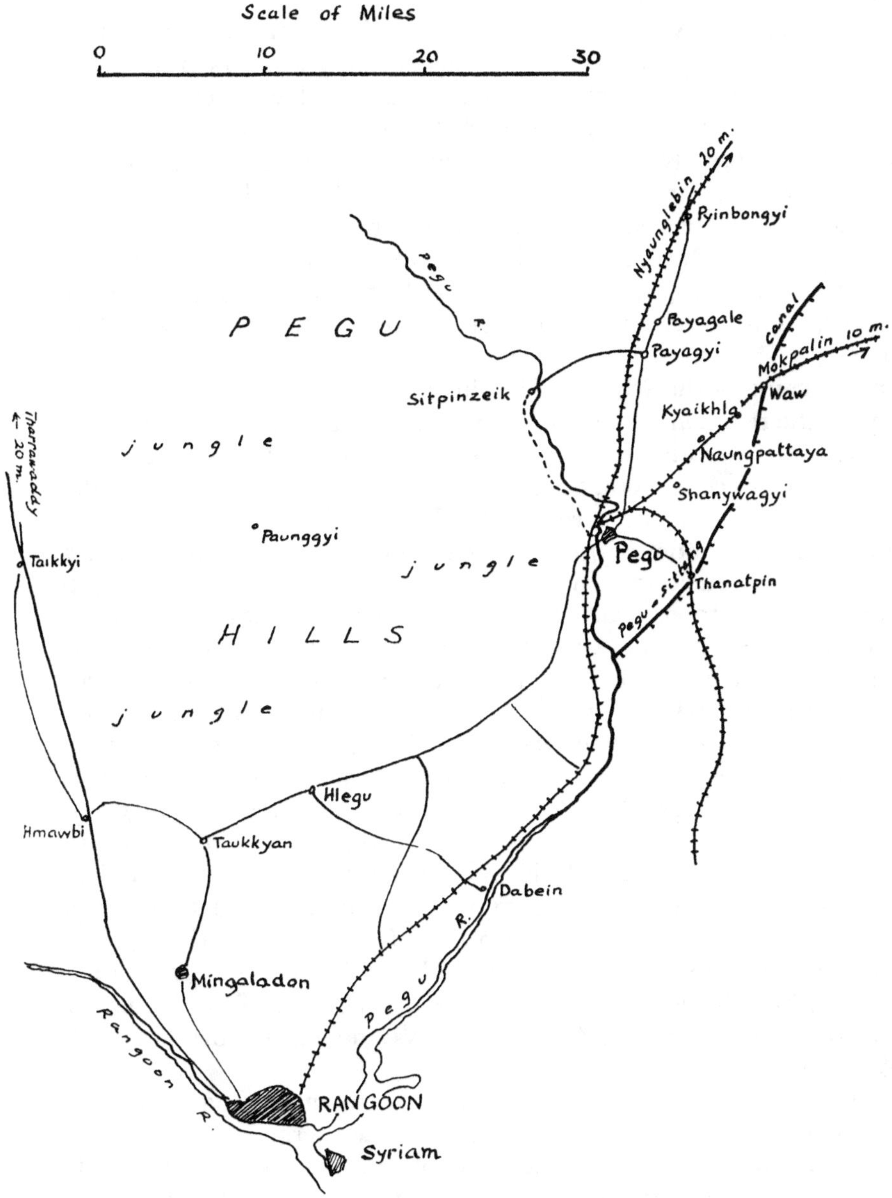

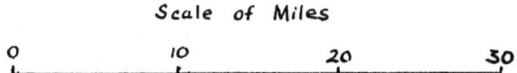

supply, and thereafter petrol and lubricants could only be provided by improvized methods of refining in the oilfields themselves. Another trouble was the loss of the heavy repair installations in Rangoon and it was only with great difficulty that vehicles in need of major repairs could be kept on the road.

But perhaps the worst feature of all was that every administrative advantage previously enjoyed by the Burma Army was now transferred to the Japanese. Although the denial scheme had been carefully thought out and thoroughly executed, the Japanese, once they could effect the necessary repairs, would be able to send to Burma, and to maintain, as many troops as they cared to make available; whereas, until the road from Assam to Burma could be built there was no possibility of the Burma Army being either reinforced or supplied, except on a very modest scale by air—and at this stage of the war air transport, at least as far as the British were concerned, was in its infancy.

The morning of the 9th was spent in maintenance and oil-changing. At 4 p.m. the regiment moved to Tharrawaddy and joined C Squadron. The enemy had made no attempt to follow up and he seems to have been fully occupied in taking possession of Rangoon and basking in the propaganda value of the great port. During the next few days the troops gradually made the most of local facilities and bamboo shelters sprang up, as protection from the mid-day sun and the dew at night.

Much of the town and of the neighbouring villages had been damaged and burnt in air attacks, but a good many houses were fit for occupation. Regimental Headquarters set itself up two or three miles north of Tharrawaddy, in a rather flimsy building, which trembled every time anyone went up or down the stairs; the heavy mess corporal, Beaney, was encouraged to move about as little as possible. Major Llewellen Palmer, now commanding A Squadron, organized a party of local inhabitants, who rigged up a pleasant and shady house of rice straw, and diet was varied somewhat by the arrival of farm produce. Some of the troops were taken for a bathe in a swimming bath owned by the Burma Oil Company and there was a general cleaning up and washing of clothes. Most of the population had gone, but the empty club provided a nice lot of books and a few chairs and glasses, and for two days the ice factory was still working.

It is not always easy to discriminate between "denial schemes" and "looting" and there are points where one merges into the other. Nobody can blame the soldier who acquires a lost dog which is only too ready to adopt a new master. Nor is it very reprehensible to use some abandoned commodity which, if it is not destroyed, would otherwise be of use to the enemy long before its rightful owner could reclaim it—such as whisky or an elephant. But niceties of distinction are apt to be overlooked in circumstances of excitement, especially when local inhabitants are suspected of being unfriendly, and a stern check had now to be imposed on any tendency to beg, borrow, or steal their more intimate belongings, such as poultry and pigs, and undue fraternisation was not encouraged.

On the 13th there was a short move northwards; but this was part of a major readjustment to the dispositions in the Irrawaddy Valley and properly belongs to the next phase of the campaign.

CHAPTER X

Central Burma

Regrouping in the Irrawaddy Valley—the tanks—dispositions round Prome—counter-stroke at Paungde—Shwedaung road block—withdrawal to Taungdwingyi.

Maps X, XI

Now that Rangoon was gone, General Alexander's next task was to hold Upper Burma. For this purpose some regrouping of the forces was necessary. A number of factors had to be taken into consideration. First there was the situation in the Irrawaddy Valley. The 17th Indian Division was reorganizing in the area round Tharrawaddy and Letpadan and reconnoitring defensive positions. It was by no means certain what the enemy would do next and, in order to divert his attention from this front, on 11th March a small operation was carried out in the Sittang valley by two battalions of 1st Burma Division to clear two occupied villages south of Nyaunglebin. This was successful, and when it was over the Burman troops of the division were withdrawn to the north, leaving the 13th Indian Infantry Brigade about Nyaunglebin. The diversion, however, could at the best have only a transitory effect, and much greater strength was needed in the Irrawaddy Valley.

For some time negotiations had been in progress for the entry of Chinese forces into Burma, and as everything was now ready for their arrival, it was decided that the Chinese Fifth Army should take over from the 1st Burma Division on the Toungoo front; this division would then move across to join the 17th Division and form the 1st Burma Corps. India was asked to provide a corps commander and staff, and Lieutenant-General Slim was flown in; owing to the lack of transport aircraft, however, the staff, services and signals had to be improvised from the army staff and units already in Burma.

The Chinese armies—the Sixth was close on the heels of the Fifth—could not arrive until the third week in March, mainly because the Burma Army had to make all their administrative arrangements, including the provision of rice. Although it would have been possible for them to take over considerably south of Toungoo, they were not permitted to operate south of that place, so the Burma Division had to withdraw slowly to Toungoo before it could hand over. Its move across to the Irrawaddy began on the night of the 21st/22nd, mostly by road and rail through Pyinmana and Taungdwingyi. One battalion marched across the Pegu Hills from Toungoo to Prome.

The dispositions in the Irrawaddy Valley were dictated to some extent by the unavoidable withdrawal in the Sittang Valley. Prome, approximately on the same parallel as Toungoo, was selected as the pivot of the 17th Division and Allanmyo for the 1st Burma Division. Each of these places was to be held by a brigade group, while the remaining brigades were to be kept mobile and prepared to act offensively. The 7th Armoured Brigade was to be in corps reserve at Tamagauk.

Finally, Army Headquarters moved to Maymyo, the centre of the civil government and the most convenient point from which General Alexander could control both the Burma Corps and the Chinese armies. The latter had been placed under his command, but the system of control was complex and cumbersome. An order by General Alexander to a Chinese army commander would first go to the American General Stilwell (who spoke Chinese and had been placed in command of the two armies) and from him to a Chinese general who submitted them to a liaison general of Marshal Chiang Kai Shek, if they were of a major nature, or issued them to the army if they were trivial. Orders involving major moves had to be referred to the senior Chinese liaison general at Lashio, who had to obtain the approval of the generalissimo at Chungking before they could come back through the same Chinese channels to the forward troops. In the intervening period the situation might have changed completely, and such a system was quite unsuited to modern war.

* * * *

The regrouping of the forces was effected without any interference from the enemy, and the respite was of great value to the troops, especially to the sorely tried 17th Indian Division. On the 12th a report was received that 1,000 Japanese were moving through the jungle east of Letpadan, but patrols sent out in that direction made no contact.

By the 13th, the 17th Indian Division was reorganized and ready to start its northward move. The 48th Brigade was to provide the rearguard, with the 7th Hussars under command. Accordingly the regiment moved to an area just north of Letpadan on the 13th and the withdrawal was to start the following morning. A dingo patrol was sent into the forest to the east of Letpadan, under Lieutenant John and accompanied by Major Kermode, an officer of the Forest Service who was attached to the regiment as liaison officer. It made contact with a Frontier Force patrol, but there was no news of the enemy. Major Kermode was useful in more ways than one, and, as he was adept at negotiating with the local inhabitants for ducks and other farm produce, several of the officers' messes were able occasionally to forget the monotony of bully beef.

In the evening, orders were issued for the 14th. The rest of the 7th Armoured Brigade and the transport were already on the move and would reach Gyobingauk during the night. In the morning the rearguard, under the commanding officer of the 1st Gloucesters, was to take up positions with the infantry astride the road about Letpadan, and the 7th Hussars deployed east of the road, facing the jungle, on the line between Letpadan and Minhla. The rest of the 48th Brigade was to entrain at Minhla during the day.

At first light on the 14th the troops had breakfast in the usual dense mist and then shook out into their positions a few miles east of the road, squadrons in the order C, B, A from right to left. By 1 p.m. the entrainment at Minhla was complete and the rearguard itself was withdrawn. The 7th Hussars moved up to Zigon, a few miles north of Gyobingauk, where the 7th Armoured Brigade was in mobile reserve.

Six days of inactivity now gave plenty of time for maintenance. A routine patrol was provided daily, one troop, with one platoon of the 1st West Yorkshires under command, going out every day at 6.30 p.m. to a road junction four miles west of Gyobingauk. No training was possible, as, with the exception of the patrol and its parent squadron, the tanks were not allowed to move about or to use their wireless for fear of detection by the enemy. Japanese aircraft were constantly flying up and down the road, evidently looking for targets as well as for information. They seemed to bomb and machine gun the most congested group of vehicles; old soldiers were not taken in by this and the 7th Hussars were never molested.

Like the sound of its name, the Gyobingauk area was somewhat unattractive. The regimental leaguer was at the end of three miles of very rough and dusty track, on rather dirty ground near a dirty village. In addition the weather was oppressively hot and there were too many snakes. Nobody knew much about snakes, so they were treated with violence when seen and with respect when not. As protection from the sun, a number of grass huts were built, in the native style, and the troops set to work to enjoy the short spell of leisure. A new interest had arisen—cock-fighting. There was keen rivalry between squadrons and some quite good birds had been collected. The best belonged to Major Davies-Gilbert of B Squadron; it was never beaten.

In war, periods of idleness usually produce a few good stories, not because more amusing things happen, but because people have more time to talk. One night in March A Squadron was disturbed, just before midnight, by a vociferous argument. The squadron leader went out in his pyjamas to investigate and found the sentry, Trooper Wright, in heated altercation with two angry officers. The colonel and the adjutant had approached the leaguer and did not know the password, so he refused to let them pass and kept his finger perilously near the trigger of his tommy gun. Trooper Wright must have recognized both officers within seconds of his challenge; as officers' mess cook, if in no other capacity, he knew them well; but he was of obstinate temperament and disposed to exploit his advantage. It was only on the intervention of Major Llewellen Palmer that peace was restored and he had the embarrassing duty of making Wright realize he was unwise and at the same time commending him for his keenness. Doubtless Wright felt that he had scored at least two bulls and one inner.

Another story which was generally believed to be true concerned the wireless of a troop of A Squadron while on patrol. On being visited by the second-in-command, the troop leader said his wireless was being interfered with by Henry Hall (a London dance-band leader) on the same frequency. The second-in-command, his thoughts evidently elsewhere, replied, "Well turn him off, boy, turn him off." He did so, and spent a peaceful day while his squadron headquarters tried frantically to get in touch with him and implored, continuously and in vain, "Report my signals." Another bull.

About this time C Squadron was coming in for a certain amount of chaff, as the result of missing the recent fighting. They were referred to as "B Echelon" which was of course meant to be insulting. It was however somewhat unfair on B Echelon, because the people who were most exposed to enemy fire when using narrow roads in the jungle were those in the unarmoured vehicles; they incurred a good many casualties at the various road blocks and ambushes. C Squadron however were not to be out of it for long, and in the next engagement had at least their full share of the fighting.

On the 20th a rumour was heard that the brewery at Mandalay was going to be closed down. For all the beer the regiment had seen since it came to Burma, this would have made no noticeable difference. Nevertheless the rumour coincided conveniently with a decision to take back three lorry loads of surplus baggage. Accordingly Major Younger set off; the baggage was dumped, and later picked up and taken on to Myitkyina, but eventually it had to be abandoned. The three lorries came back with enough beer to provide two bottles per man, not only for the 7th Hussars, but for the West Yorkshires and the Essex Yeomanry Battery, who were at the time under command; and they arrived conveniently just at the end of the next battle.

*   *   *   *

During the lull in operations, there was time to consider the merits of the "Honeys." They had had a good testing, in over a fortnight of continuous marching and fighting, and had stood up to their work remarkably well. Their mechanical performance was excellent, they gave little trouble, they never broke down, their suspension was thoroughly reliable and their rubber tracks seemed to stand up to hard wear and rough going better than steel ones. They had in fact a number of advantages over the A.13's and Crusaders with which the regiment had fought its last battle in the desert. Their weapons, too, were good, the 37-millimeter gun and the 0·3-inch Browning machine guns.

There were nevertheless several disadvantages. The turret was very cramped. The tank was built for a crew of four, the driver, the machine gunner in the hull next the driver, and two in the turret, including the commander; those in the turret had to work the gun, the machine gun and the wireless. The commander had either to load or to fire the guns. Experience in the three-man light tanks in Egypt had proved that the commander must be free from all handling of the guns except giving fire orders, as otherwise he could not control his tank. So now the hull gunner was put into the turret also to help with the guns, and his space in the hull was used for blankets and rations; the third man made the turret very cramped.

Secondly, the fuel supply was limited. Only forty gallons of petrol were carried in the tanks built into the hull, giving a cross-country endurance of only forty miles. There were two auxiliary self-sealing tanks on the outside, but in view of the air situation and the close-in fighting which might take place in the jungle, nobody liked carrying petrol in these.

Thirdly, the low-power No. 11 wireless sets with which the tanks were fitted had insufficient output to overcome track and engine interference, and inter-communication when on the move was never satisfactory.

Finally the construction of the turret was such that the commander could not get a very good view without exposing himself more than was desirable. These drawbacks, however, were trifles compared with the feeling of confidence inspired by the reliable engine and suspension.

Learning to handle the new tanks had been easy, in spite of the very short period of training in Egypt. More difficult was the tactical employment of tanks in co-operation with infantry. None of the Indian or Burman troops had ever seen a tank before and none of the British had had experience of working with them. Nor had the 7th Hussars had any practice in working in close tactical union with infantry. Dealing with road blocks in the jungle was very different from ranging over the desert with a few riflemen in trucks which were seldom more than specks in the distance.

So there was much to learn on both sides and, in the case of the Gurkhas, Indians and Burmans, there was the language difficulty as well. However everybody was keen and the tanks were always popular wherever they appeared. It was in fact difficult to conserve their mileage, as the infantry were always willing for them to run back and forth in reconnaissances or on errands where trucks would have been good enough; it had constantly to be emphasized that when the tanks had done about 4,000 miles apiece they would just lie down and die and there would be no means of reviving them.

*   *   *   *

On the 20th the 7th Armoured Brigade moved to an area north of Paungde, in the next stage of the withdrawal. Reconnaissances were carried out in the Prome area, and the country north of Prome was found to be much more thickly wooded and less suitable for the use of tanks. There was no further move until the 27th, when the 17th Indian Division completed its dispositions, as ordered, for the occupation of the Prome Area. The 7th Hussars remained under the 48th Brigade in the Paungde area until the move was complete, and at 6.15 p.m. on the 27th began the march to Wettigan. For ten miles south of Prome the road runs close to the Irrawaddy, which is in places more than a mile wide and looked its best in the bright moonlight. The air-raid damage in Prome was less conspicuous at night, but the huge and ornate temples stood out clearly on the hill-side.

At Tamagauk the regiment turned right and marched, with forest on either hand, into Wettigan, its allotted area. The time was midnight and the moon was getting low. Reconnaissance for a leaguer had not been carried out and squadrons halted along the road, one behind the other. The village was very dirty and most people sat huddled in their vehicles rather than lie on the filthy ground. At daylight the squadrons found tolerable leaguer areas in the fields near the village and prepared, in the usual way, to settle down for an indefinite period.

B Echelon was at this time between Prome and Tamagauk, nearer to the enemy than the fighting troops. This seemed rather an unusual lay-out, but it was nearer to the source of supply—the dumps at Prome—and brigade headquarters commented at the time that the enemy appeared in rear as often as in front, so what did it matter? Anxiety was in fact again being felt for the line of communication to the north, and on 27th March two squadrons of the 2nd Royal Tanks were ordered to go out the next day to patrol the road between Prome and Allanmyo. There were already signs that the enemy was about to resume the offensive, and although information was at this time founded largely on rumours, there were definite contacts on the Toungoo front and near Paungde.

On the morning of 28th March reconnaissances were carried out in the area round Prome and Tamagauk, so that as many officers as possible should know the country where they might have to operate and the route to the headquarters of neighbouring units and formations. Later in the morning Brigadier Anstice called to see the regiment and squadrons were settling down to make the best of a not very sanitary leaguer area.

The brigade commander had scarcely left when a message was received from brigade headquarters putting one squadron at thirty minutes notice to move. A few minutes later the whole regiment was put at twenty minutes notice and by 2 o'clock it was on its way back to Inma, where it had just come from. So far, information was vague, but the Japanese were said to be in Paungde and the regiment was to help the 1st Gloucesters to destroy any enemy who were in that area. This was in fact the opening movement in a diversionary offensive which coincided exactly with the next Japanese advances in the Irrawaddy Valley. The circumstances which led up to the subsequent bloody and somewhat unsatisfactory battle must be examined in some detail.

Although there had never been any doubt that the enemy would eventually resume the offensive, or that he would again employ enveloping tactics, the detailed form and scope of his next manoeuvres provided several surprises. There was more than one reason for this. First, there was no intelligence service and information from the local inhabitants was mainly fortuitous. Secondly, even the very limited number of sorties by the Royal Air Force reconnaissance aircraft ceased on 22nd March; Magwe aerodrome was badly bombed on the 21st and 22nd and a number of aircraft were destroyed on the ground; the remains of the Royal Air Force and the American Volunteer Group were then withdrawn to Loiwing in China, 400 miles away. Thirdly, contact both on the Irrawaddy and the Toungoo fronts had been broken off altogether after the withdrawal from Taukkyan and Nyaunglebin, and since then had been only spasmodic. It is by no means certain that long distance patrols of infantry who were inexperienced in the jungle would have achieved much; the enemy's superior jungle technique, about which at this stage of the war there is no question, might have led to the loss of a number of men for very little result.

The 1st Gloucesters, who were the reconnaissance unit of the 17th Indian Division, had been in occasional contact with the enemy since the episode of the Taukkyan road block and had had one notable engagement at Letpadan in which they had inflicted a number of casualties on the Japanese at small cost to themselves. The Royal Marines' river patrol had also had a successful brush with enemy craft at Henzada. But definite information was scarce and reports from local inhabitants were often vague and unreliable. In the last week of March the general line of observation ran about thirty miles south of Prome; from right to left it consisted of an improvised commando on the west bank of the Irrawaddy, the Royal Marines' river patrol, the 1st Gloucesters about Nattalin and Paungde and detachments of the Frontier Force in the woods to the east.

The attack on the airfields, already referred to, was part of the enemy's concerted plan for his renewed offensive. He now had absolute control of the air and besides giving tactical support to his land forces, he was able to bomb communications and towns in northern Burma; this caused further paralysis in the civil administration and the flight of most of the railwaymen seriously reduced the capacity of the railways.

On the ground, the enemy's first move was against the Chinese at Toungoo. On 24th March he emerged from the jungle and seized the area north of the town, which included the airfield. The 200th Chinese Division was cut off, south of the town, and despite the stout resistance of an Indian Mountain battery and detachments of the Frontier Force the enemy secured his hold; subsequent efforts by another Chinese division to dislodge him were unsuccessful. On 1st April, after a week of isolation, the 200th Division fought its way out and the new Chinese line was established about Yedashe.

The Japanese began to operate against the 1st Burma Corps on 26th March, just when it was completing the last moves in the readjustment of its dispositions. Prome was bombed on the 26th and three-quarters of the town was burnt. On the 27th reports were received of four to five thousand Japanese and Burmans on the west bank of the Irrawaddy near Tonbo; east of the river, the leading elements of the enemy were already in contact with patrols of the 1st Gloucesters south of Paungde. On this day, at the request of Generalissimo Chiang Kai Shek, General Alexander telegraphed to 1st Burma Corps instructions for an offensive to be carried out on the Irrawaddy front with a view to relieving pressure on the Chinese at Toungoo. On the 28th the Japanese attacked the 1st Gloucesters at Paungde and fighting continued all day. The corps commander considered that this was a good opportunity for offensive action and orders were issued accordingly.

It is curious to note that, by the time the plan reached the troop-leader level, the original conception of a diversionary attack had developed into a counter-offensive which would end up in Rangoon, while the Chinese were to start an offensive a day later and would end up in Pegu. This may have been attributable partly to the forecast given out at the Army Headquarters Conference on the 19th. Orders had then been issued for the occupation of the general line Prome-Toungoo and it was stated that "the intention was to take the offensive and recapture Rangoon as soon as circumstances permit." (7th Armoured Brigade War Diary.) It is more probable however that the main cause of what almost amounted to deception of the troops was the desire of each commander at each level to give them an extra boost.

Some encouragement was certainly desirable. For experienced troops however an excessive dose of "pep" was a little trying, and the contrast between the high-sounding purposes of the counter-offensive and the bloody and rather ignominious escape from an awkward situation two days later, gave rise afterwards to a certain amount of caustic comment. In particular there was a mythical "intelligence officer" somewhere among the clouds of Upper Burma, who was supposed to have announced his discovery that the Japanese were so afraid of the tanks that they would run back to Rangoon again if they saw them coming. One regimental document says "The unknown Intelligence Officer who had produced this report was to remain our bitterest enemy, and much speculation as to what he looked like and his habits in general was made by everyone." As for the Chinese offensive on the following day, this was never even contemplated; the Chinese troops at Toungoo were in serious difficulties and scarcely able to hold their own.

* * * *

At noon on the 28th there was a conference at headquarters, 17th Indian Division. The division was to undertake a local offensive to relieve pressure on the Chinese at Toungoo. The objective was Okpo, thirty miles south of Paungde. Brigadier Anstice was to command the striking force. The operation was to be carried out in two phases, for each of which troops were specifically allotted:—

Phase I—to capture Paungde on 29th March with:—
    414th Battery, Royal Horse Artillery;
    7th Hussars;
    one company 1st West Yorkshires;
    1st Gloucesters;
    2nd Duke of Wellington's Regiment;
    1st Cameronians;
    24th Field Company, Sappers and Miners.

Phase II—to advance on Okpo on 30th March with:—
    All the above, and in addition:—
    2nd Royal Tanks (less one squadron);
    one troop 1st Indian Field Regiment, Royal Artillery;
    one troop 15th Mountain Battery;
    one troop Light Anti-Aircraft;
    7th/10th Baluch Regiment;
    1st/4th Gurkha Rifles.

During the afternoon of the 28th the 2nd D.W.R. were sent forward to Inma to reinforce the 7th Hussars, who were on the way, and the 1st Gloucesters, who were already in action around Paungde; it was hoped that, with this addition, it might be possible to capture Paungde the same evening; in that case Phase II might be advanced to the 29th. The brigade commander and his headquarters, E Troop of 414th Battery and the Cameronians, were to move forward to Inma, the selected leaguer area for the 7th Hussars, so as to get there at first light on the 29th. No written orders were issued, as it was possible that Phase I would be over before they could be typed. The extra troops for Phase II were being concentrated by divisional headquarters and would not come under command of the 7th Armoured Brigade until they reached the Paungde area, sometime during the 29th. The force sounds, on paper, formidable; infantry battalions however were at barely half their strength, and the army was so lamentably short of artillery that only the eight guns of the 414th Battery Royal Horse Artillery could be made available for the operation.

At 2 p.m. on the 28th the regiment moved off. Lieutenant-Colonel

Fosdick went ahead, to find the commanding officer of the 1st Gloucesters and make a plan. The regiment marched quickly back by the route it had followed in the night. Prome looked very different in daylight; the temple was just as magnificent, but the town was badly wrecked and in places still smouldering.

Just north of Inma the regiment halted. The bridge and the diversion over the stream had both been destroyed, so there was no question of joining the Gloucesters in an attack that evening. It would take the sappers most of the night to make a fresh crossing. There was nothing to do but wait, and squadrons stood by the dusty roadside and were told about the situation in front.

The story, as generally understood, was that the Gloucesters had evacuated Nattalin at midnight and had withdrawn to a position about a mile north of Paungde. At daybreak a truck had gone back into Paungde, for the purpose of buying eggs or something, and had not returned. Sometime later the truck was seen again but this time with two Japanese in it, with a Japanese flag. During the morning the Gloucesters attacked Paungde and succeeded in entering it. They had two hours of severe house to house fighting and killed a number of the enemy, with the loss of only eighteen men. Eventually however it became apparent that the Japanese were in great strength and were constantly working round their flanks and rear, and the battalion was slowly drawn back to its original position outside the village. It was very tired and would have been in no condition to carry out another attack the same day, even if the 7th Hussars could have crossed the stream at Inma to co-operate.

Concerning the future, the intentions of the forthcoming offensive were explained to the troops in encouraging terms. It was said that the Japanese on the Irrawaddy front were of low morale and were particularly scared of the tanks. Accordingly the regiment, with a brigade of infantry, was going to attack Paungde in the morning, was then going to Okpo, and if everything went well, would soon be in Rangoon. The Chinese were starting a push on the 30th which should bring them to Pegu at about the same time.

All this was very surprising, but the optimism of the plan was infectious, and the troops were delighted at the prospect of bringing the campaign to a successful conclusion before the rains came. Once the enemy could be got on the run, he might be kept moving and be moved right out. And it was a great relief to be advancing again instead of being perpetually the rearguard. At dusk the squadrons moved off the road to leaguer in the nearby paddy fields and the men lay down for a good night's sleep in an atmosphere of confidence and hope.

At daybreak the 7th Hussars moved back from the paddy fields to the road. C Squadron were in the leading position, with headquarters just behind them, B Squadron and then A, who were to be in reserve. Soft vehicles had been reduced to a minimum, as in previous operations experience had proved that transport vehicles were always an embarrassment and often had to be abandoned. Breakfasts were eaten and everyone was waiting for the sappers to finish repairing the crossings over the stream. At 7 a.m. the brigade commander arrived and held a conference at 7th Hussars headquarters, attended by Lieutenant-Colonel Fosdick and the commanding officers of the four infantry battalions.

On the previous evening the Gloucesters had sent one company to Padigon, on the railway, to prevent any enemy advance in that direction. During the night two companies of the 2nd D.W.R., who had arrived late in the afternoon, had been sent forward to try to get into Paungde; one tried from the north-east and one from the south-west; and nothing had been heard of either since they reached their rendezvous at 3.15 a.m. Arrangements were just being made for the 7th Hussars to move forward on Paungde, when a report from the Gloucesters said that a body of Japanese, strength at least one battalion, was attacking their company at Padigon and outflanking it to the east.

A Squadron was at once sent off to Padigon, with orders to make contact with the company of the Gloucesters and then move north to Thegon, with a view to cutting off the ouflanking enemy column. At the same time one troop of C Squadron was sent off to try to find the company of D.W.R. south-west of Paungde and the regiment, with C Squadron in the lead, began its eastward move along the main road. Two separate battles now developed, one at Padigon and one at Paungde.

Major Llewellen Palmer's orders to A Squadron were simple, "Padigon flat-out." Lieutenant M. M. Stanley Evans' troop was sent first, followed by the squadron leader and second-in-command and the rest of the squadron. Within a minute the tanks were on the move, along the main road towards Paungde. Turning left at the road junction, Stanley Evans raced on at forty miles an hour. Llewellen Palmer checked for a moment, however, to have a word with Major Congreve, whose squadron was at the road junction; and learned that another Japanese column had been seen moving north, this side of Padigon.

As he moved on again, the squadron leader ordered Stanley Evans, who knew nothing of the situation near Padigon, to reduce speed; he was now approaching a coconut plantation, astride the road two miles south of Padigon, a very likely place for the Japanese force to be lying up and a dangerous bottleneck. But it was too late. Stanley Evans had been expressly forbidden to go first in his tank and Sergeant Walton was in the lead. The latter failed to hear the troop leader's wireless efforts to slow him down, and rushed through the wood at a good forty miles an hour. Stanley Evans tried to catch him up, blowing his siren, leaning far out of his turret and shouting, but still without avail. Sergeant Walton was going to Padigon and looked neither to right nor to left, much less behind him.

Nose to tail the two tanks hurtled into the wood, which was occupied by the enemy in some strength. The first sign was when a 12-pounder shell landed close to Stanley Evans' tank; neither his driver nor operator were even partially closed down. A storm of small arms fire rattled on the tanks and occasional shells fell close, but all three tanks emerged on the other side and at last Sergeant Walton was stopped.

Meanwhile the squadron headquarters tanks were closely engaged with enemy occupying another copse, just off the road to the east, who opened fire on them as they approached. The tanks drew off, with slight damage, and Llewellen Palmer took stock of the situation. Not realizing how far Stanley Evans had gone, he ordered him to come back south of the wood (which he had already passed through) with a view to finding an unopposed way round it. Stanley Evans accordingly returned, by the same way as he had gone, and through the same hail of bullets and shells, fortunately with only slight superficial damage.

A Squadron was now faced with two enemy forces, one in the wood and one in the copse. No contact had been made with the Gloucesters in Padigon, and the main enemy force which had outflanked them to the east had now passed out of reach of the squadron. It was clear that, even if tanks could break through to Padigon, the company of Gloucesters would be unable to come back through the wood.

The time had now come for the intervention of infantry and artillery. At about 9.30 a.m. a company of the West Yorkshires, with the help of A Squadron and a troop of 414th Battery Royal Horse Artillery, attacked and captured the copse east of the road. All the enemy in it were killed. Attention was then turned once more to the coconut wood.

Llewellen Palmer had asked for more infantry, but while these were on their way he made one more attempt to reach the Gloucesters with his own resources. Under cover of the 25-pounder troop, using smoke, an attack was made down the road into the wood. This time Lieutenant Barton's troop led the way. He encountered a road block, and broke through it. But he then ran into very heavy gun and small arm

Grass huts in A Squadron's leaguer near Tharrawaddy.

Sergeant Brown's crew, of B Squadron. In front, left to right, Tpr. B. Wilcox, Tpr. Chaplin and Tpr. L. Pinder. Behind, a fitter of the Light Aid Detachment, R.E.M.E.

fire at close range and was ordered to withdraw. He did so with remarkably little damage, under cover of smoke.

When the Cameronians arrived they attacked the wood, with support from A Squadron and the artillery, but were driven back with losses. A further attempt from a different angle also failed. The enemy was in considerable strength and his determined defence prevented all attempts both to interfere with the movement of his main column and to make contact with the company of the Gloucesters at Padigon. A fresh attack was being planned by Colonel Fosdick when, because of events elsewhere, the order came to withdraw.

While A Squadron was going off to deal with the situation in Padigon, the rest of C Squadron was sent off down the road towards Paungde. The troop which had been sent round the western side of the town, had not yet reported contact with the D.W.R. As the squadron advanced down the road it found a block about 600 yards east of the Padigon turning, and the leading troop came under fire from mortars and machine guns. C Squadron was ordered to clear the road block and a company of the D.W.R. was sent forward to co-operate. The tanks and the infantry moved by the more open country on the right of the road and the leading troop managed to reach the road block. This was successfully dealt with. Another troop then took the lead and entered the village at high speed. At a road junction the commander of the first tank obeyed traffic signals given by a Burman policeman and ran at once into an ambush. The crew were temporarily blinded by an incendiary grenade, but the tank was taken in tow and brought away without further damage. Fighting went on in and around Paungde for the rest of the day but the enemy could not be dislodged.

* * * *

While fighting continued round Paungde and Padigon a serious situation was developing in the rear. Early on the morning of the 29th Captain Pilkington, who was now liaison officer between the 17th Indian Division and the 7th Armoured Brigade, left Prome in a scout car, on his way to visit the 7th Armoured Brigade. Driving through Shwedaung he saw a party of men standing round a lorry in front of him. As he approached they opened fire, but he increased speed and shot past. They were in fact Japanese troops in the act of constructing a block.

The first news of enemy on the west bank of the Irrawaddy in any numbers had been received on the 27th. On the 28th the commando unit had been surprised and severely mauled by a party of Japanese disguised as Burmans and the enemy then crossed to the east bank in strength.

The neighbourhood of Shwedaung afforded perfect facilities for ambush and road-blocking tactics, as there was thick jungle on both sides of the road, which passed through a defile between the hills and the river. For troops on a pack transport basis it would not have been difficult to move round another way; but for the armoured brigade, the mechanical transport of the attached infantry and the additional transport provided for ferrying them up to Paungde, some 300 vehicles in all, the 20-foot width of tarmac, crossing many bridges and with a ditch on each side, was of vital importance. There were however no troops watching the road and the Japanese were able to set up a series of blocks without molestation.

Meanwhile at Paungde and Padigon attacks on the enemy had made little or no impression, the infantry were tired, the guns had expended most of their ammunition and no further attack was possible on a scale which would be likely to succeed. In these circumstances Brigadier Anstice asked the 17th Division for further instructions.

The troops south of Shwedaung comprised the whole of the force allotted for Phase I of the counter-offensive. The additional units destined for Phase II had not yet moved south of Prome. Brigadier Anstice was now ordered to withdraw his force to Prome, by way of either Padigon or Shwedaung, whichever offered the better prospect. As all efforts at the former had failed, he decided to break out at Shwedaung. Orders were accordingly given for the force to form up about Inma. The bulk of the transport was already in that area, most of it on the road, facing south-east. There were few places where it was possible to turn a lorry, but by very strenuous efforts, within an hour every vehicle was turned round, and most of them were sorted out in their units. This was no mean achievement, as many of the drivers were Indian. Lieutenant P. B. Stanley Evans played a conspicuous part in this manoeuvre.

The plan was for a small striking force to clear the way and the main body would then pass through. C Squadron would be rearguard. Major Pereira, commanding the 414th Battery, was placed in command of the striking force, which consisted of one troop of his battery, two companies of the Gloucesters, a detachment of engineers and B Squadron 7th Hussars. As this squadron was rather short of tanks, Sergeant Martin's troop of A Squadron was attached to B for the operation.

At 6.15 p.m. Major Pereira's force set off, with B Squadron in front. Lieutenant Geoffrey Palmer's troop took the lead, with Lieutenant Patteson's troop—one tank only—under command. It was rapidly getting dark, but there was a good moon. About two miles south of Shwedaung Sergeant Davies, in the first tank, found a lorry across the road and, as he pulled up, the enemy opened a heavy fire. D Troop Essex Yeomanry at once came into action and fired a few rounds; ammunition was now very scarce owing to the heavy expenditure at Paungde and Padigon during the day. However, this was enough, and when, a few minutes later, the march was resumed, the enemy had disappeared and the block was passed without opposition.

The next obstacle was half a mile farther on. This was a three-ton lorry across the road and on fire. It was covered by a well concealed anti-tank gun and infantry. Sergeant Davies moved off the road to the left and Lieutenant Palmer to the right and both opened fire on the block and the most likely places where the enemy might be concealed. Captain Shorten again got his 25-pounders into action and ranged them on to the targets by the light of the moon. The whole area of the obstruction was well covered with high explosive shell, and as the fire stopped the troop leader gave the order to advance.

This time Lieutenant Patteson took the lead. He edged round the block, reported that he was through and then nothing more was heard of him. The remaining two tanks followed and went on down the road. But almost immediately they came under intense fire from small arms, mortars and light field guns. A few hundred yards farther on Palmer's tank struck another road block. This was passed with difficulty and he realized that there could be no question of the regiment and the hundreds of soft vehicles driving through during the night. Palmer tried to get through to his squadron on the wireless, but found that his aerial had been shot away. He could not turn round on the narrow road in the dark, and he thought that Patteson was still ahead; so he decided to go on and, still under heavy fire, the two tanks continued along the road.

The moon was now setting and the only lights were provided by the enemy's gun flashes, incendiary grenades and tracer ammunition. The speed was a good twenty miles an hour and Palmer intended to drive through the ambush area and then to halt and get his wireless going again. He struck four more road blocks, each time the physical impact of the tank being the first indication. The tanks stood up well to this treatment. The last of the obstacles was across the road in the middle of a bridge, high above a gorge. Fortunately it was only a felled tree which had been dragged there and the tanks hurdled it without damage to themselves or the bridge.

Palmer must have covered two miles by the time he came out of the firing. He halted and again tried to make his wireless work. But both his and Sergeant Davies' sets were out of action, so he drove on to Prome and reported to the headquarters of the 17th Indian Division. At first they seemed to think he was just another candidate for the "Last Survivors' Club," but gradually it was realized that the report he made was of some consequence and the G.S.O.1 passed a message through to the 7th Armoured Brigade and ordered Palmer to remain at Prome.

Meanwhile Patteson was having a most disagreeable experience. He had only just finished sending his message saying he had passed round the block when his tank was hit by an anti-tank gun. The shot did not penetrate, but the driver lost control and the tank went down the steep bank off the road into a paddy field and overturned. The crew scrambled out. Lieutenant Patteson went one way and his crew another. They were more fortunate than he, to begin with, as they made their way to the river and found a small boat. But it was not up to their combined weight and sank in midstream. Two managed to swim ashore and arrived in B Echelon three days later, but the third was drowned.

Patteson walked straight into the Japanese. He was interrogated by an officer and encouraged to talk by kicks on the shins and knocks on the face. This had no effect however and when they got tired of asking him questions the Japanese led him back to the road and roped him to the block. Here he spent several very uncomfortable hours knowing he was bound to be shelled by the 25-pounders and, if he survived that, had every chance of being rammed by a 7th Hussars tank. His captors had also thought of these things and their delight was unconcealed.

The brigade commander had meanwhile decided that the next attack should be carried out by two companies of the Gloucesters and one of the West Yorkshires, seizing the jungle on either side of the road blocks, while two troops of B Squadron advanced down the road. The moon set soon after midnight and the attack was to take place at 2 a.m., preceded by a brisk fifteen-minute bombardment of 25-pounders.

Just before 2 o'clock the bombardment began. For Lieutenant Patteson its results were remarkable. A splinter loosened one of the ropes by which he was tied and enabled him to free himself; the Japanese took cover, and forgot to watch him, and some cattle stampeded. Still with his hands tied, he made his escape among the cattle and, taking to the paddy fields, was able to regain regimental headquarters and give a clear report on the road block and its surroundings.

The attack did not succeed and Brigadier Anstice decided to postpone further attempts until daylight. The whole force closed up as much as possible and spent a cold and uncomfortable night—or what was left of it—by the roadside. Many people managed to snatch an hour or two of fitful and uneasy sleep, but most kept half an eye on the jungle, as there was no knowing what might be lurking in it. It was not really an enjoyable situation. The brigade commander and his brigade major however were in excellent spirits. The adjutant spent part of the night sitting up and talking to them and he said they cheered him up a lot.

The plan for the next morning was simple. First the infantry, supported by 414th Battery, were to capture and hold the woods on both sides of the road block. Then the road block was to be cleared by the 7th Hussars, and the whole of the force was to pass through, 7th Hussars in the lead, except C Squadron, which was to bring up the rear. Then the attacking infantry were to be withdrawn to Prome covered by C Squadron.

At 6.45 a.m. 414th Battery opened fire, and under cover of the bombardment B Squadron moved forward to positions from which to give additional support to the attack. As soon as they opened fire the guns were engaged by enemy mortars and light automatics from their left rear. This threat was not however allowed to interfere with the artillery programme and a troop of C Squadron, with the help of the Duke of Wellington's Regiment, was able to suppress the enemy fire from this quarter on the several occasions when it recurred during the day. Those 7th Hussars who were near the gun position when this attack started were greatly impressed by the bearing of the gunners as the enemy's fire increased. Not one was seen to look over his shoulder in the direction from which the fire was coming. Even when a party of some thirty Japanese and Burmans made an unsuccessful attempt to rush the guns from a nearby copse, the drill of the detachments, as their fire was directed on the distant road block, was as smooth and unconcerned as ever.

B Squadron were led by the troops of Lieutenants Young and Parry, the troop sergeants being respectively Sergeants Cowley and Campbell. At 7 a.m. the infantry attack went in, the Cameronians, one company of the West Yorkshires and two companies of the Gloucesters, along both sides of the road, the objective being the edge of the woods half a mile beyond the road block. At the same time the tanks advanced and attacked the enemy at the block. The block was partially cleared, but Sergeant Cowley's tank was knocked out. Corporal Bowen was killed and Trooper Ashmead wounded. The latter managed to rejoin the following day and said that when he last saw Sergeant Cowley he was advancing on the enemy with a tommy gun.

After considerable fighting the attack achieved a measure of success, although the woods were not fully cleared. Firing died down, and it was decided that the main body should now take its chance and run the gauntlet of any enemy who remained in the area. This decision was the more imperative because by now the enemy's pressure in the rear had caused the column to pack more densely on the road, and vehicles were in many places nose to tail and four abreast; secondly, reconnaissance aircraft now appeared and it was expected that bombers would soon follow; thirdly, there came yet another report of enemy advancing from the rear.

C Squadron was right behind and was to come through last, protecting the withdrawal of the infantry now deployed in the woods. The breakthrough was led by B Squadron followed by A Squadron, whose tanks were mingled with the transport to provide some extra protection. Regimental and brigade headquarters followed and finally the transport and guns. As B Squadron advanced the enemy, who were still present in strength, and had merely been lying low after the attack, opened heavy and close fire.

B Squadron got through, with some loss, but every lorry that was knocked out and set on fire became one more road block. On one bridge there were two wrecked lorries, and Sergeant Hipsey's tank went back to clear them off and to hold the bridge while the column passed. His tank was knocked out and only Trooper Martin survived. Most of A Squadron were able to follow B, losing the fitter Sergeant, Bowden, and Trooper Hawkins killed, but the mounting pile of burning vehicles soon stopped movement and once more the road was blocked.

At the head of the halted column was Major Llewellen Palmer's tank, then Captain Murray Smith's, and behind these the soft vehicles of regimental headquarters, with the other headquarters tanks interspersed between them. Behind these were brigade headquarters and the rest of the transport, C Squadron being still in rear and holding off those enemy who were following up. Bombers could be expected at any minute and there was little to be gained by waiting. So it was decided to go bald-headed for the block, in the order in which vehicles now stood on the road.

The two leading tanks set off and went down the road at top speed. The principal obstacle was a large log of wood. Llewellen Palmer's tank jumped it and pushed it slightly to one side. The adjutant's tank, driven by Trooper Muxworthy, followed closely, and the way was clear for wheeled vehicles. Although the tanks were not fired on—as far as they were able to notice—the rest of the party was heavily engaged by the enemy at close range.

The first soft vehicle through was the adjutant's truck, driven by his batman, Trooper Washington, who came through without mishap and apparently quite unconcerned. The next was the colonel's car, which was hit by a Molotoff cocktail and burnt out. His driver, Trooper Frost, and batman jumped on to Mr. Brown's truck. Nearly all the vehicles were hit and one petrol lorry was destroyed, but the headquarters came through with little damage.

One of the outstanding individual actions of this episode was that of Trooper Fox. Fox was a tall, fair haired man who always seemed to take his pleasures, if any, sadly. He was a despatch rider on regimental headquarters, and as he rode through the ambush area on his motor cycle he noticed an infantry despatch rider crouching in the ditch, with his motor-cycle lying on the road above. He stopped to ask him what was the matter and on learning that the motor cycle had gone wrong, said "I know these things well, you take mine and go on and I'll put this one right." The other went on, and for the best part of twenty minutes Fox stayed by the roadside repairing the motor cycle and, as the tanks came past, standing up and pointing at the houses from which fire was coming so that they should engage the best targets. Having done the repairs he mounted and rode out, among the last to get through.

Brigade headquarters and some of the transport succeeded in passing through. But the increasing number of burning vehicles again caused a stoppage and the Japanese closed in on the road. Some of the Indian drivers managed to find diversions through the woods, but these too were quickly obstructed by burning vehicles and the Japanese seemed to be just as numerous as ever. To add to the confusion, bombing now started, and was kept up continuously for the rest of the day. There were neither anti-aircraft guns nor fighter aircraft and the enemy airmen had all their own way.

Among the body of troops still cut off, only C Squadron and 414th Battery Royal Horse Artillery were able to take any effective action to open a way out. On the north side of the block, however, there were two fresh Indian battalions, which had originally been intended for Phase II of the operation and were waiting between Prome and Shwedaung. As soon as Brigadier Anstice had found these he started making plans for an effort from that side.

Meanwhile the adjutant of the 7th Hussars was sent ahead to Prome to report the situation to divisional headquarters. He records that he was coldly received by the corps and divisional commanders, who were together, that his report seemed to evoke little interest, and that he came away rather angry and bad-tempered, but supposed that, after all, there was very little they could do about it. In this he was probably right; Brigadier Anstice was already doing all that was possible from the northern side. The two Indian battalions were sent southwards with two tanks of brigade headquarters to clear the woods near the road block. On the road the tanks were held up by a burning ammunition lorry, and the infantry were stopped by enemy fire before they reached the northern edge of the village.

On the other side of the block Major Congreve's squadron was still fighting off the enemy who were following up from Paungde, and bombing was setting more and more of the transport vehicles alight. He did all he could to re-open the way quickly, and sent Sergeant Cleere's troop to force the road block. The troop had great difficulty in passing the infantry trucks, which were all over the road and many of them blazing. However, Sergeant Cleere managed to reach the road block. Here he came under very heavy fire from mortars and an anti-tank gun and had to retire. One tank, which had tried to grapple the block and drag it away, had to be left, as it got stuck on its side in the ditch.

Major Congreve now held a conference with the two infantry commanding officers and a plan was made to attack with one company on each side of the road, while a troop of tanks rushed the block. The Essex Yeomanry gave support. But the attack made little progress, as the infantry were pinned down by machine gun fire and continual dive bombing, while the tanks were hampered by burning trucks.

It was now late afternoon, and the situation was almost desperate. The troop protecting the rear was constantly under fire from the enemy, who were working in closer and closer towards the congested mass of transport. The whole party was in danger of capture unless something could be done at once. The squadron leader asked the infantry commanding officers for a final effort. But their troops had already been fully committed, and under the impact of continuous air attack had taken cover a little deeper in the jungle. They could not be mustered for another assault. The only possible course that remained was for the tanks to break out through the road block, after one final shoot-up from the battery, for the infantry to find their way round on foot and for the soft vehicles either to take their chance or to be abandoned.

The 414th Battery Royal Horse Artillery were not to be daunted. To abandon soft vehicles meant to abandon their guns as well. For Pereira and Shorten such a course was unthinkable. They had scarcely a round left and could be of little further use in the present battle, but they would be needed again and the guns must be saved. So, in the best traditions of the Royal Horse Artillery and after the

Infantry preparing to attack the wood on the road to Padigon.

Jungle conference.
Maj. Gen. Cowan, commanding 17th India Division, with Lt.-Col. Fosdick (*left*) and Captain P. B. Stanley Evans (*right*).

fashion of the famous troop which charged through the French cavalry at Fuentes d'Onor in 1811, the battery drove out.

There was one particularly tiresome spot in the Japanese position which seemed to conceal a mortar or anti-tank gun. It was decided that one of the few remaining rounds should be used against this and that the only way to tackle it was with a 25-pounder at close range. So a gun of 414th Battery was towed up by a tank to within thirty yards of the enemy and quickly came into action; the work was demolished.

The road block was now blazing with such fury that it could not be penetrated. The leading troop of tanks however found a way round through the jungle, and over a stream. The rest of the squadron followed, with its own transport, the guns and a few of the infantry vehicles, knocking down small trees and flimsy native huts as they went. A troop of C Squadron brought up the rear.

Captain Shorten led the battery in his observation tank. After skirting round the blazing block the column regained the road, still under fierce fire, which continued for nearly a mile farther. The narrow tarmac was obstructed by numerous burning vehicles and every tree seemed to conceal a Japanese. Each time a vehicle was stopped a few Japanese would rush out and set fire to it with a Molotoff cocktail; while others would keep up a constant rifle and automatic fire. Three of the four-wheel-drive gun tractors were knocked out, resulting in the loss of two of the guns. The third gun, which had overturned, was towed out upside down by a tank. To have attempted to save the others would have led to certain loss of their detachments as they were under close automatic fire. During one hold-up Lieutenant Simcox manhandled a gun into action and fired the single remaining round into a nearby enemy post, killing a machine gun crew. One of the gunners advanced on another enemy post with hand grenades he had obtained from the infantry. Covered by these and many other acts of individual gallantry six of the eight guns came through. The casualties in the battery were severe, but it was a very gallant action and these six guns were to play an indispensable part in the remaining six weeks of the campaign.

At about 4.30 p.m. the Indian battalions which had moved south from Prome were withdrawn, covered by a squadron of the 2nd Royal Tanks; this regiment was temporarily under the 48th Indian Infantry Brigade, which now pushed detachments out to the east to guard against the enemy's threat along the railway. The 7th Hussars moved back to B Echelon's area near Tamagauk, replenished and settled down for the night.

Thus ended a venture which may have achieved the object of diverting Japanese attention from the Chinese front at Toungoo but, as the Japanese had already begun their offensive in the Irrawaddy Valley, it probably diverted none of their troops. It undoubtedly cost them a number of casualties and may have caused a few days' delay in their northward advance against the oilfields. But the cost to the Burma Army was severe. The 7th Hussars lost eleven killed and over thirty wounded. Material losses of the force were also serious, and included ten tanks, two guns and nearly three hundred transport vehicles, many of which fell into the enemy's hands intact.

It was indeed an unkind twist of fate which placed Brigadier Anstice's valuable force within the enemy's net. Only twenty-four hours earlier the whole area south of Prome had been evacuated, except by the divisional reconnaissance unit, the 1st Gloucesters. For these to slip away through the woods would have been comparatively easy. As it turned out, the enemy's encircling movement coincided exactly with the filling-up of the area with British troops, and, which was worse, with vast quantities of transport whose communications along a ribbon of tarmac were so vital and so easy to cut.

Among the losses at Shwedaung was the Senior Chaplain of the brigade, the Reverend Funnell. "Smokey"—his name, coupled with a perpetually active pipe, made this inevitable—had been with the brigade since September. He had qualities of sincerity, kindliness and serenity which endeared him to all. He would turn up in a crisis, when he might be least expected, perhaps bringing the news sheet which he prepared almost daily and often letting people listen to the news on his wireless set. As he accompanied the brigade past the block his driver was hit. Smokey managed to stop the truck and got out to go round to the other side and help the driver. But he was already dead and Smokey himself was shot dead at close range. Everyone in the brigade felt he had lost a friend.

Cowley, whose home was in Newcastle, joined the regiment as a boy, but left the Band as soon as he was eighteen. After first being staff car driver in B Squadron, he became one of the first of the Driver Operators, and was control operator of B Squadron for over two years. After Beda Fomm he became a tank commander, still in B Squadron, and was a troop sergeant at the time of his death. He won the Military Medal in July 1940 near Fort Capuzzo, and a bar in November 1941 on Sidi Rezegh aerodrome. Cowley was little more than 23 when he was killed. Always smart and keen he set the highest example in everything he did. In peace time he had been a mainstay of the regimental boxing team, and he also kept goal for his squadron at football.

Hipsey came to the regiment from the 9th Lancers in 1937. Always very smart, he was for some time officers' mess corporal before becoming a tank driver in B Squadron. When war came he soon made a name as a tank commander in the Italian campaign. He was badly wounded near Fort Capuzzo in April 1941. He returned to the regiment in the autumn, but missed Operation Crusader through being on a course. Of fine physique and bearing, Hipsey was a splendid leader, and was liked and respected by everyone.

*   *   *   *

The country round Prome consisted largely of reserved forest and, while being unsuited to tanks, was very favourable to the usual Japanese tactics of infiltration. Prome was the terminus of the railway in the Irrawaddy Valley and had consequently been the most convenient dumping ground when Rangoon was being cleared; it had been hoped that the position could be held long enough to enable the large quantities of supplies, stores and ammunition to be back-loaded to the north. But this was not to be. Preliminary arrangements for a withdrawal had been approved by General Wavell on the afternoon of 1st April, when, with General Alexander, he had visited 1st Burma Corps at Allanmyo.

The defence of the oilfields was now the first consideration. But in view of the nature of the country and the tired state of the 17th Indian Division, the latter was to be withdrawn through the 1st Burma Division's position at Dayindabo and Pyalo, to the general line Allanmyo-Kyaukpadaung. It was also foreseen that a further retirement might eventually be necessary, to the area south of Taungdwingyi. Backloading of supplies from Prome in the next few days was to continue as fast as the depleted transport situation would permit and unit transport was to draw daily requirements direct from the dumps.

The 7th Armoured Brigade headquarters and 7th Hussars were still at Tamagauk. The 2nd Royal Tanks were protecting the eastern flank of the force in Prome, and had had encounters with small Japanese detachments but had been prevented, by the nature of the country, from chasing them. The 7th Hussars had a patrol at Wettigan, also looking eastwards, and everyone was expecting another encircling movement. The inhabitants of Wettigan were busy evacuating the village and one of them, on a horse, was seen galloping away to the south, which seemed to indicate that something was in the wind. It was believed that the enemy were always anxious, above all, to know the whereabouts of the tanks, and doubtless they made full use of disaffected Burmans for this purpose. On the next morning the regiment was due to move at 7 a.m. to Allanmyo.

The conference of the commanders at Allanmyo was scarcely over when the enemy attacked the positions south of Prome. So the prospect of an uninterrupted withdrawal to the Allanmyo line had gone. At first the attacks were held, but at about midnight the enemy penetrated the positions of the 63rd Indian Infantry Brigade and passed through Prome. The situation was for some time obscure, but it was known that there were numbers of Japanese north of the town, between the Irrawaddy and the road through Tamagauk to Allanmyo.

At 1.30 a.m. on the 2nd the 7th Hussars were rudely awakened and ordered to line the road through Tamagauk, facing west. In this region the road runs through a broad belt of jungle and from 2 a.m. until daylight the tank crews spent an anxious few hours listening for the enemy. However, no Japanese appeared and at 7 a.m. the regiment marched for Allanmyo, most of the tanks being loaded to capacity with Gurkhas.

The march was uneventful, and rather unexpectedly so, because a Japanese reconnaissance aircraft was constantly flying up and down the road. For most of the way there was forest on both sides, but for one stretch the road described a series of S-bends on the open slopes of steep hills, overhanging the Irrawaddy. It was something of a relief when this part of the journey was accomplished without mishap. At about 10 a.m. the regiment and brigade headquarters arrived in the allotted area, some three miles north of Allanmyo, where B Echelon was already established. The country was like an English park, studded with large trees, and the vehicles were dispersed beneath them in unusually pleasant surroundings. The brigade was to be in corps reserve, while the Burma Division held the Dayindabo position and the 17th Division withdrew through it to the general line Allanmyo-Kyaukpadaung.

Here it had been intended that the withdrawal should cease; only the 48th Indian Infantry Brigade and the 7th Armoured Brigade (less the 2nd Royal Tanks) were to move back a little farther, to Satthwa, in corps reserve. But on 3rd April, owing to the exhaustion of the troops, it was decided that the withdrawal should continue to the general line Minhla-Taungdwingyi. The 17th Division's movement was necessarily slow, owing to the depleted state of the transport, and the 2nd Royal Tanks helped to lift the infantry, carrying, according to the brigade report, as many as twenty or thirty on a tank.

The area round Taungdwingyi was known as the dry zone. The country was rather more open and suitable for the operation of armour, but it had the disadvantage of giving greater scope to the enemy's air force. At this stage of the campaign bombing and machine-gunning were almost continuous in the forward area during daylight.

Map X
PROME

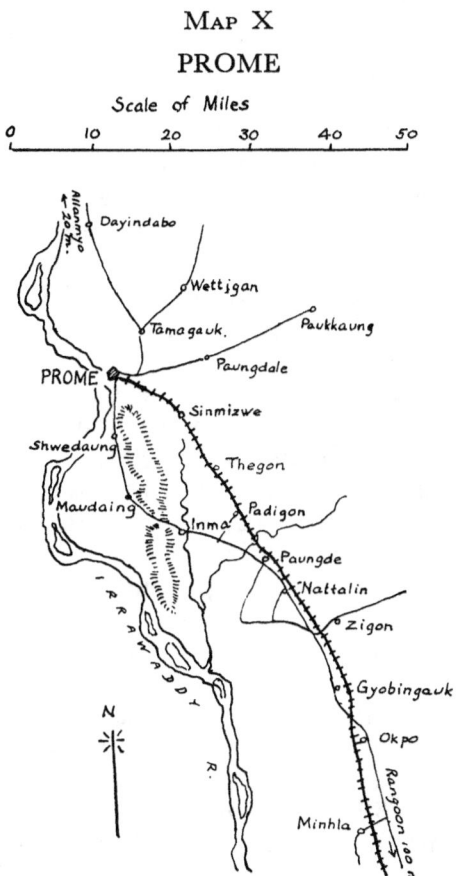

On 3rd April the 7th Hussars spent a quiet morning in their agreeable surroundings. Some went for short walks among the trees and woods, others went looking for limes. At one spot, on the bank of an attractive stream, a group of three or four officers could have been seen playing, like children, with paper boats. Nothing could have been better for the state of mind of men who had just had a rather disagreeable and unsatisfactory battle.

At about noon the order came for the withdrawal to Satthwa. This was to be a night march. The regiment moved off soon after seven and was in its new area by ten o'clock, a small, squalid village a few miles north of Satthwa. However, next morning squadrons spread out among the surrounding woods and settled down for three days of maintenance.

The brigade commander had been pressing frequently for an opportunity to do the 100-hour check which was considered essential for the Honeys. It was hoped that the withdrawal to Satthwa would give the regiment its chance, and work began. Before long quite a lot of the trees had an engine hanging in their lower branches, as well as the usual flying foxes in their upper ones. The 5th was Easter Sunday and the flying foxes had the further new experience of lusty Easter hymns. By the evening all the tanks were ready for action again.

Next day squadron officers carried out reconnaissances of the probable areas of operation and news came of the projected move to the Thadodan area. It was becoming more and more clear that an ultimate evacuation of Burma might be necessary. Rations were getting a little short and the ammunition situation was also causing anxiety. The officers discussed these things among themselves, with "cheerful defeatism," and speculated upon the possibilities of turning north-east for China or north-west for India. In the latter case, it was evident that at some time or other there would be a long walk on foot, and first thoughts were given to little personal matters such as the things that could be carried.

On the evening of the 7th the regiment marched again, and reached its destination at Wetchangan just before dark. The pace was fairly good in spite of the congestion on the road caused by withdrawing infantry and crowds of Indian refugees. The leaguer area was in a wood near a monastery.

By the night of the 7th/8th the Corps was on its new line, except one brigade of the Burma Division on the west bank of the river, which was twenty-four hours behind. The Burma Division held the right, with brigades at Minhla, Migyaungye and Nyaungyatsan. The 17th Indian Division held the left at Taungdwingyi. The 48th Indian Infantry Brigade, with the 7th Armoured Brigade in support, held the centre about Thadodan and was also to act offensively if required, under corps control. A light screen of patrols was established some fifteen miles to the south of the position, reconnaissances were carried out and plans were made to attack the enemy as he approached the position.

Conditions for the successful defence of the Taungdwingyi position were by no means ideal. The line was very extended—forty miles long—and had no depth; to make up for the shortage of troops, the

Chinese promised to send a division to take over the defence of Taungwingyi itself, but in the event they only sent a battalion; a Chinese battalion had the fire power of a British company. Secondly, the main line of communications ran parallel with and just behind the front; the track from Taungdwingyi to Natmauk along the railway was very rough and had to be repaired before it could be used, and the force was now being maintained from supply dumps at Magwe and Yenangyaung. So the 17th Indian Division at Taungdwingyi depended on the main road through Thitagauk for its supplies. Thirdly, the principal obstacle in the district, the Yin Chaung, lay behind the position and not in front of it. Fourthly, although it was fashionable to talk of Taungdwingyi as the "Tobruk of Burma"—an expression which caused supercilious amusement among the 7th Hussars —some of the essential ingredients were missing; not least among these were barbed wire and guns. For the latter there was no substitute—not even an aeroplane. But the Gurkhas had a primaeval device which took the place of barbed wire; this consisted of several rows of bamboo spikes, sunk in the ground at an angle, the sharp end facing outwards. Every position had to be prepared for all-round defence, and this type of obstacle was quite quick and easy to erect, and was used whenever bamboos could be obtained.

During the brief lull which followed the withdrawal, thoughts turned again to things beyond the immediate surroundings. News from the outside world was somewhat depressing. Two cruisers had been lost in the Bay of Bengal, including the *Cornwall*, which had escorted the *Ascanius* on part of her voyage. Colombo had had its first air attack by carrier-borne aircraft. Although the enemy had had severe losses in the attack, the idea of a Japanese fleet in the Indian Ocean was anything but pleasant. However, on 9th April the war was forgotten. Mail arrived, flown from India, the first since the regiment had left Egypt three months before; more arrived on the 10th. The difference which this made to the troops, officers and men alike, was a surprise even to the most experienced soldiers, and General Alexander commented upon it in his despatch. Even the most gloomy recovered their cheerfulness, and the feeling of the restored link with those at home put new zest into the army. From now onwards there was at least hope of another mail, although in fact none came until the army was out of Burma, nearly six weeks later.

CHAPTER XI

From Burma to India

The Taungdwingyi position—loss of the oilfields—Meiktila and Kyaukse—the Irrawaddy position—the race for Kalewa—the race with the weather—into India.

Maps VIII, XI, XII

On the afternoon of 10th April came news of the next Japanese moves in the Irrawaddy Valley. At noon on that day an enemy force estimated at one battalion was seen by an infantry patrol at Yagyidaw, seven miles south of Thadodan. A little later Sergeant Patrick Cleere's troop, patrolling to the south, rounded a bend in the road and encountered a road block. Japanese troops were standing about and, to judge by their surprised faces, had not heard the tanks coming on account of the continual noise of aircraft overhead. The two tanks had a good shoot before the enemy could get his anti-tank gun into action, but the fire then became too hot, targets had been shot down and no more enemy could be seen. The troop therefore withdrew, having obtained valuable information. The Japanese were in fact beginning their penetration through the Taungdwingyi line, on their way to Yenangyaung.

In the evening soft vehicles were sent back to B Echelon to be out of the way and the regiment closed on brigade headquarters for the night. Patrols sent southwards from A and B Squadrons made no contact with the enemy, as the going was bad and the night was dark.

At first light on the 11th patrols of the 48th Infantry Brigade were attacked by Japanese at Yewe and Songon. The enemy seemed to be trying to penetrate the main line of defence in the gap between the 13th and 48th Infantry Brigades and also near the Irrawaddy. A detachment of scout cars of the 2nd Royal Tanks was ordered to patrol the road between the two brigades and another was sent to protect the bridge over the Yabe Chaung, just to the west of the 48th Brigade's position. The 7th Hussars again sent one squadron southwards at dawn to co-operate with 48th Brigade's patrols; it was A Squadron's turn.

The squadron moved off just as it was getting light and reached Myinzu. From this point the three troops were sent farther south and squadron headquarters stayed near the village. The area was well wooded and tanks were by no means ideal for searching out the enemy.

Something, apparently human, was seen creeping along a scrubby ditch only about fifty yards from the squadron headquarters tanks, and Major Llewellen Palmer asked for infantry to come and help in the reconnaissances.

Sergeant Roberts' and Lieutenant Barton's troops meanwhile reported Songon and Kobin respectively clear of the enemy, and both villages were burnt. Lieutenant Browne opened fire on a bullock cart, suspected of concealing enemy—a quite usual Japanese ruse—but this one proved to contain only friendly Burmans and was allowed to proceed.

At about 11 a.m. some infantry arrived; the squadron headquarters then moved on to Kobin and the three troops moved farther south, into country which was more open and afforded a better view. An air attack on Kobin caused casualties to a party of refugees, but no damage to the troops. Sergeant Roberts reported Yagyidaw empty. Lieutenant Barton however saw a Honey tank manned by men in black overalls; for a time he thought it was one of the 2nd Royal Tanks, and only as it disappeared did he observe a Japanese flag and realize, too late, that the Royal Tank Regiment no longer wore black except on their heads.

At dusk the squadron withdrew. It came on to rain very heavily and although at first the cooling effect was something of a relief, everyone was very wet and cold before they reached the leaguer. The whereabouts of the Japanese was still uncertain, and a careful look-out was kept on the way through the wooded area round Myinzu. When the rain passed over the whole countryside was lit up by an ominous red glow which, with the deep contrasting purple of the hills, was beautiful in its own way, but in the circumstances too sinister to be appreciated. The regiment leaguered with the brigade headquarters, just north of the main road and four miles nearer Taungdwingyi than they had been the previous night.

On the right flank, early in the same afternoon, the 13th Infantry Brigade had made contact with a considerable Japanese force moving west through Letpanywa, apparently heading for the gap between their position and the river. A squadron of 2nd Royal Tanks was placed under the 13th Brigade, but it did not arrive in time to come into action that day.

At about 6 p.m. the Japanese began an attack on the south-west of the 48th Brigade's positions near Wetchangan. This enemy force was probably the same as had passed through Yagyidaw early the previous day. The 2nd Royal Tanks (less the squadron already with the 13th Brigade) were now in support of the 48th Brigade, to help them if possible during the night. All their soft vehicles, the 7th

Armoured Brigade Headquarters and the 7th Hussars, moved again, four miles nearer Taungdwingyi, so as to avoid being caught up in a midnight dog-fight.

The 48th Brigade managed to hold their own, and the 7th Armoured Brigade's replenishment convoy got through from Magwe, along the main road, and arrived in the new leaguer area shortly before midnight. Enemy pressure continued all night and in the early hours of the morning the 48th Brigade's positions were penetrated at one point. A counter attack at dawn, however, supported by the 2nd Royal Tanks, restored the situation.

Patrols were then sent out by the 2nd Royal Tanks. One of these found a road block of the usual pattern established at milestone 294 and another found Kokkogwa occupied by the Japanese. This village was north of the road and it was apparent that the enemy had discovered the gap between the 13th and 48th Brigades, although nobody could tell in what strength he was going through it. A plan was at once made to clear first the village and then the road block. Both tasks were carried out by the 48th Brigade, with tanks in support. The 2nd Royal Tanks had a good day, destroying two anti-tank guns, causing a number of casualties and shooting down one enemy aircraft.

The 7th Hussars meanwhile stayed concealed in the woods. C Squadron was sent out to patrol westwards towards the 48th Brigade, along the road and southwards. Other squadrons put out patrols for local protection.

B Squadron's patrol (Lieutenant John Parry's troop) somehow got into the area where Lieutenant Allen's troop of C Squadron was operating. The news of Barton's oversight of the previous day had spread quickly and nobody wanted to be caught out in the same way. Each troop leader therefore decided that the other was probably the enemy in captured Honeys. There followed an hour of cautious stalking, and reporting on the wireless. Allen's troop had a few anxious minutes when the troop leader, who had climbed a tree for a better view, got his foot lodged in a fork and stuck. However, his crew prised him out. Eventually regimental headquarters, after both squadrons had made several reports on suspected enemy tanks, realized what was happening and the impromptu manoeuvres were brought to an end without casualties on either side. It was some time before either of the officers was allowed to forget this incident.

There was no contact between the regiment and the enemy on this day but, as a precaution a road block of bullock carts was established at the 290th milestone; this was effective while it lasted, but the Burmans later removed their bullock carts while no one was looking.

Meanwhile, during the afternoon, the Japanese in Kokkogwa, who had apparently only been lying low while the 2nd Royal Tanks passed through, popped up again. They engaged the 48th Brigade positions with mortars and light field gun fire. Another attack on the village was planned, and just as it was about to start, the enemy began shelling from the Yewe direction. In view of this threat from another angle, and the tiredness of the infantry, the attack was called off. The Essex Yeomanry battery made every effort to locate the enemy's guns—he seemed to have two batteries in action—but observation was very difficult and they were not silenced.

Firing by both sides continued during the night, and at about 1 a.m. the enemy attacked the 48th Brigade, again without success. One sleepy 7th Hussar said to another "Why won't these ruddy Japs and that 48th Brigade stay still for a minute and let me get to sleep?"

*　　　*　　　*　　　*

On 13th April the 7th Hussars spent a quiet morning, with patrols out to the south and the restful role of protecting the soft vehicles of the brigade in the woods north of the road. To the west, however, there were still signs of enemy activity. Patrols at dawn saw two tanks in the Sonzu-Yewe area, almost certainly salvaged Honeys, but they got away before they could be brought to action. The road was found clear as far as milestone 300 and infantry patrols passed through Kokkogwa unmolested. Patrols set fire to Sonzu and Yewe. The only village still occupied by the Japanese seemed to be Songon, and this was accordingly shelled by the Essex Yeomanry.

Farther west, however, there was a more serious situation. The enemy had entered Migyaungye on the river bank; here there was nobody in front of them, as the 1st Burma Brigade had been moved eastwards the previous day, to deal with the column reported at Letpadywa.

The 2nd Royal Tanks were now sent off to the Yin Chaung bridge to come into divisional reserve for the 1st Burma Division, and the 7th Hussars went to take over their functions with the 48th Brigade. At 2 p.m. the 7th Hussars moved up to milestone 290 and thence southwards into some copse land just as enemy aircraft began dropping bombs. At the same time the 2nd Royal Tanks moved off down the Magwe road.

The latter had some trouble at the bridge over the chaung, which was being accurately shelled by the Japanese. But the Essex Yeomanry now had a fairly good idea of the enemy's gun positions in the Songon area, and were able to keep them more or less neutralized when necessary. In the main, however, the road was open, and the replenishing party came up from Magwe in the evening, as usual. On their way up they passed a large number of infantry withdrawing towards Magwe and there were many knocked out vehicles by the roadside, but there was no sign of the enemy, whose whereabouts, as far as the regimental officers and men were concerned, was a matter only for rumour and conjecture. Owing to the uncertainty however the guards in B Echelon, near Magwe, had been doubled; the Japanese had been reported opposite to them, just across the river.

During the afternoon a further change was ordered in the dispositions of the corps. The headquarters of the 7th Armoured Brigade was to move back to the Yin Chaung crossing and come under the 1st Burma Division. The 7th Hussars were to remain with the 48th Brigade, which was to come under the 17th Indian Division. These dispositions had been rendered necessary by the enemy's deep penetration, about which there was no longer any doubt, through the gaps in the line.

The corps commander had now come to the conclusion that, without the Chinese division which had been promised but had not arrived, he could not both hold Taungdwingyi and cover the direct approach to the oilfields. To have abandoned Taungdwingyi would have exposed the right flank of the Chinese armies, whose advanced troops were still south of Pyinmana, and would also have jeopardized the lines of communication between the Burma Corps and Mandalay. General Alexander therefore gave orders that Taungdwingyi was to be held at all costs, and the re-distribution of the troops during the next few days was directed, in so far as the enemy permitted, to this end.

The 48th Indian Infantry Brigade moved into Taungdwingyi on the 14th, covered and also carried by the 7th Hussars. Next morning B Squadron (Captain T. R. S. Thornton, M.C.) moved to join the 13th Indian Infantry Brigade which was now at Natmauk, twenty-five miles north of Taungdwingyi, on the newly established lines of communication of the 17th Indian Division. The "road" between Natmauk and Taungdwingyi consisted partly of rough cart track and partly of railway from which the sappers had wrenched up fifteen miles of metre-gauge track. It was by no means good going, but it served its purpose. One of the first convoys to use it was sent by the 7th Armoured Brigade from Magwe on the 15th. The movements of the enemy round Yenangyaung were already causing anxiety for the maintenance of the 7th Hussars, and the convoy included 200 per cent. of everything required. As the enemy was known to have crossed the Magwe-Natmauk road, a troop of the 2nd Royal Tanks escorted the party to Natmauk. The convoy arrived safely at Taungdwingyi the same evening. That however was the last connection between the 17th Indian Division and the supply centre at Magwe, and from the 16th onwards supplies came up by the even more circuitous route, from Meiktilla through Pyawbwe and Ywamun to Natmauk.

On the 16th orders were issued for harassing operations to be carried out by the 17th Indian Division on the following day. The situation on the western flank, hitherto obscure, was quickly becoming critical and assuming the well-known pattern of encirclement and road blocks.

Instructions were issued to Lieutenant-Colonel McCready, commanding the 1st/10th Gurkha Rifles, for an operation to be carried out against the flank and rear of the strong enemy forces in the Yenangyaung area. The Gurkhas were to be carried in lorries as far as Thityagauk, starting as early as practicable on the 17th. A Squadron of the 7th Hussars was placed under command and a tank patrol was to precede the infantry. Transport was to return to Taungdwingyi and to be available to pick the battalion up again on the 19th. Two days' rations were to be carried and the force was to work in guerilla fashion, destroying small bodies of the enemy, drawing away larger forces from the front of the Burma Division, but avoiding major engagements with superior numbers.

On the same day similar instructions were issued to Lieutenant-Colonel Theyre, commanding the Duke of Wellington's Regiment at Natmauk. B Squadron was put under his command and his debussing point was to be four miles west of Kyagan.

Both columns quickly made contact with the enemy. The Gurkha column from Taungdwingyi captured an enemy peace propaganda party, including a Japanese civilian and a Burman priest, with documents. Moving farther south, the column destroyed a staff car and petrol lorry and killed all the occupants. No further enemy were seen on the Magwe road and a road block was established at milestone 304. On the 19th the column was withdrawn, having suffered only minor casualties from two dive-bombing attacks. The enemy had moved too far to the north-west for effective contact to be made with his main forces.

The column from Natmauk found a road block eight miles east of Magwe. B Squadron attacked it, but there was no artillery support and no progress could be made. Sergeant Campbell's tank was hit by a bomb which contained some sort of chemical, thought at the time to be gas. The driver was put out of action, but Sergeant Campbell, although himself affected, drove the tank out. It seems probable that the gas was the usual phosphorus content of the Japanese incendiary grenade.

Neither of these harassing operations had any noticeable effect on the engagement at Yenangyaung. The situation on that flank was now extremely dangerous. The threat had been apparent as early as the 14th, when a strong enemy column had penetrated the widening gap between the two divisions and was heading for Yenangyaung. The denial scheme for the oil installations required two full periods of daylight to complete. The order was given on the 14th and by the evening of the 16th the last act, the destruction of the power station, was finished; the Japanese were then in the outskirts of the town.

By the evening of the 16th the 1st Burma Division was north of the Kadaung Chaung, which joins the Irrawaddy seventeen miles south of Yenangyaung. The 1st K.O.Y.L.I., who had been cut off at Myingun close to the river on the 14th, had fought their way back, but had had losses, which included some of their transport. The 13th Indian Infantry Brigade was now at Natmauk. The 7th Armoured Brigade, which had control only of the headquarters and two squadrons of the 2nd Royal Tanks—the other squadron was still under the 1st Burma Brigade—had covered the withdrawal of the infantry.

The 2nd Royal Tanks had had two days of severe fighting, both rearguard actions and offensive sweeps directed against a column which was believed to have passed round the eastern flank. On the 16th in particular they fought a number of actions in which they killed at least 100 Japanese for the loss of 2 tanks. They and the 1st Burma Division were now ordered to withdraw to the northwards. The depleted 7th Armoured Brigade, with its B echelon, which included some of the 7th Hussars' transport, was to move to an area some thirty miles away, where the tanks were to have three clear days for overhaul and track changing; both were overdue, but whenever efforts were made to give the necessary time some crisis seemed to arise and they would have to go into action; this was to happen again.

At 6 p.m. the move began. Yenangyaung oilfields were passed in daylight; the demolitions seemed to have been very thorough, the oil tanks were blazing fiercely and the whole countryside lay under a heavy pall of black smoke. The formidable Pin Chaung was crossed without incident just as it got dark, and brigade headquarters, with some of the transport, reached the first halting point, five miles north of the chaung, at 8.30 p.m. All went well until just before midnight. At this hour the 2nd Royal Tanks, accompanied by some 150 lorries of the Burma Division, were crossing the obstacle. The leading squadron had gone two miles north of the chaung when a tank was hit by a shell and a staff car was set on fire by machine guns. The ambush was quickly turned into a road block, with half a squadron on the north of it and the rest of the regiment, as well as the whole Burma Division, to the south.

An attempt by a detachment of the Burma Frontier Force to clear the enemy away during the night was unsuccessful and the detachment disappeared into the jungle. At first light the brigade headquarters, the half squadron which had passed through and a company of the West Yorkshires attacked from the north; the rest of the 2nd Royal Tanks attacked from the south. The attack succeeded after severe fighting, and the regiment, with a number of the soft vehicles, passed through. About a hundred of the transport vehicles, however, had to be left; their drivers had immobilized them and disappeared.

During the night a considerable enemy force had occupied the southern edge of the chaung and the northern part of the group of villages on the outskirts of Yenangyaung. The situation of the division was now serious. It began its withdrawal from the Kadaung Chaung on the 17th, but after a long march it was too tired to try to break out the same evening. Fortunately a wireless set had been sent to the division by the 7th Armoured Brigade and this was the only means of communication between the corps and the division. During the night the corps commander arrived at brigade headquarters, a Chinese regiment was sent in haste from Kyaukpadaung and a plan was made for an attack from both north and south at first light.

On the 18th the Chinese succeeded in reaching the chaung, which they were not then allowed to cross in case of accidents due to mistaken identity. The Burma Division however were held up several miles south of it. Efforts to move round by a diversionary route were frustrated by a road block, and at nightfall the division was still in a perilous position and suffering severely from want of water.

Next day a dawn attack by a squadron of tanks and one brigade against the road block failed to dislodge the enemy. The Chinese at the same time attacked across the chaung on the west of the road, but their attack went wide and was not effective.

A plan was then made for a combined attack on the road block, by the Burma Division at noon and by the Chinese half an hour later—the earliest they could manage. The Burma Division's attack failed, and the troops were so exhausted that for the time being they could make no further effort. They waited hopefully for the Chinese attack, but at 2 p.m. as there was still no sign of it happening, the divisional commander ordered the division to break out by another diversion, found by the tank squadron, and very rough and difficult.

The tanks led the way, but the leading one was soon hit by a mortar and set on fire and some of the leading lorries got stuck in soft sand. The column was brought to a standstill and inextricably jammed. The order was now given to destroy vehicles and come out on foot. In the process 4 guns of the 1st Indian Field Regiment were lost, and 250 transport vehicles. A Squadron of the 2nd Royal Tanks broke through, having lost four of its tanks in the operation.

Meanwhile at 3.30 p.m. the Chinese attack, supported by E Troop of 414th Battery and another squadron of tanks, had a fair measure of success. Some 200 of the enemy were killed and the Chinese established themselves on the south side of the chaung. The rest of the 38th Chinese Division was on its way south, and the 7th Armoured Brigade came under its command—the first time in history that British troops had been under Chinese command.

The position south of the chaung was held while the thirsty and battered troops of the Burma Division were being ferried to the rear. On the 21st the Chinese Division began to withdraw on Gwegyo, covered by a squadron of tanks and E Troop of 414th Battery. The rest of the brigade was ordered to move in the evening to milestone 29 on the road Kyaukpadaung-Meiktilla, where the 7th Hussars were to rejoin and where tracks could be changed at last. For this purpose however the location was far too exposed, and permission was obtained to send one squadron at a time from each regiment to the safer region north of Meiktilla.

During the fighting at Yenangyaung the enemy made no efforts to molest the 17th Indian Division and the 7th Hussars at Taungdwingyi. It was not realized at the time, but there was still only one Japanese division in the Irrawaddy valley, the 33rd. Although aided by a number of disaffected Burmans, this division had its hands full in the thrust for the oil-fields. There was thus a fleeting opportunity for a counterstroke against the flank and rear of the 33rd Division. But troops were not at first available, as in the vast tract of wooded country into which the elusive enemy had disappeared, even to find his main force required a large number of infantry. The Chinese could do little, as they too were contemplating an offensive on the Pyinmana front. For this offensive General Alexander had promised the loan of the 7th Hussars and Major Younger had been across to Pyawbwe and Pyinmana to reconnoitre. At first therefore the Chinese could only spare one division, the 38th, to co-operate with the 1st Burma Corps; this division was allotted by special request for the purpose of ensuring the safety of the important centre of communications at Meiktilla.

Metcalfe the Padré.

The Ava Bridge.

On the 19th, when it became clear that no offensive was possible on the Chinese front, General Alexander obtained the promise of one more division and an extra regiment; these would be placed under command of G.O.C.-in-C. 1st Burma Corps and thus enable him to form a reserve for a counter-offensive. But before they could arrive the opportunity

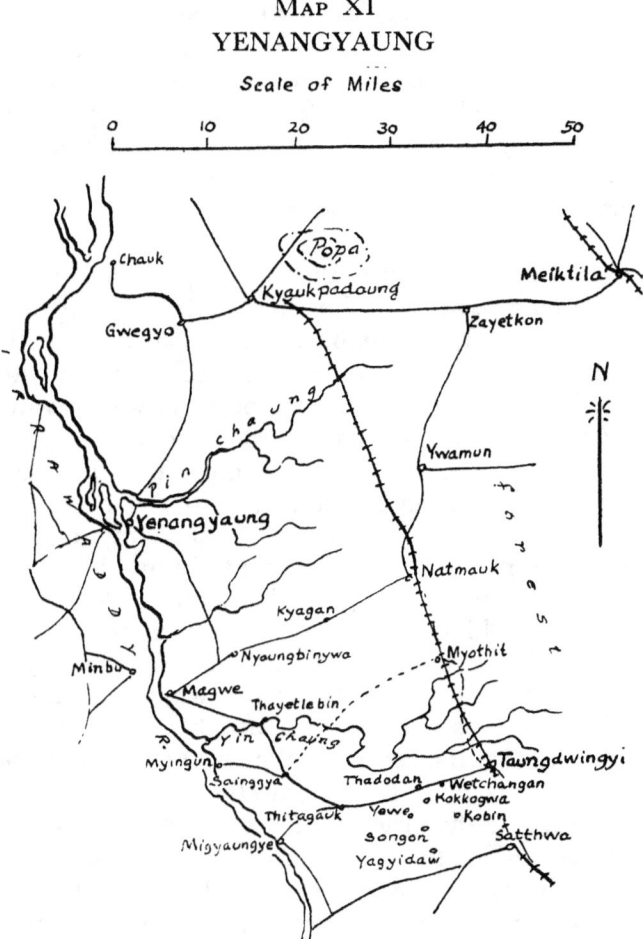

MAP XI
YENANGYAUNG

had passed; in the Irrawaddy Valley the 1st Burma Division had lost most of its transport and much of its fighting value; to the eastward the enemy's thrust from Toungoo through Bawlake and Loikaw into the Southern Shan States was threatening the northward communications of the Chinese armies on the Pyinmana front. So nothing came of the plans for either offensive and the moves carried out during the next few days were of a defensive character, designed to ensure the safety of the approaches to the Irrawaddy crossings.

*   *   *   *

As early as the end of March General Alexander had ordered his staff to prepare an appreciation of the situation which would arise if the allied armies were forced to withdraw north of Mandalay. The two principal factors taken into consideration were, first, the need to give the Chinese forces every possible assistance and secondly the gaining of time to allow India to build up her defences and to complete the two roads, from Assam to central Burma and from India to China through the Hukawng Valley. A plan was accordingly made and administrative preparations were put in hand in case it should have to be implemented.

As the movements of the forces after the loss of the oilfields are closely bound up with this plan, a brief outline must be given of its principal features. From right to left, the 1st Burma Division was to withdraw astride the Chindwin, covering the approaches to India through Kalewa; the 17th Indian Division, less one brigade, was to withdraw on the axis Mandalay, Shwebo, Katha, in order to cover the projected Hukawng Valley road; the Chinese Fifth Army was to withdraw on the Mandalay-Lashio road, accompanied by the 7th Armoured Brigade and one brigade of the Indian division; the Sixth Army in the Shan States was to withdraw partly by Puerh and partly by Lashio.

The object of sending the 7th Armoured Brigade with the Chinese was partly to stimulate Chinese resistance and partly to preserve the tanks if the allies should be driven out of Burma altogether; the road through Lashio into China was the only possible way for them to leave the country. The offer was however declined by the Chinese, who suggested, with reason, that the tanks could more usefully be employed in the less mountainous country round Shwebo.

Another modification to the original plan was made necessary by a combination of supply difficulties for the Chinese, and enemy penetration through the southern Shan States towards Lashio. If the plains south of Mandalay should have to be given up, the Shwebo area was the next rice producing area upon which to draw for Chinese rations. The provision of rice for their armies was a British responsibility and 300 lorries were permanently employed in collecting it and delivering it to divisions. Distribution within divisions was a Chinese responsibility and was carried out by a variegated mixture of porters, pack transport and impressed local carts.

The strain on the transportation services was by this time very great owing to the increasing unreliability of the railway service, the urgent need for redistribution of supplies on the projected lines of withdrawal, and the further loss of transport in the Yenangyaung fighting. Accordingly, while the Chinese Sixth Army retained the route through Lashio to China as its line of communication, the Fifth Army prepared to hold the general line of the Myitnge River and thence, if necessary, the bulk of it would fall back up the Irrawaddy Valley. One division, the 38th, would remain under 1st Burma Corps, with which it would cross the Irrawaddy and the Mu River, with the 7th Armoured Brigade under command.

It must be emphasized that at this stage General Alexander had no intention of withdrawing from Burma altogether; it would however have been strategically unwise not to have made plans for a contingency which appeared more than probable. Some of the administrative preparations had to be put in hand at once, and, in case it should be impossible to hold the Kyaukpadaung-Meiktilla area, the tactical dispositions on the next line of defence had to be related to the subsequent plan for withdrawal. He had no intention of allowing the Burma Corps to be caught in the loop of the Irrawaddy between Myingyan and Kyaukse and compelled to fight a major battle with the great obstacle at its back. He accordingly decided that the next main line of defence should be on the lower Chindwin from Monywa, thence the Irrawaddy to its junction with the Myitnge, and the line of this river north-eastwards towards Lashio. The withdrawal to this line would be ordered when it became clear that the Kyaukpadaung and Meiktilla areas could no longer be held.

For the defence of the Kyaukpadaung and Meiktilla areas General Alexander arranged his forces in two groups. On the right was the 1st Burma Corps, now augmented by the 38th Chinese Division. On the left was a force under General Lo, the Chinese Commander-in-Chief; this consisted of the 22nd and 96th Divisions and the 7th Armoured Brigade, the last named being allotted specifically for the defence of the area Meiktilla-Thazi-Pyawbwe.

The 28th Chinese Division was allotted for the defence of Mandalay and the protection of the only and vital Ava bridge, which carried the road and railway high above the Irrawaddy. This bridge is over half a mile long and, in view of the air situation which has already been explained, both the bridge and its approaches were exceedingly vulnerable. Ferries were therefore improvised, over both the Irrawaddy and the Myitnge Rivers, as an insurance against the total obstruction of the Ava bridge and as a relief for congestion at what must in any case be a dangerous bottleneck.

On 20th April orders were issued for the fresh disposition of the forces. The 38th Chinese Division was to concentrate at Kyaukpadaung, the 1st Burma Division at Taungtha and the 17th Indian Division was to withdraw from Taungdwingyi and later from Natmauk to positions north-west and west of Meiktilla, at Mahlaing and Zayetkin. The 7th Armoured Brigade was ordered to Meiktilla, where it was to come under command of General Lo. Each regiment was to send one squadron in turn to a point ten miles north of Meiktilla for track changing, and as another squadron of each had been left respectively with the 17th Indian Division and the 38th Chinese Division, the brigade's effective strength would in fact be only two squadrons; General Stilwell decided to keep it under his own direct command.

On the evening of the 21st, leaving B Squadron at Natmauk, the 7th Hussars started their march along the indifferent track northwards, to a point on the Kyaukpadaung-Meiktilla road twenty miles west of the latter. They arrived about dawn on the 22nd and rejoined the brigade headquarters, which was already there. A Squadron moved on for its overhaul and next day regimental headquarters and C Squadron moved to a point four miles west of Meiktilla. On the 24th the brigade was finally disposed five miles north of the town, whence it was to operate southwards in support of the Chinese 22nd Division. This division had been ordered to hold Pyawbwe for seven days, but it was not expected that it could do so, because the enemy were now believed to have four divisions on this front. B Squadron rejoined on this day, now commanded by Major Murray Smith. Major Davies-Gilbert had taken up a staff appointment in Maymyo and Captain P. B. Stanley Evans took Murray Smith's place as adjutant.

On the 25th a patrol of 2nd Royal Tanks on the Thazi road reported a heavy stream of Chinese troops withdrawing towards Meiktilla. The situation was somewhat obscure and the 7th Hussars were sent to a position on the Pyawbwe road, and pushed patrols out to the south. Captain Nickels of C Squadron encountered a Japanese column, which he engaged. Before the enemy could dismount from their lorries he drove along the column and caused much havoc. At least three lorries were destroyed and a number of casualties were inflicted. The enemy was stopped, but the action was not pressed to a decision as it was nearly dark. The regiment withdrew behind Meiktilla for the night.

Early next morning A Squadron, temporarily under Captain Fox, moved south. At Kadang, seven miles south of Meiktilla, the leading troop found a considerable body of the enemy, with lorries. They were at once engaged by the squadron and, being completely surprised, suffered a number of casualties before they could reach cover in a wood. Arrangements were then made for reinforcements to be sent from Meiktilla. These included a troop from both B and C Squadrons, D Troop of 414th Battery and two companies of the West Yorkshires. The two attached troops remained netted to their own squadron frequencies, which made control a bit difficult.

It was some time before the attack could be staged. However, at 5 p.m. the infantry advanced, with support from the tanks. But the enemy were now well prepared and the assault was held up. As darkness fell the West Yorkshires, having attacked three times without success, withdrew. There was some difficulty in extricating one of their platoons and their many wounded. The latter were eventually got away under the personal direction of Lieutenant-Colonel P. C. Marindin, their commanding officer. The 7th Hussars lost two tanks in these operations. Lieutenant W. H. Jackson-Stops of C Squadron, who was badly wounded, was carried a mile by his crew before they were picked up; he never recovered consciousness.

One enemy gun had been knocked out, about a dozen lorries had been destroyed and a hundred of the enemy had been killed. Although tactically the day's operations had been disappointing, this small counter-stroke had a greater effect than was at first apparent. The Japanese were firmly checked and made no further advance that day. After dark the 7th Hussars were withdrawn to Wundwin, ferrying the infantry.

Throughout the night and the next day the Chinese were streaming back from Pyawbwe and Thazi and they appeared to be in no condition to hold the Meiktilla area much longer. The approaches to the Irrawaddy crossings had to be denied to the enemy for several days yet, as Maymyo had not been evacuated. Most of the wounded had indeed gone to India, as these had been first on the priority list for every aircraft, and delay in completing the clearance was due to nothing but lack of transport aeroplanes. There were also a number of administrative units to be moved and quite a few civilians, including several ladies who did splendid work visiting the wounded and postponed their departure dangerously long.

To keep the enemy in check, the 17th Indian Division was made responsible for the defence of the Meiktilla area and the Chinese Fifth Army was to withdraw through it. The 63rd Indian Infantry Brigade was placed astride the road at Wundwin, with the 2nd Royal Tanks in support; the 48th Indian Infantry Brigade was sent to Kyaukse with the 7th Hussars. The Wundwin line was to be held until 6 p.m. on the 27th, when the 63rd Brigade and attached troops would withdraw through the 48th Brigade to the Irrawaddy bridgehead. The armoured brigade's B Echelon was ordered to Ondaw, across the Ava Bridge, but as this long withdrawal would have made maintenance very difficult, 65th Company R.A.S.C. and the non-essential unit vehicles were sent back to Ondaw and most of B Echelon was kept at Kyaukse.

On the 27th the 2nd Royal Tanks were constantly engaged with the enemy south of Wundwin. The country was unsatisfactory for armour, as it was covered with low scrub above which the vehicles were very exposed, while the enemy infantry could approach unseen. The tanks however were boldly handled and succeeding in preventing the enemy from developing any serious attack on the 63rd Brigade. Meanwhile B and C Squadrons of the 7th Hussars patrolled the railway to the east of Wundwin, on the look-out for an enveloping movement, but saw no enemy.

There then occurred a hitch in the arrangements for the withdrawal; lorries could not reach the 63rd Brigade before midnight. So the 7th Hussars were called upon to ferry back 1,800 men. The first party was picked up at 6 p.m. and, by midnight, the whole brigade had been carried back on the first stage of its withdrawal, as far as Kume. The 2nd Royal Tanks now managed to disengage south of Wundwin and transport was arriving for the infantry, so the 7th Hussars were sent on to join the 48th Brigade at Kyaukse.

The position at Kyaukse was a strong one, the main feature of which was a dominating hill giving unusually good observation. The right was protected by the river, which here spread itself in many streams over a broad valley, but the left flank was open and liable to be turned. B Squadron was put in the village, regimental headquarters and A Squadron were held in brigade reserve and C Squadron with one company of the West Yorkshires was sent northwards some ten miles to a point where it was thought the enemy might try to cut the road. During daylight A Squadron kept a patrol on the main road to the south. The Gurkha brigade was full of fight and confident that it could hold the position against all comers.

On the morning of 28th April a composite troop of C Squadron under Lieutenant D. M. Allen, who had been lent to A Squadron, was sent southwards to report whether a bridge some ten miles from Kyaukse had been demolished. Finding it intact, the troop leader sent Sergeant Kilty's tank back for a 40-gallon drum of petrol with which to burn the bridge. Sergeant Cleere was standing on the bridge and directing Kilty where to off-load the petrol when the party was attacked by four fighter-bombers.

Sergeant Cleere returned to his tank and the troop went up the road, making for the nearest cover, and bombed all the way. Lieutenant Allen was wounded, Sergeant Kilty's tank was hit, and the petrol drum was punctured and burst into flames. Cleere, with no thought for his own safety, went straight to the burning tank. Two of the crew were outside it already, although one of them was badly wounded and burned. The other two were inside and Cleere carried both to his own tank, under repeated bombing and machine-gun attacks by the aircraft, and then went back for the third wounded man. There were now no means of destroying the bridge and he withdrew the troop to squadron headquarters. For this action Sergeant Cleere was awarded a bar to his D.C.M.; in spite of his efforts, however, only one of Kilty's crew survived.

This troop was then replaced by another under SSM Ainley, which exchanged shots with a Japanese column two miles south of Kyaukse just as it was getting dark. During the night there was some shelling and several Japanese attacks were driven off. Next morning however the tables were turned, temporarily, and the 48th Brigade carried out a counter-attack, supported by B Squadron. The objective was captured and a large number of the enemy were killed. The Gurkhas were more than a match for the Japanese, who were now meeting resistance more stubborn than they had been accustomed to; after delivering several attacks on the 29th and 30th the enemy seemed to have been fought to a standstill. At 5 p.m. on the 30th the final demolitions were blown and, covered by a heavy concentration from the 414th Battery R.H.A. and the 1st Indian Field Regiment, the withdrawal to the Irrawaddy began.

The destination of the regiment was Shwebo, some sixty miles away. The march was uneventful, by the wooden bridge over the Myitnge and nearly to Mandalay. The night was dark and at intervals, where wretched refugees had collapsed and died, the atmosphere was putrid with the stench of their unburied corpses. A little before midnight the magnificent Ava Bridge was crossed and the column reached Sagaing, a mile to the north of the river. Here there was a long halt, and the regiment became thoroughly mixed up with a mass of Chinese transport.

Soon after the march was resumed came the roar of the explosions as the Ava Bridge was destroyed. The demolition was most efficiently carried out, the two centre spans fell, and the bridge remained unserviceable for the rest of the war.

Shortly before dawn the regiment reached its leaguer area near Shwebo, in pleasant, shady and park-like surroundings. Everyone was now very tired and it was hoped that there might be a short spell for rest and maintenance. This, however, was not to be, for new threats were developing against both flanks and the rear. At 3 a.m. on 1st May, C Squadron was already on the way to the scene of the next fighting, Monywa, and the whole regiment marched again the following night.

* * * *

While the forces had been withdrawing across the Irrawaddy events were moving rapidly on both flanks and it was soon evident that the new positions could not be maintained for very long. On 27th April reports had been received of a strong Japanese detachment which had crossed into the Myittha Valley between the 15th and 20th and was moving down it towards Kalemyo. The 2nd Burma Brigade was already withdrawing northwards down the Myittha Valley, and the 13th Indian Infantry Brigade, of the Burma Division, was now ordered to move by river to Kalewa and thence across to Kalemyo, as this was a most important point on the route of withdrawal to India.

On the other flank, by 29th April the fall of Lashio was clearly imminent. General Stilwell had made up his mind to withdraw the Fifth Army to the north of Katha and thence probably to Bhamo and the 96th Division was already so exhausted that he proposed to move it at once by train to Myitkyina. This left only the 22nd Division to hold the Myitnge crossings, so little more than a delaying action could be looked for on this sector. General Stilwell further asked that the 38th Division should revert to his command, to cover the withdrawal of his forces up the Irrawaddy Valley; to this request General Alexander felt compelled to accede.

By the 30th the Japanese were reported to have occupied Lashio, Hsipaw and Maymyo. So even before the last troops had crossed the Ava Bridge the enemy's movements through the Shan States were threatening communications with Bhamo and Myitkyina and the rear of the position west of Mandalay; the roads from Hsipaw to the ferries at Thabeikkyim and Male were entirely devoid of protection. Moreover a large number of casualties and refugees were on their way up the river to Katha, whence they were to be evacuated to Myitkyina by train and thence by air to India. No troops were available for the defence of Upper Burma, and all that could be spared to guard against the new threat were one squadron of the 2nd Royal Tanks for the protection of Shwebo, an important bottleneck on the route to Ye-U and India, and a few infantry patrols for observation on the east bank of the Irrawaddy.

The stocking of the Ye-U–Kalews track with supplies and water had

Kalewa.
7th Hussars on the last ferry boat to cross the Chindwin.

A cargo of Gurkhas on the road to Shwegyin.

begun some time before and some improvements were being made to the track itself so as to make it passable for mechanical transport. The stocking of supplies was estimated to take at least another ten days, and when, on the 30th, it became certain that the Irrawaddy line must soon be abandoned, the work of dumping and of evacuating the wounded was accelerated by drastic withdrawals of transport from units. Every vehicle not required to carry the absolute essentials for fighting was appropriated for the work and every article that could possibly be dispensed with was destroyed or thrown away.

The "road" was no more than a sandy track passing through Kaduna, Pyingaing and Thetkegyin to Shwegyin, on the east bank of the Chindwin, eight miles south of Kalewa. Maps were scarce, and the single copy issued to the regiment marked little but the bare names of these villages, as no detailed survey of this arid and sparsely populated area had been made. From Ye-U the track passed through numerous chaungs, some of which were dry and sandy and some wet. After Pyingaing there was a difficult hill section, with many rickety bridges constructed only of logs, brushwood or bamboo. Anyone seeing this track for the first time could scarcely have imagined a mechanized force passing that way at all.

It had been intended to continue the track from Thetkegyin to a point on the river opposite Kalewa but, owing to the difficulties of this last stretch of twelve miles, which needed a lot of rock-blasting, this part was never finished. It was for this reason that all the tanks except one and nearly all the wheeled transport had eventually to be abandoned; the half-dozen boats available for the eight-mile journey by river from Shwegyin to Kalewa could only carry one or two lorries and two jeeps each at a time and, with their long turn-round, could make little contribution to the saving of the guns and transport and none at all to the saving of the tanks.

From Kalewa a track led to Kalemyo at the southern end of the Kabaw Valley, where the Yu River joins the Myittha before their confluence with the Chindwin. Thence up the Kabaw Valley there was merely a dust track. South of Tamu various staging points, with supplies, were established by transport working from Imphal, in Manipur State. This work had also to be pressed with vigour, on account of the monsoon, which was due to break about 15th May. Once the rains started, this corner of Burma and India would become a quagmire; all movement of wheeled vehicles off the limited network of metalled roads round Imphal itself would abruptly cease.

General Alexander had hoped to be able to hold the Irrawaddy position long enough to ensure the safe evacuation of the casualties and refugees up the Irrawaddy to Myitkyina and to India through Kalewa, and to enable the latter route to be fully stocked. The casualties were eventually all cleared, as well as the vast majority of the refugees, and it was on account of these last that the eventual withdrawal of the rearguard through Ye-U was postponed so dangerously long.

On 30th April yet another threat developed, up the Chindwin river itself. The Japanese appeared at Monywa and it was realized that they had sufficient craft to take a small force upstream if they should wish to do so; this could be landed anywhere to strike at the long and tenuous line of communications with India.

For the Burma Army, with its rear threatened by both the Myittha and the Chindwin routes, the campaign had now become a race for Kalewa against the Japanese and a race for Tamu against the weather.

On the evening of 30th April a Japanese force crossed the Chindwin and attacked Monywa. This was to be the only scene of serious fighting on the Irrawaddy position. At the time there were in Monywa only 150 men of the 1st Gloucesters, providing guards. At Alon, five miles to the north-west, was the headquarters of the 1st Burma Corps, with a protective detachment and a Frontier Force Column. The Gloucesters, as usual, put up a stout resistance and General Slim organized an immediate counter-attack with the few troops in the neighbourhood.

By the morning of 1st May the town was cleared of the enemy. The situation was nevertheless serious; Monywa was on the direct route between the forces holding the Irrawaddy line west of the Mu and their line of withdrawal through Ye-U; secondly, the presence of the enemy on the bank of the Chindwin at that point prevented any possibility of moving the 13th Brigade by boat up to Kalewa, as planned; thirdly, there was no regular formation of troops to oppose the enemy's advance on the vital centre of communications at Ye-U.

All efforts were now concentrated on securing the line of withdrawal to Kalewa. At 8.45 p.m. on the 30th the corps commander ordered the 1st Burma Division to advance with all speed on Monywa, placing under its command the 63rd Indian Infantry Brigade, due to arrive by train at Chaungu early on 1st May, and the 48th Infantry Brigade at Myinmu; the latter was actually moved later by Shwebo on Ye-U. The 16th Indian Infantry Brigade were ordered to move at once via Shwebo to positions covering the southern approaches to Ye-U.

Army headquarters, on hearing of the attack on Monywa, ordered a squadron of tanks to move there at once. The headquarters of the army, the corps and the 17th Indian Division all moved to the Ye-U area and, in view of the serious situation, General Alexander arranged to hold a conference with General Stilwell at Ye-U the same evening. At this conference it was agreed that the withdrawal from the Irrawaddy position could be delayed no longer, that the 7th Armoured Brigade could not be left in support of the 38th Division, and that the latter must at once revert to General Stilwell's command.

The 7th Armoured Brigade accordingly moved to the Ye-U area during the night of 1st/2nd May.

On 3rd May the final arrangements for the withdrawals of the rearguards on the diverging lines of retreat were co-ordinated by General Alexander and General Li Jan Sun, commanding the 38th Division, which was to cover the Fifth Army's movement up the Irrawaddy Valley; the 1st Burma Corps was ordered not to withdraw its rearguard north of Ye-U until the 38th Division had passed to the north of Shwebo. Thus the Commander-in-Chief parted reluctantly with a most co-operative and gallant Chinese general, the first of his race ever to command British troops in the field and one who had earned their unstinted loyalty and respect.

The enemy's next move at Monywa took place before any of the fresh troops could arrive. When C Squadron, after a 60-mile march, reached the headquarters of the 1st Burma Division on the morning of 1st May, they found the divisional commander near what remained of his headquarters; this had been overrun in the early morning, and much of it had been lost, including parts of the staff and of the wireless equipment. Monywa town was in enemy hands. The 63rd Infantry Brigade and C Squadron moved up to the outskirts of the town with a view to attacking the next morning, and in making contact with the enemy C Squadron lost one tank, destroyed by a direct hit from a field gun.

The 7th Armoured Brigade reached the Ye-U area about dawn on the 2nd. Here there was a halt for breakfast and the march was then resumed for Budalin. The 7th Hussars and brigade headquarters continued to an area about six miles north of Monywa and B Squadron was sent ahead to make contact with C; wireless touch had already been established.

Monywa appeared to be firmly held by the Japanese and unless an alternative route could be found to the east of the town, the 63rd Brigade's line of withdrawal to Ye-U was blocked. The country was intersected by numerous banks and water-courses, most of them dry, but each one an obstacle to vehicles. Eventually, however, Lieutenant Geoffrey Palmer of B Squadron succeeded in finding a passable route and made physical contact with C Squadron. That night, after a day of desultory fighting on the outskirts of Monywa, the 63rd Brigade and C Squadron withdrew by this route. It was a difficult march and tank commanders frequently had to walk in front of their tanks to guide them over the many obstacles.

On the same day there occurred one of the most disagreeable episodes of the campaign. Lieutenant M. M. Stanley Evans' troop was on the outskirts of a small village, watching the river. As all seemed quiet, the squadron leader ordered tanks in turn to come back to squadron headquarters to replenish, leaving one tank in observation. The distance was less than a mile to squadron headquarters, and the tank on duty could be clearly seen. Suddenly Sergeant Browning was seen running towards the squadron. He reported that a group of simple looking Burmans had come up to the crew, offering eggs and chickens. While these were being discussed the Burmans had suddenly produced swords and killed the crew.

The wireless operator had been on top of the tank, both as look-out and on wireless watch. The others had been lying on a bank some yards away, Sergeant Browning separate from the rest. The attack was so sudden that two of the crew were killed before he realized what was happening. The wireless operator very gallantly went inside the tank to his wireless set, but only managed to get his call-sign through to the squadron; he was killed before he could send a message. Sergeant Browning drove off the Burmans with his revolver and then made for his squadron headquarters.

When the squadron heard this they were coldly furious. A plan was at once made to punish the murderers. A company of the West Yorkshires was to go through the village and drive out the inhabitants, the squadron was to catch the culprits as they went. Unfortunately a number of Indian refugees were taking precarious shelter in the village and fled with the Burmans across the river or into the jungle. It was tragic indeed that some of these unfortunate people, who had covered five hundred miles of their journey towards safety, lost their lives in the subsequent shooting.

In the evening C Squadron rejoined the regiment, which leaguered some twenty miles north of Monywa. The following day the 2nd Royal Tanks took over rearguard duties on the Monywa front and, of the 7th Hussars, only B Squadron was actively employed, patrolling the road between Monywa and Ye-U.

* * * *

The Burma Army was now spread round the Ye-U area and the

Map XII
MANDALAY

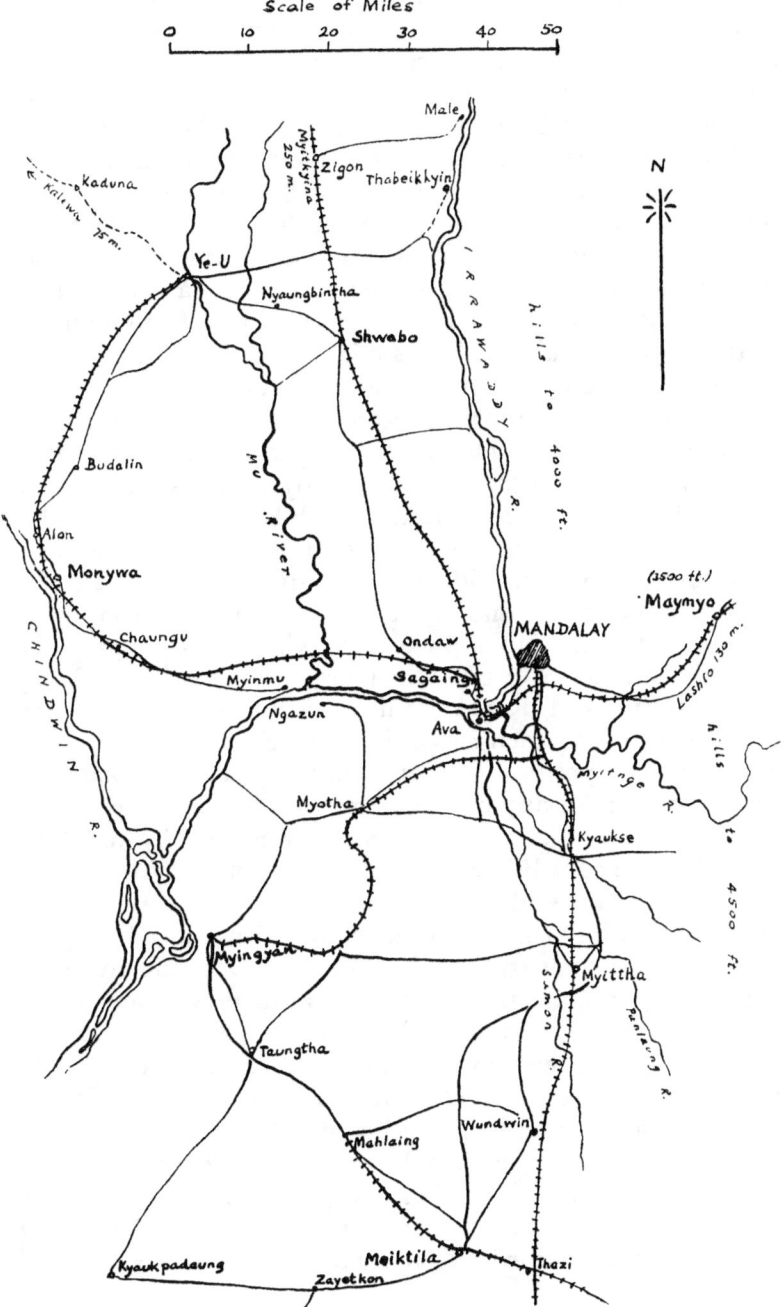

stage was set for the race for Kalewa. The Japanese had the advantage of free use of the river and, to guard against an attack in rear, a composite detachment of officers and men from the former Infantry Depot and the Bush Warfare School at Maymyo was sent to Maukkadaw, where the threat to the line of retreat was most obvious. At the same time GHQ India was asked to hasten the move of the 1st Indian Infantry Brigade from the Imphal area to Kalewa. This movement actually had to be cancelled, because the strain on local administration was so great, in trying to feed the retreating Burma Army, that no extra troops could have been maintained south of Tamu. Instead, General Alexander sent the detachment of Royal Marines, which had previously done excellent work as a river patrol, to hold a boom across the Chindwin at Shwegyin, the commander of the lines of communication was instructed to provide local protection, and India was asked to send aircraft to attack any enemy vessels seen moving up the river.

The withdrawal from Monywa began on 4th May and both tanks and transport were used to ferry infantry part of the way towards Ye-U. The Burma Division and the 2nd Royal Tanks occupied a position a few miles south of Ye-U, while the 7th Hussars moved in the evening to Kaduna, which the 63rd Brigade was to hold as the next rearguard position. During the 5th A and C Squadrons piquetted the Ye-U road, and patrols of the 2nd Royal Tanks, sent out sixteen miles to the southward, found no sign of the enemy, who was not apparently following up on this route. Next day the rearguard passed through the Kaduna position, the 2nd Royal Tanks picking up the engineer demolition detachments at each successive bridge.

The next rearguard position was at Pyingaing, a very congested area, where it was hard for any vehicle to get off the narrow track, or, once off it, to get back again. This position was held by the 48th Brigade, and when the 63rd Brigade passed through it, the 7th Hussars once more came under the 48th.

The retreat of the army continued on the 6th, 7th and 8th in conditions of ever greater congestion and difficulty. Occasionally there were vehicles passing from north to south and, as there were few places on the hilly track where vehicles could pass one another, this caused frequent hold-ups. Long columns of animal transport often limited the speed of the general movement to no more than three miles an hour. There was a constantly increasing number of broken down lorries by the roadside, some with only minor troubles, some which had gone over through drivers dropping asleep. There were hundreds of private cars and civilian vehicles of every description, abandoned by their original owners, pushed off the road, and now often tenanted by sick, dying or dead refugees. In some places the dying had crept away into the jungle. Others had lain down by the roadside and, too ill to rise again, had died where they lay, for all to see in the day time and scarcely less noticeable at night. Wending their way along this fearful hill-track, the lorries having to reverse at many of the hairpin-bends, by 9th May the last of the troops reached their destination, a few miles from the Chindwin, near Shwegyin.

An advanced party from the brigade had been sent ahead to reconnoitre the crossing facilities; this had included Lieutenant Calder and one tank of B Squadron, but it was only when the regiment arrived at Shwegyin with the rearguard that the real gravity of the situation was appreciated. A special raft had been built for vehicles, but the tank, now safely at Kalewa, had taken six hours to load and had nearly split the raft in the process. There was no question of getting any more tanks across to Kalewa and those of the 2nd Royal Tanks were already being destroyed. The single B Squadron tank was to have an adventurous career. It was driven to Imphal and later, with its turret removed, it became the command tank of the 7th Indian Cavalry. In this capacity, and with the startling name of "The Curse of Scotland," it re-entered Rangoon in 1945 with the Fourteenth Army.

Ferrying went on as fast as the few craft could—or would—proceed. From time to time enemy aircraft attacked the boom across the river and the native crews of the river steamers refused to move in daylight. Drastic measures had to be taken to keep the boats going, and guards were placed on each to prevent desertions. Output was thus increased and twenty-four vehicles a day were cleared upstream to Kalewa. On the night of the 9th/10th the men and twenty-three specialist vehicles of the 7th Armoured Brigade, less the 7th Hussars, were safely embarked. The 7th Hussars and the rearguard of the 48th Brigade were to go the next night, having destroyed all remaining vehicles.

Nobody knew exactly what the future held in store, how much walking would have to be done in the Kabaw Valley, or what the water and ration situation would be. The men were organized more or less as infantry platoons of thirty, under an officer. Everyone carried a personal weapon and ammunition, a small quantity of rations, shaving kit, and whatever personal possessions he valued most; one or two officers kept their shot-guns. Light and scarce articles of military equipment, such as field glasses and compasses, were shared out among officers and NCOs. The "denial scheme" of the vehicles and tanks was to take place at the last moment.

During the night of the 9th/10th, while the 63rd Brigade and the 2nd Royal Tanks were being carried up the river to Kalewa, the enemy landed a force of about battalion strength on the east bank and occupied some of the high ground overlooking the scrubby and broken basin of Shwegyin. The jetty was under mortar fire and the enemy was installed on several heights which seemed, on the north side, too steep to climb. The 48th Indian Infantry Brigade were still acting as rearguard and the 7th Hussars who, on the 8th, had destroyed all two-wheel-drive vehicles on account of the bad going, had moved up the last eight miles of their journey to Shwegyin.

The commander of the 17th Indian Division ordered the 48th Brigade to clear the enemy from the hills overlooking the jetty and a battalion of Gurkhas quickly formed up for the purpose. A and C Squadrons both provided fire support. Attacks on the several objectives were carried out with good effect and the Gurkhas, who fought with splendid determination, killed a considerable number of enemy. By 11 o'clock the nearest hills were cleared. Desultory firing continued until the evening, when the enemy seemed to lose heart and, beyond occasional shelling of the jetty area, fighting stopped. It was a sore disappointment to the 7th Hussars that they had to stand off during this engagement and could only use their guns at long range. But the country was quite impossible for close co-operation between tanks and infantry.

This was the last action of the campaign and the last the regiment was to see of the splendid Gurkha Brigade, with which it had been operating almost continuously since the battle of the oilfields. The Gurkha battalions, like most of the Burma Army, had been only partly trained when they arrived in the country. Like other units, they gained their training and experience in the hard school of war. The long retreat and the feeling of encirclement and isolation which seemed progressively to lower the morale of many of the troops, apparently worked the opposite way with the Gurkhas. Nothing could depress them and their high spirits were obvious—and infectious—as they formed up among the tanks for their last attacks on the heights at Shwegyin. They now felt that they had the measure of the Japanese and their happy confidence seemed to have reached its peak just when other people were most depressed. They were always ready to grin and always ready to cheer. At Shwegyin they stood up and shouted "Shabash"—a little derisively—when a solitary Wellington bomber flew over, the first British aircraft that they had seen since leaving the Tenasserim strip. They stood up and cheered again, even those who were close to the enemy, and sure of being shot at, when a Japanese gun was bowled over a precipice by a good burst from an anti-aircraft

(*Left to right*) Captains Bill Low (R.A.M.C.) and Vyvyan John, Major Ralph Younger and Lt.-Col. "Rhino" Fosdick.

A Squadron's tanks supporting the Gurkha attack at Shwegyin.

Bofors. They had earned the greatest affection, admiration and confidence of the 7th Hussars, who would have asked for nothing better than to serve alongside them for the rest of the war.

Although the enemy were held off, there was no longer any question of a move by boat to Kalewa. There was no alternative now to the rough and twisting mountain footpath, fit for nothing but mules and men. Squadrons had already prepared themselves for movement on foot, in anticipation of a long march beyond Kalewa. Nobody however had expected that the march would begin at Shwegyin.

In the evening the final destruction of the tanks and all remaining vehicles was carried out. Some were destroyed by draining the oil from the sumps and racing the engines until they seized up. One squadron lined up its tanks close together, packed the men's blankets, soaked with petrol, into the turrets, connecting each tank with its neighbour in a continuous chain; one match set light to the whole lot. The tanks were seen again by Colonel Younger during the advance of the Fourteenth Army late in 1944; none had moved, so their denial to the enemy had been completely effective.

Schwegyin was a scene of wholesale wreckage. While the tanks were being destroyed everyone opened his personal kit and spread it about so as to choose his most cherished possessions, and then set fire to the rest. Anything which might have been of use or pleasure to the enemy was wrecked and burned, whole lorry loads of stores and equipment, hundreds of vehicles and tons of ammunition.

As dusk fell every remaining light anti-aircraft gun and machine gun opened fire and spent its last round on the enemy's positions before itself being destroyed. Then the march for Kalewa began, the headquarters of the 17th Indian Division, the mule transport and miscellaneous details in the lead, the headquarters of the 7th Armoured Brigade, then the 7th Hussars, finally a battalion of Gurkhas as rearguard.

From start to finish it was a nightmare. The track was very steep, rough, narrow and ill-defined. There was room only to move in single file. The night was black and at one time or another almost everyone lost sight of the man in front of him and stumbled over the edge. Once only was this march punctuated by a humorous incident. The new "foot-sloggers" had had a good deal of advice, from the West Yorkshires, in the gentle art of marching in silence, and everyone thought he was doing quite well. Suddenly the air was rent by a resounding clatter. At Shwegyin Major Llewellen Palmer had found a grey pony, improvised a pack-saddle with ropes and blankets and tied on a number of cans of water and a bottle or two of whisky.

Something had slipped and the whole cargo hurtled merrily down the steep rocky slope, ending with a final crash in the bed of the stream below.

The march went on and the occasional whisper that Kalewa was just over the next hill always ended in disappointment, as another chaung was crossed and another hill had to be climbed. Exhaustion and thirst, for men who had scarcely ever marched two consecutive miles on their feet, became almost unbearable, and when a trickle of water was heard running in the bottom of a chaung, men went down to it and drank, despite the fearful stench of dead mules—or human bodies—which polluted the atmosphere. Gradually, as its weight became intolerable, nearly every personal possession was thrown away and only weapons and shaving kit were kept; as dawn broke it was a footsore and exhausted column which filed off the hill, down to the river at Kalewa.

The rearguard had broken contact with the enemy at 9 p.m., and there was no interference with the march. At Kalewa a paddle steamer was waiting and, covered by the 63rd Brigade and the six guns of the 414th Battery, in position on the west bank, the 7th Hussars were ferried across. By nightfall on the 11th all were over. Most of the infantry were carried in steamers farther up the river, so as to relieve congestion on the Kabaw Valley route and to take the steamers to a safer place.

*   *   *   *

The race with the Japanese had been won, but only just. The next enemy was the monsoon and this contest was just as close. All transport was now pooled and several General Purpose Transport companies were provided by the Indian formation at Imphal, both for stocking the Kabaw Valley route and for ferrying the troops. In order to increase the capacity of the transport, the 7th Armoured Brigade was called upon to provide extra drivers and nearly 200 of the 7th Hussars were employed on this task. The lorries ploughed their way along the dusty track, backwards and forwards, winding in and out among the refugees, cursed by the marching troops as they covered them with dust, blessed when they picked them up and carried them a stage or two northwards.

The march up the Kabaw Valley took a week. This is one of the most beautiful parts of Burma—steep mountain sides, luxuriantly clad in natural jungle, and forests of magnificent trees. The scenery however was not much consolation; the heat was intense, as always when the rains are about to break, the insects were abominable and everyone knew the importance of covering this last 130 miles before the dust was turned into mud and no vehicle would be able to move.

Most of the 7th Hussars were lucky enough to walk only two of the stages and to be carried in transport over the remainder. The transport was admirably organized and on the marching days one lorry was available for the regiment, to take the cooks on ahead and then to return for stragglers. In spite of increasing sickness and sore feet, very few men fell out, and a careful check was made by squadron leaders and sergeant-majors, who marched in rear of the troops.

On one fearful morning an officer and twenty men awoke to find they had been sharing a copse, no more than ten yards square, into which they had stumbled the night before, with three Indian corpses; they were refugees who had obviously been dead several days and had the unmistakable symptoms of cholera. It says much for the efficiency of the anti-cholera injections that the 7th Hussars had only two cases.

On 16th May the regiment was carried in transport for the final forty-five miles to its allotted bivouac area on the Dimapur road, not far from Imphal.

Imphal itself was no more than a straggling town of mud and bamboo huts, the centre of Manipur State, and standing in a plain some fifty miles square among the surrounding hills. The rains had now begun in earnest; the water gushed down the hillsides, the plain was a quagmire and infested with leeches.

Each man had his weapon, his shaving kit and the clothes he stood up in. Most had a waterproof sheet or a blanket. It was several days before tents could be provided and then only on a very limited scale. The Ordnance Service could do nothing to help; they had nothing to help with. The reception of the Burma Army was in fact beyond the capacity of India's hard-worked administrative machine, which was already stretched to the utmost by the calls of the Middle East. Transportation was one of the greatest difficulties. Strenuous efforts were made to speed up the turn-round of the available vehicles by improving the road from Dimapur railhead, over 100 miles away, but the transportation service was quite unable to deal with all the demands made upon it.

After three days near Milestone 116 the regiment moved on to a hillside near Milestone 108. This was no improvement. Still there were not enough tents. Sickness increased rapidly, dysentery and malaria being the most prevalent afflictions, and the camp came to be known as Dysentery Hill. At night officers and men lay cold and soaked, or walked miserably up and down to restore the circulation. By day they picked off the leeches and tried to wring themselves out a little, only to be drenched again a few minutes later. The casualty clearing stations and hospitals could only take in a proportion of the sick, and many were transported direct to railhead in unit vehicles.

To say that morale was low would be an exaggeration; but undoubtedly all were tired and many who stayed on ought really to have gone sick. Then, on 24th May, came General Wavell, a visitor who, to the 7th Hussars, was always welcome and who was, in himself, a tonic. With him were General Alexander and a number of their respective staffs. In a few words—he never used many—General Wavell thanked the regiment for all it had done in the campaign. Later, in his report, General Alexander also expressed his appreciation of the work of the 7th Armoured Brigade:

> "I must also mention here the excellent work done by the 7th Armoured Brigade, whose high morale and great fighting capacity I have frequently stressed. During the withdrawal it was necessary to take from the 7th Armoured Brigade nearly all their vehicles for use in the general pool both east and west of the Chindwin, and after their tanks and remaining vehicles had been abandoned at Shwegyin, this brigade continued to find drivers not only for the vehicles brought across the Chindwin but also to supplement the drivers of the G.P.T. Companies working north and south of Tamu. Six to seven hundred men were employed in this way. No praise is too high for the work done by this formation."

And again:

> "The value of long training as a formation and the confidence resulting therefrom was well exemplified by the 7th Armoured Brigade, which retained its cheerful outlook and fighting capacity throughout."

And later, verbally, to a former commander of the brigade:

> "Without the 7th Armoured Brigade we should not have got the army out of Burma."

*   *   *   *

In view of the Japanese threat to Imphal and Assam it was several days before a decision was reached about the place for refitting the 7th Armoured Brigade. For a time it seemed probable that the 414th Battery would have to stay at Imphal. The brigade was also warned to provide one regiment for defence of the oilfields at Digboi. The two armoured regiments tossed up for the task and, as the 7th Hussars lost, they got it. The 2nd Royal Tanks were therefore the first regiment to leave for India and they moved to Dimapur railhead on

25th May. The rest of the brigade, including the 414th Battery, moved during the next three days and finally, on 28th May, it was learned that the 7th Husaars were not needed at Digboi and next day they went too.

The journey to railhead was alarming. The lorries were driven by Indians, many of them not properly out of the "learner" category. This however did not discourage them and they took their hairpins with a light-hearted buoyancy terrifying to their passengers. Nearly every bend had evidence of a crash; sometimes only the bottom of a lorry would be visible, far down the khud-side; occasionally a wrecked vehicle would be suspended in mid air, held by a stout tree trunk. The 7th Hussars however arrived at railhead fortunately, if unexpectedly, intact.

The journey by rail was slow and, at first, very uncomfortable. Only goods trucks were available and these were very dirty. Already many thousands of refugees and troops had passed along the route. At one station, Lumding, Captain Pilkington asked the station master about the local sanitary arrangements and was informed, with a generous wave of the arm, "Sir, everywhere is the latrine."

At Ranchi the regiment detrained and stayed in camp for several days, getting together a little personal kit and clothing, and able to tidy up a bit before going on to Dhond. The last part of the rail journey took four days and was very hot. Meals were provided at the periodical halts, cooked by the Royal Indian Army Service Corps. One extra halt was made at Raipur, where tea was provided by the Women's Voluntary Service. On 11th June the brigade reached Dhond, where admirable arrangements for its reception had been made by the 50th Army Tank Brigade.

The 7th Armoured Brigade now came under command of the 32nd Indian Armoured Division. The principal function was to provide guards for the railway, at the station and at the bridge over the Bhima River. It seemed strange that such tasks should be necessary so far from the nearest enemy. But, from the Allies' point of view, things were going badly. With Japan's entry into the war and rapid advance through Asia, Rommel's advance into Egypt, and the arrival of the German armies in the foothills of the Caucasus, the end of British influence in the east had seemed to be in sight. The Congress Party in India had taken advantage of the situation; some of their leaders were arrested, but there was a widespread, though not very effective, outbreak of sabotage. This, and the accompaniment of anti-British propaganda among Indian troops, were never of serious consequence but, coming at a time when the resources of the British Commonwealth were stretched to their limit, the diversion of further British troops for internal security duties was, to say the least, an inconvenience.

The strength of the whole brigade was now only 1,500 men, and ever since reaching Imphal the rate of sickness had been going up. Even those returning from hospital were in poor physical condition. However, the effects wore off and, thanks largely to the setting up of a brigade leave camp at Bombay, by the end of July everyone was in good order again. The leave camp took 600 men at a time. The Revd. Metcalfe played a considerable part in making a success of it, and every man was there for a fortnight of bathing and entertainments.

Early in July the Duke of Gloucester inspected the brigade on a dismouted ceremonial parade.

While the regiment was at Dhond Major R. F. G. Jayne rejoined after an absence, in the United States and elsewhere, of more than a year. Major Younger spent a week as G.S.O.1 of the Eastern Army and then became second-in-command of the 3rd Carabiniers, which regiment he subsequently commanded. It was the middle of July before vehicles began to arrive. Training could then start on a few "General Grant" tanks, carriers and armoured cars. By the time that orders came for the next move the regiment was proficient with its new equipment, had absorbed and trained its reinforcements and was ready again for active operations.

In September, with the rest of the brigade, the 7th Hussars moved down to Bombay and embarked for Iraq.

PART III—ITALY

CHAPTER XII

Iraq to Italy

Iraq—Syria—Greek mutinies—back in Egypt—Mediterranean strategy—plans for Italy—the landings—winter battles—arrival in Italy—the fall of Rome—the beginning of the end—pursuit from Rome—follow-up to the Chienti.

Map XIII, XIV

Two years elapsed between the last fight of the 7th Hussars in Burma and their first in Italy. In this period they had their taste of boredom and there were not a few who felt that, for all the good they were doing, they might as well be at home.

The months in Iraq were the dreariest of all. There was shooting—black partridges and duck—for those who could get guns and cartridges. There were the usual games. But the country was dusty and colourless and by the beginning of April the heat was becoming severe. Hockey and soccer gave place to cricket. Training with General Stuart tanks, which had been issued in place of the old General Grants, was restricted, as usual, by track mileage.

As the heat increased, so did the sickness; fifty men were admitted to hospital during April, mostly with sandfly fever and malaria. The strength of the regiment was further reduced by the loss of thirty-four NCOs and men with long foreign service, who were sent home, and a draft of a hundred who were sent to the 14th/20th Hussars, also in Iraq. As a last straw, there was a scare of rabies, and the order was given for all dogs in the regiment to be destroyed; there were quite a large number of dogs at this period, and it was particularly exasperating for those owners who obeyed the order promptly that it was soon afterwards rescinded.

Early in May orders came for a move to an unknown destination. It was Iraq and its climate that had inspired Noel Coward to write his well-known song about mad dogs and Englishmen going out in the mid-day sun, and not a single 7th Hussar had any regrets about leaving it.

*   *   *   *

On 6th May the tracked vehicles were sent by rail to Basra for embarkation and next day the regiment began a six-day march by road and desert. On entering Transjordania it passed out of the

Persia and Iraq Command and came once more under Middle East Forces. Turning north in Palestine, it crossed the Syrian frontier on the 12th and went into camp at Insurriya.

Three pleasant and idle weeks were now spent by the sea before the march was resumed. On 1st June the 7th Hussars set out once more, on the 300 mile journey to Aleppo. Here the 7th Armoured Brigade came under command of the 10th Armoured Division.

The 7th Hussars were now commanded by Lieutenant-Colonel R. F. G. Jayne, D.S.O., and during this period there were several other changes of officers. Before leaving Iraq Major Congreve had been sent to a staff course at Haifa and eventually he went to a staff appointment on the headquarters of Eighth Army in Italy. Captain M. V. Argyle became adjutant and R.S.M. P. W. Brown was promoted to Lieutenant and Quartermaster. Nine new subalterns joined.

Aleppo is only a few miles from the Turkish frontier and troops stationed in the area had an operational function; if Turkey became involved in the war they would be the first to go to her support.

In the spring of 1943 the Allies were endeavouring to induce Turkey to go to war with Germany. The Turks certainly had no love for the Germans; the uneasy alliance of World War I was still fresh in their memories; they had even less love for the Italians, who had bitten off the North-African outpost of their empire in 1912. Their attitude to the British, however, was markedly friendly. As it was the British more than anyone else who had broken up the Turkish empire into a number of independent states in 1918, this seems surprising. But it was clear to the Turks that imperial expansion played no part in British designs. On the other hand there seemed to be no limit to the ambitions of Hitler. In the present conflict therefore Turkish interests would best be served by a British-American victory.

This, in simple terms, was the Turkish attitude towards Germany and Italy, but the Turks had no intention of taking part if they could avoid doing so. Nor did they any longer "feel themselves threatened." By the summer of 1943 the last Germans had been flung out of Africa; the eastern front was rolling westwards; Hitler could gain nothing by attacking Turkey.

Diplomatic and military conversations between the British and the Turks went on in the most friendly and cordial atmosphere. The Turks received tanks, guns and other equipment. They accepted training teams, they permitted the construction of fighter air strips, to enable the Royal Air Force to fly in for their protection in case of German attack or Turkish intervention in the war. But by this time the Turks had lost interest in Germany; their eyes were turned to clouds gathering on the eastern and northern horizons, a menace deeper in the past and more distant in the future than the transitory "Hitler incident." The control of an outlet to the Mediterranean had been the ambition of the Czars and remained the unaltered ambition of their successors, the Communist dictators. Turkey, firmly astride the Bosphorus, was still the obstacle, a fact of which the Turks themselves were acutely aware. Consequently, while they accepted British military help ostensibly for one purpose, they scarcely concealed the fact that they meant to conserve it for another.

At Aleppo Turkish officers attended regimental exercises and training. They cannot have been greatly impressed. The 7th Hussars had three well-worn old Sherman tanks and a number of Crusaders, now obsolete. The numerical strength of the regiment was equally uninspiring. It was more than 150 below establishment. Of those on the books eighty at a time were away at the leave camp at Beyrouth and in June about forty a day were going sick with sandfly fever. At the end of the month twelve officers and a hundred men were out of action with this complaint. Four or five days in bed were usually enough, but after that it was a week or two before normal strength and vigour returned.

The country round Aleppo was excellent for training. The roads and tracks in the mountains were very like those on the seaboard of southern Europe. Exercises included practice in convoy driving in hilly country, the passage of defiles, and clearance of minefields. In technical training the three Shermans were very valuable. The regiment was eventually to be equipped with this type of tank, and while in Syria most of the tank crews were put through a Sherman course.

*   *   *   *

On 2nd July the 7th Hussars marched south from Aleppo and went into camp at Baalbek. The Stuart tanks had now reached Beyrouth and were all allotted to B Squadron.

While at Baalbek the regiment touched the fringe of another political problem, typical of those which afflicted the exiled people of all enemy-occupied countries. Those Greeks who had escaped at the time of the German occupation had been formed into a brigade, equipped and trained on British lines, in the Middle East. The exiled King and an exiled government of mixed political persuasion were established in Cairo. The brigade was having one of its periodical mutinies and the 7th Hussars were required to play a modest part in maintaining order.

It has been said of the Greeks that if you see two together, you see two political parties. Any attempt to describe Greek politics must result in either volumes of confusion or misleading over-simplification. There is nothing simple about them, and even German invasion only momentarily mollified the inter-party bitterness. Parties themselves were torn by fierce rivalries among party leaders and their adherents, and Greeks were soon branding one another freely as traitors. Rampaging in the multi-coloured tangle was a litter of constitutional kittens, wrangling and spitting over monarchy, republicanism, communism. Even the meaning of the word "democracy," to a people whose ancestors had themselves evolved the democratic way of life and whose language had given the word to the dictionaries of civilization, was in dispute.

While the Greeks bickered among themselves over post-war settlements, almost none of them fought the Germans. Two main resistance movements were backed and supported by Great Britain with arms, food, clothing and British liaison units. One of these was republican and anti-communist. The other was frankly communist. On rare occasions, under pressure from British officers, acts of anti-German sabotage were carried out. But E.L.A.S., the larger resistance movement, had no genuine interest in anything but the establishment of a communist régime under Moscow at the conclusion of the war, and its necessary accompaniment—the liquidation of the non-communists. Their hopes of success were greatly increased after the autumn of 1943, when they acquired the weapons of the departing Italian garrison.

A foretaste of the reign of terror had begun in a small way in 1942 and the Germans had allowed the non-communist Greeks to form Security Battalions for the protection of the population. Some called them traitors and some patriots. Their military prospects against the increasing armed power of E.L.A.S. were never very bright. But to the mass of the Greek people they afforded a tiny gleam of hope, which might carry them through the anxious days of anarchy when the Germans left.

Every complexity of the situation in Greece itself was reflected in the Greek Brigade. If only it could have been brought into action against the Germans it might have proved itself an asset. It was well equipped, well trained, even in combined operations, and the Greeks do not lack courage. But until September 1944, when it went into action in Italy, no commander would have it. In consequence it had too much time on its hands, which meant too much politics, and mutinies broke out with monotonous regularity.

The 7th Armoured Brigade was involved in two of these, in the summer of 1943 and the spring of 1944. In one there was considerable fighting before the Greeks gave in. The 7th Hussars however were fortunate. In the first they were required to disarm the anti-tank platoons of two battalions, and this was effected without resistance. In the second they provided a party, with tanks, to disarm a mutinous Greek naval detachment at Kabrit on the Suez Canal, and again there was no opposition.

*   *   *   *

At the end of September 1943 the 7th Armoured Brigade left Syria for Egypt. The march through Palestine was carried out with more than the usual security measures. No contact whatever was permitted with the inhabitants and particular care was taken to prevent the loss of personal weapons. The Jewish terrorist organization was at this time showing great ingenuity in accumulating weapons and ammunition from the British, for use in the coming "war of independence." Their methods included thefts of personal weapons from officers and men and raids in which, sometimes with the aid of faked documents, they were able to drive off whole lorry loads from depots. It was some time before the scope of these activities was realized, but by now the most stringent rules were in force and the loss of a weapon involved severe penalties.

Outwardly Egypt had changed little in the past two years. The camps and the huge base organizations were still there. But the war had moved away. In October and November, 1942, the Eighth Army under General Montgomery had beaten Rommel at El Alamein, and General Eisenhower's allied forces had landed in Algeria and Morocco. After twelve days of fighting at El Alamein Rommel abandoned his Italian allies on the field and withdrew his battered Germans once more to Agheila, harassed by the Royal Air Force as they went. At Agheila and again in southern Tunisia he imposed delays on the Eighth Army, while Hitler threw reinforcing formations across the central Mediterranean in a desperate effort to save the situation in Africa. But the pressure of the Eighth Army from the east and south and the allied forces from the west was too great. As the spring advanced the Germans were forced back towards the Cape Bon peninsula. Some escaped to Europe, but the greater part were compelled to lay down their arms.

At Fanara the regiment was quickly brought up to strength in men and equipment, the latter including Stuarts, Shermans and Daimler Scout Cars. In November the 7th Hussars became the reconnaissance regiment of the 10th Armoured Division and for a time were detached from the 7th Armoured Brigade. The latter however still had two armoured regiments, as the 6th Royal Tanks, who had been left behind when the rest of the brigade went to Burma, had now rejoined.

The new role involved several changes in organization and each troop consisted of two Stuarts and two Shermans.

The winter in Egypt was a busy one. The absorption of a large number of recruits meant a lot of hard work in individual training, and even the old hands had everything to learn about modern and scientific methods of tank gunnery. The hit-and-miss shooting of the bad old days had gone for ever and the guns of armoured regiments were now used not only to engage enemy armour, but as forward artillery in close and intimate support of infantry. The new second-in-command, Major E. H. Tinker, 13th/18th Hussars, took an active part in all this training, and his wisdom and experience were most valuable.

In squadron and regimental exercises, attention was paid particularly to the passage of defiles in mountainous country, mine clearing and river crossings. Old vehicles with desert colouring were painted over with the sombre hues more suitable for Europe. New vehicles already wore the new colours. Preparation ended with a course in combined operations, the dry-shod part at Fayid, followed by the wet-shod fortnight at Kabrit.

The long period of waiting was drawing to its close. At times the months had seemed to drag, especially when men were short and equipment was scarce. Sometimes it was not easy to keep the men occupied and interested; it was then especially that the padré weighed in with his unflagging enthusiasm to supplement the efforts of the other officers. Not only was he the moving spirit in seaside camps, but he promoted many excursions and—it is said—instigated more than one military exercise in the neighbourhood of some place of historic interest.

As a guide, Metcalfe was excellent, always ready and able to explain and to answer questions. Many 7th Hussars owe to him their visits to the great monuments of the Near East—the temples and tombs of Upper Egypt, the monastery of St. Catherine on Mount Sinai, the rose-red, rock-hewn city of Petra, the massive Roman temple at Baalbek, and what is perhaps, to a soldier, the most impressive of all—the Krak des Chevaliers, fortress of the Crusaders, long since deserted, but still vast and dominating in its solitude.

On 15th April, when training at Kabrit was over, the tanks were sent to Wardian workshops for modifications and the regiment moved into bivouac at Muhaggara on the coast of the Gulf of Suez, to await embarkation. A week later the armoured vehicles left by train and the soft vehicles by road for Alexandria, and embarkation began. The officers and men of the 7th Armoured Brigade, once more the parent formation of the 7th Hussars, embarked at Suez in the liners *Champollion* and *Reina del Pacifico*.

On 27th April 1944, for the second time during the war, the 7th Hussars sailed from Suez. This time however it was not southwards and eastwards, but northwards and westwards, through the Suez Canal, out into the Mediterranean towards Europe. Even the destination was no secret—Taranto.

* * * *

The successful conclusion of the Allies' campaign in North Africa in the spring of 1943 had been followed in July of the same year by the invasion of Sicily. This was the final exploitation of the African campaigns, which had begun with the capture of Fort Capuzzo in June 1940 and ended when the last Germans escaped across the Strait of Messina in August 1943. After the capture of Sicily the Mediterranean was comparatively safe for merchant ships, and the saving of tonnage through the shortening of the sea routes to the Middle East, India and Australasia was of great consequence at this stage of the war. The wolf-pack tactics of the German submarines had not yet been mastered, and this saving in tonnage was an important factor in the build-up of the allied invasion forces in Great Britain.

Inter-allied planning had been a continuous process ever since the United States entered the war. Plans were evolved by the Allied staffs, then thrashed out and confirmed by high-level conferences attended by Mr. Churchill and President Roosevelt. Naturally there were conflicts of opinion and conflicts of interest and when the Russians were also brought into conference, as their armies closed in upon the Reich, yet further diversities of purpose were revealed.

The course of grand strategy, as determined at the many conferences, Quebec, Casablanca, Teheran, Washington, Cairo, Yalta and others, may now be studied in many works on the strategy of the war. Here we are concerned only with the campaign in Italy, the circumstances which led to it, and its place in the general scheme for the overthrow of Hitler's Germany.

That its purposes were subsidiary and its resources limited to what could be spared from other theatres, was to cause disappointment to the commanders in Italy and to their troops; too often they saw the fruits of their efforts rotting for want of pickers. There were many who scarcely realized at the time how great a part their hard fighting played in the final victory, how much their many "D Days" contributed to the success of the more glamorous D Day of Normandy, how they forced Hitler to fight not merely on two fronts, but on three, and drained away his troops while Germany was over-run. This was the appointed task of the forces in Italy, a task typical of British strategy, but only undertaken after prolonged inter-allied debate.

One broad principle had been accepted by the United States leaders from the first, and from this the President never wavered: until Germany was defeated, the European theatre would have priority over the Asiatic. This decision was something of a strain for the American staffs, especially for their naval members. The American people, and above all the American navy, were thirsting for revenge on the Japanese; Pearl Harbour had left a stain which must be wiped out. So there was always a draw towards the Pacific; at one time or another a number of troops, naval and air units were moved towards the Pacific by the United States military leaders, who were to be the sole judges of what were the minimum forces necessary for that area. The implied threat of further withdrawals was thus a powerful handle in strategical arguments, and points of difference between the respective joint staffs needed most delicate handling.

Another important combined decision was that the main attack on the Reich should be delivered across the Channel, through France. This brought out several interesting differences of strategical conception between the British and the Americans. For example, the latter liked the direct approach and were content with a head-on, head-down, frontal attack, without any diversionary operations against secondary objectives.

Secondly, the Americans were anxious to keep the British as far as possible from the Balkans; never since the 1770's had they quite got out of their system the bogey of British imperialism, and a sort of crusading spirit still impelled them to save people from the British.

At the period of these discussions there was the added stimulus of Stalin. He was thinking far beyond the present war, which was but an incident in the evolution of Russia's plan of World Domination, a mere stepping stone, to be used in the development of a grand design whose origins were to be sought long before the revolution of 1917. Stalin intended this stepping stone to take him as far westward as possible, and his present stride was to include the Balkans. He accordingly welcomed the invasion of France from the north (Operation OVERLORD) and when the suggestion was eventually made that France should be invaded from the south also (Operation ANVIL) he welcomed this too. What he did not like was any sign of allied intervention in the Balkans. On this point therefore he and Roosevelt were of one accord, though for somewhat different reasons.

The Krak des Chevaliers.

5th Troop, C Squadron, near Lanciano; Sangro valley in distance. *Left to right*, Tprs. Wilkinson, Singleton, Mayne, Corporal Russell, Tpr. Emery (and here S.Q.M.S. Trusler's memory fails).

British strategical conception was founded on a long tradition of sea-power. Britain had never had the military resources to indulge alone in head-on collisions with the armies of powerful continental states. She had had to resort to finesse and strategem, to throwing her enemies off their balance by striking at distant points, taking advantage of her sea-borne mobility. One outstanding example in her history had been the drawing off of French forces into the Peninsula, where Wellington's campaigns were a decisive factor in the downfall of Napoleon.

Churchill and his Chiefs of Staff now wished to use the allied forces still in the Mediterranean in some similar fashion; they could not be allowed to stand idle for the winter, and a campain in southern Europe would have an excellent diversionary effect for OVERLORD.

The choice was limited. An early attack on Southern France might draw too many Germans westwards, nearer to Normandy. The Balkans were too difficult for major operations and their communications too poor. An attack on Sardinia and Corsica could have no more than a limited effect. Only an invasion of the Italian peninsula seemed to offer far-reaching results. This would of itself keep a number of German formations occupied at a considerable distance both from the OVERLORD area, and from the eastern front; in this respect it would to some extent redeem the pledge for a "second front in Europe," a pledge given somewhat hastily by Roosevelt two years before. Secondly, it might bring about the collapse of Italy; this again would draw German forces southwards, to replace Italian occupation forces in southern France and the Balkans. Thirdly, it would create a threat to the Balkans; if ever the Germans were pressed back to the Venice area, their hold on the Balkans would be threatened, and even before this, they could never feel quite safe from an attack across the Adriatic against their already precarious communications. The arguments in favour of a direct assault on the Italian peninsula were used with vigour and were difficult to rebut; eventually they prevailed.

After the Washington Conference, on 26th May 1943, the Combined Chiefs of Staff issued to General Eisenhower a directive for the conduct of operations in the Mediterranean when he had captured Sicily; he would then lose a number of formations selected for OVERLORD, and the Mediterranean theatre would no longer enjoy its hitherto over-riding priority. With what was left he was to plan "such operations in exploitation of the conquest of Sicily as would be best calculated to eliminate Italy from the war and to contain the maximum number of German divisions."

Planning for Italy was soon in full swing, but it was only on

20th July that the project for attacking Sardinia was handed over to the French planners as a possible task for the future, when their forces were organized and ready. Sardinia had been attractive to the Americans. Its nearest point to Italy is 140 miles and there would have been no danger of British strategists locking up forces on the mainland of Italy, still less of any diversion in the Balkans. For precisely these reasons an attack on Sardinia would have done little to fulfil the terms of General Eisenhower's directive. Nevertheless, in spite of its patent limitations, the American predilection for the operation had been most difficult to overcome.

* * * *

Now that the attack on Italy had been firmly accepted the next problem to be settled was the time and place for the landing. The Calabrian peninsula would be the easiest place to secure a footing, as the crossing of the Strait of Messina could be supported by artillery in Sicily and would be hardly more difficult than a river crossing. The country however is mountainous, the roads bad, the little ports quite inadequate for the maintenance of a large force over a long line of communications, three comparatively narrow isthmuses afforded excellent facilities for defence, and if this were the only area selected for landings, the terms of the directive would still be unfulfilled. Something of wider scope was needed, an operation which would lead to the capture of one of the major ports—Taranto or Naples—and ultimately to an advance against Rome and the industrial areas of the north.

The major ports—Taranto and Naples—were heavily defended and —most important of all—beyond the range of fighter cover; carriers in sufficient numbers were not available and the risks of a large scale combined operation without fighter cover were too great.

The first outline plan therefore envisaged a landing by one corps of Eighth Army round the tip of the Calabrian Peninsula, to be followed a month later by another corps landing at Cotrone, fifty miles up; the latter operation was designed to hasten the break out into the plains and the advance on one of the large ports. The target date for the first of these operations was governed by availability of landing craft and the phases of the moon, and was fixed provisionally for 1st October.

On 25th July the pace was forced by an event which was not altogether unexpected. Rome radio announced the fall of Mussolini and the suppression of the Fascist party. Marshal Badoglio, who had formed a government, said "the war continues," but this deceived nobody. Italy was clearly nearing the "collapse" which had long been foreseen and in the middle of August negotiations for an armistice began. The Italians were in a quandary. Willing as they were to end the now unpopular alliance, the surrender was difficult to implement when there was nobody on Italian soil who could make it effective and, which was more important, protect the Italians from German reprisals.

Allied dates were at once put forward and the 10th Corps, planning the Cotrone operation, was to prepare itself for an alternative landing, with the United States 6th Corps, both under the Fifth Army, at Salerno. Naples was the objective.

Salerno Bay was just within range of Spitfires based on Sicily, the beaches were good, and a single, though rugged, mountain spur was the only serious natural barrier between the landing place and the great port. The date for the operation was provisionally fixed for 7th September, the determining factors being as usual the availability of landing craft and the phases of the moon.

On the news of Mussolini's fall the Germans reacted quickly. They moved troops down to the south of Italy and before the invasion began they had established one division on the coast in the Salerno area and two in the coastal belt just north of Naples. Six in all were south of Naples, including four recently evacuated from Sicily. The total number of divisions in Italy increased to nineteen. These movements were almost unmolested, as the United States Chiefs of Staff would not modify by a moment the withdrawal of forces from Eisenhower's command and on 2nd August he was deprived of four heavy bomber groups, which were despatched to the United Kingdom.

Between the first contact of the Italian emissaries on 1st August and the signing of the armistice on 3rd September, the Italians became more and more afraid of the Germans. They wished to time their surrender so that they would have to fight the Germans just a little, enough to secure acceptance as members of the United Nations, but no more. They made no difficulties about the expression "unconditional surrender," which was freely used among allied statesmen at this time. Their main anxiety was for their own protection against the Germans. Their military staffs had no conception of the problems and difficulties of combined operations and they sought assurances that the Allies would land fifteen divisions in the Leghorn area and a further force at Ancona. They could not of course be told the strength or point of the invasion, and the only concession was the promise of an airborne division, the 82nd U.S., to land near Rome and help the five Italian divisions there to overcome one German division.

Eventually, after much persuasion and while the assault divisions of the Eighth Army were landing on the Calabrian shores, the Italians signed the instrument of surrender.

The announcement of the surrender on the Italian radio was to be made the day before the landing at Salerno. Badoglio vacillated until the last moment. Even as late as 8th September, when some of the troops had been at sea for four days and the assault convoys were approaching Salerno through the swept channel, he tried to back out; he signalled that the Allied landing must prove successful before he could make his announcement. At the eleventh hour, however, pressed by a vigorous signal from Eisenhower, he made a statement on Rome radio and rather half-heartedly called on Italian troops to cease resistance to the Allies and to "resist any attack which might come from another quarter." He and the aged King then took refuge on an Italian warship.

General Alexander sums up the Italian surrender in his Despatch: "The plain fact is that the Italian Government did not decide to capitulate because it saw itself incapable of offering further resistance, nor because of any change of heart or intellectual conviction of the justice of the Allied and Democratic cause; it decided, as Italian statesmen had decided in the past, that the time had come to 'spring to the aid of the victors'."

The Germans quickly disarmed the Italian troops. Those in the Salerno area, with which we are mainly concerned, offered no resistance at all, and within the nine hours between Badoglio's announcement and the assault all coast defences were securely in German hands. The German plan at this time was to defeat any invasion forces which might land in Italy—other than in Calabria—on the beaches. If this should fail, they intended to abandon southern Italy and withdraw to the general line Pisa-Rimini.

The final Allied plan included three main landings. First the Eighth Army was to land in Calabria and advance rapidly up the peninsula; this operation was carefully and deliberately planned, but would be restricted by availability of landing craft, in which priority was given to the Fifth Army. The latter was to assault Salerno with the 10th British Corps and 6th U.S. Corps, which had previously been planning assaults respectively on Cotrone (now cancelled) and Sardinia (now a French responsibility). The Salerno landing was planned in great haste and called for a good deal of improvisation. The 82nd U.S. Airborne Division was now withdrawn from the Salerno operation and prepared for the landing on Rome. This was actually cancelled at the last moment owing to the apathy of the Italians in general and Badoglio in particular, so the 82nd Airborne Division became for the moment a wasted asset. The 1st British Airborne Division, for which there was no air lift, was to embark in warships, no longer required to give protection against the Italian fleet, and to land near Taranto, with the task of securing the port and the "heel" of Italy. It was to be followed up by other troops and a corps headquarters. This operation, mounted at the last moment and with virtually no planning at all, would eventually speed up the Eighth Army's maintenance build-up when it crossed over to the Adriatic coast.

*   *   *   *

On 3rd September the mountains round the Strait of Messina echoed to a bombardment almost as heavy as any that even the Eighth Army had known, as British and American guns in Sicily and warships on the flanks battered the area of the assaults. When the two divisions landed they found no Germans and there was practically no opposition from the Italians. Other troops followed. The leading elements advanced some fifty miles and the army began to build up its administration. Here it stayed for three weeks while the battle for a footing on the more sensitive "shin" of Italy was fought and won—but only just—by the Fifth Army.

The Salerno assault took place on the 9th September. There were four enemy battalions and a number of tanks holding the beaches and these contested every step. Within a few hours the Germans had a whole division in action and other divisions were moving on the threatened area. Every effort was made to throw the Allies back into the sea.

Both corps fought their way inland, the Americans on the right, where the mountains lay well back from the coast, penetrated farther than the British. For three days progress was fairly satisfactory, but by the 12th the Germans had been able to build up their forces more rapidly than had been hoped. They withdrew every man from Calabria, completely ignoring the threat—which proved to be non-existent—from the Eighth Army. They brought down divisions from north of Naples—a movement which could have been restricted and delayed by either the cancelled airborne operation or the vanished American bombers.

For three days the enemy launched successive counter-attacks against the tiring and depleted allied force. Some of these penetrated almost to the beaches. The navies and air forces did their best. In spite of the air risk, the battleships *Warspite* and *Valiant* were sent to supplement the fire of the warships already in the bay. The strategic bombers were turned on to enemy communications. Part of the 82nd Airborne

Division was parachuted by night into the beach-head as an emergency reinforcement.

On the 13th and 14th the situation was critical, but finally, on the 15th, the enemy gave up the struggle and began slowly to wheel back his forces to positions covering Naples and the Foggia airfields. The determination of Generals Mark Clark and Richard McCreery had triumphed. The result of this grim and, in its way, decisive battle, was in great measure due to the gallantry of the British 10th Corps and the dogged, fierce and single-minded cavalryman who commanded it.

The withdrawal was followed up vigorously by the Fifth Army and the 1st Airborne Division. The latter had landed near Taranto on the 10th. It had practically no transport, but with great enterprise and energy and inspired by the example of its ingenious commander, Hopkinson, who was killed during these operations, it managed to advance a hundred miles, harassing the retreating Germans all the way.

On the Adriatic flank the Foggia area was occupied on 27th September and by 1st October the 10th Corps, on the left, had fought its way through the mountain passes and down into Naples.

During these operations the Eighth Army moved over from Calabria to take over the eastern sector of the front, with its right on the Adriatic, its left in touch with the Fifth Army and its base area including the ports of Taranto and Bari.

*   *   *   *

The next task of the Allied armies in Italy was to secure their position. The Eighth Army on the right, while building up its administration, carried out a limited offensive designed to secure the small port of Termoli and to drive the enemy back to the Trigno, his next delaying position south of the "Winter Line." The Fifth Army on the left had fewer maintenance difficulties once Naples port was working, but in order to make Naples secure it was necessary to force the crossings of the Volturno, to advance at least as far as the Garigliano and if possible to seize the Aurunci Mountains beyond.

The Termoli operation began on 3rd October with a small combined operation, and the Volturno operation a week later. Both offensives met with heavy opposition, but eventually succeeded in pushing the enemy back.

The Germans now had a fresh directive which accounted for the obstinacy of their defence and contributed materially to the fulfilling of General Alexander's primary task. They were to stand fast on what was called their Winter Line. This was a broad defensive belt running approximately from the mouth of the Sangro on the east, including the massive Monte della Maiella feature, the Monte Cairo spur, the Aurunci Mountains and ending on the Tyrrhenian Sea about the mouth of the Garigliano. While defences were being hastily prepared the Allied advance was to be delayed as much as possible, but beyond the Winter Line there was to be no withdrawal.

This was one of many Hitlerian decisions of a similar character; from now to the end of the war he repeatedly insisted on holding every yard of ground when considerations of strategy and tactics cried out for geographical adjustments and economy of force.

In Italy the Germans had twenty-three divisions, of which, by the beginning of October, nine were actively engaged with General Alexander's eleven. In the succeeding three months the Allies would be reinforced by another six divisions, but during the same period the enemy could quickly double his forces in the south by bringing down troops from Northern Italy, where the Italian army and population were almost universally docile. Even if he did not intend to stage an offensive to drive the invaders out, he would be able to provide fresh divisions to relieve any which became battle-worn. As the Allies kept him constantly fighting, this was what he proceeded to do. The strategical result was that many more German divisions were kept occupied, on a front far removed from OVERLORD, than if they had been withdrawn to the Pisa-Rimini line, or better still, the Alps. To this extent Hitler was now a subscriber to his own downfall.

During October both the Fifth and Eighth Armies fought their way to within striking distance of the Winter Line. The weather had been abominable, and was to get much worse. All illusions about the "Sunny Italy" of the travel agencies' advertisements were shattered by the end of the month and as the troops floundered in the deep mud they had their first taste of what their fathers had known so well in World War I.

In order to keep the enemy off his balance it was necessary to keep the initiative. Offensive operations must therefore continue without waiting for the perfection of administration. Eighth Army was directed on the high ground north of Pescara, whence it was to threaten Rome from the north-east. Fifth Army was directed on Rome. A combined operation was to be launched near the mouth of the Tiber when this army had broken into the plains north-west of Cassino.

The build-up and reinforcement of the armies was being delayed above all by shortage of landing craft and the impending removal of most of those now in the theatre. Furthermore, the concentration of the Strategic Air Force at Foggia and the steel-plank all-weather construction of its airfields was competing with the army for the few which were available. The struggle for landing craft was henceforth to be one of General Alexander's foremost worries, not only for seaborne assaults but also for general administrative purposes.

The offensive was to open on the Adriatic Sector. The country here was very difficult. About every ten miles a major river ran at right-angles to the line of advance, through deep gorges and valleys, sometimes opening out into wide shingle beds, where, after a distant downpour in the mountains, the normal trickle would become a broad torrent in a matter of minutes. Intervening ridges were usually of rock and clay and intersected with innumerable streams. Against stubborn resistance, unfavourable country and bad weather Eighth Army's progress was costly and slow.

By the middle of December, after three weeks of fighting, the high ground between the Sangro and the Moro had been captured but, faced repeatedly by fresh enemy troops, Eighth Army had no impetus left for continuing its thrust to Pescara. The threat to Rome from the north-east never materialized.

The attacks of the Fifth Army had begun a few days later. By the end of December the enemy had been pressed back to his Winter Line and the system had been penetrated in places, but not broken. On this sector also the fighting was severe, and again the enemy was aided by the mountains and the weather.

The breaking of the Winter Line was going to be a hard task and the Allied armies had now to pause and re-group before renewing the offensive. The narrow and steeply corrugated Adriatic sector did not lend itself to offensive operations and even a deep penetration on that flank would reach no vital objective. The Apennines were impassable for large forces. On the extreme left the coastal road followed the sea shore round the foot of the Aurunci mountains and debouched into the Pontine Marshes, which had been flooded by the Germans. The only sector where a penetration would lead to decisive results was the Liri Valley, the direct approach to Rome.

Stretching South from the Apennines and barring the entrance to the Liri Valley is the great Monte Cairo spur, ending in the rocky promontory of Monte Cassino. This formidable bastion, crowned by its magnificent Benedictine monastery, had been regarded by the Italian General Staff as an example of an impregnable position. The Germans did their best to convert it into a fortress and took full advantage of the massive masonry of the monastery.

Ever since the landing in Italy amphibious operations had been much to the fore in planning. Resources had been limited and only one—on the east coast—had been carried out. During November however plans were made for the landing of a division at Anzio, with the Alban Hills as its objective. This operation was to take place when the advance on Rome had progressed about half way up the valley from Cassino and the main forces were thus within supporting distance.

When it became clear that the Cassino bastion could not be so easily broken, the projected landing at Anzio assumed another character. It was to be on a much larger scale and enough troops were to land to make the force self-supporting for an indefinite period. In its new character, the Anzio force might conceivably cause the enemy, with his communications threatened, to evacuate the Cassino position. It would in any case draw in more German troops, including perhaps some from other theatres.

After much juggling with the plans for overhauling landing craft, so that there should be no delay to OVERLORD, enough were made available to launch the operation on 22nd January and for its subsequent maintenance.

The battle for Rome opened on 17th January with an attack by the Fifth Army across the Garigliano. The first attacks succeeded, but the Germans reinforced rapidly and counter-attacked with fresh divisions. One of these had been the division which could most easily have moved to oppose the Anzio landing, another had been about to transfer from Italy to the eastern front. To this extent the operations succeeded, but penetration through the Gustav Line (the final defensive position of the Winter Line System) and into the Liri Valley was impossible with the resources available.

The landing at Anzio took place on 22nd January. There was almost no opposition. The only Germans in the area were a depleted battalion sent to the seaside for a rest. The Allied corps consolidated a bridgehead about fifteen miles wide and seven miles deep, but penetration inland was rather slow. In view of the failure of the frontal attacks to break through into the Liri Valley, it is doubtful whether, at this stage, any useful purpose would have been served by seizing the Alban Hills; the force there would have been dangerously exposed and any set-back would have seriously weakened the beach perimeter.

German reactions were strategically quite satisfactory. The Gustav Line was to be held intact; "The Führer expects the bitterest struggle for every yard." Kesselring was promised the equivalent of more than three extra divisions, two heavy tank battalions and extra artillery. He was to eliminate the bridgehead.

On 25th January the Anzio force endeavoured to enlarge its perimeter and on the 30th began the operation which was to have ended with the capture of Velletri on the Appian Way. Both British and American troops advanced several miles, but on 3rd February came the first enemy counter-attack against the British 1st Division, and by the 5th the whole force went over to the defensive in order to prepare against the enemy's impending counter-offensive.

Meanwhile operations continued on the main battle front. French and American troops made some progress but no impression could be made on Monte Cassino. At one time the Americans seemed likely to capture the Monastery. But the enemy reinforced this part of the front with first-class troops and the attack was defeated. In the first battle of Cassino the Allies secured a crossing over the Rapido River, but the outcome as a whole was a German success.

The Fifth Army was now reinforced by the 4th Indian Division which, with the New Zealand Division, was formed into the "New Zealand Corps." Originally intended for the pursuit, this corps was now to carry out an attack at Cassino, to be staged as early as possible, as an offset to the obviously imminent German attack at Anzio. As it happened, both attacks began on 16th February.

The Germans at Anzio mustered some ten divisions against the Allies' five. Inspired by a message from Hitler which required the "abscess to be eliminated in three days," they attacked repeatedly. By the third evening their effort was spent and they had used up their exploitation reserve in the attack. On the 19th the United States armour delivered the planned counter-attack and the situation was restored.

Before the second battle of Cassino the monastery, which was an integral part of the defensive system, was reduced to rubble by air bombardment. In spite of heavy supporting fire, however, the attack made little progress and had to be called off.

The third battle of Cassino was designed partly to clear the way for a large-scale spring offensive, which was to be timed shortly before OVERLORD, and partly to keep the enemy busy in the meanwhile, so as to prevent the withdrawal of troops from Italy. This time the United States Air Force bombarded Cassino town, which was the immediate objective. The New Zealand Division was to carry out the assault, to pass through into the Liri Valley, join hands with the Indians from the high ground above and north-west of the monastery, and isolate its garrison.

The attack was delayed until there seemed to be a prospect of three days fine weather, to dry up the mud in the Liri Valley. On the 15th March it went in. Over a thousand tons of bombs reduced the town to ruins, but the rubble obstructed tank movement and the survivors of the bombardment were still resisting. The 1st Parachute Division had now taken over the defences of the town as well as the monastery and it was probably the toughest German formation on any front. Fighting continued for a week. Most of the town was captured, the Indians took two hills which projected from the main monastery feature, and held one of them, but by 23rd March it was obvious that with existing resources there was no prospect of breaking through the defences. The third battle of Cassino had had little more tactical success than the other two.

During March a general re-grouping of the Allied armies had begun. For his next offensive General Alexander considered it essential to have a local superiority at the point of attack of three to one. He accordingly brought over the Eighth Army headquarters, to command the bulk of the British troops and the Polish Corps in the central sector. The Fifth Army shortened its frontage and was responsible for the left, in the Aurunci Mountains, and also for Anzio. The 5th British Corps was left on the Adriatic side of the Apennines, with two Indian divisions, in a containing role. By the end of April, although the overall strength of the Allies was only twenty-eight divisions against the Germans' twenty-three, the necessary superiority had been established at the point selected for the attack, and all was now ready for the battle for Rome.

It was at this stage of the campaign that the 7th Hussars landed in Italy.

*   *   *   *

On 4th May 1944 the 7th Armoured Brigade began disembarking at Taranto. It moved up at once by rail and road to the Lanciano area, where concentration was completed by the 9th. Here it came under the command of the 5th Corps, which consisted of the 4th and 10th Indian Divisions and had only a holding role in the forthcoming offensive. The corps frontage was a wide one, much of it mountainous. Detachments from the armoured regiments were allotted for the support of the various Indian brigades holding the line, but the bulk of the brigade remained in the Lanciano area.

Except A Squadron, which was detached in support of the troops holding Sector C, the 7th Hussars were bivouacked at Elici in mobile reserve. Elici was not far behind the lines, but apart from occasional light shelling, the Adriatic front was quiet and peaceful. Squadrons were harboured (the European equivalent of "leaguer") among olive groves and thin oak woodlands in one of the most beautiful parts of Italy. Snow was still deep upon the majestic Monte della Maiella, but in the foothills and the plain the corn was tall and green on the terraces among the olive trees, and slopes which were too steep even for the Italians to cultivate were carpeted with primroses and violets.

The inhabitants were co-operative and pleasant in their passive fashion, somewhat bewildered, but on the whole relieved, at their recent change of sides, and they smilingly reciprocated the natural friendliness of the British soldier. Most of the people in this part of Italy live in the towns and villages, built high up on rocky hill-tops, and clustering round the Cathedral or church which crowns the summit. From these they flock daily to their fields and, even when their villages were near the front line, they preferred to remain and to risk the occasional shell rather than chance the loss of their property to looters. The changing fortunes of the war made little difference to their peaceful lives and the natural processes of births, marriages and deaths went on as usual. One "happy event" occurred in the house where A Squadron's officers were billeted and most of the officers were involved in one way or another. One drove the Italian father in a jeep to Lanciano and brought out a midwife. Others reorganized the household. Captain Low, as the medical officer, was concerned more intimately still, and a week later the christening of the surviving twin was the occasion of a friendly little party.

For Captain Low this was only one of many acts of kindness to the Italians. The British medical profession has a long tradition of undiscriminating service to humanity. As the liberating armies advanced into Europe, unit medical officers were always ready and willing to give what help they could. Bill Low was no exception and whenever the regiment settled for a day or two in one place, those with ailments were sure to find their way to him.

Immediately on arrival in the forward area reconnaissance and training began. The latter consisted largely of range practices and target spotting, and crews were practised in carrying out their own dismounted reconnaissance in close country, on the assumption that infantry might not be available. This particular feature of tactical training was to prove very useful in the weeks which followed. At the same time several officers went off on courses and attachments to other units. Lieutenant-Colonel Jayne went to the Central Mediterranean Training Centre at Benevento, which was especially valuable for bringing new arrivals up-to-date in the latest methods of warfare.

Reconnaissances were carried out for counter-attacks in case the enemy should assume the offensive on the Adriatic front. The chances of this however were obviously receding. It was clear to all that the final assault on Hitler's Europe could not be long delayed, and the troops were thinking more about the expected advance in Italy than the repulse of improbable German attacks. But they were thinking further afield than this; the "second front" agitation, kindled by President Roosevelt two years before and sedulously fanned by the Soviet authorities and their supporters ever since—for Soviet purposes —had already penetrated to the Mediterranean. One 7th Hussar expressed the prevailing impatience when he wrote, "If this second front doesn't come very early next month, I shall make a separate peace."

On the night of 11th May the Monte della Maiella was silhouetted against the flickering glow of bombardment in the west. The Fifth and Eighth Armies had opened the battle for Rome. All night and the following day the deep, distant rumble went on, and as each day brought in news of fresh successes, preparations were pressed on for the pursuit up the Adriatic coast as soon as this should be permitted.

*   *   *   *

The plan for the offensive was simple. The Eighth Army was directed to break through the enemy's main front into the Liri Valley and advance on Valmontone. The Fifth Army was to secure the Ausonia defile and advance parallel to the Eighth Army but south of the Liri and Sacco Valleys, and the force at Anzio was to break out of the bridgehead and advance on Valmontone. This last operation was to take place on D plus 4, so that the available air support might be concentrated, first on one front and then on the other.

During the winter and spring the enemy had continued to improve his defences both on his present Gustav Line and in rear. The most important of the rearward lines was across the Liri Valley through Piedimonte and Pontecorvo, the "Hitler Line." This however could be turned by a successful break-out from Anzio, and in March work was begun on the "Caesar Line," a last-ditch position covering Rome, on a general line from north of the Anzio beach-head, through the Alban Hills and Avezzano to the Saline River near Pescara.

In the two months preceding the offensive Kesselring was grossly misled both by the concealment of actual movements and by positive deception. He was sure that the first move would be a preliminary feint on the main front, where he under-estimated the Allied strength by half; he thought the main assault would be at Anzio and also expected another amphibious landing about Civitavecchia. When the main assault opened he believed he had judged correctly and it was at least four days before he began to realize that it was not a feint. He then suffered the consequences of the faulty appreciation which had been sedulously forced upon him. The bulk of his mobile forces were spread out along the west coast and, when at last he understood his error, they were brought down and thrown in piecemeal, always too few and always too late.

On the night of 11th/12th May, to the accompaniment of a tremendous bombardment, the Fifth and Eighth Armies attacked. The enemy fought for every yard.

On the left, the Americans and the French Expeditionary Corps made good progress. They had heavy casualties, but within two days they had nearly destroyed the two enemy divisions facing them. The French Goums, launched across trackless mountains regarded as impassable, reached the Liri Valley.

The 13th Corps' assault made slow but steady progress in the Cassino sector. On the ridge above Monte Cassino the Polish Corps had an initial success, but was shelled off its objectives. Having had severe losses, it was compelled to reorganize before renewing its efforts. The next Polish attack was not to begin until the 13th Corps had cleared the entrance to the Liri Valley at the foot of Monte Cassino. This was almost done by the 16th and on the 17th the Poles were once more launched against Monastery Hill. The attack made excellent progress, although the enemy managed to keep open a narrow corridor down the rocky hillside long enough to withdraw most of the garrison. Nevertheless the 2nd Polish Corps, in its first great battle under British command, had greatly distinguished itself. On the 18th the red and white ensign of Poland, with the white eagle, floated proudly over the ruins of the Monastery.

On the left the battle was already fluid. In the Liri Valley however Kesselring still tried to carry out Hitler's directions. The Hitler Line across the Valley was manned with parts of a number of German divisions. It was a highly developed defensive position and could only be tackled by a properly mounted assault. The Canadian Corps attacked at dawn on 23rd May and by noon the following day almost the whole position had been captured and an armoured division was launched in pursuit.

Half an hour after the Canadian attack the American 6th Corps began its offensive at Anzio. The Germans were now bringing in their last reserve, the Hermann Goering Division. This consisted of good troops and as it gradually arrived the enemy's resistance stiffened. The 6th Corps made good progress but could not reach Route 6 in time to cut off the elements of Tenth Army withdrawing from the Cassino front.

On 25th May the allied armies advancing from the main front joined up with the forces from Anzio.

While the Eighth Army and the right wing of the Fifth Army fought their way forward, the 6th Corps at Anzio shifted the direction of its attack to the left. On the 26th and 27th it made progress, but next day it came up against the defences of the Caesar Line. There followed three days of heavy fighting with no appreciable result. General Clark now re-grouped his tiring troops for a final blow in the Valmontone area before the enemy could recover himself and settle down on the new line. Farther to the east Eighth Army was still fighting its way forward against stubborn rearguards in the mountainous country, and was not yet approaching the Caesar Line. However there was no reason for delaying the Fifth Army on this account.

On 30th May, before General Clark's new attack was prepared, a sudden change of fortune altered the whole aspect of the battle. Enterprising patrols from a United States division discovered that the enemy, in his efforts to bolster up the Valmontone sector, had left a 3,000 foot feature of the Alban Hills entirely unguarded. An American regiment quickly marched up in the moonlight and the rest of the division followed next day. The Caesar Line was thus penetrated at its most vital point, and the whole structure of the defence was endangered.

On 1st June the Fifth Army attacked. The enemy, although his positions had been breached in the Alban Hills and his centre was disintegrating under the blows of the Eighth Army, continued to resist fiercely. The Americans however advanced rapidly east of the Alban Hills and by the evening of the 2nd the enemy was beaten. Even the Hermann Goering Division gave up the fight. The Germans south of the Alban Hills also pulled out and escaped through Rome. The Fifth Army followed up quickly and on the 4th June United States troops reached the centre of the city.

* * * *

All through May the 7th Hussars remained in the Lanciano area and the 5th Corps made no forward move. Plans were ready for an advance, and were demonstrated to each squadron in turn on a sand table. Meanwhile the regiment had its defensive tasks, in co-operation with the 4th Indian Division, and continued its training.

On 2nd June A Squadron was ordered to take over the defence of a ridge known as the Ascigno feature from a carrier force of the Manchester Regiment. Only the Stuarts were used, organized into two troops under Captain M. M. Stanley Evans, M.C. This detachment provided the mobile element, supporting the widely dispersed defended localities held by the Indian infantry, and Stanley Evans assumed command of all troops on the hill. The front was very thinly held and in no sense continuous, but the Germans were entirely passive, and there were not even clashes between patrols.

Two days later Italian troops appeared on the Ascigno ridge, including an artillery observation post. The newly formed Italian corps was beginning to take its place on the left and more mountainous sector of the Adriatic front, where, with its limited resources, it was to play quite a useful part in the subsequent advance on Ancona. For a few days the A Squadron detachment remained in support of the Italians, a role in which it was never quite happy. The Italian organization of the defences seemed somewhat sketchy. They provided no sentries and had no controlled sanitary arrangements; this was particularly irksome to their neighbours in the very hot weather.

News of the fall of Rome reached the regiment on the evening of 4th June. This had been expected for some days, and caused little excitement. The next bit of news however was more stirring. At 8 a.m. on the 6th those whose ears were pressed to their head-phones and whose wireless sets happened to be tuned to the right frequency, heard from the B.B.C. that the Germans had put out a report that allied forces had landed in France that morning.

News came in fast during the day and many 7th Hussars wireless sets were used for purposes for which they were not intended. As far as could be gathered from the guarded phrases of the B.B.C. everything was going quite well. This was a great relief. Everyone in the Mediterranean knew the hazards of combined operations and all had felt some measure of unexpressed anxiety about the actual landings. It seemed that the initial footing had been secured and, on the quiet Adriatic sector, men went about their unexciting duties with more cheerful faces, weight off their minds and brighter hopes for the future.

The day was marked on the Ascigno feature by the arrival of four Shermans of A Squadron, which went forward to shell some houses believed to be occupied by the enemy. Many officers and tank commanders of other squadrons arrived to watch the shoot, but on this day conversation centred more on Normandy than on tank gunnery. The Germans showed no interest either. Perhaps they too felt that the end was at last in sight.

*   *   *   *

Capt. Bill Low and Maj. Richard Thornton.

A christening party near Lanciano. The group includes, *left to right*, Lieutenant E. C. F. Harding, Major T. R. S. Thornton, Lieutenant S. Agnew, Tpr. Cook (above the baby's feet) and, on the right, Captain W. Low, R.A.M.C., Captain P. B. Stanley Evans and Lieutenant J. E. Parry.

After the collapse of the Caesar Line, south of Rome, the Germans began a fighting withdrawal to the "Gothic" Line. This ran across the peninsula from about Pisa to Pesaro, generally following the summits of the Apennines in the west and centre and the Foglia River on the east. Although this line had been selected by the German staff as a possible future position at the time of the first British landings, little work had been done on it. When Hitlerian edicts required positions to be held at all costs, his generals found it was unwise to prepare other positions in rear. Now however the Gothic Line was the last natural defensive position across the "leg" of Italy. But preparations for its defence were quite inadequate and it was of the utmost importance that the allies should be held off while the strength of the main position was being developed.

On each of the many routes of withdrawal the enemy's rearguards offered stubborn resistance wherever the ground lent itself to defence. In the hilly and often mountainous country the opportunities for delaying actions were almost unlimited. At the beginning of their withdrawal German units were badly mixed up and disorganized. But by 20th June they had managed to sort themselves out and were established in some strength on a delaying position running across the peninsula, roughly east and west through Lake Trasimene, its eastern sector following the line of the Chienti River to the sea at Portocivitanova.

General Alexander was anxious to afford the enemy no respite. The Eighth Army was directed on Florence and the Fifth on Pisa. Instructions for the pursuit were issued three days before the fall of Rome and he authorized the two army commanders to take extreme risks, so that Kesselring should have no chance to recover and reorganize.

Demolitions were sure to be extensive and one of the many difficulties of the pursuing troops would be the overcoming of obstacles. In order to economise transportation stores and bridging equipment, the 5th Corps was therefore ordered not to follow up a withdrawal on the Adriatic sector. Instead, it was to hand over its sector to the 2nd Polish Corps, and to move across to the Eighth Army, while the Poles, somewhat weakened after their battle at Cassino, remained on the defensive and recuperated their strength.

On the main front the Eighth and Fifth Armies pursued with great energy, but by the tenth day their effort was spent. They were now feeling the administrative pinch of a railhead 200 miles behind the front line and it was not until 20th June that they had closed up to the Trasimene line and were ready to renew the offensive.

The administrative situation was not however the only factor which prevented General Alexander from quickly driving his armies right up to—perhaps even through—the Gothic Line. For some weeks the shadow of ANVIL—the invasion of southern France—had hung heavily over the operations in Italy. Although the decision to mount the operation was not taken until early July, the effect in Italy was felt throughout June. As a precautionary measure, all the French forces, three United States divisions and appropriate headquarters and administrative units were being withdrawn from General Alexander's command and made ready for ANVIL.

While the allies in Italy were being deprived of seven divisions for use in France, Kesselring on the other hand was being reinforced by eight divisions from elsewhere. It may thus be argued that the containing effect of the recent operations in Italy was fifteen divisions in the Allies' favour. This was an excellent strategical result and all that could have been desired, but it had disappointing consequences for the subsequent operations in Italy.

On the main front, the battle of the Trasimene line began on 20th June and lasted until the 30th. The Germans, having recovered their balance, fought hard, and resistance was especially difficult to ovecome on the British sector round Lake Trasimene itself. Still the enemy did not fall back to his main "Gothic" Line, but imposed further delay on a succession of positions covering Arezzo, Florence and Leghorn. All three towns were required, as each was to play an important part in the final assault on the Gothic line; Arezzo as roadhead and eventually railhead—the administrative base; Florence, an important centre of communications, the operational base; Leghorn was urgently needed for its port facilities in order to relieve the long and overburdened land routes which made such a heavy call on the reduced road transport resources.

The battles for Ancona, Arezzo, Florence and Leghorn were just opening when the final decision was taken about Operation ANVIL. On 5th July, General Alexander was given a fresh directive, which governed all future developments of the campaign in Italy. Briefly, ANVIL now had priority over all other operations in the Mediterranean, and this priority would last until the forces in the south of France had been built up to ten divisions. As a slight offset to the loss of seven United States and French divisions, one Brazilian and one coloured American division would reach Italy in September and October.

While telling him that the destruction of the German forces in Italy continued to be his task, the directive went on to explain how he was to do it. First he was to cross the Apennines and secure the area Ravenna-Bologna-Modena and also, if possible, Piacenza, which was an important road centre. Subsequently he was to cross the Po to the line Venice-Padua-Verona-Brescia. On reaching this line, further instructions would follow, but it was hoped that the advance of the ANVIL forces up the Rhone valley would make a thrust into north-western Italy unnecessary. All available resources in the Mediterranean, including maximum air support, would be allotted for these operations, subject however to the over-riding priority of ANVIL.

The long, far-reaching and somewhat optimistic instruction of which this is a summary, was the product of the rather cumbersome "integrated" staff of Allied Force Headquarters. It is only fair to say, however, that as the war progressed, the formulation of clear-cut military policy became more and more difficult. In the Mediterranean especially there were a multiplicity of considerations, and a heterogeneous collection of allies and co-belligerents, and by 1944 post-war politics were encroaching heavily upon the requirements of strictly military strategy.

In spite of the reduction of his forces and the loss of his priority, General Alexander succeeded in the end in fulfilling the whole of his task. In Italy the fighting was to end not, as in Germany, in a drive through the enemy's own country in which his armed forces had disintegrated, but in the surrender on foreign soil of an army which had been out-fought and out-manoeuvred by forces seldom superior in numbers or equipment to itself.

Whether the use of the seven Allied divisions in southern France was worth more than the contribution they would have made to a rapid and complete victory in Italy, whether an earlier victory here would have hastened Hitler's downfall, and what difference it might have made to the political pattern of post-war Europe, are questions which will always be controversial; what is beyond controversy however is the great diversionary value of the hard fighting which had just ended and the equally tough struggles which were to follow in the next ten months.

*   *   *   *

Soon after the fall of Rome, the Adriatic sector, which had so long remained quiet, gradually came to life. On the night of 7th June explosions were heard to the northward. They were obviously demolitions and infantry patrols quickly found that the enemy had withdrawn. In the morning the towns of Orsogna and Guardiagrele were occupied without opposition.

For the next two nights the red glow of distant fires could be seen towards Pescara, and the troops were getting impatient. The order not to follow up was now modified slightly. No full-scale pursuit was allowed, but the 4th Indian Division was ordered to prepare to move forward so as to regain contact with the enemy.

On 8th June B Squadron 7th Hussars (Major Murray Smith) was moved to a concentration area west of Ortona and was placed in support of the 7th Indian Infantry Brigade. Two days later the Stuarts at Ascigno rejoined A Squadron, and the whole regiment was on its toes. For the present however only B Squadron was to move forward.

The advance began on the 11th, and the squadron reached Ripa Teatina. On the following evening it harboured on the southern bank of the River Tavo and on the 13th entered San Angelo. Both the Tavo and the Fino were almost dry and no obstacle to movement. All bridges had been destroyed and at every crossing diversions had to be found. Mines and booby traps were cunningly concealed and tellermines were often joined together so that several detonated at once.

B Squadron spent two days bivouacked in the dusty square of San Angelo, while patrols went out to the north-west. On the 13th Lieutenant J. H. Harding took his troop across the Piomba stream and on to Atri. This was clear of the enemy, but the road just short of the town was blocked by a crater on a hairpin bend and the lip had been liberally treated with booby traps. The platoon of 4th/16th Punjab Regiment which accompanied the troop had casualties when trying to clear the mines and the party returned to San Angelo.

On the 14th Lieutenant J. C. R. Type reconnoitred the route northwards to the River Vomano. Next day the squadron moved a short distance and harboured north of the Piomba stream. The Indians had now been relieved by the Poles and armoured patrols sent out towards the Vomano River were accompanied this time by infantry of the 1st Carpathian Infantry Brigade. Lieutenant J. J. H. Browne went westwards from Cellino and Lieutenant G. M. Thompson eastwards from Atri to Pineto near the coast. The enemy was well clear and it was to be some days before the pursuing troops could worry their way over the numerous obstacles and resume contact. On the 16th B Squadron moved forward again and crossed the Vomano.

The rest of the regiment had meanwhile remained at Elici. On 15th June the commanding officer had heard that the 7th Hussars were to move with the rest of the 7th Armoured Brigade and the 5th Corps to the Eighth Army. Almost at once however this move was cancelled; the 7th Hussars were removed from the 7th Armoured

Brigade and placed under the command of the 2nd Polish Corps (Lieutenant-General Wladislaw Anders). Lieutenant-Colonel Jayne attended a conference the same afternoon and issued his orders at midnight. The regiment made an early start the next morning and

Map XIII

CENTRAL ITALY

marched along the coast, through Pescara, to harbour some three miles east of San Angelo.

At every river and stream the road was blown and some of the diversions were hard to find. Dangerous areas had been marked with tape, when they could be detected. In spite of this, however, on the 17th, A Squadron narrowly missed an unmarked clutch of four tellermines and three bombs, all wired together, in a diversion near Pineto.

A Squadron was now placed under the 2nd Carpathian Infantry Brigade, operating along the coast, while B Squadron remained under the 1st Brigade, working along the inland route. B Squadron sent two troops over the ridge from the Vomano and down the winding road to the Tordino. Crossing the river, they took different routes up the hill beyond and entered Bellante town almost together. The enemy had gone and the people, in their newly found freedom, were all ready to welcome the liberators. The reception was tumultuous, flowers, flags, surging crowds of shouting, smiling people; running hither and thither to fetch their relations and crowding round the tanks, whose crews (though they did not all confess it in their letters home) were generously embraced by the girls.

On the same day the more senior officers of A Squadron attended a conference at the headquarters of the Polish battalion which was to lead along the coast. They were most impressed by the efficiency of the proceedings and the bearing of the Poles; the colonel, a dapper little man with a pointed black beard, gave out his orders in a vigorous and concise manner which showed that he knew his job and knew his mind and, as one officer observed, the Poles clearly knew how to handle an armoured reconnaissance regiment.

At 1 o'clock the leading troops of A Squadron moved off. The crossing of the Vomano was rather slow, as one of the tanks broke through a bridge on the diversion. At Roseto, as at Bellante, the inhabitants turned out to greet the leading troops. They cheered and clapped and showered the tanks with flowers. In spite of the rain the same reception awaited the first Britons in Giulianova, Captain M. M. Stanley Evans and one man of the 7th Hussars in a dingo. They were greeted by thousands of cheering Italians, some with bunches of flowers, some with bottles of wine and some with colourful information on a wide variety of subjects—the names of the local patriots and the best restaurants, the whereabouts of escaped British prisoners, a German baroness, prominent Fascists, other Italians of doubtful reputation, and even a beautiful Jewess whose reputation was not in doubt at all.

Two troops remained in Giulianova and the rest of the squadron spent the night in Roseto. It rained in torrents and next day the rivers were badly swollen.

Soon after breakfast on Waterloo Day the Polish colonel arrived at squadron headquarters and announced that the conduct of operations on the Adriatic sector was to change. Whereas before they had been ordered not to press the enemy, now they were ordered to go for him as hard as possible.

At noon, Lieutenant E. C. F. Harding's and Lieutenant P. J. Howard-Dobson's troops from Roseto moved out, and passed through Giulianova where the other two troops remained. They crossed the Salinello and advanced rapidly to Martinsicuro at the mouth of the Tronto. Squadron headquarters followed, Major T. R. S. Thornton, M.C., driving his jeep, in which were riding Trooper Cook, the Polish liaison officer and an Italian civilian who had information about the enemy. As they crossed the diversion through the Salinello, now flowing in a broad and rapid stream, the back wheels of the jeep seemed to skid in the loose shingle, and slipped a few inches outside the marked and swept channel. This was enough, and the jeep was blown to bits on a clutch of three inter-connected tellermines. All four occupants were killed and Lieutenant Parry and one other rank following close behind in a dingo were shaken by the concussion.

The loss of a very gallant and respected squadron leader was keenly felt by the whole regiment. Richard Thornton was the elder son of an old 7th Hussar, Lieutenant-Colonel T. A. Thornton, C.V.O., who was subsequently to become Colonel of the regiment. Richard Thornton had distinguished himself greatly as a troop leader in the desert, where he had won the Military Cross, and again in Burma as squadron second-in-command. He had all the qualities of a first class fighting soldier. From his early youth, one of his outstanding characteristics was a cheerfulness and equanimity which nothing could disturb. The exuberance of the Sandhurst cadet was merged but not lost in the serious responsibilities of the squadron leader. He had the absolute trust of his superiors and the unstinted affection of his men.

On the 18th B Squadron also moved forward and reached the Tronto. Passing through Bellante, the squadron harboured near Andaramo. The troops went forward to reconnoitre crossings over the river, which was now rising rapidly.

The advance continued on the 19th. Both squadrons crossed the river and were making good progress. Soon, however, much to everyone's surprise, the order came to halt. A Squadron's leading troops had only reached Porto d'Ascoli, two miles beyond the Tronto. But before the order reached B Squadron, the whole squadron had passed down into the deep Tesino valley and up the other side, and the leading troops had reached the brink of the Aso valley beyond. The left forward troop received the joyful welcome of Montalto della Marche before it was stopped; this little town, perched high above the Aso valley, commands views of the surrounding country which are exceptional even for Italy. Five miles to the north-east the right troop reached the village of Carassai.

While A and B Squadrons had been moving forward, the rest of the regiment had remained on the Saline, not far from Pescara. The forward squadrons were now ordered back to the Saline and the 7th Hussars were then to move to a concentration area near San Vito Chietino, where the tanks were to be entrained for Venafro. The regiment was to move across to the Eighth Army.

A and B Squadrons rejoined on the 21st, after a night march. On the 23rd the regiment set off southwards along the coastal road. At Ortona the tank ammunition was handed over at an ammunition dump, and the regiment turned to follow the inland route through San Apollinare, which was reached at about noon.

Here the Commanding Officer was met by a representative from the 7th Armoured Brigade with the news that the order to halt had been a mistake; the 7th Hussars were not to cross over with the 7th Armoured Brigade, but were at once to come under the 2nd Polish Armoured Brigade. This was now near Lanciano, whence it was to move in two days time to support the 3rd Carpathian Division in the Fermo area. Fermo was nearly a hundred miles to the north and about eight miles beyond the point where B Squadron's patrols had been halted on the Aso River a few days before.

After one day's maintenance the regiment turned round and went back. The marching and counter-marching of the past fortnight, in particular this last and apparently unnecessary route march of two hundred miles, had now made it necessary for A and B Squadrons to carry out their standard 100-hour check. For this purpose there was a five-day halt at the hamlet of Centobuchi, near Porto d'Ascoli.

By the 30th all except B Squadron had moved up to join the 2nd Polish Armoured Brigade near Fermo; B Squadron followed the next day. The regiment harboured in the area north-east of Fermo and a mile from the Tenna River.

Although there had been no fighting during the month, the best of relations had been established with the Poles. General Duchs, commander of the 3rd Carpathian Division, not realizing how soon the 7th Hussars would be back with the Polish Corps, wrote a letter of appreciation when the regiment was taken from him on 20th June :—

> "It is with a deep feeling of regret that my division must part with your regiment. The 7th Hussars have made an excellent job by advancing rapidly with their "go and get it" spirit. I am extremely sorry and deeply regret the tragic death of A Squadron Commander, Major Thornton. I would be most grateful if you would convey my thanks to all officers and men of your regiment."

CHAPTER XIII

The Struggle up the "Calf"

Pursuit to the Musone—Castelfidardo and Osimo—capture of Ancona—pursuit to the Misa—battles of the Cesano—battle of the Metauro.

Maps XIV, XV, XVI, XVII

The policy of restraint on the Adriatic sector held good until 16th June. On that date General Anders had been instructed to force the pace. He was to cross the Chienti, break the enemy's line of resistance and seize Ancona. This port, like Leghorn on the west coast, was badly needed in order to relieve the transport situation.

The effect of this order has already been seen in the increased speed of advance on the 17th and 18th, just before the 7th Hussars were withdrawn from General Duchs' command. On the 20th the Poles crossed the Aso and occupied Fermo and Pedaso; next day they seized a small bridgehead over the Chienti. This however they were unable to hold, as the enemy counter-attacked in some strength.

The enemy clearly had no intention of leaving his principal delaying position on the Chienti without a fight, and General Anders realized that he must stage a full scale corps attack. Owing to the state of the rail and road communications he would be unable to complete the forward concentration of his troops and stores before early July, and the date of the operation was provisionally fixed for the 4th.

While the Germans on the main front were being driven out of the Trasimene line and the 7th Hussars were marching and countermarching along the Adriatic coast, the Polish Corps gradually closed up to the Chienti and prepared for the Ancona offensive. The 5th Kresowa Division, still far in rear, was to take its place on the left of the 3rd, and its advanced elements, an armoured regiment and one battalion, with supporting arms, reached the Chienti on a broad front from Corridonia to Tolentino on 24th June. The 2nd Polish Armoured Brigade provided armoured support for both divisions, and its headquarters and units not allotted to divisions were to be the nucleus of a corps reserve.

The Polish corps was now disposed on a frontage of thirty miles and a depth of eighty. In the process of closing up to the Chienti, on which the Germans seemed determined to stand, the Poles were faced with tremendous difficulties. In view of the wholesale demolitions, the shortage of transportation stores, the long lines of communication and the consequent strain on the limited amount of transport, and the spasmodic spates which at every river held up movement at some time or other for hours on end, the speed of their advance had been remarkable.

During the last week of June, while the tail of the corps was drawing up, reconnaissances were carried out and plans were made for the corps offensive. The general conception was an assault on the high ground across the Chienti by both the Polish divisions, their left protected by the Italians. The plan was so designed that, if all went well, or if the enemy withdrew from the Chienti before the attack, the impetus of the corps should carry it through to Ancona. In the final phase the 5th Division, directed on the axis Fillotrano-Iesi, and the 2nd Armoured Brigade, would have the principal parts.

On the 27th and 28th patrols on both divisions' fronts found the enemy thinner on the ground than usual. Evidently he was preparing, on the Adriatic sector, to conform with the movements of his forces on the rest of the Trasimene line. Before dawn on the 30th the customary explosions announced that the withdrawal had begun.

Soon after first light strong contact patrols went forward across the Chienti. Those of the 3rd Carpathian Division were in Porto Civitanova and Montecosaro by noon, and orders for the pursuit were then issued. The inland column captured Potenza Picena during the afternoon, after a short skirmish, and all the advancing troops came under fire as they moved down to the Potenza River. Enemy rearguards were holding the river, and no crossing could be forced that day.

The armoured spearhead of the 5th Division entered Macerata at 3 p.m. and before nightfall all the advanced elements of the 5th Division had reached the Potenza River. In the early hours of the morning a crossing was found unguarded and a bridgehead was established at San Leonardo, near Sambucheto.

During the night the German rearguards withdrew and at dawn the pursuit was resumed.

The enemy had now reached the main defensive line on which he intended to fight for Ancona. This ran along the high ground north of the Musone river from the sea to where it is joined by the Fiumicello stream, thence along the latter westwards.

The 15th Lancers, operating with the 5th Division, encountered heavy opposition on reaching the Fiumicello stream, opposite the village of San Biagio. Supported by only a few self-propelled guns, the lancers attacked with great dash and almost wiped out one German battalion.

They drove off a succession of counter-attacks during the night and held their position until they were reinforced by infantry. A wedge was thus driven into the enemy's main line of resistance and part of his tactical reserves were already drawn into the battle.

On the 3rd Division's front there was practically no resistance; German patrols were chased out of Loreto, and by nightfall the leading troops had crossed the Musone River. Patrols reached Crocette and the vicinity of Castelfidardo and one battalion spent the night on the slopes south of Osimo. Local civilians reported that the Germans were preparing defences on the line Castelfidardo-Osimo—thence along the Musone to the west.

On the left of the Polish Corps the Italians had conformed with the advance and by the evening of 1st July they too were up to the Fiumicello Stream, and in conjunction with the 12th Polish Lancers established a bridgehead and made contact on a wide frontage with the enemy's positions.

The pursuit phase was now over. The time had come for co-ordinated attacks on positions which the enemy clearly intended to hold. This had been foreseen, and consequently no re-grouping was required; the battle for Ancona was opened without delay.

*   *   *   *

On 1st July B Squadron had finished its overhaul and the regiment was concentrated at the little village of San Marco, near Fermo.

At 1 a.m. on the 2nd a message was received ordering the 7th Hussars to move forward to the south bank of the River Potenza; here they were to be at immediate call to take part in operations beyond the next river, the Musone, where fighting was now in progress. At 6 a.m. the regiment moved off, and marched by Route 16 (the main coast road) through Porto Civitanova to its concentration area, two miles inland and on the south bank of the Potenza River. Squadrons were in their allotted areas by 9.30 a.m.

Soon afterwards orders were received from General Rakowski, the commander of the 2nd Polish Armoured Brigade. The 2nd Polish Infantry Brigade, supported by the 6th Armoured Regiment, was to capture the Castelfidardo ridge, a dominating feature which overlooked the broad Musone Valley as far as Loreto. The 7th Hussars were then to pass through the infantry, move northwards across the Fosso Rigo stream and seize the Badia (or Abbadia) spur, which takes off from the main ridge at Osimo and runs eastwards nearly parallel with it. The object of this operation was to protect the right flank of the 1st Carpathian Infantry Brigade, which was to attack Osimo.

The Commanding Officer issued his orders at about 1 p.m. An hour later all were packed up and ready to move up to Loreto. This was a typical little Italian town on a hill top, with extensive views over the valleys on both sides. The route followed by the regiment was down to the coast and then along the main road, and the distance was only seven miles.

After a wait of nearly two hours in the bivouac area, the leading squadron moved off but, on reaching Route 16, found the traffic congestion so bad that the whole regiment was brought to a halt. The Poles were people of great persistence, and their transport drivers were determined to do their jobs and to overcome all opposition, including their own military police. The result was unfortunate for other road users and by 6.30 p.m. the head of the regiment was still a mile short of Loreto.

The Commanding Officer and one or two squadron leaders and other officers had meanwhile been at the armoured brigade headquarters, which had set itself up in a travel agency on the northern side of Loreto. Here, through a plate glass window, the battle on Castelfidardo ridge could be followed in detail and comfort. A convenient restaurant a few doors away gave an equally good view and not a bad dinner. Fighting seemed to be heavy, and in places the ridge was obscured by the smoke of numerous burning vehicles, houses and stacks.

During the afternoon it became evident that the first phase, the capture of Castelfidardo itself, would not be completed in time for the 7th Hussars to carry out their task before nightfall. The infantry and tanks were held up some distance short of their objective, and as it grew dark the bright streaks of the tracer ammunition showed clearly that no further progress was being made. At 9 p.m. squadrons moved off the road into whatever area they could find and spent a rather noisy night among the Polish artillery positions.

During the fighting on the 2nd the Poles had gained a shallow bridgehead over the Musone from the railway to a point opposite Osimo, but they had not reached the top of the ridge. On 3rd July therefore the plan was slightly altered. By noon the eastern end of the ridge had been captured by the Bobinski Group, which consisted of the 6th Armoured Regiment and 6th Carpathian Infantry Battalion, under Colonel Bobinski, the second-in-command of the armoured brigade. The 7th Hussars were now ordered forward to a conspicuous blue house beyond the river, whence they would support the next phase.

The south bank of the Musone was under spasmodic artillery and mortar fire, but the prepared crossing near the blown bridge on Route

16 did not seem to have been registered. A few shells fell on B Squadron as they moved along the track on the north bank, but caused no casualties. A long column of German prisoners passed, being marched in single file with their hands above their heads. By 3.30 p.m. squadrons were dispersed in the area north of regimental headquarters, which was established at the Blue House.

General Rakowski's plan for the capture of Castelfidardo was now issued. The Bobinski Group was to advance from Crocette and attack the town from the north-east. The 5th Carpathian Infantry Battalion was to cross the Musone south-west of the Blue House and attack the town from the south-east, its right on the Blue House-Castelfidardo road. Before these converging attacks went in, the 7th Hussars were to make sure that the area a mile west of the Blue House was clear of enemy self-propelled guns, which had been reported there in the morning. They were then to support the Bobinski Group with fire. When these two eastern attacks were under way, the 1st Carpathian Infantry Brigade was to attack from the south-west.

The first of the 7th Hussars' tasks was given to A Squadron, which advanced towards its objective at 4.45. It found no S.P. guns and at 5.15, after only slight opposition from enemy in slit trenches a mile short of Castelfidardo, established itself about a thousand yards from the outskirts of the town. B and C Squadron remained in reserve near the Blue House and regimental headquarters moved forward behind A and set itself up in a farmhouse from which there was a good view of the approaches to the town.

The Bobinski Group advanced at about 5 p.m. They met considerable opposition in the area of the brick factory a mile to the east of Castelfidardo. Two troops of A Squadron, Captain G. S. B. Palmer's and Lieutenant P. J. Howard-Dobson's, engaged the enemy in this area. The country was rather enclosed, and the pin-pointing of targets was not easy, but the fire was effective and Bobinski said afterwards that it had made the enemy withdraw.

On the left the leading elements of the 8th Carpathian Battalion reached A Squadron's forward troop on the road at about 7 p.m. The tanks supported the advance of their leading companies up to the town. Here they were checked by considerable enemy opposition. The Germans were established in the houses and, as these were generally of good solid masonry, they could not be tackled by infantry alone. The Polish infantry took cover and the company commander pointed out the targets to Lieutenant E. C. F. Harding. The latter then led his troop forward and engaged the occupied houses from below at close range. This manoeuvre was repeated several times and on each occasion with complete success. Each time the Polish infantry advanced and by the time it was dark the battalion had a firm footing on the edge of the town. After nightfall A Squadron was withdrawn to the regimental harbour area near the Blue House.

This was the 7th Hussars' first experience of close co-operation between infantry and Sherman tanks in the attack, and it had been very successful. The only casualties of the day were three men of B Squadron wounded by mortar fire.

A few bombs dropped by two enterprising enemy aircraft in the moonlight caused mild surprise and the anti-aircraft response made a lot of noise, but there were no casualties.

At 5.30 on the morning of the 5th General Rakowski with some of his staff arrived at 7th Hussars regimental headquarters and gave out his orders. First the town of Castelfidardo was to be cleared of the enemy. Secondly Osimo was to be captured by attacks from the north-east and south-east. This required that first the Abbadia ridge should be seized, north of Castelfidardo. The pattern of the day's operations was therefore very similar to that of the 4th, with Abbadia and Osimo substituted for Crocette and Castelfidardo.

The 7th Hussars were quickly on the move. A Squadron advanced on Castelfidardo with the 5th Carpathian Battalion, to carry out the first task. The town was entered at 7 a.m. and half an hour later the tanks and infantry emerged on the other side, having encountered no opposition. They pressed on westward for about a mile, when the leading troop came under small arms fire from San Sabino. This completed the first of the day's operations. The infantry remained in observation and A Squadron returned to Castelfidardo. While waiting in the town good relations were established with a concertina factory and a number of these instruments found their way into the squadron. This was not entirely to the general advantage, but, after all, it was A Squadron who suffered most.

While A Squadron were engaged in this clearing-up operation, the rest of the regiment moved along the valley road to a point south of San Sabino. The vehicles made a great dust but did not draw fire until squadrons arrived in their dispersal areas. There was then a little shelling, but it caused only one slight casualty.

At 10.30 the regiment was ordered back to Castelfidardo, along the same dusty road. Lieutenant-Colonel Jayne went ahead and joined Colonel Bobinski in a tall house at the northern edge of the town. Here there was an excellent view of the ground where the next operation was to take place. Bobinski told the commanding officer what was required, and the latter gave out his orders at the same place.

The objective was the Abbadia ridge. B Squadron was given the church tower, C the Casa Lardinelli, a large farmhouse half a mile to the left of the village, and A was to advance on the right of B. A Squadron was supposed to be under the command of the 5th Carpathian Battalion, but as Major Congreve had difficulty in connecting with the infantry, the squadron operated with the regiment. The start line was to be the Fosso Rigo stream.

The tanks, on their journey from south of Sabino, were meant to carry most of one infantry battalion, which was to take part in the attack. It took a long time to persuade the company commanders to commit their men to the care of the 7th Hussars, as this had not apparently been mentioned by the battalion commander when he was called away. Consequently two hours elapsed before a start was made.

By about 3 p.m. the tanks and infantry reached their position of assembly near Castelfidardo. Then however there was another hitch. Enemy artillery opened fire and the infantry left the tanks and took cover. They did not return, as they thought the tanks attracted the enemy's fire. This caused considerable delay. Colonel Jayne became anxious, as there were only a few hours of daylight left and he feared that the objective might not be properly occupied before dark. Accordingly he decided to carry out the attack without the infantry.

In order to reach the start line, B and C Squadrons, closely followed by regimental headquarters, had to move in line ahead along the road from Castelfidardo towards San Sabino and then swing right, down into the valley. They soon lost sight of their objectives, and did not see them again until they had climbed most of the way up the opposite ridge. At first Major Tinker, the second-in-command, was able to help squadrons in keeping direction, as in spite of the close nature of the country, he could see some of the tanks from the church tower and correct their movements by wireless. But soon all were hidden by the heavy rain and thick mist which came down over the Abbadia ridge. As they came up the hill however the squadrons once more came in sight of their objectives and drove straight for them. There was little opposition and none of the enemy waited for the tanks.

Patrols were at once sent out to the west and north. C Squadron's patrol advanced more than a mile along the ridge towards Osimo but did not make contact with the enemy. Lieutenant J. C. R. Type's troop of B Squadron went northwards from Abbadia village. He ordered two of his tanks to remain in observation close to Abbadia while he in his own tank went forward to Route 16. Near the Stazione di Osimo he found and engaged a number of German infantry, but his tank was knocked out and set on fire by a hollow-charge anti-tank grenade. He and one of the crew were killed and the rest were captured.

The Commanding Officer arrived at Abbadia on foot. His tank had twice stuck, first in a narrow lane and then in the Fosso Rigo. Infantry arrived to take over just as it got dark and the regiment withdrew half a mile south of Abbadia and harboured for the night. There was a good deal of mortar and artillery fire and A1 Echelon was ordered not to come up. Replenishment was carried out the next morning instead.

At 7 a.m. on the 5th General Rakowski issued his orders for the day. The attack on Osimo was to continue more or less as originally planned. The 7th Hussars were again to operate under command of Colonel Bobinski, whose task was to seize Point 217, a conspicuous feature half a mile outside the town, to the north-east. The capture of this would help the main attack of the 1st Carpathian Brigade and the 1st Armoured Regiment along the axis of the San Sabino-Osimo road.

Colonel Bobinski was soon to become well known to all 7th Hussars. He moved freely about among the troops, always accompanied by his poodle. Once, over the wireless, a sergeant commanding a troop referred to him as "the poodle-man," for security reasons; as Polish names are usually stumbling blocks to the British, poodle-man he remained.

Bobinski and Jayne now went off together to reconnoitre the country towards the objective. Much of this could be seen from the Casa Lardinelli, especially from its upper windows. The principal bedroom was shamefully untidy; in the absence of the lady owner, her friends or neighbours had clearly "been through" her lingerie with more haste than method. However, the room had an excellent view and this made the Casa popular both as a headquarters and as an observation post; as more and more people, especially Polish gunner officers, crowded at the windows with their maps, it promised also to become unhealthy.

The Abbadia-Osimo ridge, along which the attack was to be made, was narrow and wooded and intersected with steep ravines. There was only space for a one-squadron frontage and A was selected to lead. The Shermans of B and C were to move well up in support of A, a Polish field artillery regiment provided covering fire and a troop of self-propelled anti-tank guns moved close behind the regiment. The 4th Carpathian Battalion was to follow A Squadron closely, to occupy ground gained and to mop up. The first objective was Monte Ragano, a pronounced bulge, and the second was Point 217, a hillock on the ridge.

At the appointed hour A Squadron advanced. In the thick country the method evolved in the past few months' training worked very well. The Stuarts of each troop went in front and, when the view from the tanks was too restricted, one of the crew dismounted and reconnoitred on foot. In this way resistance was located and targets were found for the Shermans.

In the past two days the enemy had twice been surprised by tank attacks. This time his defences proved to be much stronger, especially in anti-tank guns. Against these the 4th Carpathian Battalion would have been very valuable. Unfortunately however the Commanding Officer was wounded early in the day, which seemed to make part of the battalion somewhat hesitant.

Until the present operations neither the 7th Hussars nor the Poles had had experience of close co-operation between tanks and infantry. The lack of a common language more than doubled the difficulty. Many Poles had a smattering of English and Colonel Bobinski spoke it well, but not a single 7th Hussar knew a word of Polish, and at the level of troops and platoons, and whenever there was no interpreter, the only communication was by signs.

There was a typical difficulty quite early in the attack. Major Congreve reported that he was being machine-gunned from behind. Colonel Jayne looked about and found an enthusiastic Pole with a Vickers in the grounds of the Casa Lardinelli, blazing away towards Osimo. He grinned happily when invited to stop, and went on. Colonel Jayne only succeeded in making him cease fire by driving his tank in front of the machine gun. The Pole, offended, got up and went away.

The support of B and C Squadrons and of the Polish artillery was excellent, and as each enemy anti-tank gun was encountered it was satisfactorily dealt with. It was nevertheless fortunate that the enemy anti-tank gunners did not on this occasion select very good positions for their guns, as most of them had to be overcome by the tanks themselves.

The first anti-tank guns encountered were a pair of 75-millimetres sited so as to cover two junctions on the Osimo-Abbadia road, the first where it is joined by the drive of the Casa Lardinelli, the second where a branch leads down to join Route 16 west of Osimo railway station. One of these guns was found by A Squadron's Second-in-Command, Captain M. M. Stanley Evans, in his Stuart, when he was going forward along the drive to look for the leading troop. The enemy waited until he was within a hundred yards and then opened fire. The Stuart did a wide and rapid turn and of the four shots fired only one hit was scored, which glanced off.

Lieutenant Howard-Dobson's troop quickly engaged the enemy guns. The crew of one were driven off and it was captured intact. He suppressed the other by driving his Sherman over it.

This troop then moved on towards Monte Ragano, on the slopes of which it found another pair of guns, this time 50-millimetre PAK 38. One of these was sited to fire down the main road, the other down a lane. Corporal D. J. Williams took these guns by surprise and his fire forced the enemy to abandon their weapons, which were both captured intact.

The first objective was now secured by A Squadron and the advance continued to the second. On the western slopes of the Monte Ragano the leading Stuart was hit and set on fire as it came round a blind corner. The tank commander had previously dismounted to reconnoitre, but had failed to see the enemy gun, which was cleverly concealed near a haystack in a farmyard. The farm was now engaged by Polish infantry with 2-inch mortars, but this prevented dismounted action by the tank crews. The gun was successfully removed by its crew and disappeared down the hill and into the lane leading north.

One 75-mm. in the same area had been carefully dug in and camouflaged near the brickworks. This was shelled by Polish artillery and the gun was captured without having fired a shot. Another had been placed on a bank beside a prominent house at a cross roads. No attempt had been made to conceal it, and its crew were engaged and driven away by fire from Lieutenant V. L. John's troop of C Squadron before it could open fire. The same troop discovered another gun on the southern slopes of Point 217, and engaged the crew, who were trying to tow it away. They were forced to abandon the gun and drove off in their tractor up the lane to Osimo.

The last opposition on Point 217 came from a self-propelled gun on the forward slope. This was driven off by A Squadron, who went on round the hill and by 6.30 p.m. were in position overlooking Osimo and the approaches to it from the south-east. The extremely steep slopes at the summit of 217 prevented the tanks going to the top, but about an hour later infantry arrived and occupied the point itself.

By nightfall the 1st Carpathian Brigade reached the outskirts of Osimo and fighting in the town went on all night. The 6th Polish Armoured Regiment took over responsibility for supporting the infantry on the Abbadia-Osimo ridge and the 7th Hussars were drawn back about a mile to harbour in the valley running south-east from Monte Ragano.

It had been noticed during the day that the ridges on either side of this valley were shelled repeatedly, but not the valley itself. Again the enemy artillery shelled the ridges and the neighbouring valley, but the 7th Hussars were left undisturbed except by a few enemy aircraft which flew round, apparently looking for targets in the moonlight. A Echelon and the squadron cooks' lorries came up as usual.

Casualties during the day had been surprisingly light. A Squadron had four wounded, one seriously, when the Stuart tank was knocked out on Monte Ragano. B Squadron had two killed and three wounded by shell fire. Captain P. B. Stanley Evans had been standing up in his tank, with his head out, when a shell burst on the turret, killing his wireless operator. He himself had both eardrums broken, but remained at duty. C Squadron lost a tank in the same way but without casualties.

The regiment had achieved all it set out to do, and much credit is due to the thrust and enterprise of A Squadron, who led the advance. It was perhaps lucky that the enemy did not offer more determined resistance. His anti-tank guns were supported to some extent by his artillery but not at all by infantry. In the battle for Monte Ragano and Point 217 infantry were in fact not much in evidence on either side.

Early on 6th July the Poles completed the capture of Osimo, and the task of the 3rd Carpathian Division and the Polish Armoured Brigade in this phase of the offensive was over. The 7th Hussars spent the day in rest and maintenance. In the afternoon they were ordered back to the brigade harbour area, south of Castelfidardo and on the north bank of the Musone River.

The enemy still had good observation over the Osimo-Abbadia ridge from the Monte della Crescia, three miles north-west of Osimo, and Monte Conero, south of Ancona. The move of a long column of vehicles in daylight might have brought down observed artillery fire, and the march was therefore postponed until 8.30 p.m. By midnight the regiment was in its new area.

The 3rd Carpathian Division now took up defensive positions covering Castelfidardo and Osimo. Most of the armour was withdrawn to rest and refit under its own brigade headquarters and the centre of interest now shifted to the left, the front of General Rudnicki's 5th Kresowa Division.

On the 4th July the enemy put in a heavy attack against the right sector of the 5th Division at Montoro. The two companies holding this area were forced back and a counter-attack only recovered part of the lost ground. The enemy renewed his attacks and more ground was lost. However, in two night attacks, each carried out by a battalion supported by tanks, the situation was fully restored. On the 5th the eastern end of the angle between the Musone and the Fiumicello was cleared of the last remains of the enemy and the following morning a bridgehead was established over the Musone River.

Farther to the left the Polish 6th Brigade and the Italians also attacked on the 6th July and by the 8th the 6th Brigade had also established bridgeheads across the Musone; the Germans counter-attacked and fighting continued throughout the night of the 9th/10th, but the Poles held on.

The Italian attack on Fillotrano was gallantly carried out, but did not, on the 6th, secure the town. The position was strong, and after severe house to house fighting the Germans succeeded in driving the Italians out. A second attack, supported by Polish tanks, was also beaten off. However, on the night of the 8th/9th the Germans withdrew from Fillotrano and the Italians moved forward to the Musone River.

For the moment the 5th Kresowa Division and the Italians had shot their bolt, and they too passed to the defensive, while General Anders made his plans for the second phase of the battle.

On the 9th July he informed his commanders that a pause of a few days was now necessary in order to build up stocks of ammunition and to withdraw the armour for re-fitting and maintenance. Meanwhile limited re-grouping of the forces was to be carried out. The Italians had shown some reluctance to advance beyond the Musone, and they were now to take over part of the front of the 5th Division so as to enable the latter to concentrate towards its right, with all its resources, in the area where the next assault was to be delivered.

The results of the recent operations had not been unsatisfactory. Although Ancona was still in enemy hands, the Germans had had severe losses. Some fifteen hundred prisoners had been taken, mostly from the 278th Division, and the measure of the enemy's anxiety for the Adriatic sector can be seen in the sudden switch of his dwindling air effort to the Polish front. Night attacks by up to forty aircraft were carried out between the 3rd and 7th July, but after the first night, when there was no opposition, British night fighters took such toll of the enemy that the weight of attack quickly declined. The last attack was on the night of the 10th, by one solitary bomber.

The 7th Hussars had sustained very few serious battle casualties, but one road accident was particularly unfortunate. On 7th July Major White and Captain R. Nickels, driving in a jeep, were involved in an accident in which the latter was killed. Nickels was an efficient and popular officer who had particularly distinguished himself in Burma, and he was a great loss to his squadron. White was fit for duty again in a very short time.

Map XIV
ADRIATIC SECTOR

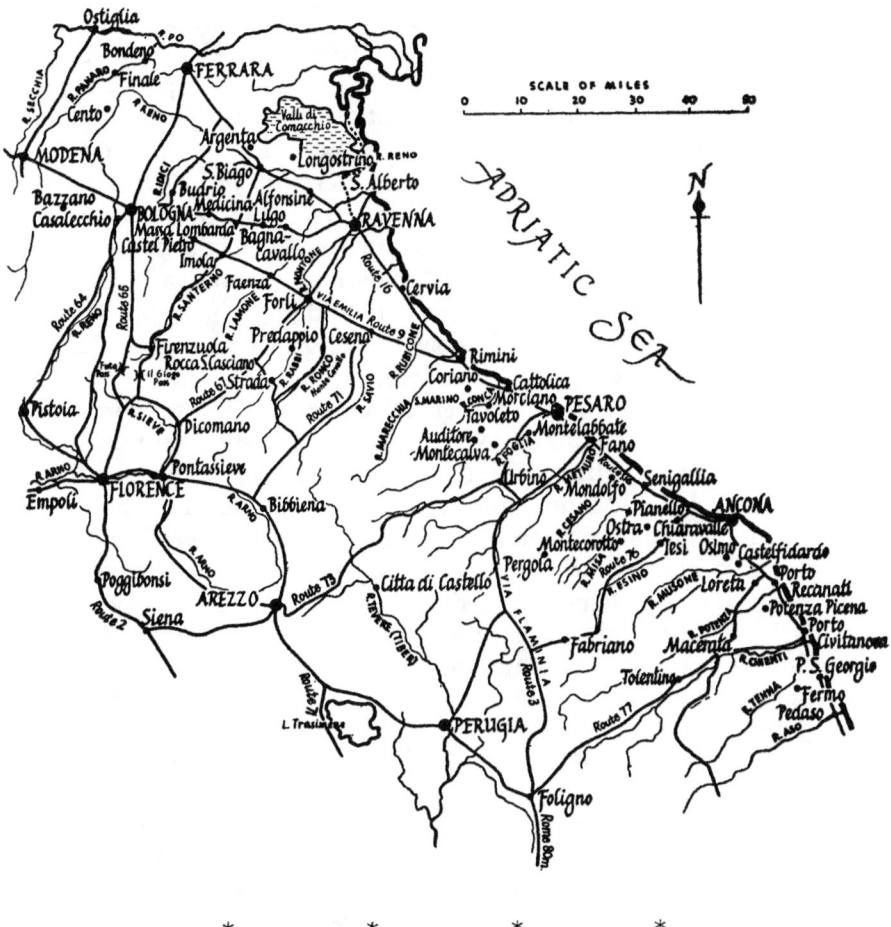

* * * *

The Germans were now in position on the "Edith" Line, covering Ancona. This ran from Numana on the coast, across Route 16 near San Biagio, up through San Stefano to the commanding feature of Monte della Crescia, thence along the high ground on the north bank of the Musone. To hold a front of some twenty miles they had no more than five thousand infantry, the 278th Division and part of the 71st; it was believed at the time that almost all were in the front line and that there was very little in reserve. The main weight of the enemy artillery was in position in the area Polverigi-Agugliano, and it was thought that the small reserve was also located about Polverigi.

The 2nd Polish Corps was now under the command of the Eighth Army (General Sir Oliver Leese). The date of the resumption of the offensive had to be related to the operations farther west, the provision of air support being the determining factor. The 13th Corps was to attack at Arezzo on the night of 14th/15th July; this action was expected to last two days, and the first date on which adequate air support could be available for the Poles was therefore the 17th.

On 14th July General Anders issued his orders. The 3rd Division was to hold its sector, astride Route 16, and to place one battalion and one armoured regiment under the 5th Division. At the same time the 3rd Division was to simulate great activity and give the impression of fresh concentrations of troops on the coastal sector. The 5th Division was to attack Monte della Crescia and exploit north-eastwards. The 2nd Armoured Brigade, less one armoured regiment, but reinforced by the 7th Hussars, 15th Lancers, 16th Infantry Battalion (from 5th Division), a self-propelled battery and a commando company, was to attack in the direction of Monte Torto and Polverigi, and on reaching the latter was to overrun the enemy's artillery and his reserves. Each division had one infantry brigade at the disposal of the corps commander. This of course somewhat reduced the scope of the divisional commanders' initiative, as a Polish division already consisted of only two brigades, but the corps commander could not otherwise have retained his own power to influence the battle; although the 2nd Armoured Brigade was in a sense the reserve for pursuit, it was to be partially committed in the opening phases, so would not all be available for exploitation.

The attack was to be supported by the whole of the corps artillery in a carefully co-ordinated programme and by the Desert Air Force. In addition the Polish reconnaissance squadron (Spitfires) was to take any opportunity of carrying out low-flying attacks.

The 7th Hussars had spent the week from the 7th to 14th July in widely dispersed bivouac areas by the River Musone. On the evening of the 14th everything was packed up and soon after dark the move began to the selected harbour area in the valley at Cura Nuova, two miles east of Filottrano. The march was carried out by night and by a rather circuitous route, so that it should be neither seen nor heard by the enemy, who were encouraged to expect the armour to be used near the coast.

The advanced party selected well concealed areas for squadrons in the steep little ravines near Cura Nuova where they were hidden even from the Monte della Crescia. The sky was overcast, and heavy rain would have made movement off the road very difficult, but fortunately there was no more than a shower. The advanced party sat patiently, as advanced parties so often do, by the roadside in the dark, eaten by mosquitoes and on one occasion nearly attacked by a Polish patrol. Eventually, just as dawn was breaking, the head of the regiment appeared.

It had not been a long march, but the roads and lanes were steep and narrow and halts frequent. This is far more tiring than long and continuous movement, and even the best of tempers become frayed. However, breakfasts were soon ready and after a couple of hours' sleep everyone was fresh again.

At 9 a.m. on the 15th, Lieutenant-Colonel Jayne attended a conference at which General Rakowski outlined his plan of attack for the 17th. The 6th Polish Armoured Regiment on the right and the 7th Hussars on the left were to capture first the Monte Torto spur, the objective being a prominent hill about a mile and a half north of the river. The second objective, another mile and a half beyond, was the road running along the crest of the main ridge from Croce di San Vicenzo to Monte Bogo. When the second objective had been captured and consolidated, the brigade was to pass a strong pursuit group through to Polverigi and Agugliano, and thence to exploit as far as possible towards the Esino River. In the initial phase, the Krechowieski and Poznan Lancers were to be in reserve.

The position of assembly was in a valley a mile north of the regiment's present area, just short of the river, but covered from the enemy's view by a steep ridge. The routes to the assembly position and onwards to the selected crossing place over the River Musone, were improved by the Polish engineers, who bull-dozed the worst corners of the lanes and, in conjunction with officers of each squadron of the 7th Hussars, taped the routes to the crossings. The river itself was the start line.

The crossing of the Musone and the left flank of the regiment as it advanced up the slopes beyond, were to be covered by a small preliminary operation in which a squadron of the 1st Lancers and two companies of Polish Commandos were to seize the village of Case Nuove, half a mile north-west of the crossing place, and a few surrounding farms, which were thought to be held by the Germans.

On the morning of the 16th the commanding officer took the squadron leaders to two observation posts from which the line of advance to the first objective could be clearly seen, and gave out his orders. The regiment was to seize the first objective on a two-squadron front, with B on the right and A on the left. C Squadron and the two companies of the 6th Polish Battalion, of which one was in Bren carriers, were to remain in the regiment's position of assembly until the first objective had been taken. The Stuarts of A Squadron were also to be left behind, as it was expected that the attack would meet heavy artillery fire and that the Stuarts, primarily of use as the reconnaissance elements in an armoured reconnaissance regiment, would be more vulnerable than useful. Arrangements for the supporting fire of the artillery and close support by a battery of the 7th Regiment of the Polish Horse Artillery were explained in detail.

The same afternoon squadron leaders took their troop leaders up to see the view, and each one was shown his objective, the particular areas he was to smother, and all that could be foreseen of the possible developments on his flanks. At nightfall one officer of each of the leading squadrons met the sappers who were preparing the river crossings, so that they might guide their squadrons to the right point.

Thus everything was laid on for the final attack which was to secure Ancona. The planning, preparation, timing and execution of this operation, and the issue of orders at each level, were models of competent and efficient command and staff work. For eighteen months the 2nd Polish Corps had been training with enthusiasm. Although the corps included many old soldiers, every unit and formation, except those which had been in the Carpathian Brigade Group at Tobruk, had started from scratch. The Poles had already distinguished themselves in one difficult and gallant action at Monte Cassino. Now General Anders conducted his own independent battle, and the careful planning and determined execution of the attack on Ancona were of an order which showed that the corps was at the highest level of formations in Italy—a level from which it never flagged until it was broken up after the war.

At 5 a.m. on the 17th the 7th Hussars moved forward to the position of assembly, where squadrons were in position soon after 6. The 1st Lancers squadron and commando companies crossed the river at 7 and in less than half an hour had cleared Case Nuove.

At 7.20 first A Squadron and then B advanced over the low ridge screening them from the Musone and passed over the river at the prepared crossing. The leading troops of both squadrons made straight for their objectives. They met little opposition, and soon after 8 o'clock were well established on the Monte Torto. A few infantry posts were mopped up and prisoners taken, for a loss of one man mortally wounded. This was Sergeant McGuinness, a tank commander of B Squadron, who was hit by a machine gun bullet while doing a reconnaissance on foot. During the attack the leading squadrons were not engaged by the enemy's mortars or artillery, which only opened on Monte Torto some time after it had been captured.

C Squadron, the infantry companies and the Stuarts of A and B Squadrons had meanwhile remained in the assembly area. The enemy shelled the area of the river and the line of hills to the south of it, but not the valley where the regiment was concealed.

At about 8.30 the Commanding Officer decided to move C Squadron and the infantry up to consolidate Monte Torto and prepare for the advance to the second objective. As the troops crossed the ridge, they at once came in view of the enemy's observation posts and he switched his fire accurately to the river crossing. A Bren carrier was unfortunately knocked out in the river and blocked the passage. The fire was heavy and the way could not be cleared until about 10.30, when it died down.

While the reserves were closing up, Lieutenant-Colonel Jayne and Major Fox, the squadron leader, went up to Monte Torto to reconnoitre the ground for C Squadron's advance to the second objective. Before this operation could begin, however, it was necessary to wait for the 6th Armoured Regiment on the right to come up to their first objective, as their assault on Croce di San Vicenzo was to take place at the same time. Their advance had been held up by S.P. guns just east of Croce di San Vicenzo, and one of these had also knocked out a Stuart tank of B Squadron on the forward slopes of Monte Torto—fortunately without injury to its crew.

At about 1 p.m. C Squadron's advance began, along the western slope of the ridge which leads up from Monte Torto to Croce di San Vicenzo. The leading troops met little opposition at this stage, but had some difficulty in finding a way round the head of the Torto ravine, which is very steep. Eventually, by moving up to within a few hundred yards of Croce di San Vicenzo, they reached the crest of the ridge, where they turned left. The going was rough and one Sherman cast a track. A composite troop of three Shermans now took the lead, and entered the grounds of a prominent red-brick house with white stone facings, the Palazzo Mainardi. From here enemy transport could be seen moving north down the hill from Polverigi towards the Esino and a long-range shoot by the Shermans sped them on their way.

The troop then moved up to the knoll above the brick-works, half a mile east of Monte Bogo, which was the final objective. At about 4 p.m. the rest of the squadron moved up to positions on the same feature and prepared for the final phase.

While C Squadron was moving northwards up the ridge to capture the eastern end of the objective, A Squadron had been ordered to attempt to reach Monte Bogo by a direct assault across the Valle di Monte Torto. It moved off about 1.30 p.m., just in time to escape the concentrated shell and mortar fire which the enemy now brought down on Monte Torto. The Italians on the left had in fact failed to take their objectives, the high ground at Rustico, and had barely succeeded in gaining a footing on the north bank of the Musone. So the left of the 7th Hussars was entirely exposed.

This fire caused several casualties. The commanding officer's tank was hit and his driver wounded; he was lifted out of the tank and while another member of the crew was attending to his wounds, both were killed. Some time later two men of B Squadron were killed while trying to bury them. The firing continued intermittently until the late afternoon and three other men of B Squadron were wounded.

After attempting to find a crossing over the Valle di Monte Torto, A Squadron eventually reported that it was impossible for tanks owing to the steep slopes, which the Shermans could not climb. It was therefore ordered to follow the route taken by C, round the upper end of the valley and on to the ridge near the Palazzo Mainardi. Here two troops took up positions for harassing the enemy retreating from Polverigi to the Esino.

The troop leader of another troop, Lieutenant E. C. F. Harding, carried out a dismounted reconnaisssance in front of his tank in the grounds of the Palazzo Mainardi and suddenly encountered a German officer stepping through a hedge. The German had a machine pistol slung over his shoulder, but at once put it down when threatened with a revolver. Unlike Harding, he did not realize that the revolver was not loaded. He turned out to be a staff officer of the regiment (brigade) which was holding this sector, and he had come to bring orders to the forward troops who were supposed to be holding the ridge.

After the arrival of A Squadron on the crest, C advanced to complete the capture of Monte Bogo, which was occupied without opposition by about 5.30 p.m. About an hour later Monte Bogo was shelled fairly heavily from the west and there were some indications that this was Italian artillery. A number of shells failed to explode and this recalled the old days at Fort Capuzzo, when dud shells often bounced harmlessly over the desert. There were no casualties, and after dark the squadron was ordered back to the regimental harbour just south of the Croce di San Vicenzo.

With the capture of Monte Bogo, the 7th Hussars' part in the operation was over. After an all-night journey on a road jammed with traffic of every kind, the A1 Echelon arrived at daybreak to replenish the regiment.

Elsewhere on 17th July operations had progressed equally well. The 5th Kresowa Division, delivering the main blow immediately on the right of the 2nd Armoured Brigade, began its attack at 6.20 a.m. The 5th Wilno Brigade Group included four armoured regiments and four battalions. At 6.25 three hundred guns opened a bombardment which lasted only ten minutes. The first objectives about San Paterniano were only captured, after a bloody fight against skilful opposition, at 8.20. The enemy, ensconced in and around the houses, held his fire until the infantry were at close range and caused heavy casualties. Eventually however the posts were reduced by tank and artillery fire and by the PIATs of the infantry.

Before the attack on the final objective could be mounted, fresh troops had to be bought forward. The second phase opened at about 10 a.m., and between 12 and 1 the whole ridge from San Stefano to Monte della Crescia was in Polish hands. The 5th Division's attempt to exploit towards Offagna was stopped by vigorous enemy resistance, so the divisional commander ordered the 5th Brigade to capture it during the night. Accordingly part of a battalion moved silently forward and at 3 a.m. found the village unoccupied.

The exploitation envisaged by the corps commander had already begun when, soon after the capture of Monte Bogo, Colonel Bobinski had been sent forward towards the Esino with an armoured force from the 2nd Armoured Brigade. At the same time General Anders, who had maintained close control of the battle from his command post at Monte Fano, had moved forward the 6th Lwow Infantry Brigade and placed it under command of the 2nd Armoured Brigade, whose commander, General Rakowski, was to conduct the pursuit.

The German troops who had been holding the sector of the attack were now in complete confusion. During the night the 15th Lancers captured a battalion headquarters near Agugliano and a number of stragglers were picked up. In the morning however both the main pursuing columns, the 6th Brigade on the right and the 15th Lancers group on the left, encountered strong resistance on the high ground south of Route 16, between Ancona and the Esino River. The enemy had established flank guards which managed to hold out long enough to enable the bulk of his forces on the coastal sector to withdraw behind the Esino.

The 6th Brigade had a fierce fight near Torette a Mare, two miles west of Ancona. The 15th Lancers Group had another, at Castelferreti, two miles from the mouth of the river; in this encounter a hundred prisoners and six guns were captured. Near the mouth of the River Esino the same column caught a reinforcing enemy battalion in the act of debussing, and the Germans fled back to the river. This was the last enemy resistance south-east of the Esino, over which a crossing was quickly effected at Chiaravalle.

While these engagements were taking place near the coast, the rest of the 2nd Armoured Brigade was moved forward to the Agugliano area, in reserve. The 7th Hussars marched soon after mid-day to the near-by village of Castel d'Emilio.

In the two days of fighting the enemy had been thoroughly beaten. He lost eight hundred prisoners, had about the same number killed and over two thousand wounded. Ten tanks and S.P. guns were captured, forty field and anti-tank guns and a quantity of lesser weapons. But most important of all was the capture of Ancona port. Demolitions were extensive, but the work of repair was begun at once and by the 23rd the first ships arrived and began to unload.

The opening of Ancona gave fresh administrative impetus, not only to the Adriatic sector, which now lost its character as Cinderella of the Italian front, but to the Eighth Army as well. The latter was able to open a new line of communication, which carried a large proportion of its supplies, from Ancona, along Route 76, through Iesi and Fabriano.

* * * *

Although the first ships entered Ancona on 23rd July, it was 6th August before the Polish Corps managed to reorganize its long line of communications and shift its base from Ortona and Porto San Georgio to Ancona. In the intervening period only limited forces could be maintained forward, in contact with the enemy.

On the 19th July orders were issued for pursuit to the River Misa. Each infantry division was to provide one pursuit detachment. On the right "A" Detachment, from the 3rd Carpathian Division, was to move by Route 16 on Senigallia and seize a crossing over the River Misa. On the left "B" Deatchment, from the 5th Kresowa Division, was to move through Morro d'Alba to Ostra, to cover the left flank of "A."

Both detachments were of similar composition. "B," with which the 7th Hussars were concerned, was commanded by Lieutenant-Colonel W. Stoczowski, Second-in-Command of the 6th Lwow Brigade. It consisted of C Squadron 7th Hussars, the 12th Podolski Lancers, 15th Battalion, 5th Field Regiment and a medium battery. C Squadron moved forward the same afternoon to a harbour area just south of the Esino.

On 20th July C Squadron moved off at 8 a.m., crossed the Esino and joined the 12th Lancers at Monte San Vito, three miles west of Chiaravalle. Stoczowski's "A" Detachment used two routes forward to the Misa, the northern through Morro d'Alba and Filetto, the southern through Monsano and Belvedere Ostrense to Ostra. One troop of C Squadron was sent off with a squadron of the 12th Podolski Lancers to reconnoitre the southern route, and found Monsano and San Murcello clear of the enemy.

On the northern route the enemy had taken up positions about Filetto and Ostra, on the high ridge between the Misa and the Fosso Traponzo. The latter is a tributary of the Esino which, in its upper reaches, runs in a deep, narrow valley, parallel with and barely two miles from the Misa.

The enemy had destroyed the bridges over the Traponzo between Morro d'Alba and Filetto, and shortly after mid-day two troops of C Squadron were sent off to find an alternative crossing farther to the east. One troop took up a covering position while the other, Lieutenant J. B. Dunlop's, went down to the river. A crossing place was found, and the troop moved over and up the opposite ridge to a point about a mile east of Filetto. Here it came under shell fire, and eventually withdrew across the Traponzo. At nightfall all troops returned to the squadron harbour at Monte San Vito.

"A" Detachment, on the coast, had also advanced during the afternoon nearly to Marzochetta, and likewise found the enemy in position south of the Misa.

On the 21st "A" Detachment had several skirmishes in the morning, but found the enemy unexpectedly strong and gains during the day were small. "B" Detachment spent the day in reconnaissance of the enemy's positions, much of this being done by C Squadron.

At 7.30 a.m. the squadron, less Lieutenant Dunlop's troop, moved from Monte San Vito towards Belvedere Ostrense, in order to support the reconnaissances towards Ostra. From Belvedere there are two alternative routes to Ostra. The eastern route, running gradually down to the Traponzo, and thence steeply up the other side, was in full view of the enemy and the leading troop came under shell fire and was withdrawn. One Sherman had a sprocket and track smashed and had to be left. The other route was then tried, less steep than the first, round the head of the valley. This road also was in view of the enemy and again the leading troop was stopped by shell fire.

The Squadron now attempted to reach Ostra with one troop on each side of the road. The troop on the left of the road had trouble in the heavy going—there had been a good deal of rain—and one Stuart was bogged and had to be left. The other troop worked its way to within two miles of Ostra, and shot at several houses occupied by the enemy on a ridge short of the town. Four prisoners were taken. At nightfall the troops withdrew and the squadron harboured at Monsano.

Meanwhile Lieutenant Dunlop had been sent off to the right flank, where he had operated the previous day. At about 4 p.m. he supported an attack by the 1st Lancers of "A" Detachment on the ridge to the east of Filetto. This attack was stopped by heavy anti-tank and artillery fire, and at nightfall Dunlop was ordered back to the squadron. On re-crossing the Traponzo the troop came under anti-tank fire from Filetto and one Sherman became bogged in the stream.

As the result of the reconnaissances on the 21st, Colonel Stoczowski made a plan to attack Ostra on the 22nd. The 15th Battalion was to attack frontally, with C Squadron advancing level with it, on its left. The 12th Podolski Lancers were to encircle the town by the south and west and to provide a detachment to protect the right of the battalion against interference from the direction of Filetto.

At 7.30 a.m. the squadron left Monsano for Belvedere, and at 8.30 two troops set off astride the westerly road, heading for the town. On the ridge near the head of the Traponzo stream, the left troop's leading Stuart was hit by an Ofenrohr (rocket launcher) and it was apparent that the enemy was in strength.

C Squadron was now brought back to Belvedere, and ordered to support the attack down the eastern road to Ostra, where the infantry and some of the 12th Lancers were already held up by shell fire. One troop moved on the right of the road, one on the road (Lieutenant G. O. W. Williams) and two on the left. Williams was within two hundred yards of the Traponzo when he came under accurate anti-tank fire from the ridge south of Ostra. The squadron was now halted and Williams' troop, as it drew back out of the enemy's fire, lost one Sherman which ran into a morass. No further progress was made by the infantry either, and at nightfall the squadron was ordered back to its previous night's harbour area.

The enemy's delaying position at Ostra and Filetto was too strong for the pursuit detachments to tackle, and no further attempt was made. On the 23rd C Squadron remained at Monsano. The two Stuarts were burnt out by the enemy on the night of 22nd/23rd July, but the two Shermans were subsequently recovered. Casualties had been only two, both wounded and neither seriously.

On the 23rd B Squadron relieved C at Monsano, with the task of counter-attacking if the enemy should advance.

The corps commander now ordered the two infantry divisions to build up the forward troops in their respective sectors to the strength of a brigade each, while the 2nd Armoured Brigade, less the squadron of the 7th Hussars operating with the 5th Division, was to be held in reserve about Agugliano.

These readjustments had hardly taken effect when, on the night of the 25th/26th, the enemy left his positions on the Filetto-Ostra ridge and withdrew behind the Misa. Patrols followed up at once and found him holding the north bank of the river, and the bed of the river itself was obstructed with numerous minefields. During the 26th advanced

Map XV

BATTLES FOR ANCONA

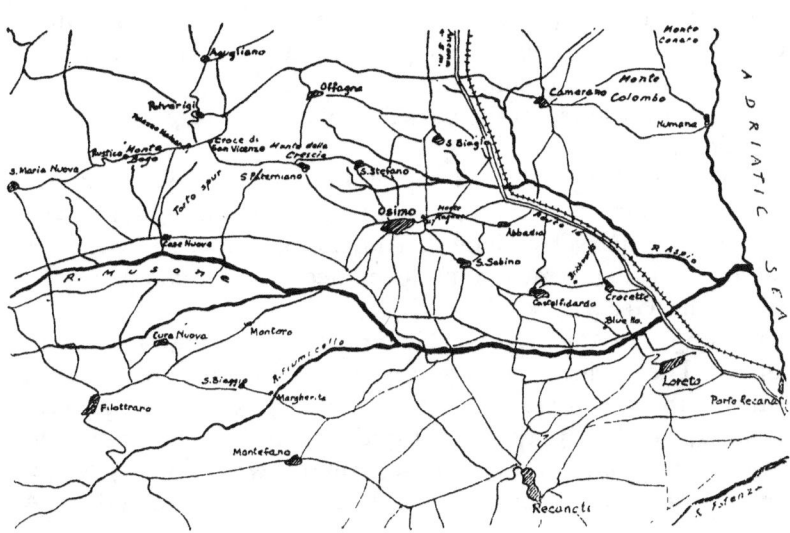

elements of the corps reached the Misa at Senigallia and Pianello, and the Maiella Group of Italians occupied Montecarotto.

On the last few days of July the Germans carried out several raids on the Italian sector and, as the Poles were not yet ready to resume the offensive, the forward troops took up defensive positions on the high ground south of the Misa.

While C and then B Squadrons were operating with the pursuit columns, the rest of the regiment spent more than two weeks in the 2nd Armoured Brigade's area near Agugliano. B Echelon joined up and the regiment made itself reasonably comfortable in agreeable surroundings.

A certain number of men were able to bathe in the sea each day and most friendly relations were established with the neighbouring Poles. A number of officers were entertained in the regimental mess, including General Rakowski and Lieutenant-Colonel Bobinski, and the 7th Hussars were especially pleased at the award of a Military Cross to 2nd Lieutenant Anzrej Liebich of the 7th Horse Artillery Regiment, whose gallantry and efficiency had been conspicuous both at Osimo and Monte Torto.

The regiment was represented on three ceremonial occasions during this period. On 22nd July a composite troop of Roman Catholics under Lieutenant J. J. H. Browne attended a High Mass at Loreto Cathedral in commemoration of the officers and men of the Polish Corps who fell in the Ancona campaign. Next day a composite troop of A Squadron under Lieutenant P. J. Howard-Dobson took part in a parade at the sports ground at Ancona, to celebrate the capture of the port. General Sosnkowski, Commander-in-Chief of the Polish Armed Forces, took the salute at the march past. Generals Alexander and Leese both congratulated Lieutenant Howard-Dobson, as the representative of the 7th Hussars, on the part the regiment had played in the recent operations.

On 26th July the King reviewed representatives of the 2nd Polish Corps at Castiglione del Lago. Lieutenant-Colonel Jayne was presented to His Majesty by General Anders, and was subsequently congratulated on the regiment's performance in the campaign by General Leese and General Sosnkowski.

At the end of July Major E. H. Tinker left to command the 48th Royal Tanks. The regiment was very sorry to see him go. During his six months with the 7th Hussars he had not only been of the greatest help in training, but had played a conspicuous part in many of their battles as well. His place as second-in-command was taken by Major J. Congreve, D.S.O., and Major A. E. White took command of A Squadron.

On the night of 3rd/4th August the enemy withdrew from the north bank of the Misa to the high ground between that river and the Cesano. On the 4th the 3rd Carpathian Division made contact with his main position and the forward troops of the 5th Division crossed both the Misa and its tributary the Fenella.

Next day the 3rd Division's pursuit columns attacked, but made no progress against the determined opposition. Farther to the left the pursuit column of the 5th Division, consisting of the 15th Battalion and B Squadron of the 7th Hussars, supported by the 5th Field Regiment, was directed on Monterado.

Lt.-General Anders presents Lt.-Colonel R. F. G. Jayne, D.S.O., to the King, July 1944.

Three captains—Phil Barton, Michael Stanley Evans, "Shorty" White.

Shortly before noon the advanced patrols found the enemy rearguards in position north of Ripe, and the column halted along the road just north of the Fenella crossing. The road at this point was thought to be out of sight of the enemy and crews dismounted. Soon, however, shelling began and they were ordered to mount. While getting into his turret Lieutenant J. J. H. Browne was hit by a small shell splinter in the stomach; he died of his wound two days later.

B Squadron was now given the task of helping the infantry to secure the ridge overlooking Ripe from the north. Enemy observation posts and snipers had been located on this ridge and Lieutenant G. M. Thompson's troop of Shermans went forward to engage them. He shelled selected targets along the ridge between two conspicuous farmhouses, one pink and one white, and when the infantry advanced they found that the enemy had gone. That, however, was the limit of the advance for the day. When the Poles crossed this objective, they came under heavy fire from the next ridge, and reconnaissances revealed that the Germans were in considerable strength along the high ground from Corinaldo to the sea.

*   *   *   *

On 4th August the Poles, with their bridgeheads established across the Misa, were still twenty miles short of the Gothic Line, which on this sector followed the high ground to the west of the River Foglia and reached the sea near Pesaro.

For reasons which will be explained later the centre of strategical interest was now gradually shifting from the mountainous centre to the apparently less difficult country on the right. It seemed that the Po plain could be reached more easily by passing around instead of through the Apennines.

The Gothic Line had still to be breached, and if the Eighth Army's main blow was to be delivered on the right it was essential that the Poles should secure a jumping off place much nearer to the objective. The assault, when launched, must not only reach the main defences, but have enough impetus to break clean through. It was therefore essential to seize and hold crossings over the Metauro and to secure as much as possible of the undulating country towards the River Foglia beyond.

The Metauro was some fifteen miles ahead, and the intervening country was of the same monotonous pattern as it had been all the way up the Adriatic coast; the only difference was that, after turning the bend of the "calf" at Ancona, all the rivers and ridges ran from south-west to north-east. The enemy was, as usual, holding a strong delaying position between two rivers, this time the Misa and the Cesano.

Once more a pause of a few days was necessary, while the 2nd Polish Corps adjusted its dispositions and brought forward its supplies. Once more the plans, preparations and execution of the operation were carefully co-ordinated and controlled by the corps commander and once more they bore the stamp of his courageous and competent military leadership.

The Polish positions beyond the Misa as well as the river crossings were generally overlooked by the Germans and subjected to a good deal of sniping and shell fire, which was depressing for the troops and interfered with their supplies. However, there were only four days to wait.

On 6th August, General Anders issued his orders. His intention was to break the German resistance on the ridge and advance to the Cesano. The date was fixed for the 9th.

The leading brigades of the two divisions were to attack side by side on a narrow frontage. The 3rd Division's objective was the Santa Lucia cemetery, a mile east of Ripe. Thence it was to exploit north-eastwards and roll up the enemy's position towards Scapezzano The 5th Division's objectives were Point 208 a mile east of Monterado, and la Croce, a high point on the ridge halfway between Ripe and Monterado.

The left of the corps was to be covered by the Italians, who were to contain the enemy in the Corinaldo-Castelleone di Suasa sector, and the 12th Podolski Lancers were to form the link between the 5th Division and the Italians, in the area between Ripe and Corinaldo.

The 2nd Armoured Brigade was to be in corps reserve, less two regiments. Of the latter, the 7th Hussars were allotted to the 5th Division.

Each division was to be supported by its own divisional artillery. The Army Group, Polish Artillery, reinforced by two British medium regiments, was first to bombard the la Croce ridge, then to turn to the enemy's artillery and selected points on the infantry objectives. Air attacks were to be made on enemy batteries which were beyond the range of the guns. A heavy anti-aircraft regiment was to keep the crossings of the Cesano under fire throughout the attack.

Between 6th and 8th August final dispositions were taken up. Owing to the enemy's good observation, most moves had to take place at night, and most of them on the night of 8th/9th August, just before the attack. Such armour as was not to be used in the first assault was kept well in rear until after the attack had begun.

General Rudnicki, the commander of the 5th Kresowa Division, gave out his orders with impressive lucidity and he himself inspired great confidence. The 5th Wilno Brigade, with the addition of the 16th Battalion of the 6th Lwow Brigade, was to carry out the 5th Division's attack. The advance was to be on two axes, one squadron of 7th Hussars, with one troop of M.10's (self propelled anti-tank guns) under command, being allotted to each axis.

On the right, the 16th Battalion, followed by the 14th and supported by A Squadron, was to advance by Point 208 on Francavilla. On the left the 15th Battalion, followed by the 13th and supported by B Squadron, was to advance by Ripe, la Croce and Monterado to seize the Cesano crossings. C Squadron was to be with the 6th Lwow Brigade in reserve in the Filetto area. Tactical regimental headquarters was to be alongside the divisional commander at his command post on the ridge between the Misa and the Fenella stream, two miles south of Ripe. This command post was carefully selected, dug in and prepared, and had an excellent view of the battlefield.

B Squadron, which had reverted to regimental command on the 7th, had been left well forward south of Ripe, so did not have to move. It was bivouacked among pine trees in the grounds of a large country house and had spent a few pleasant days without even the inconveniences of shell fire. On the morning of the 8th the rest of the regiment marched from Agugliano, where it had been resting for over a fortnight. There was some delay at the Esino crossing and again in Chiaravalle, and a certain amount of misunderstanding, between the leading tanks and the Polish military police, about the direction the regiment should take. Some delay was also caused by tanks breaking down; they had been standing too long in the rain and were not running smoothly. One of A Squadron's Stuarts stopped in the main street of Morro d'Alba and held up those in rear for some minutes.

At Ostra C Squadron branched off to its harbour area at Filetto. The rest of the regiment moved on two miles to the Casino area, in the Misa valley. All squadrons were in their allotted areas by 1 o'clock, and B Echelon arrived a few hours later.

In the afternoon Major White and the officers of A Squadron went to the 16th Battalion for a conference and reconnaissance. Later in the evening the squadron leader and second-in-command visited B Squadron near Ripe. Here there was a certain amount of shelling, and one officer noted afterwards, "Shells were dropping annoyingly near at intervals; it is odd that different people duck each time; young X got kicked by George for ducking, so Y got behind George so that he could flinch with impunity; Z didn't stir for any of the shells, but got right down when a 3-tonner started up twenty yards away."

"George" was of course the squadron leader, Murray Smith. His disregard for shell-fire was no less remarkable than his gift of invariably radiating confidence, a gift which had been of particular value to the regiment during some of the more critical episodes of the Burma campaign.

The enemy must have seen something of the forward move of the 7th Hussars, and during the afternoon there was spasmodic shelling of the harbour areas; there were no casualties.

After dark A Squadron moved up to Santa Lucia, close to the 16th Battalion. Both forward squadrons spent the night alongside the battalions they were to support next day.

The attack up the left axis was timed for 7.30 and on the right axis, where the first objective was closer, for 8 o'clock.

The 15th Battalion started from the line of the high ridge just north of Ripe and from Castel Colonna. The enemy's position was on the rather higher ridge about a thousand yards to the north. B Squadron supported the attack with two troops, organized as one troop of four Shermans, under S.S.M. Davies, firing from positions on the ridge just west of Ripe. All Stuarts had been left behind in the harbour area, as there was no place for them in a set-piece attack.

The infantry quickly reached the first ridge, which they took without much difficulty. At 8 a.m. they began to move forward against la Croce. As S.S.M. Davies could not support them on to la Croce from his original position, he led his composite troop forward, intending to give support from the next ridge.

The tanks had moved a few hundred yards down the slope when all at once they were fired on from several different directions by anti-tank guns, which had hitherto been silent, on the left flank. Three of the four tanks were quickly knocked out. Two were set on fire, and the explosion of the ammunition blew the turret half off one and completely off the other. The third received three hits, none of which penetrated, and it was later recovered. S.S.M. Davies was wounded, but the rest of his crew were unhurt; in another tank the lap-gunner was killed, but the others escaped before the ammunition exploded; in the third the turret was penetrated by three shots; the commander, Sergeant Andrews, the gunner and operator were all killed, but the driver and lap-gunner got out before the tank blew up. The fourth tank escaped down the ravine into cover and managed to rejoin the squadron.

As the infantry advanced towards la Croce they met stiffer opposition, and at 9 a.m. the rest of B Squadron moved forward along the high ground on the left of the Ripe-la Croce road. They were evidently observed by the enemy, who brought down heavy artillery fire. Lieutenant Thompson's troop managed to work its way forward to the ridge a few hundred yards short of la Croce. Here it spotted an enemy S.P. gun partly hidden by a haystack in a farmyard on the la Croce feature. After firing a few rounds at the gun and getting no response, the troop advanced and captured the gun crew, who said they had run out of ammunition.

The infantry then occupied la Croce with little difficulty.

On the right the 16th Battalion was equally successful in reaching its first objectives. A Squadron took up positions soon after 7 o'clock, ready to support the attack with fire. The first objective, Point 186, was less than a thousand yards from the start line and was taken without opposition. Just after 8 o'clock A Squadron moved up to Point 186 in order to support the attack on Point 208. Two troops on the left of the road covered the area to the left of Point 208 and the road running along the ridge to la Croce, while two others on the right faced north-eastwards.

A little before 9 the infantry advanced on the objective. It appeared that they were meeting little opposition, but soon a report came in to say that Point 208 was very strongly held, and the battalion commander asked that tanks should be sent forward. Although it was explained that their support would be much more effective from Point 186, the battalion commander still pressed his appeal. They were not however sent up until the infantry had secured their objective, soon after 9 o'clock.

Four troops of A Squadron then went forward to positions on the reverse slope of Point 208, in case of counter-attack. This was not long delayed. At about 11 a.m. the 16th Battalion reported that enemy infantry and tanks were about to attack and the forward elements of the battalion withdrew behind the crest, close to A Squadron's tanks.

For some time nothing happened, but eventually three enemy SP guns appeared over the hill. They were Italian Semoventes, mounting a 105/25 gun on an M.15/42 chassis. Two were quickly knocked out by the Polish S.P. guns attached to the squadron. Both blew up and pieces were scattered over a wide area. The third escaped down the road to Francavilla.

Soon afterwards another S.P. gun was spotted, on the left flank, by Corporal Clare. It was trying to climb up the bank off the road between Point 208 and la Croce, but the slope was too steep and it stuck. Clare's first shot penetrated the chassis behind the driver's compartment; this set the ammunition on fire and the crew abandoned the gun. It was an 88-millimetre PAK 43, or "Hornet," belonging to an Army anti-tank unit recently sent to support the 278th Division, and the most formidable enemy weapon that the 7th Hussars had yet encountered.

At about mid-day the 16th Battalion re-occupied Point 208 and advanced north-westwards to a road junction two hundred yards beyond. From here there was a good view over Francavilla to the north and Monterado to the west. Two troops of A Squadron moved up to the same area, to cover the Francavilla road.

While here an air-burst shell caused three casualties. Trooper Eddis, inside his turret, was killed; Corporal Clare and Trooper Thomas were wounded.

At about 3 p.m. another enemy Hornet was seen in the valley to the right of Francavilla. Both troops opened fire, but observation was difficult owing to the undergrowth and small trees in the valley. It was also engaged by the 1st Lancers of the 3rd Division, from a point farther along the ridge to the east. Eventually the Hornet was brought to a halt on the track leading up to Francavilla. It had been hit several times, probably by both regiments, its left sprocket and track were shot away, the ammunition was set on fire and the explosion which followed blew off the rear and side shields.

Early in the afternoon the 16th Battalion advanced on Francavilla. They met only sporadic mortar fire, and at about 3.15 p.m. they asked for some tanks of A Squadron to move down to Francavilla to support an attack from that direction, along the saddle of the ridge, to Monterado.

At 3.30 Lieutenant Howard-Dobson's troop moved forward from behind Point 208, making for Francavilla. As soon as the troop started to move along the hillside just below the Francavilla road, it came under long range armour-piercing fire. Several shots hit the front of Howard-Dobson's tank, without penetrating, and he continued forward to a group of trees in a slight hollow, where he would be out of sight of the enemy anti-tank gun. The trees however had evidently been registered, as the Germans immediately opened heavy and accurate mortar fire. Howard-Dobson now decided to return behind the ridge, and reversed back the way he had come.

As he cleared the trees, the gun covering the open ground again opened fire. This time a track was broken and the tank was brought to a halt. Mortaring began again and, as the crew dismounted, all except Howard-Dobson were wounded. They managed to get back over the ridge, and only one, Lyndon, was seriously hurt.

The enemy then engaged the Sherman with an 88-millimetre at

long range, presumably intending to set it on fire. Only one shot scored a hit; this did not explode, but passed into the turret and, owing to the tilt of the tank, clean out through the hull on the other side. The tank was subsequently recovered.

After this episode the Polish infantry were persuaded not to ask for tanks to be sent to places on the forward slopes of the ridge, where they would be unduly exposed to anti-tank guns.

The 16th Battalion, on the Francavilla axis, had made more progress either than the 3rd Division on the right or the other part of the 5th Wilno Brigade on the left. At 5.30, in order to assist the advance of the latter, A Squadron was asked by the commander of the 16th Battalion, to move all his tanks up to the road junction east of la Croce, where two troops were already established. From a hill a little farther to the west he could then support an attack on the left axis by the 13th Battalion, who were to pass through the 15th Battalion on la Croce and capture Monterado.

A Squadron moved up to the hill and came into position. While it was waiting for the attack to begin, an officer of the 16th Batalion came up to the squadron leader and pointed out to him an enemy S.P. gun halted in a lane just south of Monterado cemetery. Its rear was turned towards the squadron and it presented a perfect and apparently unsuspecting target, at a range of about 1,500 yards. Lieutenant E. C. F. Harding was ordered to engage it.

His gun was already loaded with a high explosive round, and he decided to fire this before loading an armour piercing shot. The aim was perfect. The enemy gun was at once enveloped in flame and smoke, as the H.E. shell had set the ammunition on fire. Like all good Hornets, as it later proved to be, it blew up.

The attack of the 13th Battalion from la Croce on Monterado did not take place as soon as expected, as the Poles could not complete their arrangements in time. Having waited until after dark, A Squadron then withdrew to harbour near the point where it had spent the previous night. At 11 p.m., when the attack went in, Monterado was found unoccupied; the enemy had slipped away under cover of the darkness and rain, and withdrawn behind the Cesano.

Throughout the day B Squadron had done its best to support the 15th Battalion in the la Croce area. But each time the tanks showed themselves to the north of the ridge they came under anti-tank fire, and while they were behind it they were often shelled. Eventually, at nightfall, the squadron was withdrawn to its harbour area near Ripe.

C Squadron was now brought up from Filetto and sent forward to harbour near B, from whom it was to take over on the following day.

All squadrons had a disturbed night; there was occasional shelling and heavy rain fell. There were many who felt the loathsome but not unusual chill of cold water coming through the blankets from below, which invariably meant the end of sleep for that night.

On the morning of the 10th A and C Squadrons each sent one troop forward to la Croce ridge. They had nothing to do, however, as the enemy had pulled back behind the Cesano during the night. His withdrawal was unmolested, as the weather made both patrolling and pursuit exceedingly difficult in the darkness.

On the 10th all squadrons remained where they were, but during the next three days B and C Squadrons, which were rather near some of the Polish artillery positions and therefore liable to be shelled, made short moves to healthier places.

Casualties, in the last two months, had been fairly heavy and a reinforcement of two officers and twenty men, which arrived on the 12th, the first since leaving Egypt in April, still left the regiment much below strength. Precedence was of course given to completing the Sherman crews, as there was little use for the Stuarts in these operations.

On the 10th both Polish divisions crossed the Cesano. The 3rd Division on the right secured a bridgehead on the north bank, and made contact with the enemy holding the high ground about San Sebastiano. On the 5th Division front, the 15th Battalion, which had passed through the 16th, was unable to retain its footing beyond the river. Farther to the left the 12th Lancers found Monteporzio unoccupied, but no bridgehead was established.

In one respect the operation had been disappointing. Owing to the enemy's strong resistance, the 2nd Corps had used up its energy before it reached the Cesano. As the enemy clearly intended to fight another delaying action south of the Metauro, another pause was now necessary for re-grouping.

Before the next battle the 7th Hussars had a week of maintenance and rest. As usual, bathing parties were organized, this time at Senigallia. The town was deserted, and the sea a long way out over the very flat beach, but even if conditions were not ideal, a bathe was always refreshing.

* * * *

The battle for the Metauro was the last preliminary operation before the attack on the Gothic Line, and its form was to a great extent dictated by the requirements of the 1st Canadian and 5th British Corps in the forthcoming offensive. These were to attack on the left of the Polish Corps, and to jump off from approximately the line of the

Metauro. It was therefore desirable to seize crossings over the Metauro on a wide front.

Time was important, as the opening of the Eighth Army's offensive must not be delayed. The choice of the point of attack was not difficult. On the left, the area of Orciano di Pesaro had certain advantages, as the ridges ran generally parallel to the line of attack; they were steep, however, and not very easy for tanks, and extensive

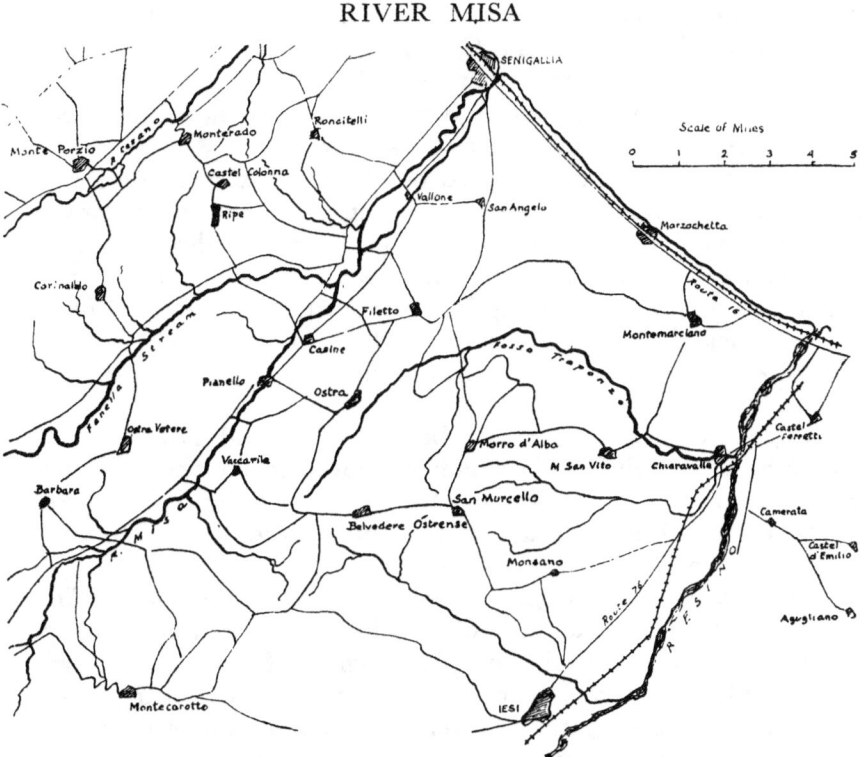

MAP XVI
RIVER MISA

NOTE: In order to simplify sketch maps, innumerable small roads and lanes are ommitted.

re-grouping would be necessary for an attack on this sector. In the centre there were two main ridges across the line of advance, separated by the upper reaches of the Rio Maggiore, and on both of these the enemy might have fought prolonged delaying actions. The right flank, in the area of Mandolfo and San Costanzo, was better tank country and less time would be needed to stage the attack in this area. This sector was therefore chosen.

General Anders decided to attack in two phases. First the 3rd

Carpathian Division was to advance to San Costanzo. Then the 2nd Armoured Brigade, which was to include the 7th Hussars, was to attack westwards along the ridge, to Montemaggiore. Both attacking formations were reinforced at the expense of the 5th Division; the 6th Lwow Brigade was attached to the 3rd Division and a battalion of the 5th Wilno Brigade was attached to the 2nd Armoured Brigade. With what was left, the 5th Division was to simulate a crossing of the Cesano near Monterado.

The left of the corps was to be protected by the Cavalry Group, partly of Polish armoured units, with one British re-horsed cavalry regiment and the Italian Maiella Group. This force was to demonstrate along the axis Corinaldo-Orciano di Pesaro. Farther to the left the rest of the Italians were also given an offensive task, but their capabilities were limited by shortage of transport.

A cover plan was carefully worked out in order to encourage the enemy to expect an attack in the Orciano sector. Squadrons of tanks, guns and transport were moved conspicuously in that direction and surreptitiously brought back. Patrol activity was reduced on the right and intensified on the left. Deception was to continue until the opening of the attack, and even the corps artillery bombardment was to open, an hour before zero, on the front where the attack was not to take place.

The re-grouping was carried out between 13th and 17th August. On the 15th, after nightfall, the regiment moved to Ponticelli, on the north bank of the Misa, not far from Senigallia. Here it spent three uneventful days waiting to play its part in the second phase of the operation.

The attack was due to start early on the morning of the 18th. The assault was to be on two axes, and the leading battalions were already across the river in their forming up places when, at 4 a.m., it started to rain. The Cesano quickly became a torrent. Mine clearing work was stopped, the leading battalions were cut off and none of the tanks had yet crossed. In consequence the attack was postponed until the following day.

On hearing this, however, one of the battalion commanders asked permission to attack at once, as he felt that this was less risky than waiting where he was. General Anders accepted his view and the attack by both brigades, each with one battalion, began at noon. It had now stopped raining.

The 5th Battalion on the right quickly drove in the enemy's covering troops, but had a stiff fight for its first objective. This was captured at 3 p.m., and the battalion at once pressed on towards the second.

By about 7 p.m. it was joined by the tanks, which had managed at last to cross the river, and by dusk had captured the eastern end of the second objective, four miles north of the river.

The left brigade's leading battalion only managed to reach its first objective during the night, after heavy fighting.

On the 19th both brigades continued their attacks. Neither reached the Metauro that day, but before nightfall the San Costanzo-il Vicinato ridge was secured; this gave the 2nd Armoured Brigade its jumping-off place for the attack along the ridge towards Montemaggiore.

Soon after mid-day on the 19th the 2nd Armoured Brigade moved forward across the Cesano and part of the corps artillery moved into the Mandolfo area, in order to give better support in the second phase. The 7th Hussars reached their harbour area, a mile south-east of il Vicinato, just before dark and, in view of the uncertain situation on the south bank of the Rio Maggiore, made tactical dispositions for the night. C and A Squadrons were to the south-west of the road, regimental headquarters and B Squadron, which was in reserve, were to the north. The attached carrier-borne company of the 17th Battalion was put under C Squadron, to guard against interference from across the Rio Maggiore. The only sign of enemy activity on the far bank however was one mortar bomb, which wounded two of the Polish infantrymen. On the following day there was no firing at all.

On 20th August the 6th Polish Armoured Regiment supported an attack by two companies of the 17th Battalion against Monte Rosario, where the enemy was holding a steep and narrow ridge; this runs at right angles to the main San Costanzo-Cerasa feature and was the strongest natural position left to him south of the Metauro.

Originally it was hoped that the ridge would be captured quickly, and a special force was formed and held ready to make a dash for the Metauro crossings. This was commanded by Major M. Fox, and consisted of his own C Squadron of the 7th Hussars, and a squadron of the 15th Poznanski Lancers, the reconnaissance regiment of the 5th Division. But it soon became clear that the enemy was going to contest his position vigorously. Every available gun of the Polish artillery supported the attack, which began at 7.30 a.m. The Germans also used every weapon they had, including tanks and Hornets, and supported the defence with their artillery in position across the river.

The fight went on until well into the night. After a prodigious expenditure of ammunition on both sides, the 6th Armoured Regiment took the objective at about 6 p.m., but it was past midnight when the infantry had finished mopping up.

"Foxforce" had meanwhile been disbanded, and the 7th Hussars were required to continue the assault the following day. After dark the regiment moved a short distance forward, to a concentration area in the deep valley just south of San Costanzo, where it had a quiet night.

At 6.45 a.m. the Commanding Officer went to brigade headquarters for a short conference, followed by a reconnaissance of the high ground west of Monte Rosario. This feature was to be the start line for the day's advance, and the objectives were first the hill at San Filippo and then the Casa Monte San Giovanni, the high point at the northern end of Piagge village. The 15th Lancers were to operate on the right of the 7th and both armoured regiments were to be supported by companies of the 17th Battalion.

There was little information about the enemy on the axis of the attack and it was uncertain whether Cerasa was held or not.

At 8.30 the regiment was ordered forward to a position of assembly. The road from Costanzo to Piagge runs along the crest of the ridge, and any movement along it or to the north of it was likely to draw fire. So the regiment moved south of the road on the upper slopes of the Rio Maggiore valley. C Squadron was in the lead, followed by regimental headquarters. The ridge was too narrow to allow more than one squadron abreast.

When due south of Monte Rosario there was a halt, while a patrol of the 15th Lancers reconnoitred Cerasa. This was reported clear, but after the tanks had gone through, some enemy infantry in the village opened fire on the infantry. The 7th Hussars were then ordered to send one troop to help a squadron of the 15th Lancers which was ordered to clear Cerasa; a troop from B Squadron was sent. By 11.30 the village was clear and C Squadron's advance began.

The subsidiary ravines and ridges on the northern slopes of the Maggiore valley were very steep and difficult, but C Squadron advanced from ridge to ridge and made gradual progress. In the valley south of San Filippo two Stuarts and one Sherman were hit by anti-tank fire and had to be abandoned; the two Stuarts were subsequently recovered.

By 2 p.m. one troop had succeeded in reaching the spur west of Rio San Filippo, covered by another on the spur behind and two more on the southern side of the San Filippo hill itself. These last two met immediate and heavy shell-fire from guns of large calibre, as soon as they showed themselves above the crest, and they remained under cover of the hill for the rest of the day.

Meanwhile the 15th Lancers' squadron and the detached troop of B Squadron, accompanied by infantry of the 17th Battalion, worked forward along the northern slope of the Cerasa-Piagge ridge. They encountered opposition on the spur north of San Filippo and B's troop took up a position near Cerasa cemetery in order to give support. But the infantry commander preferred to trickle forward without the fire of the tanks, as he considered that they might draw attention from the enemy artillery on the other side of the river.

For the attack on the final objective, Casa Monte San Giovanni, A Squadron passed through C and took up a position on the spur

MAP XVII
RIVERS CESANO AND METAURO

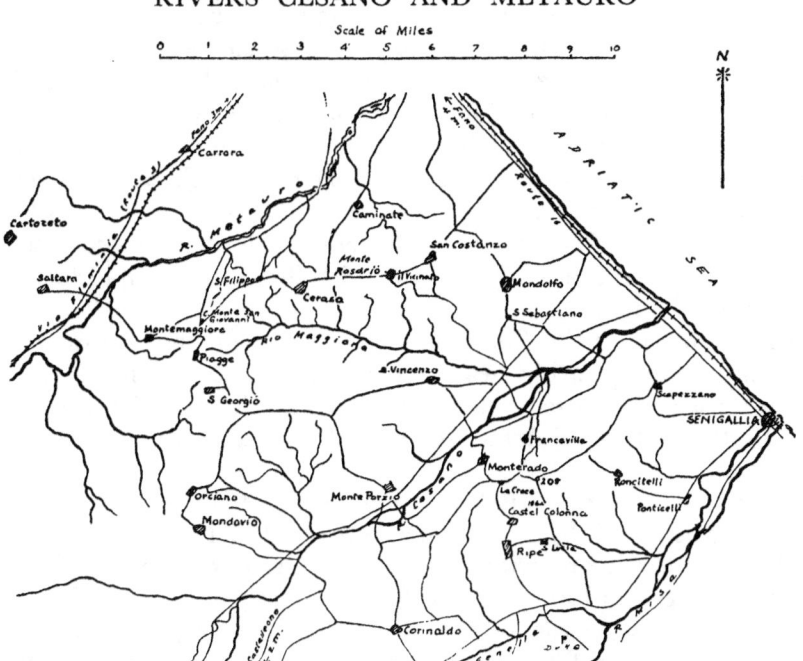

running west of the Rio di San Filippo, from which it dominated the objective and three smaller intervening spurs. The plan was to attack with B Squadron, supported by the fire of A and if necessary also by the Polish field artillery which the regiment had on call.

The attack started at 6.30 p.m. and when the two leading troops were on their way the squadron leader called for the supporting fire. This was very effective and the squadron reached its objective without difficulty at about 7 p.m. The only two anti-tank guns, 75-mm. PAK 40's, had been spotted by A Squadron and destroyed before they could engage B.

Some time later, B Squadron was engaged by anti-tank guns and mortars in the Piagge area, a thousand yards to the south. Here there was still a detachment of Germans, which had hitherto held up the advance of the 5th Wilno Brigade on the left. B Squadron returned the fire but as the situation on that flank was still obscure, the regiment was ordered not to fire on Piagge as the Wilno Brigade might be too close to it on the other side. During the night this brigade actually by-passed it and reached Monte San Giovanni.

At about 8 p.m. A Squadron was moved up to reinforce B on the objective and one company of the 17th Battalion, under command of the 7th Hussars, was brought up to protect the tanks until more infantry came to occupy the ridge. This company was not able to give protection in the broken country and the language difficulty at night created a danger of its own. One troop of A Squadron was fired on by enemy infantry with bazookas and B was subjected to a good deal of sniping. In order to avoid night skirmishing in which tanks are at a serious disadvantage and may easily be stalked, the commanding officer decided to withdraw the regiment to the next ridge. This movement was completed by midnight.

At first light on the 22nd a troop was sent to Monte San Giovanni and made contact with the infantry of the 5th Brigade, who had taken it over during the night.

During the morning the 6th Armoured Regiment passed through to assist in forming a bridgehead across the Metauro and the 7th Hussars were withdrawn to Cerasa cemetery and, later in the day, to the area allotted to the 2nd Armoured Brigade on the north bank of the River Cesano.

Farther to the east the 3rd Carpathian Division had reached the Metauro near its mouth by the evening of the 20th. During the night of the 21st/22nd the enemy withdrew across the river on the rest of the front and the Poles and Italians everywhere closed up to the south bank.

The results of the battle of the Metauro were very satisfactory. Space had been gained for the assaulting divisions to form up within measurable distance of their objectives. Severe losses had been inflicted on the enemy. The 278th German Division and 71st Division left 300 dead on the field, 270 prisoners were taken, and the former division was now so weakened that it had to be relieved by the 1st Parachute Division. The enemy had already moved this division over to the Adriatic sector, but had not intended to use it until driven back to the Gothic Line. Troops who had been earmarked as the garrison of the Gothic Line were in fact being used in delaying positions behind the Metauro, and there was consequently a reasonable chance that they might be overwhelmed before they could enjoy the advantages of their carefully prepared fortifications.

CHAPTER XIV

Round the Apennines

Autumn strategy—last operations with the Poles—preparations for the break through—first engagements round Croce—the 13th September—advance to the Marecchia—end of the Gothic Line battles.

Maps XIV, XVIII, XIX

While the Poles had been struggling up the "calf," the Eighth and Fifth Armies had fought hard in the centre and on the left for the possession of the port of Leghorn and the towns of Arezzo and Florence. The French celebrated 14th July—the storming of the Bastille in 1789—by capturing Poggibonsi, on the direct route from Siena to Florence; this was their last major action in Italy. On the 16th the Eighth Army captured Arezzo and on the 19th—the day after Ancona fell to the Poles—the Americans entered Leghorn.

Florence was a tougher proposition; while declaring it an open city, the Germans occupied successive delaying positions just to the south of it. When forced from the last of these, they withdrew at least three of their divisions through the city itself. Of the many bridges, they spared only the weak and useless Ponte Vecchio; instead of blowing it up they blocked its approaches by demolishing the ancient buildings at both ends.

The destruction of the other bridges deprived the world of several of the gems of its architecture. If the Germans had themselves respected Florence as a declared open city, the Allies might have conformed, but as the local commander could scarcely have avoided using the routes through Florence, his demolitions, though regrettable, would seem, from the purely military point of view, to have been justifiable.

Florence was entered on 4th August. Although the allied armies were not yet in contact with the main defences of the Gothic Line, they were now at last within striking distance.

Preliminary operations were still necessary on both flanks, in order to secure jumping off positions for the main assault. While the Poles on the Adriatic flank were forcing their way to the Metauro, the Fifth Army on the left crossed the Arno above Pontedera and made some headway towards Pistoia and Lucca.

General Alexander had originally hoped that his offensive operations after the fall of Rome would carry him not only up to but through the Gothic Line, in one motion, and perhaps across the Po as well. The decision about ANVIL however so reduced his forces that the impetus of the advance could not be maintained, and it soon became clear that there would have to be a pause while a full-scale attack was prepared. Partly in order to reduce the length of the pause, his first plan was for the two armies to attack side by side, in the centre of the front, where their main weight was already concentrated. They were to penetrate the Gothic Line between Dicomano and Pistoia, thrust over the Apennines to the general line Imola-Bologna-Modena, complete the destruction of the enemy south of the Po and finally to secure crossings over the river at Ferrara and if possible at Ostiglia as well.

As it now seemed unlikely that the Allies would be strong enough to exploit far beyond the Po, and as the destruction of the enemy before he could cross it had now become an integral part of the plan, the air forces were ordered to put into execution a project which had first been studied after the fall of Rome. This was the destruction of six bridges over the river.

Marshalling yards, which the Royal Air Force had often selected as targets, from the beginning of the war, had been easy to hit, and consequently attacks on them were always reported as successful; but the damage was quickly repaired and very little dislocation was caused. When this fact was eventually accepted, a new and more satisfactory system of strategical bombing was evolved. This aimed at creating lines of "interdiction."

The Po was now selected as a line of interdiction and the original plan was extended to include all the bridges over the river and in addition an important viaduct east of Genoa. Thus not only would the enemy's supply position be seriously affected, but when he was driven from the Gothic Line he would be forced back against a bridgeless river.

Between 12th and 15th July medium bombers succeeded in damaging every bridge. When the destruction was not considered adequate, attacks were continued until, by the 27th, all bridges over the Po from Torreberetti, forty miles north of Genoa, to the sea were thoroughly wrecked.

On 4th August the plan of attack of the two armies was re-cast and, as described in the previous chapter, important preliminary operations had in consequence to be carried out by the 2nd Polish Corps. Four principal factors brought about the change. First, an assault in the centre would lead through the most heavily defended part

Polish artillery crossing the Metauro, on 28th August 1944.

A tank of the 7th Hussars on the heights overlooking Pesaro, 31st August 1944.

of the Apennines; secondly the loss of the French corps had deprived the Allies of their only mountain formations; thirdly, the Eighth Army still consisted largely of troops who had fought in the desert and for whom the plains round Ravenna and the Via Emilia had a peculiar psychological attraction, and fourthly, with the capture of Ancona all the major difficulties of maintenance on the Adriatic front had melted away.

The new plan left the scope and objects of the offensive unaltered, but the direction of the main blow by the Eighth Army was changed from the centre to the extreme right. When this was well under way and the enemy, whose lateral communications were infinitely better than those of the Allies, had weakened his centre to bolster up his left, the Fifth Army was to attack up the Florence-Bologna axis.

The Fifth Army, now somewhat depleted by the withdrawal of divisions for ANVIL, was reinforced by the 13th British Corps. Each army had formations in reserve but there was no Army Group reserve under General Alexander's own hand. In a sense, however, the Fifth Army itself was a general reserve, which he would launch at the time judged by himself to be most propitious.

The change of direction involved two major feats of military gymnastics, one operational and the other administrative. The latter was the moving of the Eighth Army across the difficult mountain roads to the Adriatic Sector.

Only the 10th Corps, consisting of the 10th Indian Division and a mixed brigade composed partly of dismounted armoured car regiments (some of whom were partly re-mounted on mules and horses) was left in the mountains, linking up with 13th British Corps on the right of the Fifth Army. The move of the rest of the Eighth Army began in great secrecy on 15th August. The Canadian and the 5th Corps, by a triumph of organization, completed their move on the 21st. This was just four days before D Day, which had been fixed for the 25th. The New Zealand Corps, which was to remain in army reserve, moved a day or two later.

The other feat was the switching of enemy interest from the Adriatic to the left centre. This called for all the ingenuity of the operational staff and the deception team, which, since the conception of the original plan, had been working hard on the Adriatic and now had to put all its works into reverse.

The Fifth Army played a major part in simulating strength and the enemy was, as usual, thoroughly misled. When he discovered that there were other troops behind the Poles he believed that this was only a sign of the expected relief of the Polish Corps resulting from its heavy losses in the Ancona battles. As usual, the main offensive had been in progress for several days before the enemy Commander-in-Chief realized his mistake. On this occasion, however, he was able quickly to adjust his dispositions, as the only two points where it was reasonable for him to expect attacks were connected, on his side of the front, by short and excellent communications.

Against the enemy's total of twenty-six German divisions and two Italian in Italy, the Allies mustered twenty, with eight additional brigades. The enemy formations were fairly well up to strength, as they had received 60,000 reinforcements in the past three months.

By 23rd August the Eighth Army was poised, ready for the attack. The 2nd Polish Corps, with 3rd and 5th Divisions in the line, was on a front of about seven miles on the extreme right, along the Metauro River. Next, on a narrow front of just over two miles, covered by a screen of Polish units, was the Canadian Corps of the 1st Infantry and 5th Armoured Divisions supported by a British tank brigade. To the west, covering about twenty miles of front, was the 5th Corps, with the 46th and 4th Indian Divisions in the line, and the 1st Armoured, 4th and 56th Infantry Divisions and two armoured brigades in reserve. The weak 10th Corps was on the extreme left in the mountains and the New Zealand Corps, which was shortly to be joined by the Greek Mountain Brigade from the Middle East, was moving across the mountains to the Iesi area, in army reserve.

The plan of attack provided for an assault by three corps abreast. The Poles were to seize the high ground north-west of Pesaro; this was all they would be able to do in their present weak state, and after completion of this task they were to revert to army reserve. The Canadians in the centre were to seize the high ground west of Pesaro and from there, squeezing out the Poles, to continue their thrust through Cattolica on the main road and on to Rimini. The 5th Corps was to advance on an axis west of Rimini, directed on Bologna and Ferrara.

The attack went in an hour before midnight on the 25th and by dawn on the 26th all the five assaulting divisions were deep across the Metauro River, more or less without opposition. The Germans had been caught in the middle of a rather complicated withdrawal and regrouping movement; the 278th Division was withdrawing through the 1st Parachute Division, and was to relieve the 5th Mountain Division in the centre of the line, which in turn was to be sent to the French frontier.

The fact that the enemy was falling back voluntarily doubtless concealed from him the great weight of Eighth Army's attack, which he mistook for another follow-up attack similar to those delivered so many times by the Poles. The secret concentration of Eighth Army was a complete surprise and, as the front was still twelve miles south of the main defences, he probably expected that no formal offensive would be launched until this distance had been substantially reduced. It was not until 29th August that the commander of the LXXVIth Corps realized that a serious break-through was intended.

By the 30th elements of the Canadians and the 5th Corps had crossed the Foglia and captured the advanced positions of the Gothic Line before the enemy had time to man them. On 31st August and 1st September further advances secured a stretch of the main position twenty miles long from the coast to Monte Calvo. The works were not manned and many of the minefields were still carefully marked and set at safe. On the night of 1st September the parachutists, who had all initialled an order from Kesselring, stating that the Gothic Line was the last hope in Italy before the Brenner Pass and that they were to hold their positions for three weeks, pulled out of Pesaro and raced back behind the Conca; they thus narrowly avoided being surrounded by the Poles.

Once he realized the danger to his left, Kesselring acted quickly. On the 29th the first brigade of 26th Panzer Division, brought across from west of Empoli, was in action on the Foglia, and the rest of the division arrived soon afterwards. The 98th Division was committed on the same day. Between 4th and 6th September the 29th Panzer Grenadier Division, the last reserve, was in action; on the same day the move of the 5th Mountain Division to France was held up and some of it was sent back into the line.

By 2nd September the Canadians were over the Conca and the 5th Corps was about to pass the 1st Armoured Division through in a dash for the flat country beyond. There was, however, just one more ridge to cross. This ridge, on the summit of which stands the village of Coriano, is the last and one of the most pronounced of the spurs leading down from the Apennines to the shores of the Adriatic. Aided by his communications, Kesselring was able to man it, just in time, with three of his best divisions, 1st Parachute, 26th Panzer and 29th Panzer Grenadier. From 5th to 7th September they were aided by torrential rain, and they resisted all attacks until the 12th September, both on the ridge itself and on its southern flank at Gemmano.

Meanwhile on the rest of the front, in order to economise manpower, Kesselring drew back his diminished forces to the Gothic Line itself. This movement was carried out on a timed programme and was followed up by the 10th Corps and the Fifth Army. Lucca was occupied on the 6th and Pistoia on the 12th. During this withdrawal Kesselring moved yet another division from the centre to his left, and on the 9th it seemed that the centre had been denuded as far as it was ever likely to be. Eighth Army was temporarily stuck, and would need a few more days' preparation before its attack could be renewed. The time had in fact come for the launching of Fifth Army, and this fresh blow was timed to coincide with Eighth Army's assault on the Coriano ridge.

All Fifth Army's preparations were completed by 8th September. On the front selected for the attack the enemy was still holding the hills north of Florence and a preliminary attack on these positions was to be carried out by the 8th Indian Division. All four assaulting divisions of the United States 2nd Corps were then to pass through the British 13th Corps to carry out the main attack.

At the last moment this plan had to be slightly modified on account of the enemy's voluntary withdrawal, which was quickly followed up by the 2nd Corps. Once more the enemy commanders misjudged the situation. Just as they had failed to appreciate the weight of Eighth Army's thrust when they were withdrawing from the Metauro, so they failed at first to recognize the significance of the present blow at their centre. It was only on the 12th, when the Americans captured the strong position of Monte Calvi, that Kesselring at last understood that this was an attack not merely to gain contact with the line, but to break through it.

Eighth Army's attack on the Coriano ridge was fixed for the night of the 12th and Fifth Army was to assault the main Gothic Line positions in the centre in the early hours of 13th September.

*   *   *   *

The 7th Hussars had had no important part to play in the opening phases of the Gothic Line battles. From 22nd to 30th August the regiment remained in its shady harbour areas near the Cesano. There was plenty of time for maintenance, and bathing on the beaches near the mouth of the river was a great luxury in the exceptionally hot weather.

On 26th August the Polish Corps made up a special force for exploitation, named CAVFORCE, consisting of the Household Cavalry Regiment, B Squadron 7th Hussars, the 3rd Carpathian Lancers and the 12th Podolski Lancers. B Squadron moved forward on the 28th to join the 12th Lancers at Monte Rosario, and accompanied them the next day to San Andrea. Here the squadron remained in reserve for four days.

On the 31st, conforming with the move of the 2nd Polish Armoured Brigade, the rest of the regiment moved to a concentration area near

Carrara, just north of the Metauro. It was not however to be engaged in any further operations under the Polish Corps, and on the 2nd September, with the exception of B Squadron, the 7th Hussars passed under command, once more, of the 7th Armoured Brigade.

B Squadron remained with CAVFORCE, which was commanded by Colonel Bobinski. On the 1st September the squadron sent two

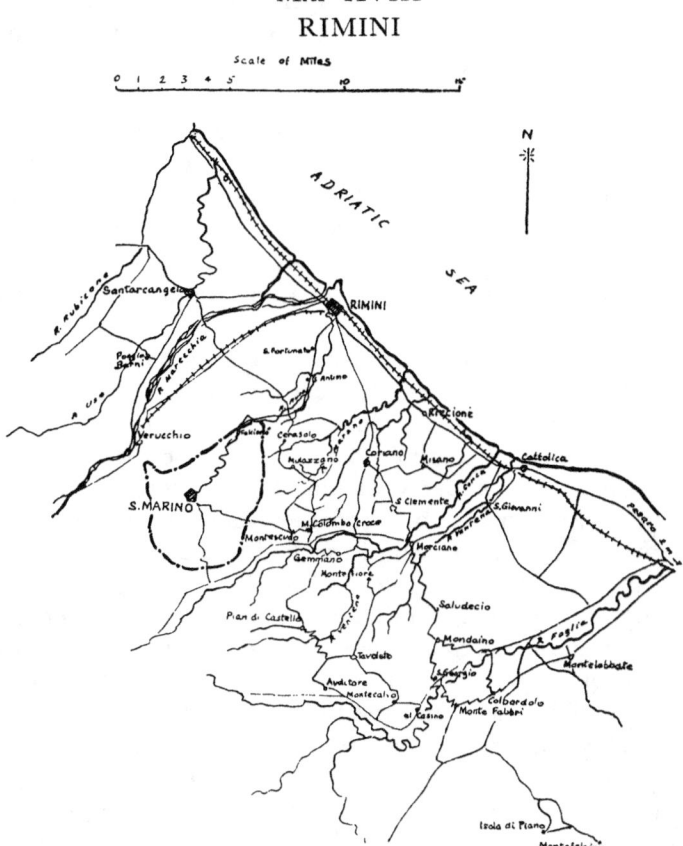

Map XVIII
RIMINI

troops forward to positions from which support could be given to patrol on the outskirts of Pesaro and along the Foglia River if the enemy should counter-attack. These troops were withdrawn at dusk and the next morning two others went out on the same task and also spent an uneventful day.

On 3rd September B Squadron took part with the 12th Podolski Lancers in their advance through the Gothic Line. The task was to clear up any enemy remaining along the Route 16 axis south of Cattolica, beyond which the Canadian Corps was to exploit across the River Conca. From San Andrea the column moved down the slope towards Pesaro, with a troop of the 12th Lancers and Lieutenant J. H. Harding's troop of B Squadron in the lead, followed closely by the Lancers' tactical headquarters.

A succession of obstacles barred the way, but these were soon overcome. The first was a deep ditch on the south side of the Pesaro-Montelabbate road. The leading troops and tactical headquarters moved into Pesaro and found a detour, and the Foglia was crossed soon after mid-day.

On the northern bank of the river was a deep mine belt; the engineers, after some searching, eventually found a lane, which the Germans had left still signposted and wired off, and the column passed safely through. An anti-tank ditch beyond the mine belt was crossed by the bridges which the enemy had left intact, and just beyond was Route 16 along which the whole column formed up at about 2 p.m., with its head at the village of Santa Maria.

The advance continued along the road. There was a check at a bridge about four miles on, when the leading Polish troop reported signs of an enemy counter-attack. Harding put his troop into position to hold the bridge, but no counter-attack developed and the only Germans discovered were a party of ten, hiding under the bridge. They were a demolition party, but had been deterred from carrying out their task by the sudden arrival of the Podolski Lancers.

The column moved forward again, and at Ponte del Colombarone, three miles short of Cattolica, the leading troop and Harding met a patrol from a Canadian reconnaissance regiment. There was now a brief interval for celebration and the exchange of hospitality, but this took only a matter of minutes, and the two leading troops, British and Polish, were quickly moving off on another job. Going back down Route 16 they were ordered to bring in some German stragglers reported in the area of Santa Marina, a village on the high ground near the coast, north of Pesaro. Harding took up a position west of the village, to give support, if necessary, to the troop of Lancers. The latter moved in and rounded up the Germans.

Harding then returned to B Squadron, now about two miles east of where he had met the Canadians. A number of German stragglers kept coming in to give themselves up, but otherwise the squadron had an undisturbed night.

Next day the 12th Podolski Lancers and B Squadron moved back to Rosciano, two miles south-west of Fano. The Poles had completed their task and were now being withdrawn into army reserve in the Fano area.

B Squadron was expecting to rejoin the regiment, but in the evening orders were received to stay at Rosciano and await instructions from Eighth Army. These arrived next day. On 6th September the Squadron handed over its Shermans to the 5th Canadian Armoured Brigade and its Stuarts to the Forward Delivery Squadron. On the 7th it started on a long march over the mountains, to join the 3rd Hussars for training with DD (amphibious) tanks at Lake Bracciano, near Rome.

* * * *

While B Squadron was taking part in the final phases of the Polish corps' operations, the rest of the 7th Hussars were involved in the preparations for a pursuit into the Po valley.

At 8 a.m. on 2nd September Lieutenant-Colonel Jayne and Major Congreve left Carrara for the headquarters of 5th Corps. The 7th Hussars, now consisting of only two squadrons, marched at 1 p.m. to join the 7th Armoured Brigade. The route led by steep and narrow roads over many ridges and ravines and in the evening the regiment reached its harbour area south-west of Monte Fabbri.

The 7th Armoured Brigade, under Brigadier O. L. Prior-Palmer, was being organized as a pursuit force of all arms; its task was the protection of the left of 1st Armoured Division, which was to debouch across the Foglia River into the plains north of the Marecchia.

It had been expected that the pursuit would begin on the morning of the 3rd. This however proved to be an over-optimistic forecast. The enemy were still holding Tavoleto and Auditore in strength. These two little mountain towns, although six miles away, had a commanding view of the western slopes of the Monte Fabbri feature, where the 7th Hussars were in harbour. Even if it had been realized that there was any danger, movement in the harbour area was restricted by a heavy downpour in the early hours of the morning.

Shortly before 1 o'clock men of headquarters and the two squadrons assembled round their respective cooks' lorries for dinners. These had just started when the Germans opened up with their artillery on the whole area. One man of regimental headquarters was killed and another wounded. A Squadron suffered the most severely. Lieutenant R. S. Dale Harris was killed. The squadron leader, Major A. E. White, and second-in-command, Captain M. M. Stanley Evans, and seven other ranks were wounded, Major White severely. Stanley Evans had to be evacuated because he was temporarily unable to sit, but he lost no time and was back in a week. Major White was a great loss to the 7th Hussars. He had joined in the desert and distinguished himself in all the subsequent actions of the regiment.

C Squadron and B Echelon were farther from the road and did not come under fire, but when the shelling died down all the regiment moved out of sight behind the hill. A further outbreak of shelling in the afternoon caused no damage to the 7th Hussars, but the 2nd Royal Tanks, who had also been shelled in the morning, had several more casualties.

During the day a reconnaissance was carried out to the crossing of the Foglia at the ford south of San Georgio, a small hamlet two miles east of Monte Calvo. At dusk the regiment joined the 7th Armoured Brigade column, which crossed the river, turned left at San Georgio and harboured for the night at El Casino, two miles farther to the south, tucked away in the deep Foglia valley, and comfortably under the lee of the Monte Calvo.

The 4th was spent at El Casino, at three hours' notice to move. At 7.30 p.m. the Commanding Officer attended a conference at which the brigade commander gave orders for a move forward to a concentration area near the Marano, which is the next river north of the Conca, beyond the Coriano ridge.

The enemy were still holding the Tavoleto ridge; this runs north and south between two rivers, both of which are called the Ventena, that lying to the west being a tributary of the Conca and the other a river in its own right, running into the sea near Cattolica. The ridge was to be attacked by the 4th Indian Division during the night. Farther to the right the enemy was thought to be withdrawing on the front of the 56th Division, and the 167th Brigade was to cross the Conca and march by night to the Marano, which it was to reach at dawn.

The 7th Armoured Brigade, less the 6th Royal Tanks and a squadron of each of the other two, the 2nd and 8th Royal Tanks, was to move by two routes to the Marano, starting at 4 a.m. on the 5th. A Squadron 7th Hussars was placed under 2nd Royal Tanks on the right, C Squadron under the 8th, on the left. The rest of the brigade was to follow the 2nd Royal Tanks.

The progress of the infantry during the night was disappointing and, in the early hours of the 5th, the move of the 7th Armoured Brigade was postponed. At 6 a.m. units were put at one hour's notice.

The concentration area given in the orders of the previous evening proved to be well behind the enemy's lines, so the move, when it happened, was necessarily a short one. At 10.15 a.m. the column set off along the main road to the San Georgio cross-roads and then up the long, winding road to Mondaino, on the line of hills which dominates the Foglia valley from the north. From Mondaino the road descended the more gradual northern slopes through Saludecio to the more eastern of the Ventena Streams. The two regimental groups halted on the western bank while the brigade and the 7th Hussars' headquarters harboured east of the stream.

At 7 p.m. on the 5th Brigadier Prior-Palmer gave out his orders for the following day. The 168th Brigade were now in process of attacking San Savino, and the 168th and 169th Brigades were to advance towards the River Marano during the night. The intention of the 56th Division commander was to advance on the 6th with the 7th Armoured Brigade group in the lead. The specific task of the brigade was to seize the crossings over the River Uso between Santarcangelo and Poggio Berni. The composition of the right and left columns remained as it was, but each column was given in addition one infantry battalion, one field regiment and one field company Royal Engineers; an Air Support Control Tentacle was allotted to the brigade.

The essential condition before the advance could begin was that San Savino and Croce should be captured. At 3 a.m. the attacking infantry reported that they had taken both, and that a few pockets still holding out would be cleared by dawn. Shortly afterwards the advance of the 7th Armoured Brigade group was fixed for 6 a.m.

At 6 a.m. on the 6th the advance began. Leaving the harbour areas on the Ventena, the brigade passed through Morciano, where it crossed the Conca by the bridge which the Germans had surprisingly left intact, and thence westwards by two parallel routes just north of the river.

The 2nd Royal Tanks, moving along the ridge, soon discovered that Croce and San Savino were again in enemy hands.

The enemy's forward positions had been correctly located by the infantry with their patrols and during their attacks of the last two days and nights. It was also correctly appreciated that he had no considerable number of anti-tank weapons, tanks or mines. There had however been a false reckoning of his intentions and, not for the first time in the Italian campaigns, the formations built up and designed for exploitation found themselves fighting the break-in battle instead.

The Germans, having withdrawn under pressure from Tavoleto and Auditore, were now established on a line running from the sea at the mouth of the Marano, along the river for about three miles, then southwards along the steep and narrow Coriano ridge to la Croce, high above the Conca valley. South of the latter river, they held the ridge on which stand Gemmano and Pian di Castello. The tiny mountain republic of San Marino lay three or four miles to the west of the German flank. The natural strength of the position and the determination of the defenders made up for their shortage of mines, tanks, bazookas and anti-tank guns.

The German command in Italy was now fully conscious of the threat to its left. In view of the rapid progress of the Allies through southern France, the eastern flank in Italy had assumed an even greater importance. If they were driven off the Apennines, the Germans would have to withdraw north-eastwards, pivotting on their left. Every effort had therefore to be made to hold Rimini and to prevent the Eighth Army debouching into the Emilian plain. The battle which had just begun was consequently one of the most fiercely contested in the whole war and resulted in considerable casualties on both sides.

*   *   *   *

By the time the 7th Armoured Brigade crossed the Conca it was clear that there was no immediate prospect of a rapid exploitation to the Marecchia. The immediate and pressing problem was how to deal with the enemy on the Coriano ridge.

On hearing that San Savino and Croce were still in German hands, the brigade commander ordered both the 2nd and 8th Royal Tanks to deploy, to make contact with the leading infantry and to reconnoitre forward.

On the immediate right of the 56th Division was the 1st Armoured Division. The 2nd Royal Tanks now made contact with Shermans of the 2nd Armoured Brigade, of the 1st Armoured Division, who were about to deal with San Savino. At about 9.30 the 2nd Tanks and the 167th Brigade reached Croce, and by noon it was reported clear of the enemy.

The Germans had excellent observation down the Conca Valley from Monte Colombo and Gemmano, and movement along the roads on the north bank always drew fire. Fortunately an Italian civilian reported the position of three troops of 88-millimetre guns, south-west of Gemmano. These were engaged at intervals by the artillery with the 7th Armoured Brigade and to some extent neutralized.

At about noon shelling and mortaring were particularly heavy. In A Squadron Lieutenant S. W. Agnew was wounded and shortly afterwards the squadron was moved a few hundred yards, to an area which afforded better concealment. C Squadron, which was farther forward, was under shell fire for much of the day, but the crews remained in their tanks and there were no casualties.

At 1 o'clock the enemy delivered a strong counter-attack on the

San Savino-Croce ridge. This was repulsed and the enemy lost heavily. Fighting went on all the afternoon, but no further counter-attack developed until after dark, when the armoured units had been drawn back. Both A and C Squadrons of the 7th Hussars had been in reserve all day.

There was heavy rain during the night and in the morning the ground was very difficult for tanks. Nevertheless 7th September was another day of hard fighting on both banks of the Conca, the 56th Division still endeavouring to force its way up both sides of the valley. A and C Squadrons had a quiet day still in reserve, but both the 2nd and 8th Royal Tanks were continually in action.

At 7.40 a.m. the 2nd Tanks reported that the enemy were back in Croce, this time with at least three self-propelled guns. Two hours later the infantry recaptured Il Palazzo, and a troop of tanks was sent up to support them.

The 56th Division's plan for the day was to attack Croce with the 168th Brigade supported by the 2nd Tanks, and Gemmano with the 167th Brigade supported by half a squadron of the 8th Tanks. The capture of both was to be completed by 5 p.m. and the 169th Brigade was later to take Monte Colombo, supported by the remainder of the 8th Tanks.

Croce was re-taken by 5 p.m.; casualties were heavy, and the losses of the 2nd Tanks included one squadron leader killed. Gemmano was not taken until 8.30, and the attack on Monte Colombo had of necessity to be postponed.

During the night the enemy succeeded in penetrating the positions of the infantry holding Croce and Il Palazzo, but were driven out again. On the other side of the river fighting continued in Gemmano, which the Germans re-occupied.

On the 8th there was another counter-attack on Croce. This was beaten off after heavy fighting, in which the 2nd Tanks knocked out one S.P. gun but themselves lost four Shermans. The enemy showed every intention of recovering Croce and fighting and shelling went on all day, both the armoured regiments being involved.

In this battle the 2nd Tanks had lost especially heavily. They had fought with the same gallantry and dash for which they had been conspicuous in all their engagements, ever since Sidi Barrani. Although they were now to be relieved, they were only to have a very temporary respite.

At 3 p.m. A and C Squadrons reverted to regimental control and the 7th Hussars were ordered to take over from the elements of the other two regiments in the Croce and Il Palazzo area. Two troops of the

330th Anti-Tank Battery of the 93rd Anti-Tank Regiment were placed under command.

After dark the regiment moved forward and both squadrons were in position by 11 p.m. A Squadron harboured at Casa Ramondo and C at Il Trebbio. At the same time the 167th Brigade, which had been operating astride the Conca, was withdrawn into reserve. The 168th Brigade became responsible for the front north of the river and the 169th (Queen's) south of it, in the Gemmano area.

Shortly before dawn on the 9th the 1st Battalion, The Welch Regiment, which had taken over Croce during the night, sent a company forward to Casa Menghino, a farmhouse on a rise half a mile west of Croce. Farther to the right the 1st Battalion, The London Scottish, sent a company forward to occupy Il Palazzo, about a quarter of a mile north of Casa Menghino. C Squadron was ordered to support these companies, each with one troop, and two troops were accordingly sent forward from Croce.

The two troops had nearly reached Casa Menghino and Il Palazzo when they were unaccountably ordered to come back to Croce, and to take up a position on the ridge running northwards from Il Trebbio to Point 168.

The decision to withdraw the two troops of C Squadron proved to be unfortunate. At about 10 o'clock the enemy counter-attacked Casa Menghino and succeeded in driving back the company of 1st Welch into Croce. This thrust also threatened the rear of the company of London Scottish at Il Palazzo, which was now practically surrounded. The London Scottish asked for tank support, to enable the company to disengage and withdraw to their main position on the Point 168 ridge.

C Squadron were accordingly ordered to send two troops forward to help, moving by the Croce-Casa Menghino road; no other line of approach was possible, as the slopes on the direct line from Croce to Il Palazzo were too steep.

The first troop debouched from the village, and Lieutenant J. S. H. Skrine, in the leading Sherman, was just descending the steep bank on to the road when an enemy tank in Casa Menghino opened fire. Rather than reverse back up the slope into the cover of the village Skrine turned sharp left, downhill. Passing rapidly through some startled German infantry in position on the slopes below Croce, he reached the road along the River Conca at Molino Vanni and then turned north to rejoin C Squadron on the Trebbio ridge. The attempt to relieve the infantry at Il Palazzo by a sortie from Croce was then abandoned.

C Squadron's third and last action of the day was a demonstration. Four tanks were sent forward to the crest of the ridge north of Point 168 so that they might draw fire and make the enemy reveal his anti-tank defences. The enemy however would not play his part in the game and the tanks were withdrawn.

A Squadron spent most of the day in Croce, with two troops in support of the infantry holding the village. They had three tanks damaged by shell fire, which was at times heavy, but there were only two slight casualties, both of whom remained at duty. The three tanks were recovered, the damage in all cases being cast or broken tracks.

A Squadron took no active part in the fighting until an hour before dusk. The enemy's comparative quietness since the early afternoon suggested that he might have withdrawn, and it was therefore decided to attempt to re-occupy the Casa Menghino area with C Company of the 1st Welch, supported by two troops of A Squadron. The attack was quickly successful and the objective was gained against only slight opposition, chiefly from mortars.

After dark both squadrons withdrew to harbour behind the positions, A Squadron in the re-entrant between Casa Ramondo and Cevolabbate and C behind the San Savino-Trebbio ridge.

Sunday 10th September brought a lull in the fighting. Before dawn both battalions drew back their forward companies. The London Scottish company at Il Palazzo had had severe casualties. The enemy made no attempt to retake Il Palazzo or Casa Menghino, and the latter was re-occupied by a company of the Welch during the afternoon. One troop of A Squadron stood by to support the infantry at Croce, but the day passed without incident.

On the 11th the enemy re-occupied Il Palazzo, but did nothing about Casa Menghino, where the Welch remained in their positions. A Squadron again sent a troop to support the infantry at Croce; two enemy tanks which approached Croce during the afternoon were set on fire by the artillery before they came within range of the Shermans' 75's.

C Squadron spent the day in harbour. One troop was sent up to the Point 168 ridge to engage some enemy infantry reported to be in caves near Il Palazzo. At nightfall another troop was sent up to relieve a squadron of the 9th Lancers, which was in support of infantry on a small hill overlooking San Savino from the south. The enemy held the western slopes of the hill along the line of the road and also San Savino itself.

There had been some shelling during the day, but no serious fighting.

During the night the 169th (Queen's) Brigade, which had handed over the Gemmano sector, south of the Conca, to the 138th Brigade of the 46th Division, relieved the 168th Brigade in the Croce area.

The 12th was another quiet day and the enemy still kept at a distance. At first light Major Fox sent a second troop of C Squadron up to the hill overlooking San Savino and a third was kept in readiness in the harbour area at the Sorgenti Minerali. Although the two troops in observation had an uninterrupted view over the enemy's positions from San Savino to Passano, no movement could be seen.

A Squadron sent one troop to the Trebbio area, to support the infantry at Croce, but here also everything was quiet except for occasional harassing fire from the enemy artillery. The squadron headquarters came under mortar fire once during the morning, and was fortunate in having only one man wounded.

During the afternoon the Commanding Officer attended an "order group" conference at the headquarters of the 169th Infantry Brigade (Brigadier Smith-Dorrien). At this conference orders were given out for an attack which was to take place the following morning. This marked the resumption of the offensive by the Eighth Army, synchronized with the opening of the Fifth Army's assault on the Gothic Line in the centre.

*   *   *   *

The conference at the headquarters of the 169th Brigade on 12th September was assembled in the middle of the afternoon. If all had gone well it might have ended in time to allow for adequate reconnaissances to be carried out. Unfortunately, however, the brigade commander was summoned to the telephone more than once for prolonged conversations with divisional headquarters. Not only did these interruptions tend to confuse the issue of orders, but they prolonged the conference until it was nearly dark and there was not time for reconnaissance at all. This probably accounted for some of the mistakes and misunderstandings which marred the co-operation between the 7th Hussars and the infantry on the following day.

The Eighth Army was to attack all along the front. On the 5th Corps sector, with which we are concerned, the 1st Armoured Division was to attack on the right of the 56th and the 46th Division on the left. The 1st Armoured Division was to capture the San Savino-Passano ridge. The 46th was to complete the occupation of the Gemmano feature and then, crossing the Conca, to seize Montescudo and Monte Colombo.

Between these two divisions the 56th Division's assault was to be carried out by the 169th Infantry Brigade, supported by two regiments of the 7th Armoured Brigade. On the right the 2nd/6th Queens, supported by the 2nd Royal Tanks, were to clear the Fabbri ridge from Il Palazzo, their starting point, to La Serra. On the left the 2nd/5th Queens, with C Squadron 7th Hussars under command, were to advance from Casa Menghino to capture the ridge, half a mile farther west, running northwards from Casa di San Marco.

C Squadron (Major Fox), with eleven Shermans, was to move forward shortly before dawn to Casa Menghino and was to support the 2nd/5th Queens from there to Casa di San Marco. A Squadron (Major M. M. Stanley Evans), under regimental command, with eight Shermans, was to provide supporting fire from Croce, in close co-operation with a forward observation officer of the 15th Field Regiment. In the interests of secrecy, there was to be no move before an hour after last light. Zero was to be at the first streak of dawn.

In order to reach Casa Menghino in time, C Squadron left its harbour area at 4.30 a.m. and moved up to Croce by the narrow track from Il Trebbio. Squadron Sergeant-Major P. Cleere's troop was in the lead, with Sergeant Aitchison's tank in front. The first three troops, six Shermans in all, went on through the village and were about half-way to the cemetery, in line ahead along the road, when a number of Spandaus opened fire in their direction. As it was still completely dark, the squadron halted, headquarters and the reserve troop remaining at Croce and the three leading troops where they were on the road.

An officer of the Queen's now came up to Cleere and told him that his own company's forward positions were only a hundred yards ahead, and the Germans only a hundred yards beyond that; he also asked Cleere if he could stop the 2nd Tanks, to the right rear, from firing into his company. This message was passed back, but whether it was the 2nd Tanks or another battalion of the Queens is by no means certain.

A Squadron had meanwhile moved up by a track from Trebbio cross-roads which makes a wide sweep to the south before entering Croce. Near Croce one of A's troops was fired on by bazookas or "Faustpatrones," but these cannot have been within effective range, as one projectile struck a tank without damaging it.

Enemy infantry had evidently penetrated during the night in several unexpected places in the Croce area, and it was clear that some modification of the plan would be necessary. In particular, there was no possibility of the tanks and infantry being ready and together on the stipulated start-line by dawn, and it was uncertain whether the infantry were even in possession of the start-line at all. In fact they were not.

Major M. M. Stanley Evans, now in command of A Squadron, remained at Croce, where his observation post was established with the artillery officer, and ordered his two troops back to Trebbio, where he meant them to wait until the situation was cleared up.

C Squadron remained where it was until daylight, when the two leading troops moved forward, this time without the spandau fire, to help the infantry in clearing Casa Menghino. This took a considerable time. Eventually, by about 8 o'clock, a good many prisoners had been taken and all opposition in the area eliminated, so the rest of C Squadron moved up to the position from which the attack was to have started at first light.

Enemy infantry could still be seen retiring across the re-entrant separating Casa Menghino from Casiccio, half a mile away. The Queens however were not ready to follow up immediately and the enemy were able to escape.

Two of C Squadron's tanks had been bogged, in the semi-darkness, between Croce and Casa Menghino and a third had developed engine trouble. This left the squadron with only eight serviceable tanks, of which the headquarters required its own two and the others were in three troops; one troop of three under Captain G. O. Williams, one of two under Lieutenant J. B. Dunlop and the third, of one tank only, Squadron Sergeant-Major P. Cleere, D.C.M.

At 9 o'clock the squadron was formed up on the starting line and waiting for the infantry. It was then told that the infantry were already advancing to attack. There was no sign of any such advance but C Squadron was nevertheless ordered to advance on its objective, the Casa di San Marco.

Dunlop's troop led, followed by Williams', and then Cleere. At the head of the re-entrant which divides Casa Menghino from Casiccio, Dunlop came upon a number of German infantry, dug in and well concealed among the scrubby bushes on the slope. There was no sign of the Queens and evidently, if they had advanced at all, it was not in this direction.

C Squadron's troops then set to work, seeking out and clearing up the enemy's positions. For a time the tanks had all their own way. Some of the enemy had bazookas. These resisted for a time, and one fired three shots at Cleere's tank, all of which missed. His machine gun jammed and, as the 75-mm. could not depress enough to engage the man with the bazooka Cleere shot him from the turret with his Thompson sub-machine gun.

It was a misfortune that no infantry came forward to help. Some of the prisoners were sent back escorted by a tank from Captain Williams' troop. More were sent back with S.S.M. Cleere, some of them carried on his tank, when he was sent to fetch up more ammunition. Others undoubtedly slipped away in the scrub and made their way back beyond the ridge. But of greater importance still was the opportunity of gaining the Casa di San Marco ridge while the enemy were still disorganized and while it was not apparently held in much strength. The objective was only a few hundred yards beyond the area where C Squadron was mopping up the enemy defended locality, but the infantry did not come, and the fleeting chance was passing.

After an hour or so in the area, the four tanks suddenly came under heavy fire from anti-tank guns which the Germans had moved up on to the San Marco ridge. The squadron leader asked for artillery support, to cover the withdrawal of the tanks to Casa Menghino, but for some reason only a few rounds were fired at the enemy guns.

Three of the tanks were quickly knocked out. Captain Williams' was penetrated the moment it began to move back. He was severely wounded and his gunner and operator, the former the brother of S.S.M. Cleere, were both killed.

Seeing his troop leader's tank knocked out, Sergeant E. Carpenter dismounted from his tank and ran over to find out the damage. The driver had succeeded in helping Captain Williams out of the turret and down to the ground, before setting off to fetch help. Carpenter then dragged Williams, who was too heavy to be carried by one man, to the shelter of a house near the road, and went back to his own tank to fetch another man to help. At the same time he ordered his own tank back to Menghino with the rest of the crew. On the way it was knocked out by a round through the engine; the lap gunner was killed and the other two were wounded.

The two wounded men were picked up by Lieutenant Dunlop, who put them on to his tank. He sent this back to squadron headquarters to report the situation, while he himself set out on foot to look for his other tank, which had reported that it was stuck. After searching for it for some time without success, he returned to his squadron headquarters at Casa Menghino.

Here he was met with the news that his own tank also had been knocked out on its way back, and the crew were not sure which way they should go to reach squadron headquarters. Dunlop therefore set off again on foot, to find the crew of his own tank. This was on the southern side of the ridge, two or three hundred yards below the cemetery. The enemy was now in occupation of the lower slopes and

Lieutenant Dunlop fell, severely wounded by a sniper's bullet, as he approached the tank.

Lieutenant Skrine then took out the C Squadron ambulance Stuart and brought in Dunlop, who died later in hospital, and the crew of his tank. Williams was brought in by A Squadron's ambulance Stuart, under cover of a smoke screen laid down by A Squadron and the artillery.

The crew of the fourth tank had at first to be posted as missing, except the lap gunner, who found his way back to the squadron on foot. The tank was in fact bogged, and then knocked out, on the south side of the road, whereas Dunlop had looked for it on the north side. All the other four members of the crew had been killed.

While C Squadron was carrying out this expensive withdrawal, A Squadron moved up to support the infantry holding the ridge between Il Palazzo and Casa Menghino. Here they remained all day. The enemy made no counter-attack, and it was estimated that he was already thinning out, before withdrawing that night to positions behind the Marano.

At nightfall A Squadron withdrew two hundred yards, to harbour just north of the cemetery. C Squadron handed over their four remaining Shermans to A Squadron crews and then went back, with their Stuarts, to join B Echelon at the Ventena.

The 7th Hussars' tactical headquarters had moved up to Croce in the early morning. Soon afterwards it was ordered by the brigade commander to move back to the Casa Ramondo, where it would be close to his own headquarters. Lieutenant-Colonel Jayne was, in fact, acting as tank adviser to the brigadier.

The northern slopes of the Conca Valley were fully exposed to the enemy on the Gemmano feature and every movement in the Croce-Casa Ramondo area drew fire. In these circumstances the exercise of command was exceedingly difficult. Early in the day the lack of co-ordination was felt among the forward troops; and it was particularly unfortunate that the brigade commander, who alone could have established control of the battle, was killed in one of the first outbursts of shelling. Thereafter the prevailing uncertainty was aggravated, and there was a conspicuous absence of personal intervention by higher formations.

On the right flank things had gone much better. The 2nd Royal Tanks advanced at the appointed hour, San Savino, on their right flank, being masked with smoke. By 7.45 the leading squadron was on the Fabbri ridge, busy mopping up enemy posts and trying to dispose of the many prisoners, who were eagerly surrendering. The 2nd/6th Queens were coming up the ridge, having been checked two or three times by pockets of Germans by-passed by the tanks. Half an hour later the infantry were firmly established on the objective and three hundred prisoners had been taken.

In spite of this success, however, no immediate exploitation was possible, as the enemy still had positions in the valley beyond the Fabbri ridge, of which the forward slopes were very open. Movement forward over the ridge at once drew shell fire, and the infantry and tanks made no further advance.

For the 7th Hussars 13th September had been a day of sharply contrasted success and disappointment. A number of the enemy had been killed and still more had surrendered, but it was nevertheless impossible to look back on the day's achievements—and losses—with satisfaction.

* * * *

During the night of 13th/14th September the 168th Brigade took over from the 169th, and the 8th Royal Tanks took over from the 2nd. The plan for the 14th was to renew the attacks; the 1st London Scottish and 8th Tanks were to take the Sensoli ridge; the 1st Welch and 7th Hussars were to take Casiccio and exploit to Monte Colombo.

During the four hours before first light the enemy brought down very heavy shell fire on the Casa Menghino area, doubtless to cover his disengagement. A Squadron were sleeping in their tanks, as a precaution, and the only casualties were the two sentries who were outside when the shelling began; both were slightly wounded.

At first light the two troops went forward again to support the infantry on the Palazzo-Menghino position. The 1st Welch however had already followed up the enemy's withdrawal and one company had taken Casa di San Marco without much opposition. Lieutenant G. J. Iles' troop was sent off to support this company, while Lieutenant J. E. Parry's remained at Menghino to give covering fire if required.

Advancing on the south side of the road, Iles' leading tank was almost immediately fired on from the direction of Monte Colombo and had its track broken. None of the crew were injured and all made their way back to squadron headquarters on foot. The other two Shermans then crossed over to the northern side of the ridge, where the going was much more difficult and whence it was impossible to see the point they were making for. From Parry's position at Menghino however he could see both Iles' troop and their objective, and he was able to direct them to the Casa di San Marco by wireless. It had nevertheless taken Iles the best part of an hour to reach his destination, where he joined up with the infantry.

At about this time Lieutenants E. C. F. Harding and P. J. Howard-Dobson arrived at A Squadron's headquarters, bringing up the four surviving tanks of C Squadron, now transferred to A, and one replacement tank from the light aid detachment. Harding was sent straight on to San Marco, taking with him some ammunition for infantry.

Meanwhile the 1st Welch, after Iles' arrival at San Marco, moved on northwards towards Casiccio. They were soon held up by machine gun fire coming from the southern end of the village. The houses where these spandaus were in position were engaged by Iles' two tanks and the infantry then had no difficulty in occupying the village. A number of dead Germans were found in the houses which had been shelled and several prisoners were taken.

Iles' troop then moved a few hundred yards north, to take up a position of observation in the Casiccio area, while Harding's troop, which had just arrived at San Marco, took over observation on the left flank towards Montescudo and Monte Colombo. Both troops spent the rest of the day in observation and ready to support the 1st Welch, who were consolidating.

At about 11 o'clock a German "Panther" was seen moving off westwards from Monte Colombo. A battery of Nebelwerfers was also observed in action near the top of Monte Olivo, and two hours later was engaged by the artillery and Kitty-bombers. This battery was shooting into the Rio di Valiano valley, between Casiccio and the Chiesa Nuova—Monte Tauro ridge, presumably providing defensive fire for the enemy screen on that ridge.

To the right of the 1st Welch the 167th Brigade, supported by the 8th Royal Tanks, had also made satisfactory progress. Advancing from the Fabbri ridge, which had been captured the previous day, they drove back the enemy's screen on the Chiesa Nuova—Monte Tauro ridge. By last light the Marano had been reached on the whole front as far inland as the area of Trarivi. The enemy however continued to hold Montescudo until after nightfall and Trarivi for a further thirty-six hours.

At about 8 p.m. A Squadron was withdrawn and began to march back to Ventena, where the regiment was concentrated in reserve. Except B Squadron, at Lake Bracciano, the whole regiment was again together, including B Echelon and the light aid detachment. Consequently it was possible, during the 15th, to carry out a much needed refit and reorganization.

The battle continued unabated on the 15th. On the right the Canadians were well across the Marano and they entered San Lorenzo. The 4th Division captured San Patrignano. The 1st Armoured

Division seized La Tomba and Point 186. On the left the 46th Division took the Montescudo—Trarivi ridge, but the enemy managed to hold Point 475, the hill overlooking Montescudo from the west, and also Trarivi village.

The next operation was to be a night attack on the front of the 56th Division, in which the 167th Brigade, supported by the 2nd Royal Tanks, was to capture the Mulazzano feature.

The Mulazzano ridge was not entirely in the hands of the 167th Brigade until the afternoon of the 16th. Meanwhile the 7th Hussars had been ordered forward to Ajello, a mile east of San Savino, where they arrived, still in reserve, at 5 p.m.

On the 17th the 167th Brigade were to continue their attacks, the objective being the Cerasolo ridge. A battalion of the 168th Brigade was to secure their left flank by seizing Monte Olivo.

On this day the 7th Hussars again moved forward, first into the next valley to the west, between San Savino and the Fabbri ridge, then immediately on again, by the 56th Division axis, to la Colombarina, on the eastern side of the ridge overlooking the Marano at Chiesa Nuova.

The enemy were still, at this time, holding Point 475 above Montescudo, and Trarivi, and thus denied to the 56th Division the only main road leading to the Marano in this sector. The divisional "axis" was therefore a series of narrow, steep, and tortuous lanes which were not wide enough for vehicles to pass one another except at rare intervals, and yet the route had to carry both the "up" and the "down" traffic. One of the passing places was the short stretch of the Coriano-Trarivi road at Casa Belina, but there was only half a mile of this luxury before the route turned off into another lane, across the Valiano stream and up the steep hill to Colombarina.

It was late in the afternoon of the 17th when the regiment reached its harbour, and the commanding officer was then given his orders. During the night the 168th Brigade, with the 7th Hussars in support, was to relieve the 167th Brigade on the Cerasolo ridge.

A Squadron (Stanley Evans) was chosen to take over from the squadron of the 2nd Royal Tanks on the Cerasolo ridge. Two troops, each of four Shermans, were sent forward at once to the Mulazzano ridge, so as to be able to move up quickly to join the infantry at daybreak. A Squadron headquarters joined the combined 168th Brigade and tactical 7th Armoured Brigade headquarters, five hundred yards east of Chiesa Nuova. Regimental headquarters and C Squadron remained at La Colombarina.

Before first light on 18th September the two advanced troops moved up to join their respective battalions, Lieutenant Howard-Dobson to the London Scottish on the Cerasolo ridge near the cemetery, Lieutenant Iles to the 1st Welch on Monte Olivo. Squadron and regimental headquarters moved up with headquarters of the 168th Brigade to Casa Ferri, on the southern side of the Mulazzano ridge.

One of Howard-Dobson's tanks had engine trouble, so he was left with only three. With these he arrived in time to help the London Scottish in the first of their operations. While it was still dark they had sent a company forward with orders to cross the Ausa stream and secure Casa Tramontana on the far side. At first light this company reported that it was being fired on by a spandau in its rear, somewhere about Casa Marago. This was on the northern slopes of the Cerasolo ridge and only a few hundred yards in front of Howard-Dobson's troop. He accordingly searched for the post, found it and helped another company of the battalion to clear it up. A dozen prisoners were taken, with an under-officer. About the same time other Germans were seen away to the left, making their way down into the valley of the Ausa.

The leading company of the London Scottish had now taken up a position in the deep ditch known as the Fosso l'Ausello, a few hundred yards short of the Ausa, and Howard-Dobson moved forward to Casa Battaglini, where an isolated knoll afforded the only cover north of the Cerasolo ridge. Here he remained in observation for six hours, but the only movement he saw was the arrival of some Churchill tanks at San Antimo, to the right, on the north bank of the Ausa.

At about 3 p.m. the company in the Ausello ditch was ordered to cross the Ausa towards Monte dell'Arboreta. Before they moved forward, Howard-Dobson shelled likely German positions, including Casa dell'Ospedale on Route 72, the main road lying between the London Scottish and the stream. As the infantry advanced, a number of Germans came out of the houses in this area and gave themselves up.

The infantry crossed the Ausa under mortar and machine gun fire, and secured a bridgehead up the slope beyond. Howard-Dobson at once went forward to reconnoitre positions from which to support them against a counter-attack, and possible crossing places over the river. He found a crossing place, but there was no suitable supporting position in the bed of the stream, and if he had crossed and placed his troop among the forward localities, the tanks would have been very exposed and would undoubtedly have drawn artillery fire on the infantry. Consequently he moved his troop back to a position near Battaglini.

His tanks were scarcely in position when down came the enemy's artillery fire. He therefore withdrew his troop to the Cerasolo ridge, from which he could cover the infantry without exposing his tanks. Towards nightfall the Commanding Officer of the London Scottish came to him and thanked him for his work during the day, told him to go behind the Mulazzano ridge to harbour for the night, and be back in the morning by 5 o'clock.

Lieutenant Iles, farther to the left, had a less eventful day, spent in observation, in a hull-down position on the northern side of Monte Olivo. He too was drawn back at nightfall, to harbour half way between Monte Olivo and Mulazzano.

The 19th September was the last day of fighting for the 7th Hussars in this battle. At first light the same two troops went back to their positions of the previous evening and made contact with their respective battalions. Both had advanced their leading companies during the night. The London Scottish had moved out of their bridgehead across the Ausa at Il Benefizio and seized the Casa Tramontana ridge. Their leading company was counter-attacked at first light, and Howard-Dobson was sent forward straight away, crossing the Ausa at the point he had reconnoitred the previous day.

He arrived at Il Benefizio at about 6 a.m. and found a squadron of the 8th Tanks which was advancing northwards towards the enemy's main position, which lay along the ridge from Ceriano to San Fortunato and Rimini. Moving forward from ridge to ridge and shelling all likely German positions before each bound, this squadron reached the Casa Tramontana ridge at about 8 o'clock. Howard-Dobson followed it up to this point and then left his troop behind the ridge while he went forward on foot to find the company commander of the London Scottish at Point 150. The company had beaten off the counter-attack and the company commander was satisfied that he was firmly established. In consequence the troop of 7th Hussars remained out of sight behind the ridge, in order not to draw artillery fire on to the infantry.

At about 10 o'clock the 1st London Irish Rifles, between Casa Tramontana ridge and the Fosso Baricello, reported that they expected a counter-attack. Howard-Dobson's troop was at once ordered to move across to support them. No counter-attack developed, but the troop was able to deal with a very troublesome spandau in a house at Point 100. While Howard-Dobson engaged this at a range of five hundred yards over the heads of the London Irish Rifles, Iles took it on from Falciano at a range of 1100. The Germans abandoned their position and withdrew up the hill under a brisk fire from both tanks and infantry.

Iles had one more shoot, at an enemy post in a house east of the chapel at Marignano, during the afternoon. Apart from this there was no further activity and both troops were withdrawn at nightfall. A Squadron then rejoined the regimental headquarters and C Squadron at Casa Ferri, south-east of Mulazzano, where they had moved during the afternoon.

The regiment had already been informed that at the conclusion of the present operations it would follow B Squadron to Lake Bracciano for amphibious training. On the 19th, when it was ordered back to Casa Ferri in reserve, the Commanding Officer was told that its last task, before leaving, would be reconnaissance of the crossings of the Marecchia. Both A and C Squadrons were now under-strength in tanks and tank-crews, so Lieutenant-Colonel Jayne decided to form a composite squadron.

There was always a chance that the period with the 7th Armoured Brigade might be unexpectedly prolonged, and that the reconnaissance role might be of even greater importance in the low country beyond Rimini. The squadron was therefore organized on the lines of the armoured reconnaissance regiment, with five troops, each of two Shermans and two Stuarts. Major Llewellen Palmer was given command. He had just returned to the regiment after an absence, in hospital, of two months. This was due to severe burns, when he had inadvertently thrown a match into a ditch in which there was an accumulation of waste petrol; this had been used, quite improperly, for cleaning a gun. Seeing his clothes alight, S.S.M. Cleere, who had already experienced trouble with petrol fires in Burma, with great presence of mind threw him to the ground and extinguished the flames.

The break-through which had been hoped for during the afternoon was not achieved. The enemy had a number of S.P. guns and tanks operating in the area south of the Marecchia, which held up the 8th Tanks and prevented the infantry from making any considerable progress in the face of repeated counter-attacks. After dark the weather also intervened on the enemy's side. It rained in torrents. Under cover of the weather the enemy broke contact all along the Adriatic front, and by dawn his last detachments were back behind the Marecchia.

On the 21st it rained intermittently and there was no activity except local patrolling. The regiment stayed damply at Casa Ferri and Vecciano ford throughout the day, on the north bank of the river, while B Echelon was moved up to a point only three-quarters of a mile away, south of the river. The movement of M.T. on the clay-covered and slippery roads was practically impossible. The officer

Broken bridge over the Marecchia.

"The weather intervened."

commanding Headquarters Squadron, Major P. B. Stanley Evans, showed much determination—even to the point of obstinacy—in his endeavours to replenish the fighting echelon; his final offer to cross the river drew from the adjutant the reply "No thank you. In any case you couldn't get here except by mule—and you have only one of those, as far as I know!"

On 22nd September the order was received to move to Lake Bracciano. The roads were still impossible until late in the afternoon,

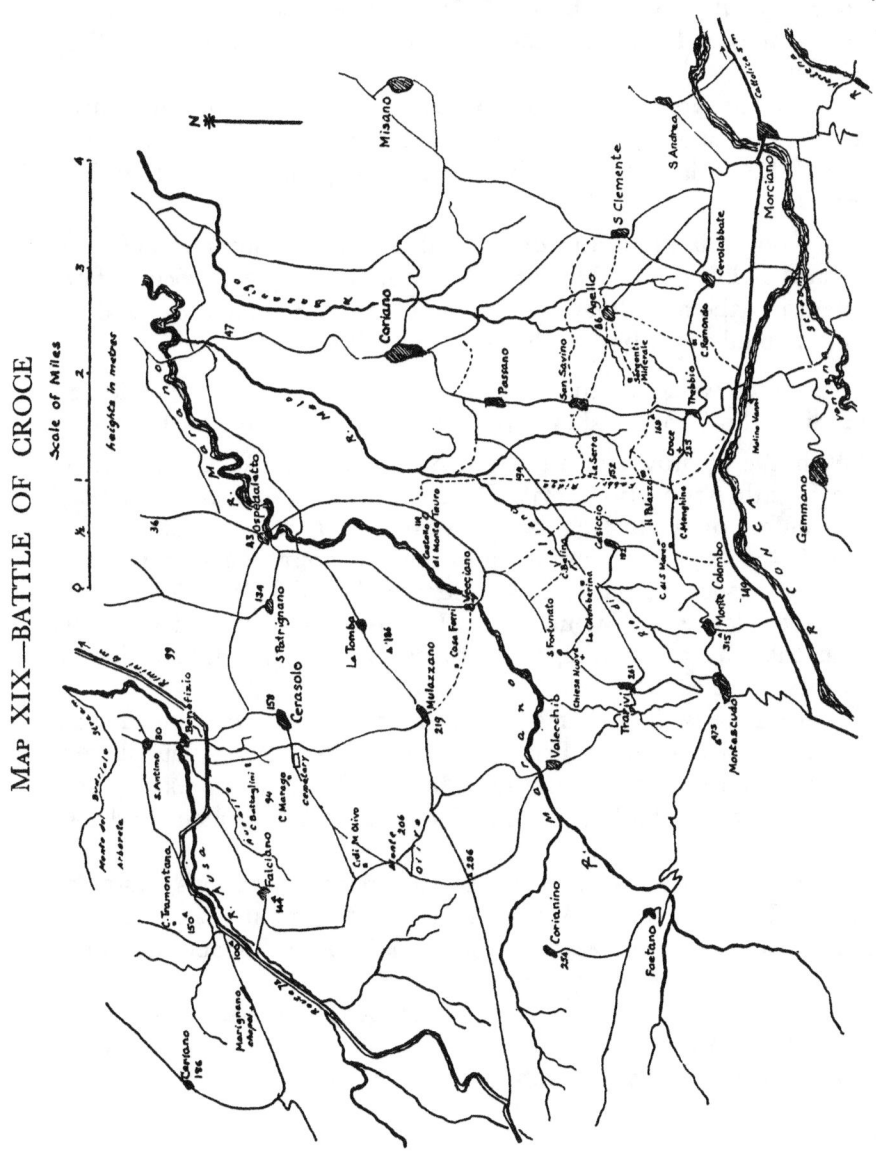

Map XIX—Battle of Croce

so the tanks were not handed in to the forward delivery squadron until the following morning. On the 24th at 4 a.m. the march began. On this day the route lay through Fano, Senigallia and Iesi, and many places with memories of the 2nd Polish Corps. On the 25th there were mountains and deep valleys all the way, the tremendous gorge of the Nero River being especially impressive. At 6 p.m. the column reached Vigne di Valli on Lake Bracciano and was quartered in a former Italian Air Force barracks.

For operational purposes the 7th Hussars were now under command of Allied Armies in Italy and they were administered by Rome Allied Area Command.

As the 7th Hussars passed from the command of the Eighth Army, the Army Commander, Lieutenant-General Sir Oliver Leese, Bart., K.C.B., C.B.E., D.S.O., sent the following message to the Commanding Officer:—

"My congratulations to you and all ranks of your regiment on your hard fighting and fine support of the infantry at Croce. The regiment may be proud of its part in a great and hard-fought victory. With my thanks and best wishes to you all."

Another most welcome eulogy was received from General Anders, commanding the 2nd Polish Corps, dated 10th October, 1944:—

"With the approval of Lt. Gen. Sir Oliver Leese, Commander of the Eighth Army, my Corps Order No. 117 dated 9th October, 1944, confers on your Regiment authority for the wearing of the Polish Corps sign in commemoration of your Regiment's distinguished services shoulder to shoulder with 2nd Polish Corps.

"In accordance with your wishes I shall forward two plaques, as soon as they are completed, to be placed in both the Officers' and Sergeants' Messes.

"I once more wish to thank you most fervently for the magnificent work of your Regiment. From June to August, 1944, you played your part in the battles on the Adriatic Coast in an exemplary manner true to the highest traditions of your fine Regiment and the British Army.

"Your work and co-operation in the many operations, notably those for Monte Torto, Monte la Croce, Monterado and Cerasa will live as fine examples of heroism and successful action under difficult and trying circumstances.

(Signed) W. ANDERS,
Lt.-Gen.

To Officer Commanding
    7th Queen's Own Hussars."

The battle on the 18th and 19th September had been part of another full-scale attack by the Eighth Army. The main weight of this blow was on the right, where the New Zealand Division was now brought in. After a desperate three-day struggle San Fortunato was entered on the 20th and the same night the Greeks, under command of the 1st Canadian Division, fought their way into Rimini.

When the Germans withdrew behind the broad and swollen Marecchia, they spared only one bridge, that built by Tiberius nineteen centuries ago. Over this passed, among others, the New Zealand division, most of them descended from a race which had provided slaves for ancient Rome and others of a race which the Romans had never even dreamed of.

As patrols were pushed forward on the 21st to regain contact, it became all too clear that during the winter, at any rate, mud and water courses would be more formidable obstacles than the Apennines. The Emilian plain consists largely of land reclaimed, over a period of centuries, from the sea. Between the rivers and streams marked on the map, the intervening spaces are a network of ditches and drains, each of them an obstacle to the movement of a mechanized army. When in spate many of the rivers flow at a level above that of the surrounding country, which has sunk through being drained, and are only kept in their courses by high artificial banks on both sides.

By the 21st the enemy facing Eighth Army, the greater part of Kesselring's forces, was almost overcome. It was now the weather, rather than German resistance, which brought this hard won battle to an inconclusive ending on the very threshold of victory.

In the centre of the front the Fifth Army's offensive on the Gothic Line had begun on 13th September. The main thrust was made up the Firenzuola road, where it was thought that the defences on the Giogo Pass were less formidable than at the Futa Pass, on the direct road from Florence to Bologna. The first breach on this sector was not made until the 15th when, after a night advance across the trackless mountains, the 8th Indian Division broke into the line.

By the 18th both the 13th British and the 2nd United States Corps were firmly established on the watershed of the mountains. From there onwards the grain of the country alters. On the south side of the Apennines there is a tangle of mountainous ridges and deep gorges, of which many run at right angles to the front. From the summit onwards however the rivers run consistently parallel to one another in a north-easterly direction. Their valleys are usually narrow and the intervening ridges steep, thus seriously limiting the areas available for the deployment of artillery and mechanized units. The descent to the plain of Emilia is so gradual that there was little advantage in the fact that the army was at last fighting, according to the map, "downhill." The many peaks and commanding features still gave the enemy excellent observation for his successive defensive positions.

The Germans were resisting stubbornly and when, at the end of the month, the effort of the Fifth Army was temporarily spent, its forward troops were still twenty-five miles short of Bologna.

Meanwhile the Eighth Army struggled on, crossed the Marecchia, and drove the enemy behind the Uso. The Germans were not in very good order and the advance continued until 29th September by which time the whole of the east bank of the Fiumicino, or Rubicon, had been cleared. Then came the rain. It poured in torrents for four days on end and once more the enemy had a much needed respite. The Fiumicello, normally a mere trickle, became a rushing river, impossible for patrols to cross. The Uso and Marecchia came down in spate behind the forward troops and stopped all movement of reserves and supplies in the army's rear.

Eighth Army's offensive was to have been resumed on the night of 6th/7th October, weather permitting. The weather did not permit. Movement in the plains was paralysed by a further outbreak of torrential rain.

General McCreery, who now commanded the Eighth Army, had spent some months operating with light forces in the mountains. He knew the Apennines well, their advantages as well as their difficulties, and he now started a series of manoeuvres in which the enemy's river line positions were turned successively by thrusts across their upper reaches.

First the 10th Indian Division exploited its bridgehead over the Rubicon, and on 7th October captured Monte Farnero. By the 16th the Canadians and the 5th Corps had both reached the Pisciatello. Next day the 2nd Polish Corps, which had taken over the mountainous sector on the left of the 5th Corps, began an attack in the direction of Rocca San Casciano, on Route 67. They made good progress, and by the 21st had captured Strada, in the valley of the Rabbi, but could not drive far enough through to secure the use of Route 67 as an extra means of lateral communication.

Farther to the right 5th Corps entered Cesena and seized a bridgehead over the Savio on Route 9, the Via Emilia, and in the foothills the 10th Indian Division seized and consolidated two more bridgeheads over the same river. By 21st October there were no Germans east of the Savio except at Cervia, on the coast.

In the next stage of the offensive the Eighth Army attacked with the 5th Corps astride and south of Route 9 and the Poles northwards down the valley of the Rabbi. The objective of both was Forli. The attacks began on 22nd October and both thrusts met heavy resistance. On the 24th however the enemy began to withdraw, his only voluntary withdrawal on this part of the front. This was made necessary partly by the loss of Monte Cavallo to the Indians, by which the flank of his positions on the Savio was turned. This however was not the only reason. In order to meet the Fifth Army's threat to Bologna three of the best German divisions, the 29th and 90th Panzer Grenadier and 1st Parachute, had been successively taken away from the Adriatic sector, which was so far denuded of troops that its line had of necessity to be shortened. Accordingly the enemy drew back to the Ronco.

By the 25th the Canadians and the 5th Corps were in contact with the new line and a few small bridgeheads were established across the river. But on the 26th the heavens opened again. All bridges over the Savio, in the immediate rear of the forward brigades, were swept away and the small detachments with footholds across the Ronco, cut off from support, were all wiped out. Only the Poles managed to continue their advance, and by the 27th had captured Predappio, Mussolini's birthplace.

The situation and the weather remained unchanged until 31st October when the 5th Corps pressed the Germans back to a switch line from just west of Forlimpopoli to the Rabbi at Grisignano.

Meanwhile the Fifth Army, at the beginning of October, had shifted the weight of its offensive to Route 65, the direct road to Bologna. General Clark kept up his offensive throughout the month, occasionally gaining fresh impetus by attacking with carefully rested reserves, and gradually advancing at the rate of a mile or so a day. The enemy resisted tenaciously at every point, encouraged, on 6th October, by another personal message from Hitler, which was read out to the troops; the Apennine position, like others before it, was to be held at all costs. The weather too was in his favour, as there were few fine days and sometimes rain fell continuously for two or three days on end.

On 15th October, Livergnano, only twelve miles from Bologna, was captured after a six-day struggle. Between the 20th and 24th the battle reached its climax. British and American troops fought their way to within four miles of Route 9 to the east of Bologna, and to within eight miles of the city itself. But the weather—snow, rain and mud—and the three best German divisions in Italy, together barred the way to the exhausted Fifth Army. On 27th October the offensive was suspended.

This marked the end of the Gothic Line battles. The operations which followed and the plan for the winter campaign no longer aimed at achieving a local victory in Italy, but were of limited scope, and essentially subordinate to the grand design of world strategy.

CHAPTER XV

A Watery Winter

The winter plan—problems in aquatics—in the infantry's boots—
offensive on the Lamone—the Senio sector.

Maps XIV, XX

The plans for the winter campaign in Italy had to be closely related with events in Western Europe, where the progress of the invading armies had not come quite up to expectations. Instead of throwing the whole of his weight into a concentrated and penetrating thrust by the 21st Army Group in the vital north, General Eisenhower had spread his effort widely on several sectors of the front. The extent to which this broad-front strategy may have delayed the final victory and its effects upon the re-drawing of national frontiers in Eastern Europe need not be considered in detail here. As far as the campaign in Italy was concerned, the task of the allied forces remained unaltered and plans for the continuance of operations were still governed by the needs of the West. There was, however, one new factor, which had been foreseen as a possibility in the summer and a probability in the autumn, and by October had become a certainty. The war in Europe would not be finished in 1944.

The prospect of serious fighting in 1945 accentuated the importance of the shortages of men and ammunition which had been causing anxiety for some time. Both the British and the American armies were affected. As a safeguard therefore, in order to provide for a spring campaign, the scope of any winter operations in Italy had to be strictly limited.

The shortage of men was felt most in the infantry. Already the 1st Armoured Division had been broken up and many of its men used as reinforcements. Infantry battalions had been reduced to three companies. Anti-aircraft units had been converted to infantry. By personal intervention with General Eisenhower, when all other channels had failed, General Alexander obtained from him an extra allocation of American reinforcements really intended for the West.

The ammunition shortage was due to a world-wide falling off in production and there was no quick remedy. Both British and American troops were affected, and neither would be able to maintain an offensive at full blast for more than two or three weeks during the winter and another fortnight in the spring. Even these brief periods of intensive fighting would only be possible if rigid economy were practised in the intervening months.

With these limitations added to his existing lack of superiority in numbers, General Alexander planned his winter campaign. In order to ensure the maximum of co-operation with the West he placed four alternative courses before General Eisenhower and accepted his choice.

One project had always loomed large and attractive in the mind of General Alexander—the shifting of half his forces from Italy to the Dalmatian coast. Of all the feasible alternatives, this would probably have drawn the most German divisions away from France. But until the Po was crossed, there would be little chance of an army from Dalmatia being able to join up with an army from Italy before the enemy could bring to bear enough troops to stop both. There were however greater objections than this—the objections of Tito and Moscow.

Russian influence in Jugoslavia had increased noticeably since the Red Army entered Belgrade on 20th October. The partisans still welcomed British arms and supplies and they eagerly accepted the support of the Royal Air Force, who bombed and rocketed selected targets, usually German but occasionally and unwittingly the houses of "collaborators." At first they welcomed British land forces as well; in the past year a number of raids had already been carried out against German detachments in the islands and on the mainland. But when a British force of 2000 men with 40 guns was sent into Montenegro, at their invitation, to help them to destroy 2 German divisions which were cut off, they found that the British soldier, naturally friendly, was far too popular with the people of Jugoslavia. The attitude of the Partisan leaders became first unco-operative, then impolite and eventually hostile. They asked for the guns to be taken away, they said they had only agreed to 20 and the British had no right to send 40. They "arrested" patrols and small raiding detachments. They placed guards near His Majesty's cruisers in the Dalmatian ports and refused to allow the sailors ashore. They no longer took an interest in the military strategy of the war with Germany. They merely wanted the Germans to go, armed or unarmed mattered not at all, so that they could consolidate their political position and establish a communist state.

In this, of course, they had the full support of Moscow, whose eyes were turned not only to the Mediterranean port of Trieste, but to the whole of the region north and east of the Adriatic. A British army operating in this area would not have suited them at all. In the circumstances, any project such as General Alexander had in mind would have met with constant and unremitting obstruction and it is doubtful whether it could have achieved anything at all.

The second suggestion was to transfer forces from Italy to France. This was discarded because there were enough divisions available already, and the build-up in France was restricted only by the capacity of the communications.

The third alternative was a continuation of the present offensive in Italy up to the limits set by exhaustion and material shortage. Such a course would offer no spectacular local profits, but would keep up the process of suction towards the south.

The fourth and last proposal was to stop the offensive now and build up for its renewal at a later date.

General Eisenhower chose the third plan, and, loyal to his interpretation of his main task, General Alexander prepared for the resumption of the offensive in Italy at the first possible moment.

Meanwhile the Eighth Army, taking advantage of every brief spell of fine weather, continued its efforts along Route 9. On 31st October the Ronco was crossed, but owing to another break in the weather Forli was not occupied until the 9th. Then there was a week of fine weather during which the enemy was forced back to the line of the Montone and Cosina. This opened Route 67. A further offensive by the 5th Corps and the 2nd Polish Corps reached the Lamone but the weather prevented exploitation to Faenza.

While the Eighth Army, by the end of November, had fought its way to the Lamone, the Fifth had managed to arrange a brief spell of rest for most of its formations. This had been difficult, as the front, from east of Bologna to the Tyrrhenian Sea, was very extended and only a few troops could be spared at a time.

The winter offensive was to be launched on 7th December, or as soon afterwards as practicable. The governing factor was to be the prospect of an adequate spell of dry weather.

General Alexander stated his intention, "To afford the greatest possible support to the Allied winter offensive on the western and and eastern fronts by bringing the enemy to battle, thereby compelling him to employ in Italy manpower and resources which might otherwise be available for use on the other fronts." There was no intention of striving for an immediate victory over the Germans in Italy, and both the armies were merely ordered forward along the axes where they were already operating, the Eighth up to and if possible across the Santerno, while the Fifth was to attack northwards to the general line Castel San Pietro-Bologna.

It proved impossible, after all, to launch this offensive. Fine weather never came to stay, but in the few short dry spells the Eighth Army managed to improve its position slightly. Both sides settled down to an uncomfortable winter, with no great changes in the strength or dispositions of either.

The Germans were still determined to hold all their ground. Although two divisions were sent away in November to meet a crisis in Hungary, they were immediately replaced. One of the replacing divisions came from Norway, and passed through Western Germany while von Rundstedt's Ardennes offensive was at its height, without being drawn into it. By holding on to his very extended line, however, with his right rear now threatened from France, Kesselring gave the Allies one more chance to defeat him south of the Po. This was a hope which they had failed to realize in the autumn. In the spring, after so much hard fighting and so many disappointments, they were at last to reap their reward.

* * * *

At Vigne di Valli the 7th Hussars were in barracks for the first time since leaving Dhond, almost two years before. The return to comparative civilization was a welcome change, and all the more so, as the last few days of September were very wet and stormy. Limited training began, but until the lake calmed down the tanks could not "swim." The opportunity was therefore taken to send leave parties daily to Rome, which everyone was anxious to visit.

This was the first undamaged city that the troops had seen in Italy, and during the stay on Lake Bracciano it proved a great attraction. No praise could be higher than the entry in the regimental war diary, which might perhaps have surprised the inhabitants of the Eternal City if they could have read it: "After Taranto and Ancona, Rome seemed almost a second Cairo."

On 1st October, Major-General H. L. Birks, D.S.O., head of the Royal Armoured Corps directorate at G.H.Q. Allied Armies in Italy, came down to discuss reorganization. The regiment was once more to be on the "armoured regiment" establishment. This meant that several officers were superfluous and a few were posted away. But there was still a shortage of men, especially of tank drivers, among whom casualties had been particularly heavy.

The "Python" scheme (repatriation of those who had been some years abroad) operated for officers as well as for men. During the month the Commanding Officer and the medical officer were both sent home. The latter, Bill Low, had been with the regiment since October, 1940, before the Wavell campaign. This was an exceptionally long time for a medical officer to stay with one unit. He inspired great confidence and was universally popular. He was missed not only for his personal and professional qualities, but for his skill on the football field, where he had been the central figure of many regimental victories during the past four and a half years.

Lieutenant-Colonel R. F. G. Jayne, D.S.O., had commanded the regiment for over two years, during long periods of boredom as well as in the recent battles. For his services in Italy he was awarded a bar to his Distinguished Service Order.

Major J. Congreve, D.S.O., was promoted to take his place. A little later Major N. M. H. Wall, M.C., returned to the regiment as second-in-command. Towards the end of the month Captain P. N. Cardew, R.A.M.C., was posted to the regiment as medical officer.

As regards the other ranks, the effect of the "Python" scheme was even more serious. Already several large drafts had been sent home, and with the exception of a few determined die-hards, almost all the original pre-war 7th Hussars had gone. After so many years abroad it is scarcely surprising that so few elected to remain when they were given a chance of serving nearer home. These transfers however did not diminish the spirit of the regiment or impair its traditions. The most serious effect was the reduction in overall numbers, as replacements were not available and the regiment remained under strength for the rest of the war.

Training in DD tanks was a novel experience. DD stands for "duplex-drive." When waterborne, the drive was transferred to two propellers and the tracks again came into play when the tank reached a depth of about nine feet of water on the opposite bank. Buoyancy was obtained by the water-tight structure of the hull and a canvas screen which was erected before entering the water. Steering was the main difficulty, and a good deal of practice was needed before a straight course could be kept.

Lake Bracciano had its full share of the foul Italian weather, and, as the tanks could only swim when the lake was calm, there was a good deal of waiting about. There were a number of visits by senior officers. Great things were expected of the DD tank and many of the commanders who were faced with the problem of crossing the watery plains of the Po and the Adige came to Bracciano to see—and to steer—for themselves. So, perhaps, did the ghost of the notorious John Mytton, who had joined the regiment as a cornet just after

Waterloo and, after a career more colourful than useful, died in the Fleet prison a few years later. The antics of the 7th Hussars on Lake Bracciano must have seemed almost as fantastic as his own.

Although C Squadron were not destined to have DD Shermans immediately, they were given practice in swimming. Their particular task was rafting, and in this they were trained by a troop of the 3rd Field Squadron. The rafts were class 40, i.e. capable of carrying a 40-ton load, and therefore a normal Sherman.

On 21st October the regiment began its move back to the Adriatic, where it was to come under the 9th Armoured Brigade (Brigadier R. B. B. B. Cooke, C.B.E., D.S.O.). The tanks were carried on transporters. They had a difficult journey through the mountains, as many of the bridges were not strong enough to take transporters and tanks together, and at these the tanks had to be unloaded. By the end of the month the regiment was concentrated in the area Belvedere-Ostra, in comfortable billets.

The 9th Armoured Brigade was now being re-constituted. It was characteristic of most armoured divisions and brigades during the war that they fought sometimes for several years with the same regiments under command and then, quite suddenly, it seemed that all the units were put into a hat and drawn out in a new order.

The remote and mysterious "they" were not always quite so whimsical as this, and somewhere or other a logical reason could probably be found for most of the changes. Before el Alamein there had been a deliberate intention to break up and break down some of the old desert traditions, especially that of excessive mobility—whether of the eastward or the westward variety. Now, in the autumn of 1944, the armies in Italy were faced with a particular problem which had never confronted them on such a scale before—the crossing of large rivers and extensive flooded areas.

The 7th Hussars had been attached to the Poles and then returned to the 7th Armoured Brigade as a fourth regiment, their place in the brigade having been taken by the 8th Royal Tanks. The 7th were therefore an obvious choice for the new role.

During October and November the 9th Armoured Brigade lost its two yeomanry regiments, which were sent back to the United Kingdom. The 3rd Hussars had already been given amphibious training at Bracciano; two of their squadrons were equipped with DD Valentines and the third with normal Shermans. The 7th Hussars had two squadrons of DD Shermans and one of ordinary Shermans. Besides these two DD regiments the brigade became the parent formation of three armoured car regiments and was responsible for their command

and training during periods when they were not allotted to other formations for operations.

Emphasis was thus laid upon pursuit and the crossing of rivers. In particular, the brigade was planning for the crossing of the Po.

In November the 4th Hussars were placed under command, and at the same time another innovation was introduced. Experience in Italy had proved that on numerous occasions attacks had lost their impetus and captured ground had been lost, through the difficulty of infantry in keeping up with tanks. One squadron of the 4th Hussars therefore carried out experiments and training as a Sherman carrier squadron. This consisted of three troops each of fourteen turretless Shermans, or "Kangaroos." The troop could carry a company of infantry and the squadron a battalion. The infantry were not to fight from the carriers, but to be disembarked on their objectives, and the carriers would then be available for another lift.

Another strange vehicle which eventually came to Italy was the "Landing Vehicle, tracked." This was an armoured amphibious troop carrier, specially designed for operating in shallow water and mud. It had already been used in France under the name of Buffalo, but in the Italian theatre it was called a "Fantail." It could carry both troops and guns, and a 25-pounder could be mounted so as to fire from it both ashore and afloat.

Other amphibians intended for the Po Valley were jeeps and DUKWs. The latter, commonly referred to as ducks, had already been used extensively in Italy, at Anzio and elsewhere. They were unarmoured load carrying vehicles, capable of carrying two and a half tons. When waterborne they were driven by a propeller and on reaching the shore the wheels took the ground and drove them inland. On land they could move at a fair pace and could deliver their load wherever it was required, but they were rather broad and ungainly, and a nuisance on narrow roads.

The particular problem of crossing the Po was studied with the headquarters of the 1st Canadian Corps. A mass of detailed information was available and this was supplemented by air photographs. One of the difficulties was that the enemy could change the character of much of the country overnight, if he should wish to do so. From Ferrara downwards the river level is above that of the surrounding country, which could easily be turned into a vast lake, generally shallow, but with a muddy bottom intersected with deep and undistinguishable ditches.

The approaches to the river itself were not generally difficult, but launching sites in most places required a little engineer work on the bank itself. The most delicate phase of the proceedings was the landing on the far bank. A muddy bottom made this almost impossible, as the tracks of the DD tanks buried themselves so far in the mud that the tank bellied down and stuck. Good firm sand was the best, and fortunately many stretches of the river had extensive sandy beaches. The banks themselves however usually had to be excavated, to allow the tanks to be launched, and the Engineers had again to be used to make lanes up the bank beyond, which was in places vertical, and through the flood banks.

The DD Shermans took a little time to prepare for swimming. When the canvas sides were erected they were very vulnerable to fire of all kinds, and the tanks were unable to protect themselves, as the turret had to be pointed to the rear and the gun could not be fired. For a period, therefore, until the tank had reached the far bank and lowered its screens, it made no positive contribution to an assault crossing.

A further limitation was the speed. As the maximum sea-going speed of the Sherman was four knots, it was difficult to maintain control or be reasonably sure of landing at the right spot, if the river was running at more than two, or at the most three knots. The fastest flow recorded for the river in the winter months was four, but this was very unusual, and it was generally between one and a half and two and a half, so there was a good chance that conditions would be satisfactory. The DD Valentines had a similar performance to the Shermans and similar limitations.

* * * *

After leaving Bracciano the 7th Hussars had a long period of inactivity. The weather was consistently unpleasant, and this limited outdoor training and football. Even Shermans fitted with "platypus grousers" (metal fins attached to the tracks to give a better grip in deep going) became bogged in the uncompromising Italian mud.

During November, C Squadron was equipped with DD Valentines taken over from the 3rd Hussars, in place of normal Shermans.

The "python" scheme took its usual toll, its November diet including Lieutenant and Quartermaster P. W. Brown; his place as quartermaster was taken by Lieutenant W. J. Lockwood, who rejoined the regiment after an absence of six years. In the following month the Stanley Evans brothers left for home. These two non-regulars had served in the regiment for over four years, during which time they never missed an engagement. Both distinguished themselves as troop leaders. Peter then became Intelligence Officer and Adjutant in

Burma and, after losing his hearing when second-in-command of B Squadron in Italy, was given command of Headquarters Squadron. Michael eventually rose to command A Squadron in which capacity he played a conspicuous part in the severe fighting at Croce.

By December, only six regular officers remained. It says much for the spirit of the regiment that, whereas it adopted the non-regulars into the regimental family, the non-regulars themselves quickly absorbed the regimental traditions and were second to none in upholding them.

Among others who rejoined in the early part of the winter were Captain the Hon. D. R. C. Chichester, who became second-in-command of B Squadron, and Squadron Sergeant-Major J. Wilson, who became Regimental Sergeant-Major. Both these had been captured at Sidi Rezegh and had escaped from enemy-occupied Italy during the summer of 1944.

Usually, during the lull after a period of severe fighting, the keeper of the regimental war diary had the satisfaction of entering up a list of awards. In the autumn of 1944 however no such list appears. It seems certain that somehow or other, at about this time, a batch of recommendations went astray.

So peaceful and static were the conditions at Ostra that A Squadron and the Sergeants' Mess held dances, to which a number of the local Italians were invited. Pantomimes were planned and it looked as if Christmas would be celebrated with traditional festivities.

All illusions of this nature were shattered on 10th December. On that day Major Wall attended a conference at the headquarters of the 9th Armoured Brigade at which Brigadier Cooke outlined the new plan. The brigade was to take over the sector of the front from Route 16 to the sea, now held by the Canadians, and to protect the right flank of the Canadian Corps. The latter, with a shorter front to hold, would then renew its attacks, aimed at reaching the River Senio north of Bagnacavallo. The brigade was to operate dismounted and the tanks were to be left at Ostra, in charge of the technical staff.

On the 11th the advance party met the brigade reconnaissance party in Ravenna and was shown the 7th Hussars area, which included Madonna del Albero and Molinaccio respectively three and five miles south of Ravenna. The regiment marched early next morning and arrived about the middle of the day. Squadrons were billeted in houses by the roadside, headquarters in Madonna del Albero, A between the two villages, B in Molinaccio and C just beyond.

Two days were spent in reconnaissance. The 7th Hussars were to take over the centre sector of the brigade front from the Governor-General's Horse Guards. On the right would be the 27th Lancers and on the left the 12th Lancers. The right boundary was the Ravenna—San Alberto road, inclusive to the 7th Hussars; the left was the River Lamone from Route 16 to where it bends sharply eastwards half a mile south of Conventello thence, exclusive, Conventello and the road northwards towards San Alberto.

This gave the regiment a frontage of 6,000 yards, but the extreme left, including the village of Torri, was held by the 2721 Squadron of the R.A.F. Regiment, which was to come under command. The rest of the front was to be held by A Squadron on the right and B in the centre. C was to remain in reserve. Regimental headquarters, and the headquarters of A Squadron, 4th Hussars, were to be set up in the houses near the church at Camerlona. This squadron, consisting of three troops of Shermans, was placed under command of the regiment; two of its troops were allotted to A Squadron and one to the 2721 Squadron R.A.F. Regiment.

The 50th (Self-Propelled) Battery of the 20th Field Regiment was in support, and two observation posts were set up, one with the right forward troop of A Squadron and one with the forward flight of 2721 Squadron.

Among many unusual experiences, the 7th Hussars now had to rely principally on line communication and telephones. A number of lines had already been laid by the Governor-General's Horse Guards, and these were supplemented by others until all troop and most section posts, as well as the supporting artillery, were connected up.

The regiment also took over a number of partisans in the area. These were in the habit of going and coming more or less as they pleased, whether on "patrols" of their own into the enemy lines, or for a "rest" in Ravenna. However, when the regiment had taken over, an Italian liaison officer arrived to help in organizing the partisans. In order to increase their usefulness and obtain better control of them, a certain number were allotted to each squadron, and thence suballotted to troops. In this way a troop and its partisans got to know one another, and "leave" was granted when the troop was out of the line. Reliable partisans were used on patrol and as sentries, and were given cigarettes and clothing, and the unreliable were sent away.

In the early hours of the 15th A and B Squadrons moved forward in the darkness to take over their appointed positions. Owing to careful reconnaissances during the day, the relief went smoothly and was complete an hour before dawn. By first light the Governor-General's Horse Guards had disappeared to the rear.

A Squadron had one troop post forward, near the River Lamone, and two along the Fossa Carlina, a broad dyke which joins the sea at

Porto Corsini. 2721 Squadron had two flights forward, in the village of le Torri. Most troops had section posts in front of their main positions and all posts were in houses or farm buildings.

During the 15th and the night of the 15th/16th, all was quiet. Patrols were limited to making contact between neighbouring posts and none were sent forward to reconnoitre the enemy's positions. Next day, however, patrolling was more active. Partisans, who had been behind the enemy lines on the 15th, brought back reports of an impending withdrawal. Such a movement must clearly be watched for, but this was not the only reason for patrolling, which is the normal procedure for "infantry" holding a position; it is only by frequent patrolling that they can find out changes in the enemy's dispositions.

Two patrols were sent from A Squadron. The right hand one came under machine gun fire from an enemy post covering the blown bridge over the Lamone on the San Alberto road. As it withdrew mortars also opened up with accurate fire and it was fortunate in having no casualties.

Farther to the left Lieutenant G. J. Iles led a section patrol, accompanied by a partisan who had crossed the river the day before and reported that the enemy in a post on the far bank were ready to come across and surrender. Iles put his section in a position to cover the partisan while he crossed again. This time, however, when he presented himself at the entrance to the dug-out the Germans had changed their minds. An argument ensued; he shot one and the others bolted. He then re-crossed the river, bringing the paybook of the dead German, an artillery N.C.O. of the 114th Jaeger Division. Iles' bren gun exchanged shots with another enemy post, but there was no visible damage on either side, and the patrol withdrew.

B Squadron's patrol was provided by Lieutenant Herbert's troop. This also came under fire and withdrew to its post without loss. All three patrols had thus adequately fulfilled their tasks.

During the following night the 2721 Squadron R.A.F. Regiment was relieved by the 2788, which took over the same positions.

Patrolling continued each day and night, and there were usually exchanges of shots with enemy on the opposite bank of the river. Partisan patrols sometimes spent a day or two behind the enemy's lines, and his dispositions were eventually known in considerable detail. The Germans covered the crossings of the river throughout its length and, as their posts were in deep dugouts along the far bank, they were almost immune from artillery fire. Patrols which crossed the river also discovered that the enemy posts could cover the flat fields behind the river bank.

Troop post on the Lamone, December 1944; Lieutenant J. H. Harding, Tprs. S. Levi and S. Amer.

Field-Marshal Lord Alexander with R.S.M. "Tug" Wilson and Lt.-Colonel J. Congreve, D.S.O., O.B.E.

Before dawn on the 20th Lieutenant Howard-Dobson's troop set forth to occupy the Casa Melina. This was an isolated farmhouse on the far side of the Lamone marshes. It had several times been visited by partisans, who had found it unoccupied, and the 7th Hussars meant to use it as a patrol base. With his fifteen men and five partisans Howard-Dobson crossed the flooded area east of the Ravenna-San Alberto road in boats and landed not far from the house, which was found empty.

Patrols sent out during the night gained valuable information about movements of horse drawn transport and reliefs by tracks from San Alberto to the posts along the river bank, and about enemy dispositions. But the enemy evidently got information too, about Howard-Dobson, probably from a partisan who had gone astray; early on the 21st he began shelling the Casa Melina from the north with 75-mm. infantry guns at a range of only 800 yards. The value of the Casa Melina as a patrol base had now gone, so Howard-Dobson's party took to its boats and slid away among the reeds, eventually rejoining A Squadron without mishap.

Also on the 20th, two miles farther to the left, Corporal Collins crossed the Lamone before it was light, with a wireless set, and installed himself in a farmhouse behind the enemy's lines. This had been reported by partisans as unoccupied, and so, for a time, it proved to be. The inhabitants were friendly, but clearly nervous, and not without reason. When sitting down to a meal with the Italians in the afternoon, Collins saw a German patrol coming towards the house. He went upstairs and hid until they had gone, but re-crossed the river that night.

Those troops who were out of the line celebrated Christmas with turkey, plum pudding and beer. C Squadron however had their celebration all together on the 24th before going into the line between A and B Squadrons.

On the 26th the 4th Hussars were withdrawn and 7th Hussars squadrons each formed a tank troop to support their own "infantry" troops. The 2788 Squadron was also taken out of the line; B Squadron therefore side-stepped to the left and took over its sector with one troop and a post of partisans.

It was not only the 7th Hussars who patrolled at night. The enemy, too, sent patrols across the river, and these occasionally made contact and exchanged shots with the forward troops. In general, however, the front was quiet until early in the new year, when a local offensive by the 5th Canadian Corps brought about a partial withdrawal of the Germans.

On 1st January orders were issued for an offensive by the 5th Canadian Armoured Division. The direction of the attack was north-eastwards, striking across the rear of the enemy holding the line of the lower Lamone. The first of four successive objectives was Conventello and the last was San Alberto; exploitation was to be pressed to the mouth of the River Reno.

The 9th Armoured Brigade now consisted of four cavalry regiments, two field regiments (S.P.) and two infantry battalions. Its task was to help the operations of the Canadians by increasing pressure all along the front and closely following up any enemy withdrawal.

On the 1st the enemy were still improving their defences, and several parties were seen digging. One of B Squadron's patrols saw two drunken Germans reeling about near one of their posts beyond the river, having a wonderful New Year's day, but out of range of its tommy-guns.

The attack of the 5th Canadian Armoured Division began at daybreak on the 2nd. At noon the leading troops were just south of Conventello, and by the evening had fought their way nearly to La Barca, where they were held up by an enemy Tiger tank. The Germans were fighting fiercely, as usual.

Throughout the day patrols of all squadrons of the 7th Hussars kept contact with the enemy positions along the Lamone, and the enemy showed no sign of withdrawing until, just before dark, a patrol of C Squadron found the railway bridge area unoccupied. The enemy was, rather naturally, more vigilant and responsive than usual and Lieutenant J. H. Harding's troop of B Squadron in le Torri was heavily shelled and mortared at intervals.

Major Murray Smith ordered Harding to cross the river next morning at a point 150 yards west of the Torri bridge and make contact with the enemy and with the right of the Canadians beyond the river. He crossed at 5 a.m. under fairly heavy fire. Lance-Corporal Gregg was wounded by shell fire, and died later, but there were no other casualties. By 8 a.m. the troop was firmly established beyond the river and patrols were sent northwards. One advanced nearly a mile to the hamlet of Grattacoppa. Another made contact with a unit of the 5th Canadian Armoured Division.

During the afternoon Murray Smith moved a second dismounted troop and his tank troop across the river. There was, however, no contact with the enemy. The leading Canadian troops were still making progress and by nightfall the 5th Canadian Armoured Regiment had reached a point two miles north of Harding's positions. Elsewhere the situation on the 7th Hussars' front remained unchanged.

At about 3 a.m. on the 4th the Germans made an unexpected and heavy counter-attack against the 60th, on the left of B Squadron. The 7th Hussars stood-to, but were not involved in the fighting. The general direction of the attack was from Alfonsine towards the bend in the Lamone near le Torri.

At first the Germans had a fair measure of success, and almost reached the river bank to the left rear of B Squadron. By this time however their casualties were very heavy. The 60th held firm and both the 12th Lancers and a tank troop of the 4th Hussars took heavy toll of the enemy. The 60th then mounted several local counter-attacks and by 9.30 the German attempt to cut off the Canadians in the San Alberto area—for such it was—had been totally and expensively defeated; by noon the 60th had counted ninety prisoners and more were coming in. A captured operation order showed that the attack was carried out by an SS Regiment (of three battalions) with supporting troops; the first objective had been Conventello and the second was the road between le Torri and Grattacoppa.

Meanwhile the Canadians had made further progress and had advanced during the morning from San Alberto to the bridge over the canal a mile to the south-east, which they captured intact. This placed the Germans opposite the 7th Hussars in a precarious position. In order to take advantage of this situation A Squadron was ordered to send a strong fighting patrol to seize two farmhouses which the enemy were known to be occupying in the fenland.

Lieutenant Iles' troop of A Squadron carried out the operation, accompanied by a forward observing officer of the 50th Field Battery. At 2 p.m. the troop crossed the lock gates on A Squadron's front and, covered by an artillery concentration, advanced on the first farmhouse. When the leading sections were about two hundred yards short of the objective the artillery stopped firing and four Germans emerged to give themselves up. There were several dead in and around the house, but the rest of the enemy had slipped away. There were no British casualties.

The second objective was half a mile farther to the east, and Iles withdrew his troop across the Lamone to re-organize before making his second attack. This time he crossed the river about 1,000 yards east of the lock gates and once again advanced under cover of the supporting artillery. When the troop was about three hundred yards from the objective a partisan called out in German to the enemy and invited them to surrender. There was no response and, as a machine gun post could be seen in the farmyard, a tank, firing from the high bank south of the Lamone, engaged the area of the machine gun and set the stacks on fire. Some of the enemy were seen running into the farmhouse, which was then engaged with armour-piercing shot.

Under cover of this fire Iles advanced and reached the buildings without being shot at. There were still a number of the enemy about and some in the slit trenches round the farm were disposed to resist. There were several clashes before the area was finally cleared, and one partisan and three Germans were killed. Six prisoners were taken, including the officer commanding the company.

While these prisoners were being disarmed and searched, Iles saw a party of four armed Germans marching away under a red-cross flag. This was a good idea, no doubt, but a flagrant mis-use of the Geneva emblem. Iles accordingly opened fire with a bren gun and killed all four. At dusk the troop withdrew across the Lamone.

Elsewhere along the front the usual patrols had found the enemy still in position, but on the night of the 4th/5th he withdrew on the whole sector. All squadrons followed up the next day, but no contact was obtained with the enemy, who had filtered away to the westward, rather than risk being pinned against the great lagoon to the north.

On the 6th the weather broke once more. There were three days of torrential rain which entirely prevented exploitation.

* * * *

On 8th January the 9th Armoured Brigade re-adjusted its dispositions and the 7th Hussars were given a new sector to defend. This lay on the bank of the Munio canal, which runs from south-west to north-east, parallel with and a mile short of the River Senio. The 60th were on the right, with their right on Route 16 near Alfonsine, the 1st Welch, of the 56th Division, were on the left of the 7th Hussars.

The regiment held a sector about two miles in extent, with A Squadron on the right and B on the left. C Squadron remained in reserve until the 12th, when it sent one troop forward to come under command of B. Two days later C Squadron took up a position on the left of B. On its left C was in contact with the 27th Lancers, who had relieved the 1st Welch and enabled them to side-step slightly to the west with their left on the banks of the Senio.

Each squadron was supported by its own tank troop, and patrolling was active by day and night. Defences were developed and the 7th Hussars even found themselves putting up barbed wire round their posts—a most unusual proceeding for an armoured regiment. There was little interference from the enemy. A few night patrols were driven off, but the greatest nuisance was the frequent mortaring and occasional sniping by S.P. guns.

Patrols moved well forward up to the Senio and lay up sometimes for several hours observing enemy movements and listening to German voices at close quarters in the occupied buildings. One patrol of Lieutenant Herbert's troop, consisting of Corporal P. J. Presnall and three men, was ambushed by the Germans and all four were posted as missing. Presnall had been ordered to cross the ditch in front of the troop position in the dark and, as soon as it was light enough, to make his way through the vineyards to a point overlooking the Rosetta road. From there he was to observe enemy positions and movements for about fifteen minutes and then return.

Herbert saw the patrol working forward in pairs through the vineyard. He was watching two of them crawling the last few yards to their view point when they both suddenly flattened themselves on the ground and remained still. All was silent, but they had evidently seen something which made them stop. After about twenty minutes they began to move back to the cover of the vineyard. At once a spandau opened fire. Nothing more was seen of the patrol, but a few minutes later five Germans came into view, following up the two men. Lieutenant Herbert engaged them with his bren gun, and they disappeared among the vines. Firing was heard for a few minutes afterwards, and a little later men were seen moving along the Rosetta road —possibly the Germans and their three prisoners. The fourth man, Trooper C. T. P. Mathew, had been killed.

On the evening of the 25th a patrol from A Squadron lay up in an unoccupied German dug-out and watched a German sentry on a plank bridge only twenty yards away. He was relieved every hour and they hoped to capture the next sentry who came on duty. Unfortunately however they were seen by other Germans 200 yards away and the alarm was raised. As they withdrew they shot the sentry and wounded one other German, but one man was killed by spandau fire.

Next day A Squadron had one man killed at a post on the Munio which was frequently shelled by mortars. Just after dark another troop was approached by an enemy patrol; the sentry opened fire, killed one German and scattered the rest.

On the 28th squadrons were informed that they would be coming out of the line on 1st February. The experience of being infantry was at last coming to an end.

During this period the DD tanks had been handed in. B and C Squadrons were now to be equipped with normal Shermans, while A Squadron would have "Kangaroos." This meant an increase in A Squadron's establishment to 220 men. Fortunately a large draft had recently arrived, but in spite of this B and C Squadrons were still considerably below strength. In fact the regiment never operated with Kangaroos and A Squadron was eventually equipped like the other two.

The last few days of January were quiet except for a little mortaring. Officers and N.C.O.s of the 10th Hussars came up to reconnoitre the 7th Hussars' sector, which they were to take over, and a few of them went out with patrols. The relief took place in daylight on the 1st and at 7 a.m. on the 2nd the sector passed to command of the 10th Hussars.

The seven weeks in the line had been a new and perhaps a valuable experience for the 7th Hussars. It afforded some excitement, some monotony and, in the watery, cold and adhesive conditions, a due measure of sympathy for the "P.B.I." Few, if any, were sorry to see the last of the Lamone marshland and the brimming dykes round the Senio, and it was a tired but cheerful lot of troops who crowded into the lorries going back to Pesaro.

In casualties the regiment had been fairly fortunate, considering the enterprising patrol work which had been kept up all the time. Five men were killed, mostly in the last few days, but there were no officer casualties except Major Llewellen Palmer, who accidentally broke his ankle. In Italy Tim Palmer's luck was clearly out, and his accidents deprived him of a share in several of the regiment's engagements. However, he had had his full share of fighting—and luck— in the desert and Burma. When he had recovered he went back to the United Kingdom to attend a course at the Staff College.

In the middle of February tanks were issued and A Squadron started its special training with Kangaroos. A regimental leave camp was started on Lake Bracciano, but was not a great success as accommodation stores could not be obtained. However, this did not matter much, as by the end of the month the 7th Hussars had handed in all their tanks once more, including the Kangaroos, and were back at Vigne di Valli, on Lake Bracciano, for re-training with DD Shermans and Valentines.

March passed quickly and pleasantly. The work was hard, but Rome was near, and so, at last, was the day when the DD Sherman was to prove its worth. The regimental diary records:—

"This month has been a very colourful one for the regiment, as we have been inspected by no less than a Field-Marshal, one major-general and a fleet of brigadiers. Each of these personalities has been taken for a 7th Hussar pleasure trip on the Lago di Bracciano and in most cases, including the field-marshal, took a turn at the tiller and realised how difficult it was to steer anything like a straight course with a DD Sherman. In spite of all these operations, none of our Shermans are missing."

Swimming round and round the lake was now too simple, and troops and squadrons could even keep their stations when moving in formation. As a final test of the technique of river crossings, already very carefully thought out by the commander and second-in-command of the 9th Armoured Brigade, each squadron was sent in turn to a

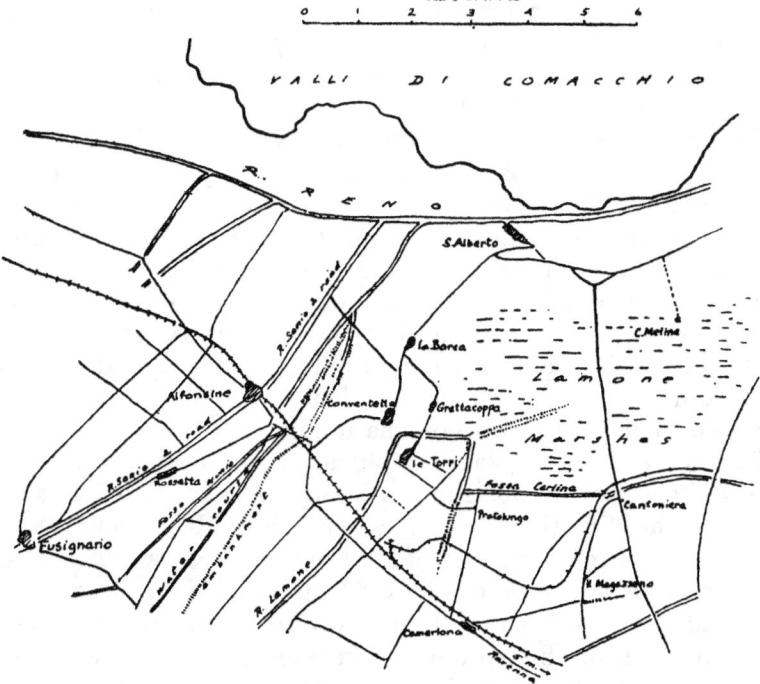

Map XX
MOUTHS OF THE LAMONE AND SENIO

Note.—This sketch is greatly simplified. The country is intersected by watercourses and flood banks and most banks also serve as tracks.

selected spot on the Tiber near Civita Castellana. Much preparatory work had to be done by the Royal Engineers, who bull-dozed the banks and erected camouflage nets round the area to give some degree of protection from prying eyes. The crews came back from these exercises full of confidence.

The regiment was now equipped entirely with DD Shermans. It was fairly well up to strength, and every man was thoroughly keyed up for what he knew to be the final episode of the war in Europe.

CHAPTER XVI

The Battle of the Po Plains

Plans for the spring—the final offensive—pursuit—A Squadron—B Squadron—C Squadron—regimental headquarters—contribution to victory—the peace—the return.

Maps XIV, XXI

General Mark Clark's plan for the spring was based essentially on General Alexander's original autumn plan which, through shortage of troops and excess of water, could not be carried to its conclusion. Once again the object was to destroy the greatest possible number of the enemy in the area south of the Po.

One of the significant features of the country was the River Reno. This rises fifty miles south of Bologna and runs at first just east of north, past the western outskirts of Bologna and on for a further twenty-five miles. At this point, only ten miles from the Po, the Reno doubles back sharply to the south-east, past Argenta, and thence eastwards, just south of the Valli di Commacchio, and into the sea. In the last seventy miles of its course, the Reno receives all the rivers and streams running down from the mountains east of Bologna, including the Senio and the Santerno, each of which was a serious obstacle to any westerly advance of the Eighth Army on Bologna itself.

The Fifth Army was well placed to advance northwards down the left bank of the upper Reno, thus avoiding the strong defences of Bologna. For the Eighth Army however the problem was more complicated. For twenty miles inland from the sea, a northward advance across the Reno would be blocked by the Valli di Commacchio, the largest and most southerly of the shallow lagoons in the Po delta. Bastia was therefore the first promising crossing place. Here again, however, there would be no plain sailing after seizing the crossing. The enemy had already, by flooding, brought the Commacchio lagoon to within two miles of the Bastia-Argenta road, which runs along a causeway, and he had cut the dykes north of the Reno on the other side of the road. If the enemy could hold the narrow Argenta gap, some three miles wide and six miles deep, he could bar the way to Ferrara indefinitely. This was a most important strategical consideration. In case of a general withdrawal, it was on the Argenta gap that he would have to pivot, while his right swung back, from Genoa and the French frontier, towards Lake Garda. It was therefore certain that the gap would be stubbornly defended.

The date of the offensive was fixed for 9th April. The object was to destroy the enemy south of the Po. The plan was first to envelop his left with the Eighth Army and, when his reserves had been drawn in that direction, to strike at his centre with the Fifth. It was hoped that successive thrusts on both flanks would then destroy a great part of the enemy in the loop of the Reno and the rest before they could cross the Po.

One of the great advantages of a two-handed punch, with an interval of a few days in between, was that the full strength of the Strategic Air Force would be used for each operation in turn. The potential weight of the air attack in Italy had now reached overwhelming proportions. Not only could a breach be blasted in front of each attacking army, but all movement of enemy troops in daylight could be practically stopped. Farther in rear, a programme of interdiction on key points of the already battered and twisted railway systems of the north would seriously impede any contemplated movement of reserves or supplies into the vital area.

Eighth Army's attack was to be preceded by three preliminary operations on the extreme right. These were all to be carried out by the 56th Division, which now included the 24th Guards Brigade, 9th Armoured Brigade, 2nd Commando Brigade and 28th Garibaldi Brigade of partisans, as well as its own three infantry brigades. The first operation was the seizure of the southern half of the spit of land between the Valli di Commacchio and the sea, in order to strengthen control of the south-eastern part of the lake. The second was the occupation of the islands, in the lake, as a patrol base. The third was to capture an area about three miles square, beyond the Reno, north west of San Alberto, so that the Reno might be bridged and launching sites prepared for the Fantails.

The completion of these operations would pave the way for an amphibious assault across the flooded areas to Argenta, and while this was being prepared, the main attack of the Eighth Army was to be opened, higher up the Senio. The 5th Corps was to assault with two divisions, the 8th Indian on the right and 2nd New Zealand on the left. On D Day they were to seize the area in the loop of the Senio round Lugo. Next day they were to cross the Santerno and secure a large bridgehead. The 78th Division was then to pass through and attack Bastia from the south, while a brigade of the 56th attacked it from the east, across the floods. The Italian Cremona Group and the 8th Indian Division were then to mop up any enemy remaining south of the Reno in this area and come into corps reserve. The New Zealanders would either advance on the left of the 78th Division, or move westwards on Budrio, according to circumstances.

The 2nd Polish Corps was to attack on an axis north of the Via Emilia, with a view to co-operating with the Fifth Army in the capture of Bologna and preparing the way for the direction of 5th Corps' attack to be switched to the west if the Argenta gap should prove impregnable.

The Eighth Army had two corps headquarters controlling lightly held defensive positions in the hills, the 10th and the 13th. Only the latter contained a complete fighting formation, the 10th Indian Division, and with this it was to be ready to move into the plains on the left of the 5th Corps and to assume command of the New Zealand Division as well. In Army reserve were the 6th Armoured Division and the 2nd Parachute Brigade.

The Fifth Army was also to carry out one preliminary operation, on its extreme left, on D minus 4. Its main assault was to be delivered on a day to be selected by General Clark, probably D plus 3. The 4th Corps, which included the 1st Brazilian Division, was to attack down the valley of the Samoggia, directed on Bazzano. Thirty-six hours later the 2nd Corps was to attack on the right of the 4th, directed on Praduro, and thence down the Reno. One of its four divisions was the 6th South African Armoured. One division remained in army reserve.

In the next phase, not more than one division was to enter and secure Bologna. The two corps were to advance side by side, to cut Route 9 west of the city, and then, leaving Modena to the west, drive through to the Po on the frontage from Bondeno to Ostiglia. It was hoped that on reaching Bondeno the 2nd Corps would be able to make contact with the Eighth Army, thus completing the encirclement of the enemy still south of the Po. The 4th Corps would then be able to cross the river, advance on Verona and cut off all enemy troops remaining in north-western Italy.

As much trouble was taken in preparing the cover plan as with the real one, and once again the enemy was thoroughly deceived. This time the threat was directed against the Adriatic coast north of the Po. The Royal Navy pointed out that a landing in this area was quite impossible, but the enemy had several times shown his ignorance of amphibious warfare and its possibilities, and it was not unreasonable to expect that he would show it once more; he did. In February one German division and various odd detachments were stationed on the coast in the "threatened" sector. Then a corps headquarters was allotted and in the last week of March the excellent 29th Panzer Grenadier Division was moved from central reserve near Bologna to the area between Venice and Treviso. This was a triumph for the cover plan staff and besides occupying a large number of troops in areas far removed from the impending battle, their transportation over such great distances made serious inroads on the enemy's diminishing stocks of fuel.

On 23rd March General Vietinghoff returned from the eastern front to Italy to take over from Kesselring, who, after three and a half consecutive years in Supreme Command in the Mediterranean, had now been appointed Commander-in-Chief West.

Vietinghoff had twenty-three German and four Italian divisions. This gave him a slight superiority in land forces over the Allies, who had seventeen divisions, ten independent brigades (of which four were armoured) and four Italian Combat Groups. His scanty air force however could not be reckoned as an asset, and his mobility was severely restricted by shortage of fuel.

The German land forces in Italy were undoubtedly the best and most coherent of all the German Army Groups. By this time the forces in the West consisted of scratch battle-groups which were divisions only in name. But in Italy the divisions were well up to strength, well trained, and still of first class morale. Neither the bad news, as the Allies advanced into Germany, nor the overwhelming allied superiority in the air, nor the propaganda of the Political Warfare Executive, had any noticeable effect on the spirits of the Germans in Italy, and they fought to the finish.

If the German high command had ever entertained plans for a National Redoubt in the mountains of southern Germany and Austria, the prospect of ever putting them into effect was now shattered by Hitler. The order to hold the present positions still stood. As the day of the offensive approached, General Herr, commanding the Tenth Army, proposed a plan for a "false front" manoeuvre. His idea was that twenty-four hours before zero (which he had judged with commendable accuracy), when the Allies' complicated air and artillery plans had been prepared in great detail, and all was ready for the attack, the Germans should withdraw behind the Santerno under cover of a heavy artillery bombardment. If this plan had been carried out the assault would have fallen on a deserted area, with great waste of effort and ammunition; there would consequently have been considerable delay in regaining contact, reconnoitring the new German positions and mounting a fresh offensive.

When Vietinghoff put this proposal to the Führer, like all others of this nature it met with a flat refusal; not even the smallest tactical withdrawal would be tolerated. General Alexander comments:—

"This was the real danger of the German situation. To be forced to give battle south of the Po meant that defeat would inevitably be a disaster which no degree of mobility could modify. The position of a Commander-in-Chief tied hand and foot by such irrational dictation was a hollow and powerless dignity; all that was left to Vietinghoff was to await the Allied attack in the mood in which the French generals advanced to Waterloo, 'without fear and without hope'."

* * * *

All the preliminary operations were successful. On the night of 1st/2nd April the 2nd Commando Brigade landed on the spit north of the Reno mouth and took nine hundred prisoners. In this operation the fantails caused some anxiety for their future use against Bastia; the lake was very shallow and they all stuck in the mud. Confidence in them was restored on the 6th however, when the 56th Division attacked and captured the wedge of land north of the Reno near San Alberto; the fantails were then tried over the inundated ground and found to behave perfectly. The occupation of the islands by the Special Boat Service was also successful, and these small-scale raiders kept up continuous observation of the enemy's flank and rear throughout the offensive.

The Fifth Army's preliminary attack on the west coast had even more success than had been expected, as it drew in the 90th Panzer Grenadier Division from the central reserve. This left Vietinghoff with only just over half a division in his hand when the main blow fell.

For an hour and a half in the early afternoon of the 9th April 825 bombers of the Strategic Air Force dropped 175,000 fragmentation bombs on a broad belt of country which contained the enemy's reserves and gun areas on the front chosen for the Eighth Army's attack. At the same time 1,000 medium and fighter bombers from the Desert Air Force and the XXIInd Tactical Air Force attacked individual targets, selected beforehand, including headquarters, gun positions and mortar sites, and any other target seen moving on roads in the battle area.

Soon afterwards the 5th Corps began a series of five "false alarm" bombardments. Each lasted for forty-two minutes, but, instead of the expected tank and infantry attack, fleets of fighter-bombers then came down to attack targets close in front of the assaulting divisions, especially the western flood-banks of the Senio. After ten minutes of this, the bombardment was repeated, then ten minutes more of fighter-bombers, and so on, until 7.20 p.m. Then, as the sixth bombardment stopped, the fighter-bombers did a dummy run along the river. This was the signal for the attack.

Flame-throwing tanks led the assault. The light was already fading and the jets of orange flame and dense black smoke mingled with the dust of the bombardment as they burned and suffocated the Germans in their deep dugouts on the flood-bank. The infantry followed closely and they too were swallowed up in the dust and smoke and the gathering darkness.

The Polish Corps attacked at the same time, but they had started some way back from the Senio, and were delayed by deep minefields. However, by the morning of the 10th the 3rd Carpathian Division was across the Senio. All this day there was heavy fighting on the fronts of both corps. Fighter-bombers and medium bombers were on call throughout the day. One German divisional commander commented afterwards in his report that even single runners were attacked; individual tanks were attacked by as many as fifteen aircraft in quick succession.

On the 10th the Strategic Air Force made another gigantic effort. Over 1,200 bombers and fighters attacked a strip seven miles long, astride the Santerno river on the front of both corps.

By the morning of 11th April the enemy on 5th Corps front was back on the Santerno and during the night all three assaulting divisions secured shallow bridgeheads across the river. On the same day the enemy's 98th Division was finally overwhelmed by the New Zealanders, who captured the town of Massa Lombarda in the afternoon, while the divisions on each flank improved their bridgeheads. The first phase of Eighth Army's plan was successfully completed.

On the right, the second phase had already begun. The 56th Division had landed one brigade in fantails at Menata, three miles behind the enemy's forward positions. The Germans were completely surprised, as they had thought that the floods gave them perfect protection.

Longastrino was captured on the first day, and this opened an overland route for a second brigade and some tanks. But the enemy fought hard for Filo on the 12th, when they withdrew to the gap in the floods between Bastia and Argenta. On the 13th the 24th Guards Brigade crossed the floods and attacked towards Bando and Argenta.

Meanwhile the other end of the 5th Corps pincers was also closing on the Argenta gap. The 78th Division had broken out of the Santerno bridgehead and on the 14th seized the bridge over the Reno at

Bastia before the enemy had succeeded in completely destroying it. They could not advance far into the gap, however, as the enemy held Bastia village with great determination.

By this time Vietinghoff had realized that no attack was coming against the coast north of the Po. He brought the 29th Panzer Grenadier Division back across the Po, under heavy air attack, and threw it into the corridor south of Argenta. He also withdrew from the salient south of Imola, and thus gave himself two divisions to play with; these however were quickly committed, one of them to replace the shattered 98th.

Eighth Army's westerly thrust continued. The Poles took Imola. The New Zealanders, who were now, with the 10th Indian Division, under command of the 13th Corps, reached and crossed the Sillaro. By the 14th, when the Fifth Army's assault began, the Eighth Army had reached the Sillaro on a broad front, from its confluence with the Reno near Bastia, almost to the Via Emilia.

The opening of the Fifth Army's attack was delayed by bad flying weather until the 14th. On the first morning the 4th Corps attacked, covered only by 500 aircraft of the tactical air force. The main air effort was kept for the following day when the 15th Air Force made its record effort of the war. Besides dropping 800 tons of bombs on communications in the rear areas in northern Italy, it dropped over 1,500 tons on targets just ahead of the Fifth Army's thrust.

At 10.30 p.m. on the 15th the 2nd Corps went in, on the right of the 4th, down the eastern side of the Reno. The enemy, in his strong mountain positions, resisted vigorously, but in vain. On the 17th and 18th, hammered on these two days by 2,700 tons of bombs, he was driven off the last three peaks barring the way to the plains, ten miles south of Bologna. Almost every building in the area of the Fifth Army's offensive was reduced to rubble or damaged by these devastating air attacks.

On the 18th General Truscott put in his reserve division, the 85th, at a point where the stubborn 334th German Division had been much reduced by casualties, and its neighbour to the west, the 94th, had practically collapsed. The enemy too put in their last reserve, part of the 90th Panzer Grenadier Division. This had already lost most of its armour in a tank versus tank battle, and could have but little effect.

On the morning of the 20th the United States 10th Mountain Division broke out of the mountains and in the afternoon crossed the Via Emilia. A little later the 85th and part of the South Africans were in Casalecchio, two miles south-west of Bologna. The Fifth

Army was now advancing through the plains, and the first and most difficult part of its task was accomplished.

On the Eighth Army's front the 5th Corps continued to attack northwards, and the 10th and 2nd Polish Corps westwards. Both met exceptionally stubborn resistance. In the Argenta gap a setpiece attack had to be staged by the 5th Corps, the 56th Division attacking from the east and the 78th from the south. The battle began late on the 16th, supported by a very heavy air attack. The Germans fought desperately, even when surrounded, and it was late on the 18th when the last prepared positions, north of the gap, fell to the 78th Division.

On the left of the army's front the New Zealanders and the Poles made good progress towards Bologna. The Poles were opposed by the 26th Panzer Grenadier Division and had some of the bitterest fighting they had experienced since Cassino. However, on the night of the 18th both the New Zealand Division and the Poles reached the Idice, the last river before Bologna.

As early as 14th April, before the Fifth Army attack began, Vietinghoff realized that his only hope of keeping his armies intact lay in an immediate withdrawal to the Po. His representations to Hitler's headquarters were turned down in the usual abrupt and menacing fashion. He received Jodl's answer on the 17th:

> "All further proposals for a change in the present war strategy will be discontinued. I wish to point out particularly that under no circumstances must troops or commanders be allowed to waver or to adopt a defeatist attitude, as a result of such ideas apparently held in your headquarters. Where any such danger is likely, the sharpest counter-measures must be employed. The Führer expects, now as before, the utmost steadfastness in the fulfilment of your present mission, to defend every inch of the North Italian areas entrusted to your command. I desire to point out the serious consequences for all those higher commanders, unit commanders or staff officers who do not carry out the Führer's orders to the last word."

By 20th April the situation was already hopeless, and nobody knew it better than Vietinghoff. The stubborn resistance of the German troops along the whole front had cost them so much that there was no longer the faintest hope of saving his armies. In his reply to Jodl he spoke of his unshakable will to hold the Italian front to the last, but said he had decided to abandon the policy of strategic defence and to adopt a mobile strategy. The same day he ordered a general withdrawal to the Po.

The situation in the German centre was now chaotic. The 1st Parachute Corps fell headlong into the net prepared in General Clark's original plan. It retreated in good order into the most northerly part of the Reno loop. Another division from south of Bologna retreated rapidly into the same area, and a fourth went back to the area north of Cento, between the Reno loop and the Panaro. Meanwhile the 6th British Armoured Division had advanced north-westwards from Argenta up the left bank of the Reno, and the 6th South African Division northwards from Casalecchio down the same bank of the Reno. They met at the appropriately named town of Finale on the 22nd. All four German divisions were thus surrounded and annihilated.

On 21st April the Poles entered Bologna from the east, two hours before the United States 34th Division from the south-west. Farther to the left the 10th United States Mountain Division covered forty-five miles in two days, and on the night of the 22nd reached the Po at San Benedetto. On this part of the front the enemy seemed to have disintegrated altogether and surrenders were wholesale.

On the morning of the 23rd the Eighth Army also reached the Po, when the 8th Indian Division, outflanking Ferrara to the west, arrived at Pontelagoscuro.

The count of prisoners so far was 35,000 and captured documents subsequently showed that the Germans reckoned their killed and wounded up to this date at 32,000. In the fortnight of fierce fighting every German formation had been severely battered, some had been wiped out, all had lost their heavy weapons and tanks, some abandoned on the river bank, some farther south, when they ran out of petrol. Of the men who arrived on the north bank of the Po, a number, who had had to swim, were without even their personal weapons. The battle was won. Beyond the river it would be a pursuit.

* * * *

The Eighth Army had made every possible arrangement to ensure that there should be no delay when the moment for the pursuit arrived. On the day the offensive opened, the 7th Hussars began to move from Lake Bracciano to a concentration area in the wooded country at Camerlona, north-west of Ravenna. This was familiar ground, and the mud of the previous Christmas was still fresh—and glutinous—in the memory.

A Squadron was at once placed under command of the 9th Armoured Brigade, in the 56th Division, but the rest of the regiment remained for a time under Eighth Army's direct command. This however did not mean that it had no connection with the 9th Armoured Brigade, which was still its parent formation and responsible for its welfare.

This versatile headquarters however had wider responsibilities than that. Although he had not commanded the troops operating round the Valli di Commacchio, Brigadier Cooke controlled the two fantail units, the 755th Tank Batallion (United States) and the "R.A.S.C. Fantail Regiment." He assisted in the planning, training, launching and water-borne maintenance of all these inland amphibious forces, with functions appropriate to a kind of "Senior Naval Officer, Inland Squadron." In this he was assisted by a naval staff officer, Commander Hudson, R.N. Brigadier Cooke was also responsible for advice and help in planning the various crossings of the Po on the Eighth Army front, a problem which he had examined in great detail ever since the previous autumn.

The concentration was complete by 14th April. The 7th Hussars then spent a busy week fitting Platypus Grousers to all the fifty-four tanks.

On the 20th the 9th Armoured Brigade, which now had the whole regiment under command, issued orders for the 7th Hussars, R.A.S.C. Fantail Regiment, 42nd Field Company and 1st Field Troop, Royal Engineers, and two sections of the 166th Light Field Ambulance, to move to a concentration area north of the Argenta gap. On the following afternoon the wheeled vehicles moved up through Argenta to Benvegnante, eight miles beyond, and the tanks came up by transporter the same night. The work of the transporters and their drivers was beyond praise. There were many delicate and vulnerable spots on a DD tank, including the screens and the propellers, but scarcely any damage was done.

The crossing of the Po was carried out on a wide frontage and the 7th Hussars played a leading part on the whole front of the Eighth Army. Lieutenant-Colonel Congreve and his regimental headquarters had the task of directing the technical side of the river crossing on one sector of the front. All the squadrons were allotted to divisions.

A Squadron, now commanded by Major M. V. Argyle, who had been adjutant for the past year, was placed under command of the 56th Division, B Squadron went to the 8th Indian Division and C to the 6th Armoured. One troop of C Squadron, first Lieutenant Burt's and then Lieutenant Rawlings', was detached and came under the 2nd New Zealand Division. Squadrons did not meet again until the pursuit was over, and in less than a week the regiment was to find itself spread round the head of the Adriatic, with its extremities 150 miles apart.

A Squadron was the first to move. At 7 a.m. on 23rd April, with a detachment of the 1st Field Troop, R.E., it started for Copparo. The march, although not more than twenty-five miles, took fourteen hours, as there were frequent hold-ups, and much congestion on the roads. Major Argyle had gone ahead to attend a conference at the 169th Infantry Brigade headquarters.

The 169th (Queens') Brigade was to cross the Po about two miles west of Crespino and establish a bridgehead on the north bank. The timing of the operation would depend on the progress of the 56th Division up to the river, and would probably be about twelve hours after the leading elements reached the south bank.

The 2/6th Queens were to make the assault, carried by Z Squadron of the R.A.S.C. Fantail Regiment and supported by A Squadron, 7th Hussars. The crossing was to be made on a frontage of one fantail troop, in the following order :—

> 1st Troop—two infantry companies, artillery forward observation officer, Royal Engineers with mats, and one officer of the 7th Hussars, with two other ranks and No. 48 radio-telephone set, to reconnoitre DD landing sites on the north bank.
>
> 2nd Troop—two infantry companies.
>
> 3rd Troop—battalion headquarters and battery commander.
>
> 4th and 5th Troops—Royal Engineers and stores.

A Squadron 7th Hussars was to take the water after the last fantail troop. The task of the squadron was to give maximum support to the 2nd/6th Queens.

The start line was to be the southern flood bank of the Po. On launching, each troop of fantails was to form up in the water in line abreast, with the wings set back. The leading troop, but no other, was to fire at the enemy bank with all guns that could bear, as the fantails came in to land. The infantry were to disembark at the northern flood bank and the fantails were then to clear the landing points to the east, re-launch, and land on the home bank about a mile down stream. They would then be available for ferrying the rest of the brigade. All routes, outward and homeward, were to be marked with lights and signs.

Preparation of the launching and landing sites on the home bank was the responsibility of the engineers of the 56th Division, but the 1st Field Troop, which had been through all the training of the fantails, was responsible for giving advice on the slopes. Four gaps in the flood bank and four landing slips in all were to be prepared.

The artillery were to co-operate by firing marker shell or Bofors tracer along the course of the assaulting craft from five minutes before H hour to H plus 15 minutes. From H plus 15 minutes onwards they were to fire tracer from south to north along the 33 easting grid line. Preparations were made to cover the crossing with smoke, but only if this should prove necessary.

The amphibious proceedings were to be under the general control of Colonel H. R. B. Foote, v.c., d.s.o., second-in-command of the 9th Armoured Brigade.

Throughout the 24th April an assorted collection of German battle groups held off the leading troops of the 56th Division, in an effort to gain time for the disorganized remnants in the Ferrara area to make their way across the Po. It was not until dawn on the 25th that the leading infantry reached the river. On arrival they judged that the north bank was only lightly held, and it was decided that the crossing should be made in daylight that same evening, at 7 p.m.

The day was spent in reconnaissance and, during the afternoon, work on the approaches and launching sites went ahead with great speed. At 3.30 the Squadron left its concentration area and moved up to the flood bank at the northern edge of the village of Alberone, a few hundred yards from the river. Owing to the congestion on the narrow road this march of only six miles took two and a half hours. There was consequently only time for a very hurried meal before H hour. Then the squadron, in line ahead under the bank, erected the screens, and all was ready.

Precisely at 7 p.m. the leading wave of fantails crossed the start line and the operation was launched. All went well and there was no opposition. Within a few minutes Lieutenant S. Ingram, who had crossed with two other ranks in the leading wave, reported by wireless that the selected landing site was satisfactory.

The squadron moved through the flood bank in line ahead and into the river at the most western of the four launching sites. The river was swift, and it was therefore important to enter it well upstream of the landing place on the opposite bank.

Sergeant Johnson's tank was in the lead, and when this was safely across the troops followed in quick succession, Lieutenant Agnew's, Captain Barton's, Lieutenant Argue's and Lieutenant Iles'. Two tanks stuck in the mud, but rejoined their troops within thirty minutes. There was only one serious casualty; Lieutenant Argue's tank struck an underwater obstruction and sank like a stone. All the crew reached the shore safely, except one man who could not swim. He owed his life to the quickness and presence of mind of Colonel Foote. Seeing a body drifting downstream, Foote launched a rubber dinghy, rowed out, and pulled the man ashore. He was unconscious, but recovered with artificial respiration.

The 2nd/6th Queens lost no time, and two companies were quickly on the move northwards from both flanks of the bridgehead, D on the right, with 2nd and 4th Troops of A Squadron, A on the left, with 1st and 3rd Troops. Squadron headquarters were with battalion headquarters, in farm buildings half a mile north of the crossing place. There was very little opposition on either flank, and a steady trickle of prisoners kept coming in all night.

By dawn the left column was in Pontecchio. With 1st and 3rd Troops in the lead, the advance continued. The bridge over the Tartaro, a mile north of Pontecchio, was captured intact and by 8 a.m. Route 16 was reached, at a point two miles south of Rovigo. Here the 2nd/5th Queens, brought forward in lorries, took over the advance from the 2nd/6th.

There was some delay while A Company of the 2nd/5th mounted the tanks and netted their wireless sets. At 11 o'clock they advanced, with 3rd Troop in support, to seize the bridge over the Adige at Anguillara.

A similar relief had taken place on the right, and C Company of the 2nd/5th Queens had already passed round to the east and north of Rovigo, directed on the area of the bridge over the Adige at Boara, on Route 16; the bridge itself was known to have been destroyed. This column failed to reach its objective, mainly because of the large numbers of Germans to the north-west of Rovigo. Most of these wished to surrender, but not all, and the mopping up took a long time.

A Company, which had now become the right hand column of the 2nd/5th Queens, were just approaching Mardimago, the village half way between Rovigo and Anguillara, when they ran into a well organized rearguard position. This was held by some 200 Turcomans, supported by four 75-millimetre horse drawn anti-tank guns. A Company and the tanks attacked this position immediately. Three of the guns were captured and the fourth was knocked out by Captain B. P. Barton's tank at close range.

The Commanding Officer of the 2nd/5th Queens had meanwhile arranged for fighter-bomber support, and the forward troops were withdrawn 300 yards for safety. Unfortunately however the fighter-bomber attack was cancelled owing to a more urgent need elsewhere, so there was a little delay before the battle was renewed. There was then only slight resistance, mostly from mortars, and at last light the leading infantry were at the edge of Mardimago village. The two troops had had a good deal of shooting and a number of prisoners were taken.

During the night a few Churchills of the 48th Royal Tanks arrived at Rovigo and took over from 2nd and 4th Troops in that sector. A Squadron was concentrated in a disused and battered warehouse in Rovigo and spent the last few hours of the night in great discomfort and pouring rain, which the warehouse roof made no pretence of keeping out.

The first thing to be done on the morning of the 27th was to check the screens of the Shermans, as it was expected that the Adige would have to be crossed during the day. Only five of the tanks were found to be fit for swimming, but it was hoped that three more could be repaired within twenty-four hours. In conditions of pursuit, perfection is out of place and the squadron's resources were considered adequate for the crossing of the Adige.

This was to be carried out by the 2nd/7th Queens. Planning was naturally more sketchy than for the crossing of the Po; there were no air photographs, the fantails were not expected to arrive until the evening, there were few sappers available and only one battery of 25-pounders had so far been ferried across the Po.

During the morning Major Argyle made a reconnaissance of the river and found a suitable crossing place for DD Shermans at Pioppe, about two miles north-east of the bridge on Route 16. A little engineer work was needed on the approaches and the river bank. A platoon of the 2nd/7th Queens was therefore sent across to hold a small bridgehead and Lieutenant Iles, with the attached sappers and a few men of A Squadron, prepared launching sites. There was a little sniping, and an officer who had come up from the 2nd/7th Queens was killed while standing next to Iles, but the work was finished by 7 p.m.

The launching sites for the fantails required a little longer, but by 10.30 p.m. all was ready for the crossing. The plan was for the 2nd/7th Queens to cross in fantails, supported by 2nd and 4th Troops of A Squadron with the five fit Shermans. They were then to swing left, to where Route 16 crosses the river, and clear up any pockets of enemy round the broken bridge. The 2nd/5th were then to cross near the bridge and take up the pursuit, supported by the same two troops. The column was to avoid pitched battles, to skirt round defended localities, tending always towards the Adriatic coast and Venice; it was not to stop for prisoners.

As fire support for the crossing was very limited, 3rd Troop collected all the smoke in the squadron and covered the flanks of the 2nd/7th

Queens with a smoke screen as they went over. At 11 p.m. the five Shermans swam the Adige without mishap and accompanied the battalion to its objective. All other tanks which could not immediately be repaired were placed in position about a mile south-east of Boara bridge, so as to provide fire support for the advance moving up Route 16 if required.

All operations went according to plan. During the morning of the 28th three more Shermans and two DD Valentines swam the Adige and advanced to Monselice, where they discovered that the main body was already well ahead on a parallel route farther to the eastward. As there was no prospect, for the time, of getting more tanks across the Adige, the crews of 1st and 3rd Troops, which were fairly fresh, were sent up to take over the tanks of 2nd and 4th.

At nightfall the battalion headquarters of the 2nd/5th Queens were at Conselve, but the leading companies were many miles ahead and off all their maps. The six Shermans with them were short of diesel fuel, and two Valentines, sent up with fuel, were immediately sent back for more.

At 9 p.m. Major Argyle also arrived, with more fuel. The leading company was now held up at the bridge over the canal near Brenta village, only three miles from the south-west corner of the great Venice Lagoon. Partisans reported that the area of the bridge was held by the Germans in strength, some said three and some eight hundred. Most of them wished to surrender and negotiations were in progress. The company commander, however, was not to be delayed for negotiations. A company attack was launched at 11.15 p.m.; it met with only weak resistance, and succeeded in crossing the canal.

Nobody quite knew where they were, but the company commander felt certain that he was not yet across the Brenta River. He therefore ordered an early start the following morning, hoping to get over before first light.

At 3 a.m. on the 29th the advance was resumed. At 9 o'clock Argyle came up to the leading troops, which had reached Pontelongo, with two tanks carrying half of A company of the 2nd/5th Queens. The screens of the DD Shermans, when in the lowered position, greatly increased the carrying capacity of the tanks, and each one could take a complete platoon.

There was a check at Dolo, which was held by 200 Turcomans with small arms, spandaus and bazookas. The partisans had several casualties and the Queens, as they cleared up the resistance, lost two carriers. One of the tanks had a narrow escape as a bazooka exploded on the ground just beside it.

THE BATTLE OF THE PO PLAINS

The bridge over the canal in Dolo was found intact and a number of prisoners were captured in the village. The column resumed the advance, turned right along the main road, and swept on for Venice. The pace however was not fast enough, and the leading troops of the New Zealand Division caught up, from Padua. An argument ensued about which force should lead, and went on for nearly half an hour. The New Zealanders were heading for Trieste, and they had two strong cards to play. First, they had maps, and secondly they had wireless contact with higher formations. So they were allowed the position of honour.

During the argument two Valentines came up with 400 gallons of diesel fuel. After replenishing, the tanks and the Queens followed the New Zealanders. At Mestre the New Zealanders kept straight ahead, and the Queens column turned off down the causeway into Venice. The Commanding Officer of the Queens received the surrender of the port and A Squadron moved into leaguer in the docks area.

An hour later B Squadron arrived, also the remaining tanks of A Squadron and the rest of the 2nd/5th Queens.

*   *   *   *

B Squadron's experiences had been very similar to those of A. At 1 p.m. on 25th April the Squadron, under the 8th Indian Division, moved to an assembly area about three miles north-west of Ferrara. Here it was equidistant from the two possible crossing places over the Po, the right one just above the bridge on Route 16 and the left just above Occhiobello. Camouflage was taken off the screens and it was expected that the river would be crossed the same evening, at the lower of the two selected places.

The plan for the crossing of the 8th Indian Division was similar to that of the 56th, and the amphibious side was controlled by Lieutenant-Colonel J. Congreve. The Royal Fusiliers began crossing at 9 p.m., but were soon stopped, as the river bank collapsed. A few more flights of fantails managed to get over, but the bank was now quite unsuitable for Shermans. Major Wall was sent at once to the western site near Occhiobello, and B Squadron followed. Under Wall's direction, launching sites and approaches were prepared and after some hours of strenuous manual labour were ready by about 3.30 on the morning of the 26th.

At that hour B Squadron moved forward from its assembly area to the river bank and began to cross. The landing point was nearly half a mile downstream, on a good firm sandbank. Just as it was getting light Lieutenant J. H. Harding's troop entered the water, followed closely by the remainder, and all seventeen tanks landed safely on the other side. Three troops went forward at once to join the forward companies of the Royal Fusiliers, who were moving north-eastwards. All three troops patrolled north-eastwards towards the crossings of the Tartaro or Canale Bianco. This is the river which flows between the Po and the Adige, connected by many minor watercourses with the former and less frequently with the latter; one of its more tiresome habits was changing its name at intervals as it got nearer the sea. None of the troops made contact with the enemy and all except one concentrated at Fiesso for the night.

Early in the morning the squadron moved forward again and crossed the Canale Bianco. Screens had to be raised, although there was not enough water to float the tanks and they trod their way over on the bottom. Two fantails made a dump of diesel fuel on the far bank, and each tank went forward with seventy-five gallons on its back.

The first opposition was encountered at Roverdicre, two miles west of Rovigo. The 5th Gurkhas attacked, with a company moving on each side of the by-road which runs northwards to the left of the Ferrara—Rovigo railway. 1st and 2nd Troops supported the attack, one on each side of the road. The opposition melted away, and the two troops then had a shoot against enemy moving on the Rovigo-Lendinara road, and advanced with the Gurkhas nearly to the Adige. The squadron leaguered in Roverdicre.

B Squadron crossed the Adige on the 28th. One tank failed to land owing to clutch trouble, but was pulled out and caught up later. The Squadron had now crossed all three rivers and had encountered almost no opposition. The 29th was simply a gallop for Venice. At 5.30 a.m. a company of Mahrattas mounted the tanks and all seventeen set off along Route 16.

At Battaglia the squadron ran into the advanced column of the New Zealand Division. This caused some delay as, although the road was a wide one, the tanks were wide too, and there were signs of a competitive spirit abroad now that the winning post was in sight. However, Major Murray Smith took a lot of stopping, and the tanks sped on through Padua. Some of the New Zealanders had been through just before, but the welcome was none the less enthusiastic. The route to Venice lay along the Autostrade, and the tanks made the most of the good going. The Mahrattas, a race with a magnificent martial background, were as keen as anyone to be first in Venice, but A Squadron and the Queens had won by an hour. B Squadron however had one consolation; they spent the night in the Piazzale

Fantails taking the 56th Division across the Po on 26th April. A Squadron crossed here.

A 7th Hussars DD Sherman tank crossing the Adige on 29th April.

Roma instead of the docks; the amenities were about equal, but it sounded better.

*   *   *   *

The 6th Armoured Division had closed up to the Po a little earlier than the divisions on its right, and Major Marcus Fox, squadron leader of C, had reconnoitred the bank very carefully. On the 24th, while the squadron moved forward to a position of assembly south-west of Ferrara, he attended a conference at the headquarters of the 24th Guards Brigade and learned that he was to operate with the 3rd Grenadier Guards.

At this conference he met General Freyberg, commander of the 2nd New Zealand Division, who asked for the loan of one troop of DD Shermans to cross with his division, to the left of the 6th Armoured. Lieutenant M. C. Burt's troop was accordingly detached for this purpose.

The two divisions were to cross at the same hour, 1 a.m. on the 25th, some twenty-four hours earlier than had been expected.

It was a rush, and the squadron had a long and difficult march in the dark to the assembly area at Porporana. It arrived there at about 10 o'clock and half an hour later was ready to take the water. This was no small achievement on the part of the squadron leader.

The Grenadiers' plan was to seize a shallow bridgehead, and throw out their No. 3 Company forward and to the right, to protect the bridgehead during the night from the direction where the enemy might be. 1st Troop of C Squadron (Lieutenant Young) was to support this company, and the rest of the squadron was to harbour a few hundred yards north of the landing point.

The plan for the crossing was very similar to that of A Squadron, already described. Lieutenant J. J. Gledsdale crossed in the leading fantail at about 12.45 a.m., to mark the landing place with lights; the tanks crossed immediately after the first three companies of Grenadiers, Lieutenant Young in the lead. A few Verey lights were seen beyond the river, but probably a good way off, and there was no opposition. As the river at this point was only nine feet deep, the tanks were never water-borne. All landed safely and, after some difficulty in finding a way over the flood bank, reached the concentration area.

At dawn Lieutenant Young's troop came under command of the Welch Guards. In the afternoon it was ordered up to Runci, four miles north of the Po, and here the Commanding Officer of the Welch Guards came to meet it. He led it in his jeep to the bridge over the Tartaro at Castel, to see if this was intact. The bridge was intact, but not for long; it was blown as the leading tank was just about to cross it. The demolition party was promptly wiped out and the rest of the squadron moved a few miles forward, but there was no further action that day.

Meanwhile, to the left, Lieutenant Burt had trouble at the New Zealand crossing. One of his tanks was sunk and two were badly stuck on a sandbank in the river. On the 26th Lieutenant Rawlings was sent with his troop to the New Zealanders, who had by this time occupied Badia, on the Adige. He remained with them to the end of the campaign, and did not see his squadron again for ten days.

The rest of the squadron, with the 2nd Rifle Brigade, was formed into a column called Nick Force. This column advanced at 6 p.m. on the 26th and two hours later the leading troops were only a mile from the Adige, east of Badia. The force then began clearing the area south of the Adige to the east, where a number of enemy were still holding out. One company was sent to capture Saguedo; it met with fairly strong resistance which was not overcome until the following morning. Cavazzona also had to be attacked and when the infantry got into difficulties Lieutenant Skrine's troop was sent in and, with infantry help, captured the village. In the evening C Squadron concentrated south of the Adige, about two miles north-west of Lendinara.

Next morning Lieutenant Burt, who had returned from the New Zealand Division, had another stroke of bad luck. As he crossed the Adige in support of a company of the Rifle Brigade, one of his tanks cast a track and the other two stuck in the mud ten yards from the far bank. The crossing place had looked perfectly satisfactory, but Burt's luck was clearly out.

Except for Rawlings' troop, this was the limit of C Squadron's advance until the campaign was over.

The other squadrons of the 7th Hussars went farther, but C could at least claim to have been the first across the Po and, with one troop, first over the Adige as well. That they stopped at the Adige was not due to any lack of enterprise on the part of either C Squadron or the 6th Armoured Division. The advanced elements of three infantry divisions were already riding a finish—and rather a foul one at that—along a single road and the 6th Armoured was held sternly in check.

Meanwhile Lieutenant Rawlings, with 4th Troop of C Squadron, was well up in front. At 2 p.m. on 26th April he was informed that he would cross the Adige that night with the New Zealanders. He had only two tanks fit, and one from 1st Troop was given him as a third. For the crossing he was placed under the 20th New Zealand Armoured Regiment, at Badia. He himself went over in a boat after dark, with a few engineers, to find a suitable landing place, and the troop crossed at 4 a.m. One tank had mechanical trouble, but rejoined during the morning.

Early in the afternoon a detachment was formed, consisting of two tanks of Rawlings' troop with five New Zealand jeeps, to reconnoitre the route for the division over the many water courses. Sergeant Edwards, in the leading tank, found that the bridge over the Dugale, about three miles north of Badia, was mined. He cleared the mines and a mile farther ahead came under machine-gun fire. This soon stopped and a party of Germans surrendered. However, there was stronger opposition ahead. A troop of 12th Lancers had now joined the party, which split, in order to encircle the enemy pocket. As he closed in on the enemy, Sergeant Edwards' tank cast a track in a very narrow lane. The tank was under small arms fire, but was taken in tow by the other tank and pulled out. It was now beginning to get dark and Edwards was ordered back to the Adige, just north of Badia.

On the morning of the 28th a column was formed, to lead the advance of the New Zealand Division. It consisted of an infantry battalion, two troops of the 20th New Zealand Armoured Regiment and Rawlings' troop. At 10 o'clock it moved off north-eastwards, through Este and Monselice and along Route 16 for Padua. Four miles short of the city a check was caused by German snipers. These were well concealed and caused casualties to the infantry. However, they melted away and at 6 p.m. the advance was resumed.

Padua was entered at 11 p.m. It had been liberated by partisans, but there was still shooting going on in the streets. This continued the following morning, and the New Zealanders had a few street skirmishes before passing through on the Venice road. The route from the bridge over the Brenta on to the Venice autostrade was reconnoitred by Rawlings, and the pursuit continued. One tank had to be left behind with clutch trouble, but the column reached Musile, twenty miles north-east of Mestre, along Route 14.

The 30th was spent in rounding up Germans in the Musile area, each of the armoured troops co-operating with a company of infantry.

At 5 a.m. on 1st May the column set forth again, forded the Piave seven miles south-east of Musile, made its way back on to Route 14 and drove straight for Trieste.

Rawlings' own engine now gave trouble, and it must have been something of a strain for him to resist the urge to mount his one remaining tank. However, he let the other go on, commanded by Sergeant Edwards.

Edwards entered Trieste with the New Zealand column on the same night, having covered ninety-seven miles in one day. From the opposite side, across the Istrian Peninsula, arrived a patrol of the Long Range Desert Group. Thus there came together at the head of the Adriatic, detachments of several units which had all seen their first active service in the early Middle East campaigns. Since then their diverse courses had taken them to Greece, Burma, the middle of the Sahara, Tripolitania, Tunisia, Iraq, Syria, Palestine, Albania and Jugoslavia. Now they met again, in the van of the pursuit, just as the German Reich crumbled in ruins about its creator.

*　　　*　　　*　　　*

At the end of the pursuit eighteen of the fifty-seven tanks were still fit for swimming. All the rest except one, which was at the bottom of the Po, were recoverable, and most of them needed only repairs to the canvas. There had been no casualties to officers or men of the 7th Hussars, except to A Squadron's non-swimmer, who soon recovered. In this the regiment was very fortunate, as there had been several brisk brushes with pockets of Germans.

The Italians in all the towns and villages greeted the tanks with enthusiasm and much clapping of hands as they rolled past. The Italian Committee of National Liberation had proclaimed an uprising on 25th April. This in some measure cleared the way for the pursuit on the fronts of both armies, as there were several attacks by partisans on German installations and isolated groups in the rear areas. By the time the leading troops of the two armies reached Vicenza and Verona these cities were already under partisan control.

On the 29th regimental headquarters, which had been kept informed of the progress of operations by a special wireless link with each squadron, moved up to Monselice. There was much rejoicing in the town and in the house opposite the headquarters billet the local partisans beat up a so-called Fascist and then came to ask Lieutenant-Colonel Congreve if he would care to deal with him. The Commanding Officer declined to intervene and later it was understood that he had been shot.

On the 30th the headquarters moved twenty miles eastwards to an area about six miles from the mouth of the Brenta. A and B Squadrons moved out of Venice into Mestre, where they were later joined by regimental headquarters. Although the capitulation had been signed, hostilities did not end until 2nd May. However, there was no more fighting, and the only Germans seen were bewildered wanderers seeking to surrender.

By 8th May Rawlings had rejoined from Trieste and the rest of C Squadron from the Adige, and the whole regiment was concentrated at Mestre.

*   *   *   *

Map XXI
ARGENTA TO VENICE

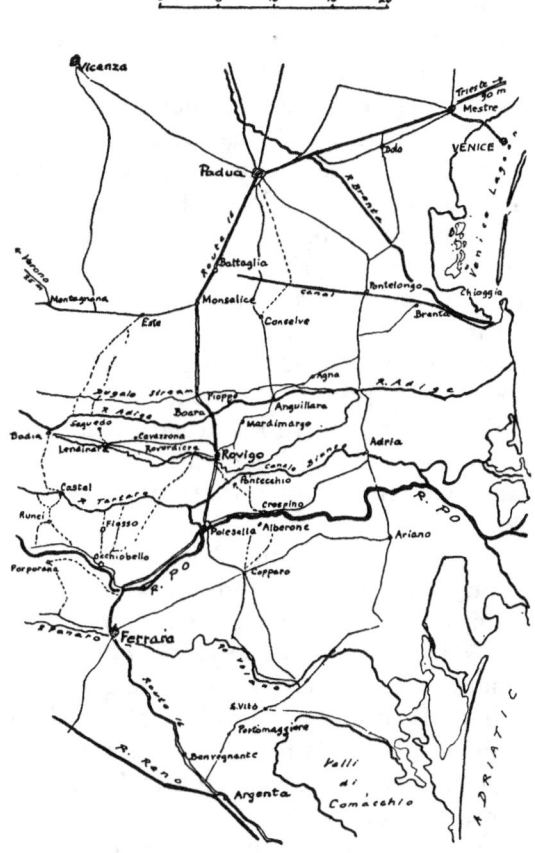

From the date of its first conception, the campaign in Italy was subordinate and preparatory to the great invasion from the west. It is in this light that its results must be measured and not in terms of time or space.

The Salerno landings preceded those in Normandy by nine months. From its very beginning the campaign in Italy was a constant drain on German resources which might have turned the scale elsewhere. This was General Alexander's task, and the supreme directors of allied strategy took care to see that he was never given more troops than were barely necessary for its fulfilment.

At the crucial moment, when the Normandy landings were about to take place, there were twenty-five Germans divisions in Italy, nineteen in the Balkans and eleven in the south of France. All those in Italy and a proportion of those in the Balkans and the south of France were being contained by the allied threat, actual or potential, in the Mediterranean, and mainly by the armies in Italy.

Only once, just before the invasion of France, did the allied formations exceed in number those of the German. Such good use was made of this temporary superiority that the enemy brought down eight more divisions from other theatres. In casualties, too, the drain was greater upon the Germans. In the twenty months of fighting, according to the Germans' own figures, they lost 536,000 men; this does not include those who surrendered after the capitulation. In the corresponding period the Allies lost 312,000.

The Allied Armies in Italy never had the thrill of a victorious advance into the heart of Germany. From start to finish they struggled against a stubborn and fanatical foe, who had to be driven from one mountain range to another, from one river to the next, and whose resistance never seemed to weaken. They were rewarded in the end, however, as their final victory was beyond anything which had been required or expected of them and, which is most important of all, they fulfilled their appointed task.

The last and greatest battle, the Battle of the Po Plains, was brilliant both in conception and execution, and ended in the classic defeat and destruction of the main German forces in Italy. Whether or not this was the Eighth Army's greatest, it was certainly not its most vaunted victory, and the honours were shared with its neighbour on the left. But it undoubtedly had the quality of finality, of which one element at least had been lacking at El Alamein. This time all the elements were there. First, the Germans were beaten in battle; then a great part of their best fighting troops were surrounded and annihilated on the field, and lastly the victory was completed by a bold and relentless pursuit.

The formal and triumphant conclusion of the campaign was the signing of the instrument of surrender in Caserta Palace. This was the first of the series of German capitulations, and took place just as the leading tanks of the 7th Hussars were racing down the Venice causeway.

* * * *

On 28th April the bodies of Mussolini, his once beautiful mistress, and two of his associates, were exposed to the public gaze in a square in Milan. The Duce had been recognized as he sought to escape to Austria; all the party had been seized, and were to be taken for trial. One partisan however took no chances. He led out Mussolini and his mistress and executed them himself, the lady first, as she tried to shield Mussolini. The partisan, however, was shot too, by his friends, for cheating the Italian people of a more spectacular finale for their dictator.

Thus died the Italian dictator, a few days only before his German counterpart. The latter however married his mistress, before shooting her and himself in his Berlin underground headquarters. This was on 30th April, when Russian tanks had already entered the city. Their bodies are believed to have been burned in the garden of the Chancellery, and no trace was ever found.

The deaths of the leaders were no more than a symbol of the downfall of their dictatorships. The real victory was to be measured rather by the extent to which the people who had chosen—or tolerated—them, realized that the way of the aggressor does not pay. Their armed might had been destroyed in battle and they were for the time being at the mercy of those whom they had sought to enslave.

Even in this moment of triumph however there were the seeds of misery. There were many countries and many exiled peoples for whom the war was no more than half won. Troops of the British Commonwealth, Nepal, the United States, France, the Netherlands, Belgium, Brazil, Norway and Denmark, could return home. But there were others who could not, prominent among them being the staunch friends of the 7th Hussars, the 2nd Polish Corps.

Most of the men of this splendid formation had been captured in 1939 by the Russians, during their invasion of Poland from the east, when the Polish Army was in the last agonies of its struggle against the Germans. When they had spent more than two years in the slave camps and prisons of the Soviet Union, the personal intervention of Churchill with Stalin had procured the release of a quarter of a million souls, men, women and children, who were then herded across the central Asian wastes and the Caspian Sea into Persia.

These were barely one-sixth of the total number of Poles who had been made prisoners or deported from the eastern regions of Poland by the Russians. Of the rest, no more was heard. It was General Anders who, on his release from the Lubljanka Prison, organized and led the exodus, and then raised the 2nd Polish Corps from the veterans, young men and women who came out with him. He was naturally revered and loved by every man, woman and child in the vast throng; they regarded him in the same light as the children of Israel had regarded Moses, though perhaps with more gratitude. He was leading them to a promised land—their own.

The war was in its last few months however when all their illusions were shattered. At the Yalta Conference the eastern quarter of Poland was signed away to Russia, and this included the homes of a great number of Anders' quarter million. To these it was little consolation that the new Poland should acquire German territories in the north and west, and still less when they learned later that the new Poland would be in the hands of mere puppets of the all-powerful Soviet Union. There were of course many who felt able to face the new conditions and were persuaded to return. Others knew too well that the new Poland had nothing to offer them except death, or a renewed exile to Siberia.

It seems strangely tragic that this fine and virile race, who had done more than any other to save Christian Europe from the ravages first of Genghiz Khan and then of the Turks, who had later suffered successive partitions at the hands of Prussia, Russia and on one occasion Austria too, and who had fought staunchly and loyally against Hitler since 1939, should again be sacrificed on the altar of political expediency. In 1939 Great Britain and France had gone to war in defence of Poland against German aggression. When the German problem was almost settled, however, Russia was able to draw the iron curtain across Europe, with Poland on the wrong side. Once more, for the Poles, the torch of freedom was extinguished.

It was not only the Poles who were exiled from their native country. Scattered over the Continent were hundreds of thousands of displaced persons of many races, some who had been deported for slave labour by the Germans, others who had fled before what they conceived to be the greater menace from the east, and whose countries were now under Soviet occupation. These too became a charge upon the victorious United Nations, whose political problems in peace were to prove no less difficult than their military problems in war, and caused infinitely greater acrimony among them in discussion.

* * * *

In October 1946, after a period of occupation in north-eastern Italy, on the fringe of the iron curtain, where the problems of post-war Europe were manifested to the full, the 7th Hussars crossed the Alps and passed through Austria into Germany. As they left Italy, the friendly vine and olive growing countryside seemed to smile its farewell in sunshine.

For the 7th Hussars there was no dramatic homecoming, to a county

B Squadron carrying infantry of the 8th Indian Division in the pursuit.

B Squadron in the Piazzale Roma at Venice.

town, with flags flying and drums beating. There were officers and men from nearly every county of the British Isles, and each, as his turn came for release, melted quietly into his job and his family life. Some had tales to tell, others kept their memories to themselves, memories of success, disappointment, laughter, and a task well done. The unpleasant and sordid experiences of war were gradually dimmed by time, but the sharing of common hardships and dangers, and a great common achievement, left with each man a sense of comradeship which neither time nor distance can destroy.

Roll of Honour

of the

7th QUEEN'S OWN HUSSARS

1939-1945

Lieutenant-Colonel
F. W. BYASS, D.S.O., M.C.

Majors

G. D. HILL
W. T. KEVILL-DAVIES, M.C.

T. R. S. THORNTON, M.C.
THE HONOURABLE S. N. ASTLEY

Captains

P. PITMAN-BUTLER
R. C. WATSON

J. M. NAPIER, M.C.
R. NICKELS

Lieutenants

E. GLENDINNING, M.M.
H. R. D. PEGLER, D.C.M., M.M.
J. B. DUNLOP
R. S. DALE HARRIS

J. C. R. TYPE
A. A. SMITH
J. L. C. WILLIAMS
J. J. H. BROWNE

W. E. F. WINNEY

2nd-Lieutenant
W. JACKSON-STOPS

Warrant Officer
L. E. SWAIN, M.M.

Sergeants

P. H. ANDREWS
H. BOWDEN
J. CAMPBELL
C. E. CHADWICK
J. T. D. CORNWELL
D. COWELL
A. V. COWLEY, M.M.
R. HIPSEY

J. J. KILTY
W. H. LOVETT
P. McGUINNESS
M. MURPHY
J. W. SCOTT
L. STANIFORTH
T. J. THOMPSON
A. G. WALFORD

A. D. J. BOUGHEN

Corporals

W. E. Dalton	L. Muxworthy
W. A. Dougan	S. Rankin
W. S. Fabry	J. Stowell
C. Inston	J. T. Tillyer
J. McLelland	J. Weaver

Lance-Corporals

J. T. Bedson	P. W. Kenton
E. F. Cleere	S. Lee
G. Delace	W. Lewis
C. R. P. Gregg	F. J. Warren
	H. G. Smith

Troopers

E. Ashbridge	C. Hawkins
H. Atack	A. M. Hiller
D. Barker	J. R. Hobbs
F. G. Barlow	K. Holden
R. Barratt	J. Hollobon
J. Beardshaw	E. L. Holloway
G. F. Bennett	J. H. W. Howard
R. St. J. Bingham	H. N. Hunter
H. Brader	D. H. Ingle
R. A. Campbell	R. Jackson
L. R. Carvell	C. R. Jones
R. J. Casson	R. E. Jones
A. P. Clarke	P. M. Joy
S. Cook	J. J. Kay
E. Cooney	W. C. Kibble
T. Copley	J. Kilner
D. J. Crone	A. Lobban
E. Davenport	F. W. Marsh
G. H. Deans	C. T. P. Mathew
A. H. Deighton	G. H. Matthews
J. A. Dodge	J. McCowen
L. W. T. Eddis	G. D. McGregor
H. Field	E. Meddowes
R. P. M. G. Freyne	E. D. Merriman
J. E. A. Gillespie	R. N. Payne
K. S. Glenn	S. Plumb
L. Graham	T. H. Poole
J. Gratty	F. W. G. Povey
G. W. Gray	L. Read
J. Harris	W. J. Redwood
J. Harrison	C. J. Reep
F. Harrison	C. Rhodes

F. S. ROBERTS
W. W. ROBERTS
G. L. ROBSON
S. J. ROCHE
W. H. ROWLEY
C. L. RUSHBROOKE
V. SHAW
H. SHIRT
W. E. SIMMONS
H. SKINNER
G. D. SLATER
E. W. J. SNEED

E. SMITH
T. W. SMITH
P. W. J. SPACKMAN
J. A. STEELE
S. R. STEWART
D. L. WALLINGTON
B. G. WATERSON
L. A. WAY
V. N. WEAVING
L. WEBB
C. S. WILKINSON
W. E. WORNER

F. H. WRIGHT

Honours and Awards 1937-45

Knight Commander of the Order of the British Empire
Major-General B. O. HUTCHISON　　Major-General M.O'M. CREAGH

Companion of the Order of the Bath
Major-General B. O. HUTCHISON　　Major-General R. K. HEWER

Commander of the Order of the British Empire
Brigadier B. O. HUTCHISON　　Colonel R. K. HEWER

Distinguished Service Order
Lieutenant-Colonel F. W. BYASS
Major R. B. SHEPPARD
Major R. F. G. JAYNE (with bar)
Major J. CONGREVE
Lieutenant-Colonel R. YOUNGER
The Reverend N. S. METCALFE (Royal Army Chaplains Department)

Officer of the Order of the British Empire
Colonel G. FIELDEN
Lieutenant-Colonel R. B. SHEPPARD
Lieutenant-Colonel J. CONGREVE
Lieutenant-Colonel N. L. L. PALMER
Lieutenant-Colonel R. C. JONES

Member of the Order of the British Empire
Major C. G. DAVIES-GILBERT
Lieutenant S. A. BLAKE
Lieutenant G. F. DUNSCOMBE
Squadron Sergeant-Major R. H. BUTLER

Military Cross
Lieutenant D. C. G. SEYMOUR-EVANS (with bar)
2nd-Lieutenant R. D. G. OATES
Lieutenant W. T. KEVILL-DAVIES
Lieutenant G. W. MURRAY SMITH (with two bars)
Lieutenant J. M. NAPIER
Lieutenant C. T. LLEWELLEN PALMER (with bar)
Major R. YOUNGER
Lieutenant T. R. S. THORNTON
Major N. M. H. WALL
Lieutenant M. FOX
Lieutenant M. J. E. PATTESON
Lieutenant M. M. STANLEY EVANS
Lieutenant G. S. B. PALMER
Lieutenant J. E. PARRY
Major M. V. ARGYLE
Captain E. C. F. HARDING
Captain B. P. BARTON
Captain J. S. H. SKRINE

HONOURS AND AWARDS

Distinguished Conduct Medal

Trooper J. R. Barlow
Corporal H. R. D. Pegler
Squadron Sergeant-Major W. C. Marshall
Corporal S. Browning
Sergeant P. Cleere
Trooper N. Hemstock

Military Medal

Corporal H. R. D. Pegler
Sergeant A. V. Cowley (with bar)
Troop Sergeant-Major H. G. Hatherall
Sergeant E. Glendinning
Squadron Sergeant-Major L. E. Swain
Sergeant A. E. Widdowson
Lance-Sergeant A. Spreadbury (Royal Signals)
Trooper J. Bell
Sergeant F. D. J. Austin
Sergeant F. W. Harding
Trooper T. Glenn
Sergeant S. Roberts
Corporal D. R. R. Collins
Trooper W. Brennan
Sergeant C. Campbell
Sergeant N. S. Davies
Trooper A. Campbell
Trooper W. A. Crewes
Sergeant D. J. Williams
Trooper H. M. Brown
Squadron Sergeant-Major M. J. O'Connor
Corporal J. Holmes

British Empire Medal

Sergeant I. S. Hyde

Mentioned in Despatches

Lieutenant-General Sir Balfour O. Hutchison (five times)
Major-General R. K. Hewer (four times)
Major-General Sir Michael O'M. Creagh (twice)
Colonel G. Fielden
Colonel R. B. Sheppard (twice)
Lieutenant-Colonel F. W. Byass
Lieutenant-Colonel F. R. C. Fosdick (twice)
Lieutenant-Colonel R. F. G. Jayne (twice)
Lieutenant-Colonel J. Congreve (three times)
Lieutenant-Colonel N. M. H. Wall (twice)
Lieutenant-Colonel R. C. Jones (twice)
Major G. D. Hill
Major W. T. Kevill-Davies
Major J. F. Astley-Rushton (twice)
Major G. G. Hill
Major G. Price
Major R. N. Dayer-Smith
Major J. P. McDonagh
Captain P. Pitman-Butler
Captain F. N. St. J. Fairhurst
Captain V. L. John
Captain G. S. B. Palmer
Captain W. Chowns
Captain M. M. Stanley Evans
Captain P. B. Stanley Evans
Captain C. G. Dean
Captain D. M. Allen
Captain H. P. M. Calder (twice) (Royal Electrical and Mechanical Engineers)
Captain P. J. Howard-Dobson
Captain J. A. Nasmyth
Captain F. H. P. G. Barker
Captain R. W. Herbert
Captain R. B. Higham
Lieutenant W. E. F. Winney
Lieutenant G. J. Iles
Lieutenant W. Huckin
Lieutenant The Hon. S. N. Astley

Lieutenant A. E. Weatherall
The Reverend N. S. Metcalfe (twice)
 (Royal Army Chaplains Department)
Lieutenant P. W. Brown
Lieutenant W. J. Lockwood
Squadron Sergeant-Major G. E. Ellis
Squadron Sergeant-Major J. W.
 Mathews
Squadron Sergeant-Major M. J.
 O'Connor
Mechanist Quartermaster-Sergeant
 W. F. Webb
Mechanist Quartermaster-Sergeant R. F.
 Smith
Squadron Quartermaster-Sergeant B.
 Welburn
Squadron Quartermaster-Sergeant R.
 Hill
Sergeant H. Cartwright
Sergeant J. G. Connelly
Sergeant E. P. Jones
Sergeant J. O'Brien
Sergeant M. J. Martin
Sergeant D. A. Gowan
Sergeant J. McAlpine
Sergeant T. T. Prior
Sergeant A. M. Shaw
Sergeant F. L. Stevens
Sergeant C. W. R. Swan

Sergeant J. Wilson
Sergeant B. Hutchinson
Sergeant L. Martin
Lance-Sergeant C. B. Bradbury
Lance-Sergeant P. Brazier
Lance-Sergeant S. Clark
Lance-Sergeant I. G. Ellis
Lance-Sergeant J. F. Johnson
Corporal E. G. Arnold
Corporal W. A. Ashworth
Corporal E. Breaks
Corporal G. C. Clare
Corporal I. Clode
Corporal J. Holmes
Corporal R. D. Jones
Corporal F. L. Morris
Corporal W. J. Terry
Corporal F. Whitehouse
Lance-Corporal C. R. Crane
Lance-Corporal H. W. R. Sollitt
Lance-Corporal W. S. Wride
Trooper H. Bridges
Trooper G. Chaplin
Trooper J. H. Duxbury
Trooper A. Pye
Trooper G. C. Robbins
Trooper E. H. Robinson
Trooper A. Smith
Trooper T. Steele

U.S.A. Legion of Merit
Lieutenant-Colonel R. C. Jones

U.S.A. Silver Star
Captain P. J. Howard-Dobson

U.S.A. Bronze Star
Captain G. J. Iles   Sergeant F. L. Stevens

Polish Virtute Militari
Lieutenant-Colonel R. F. G. Jayne   Captain P. J. Howard-Dobson

French Croix De Guerre
Lieutenant-Colonel M. C. S. Phipps   Lieutenant-Colonel R. C. Jones

Index

Abbassia: 13, 94, 187
Abrahams, Tpr.: 224
Abyssinian War: 9, 10
Adige River: 412, 438, 439; A Sqn. crosses, 440; B Sqn. crosses, 442; C Sqn. crosses, 444–5
Agheila: 90, 95–6, 114
Agnew, Lt. S. W.: 388, 437
Ainley, S.S.M.: 289
Air Force—
  Desert: 352, 430–3
  Strategic: 427, 430–3
  XXIInd Tactical: 430–3
Aitchison, Sgt.: 393
Alamein: *see* El Alamein
Alam el Rimth: 61–4
Alexander of Tunis, Field-Marshal the Earl, K.G., G.C.B., G.C.M.G., C.S.I., D.S.O., M.C.: 220, 222, 226, 236, 238–9, 242, 246–7, 254, 269, 273, 278, 282–5, 290–1, 293, 296, 302, 318, 320–2, 325, 331–3, 362, 378–9, 408–10, 426, 430, 448
Allen, Capt. D. M.: 93, 179, 237, 239, 276, 288–9
Allied Armies in Italy: 404, 411, 448
Allied Force Headquarters: 333
American Volunteer Group: 201, 253
Amiriya: 55, 111–2, 124–5
Ancona: 330, 332, 339–41, 350–1, 354; capture of, 357–8
Anders, Lt.-Gen. W.: 335, 339, 350, 352, 354–5, 362, 364, 371–2, 404, 449–50
Andrews, Sgt. P. H.: 366
Anglo-Japanese Treaty: 195
Anstice, Brig. J. H., D.S.O.: 186, 206, 211, 252, 257, 260, 262, 265–6
Antelat: 84, 86
Anzio: 323–5, 327–9
Aosta, Duke of: 113, 137
Arab Legion: 51
Argue, Lt.: 437
Argyle, Maj. M. V., M.C.: 308, 435–6, 439–40
Armies—
  British—
    Eighth: formation of, 137; *see* Operation Crusader; at El Alamein, 311; in Italy, 318–23, 325, 327–9, 331, 334, 338, 352, 358, 377, 379–80, 382, 385, 388, 392, 404–6, 410–1; Battle of the Po Plains, 426–35; 448
    Fourteenth: 297, 299
  Burma—
    Burma Army: 221–2, 224, 244, 246, 292

Armies—(cont.)
  Chinese—
    Fifth: 246, 284–5, 287, 290, 293
    Sixth: 246, 284–5
  German—
    Tenth: 328, 429
  United States—
    Fifth: 317–25, 327–9, 331, 377, 379, 381–2, 392, 405–7, 410, 426–8, 430, 432–3
Ascanius, S.S.: 208–10, 273
Ashmead, Tpr.: 263
Astley, Maj. the Hon. S. N.: 86, 125
Astley-Rushton, Maj. J. F.: 23, 46, 66
Athlone, H.R.H. Princess Alice, Countess of, G.C.V.O., G.B.E.: 9
Athlone, Maj.-Gen. the Earl of, K.G., P.C., G.C.B., G.M.M.G., G.C.V.O., D.S.O.: 9
Auchinleck, Field-Marshal Sir Claude, G.C.B., G.C.I.E., C.S.I., D.S.O., O.B.E.: 123–4, 137
Austin, Sgt. F. D. J., M.M.: 93, 186
Australian Forces—
  anti-tank guns with B Sqn.: 108–9
  2nd/7th Royal Aust. Arty. Regt.: 131
  see also Divisions, Brigades
Ava Bridge: 285, 288–90
Azziziya: 60–2

Badoglio, Marshal: 316, 318
Bancroft, L/Cpl. H.: 45
Bardia: 20, 26, 29, 30, 32–3, 41–3, 45; capture of, 65–74; 98–9, 136, 150, 172, 186
Barlow, Tpr. J. R., D.C.M.: 80, 81, 93
Barr, Cpl.: 234
Barton, Capt. B. P., M.C.: 93, 229, 258, 275, 437–8
Basra: 116–17
Beaney, Cpl.: 244
Beda Fomm: 76; Battle of, 86–91
Bedawin: evacuation of, 55; at Beda Fomm, 89
B.E.F.: evacuation from France, 25
Belgium: resistance of, 23
Bell, Tpr. J., M.M.: 93
Benghazi: 20, 86, 88, 91, 96, 99, 186
Benson, Maj. W. A. (Northumberland Hussars): 176–7, 179
Beresford-Peirse, Lt.-Gen. Sir Noel M. de la P., K.B.E., C.B., D.S.O.: 120
Bir el Gubi: 27, 34, 143, 149, 151, 165, 185
Bir el Kenayis: 51, 54–5
Bir el Khreigat: 34, 103, 128
Bir el Telata: 26, 104, 129

459

INDEX

Bir Enba: 58–60, 65, 104, 106
Bir Sheferzen: *see* Sheferzen
Birks, Maj.-Gen. H. L., c.b., d.s.o.: 65–6, 78, 411
Blake, Lt. & Q.M. S. A., m.b.e.: 92, 125
Blenkinsop, L/Cpl.: 81
Bobinski, Col.: 342–4, 346–7, 357, 362, 383
Bologna: 378–9, 405–7, 426, 428–9, 432–4
Bonham-Carter, Maj. J. (R.T.R.): 240
Bowden, Sgt. H.: 264
Bowen, Cpl.: 263
Bracciano, Lake: 385, 398, 402–4, 411–3, 415, 424, 434
Brennan, Tpr. W., m.m.: 179
Bridges, Tpr. H.: 229
Brigades—
  Australian—
    19th Infantry: 73
  British—
    Heavy Armoured: 19
    Light Armoured: 12, 15, 19, 20
    1st Armoured: 114
    2nd Armoured: 388
    3rd Armoured: 92, 119, 121, 137
    4th Armoured: 19, 26, 28, 34, 38, 45, 54, 58, 60, 64–6, 71–4, 76, 78, 82–7, 90, 92, 121–2, 137, 141–2, 149–82
    7th Armoured: 20, 23, 45, 54, 58, 64–6, 72–4, 82, 84, 87, 90, 121–2, 125–6, 128–30, 141 *et seq.*; 206, 211, 217, 221, 226, 230–1, 237–8, 247–8, 251, 255, 259, 262, 269, 272, 276, 278, 280–2, 284–6, 293, 297, 299, 302; 308, 311, 313, 325, 334, 338, 383, 385–8, 393, 413
    9th Armoured: 413, 416, 420, 422, 425, 427, 434–5, 437
    22nd Armoured: 130, 141, 143, 149–82
    1st Army Tank: 133, 137–8, 143, 172
    32nd Army Tank: 137–8, 163
    50th Army Tank: 303
    Cairo Cavalry: 8
    2nd Commando: 427, 430
    22nd Guards: 97, 106–8, 121–2, 137, 141
    24th Guards: 427, 431, 443
    22nd Infantry: 23
    23rd Infantry: 163
    138th Infantry: 392
    167th Infantry: 386, 388–90, 398–9
    168th Infantry: 387–90, 392, 397, 399, 400
    169th Infantry: 387, 389–90, 392–3, 397, 435
    2nd Parachute: 428
    Support Group (7th Armd. Div.): 21, 33, 40, 51, 53, 71, 74, 83, 87, 97, 99, 108–9, 129, 141, 148–82
  Burma—
    1st: 277, 280
    2nd: 290

Brigades—(cont.)
  Canadian—
    5th Armoured: 385
  Greek—
    Mountain: 309–11, 380, 405
  Indian—
    5th Infantry: 118
    7th Infantry: 171, 334
    11th Infantry: 121
    13th Infantry: 246, 274–6, 278, 280, 290, 292
    16th Infantry: 205, 221, 292
    29th Infantry: 137
    46th Infantry: 205
    48th Infantry: 205, 226, 230–1, 233–4, 240–1, 247–8, 251, 267, 272, 274–8, 287–9, 292–3, 296–8
    63rd Infantry: 221, 230–1, 238–40, 270, 287–8, 292–3, 296, 298, 300
    3rd Motor: 96
  Polish—
    2nd Armoured: 338–41, 349, 352, 357–8, 361, 364, 372–3, 376, 382
    Carpathian Bde. Group: 137, 163, 354
    1st Carpathian Inf.: 336, 341, 343, 346, 348
    2nd Carpathian Inf.: 336, 341
    5th Wilno Inf.: 357, 365, 369, 372, 376
    6th Lwow Inf.: 350, 357–8, 365, 372
  South African—
    1st Infantry: 171
    2nd Infantry: 137
    5th Infantry: 151–2, 162, 167–9
Brink, Maj.-Gen. G. E., c.b., c.b.e., d.s.o. 174
Brown, Tpr. H. M., m.m.: 68, 93
Brown, Lt. & Q.M. P. W.: 265, 308
Brown, Sgt.: 228
Brown, Lt. P. W.: 415
Browne, Lt. J. J. H.: 275, 334, 362–3
Browning, Sgt.: 294
Bugbug: 26, 54, 60, 64, 100, 104, 106–8
Bulgaria: German hold on, 113
Burt, Lt. M. C.: 435, 443–4
Byass, Lt.-Col. F. W., d.s.o., m.c.: 22, 36, 42, 61–2, 64, 79, 81, 90, 93, 144, 152, 155, 157–8

Caesar Line: 327, 329, 331
Calder, Capt. (R.A.O.C.): 46, 113, 182, 212, 214, 297
Cameron, Capt. A. I. C.: 15, 22, 97
Cameronians, 1st Bn.: 217, 223–4, 225–7, 233–5, 255, 259, 263
Campbell, Sgt. C., m.m.: 263, 279
Campbell, Maj.-Gen. J. C., v.c., d.s.o., m.c.: 98–9, 104, 150, 154, 159, 170
Canadian Forces—
  5th Armoured Regt.: 420
  Governor-General's Horse Guards: 416–7
Canby, Tpr.: 101

INDEX

Capuzzo: 23, 26–9, 31–5, 38, 40–4, 48, 52, 66, 70, 97, 99–101, 104, 110, 120–2, 172
Cardew, Capt. (R.A.M.C.): 412
Carpenter, Sgt. E.: 395
Carr, Brig. W. G.: 130
Cassino: 321–5, 328, 331
Caunter, Brig. J. A. L., C.B.E., M.C.: 13, 21, 28, 78, 90
Cesano River: 364–5, 369, 370, 372–3
Charing Cross: 11, 13, 124
Chiang Kai Shek: 201, 247, 254
Chichester, Capt. the Hon. D. R. C.: 55, 146, 416
Chindwin River: 203, 285, 291–2, 296–7, 300
Chinese Forces: 242, 246, 254; intervention near Yenangyaung, 281–2, 283; *see also* Armies, Divisions
Churchill, Rt. Hon., later Sir Winston S., K.G., P.C., O.M., C.H.: call to the Nation, 25; 32, 198, 313, 315, 449
Clare, Cpl. G. C.: 229, 367–8
Clark, Gen. Mark (U.S.): 320, 329, 407, 426, 428, 434
Clarke, Tpr. A. P.: 234
Clarke, T.S.-M.: 37
Clayton, Tpr.: 101
Cleere, L/Cpl. E. F.: 395
Cleere, R.S.M. P., D.C.M.: 75–6, 87, 93, 266, 274, 288–9, 393–5, 402
Coldstream Guards, 3rd Bn.: 53, 59, 94, 97
Collins, Cpl. D. R. R., M.M.: 419
Colombo: atmosphere, 209–10; air attack, 273
Columns: usefulness of, 105–6
Combe, Maj.-Gen. J. F. B., C.B., D.S.O.: 29–31, 65–6, 85, 87, 89, 96
Congreve, Lt.-Col. J., D.S.O., O.B.E.: 16, 72, 75, 113, 126, 144, 155, 171, 175–6, 183, 186, 220, 238, 257, 266, 308, 345, 347, 362, 385, 412, 435, 441, 446
Connelly, Sgt. J. G.: 125
Cook, Tpr. S.: 337
Cooke, Maj.-Gen. R. B. B. B., C.B., C.B.E., D.S.O.: 413, 416, 435
Cookson, Maj. J. C., D.S.O. (Northumberland Hussars): 176
Cooney, Tpr. E.: 43
Cornwall, H.M.S.: 273
Corps—
  British—
    5th: 325, 329, 331, 334, 370, 379–81, 392, 406–7, 410, 427–8, 430–1, 433
    10th: 317–8, 320, 379–81, 428, 433
    13th: 84, 137, 141–2, 148–9, 151, 171–3, 328, 352, 379, 382, 405, 428, 432
    30th: 135, 137–8, 141–2, 148–150, 161, 172–6, 185
  Burma—
    1st: 246–7, 253–4, 269, 272, 278, 282–3, 285, 292–3

Corps—(cont.)
  Canadian—
    1st: 328, 370, 380–1, 384, 398, 406–7, 414, 416, 419
  French—
    Expeditionary: 328, 379
  German—
    Africa: 136, 143–4, 163, 172–3
    LXXVIth: 381
    1st Parachute: 434
  Italian—
    (co-belligerent): 330, 350, 356, 361, 372, 427, 429
    Mobile (enemy): 136, 142
  New Zealand: 324, 379–80
  Polish—
    2nd: 328, 331, 335, 339, 341, 352, 354, 358, 362, 364, 370, 378, 380, 382–3, 404, 406, 410, 428, 431–3, 449
  United States—
    2nd: 382, 405, 428, 432
    4th: 428, 432
    6th: 317–8, 328
Cossins, Tpr.: 101
County of London Yeomanry, 3rd & 4th: 130, 170
Cowan, Maj.-Gen. D. T., C.B., C.B.E., D.S.O., M.C.: 224
Cowley, Sgt. A. V., M.M. 45–6, 186, 263, 268
Creagh, Maj.-Gen. Sir Michael O'M., K.B.E., M.C.: 16, 21, 84–5, 121–2
Crete: German invasion, 113, 115–6
Crew, Sgt.: 183
Croce, Battle of: 387–403
Crone, Tpr. D. J.: 155
Crüwell, Gen. (German): 136
Cunningham, Gen. Sir Alan G., G.C.M.G., K.C.B., D.S.O., M.C.: 137, 140, 148, 183
Cyprus: 117

Dale Harris, Lt. R. S.: 385
Danzig: 12
Davenport, Tpr. E.: 76
Davies, S.S.M. N. S., M.M.: 234, 261–2, 366
Davies-Gilbert, Maj. C. G., M.B.E.: 13, 16, 125, 223, 248, 286
Davy, Brig. G. M. O., C.B., C.B.E., D.S.O.: 121, 126, 175, 186
Dean, Capt. C. G.: 16, 46, 125, 212, 223
de Beer, Capt.: 168
de Gaulle, Brig. Gen. (French): 117
Derna: 21, 77, 79–80, 82, 96, 99
Divisions—
  Australian—
    6th: 70–1, 74, 114
    7th: 117–8
    9th: 119, 137
  Brazilian—
    1st: 332, 428
  British—
    1st Airborne: 319

Divisions—*British*—(cont.)
  1st Armoured: 137, 380–1, 385, 388, 392, 398, 408
  2nd Armoured: 96, 114
  6th Armoured: 428, 434–5, 443–4
  7th Armoured: 23, 26, 48, 51, 58, 71, 74, 84–5, 90, 120–1, 125; in Operation Crusader, 137 *et seq.*
  10th Armoured: 308, 311
  Cavalry: 118
  4th Inf.: 398
  6th Inf.: 23, 118
  7th Inf.: 14
  46th Inf.: 380, 392, 399
  56th Inf.: 386, 388–9, 392, 399, 422, 427, 430–1, 433–7, 441
  70th Inf.: 137, 150–4, 163, 172–3, 185
  78th Inf.: 427–8, 431, 433
Burma—
  1st: 205, 219, 221, 224, 236, 242, 246–7, 269–72, 277–84, 286, 292, 296
Canadian—
  5th Armoured: 380, 420
  1st Inf.: 380, 405
Chinese—
  22nd: 285, 290
  28th: 285
  38th: 282, 285–6, 290, 293
  96th: 285, 290
  200th: 253
German—
  Hermann Goering: 328–9
  71st Inf.: 351, 376
  94th Inf.: 432
  98th Inf.: 381, 431–2
  278th Inf.: 350–1, 368, 376, 380
  334th Inf.: 432
  114th Jaeger: 418
  90th Light: 136, 162, 169
  5th Mountain: 380–1
  15th Panzer: 151, 160, 162
  21st Panzer: 127, 136, 142, 151, 160, 162, 178, 184
  26th Panzer-Grenadier: 381, 433
  29th Panzer-Grenadier: 381, 407, 429, 432
  90th Panzer-Grenadier: 407, 430, 432
  1st Parachute: 325, 376, 380–1, 407
Indian—
  4th: 57–8, 60, 64, 125–7, 137, 171–2, 184, 324–5, 329, 334, 386
  8th: 382, 405, 427, 434–5, 441
  10th: 325, 379, 406, 428, 432
  17th: 201, 214, 221, 224, 231, 242, 246–7, 251, 253, 259–60, 262, 269–70, 272, 278–9, 282, 284, 286–7, 292, 298–9
Italian (*hostile*)—
  17th Inf.: 84
  27th Inf.: 84
  60th Inf.: 84
  Savona Inf.: 171

Divisions—*Italian* (*hostile*)—(cont.)
  Ariete Mobile: 142–3
  Trento Mobile: 143
  Trieste Mobile: 142
New Zealand—
  2nd: 114, 137, 171–2, 185, 324, 405, 427–8, 431–3, 435, 441–6
Polish—
  3rd Carpathian: 338–41, 349, 352, 358, 362, 364, 369–72, 380, 431
  5th Kresowa: 339–40, 349–50, 352, 357–8, 362, 364–5, 370, 372–3, 380
South African—
  6th Armoured: 428, 432, 434
  1st Inf.: 126, 137–8, 141, 148–9, 151, 173–4
United States—
  82nd Airborne: 317
  34th Inf.: 434
  85th Inf.: 432
  10th Mountain: 432, 434
Douglas, Brig. A. S. G.: 108
Doyle, Cpl.: 155
Duchs, Maj.-Gen. (Polish): 338–9
Duke of Wellington's Regt.: 238, 255, 257, 259, 263, 279
DUKW: 414
Dunlop, Lt. J. B.: 359–60, 394–6
Durham Light Infantry, 2nd Bn.: 73–5, 98

Eddis, Tpr. L. W. T.: 368
Edwards, Sgt.: 445–6
Egypt: military occupation, 5–6; voyage to, 6–8; departure from, 208; return to, 311–3
Eisenhower, Gen. of the Army Dwight D., HON. G.C.B., HON. O.M., D.S.M. (U.S.), etc.: 311, 315–6, 408–10
El Adem: 27, 72, 119, 134, 150, 153
El Alamein: 105, 137, 311
El Duda: 120, 152–4, 163
Erskine, Maj.-Gen. I. D., C.B., C.B.E., D.S.O.: 97
Essex Yeomanry: *see* Royal Horse Artillery, 414th Bty.

Fabry, Cpl. W. S.: 37
Fairhurst, Capt. F. H. St. J.: 125
Fantail: 414, 430–1, 435–42
Fielden, Col. G., O.B.E.: 15, 22, 29, 35–6, 57, 208
Foggia: 320, 322
Foote, Maj.-Gen. H. R. B., V.C., D.S.O.: 437–8
Fort Capuzzo: *see* Capuzzo
Fort Madalena: *see* Madalena
Fosdick, Lt.-Col. F. R. C.: 124, 129, 144, 156–7, 170, 178, 182–3, 186, 191, 216, 239–40, 256–7, 259
Fox, Maj. M., M.C.: 87, 89, 179, 182, 186, 286, 355, 373–4, 392–3, 443

INDEX

Fox, Tpr.: 265
France: defeat of, 23–5; armistice, 32
Francis, Capt. S. C., D.S.O. (West Yorks Regt.): 229, 234
Free French: 54, 117–8
Freyberg, Lt.-Gen. Sir Bernard, later Lord F. of Wellington, New Zealand, V.C., G.C.M.G., K.C.B., K.B.E., D.S.O.: 443
Friend, Maj.-Gen. A. L. I., C.B., C.B.E., M.C.: 8
Frost, Tpr.: 265
Funnell, the Revd.: 268

Gabr Saleh: 52, 142, 148–9, 152, 162, 174
Gairdner, Lt.-Gen. Sir Charles H., K.C.M.G., C.B., C.B.E.: 31, 33, 40–1, 43
Gambier-Parry, Maj.-Gen. M. D., C.B., M.C.: 96
Gambut: 66, 73, 119
Gazala: 78, 142
Gebel el Akhdar: 17, 76
Gerawla: 22, 129
German Forces: arrival in Africa, 95
Ghot Breiber: 79–80
Gledsdale, Lt. J. J.: 443
Glendinning, Lt. E., M.M.: 93, 174, 214, 225, 230
Glenn, L/Cpl. T., M.M.: 186
Gloucester, Maj.-Gen. H.R.H. The Duke of, K.G., K.T., K.P., G.C.B., G.C.M.G., G.C.V.O.: 304
Gloucestershire Regt., 1st Bn.: 217, 248; in operations round Paungde, 252–63
Goschen, Maj. G. W., M.C.: 47, 61, 64
Gothic Line: 331–2, 363, 370, 376–8, 381, 392
Gott, Lt.-Gen. W. H. E., C.B., C.B.E., D.S.O., M.C.: 12, 51, 99, 102, 148, 150–2, 160–1, 184, 207
Gowan, Sgt. D. A.: 66, 125
Gray, 2/Lt. L. H.: 16
Gray, Capt. P. V. (Cameronians): 223, 235
Graziani, Marshal (Italian): 32, 87
Greece: Italian invasion, 56; German invasion, 113–16; politics, 309–11
Greek Forces: see Brigades
Gregg, L/Cpl. C. R. P.: 420
Grenadier Guards, 3rd Bn.: 443
Guns—
  British—
    25 pdr.: as anti-tank weapon, 139, 183–4
    2 pdr.: value and use of, 111, 132–3, 143
  German—
    50-mm.: 138–9
    88-mm. A.A.: 122, 138
    88-mm. PAK 43 (Hornet): 368–9, 373
Gurkhas: 220, 230, 233, 270, 298–9
Gurkha battalions—
  1st/4th: 255
  5th: 442
  1st/10th: 239, 279

Gustav Line: 323, 327
Guthrie, Lt.: 88

Hancock, Tpr.: 218
Harbord, Maj. G.: 45
Harding, Lt. E. C. F., M.C.: 337, 343, 356, 369, 398
Harding, Sgt. F. W., M.M.: 101–3, 125
Harding, Lt. J. H.: 334, 384, 420, 442
Hatherall, T.S.-M. T. H. G., M.M.: 43, 93
Hawkins, Tpr.: 264
Headquarters—
  British Troops in Egypt: 13, 19
  Western Desert Force: 23, 112
Helfaya Pass: 53, 94, 97, 100, 104, 107, 109, 121–2, 172, 186
Helwan: 92
Herbert, Capt. R. W.: 418, 423
Herr, Gen. (German): 429
Hewer, Maj.-Gen. R. K., C.B., C.B.E.: 208
Highland Light Infantry, 2nd Bn.: 33
Hill, Maj. G. D.: 16
Hipsey, Sgt. R.: 73, 101, 264, 269
Hitler, Adolf: relations with League of Nations, 9–10; attitude to Turkey, 308–9; reinforcement of Africa, 311; strategy in Europe, 314, 321, 324, 328, 333, 407, 429, 433; death of, 449
Hitler Line: 327–8
H.M. King George VI: 362
Hobart, Maj.-Gen. Sir P. C. S., K.B.E., C.B., D.S.O., M.C.: 12–3, 16
Horsecroft, Tpr:. 175
Household Cavalry Regt.: 382
Howard-Dobson, Lt. P. J.: 337, 343, 348, 362, 368, 398, 400–1, 419
Huckin, 2/Lt. W.: 16, 72–3, 80
Hudson, Comdr. (R.N.): 435
Hugh-Jones, Brig. N., M.C.: 230–1
Hull-down positions: 52
Hunt, Sgt.: 219
Hussars—
  3rd: 56, 64–5, 77–9, 82, 85, 88–90, 92, 107, 110, 385, 413, 415
  4th: 114, 414, 417, 419, 421
  8th: 13, 20, 45, 73, 76, 94, 157
  10th: 424
  11th: 11, 22–3, 26–7, 30–1, 33–4, 46, 53, 64–6, 74, 77, 84–5, 99, 102–3, 106–7, 121, 135, 153, 170
  14th/20th: 307
Hutchison, Lt.-Gen. Sir Balfour O., K.B.E., D.S.O.: 123
Hutton, Lt.-Gen. Sir Thomas, K.C.I.E., C.B., M.C.: 220, 238

Iles, Lt. G. J.: 397–8, 400–2, 418, 421–2, 437, 439
India: Japanese threat, 200
Indian Forces—
  7th Cavalry: 297

Indian Forces—(cont.)
  Central India Horse: 121
  1st Field Regt.: 221, 255, 282, 289
  24th Fd. Coy., Sappers and Miners: 255
  7th/10th Baluch Regt.: 255
  2nd/13th Frontier Force Rifles: 238
  Mahratta Light Infantry: 442
  4th/16th Punjab Regt.: 334
  1st/11th Sikhs: 239
Ingram, Lt. S.: 437
Iraq: rising in, 113, 116–8; 7th Hussars in, 304, 307–8
Italy: at war with, 25; plans for invasion of, 313–6; surrender, 316–8; invasion of, 319 et seq.

Jackson, Tpr. R.: 66
Jackson-Stops, Lt. W. H.: 287
Japan: ancient history, 191–2; European contacts, 192–3; isolationism, 193–4; new era, 194–6; the League and the Axis, 196–7; Pearl Harbour, 198; swarms over Asia, 198–9; the army, 199–200
Jarabub: 27, 33, 38, 94, 135, 141
Jayne, Lt.-Col. R. F. G., D.S.O.: 30, 61–2, 80–1, 93, 304, 308, 326, 335, 344–7, 353, 355, 362, 374, 385, 396, 402, 411–2
Jebel: see Gebel
Jodl, Gen. (German): 433
John, Capt. V. L.: 93, 180–1, 212, 247
Johnson, Maj. (D.L.I.): 75
Johnson, Sgt.: 437
Jones, Sgt. E. P.: 125
Jugoslavia: obstruction to Allies, 409–10

Kabaw Valley: 291, 297, 300–1
Kalewa: 284, 290–2, 296–300
Kangaroo: 414, 423–4
Kermode, Maj.: 247–8
Kesselring, Marshal (German): 323, 327–8, 331–2, 381–2, 405, 411, 429
Kevill-Davies, Maj. W. T., M.C.: 15, 18, 125–6, 143, 183, 216, 232
Khamsin: 22
Kilty, Sgt. J. J.: 288–9
King, T.S.-M.: 43
King's Dragoon Guards: 119, 135
King's Own Yorkshire Light Infantry: 238, 280
King's Royal Rifle Corps (The 60th): in the desert, 12, 26, 29, 33, 60, 87, 98–9, 104, 152, 159, 166; in Italy, 421–2
Kut el Amara: compared with Tobruk, 118–19

Lamone River: 410; 7th Hussars holding of, 417–25

Lancers—
  9th: 391
  12th: 130, 417, 421, 445
  27th: 416, 422
Laverack, Lt.-Gen. Sir John D., K.B.E., C.B., C.M.G., D.S.O.: 211
League of Nations: weakness over Abyssinia, 5, 9, 10; weakness over Manchurian episode, 195–6
Leaguering: 14
Leathwood, Tpr.: 218
Lee, L/Cpl. S.: 132
Leese, Lt.-Gen. Sir Oliver W. H., Bart., K.C.B., C.B.E., D.S.O.: 352, 362, 404
Lewis, L/Cpl. W.: 37
Li Jan Sun, Gen. (Chinese): 293
Liebich, 2/Lt. A., M.C.: 362
Littlewood, Tpr.: 241
Llewellen Palmer, Maj. C. T., M.C.: 41, 45, 62, 66, 75, 80–1, 88, 99, 102, 107, 125, 165, 212, 257–8, 274, 299, 402, 424
Lloyd, Brig. L. S., C.B.E., M.C.: 162
Lo, Gen. (Chinese): 285–6
L.O.B. (left out of battle): 21
Lockwood, Lt. & Q.M. W. J.: 415
London Irish Rifles: 401
London Scottish: 390–1, 397, 400–1
Long Range Desert Group: 137, 446
Longworth, Capt. (R.T.R.): 159, 166–7
Loraine, Sir Percy L., Bart., G.C.M.G.: 20
Low, Capt. W. (R.A.M.C.): 57, 75, 182, 225, 241, 326, 411–2
Lowe, S.S.M.: 167, 183
Lyndon, Tpr.: 368

Maadi: 15, 18, 21, 22
McCready, Lt.-Col. D. D. M. (Gurkhas): 279
McCreery, Gen. Sir Richard L., G.C.B., K.B.E., D.S.O., M.C.: 320, 406
MacGill, Lt.: 186
McGuinness, Sgt. P.: 354
Madalena: 27–8, 31, 65, 145, 179
Magill, Cpl.: 76
Mail: 51, 273
Manchester Regt.: 329
Maletti, Col. (Italian): 58, 63
Mansell, Tpr.: 234–5
Mansfield, B.S.M. (Essex Yeomanry): 235
Marlow, Cpl.: 227
Marindin, Lt.-Col. P. C., M.C. (West Yorks Regt.): 287
Marsh, Maj. J., M.C. (R.T.R.): 124
Marshall, S.S.M. W. C., D.C.M.: 179, 186
Martin, Sgt. L.: 125, 260
Martin, Tpr.: 264
Mathew, Tpr. C. T. P.: 423
Matruh Mobile Force: 11
Mechanization: 3, 4, 8
Mechili: 76–83, 92, 96–7, 142, 150, 186
Mena: 92–3, 111–2

INDEX

Mersa Matruh: 11–15, 22, 51–2, 54, 57–9, 94, 97, 110–2, 125–7
Messervy, Gen. Sir Frank W., K.C.S.I., K.B.E., C.B., D.S.O.: 121–2
Messina, Strait of: 313, 316, 319
Metauro River: 363; battle for crossings, 370–80
Metcalfe, Revd. N. S., D.S.O.: 57, 209, 214, 234–6, 312
Mills, 2/Lt. A. P.: 93
Mirrlees, Maj.-Gen. W. H. B., C.B., D.S.O., M.C.: 12
Misa River: 358–9, 361–4
Mokpalin: 205–6; disaster at, 214–6
Montgomery of Alamein, Field-Marshal the Viscount, K.G., G.C.B., D.S.O.: 311
Monywa: fighting around, 290–6
Morshead, Lt.-Gen. Sir Leslie J., K.C.B., K.B.E., C.M.G., D.S.O.: 119
Moubray, Lt.-Col. J. (Coldstream Gds.): 97
Msus: 84–5, 87, 92, 96
Murphy, Sgt. M.: 175
Murray Smith, Maj. G. W., M.C.: 44, 66, 86, 93, 104, 107, 178, 182–3, 186, 239, 241, 263–5, 286, 334, 366, 420, 422
Musaid: 37, 40, 52–3, 97–8, 100, 121, 172
Musone River: crossing of, 340–53
Mussolini, Benito: ambitions in Africa, 9; relations with league, 5, 10; war of nerves, 20–1; fall of 316–7; 407; death of, 448–9
Muxworthy, Tpr.: 264
Mytton, Lt. John: 412

Napier, Capt. J. M., M.C.: 66, 68, 93, 98, 102–4, 110, 125, 155
Naples: 316–7, 320
Navigation: 17–8
Neame, Lt.-Gen. Sir Philip, V.C., K.B.E., C.B., D.S.O.: 95–6
Neumann-Silkow, Gen. (German): 136
New Zealand Forces—
  20th Armoured Regt.: 444–5
  see also Divisions
Nibeiwa: 56, 58–60, 63–4
Nickells, Capt. R.: 93, 102–3, 108, 167, 237, 286, 350
Normandy: *see* Operation Overlord
Norrie, Lt.-Gen. Sir C. Willoughby M., K.C.M.G., C.B., D.S.O., M.C.: 137, 142, 148, 151, 184–5
Northumberland, Capt. the Duke of (Northd. Hussars): 176–7
Northumberland Hussars: 176–9

Oates, 2/Lt. R. D. G., M.C.: 15, 42, 43
O'Brien, Sgt. J.: 125
O'Connor, Gen. Sir Richard N., G.C.B., D.S.O., M.C.: 23, 59, 73, 84, 90, 96, 140

Operations—
  ANVIL: 314, 332–3, 378–9
  BATTLEAXE: 120–3, 136
  CRUSADER: 134 *et seq.*; troops available, 137; comparison of armour, 138–9; plan, 139–43; enemy dispositions, 143; opening moves, 143–6; Battle of Sidi Rezegh, 147–171; Sheferzen, 173–82; end of campaign, 183–6
  OVERLORD: 314–5, 321, 323; news of the landings, 330; related to operations in Italy, 408–11, 448

Palmer, Capt. G. S. B., M.C.: 145, 183, 225, 234, 260–2, 293, 343
Palmer, Lt.-Col. N. L. L., O.B.E.: 22
Panzer Gruppe Afrika: 136
Parry, Lt. J. E., M.C.: 93, 263, 276, 397
Partisans—
  Italian: 417–8, 421–2, 440, 445–6
  Jugoslav: 409
Patterson, Sgt.: 224
Patteson, Lt. M. J. E., M.C.: 93, 183, 186, 224, 260–2
Paungde: 255–7
Payne-Gallwey, Lt.-Col. L. P., O.B.E., M.C.: 15
Pearl Harbour: 191, 198, 314
Pegler, Lt. H. R. D., D.C.M., M.M.: 37, 101, 125
Pegu: fighting around, 214–36
Pegu Hills: 204, 224, 236
Pereira, Maj. T. (Essex Yeomanry): 233, 260, 266
Phillips, Cpl.: 156
Phipps, Capt. M. C. S.: 125
Pilkington, Lt. A. H. L. A.: 87, 183, 259, 303
Pisa-Rimini Line: 318, 321
Pitman-Butler, Capt. P.: 16, 29, 33, 37, 44–5
Pivot Group: 12
Platypus Grousers: 415, 435
Po, River: destruction of bridges, 378; 409, 411; plans for crossing, 414; Battle of the Po Plains, 426 *et seq.*; A Sqn. crosses, 436–8; B Sqn. crosses, 441–2; C Sqn. crosses, 443–5
Poland: partition of, 12; invasion, 14, 20; freedom extinguished, 449–50
Polish Forces—
  Armour—
    1st Armd. Regt.: 346
    6th Armd. Regt.: 341–2, 353, 355, 373, 376
      1st Krechowieski Lancers: 353–4, 360, 368
      3rd Carpathian Lancers: 382
      12th Podolski Lancers: 341, 358–60, 364, 370, 382–4
      15th Poznanski Lancers: 340, 352–3, 357, 374

Polish Forces (cont.)
Artillery—
   7th Horse Arty. Regt.: 354
   5th Regt.: 358, 362
Commandos: 353–4
Infantry—
   4th Carpathian Bn.: 346–7
   5th Carpathian Bn.: 343–5, 372
   6th Carpathian Bn.: 342, 354
   8th Carpathian Bn.: 343
   13th Bn.: 369
   15th Bn.: 358, 360, 362, 365–6, 369–70
   16th Bn.: 352, 365–70
   17th Bn.: 373–4, 376
   See also Brigades, Corps, Divisions
Pratt, Cpl.: 74
Presnall, Cpl. P. J.: 423
Prince of Wales, H.M.S.: 198
Prior-Palmer, Brig. O. L., D.S.O.: 385, 387
Prome: operations around, 251–71
Pye, Tpr. A.: 125
Python Scheme: 412, 415

Queen's Regt.—
   2nd/5th: 393, 438–41
   2nd/6th: 393, 396, 436, 438
   2nd/7th: 439

Rabia: 56, 64, 127–8
Rakowski, Maj.-Gen. (Polish): 341, 343–4, 346, 357, 362
Ram, Cpl.: 43
Rangoon: 209; arrival, 210–14; threat to, 214, 220; to be evacuated, 221; to be held, 222; evacuated, 236–7, 240
Rash, Maj. E. D. (R.T.R.): 80
Rashid Ali: 116–17
Rawlings, Lt.: 435, 444–5, 447
Reed, Maj. (U.S.): 110
Reno, River: 420, 426–8, 430–2, 434
Repulse, H.M.S.: 198
Rifle Brigade, 2nd Bn.: 19, 34, 40, 78–9, 85, 108–9, 131, 144, 147, 152, 159, 444
Road blocks: Pegu, 230–6; Taukkyan, 237–41; Padigon, 258–9; Shwedaung, 259–69; Yenangyaung, 280–3
Roberts, Sgt.: 275
Robson, Tpr. G. L.: 179
Rome: 316–7, 321–3; fall of, 330–1; 333, 411
Rommel, Field-Marshal (German): 95, 105, 136, 140, 152, 164, 173, 180, 185–6, 311
Roosevelt, President Franklin D.: 198, 313–4, 327
Royal Air Force: 26, 28, 33; cover for troop concentration, 60; attacks Italian "circus," 71; absent from Beda Fomm, 87; tactical co-operation with army, 128; in Burma, 201; withdrawal to China, 252–3; re-appears, 298; in pursuit of Rommel, 311; in Italy, *frequent references, including* strategical co-operation, 378; tactical co-operation, 398; aid to Jugoslavs, 409; *see also* Air Force
Royal Air Force Regiment—
   2721 Sqn.: 417–8
   2788 Sqn.: 418–9
Royal Armoured Corps Depot: 57
Royal Army Medical Corps—
   2nd/3rd Fd. Amb.: 12
   166th Light Fd. Amb.: 435
Royal Army Ordnance Corps: 46, 163
Royal Army Service Corps—
   Fantail Regt.: 435–6
   No. 5 Coy.: 12
   No. 65 Coy.: 288
Royal Artillery—
   Royal Horse Artillery—
      3rd Regt.: 11, 19, 33, 98
      4th Regt.: 19, 33, 65–6, 78–9, 81, 100
      C Bty.: 19, 26, 30, 35, 36, 44–7, 53, 61, 64, 85, 89, 102
      D Bty.: 59, 62, 82, 86, 88, 100–2
      F Bty.: 12, 54, 87–8, 98, 100–1, 107, 135, 154, 156, 158, 162, 183
      J Bty.: 19, 26, 30–1, 40
      P Bty.: 13
      DD (Jerboa) Bty.: 146–7, 156, 158
      414th Bty. (Essex Yeomanry): 206, 216, 223, 225–6, 230–5, 238–40, 250, 252–267, 277, 282, 287, 289, 300, 302–3
   Anti-Aircraft—
      1st Lt. A.A. Regt.: 175
      155th Lt. A.A. Bty.: 78
   Anti-Tank—
      93rd A/Tk. Regt.: 390
      95th A/Tk. Regt.: 206
   Field—
      8th Regt.: 109–10
      15th Regt.: 393
      20th Regt.: 417
      1st Indian Regt.: 221, 255, 282, 289
   Mountain—
      15th Bty.: 255
Royal Electrical and Mechanical Engineers: 163
Royal Engineers—
   42nd Field Company: 435
   2nd Field Squadron: 29, 33, 75
   3rd Field Squadron: 413
   1st Field Troop: 435–6
Royal Fusiliers: 441–2
Royal Marines: 253, 296
Royal Navy: 6, 58, 198, 209–10, 273
Royal Scots Greys: 118
Royal Tank Regiment—
   1st: 11, 12, 19, 20, 45, 53, 87, 125
   2nd: 56, 60, 64–5, 68, 75, 78–81, 87–90, 111–12, 122, 124, 145, 147, 152, 154, 158–60, 166–7, 171, 206, 216, 218–23, 226, 231, 238–41, 252, 255, 267,

INDEX 467

Royal Tank Regiment—2nd; (cont.) 269–70, 274–82, 286–8, 290, 294, 296–8, 302, 386–9, 393, 396–7, 399
3rd: 114
6th: 8, 19, 26, 35, 40, 51, 60, 62, 76, 127, 145, 147–8, 152, 159, 166, 180, 312, 386
7th: 56, 58, 71, 74, 119
8th: 386, 388–9, 397–8, 402, 413
48th: 362, 439
Rudnicki, Maj.-Gen. (Polish): 349, 365
Rumania: German hold on, 113
Russell, Brig. H. E.: 11, 16, 121, 126
Russia, see U.S.S.R.
Russo-German Non-Aggression Pact: 12

Salerno: 317–20
Salt marsh: nature of, 107
Salum: 23, 27, 29, 33, 52–3, 97, 104, 109, 120–1, 141, 172
Scobie, Lt.-Gen. Sir Ronald McK., K.B.E., C.B., M.C.: 141, 163
Scots Guards, 2nd Bn.: 107–8, 170
Scott-Cockburn, Brig. J., D.S.O., M.C.: 161
Senussi: 8
Seymour-Evans, Maj. D. C., M.C.: 29, 32, 43, 61, 81, 126, 145, 155, 186
Sheferzen: 69, 128, 131–2, 153, 178, 180
Sheppard, Lt.-Col. R. B., D.S.O.: 22, 79, 81, 92, 93
Shwedaung: battle around, 259–69
Shwegyin: 291, 296–8
Shorten, Capt. N. (Essex Yeomanry): 224, 238, 261, 266–7
Sicily: invasion of, 313
Sidi Azeiz: 27–30, 34, 38, 41–3, 45–6, 48, 52, 66–7, 70–2, 97–9, 172
Sidi Barrani: 8, 11, 22–3, 26, 32; Battle of, 54 et seq.; 94, 106, 172
Sidi Omar: 26, 28, 52, 65–9, 97, 100, 122, 132, 141, 171, 181
Sidi Rezegh: 120–1, 130, 132, 134, 141–2; Battle of, 145–174
Sidi Saleh: 85, 87
Simcox, Lt. (Essex Yeomanry): 267
Sims, Tpr.: 43
Sinclair, Lt.-Col. C., M.C. (Rifle Bde.): 145, 148
Singapore: 198–9, 209; surrender of, 210
Skrine, Lt. J. S. H., M.C.: 390, 396, 444
Slim, Field-Marshal Sir William J., G.C.B., G.B.E., D.S.O., M.C.: 246, 292
Smith, Lt. A. A.: 230
Smith-Dorrien, Brig.: 392
Sofafi: 56, 64–5, 104, 106, 127, 129
Solomon, Tpr.: 218
Sosnkowski, Gen. (Polish): 362
South African Forces—
  Armoured Car Regts.—
    4th: 127, 131–2, 135, 153, 167
    6th: 137
  See also Brigades, Divisions

Spreadbury, L/Sgt. A., M.M. (R. Signals): 93–4, 110
Stalin, Joseph: 314, 449; see also U.S.S.R.
Stanley Evans, Maj. M. M., M.C.: 57, 73, 81, 180–1, 223, 228–9, 232, 239, 257–8, 294, 330, 336, 347, 385, 393–4, 399, 415–16
Stanley Evans, Maj. P. B.: 57, 75–6, 80, 102, 109, 125, 155, 175–6, 179, 212, 216, 227, 241, 260, 286, 349, 403, 415–6
Steele, Tpr. T.: 125
Stevens, 2/Lt. P. J.: 93
Stillwell, Gen. (U.S.): 247, 286, 290, 293
Stoczowski, Lt.-Col. W. (Polish): 358–60
Strickland, Tpr.: 180
Suez Canal: 5, 6, 10, 13, 21, 116, 313
Sümmermann, Gen. (German): 136
Swain, S.S.M. L. E., M.M.: 46, 101
Syria: campaign in, 113, 116

Tactics: frontier operations, 47–8; British and German compared, 105, 183–5
Tanks: influence on strategy, 105; German strength, 138, and losses, 151; strengths after Sidi Rezegh, 159, 167; night engagement, 177–9
Tanks—
  American—
    Gen. Grant: 304, 307
    Gen. Sherman: 309, 311, 312; in Italy, 330, 344 et seq.; see also Tanks, DD
    Gen. Stuart (Honey): 139, 157, 175 et seq.; in Burma, 207, 250–1, 275, 277; 307, 311, 312; in Italy, 329 et seq.
  British—
    A.9 cruiser: 19, 112, 126, 129
    A.10 cruiser: 19, 56, 112, 113, 124, 126, 129, 157, 174–5
    A.13 cruiser: 56, 111–12, 124–6, 129, 174
    A.15 cruiser (Crusader): 129, 143, 174–5, 309
    Mark III light: 11
    Mark VI A light: 11
    Mark VI B light: 11, 56
    Matilda, infantry: 56, 58, 63, 71, 74, 138
    Valentine, infantry: 164; see also Tanks, DD
  DD: 385, 412–5, 424–5; in the pursuit, 435 et seq.
  Dummy: 73–4
  German—
    Mks. II, III, IV: 138–9
    Panther: 398
    Tiger: 420
  Italian—
    C.V.3 light: 30–2, 170
    M.11 medium: 41
    M.13 medium: 80, 88–90, 92, 138, 170

Taukkyan: 221; fighting around, 237–41
Taranto: 313, 316, 325
Taungdwingyi: 272–4
Thermos bomb: 53, 84–5
Theyre, Lt.-Col. S. M. C.: 279
Thomas, Lt.-Col. R. H.: 225
Thomas, Tpr.: 368
Thompson, Lt. G. M.: 334, 363, 367
Thompson, Sgt. T. J.: 81
Thornton, Col. T. A., C.V.O.: 337
Thornton, Maj. T. R. S., M.C.: 15, 45, 175, 186, 234, 278, 337–8
Tinker, Maj. E. H.: 312, 345, 362
Tito, Marshal: 409
Tobruk: 20, 26, 30, 32, 65; captured, 70–6; 82, 92; decision to hold, 96–7; investment, 98, 99, 112; siege, 118–20; attempts to relieve, 120–2; 136–7; plan for relief, 141–3; 144, 150–1, 154; sortie, 163–4; 166, 172–3
Trasimene Line: 331–2, 339–40
Trieste: 441, 445–6
Trigh Capuzzo: 27, 66–7, 142, 144, 147–50, 152–3, 159, 172–3
Trigh El Abd: 151–3, 172–4
Truscott, Gen. (U.S.): 432
Tummar: 58, 63
Turkey: attitude to war, 308–9; liaison with, 309
Type, Lt. J. C. R.: 334, 345

United States of America: early contact with Japan, 194; attitude to Japan and Britain, 198; at war, 198; strategy, 313–16
United States Forces—
  755th Tank Bn.: 435
  See also Armies, Brigades, Corps, Divisions
U.S.S.R.: partition of Poland, 12, 13; German invasion, 115, 117; relations with Japan, 196; strategic purposes, 313–15; influence on Jugoslavs, 409; domination of Poland, 449–50

Venice: 429, 441–2, 445–6, 448–9
Vichy French: 118
Vietinghoff, Gen. (German): 429–30, 432–3
von Ravenstein, Gen. (German): 136

Wadi el Kharruba: 60–2
Waite, Cpl.: 62
Walford, Sgt. A. G.: 165
Wall, Lt.-Col. N. M. H., M.C.: 15, 36, 160, 162, 186, 412, 416, 441
Walsh, L/Cpl.: 156
Walton, Sgt.: 228–9, 258
Washington Treaty: 195
Washington, Tpr.: 265
Watkins, Brig. H. R. B., C.B.E., D.S.O., M.C.: 12, 16
Watson, Capt. R. C.: 15, 155, 186
Wavell, Field-Marshal The Earl, P.C., G.C.B., G.C.S.I., G.C.I.E., C.M.G., M.C.: 4, 64, 96, 113–4, 117, 120, 122–3, 206, 209, 211, 220, 222, 226, 269, 302
Weatherall, Lt.-Col. N. E.: 8
Weaver, Cpl. J.: 165
Weaver, Sgt.: 179
Webb, Tpr. L.: 30
Welch Guards: 443
Welch Regt., 1st Bn.: 390–1, 397–8, 400, 422
West Yorkshire Regt., 1st Bn.: 217, 219–21, 225–6, 228, 233, 248, 250, 255, 258, 262–3, 281, 287–8, 294, 299
White, Maj. A. E.: 16, 131, 165, 212, 350, 362, 385
Whitehouse, Cpl. F.: 125
Widdowson, Sgt. A. E., M.M.: 93, 104
Williams, Cpl. D. J.: 348
Williams, Capt. G. O.: 360, 394–5
Williams, Lt. J. L. C.: 57, 146, 157
Williams, Sgt.: 228, 230
Williamson, Capt. W. H. (Northumberland Hussars): 178
Wilson, Field-Marshal The Lord W. of Libya, G.C.B., G.B.E., D.S.O.: 21, 95, 114, 117
Wilson, R.S.M. J.: 113, 186, 416
Winney, Lt. W. E. F.: 125
Winter Line: 320–3
Withers, Lt.-Col. H. C., M.C. (R.H.A.): 54, 87–8
Woodcock, Cpl.: 81
Wright, Tpr.: 249

Yalta: 450
Yenangyaung: 220, 222, 274, 279; fighting around, 280–3
Young, Lt.: 225, 238, 263, 443
Younger, Brig. R., D.S.O., M.C.: 16, 66, 82, 94, 99, 101, 104, 125–6, 131, 145, 156, 217, 231, 249, 282, 299, 304
Yoxall, Tpr.: 76
Yule, Maj. G. (R.T.R.): 174

www.ingramcontent.com/pod-product-compliance
Lightning Source LLC
Chambersburg PA
CBHW052040220426
43663CB00012B/2385